MIKE BAZLEY & PHIL HANCOCK

CONTEMPORARYACCOUNTING

SIXTH EDITION

THOMSON

Australia · New Zealand · Canada · Mexico · Singapore · Spain · United Kingdom · United States

Level 7, 80 Dorcas Street
South Melbourne, Victoria
Australia 3205

Email: highereducation@thomsonlearning.com.au
Website: www.thomsonlearning.com.au

First published by Thomson in 2004
This edition published in 2006
10 9 8 7 6 5 4 3 2 1
10 09 08 07 06

Copyright © 2007 Nelson Australia Pty Limited.

COPYRIGHT

Reproduction and Communication for educational purposes
The Australian *Copyright Act 1968* (the Act) allows a maximum of one chapter or 10% of the pages of this work, whichever is the greater, to be reproduced and/or communicated by any educational institution for its educational purposes provided that the educational institution (or the body that administers it) has given a remuneration notice to Copyright Agency Limited (CAL) under the Act.

For details of the CAL licence for educational institutions contact:

Copyright Agency Limited
Level 19, 157 Liverpool Street
Sydney NSW 2000
Telephone: (02) 9394 7600
Facsimile: (02) 9394 7601
E-mail: info@copyright.com.au

Reproduction and Communication for other purposes
Except as permitted under the Act (for example a fair dealing for the purposes of study, research, criticism or review) no part of this book may be reproduced, stored in a retrieval system, communicated or transmitted in any form or by any means without prior written permission. All inquiries should be made to the publisher at the address above.

Copyright owners may take legal action against a person who infringes on their copyright through unauthorised copying. Enquiries should be directed to the publisher.

National Library of Australia
Cataloguing-in-Publication data

Bazley, M. E. (Michael E.).
Contemporary accounting.

  6th ed.
  ISBN 0 17 012975 6.
  ISBN 978 0 17 012975 6.

  1. Accounting – Australia – Textbooks. I. Hancock, Phil.
  II. Title.

657.0994

Editor: Megan Stansfield
Project editor: Chris Wyness
Developmental editor: Elizabeth Male
Publishing editor: Tony Hey
Publishing manager: Michael Tully
Indexer: Neale Towart
Text designer: Olga Lavecchia
Cover designer: Olga Lavecchia
Cover image: Masterfile
Typeset in Rotis Semi Serif 10/14pt by Sun Photoset
Production controller: Ruth Coleman
Printed in China by CTPS

This title is published under the imprint of Thomson.
Nelson Australia Pty Limited ACN 058 280 149 (incorporated in Victoria)
trading as Thomson Learning Australia.

The URLs contained in this publication were checked for currency during the production process. Note, however, that the publisher cannot vouch for the ongoing currency of URLs.

CONTENTS

19 Accounting for decision making: with and without resource constraints 595

20 Budgets 634

21 Performance measurement and the balanced scorecard 666

Appendices

PREFACE

Contemporary Accounting, sixth edition, is designed to provide an introduction to accounting for students at universities and similar tertiary institutions. It is intended to cover the requirements of a one-semester course in accounting at the undergraduate and MBA level for both accounting and non-accounting majors. We believe that the approach to financial accounting taken in this book will provide a solid foundation on which accounting majors will be better able to understand the bookkeeping function. It also provides an excellent overview of the accounting function in business for non-accounting majors. The implications of accounting policies on managers are discussed wherever relevant throughout the book.

This book has been written with the objective of conveying an understanding of accounting without introducing unnecessary technical terminology and procedures. Rather, it builds on basic concepts to provide a clear understanding of financial statements, their uses and limitations. Accounting terms and concepts are defined according to the official pronouncements. In July 2002, the Financial Reporting Council in Australia decided that from 1 January 2005, Australia would adopt International Accounting Standards. In July 2004, the Australian Accounting Standards Board issued the Australian equivalents of International Financial Reporting Standards (AIFRS). Therefore, in this edition we have used the terminology consistent with AIFRSs. The accounting concepts used in the AASB *Framework for the Preparation and Presentation of Financial Statements* (2004) provide the conceptual basis of *Contemporary Accounting* and are used to analyse various issues in accounting.

We have included in the text extracts from some annual reports to illustrate contemporary accounting practices. Also included is the 2005 half-yearly financial report of Woodside Limited. This half-year report is one of the first to be prepared using the new AIFRS. This report appears in Appendix 1 and students are referred to it frequently throughout the text. Due to the timing of the sixth edition, we were not able to include an AIFRS annual report as we have done in the previous five editions.

To introduce accounting techniques and principles such as duality, we have used worksheets based on the balance sheet equation. Students develop an understanding of concepts such as assets, liabilities, equity, income, revenues and expenses and see how financial statements are prepared. This approach avoids the problems often experienced by students in trying to understand debits and credits.

Chapters 1 to 14 provide an introduction to financial accounting where the needs of external users are most important. Chapters 15 to 21 look at the needs of internal users and provide an introduction to management accounting. A one-semester MBA course in financial accounting is likely to cover all the material in Chapters 1 to 14.

In each chapter learning objectives and key concepts are identified and highlighted throughout the chapter. Review exercises are also included in each chapter and solutions are provided at the end of the chapter. Additional review questions and problems are provided at the end of each chapter.

The problems are listed in order of difficulty. The more difficult problems are primarily intended for use in MBA courses (and these are indicated in each chapter), but instructors of undergraduate courses may also find them useful. The ethics case studies are intended for all students and are well suited to group discussion. We recommend that students refer to the comprehensive glossary as they work through the book.

Contemporary Accounting has been written in a manner which students find easy to read. The response to the first five editions of this book has been very positive. However, there are several changes in the sixth edition of the book. These changes have been made in response to comments from users of the book, and also in response to changes occurring in education and business.

Summary of major changes

- Pedagogical changes – The learning objectives for each chapter are now referenced throughout the chapter. The end-of-chapter summaries have been rewritten as a summary relating to each learning objective. We have also included review exercises throughout each chapter, with solutions at the end of the chapter. This enables students to test their understanding of issues as they read through each chapter.
- Chapter 2 is a revised chapter on the financial reporting framework in Australia. It incorporates the material on the role of the auditor from Chapter 13 in the fifth edition. The Australian approach to the adoption of the Australian equivalents to International Financial Reporting Standards is explained.
- Chapter 3 has been amended to include some discussion on fair value measurement – given its importance in AIFRS.
- Chapter 4 has been amended to replace the term 'statement of financial position' with 'balance sheet'.
- Chapter 5 has been amended to replace the term 'statement of financial performance' with 'income statement'. The statement of changes in equity (SOCE) has also been added to Chapter 5. The purpose of the SOCE is to report all changes to equity that are taken directly to the equity section of the balance sheet together with the profit or loss for the period (therefore showing the total changes to the equity for the period). We have also included a brief discussion on the future of the performance reporting statement.
- Chapter 7 has been revised to include commentary about the valuation rule for the inventories of a not-for-profit entity.
- Chapter 8 has been revised to include discussion about the use of trade credit.
- Chapter 9 has been revised to include discussion about the treatment of intangible assets in accordance with AASB 138 *Intangible Assets*.
- Chapter 10 has been revised to include details about the classification of preference shares and other financial instruments under AIFRS. More explanation is also included about the meaning of short-term, medium-term and long-term sources of finance.
- Chapter 11 has been revised to include the statement of changes in equity as one of the financial statements produced by a company.
- Chapter 13 is a substantially revised chapter. As mentioned earlier, the section on the external auditor has been relocated to Chapter 2. The section on corporate governance has been updated. Also included in Chapter 13 is a new section on triple bottom line reporting. A triple bottom line report refers to the publication of economic, environmental and social information in an integrated report.
- Chapter 14 has been revised and the section on ratio analysis has been rewritten. Comparison of ratios between Coles Myer and Woolworths are also added. The statement of changes in equity has also been included in this chapter.

- Chapter 21 has been revised and now includes a new section on the Economic Value Added (EVA®) method as another way of measuring performance.
- The 2005 half-yearly report of Woodside Limited is included in Appendix 1. Reference is made to the Woodside financial report throughout the financial accounting section of the sixth edition, enabling readers to acquire an appreciation of the financial report of a real company. There are questions relating to the report at the end of most chapters relating to financial accounting. The questions are intended to encourage students to read and familiarise themselves with financial reports. In the previous five editions we have included the annual financial statements of Woolworths Ltd. Because we wanted to include a set of AIFRS financial statements, we had to use the half-year report for a company with a 31 December year-end, due to the timing of the sixth edition. Woolworths Ltd does not have a 31 December year-end.
- Newspaper articles have been updated in most chapters to illustrate the various topics discussed in the book. Reference to newspaper articles adds realism to the subject matter and interest for students.

RESOURCES GUIDE
FOR THE STUDENT

As you read this text you will find a wealth of features in every chapter to help you master introductory accounting concepts and relate those concepts to business applications. Please take note of the following features:

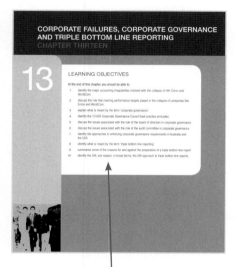

Learning objectives

Are listed at the start of each chapter and give a clear sense of what you will learn in each chapter. These objectives are now also referenced throughout each chapter to enhance your learning of the key concepts they represent.

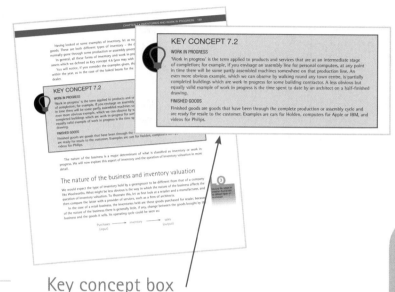

Key concept box

Key concept boxes within each chapter bring special attention to important points, and provide precise definitions

Case studies/newspaper articles

Case studies and *newspaper articles* are included throughout to help you relate your study of introductory accounting to the real-world business environment

Ethics case studies

Provides real world examples and dilemmas to aid
understanding of ethics in accounting

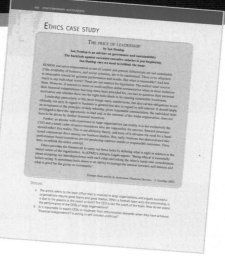

Review Exercises

In-chapter review questions, with solutions at the end of each
chapter, enable you to test your comprehension of key concepts
as you work your way through each chapter.

Appendix

The 2005 half yearly financial report of Woodside Ltd is
included as a reference. This report is fully compliant with
IFRS and includes a statement of changes in equity (author
to confirm). Reference is made to this report throughout
the financial accounting section of this text enabling you
to acquire an appreciation and become familiar with of the
financial report of a real company - questions relating to this
report can be found at the end of most chapters.

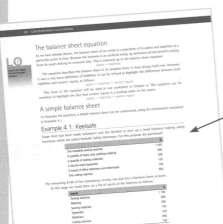

Worked examples

Worked examples will guide you through important concepts

Glossary

A full list of key terms is also available in the glossary, which can be found at the back of the book.

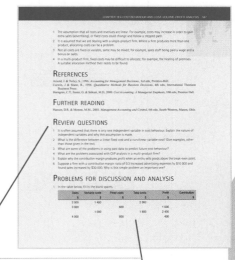

At the end of each chapter you'll find several learning tools to help you review the chapter and key concepts. The aim of these end-of-chapter tools is to help you extend your learning.

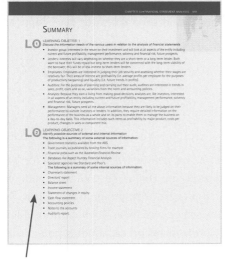

Summary

End-of-chapter summaries provide a review of each chapter's important concepts. Each summary has been written in respect the learning objectives of each chapter to further enhance your understanding of key concepts and issues.

Review questions

End-of chapter review questions enable you to test your comprehension of the key concepts in the chapter.

Problems for discussion and analysis

End-of-chapter problems for discussion and analysis are graded in order of difficulty with the more difficult questions being labeled more suitable for MBA than undergraduate students.

www.thomsonlearning.com.au/higher/accounting/bazley/6e
For updates and news relating to *Contemporary Accounting* sixth edition, please go to the companion website.

RESOURCES GUIDE
FOR THE INSTRUCTOR

Thomson Learning is pleased to provide you with an extensive selection of electronic and online supplements to help you lecture in introductory accounting. These resources have all been specifically developed to supplement *Contemporary Accounting*, sixth edition

WebCT and Blackboard Content

Thomson has developed unique content, which can be placed onto either *WebCT* or *Blackboard* platforms through a cartridge supplied free to adopters. This original content includes objectives and summaries for each topic and practice tests.

ExamView Testbank CD ROM

ExamView helps you create, customise and deliver tests in minutes for both print and online. The Quick Test Wizard and Online Test Wizard guide you step by step through the test-creation process. The program also allows you to see the test you are creating on the screen exactly as it will print or display online. With ExamView's complete word-processing capabilities, you can add an unlimited number of new questions to the bank, edit existing questions and build tests of up to 250 questions using up to 12 question types. You can now export the files into Blackboard or WebCT.

Solutions Manual and PowerPoint Presentation on CD-ROM

This CD-ROM includes solutions to all problems in the text. Also included on the CD-ROM are PowerPoint presentations to accompany *Contemporary Accounting* 6E that reinforce key accounting principles. You can use this presentation as is or edit it to your own requirements.

ACKNOWLEDGEMENTS

We wish to express our appreciation and gratitude to the following people who have contributed in some way to the development of this book: Professor Alan Davison for his support and encouragement; Professor Christine Jubb for helpful suggestions on the content of the sixth edition; Peter Robinson for providing questions on the balanced scorecard; Colette Larsen and Lesley Murrish for the unenviable task of typing many drafts of the very first edition of the book; and to our wives Pam Bazley and Jenny Hancock for their patience, and for proofreading early versions of the very first edition of the book.

We would also like to express our appreciation for all the reviewers who have provided helpful comments and suggestions: Paul Kenny, *Flinders University*

Rebecca Tan, *ANU*

John Doyle, *Notre Dame*

Mary Dunkley, *Swinburne*

Frank Westerman, *Manukau (NZ)*

Rafiuddi Ahmed, *JCU*

We also acknowledge our debt to Aidan Berry and Robin Jarvis, the authors of *Accounting in Business Context* published in the UK. This book was originally based on the British text, although the two books are now significantly different. Responsibility for the opinions expressed and for any errors in this book is entirely our own.

Phil Hancock
Graduate School of Management
University of Western Australia

Michael Bazley
Retired

The authors and publisher would like gratefully to credit or acknowledge permission to reproduce the following:

'Leaders – it's time to close the greed gap', Editorial Opinion, *The Age*, 14/2/03, p. 667; From *Ethical Issues in the Practice of Accounting, 1e* by Albrecht. © 1992. Reprinted with permission of South-Western, a division of Thomson Learning: www.thomsonrights.com, p. 22; © Australian Stock Exchange Limited ABN 98 008 624 691 (ASX) 2002. All rights reserved. This material is reproduced with the permission of ASX. This material should not be reproduced, stored in a retrieval system or transmitted in any form whether in whole or in part without the prior written permission of ASX., pp. 306, 397–8; 'Willpower the key to budgeting' by Kathy Bowler, CPA Australia Manager of Financial Planning, Adelaide Advertiser, 18/11/02, Copyright CPA Australia. Reproduced with the permission of the copyright owner and acknowledgment of the author, Ms. Kath Bowler, p. 646; David Brearley, 'Swallowed by $5bn liabilities gap – HIH – the findings', *The Australian*, 14/1/03, pp. 392–3; 'Obsession with performance leads to accounting scandals' by Larry Chao, *The Nation*, Thailand, 23/9/02. By permission of *The Nation Newspaper*, Thailand, pp. 394–5; © Commonwealth of Australia 2004. All legislation herein is reproduced by permission but does not purport to be the official or authorised version. It is subject to Commonwealth of Australia copyright. The *Copyright Act 1968* permits certain reproduction and publication of Commonwealth legislation. In particular, s.182A of the Act enables a complete copy to be made by or on behalf of a particular person. For reproduction or publication beyond that permitted by the Act, permission should be sought in writing from the Commonwealth available from the Australian Accounting Standards Board. Requests in the first instance should be addressed to the Administration Director, Australian Accounting Standards Board, PO Box 204, Collins St. West, Melbourne, VIC 8007, pp. 96, 98; Extract from Submission to Parliamentary Joint Committee, 2005, Copyright CPA Australia and the Institute of Chartered Accountants in Australia. Reproduced with the permission of the copyright owners, p. 410; James Doran, 'Man Utd takes a beating', *The Times*, 2/9/00, pp. 53–4; Mark Drummond, 'Banking and finance: investors eye BankWest bad debts', *AFR*, 19/12/02, p. 245; Steve Dunbar, 'Good credit process vital in cash flow management', *Otago Daily Times*, 24/10/05, pp. 220–1; Ian Dunlop, 'The price of leadership', *AFR*, 11/10/02, p. 692; Mark Fenton-Jones, 'Board of Ethics to help accountants do right thing' (3/11/05), 'Coming to grips with the IFRS' (23/9/05), 'Beyond the balance sheet: finding a company's value' (24/9/02), 'Don't let cash take a holiday' (15/11/05), *AFR*, pp. 24, 41–3, 107, 360–1; Leon Gettler, Senior Business Journalist at *The Age*, 'Ethics are popular, not always practiced' (7/705), 'It all comes down to bank ability' (28/10/02), *Sydney Morning Herald*, pp. 10–11, 485–6; Peter Gosnell & Joe Hildebrand, 'Cough up Hardies or we'll make you – Premier says there are no obstacles to deal', *Daily Telegraph*, 22/11/05, pp. 417–18; Matthew Hart, 'Bad debts slow CBA recort of $1.204b', *The Courier-Mail*, 14/2/02, pp. 227–8; Louise Hattam, 'Tax penalty plea', *Herald-Sun*, 15/7/02. By permission of the *Herald and Weekly Times*, pp. 372–3; Andrew Heathcote, 'Coca-Cola bites the bullet', *BRW*, 26/5/05, p. 81; Mark Henderson, 'Dome "will not break even"', *The Times*, 14/1/00, p. 579; Elizabeth Knight, 'Inventiveness in inventories', *Sydney Morning Herald*, 9/9/01, pp. 204–5; Andrew Main, 'Governance council chief warns of audit upheaval', *AFR*, 19/2/03, p. 401; Sue Mitchell, 'Big savings from systems to replenish the shelves', *AFR*, 24/2/04, pp. 192–3; Lauren Mulhall, 'Reaping rewards', *The Courier-Mail*, 24/8/02, pp. 670–1; Geoffrey Newman, 'Bad debt forces angry ANZ to take another $50m hit', *The Australian*, 19/6/04, p. 244; News Limited, 10/7/02, p. 87; Katrina Nicholas, 'Suncorp monitors the bozo layer', *AFR*, 17/7/01, pp. 545–6; Anne O'Donnell, 'Investing for a better world', *The Canberra Times*, 19/2/05, pp. 404–6; Wall Street Journal by Mitchell Pacelle. Copyright 2002 by DOW JONES & COMPANY, INC.. Reproduced with permission of DOW JONES & COMPANY, INC. in the format Textbook via Copyright Clearance Center, pp. 391–2; John Parsons, 'Missing measure leaves NAB floundering', *AFR*, 27/5/05. Resource Alternatives Australia/Australian Productivity Council www.apcouncil.com.au, p. 681; Ian Porter, 'BHP Steel's gearing under 20%

"sensational"', *The Age*, 12/4/02, p. 300; Ian Ramsay, 'Public show and tell is the way to incentivise directors and their companies to behave nicely', *The Age*, 21/7/05, pp. 416–17; Jane Schulze, 'Media to feel IFRS cut the deepest', *The Australian*, 10/1/05, pp. 269–70; John Shanahan, 'Panic will ruin good prospects', *BRW*, 13/11/03, pp. 296–7; Wall Street Journal by Rebecca Smith. Copyright 2002 by DOW JONES & COMPANY, INC., Reproduced with permission of DOW JONES & COMPANY, INC. in the format Textbook via Copyright Clearance Center, p. 308; 'Measuring profit with EVA highlights performance' by G. Bennet Stewart and A. Thompson, *The Nation*, Thailand, 11/11/02. By permission of *The Nation Newspaper*, Thailand, pp. 677–8; Paul Tomasch, 'Telco boss unfazed by dud figures, court told', *The Courier-Mail*, 10/2/05, pp. 389–90; Paul Thompson, 'SIA profit due to depreciation', *Business Times Singapore*, 25/4/02, pp. 18, 265–6; Joanna Tovia, 'Decoding the mumbo jumbo – secrets of reading company reports', *The Courier-Mail*, 7/12/02, pp. 456–7; Kath Walters, 'Audit is the pot of gold', *BRW*, 10/4/03, pp. 60–1; Leonie Wood, 'Retailers rebound on Woolies' whopper', *The Age*, 29/8/00, pp. 514–15; Hui Yuk-min, 'Professional ingredient in recipe for success', *South China Morning Post*, 30/8/00. Reproduced by permission of the *South China Morning Post*, pp. 329–30.

Every attempt has been made to trace and acknowledge copyright holders. Where the attempt has been unsuccessful, the publishers welcome information and would redress the situation.

INTRODUCTION TO ACCOUNTING
CHAPTER ONE

1

LEARNING OBJECTIVES

At the end of this chapter, you should be able to:

1   understand what is meant by the term 'accounting'

2   explain the difference between management accounting and financial accounting

3   identify who the main users of accounting information are, and the main purposes for which the information is used

4   identify the limitations of accounting information

5   discuss the factors that influence the choice of accounting systems for different types of organisations

6   explain what is meant by the term 'economic consequences' and relate this to the choice of accounting policies

7   discuss the importance of ethics in accounting, and business in general

8   explain what is meant by ethical behaviour

9   identify the factors that should help determine appropriate ethical behaviour for accountants

10   identify career opportunities for accountants.

Introduction

This chapter discusses the role of accounting, its uses and its users. It will also give you an appreciation of the role of accounting within a business organisation and in its dealings with others. We introduce some ideas about the ways in which accounting helps managers to meet business objectives by, for example, providing the information necessary to make a decision about buying or renting premises. The way in which the size and type of the organisation affects its accounting will be discussed. For example, in a small family restaurant the accounting requirements are much less complex than in a large business such as Westpac Banking Corporation. Another factor that both affects and is affected by accounting is the commercial environment. The influence of the commercial environment on accounting can be through government legislation such as the adoption of a new corporations act or through the introduction of a Goods and Services Tax (GST). Besides government action, accounting can be affected at this level by changes in technology. For instance, the introduction of information technology has allowed accounting information to be provided quickly and efficiently, thus enabling different decisions to be made than might otherwise have been the case. In addition to accounting in the business sector, we also briefly discuss accounting in the public and not-for-profit sectors. Finally, we look at the limitations of accounting information. As with most sources of information, there are imperfections. From this brief résumé we can see that the accounting activity interacts with all levels of business.

Accounts are normally seen as a series of figures, which may give the impression that they are only a form of commercial arithmetic. These figures are, in fact, a convenient way of summarising and reporting information that would be indigestible in narrative form. If you were asked to provide a report that gives details of the value of everything you own, it would be simpler to use figures to represent the value, rather than words. The value of some things (i.e. good health, lead-free petrol or a qualification such as a degree) is difficult to express in numerical terms. These examples do not lend themselves to numerical analysis, but this has not stopped people assigning a monetary value to them.

In order to understand the role and importance of accounting in the context of business organisations, it is necessary to decide what accounting means. If you were to look up the word 'account' in *Roget's Thesaurus* you would be directed to words such as 'report' and 'narration'. Further investigation would reveal that it is also referred to as 'commercial arithmetic', 'double-entry bookkeeping' and so on. These alternatives imply totally different things: a report is something that conveys information for a particular purpose, while commercial arithmetic implies a mechanical exercise following agreed rules or principles.

Besides problems about what accounting can and should document, other issues need to be considered; for example, whether numerical format is the best format. We also need to consider whom the report is for and what its purpose is. For instance, you may give different accounts of your car's capabilities to a prospective buyer and to a mechanic to whom you have taken it for repairs. In both cases the description could be true, but the prospective buyer may be given general details about the car's performance and exterior finish while the mechanic is told all the problems requiring attention. So we can see that the question of defining accounting has many facets: what you report, how you report, to whom you report and for what purpose you report. We shall look at these issues in more detail later in this chapter. First, in order to get a better idea of what accounting is generally understood to be about, let us examine some definitions contained in the accounting literature.

What is accounting?

There are a number of definitions of accounting and they have changed over time in response to the changing accounting environment. One definition that has stood the test of time is that given by the American Accounting Association in *A Statement of Basic Accounting Theory* (also known as *ASOBAT*), which defines accounting as:

LO 1

Understand what is meant by the term 'accounting'

> the process of identifying, measuring and communicating economic information to permit informed judgement and decisions by users of the information. [1966, page 1]

First, this definition states the purpose of accounting. Second, it states that accounting has a number of components – some technical (such as measuring the data), some analytical (such as identifying the data), and some that require further information (such as the communication of this economic information to users: who are these users and what form does this information take?). Finally, the definition implies that the information has value in the decision-making process. The definition assumes that economics concerns any situation in which a choice must be made involving scarce resources.

Another definition was offered by the American Institute of Certified Public Accountants (AICPA), in the 1973 Trueblood Report (titled *Objectives of Financial Statements*), which looks to the role of accounting in decision making. The report lists 12 objectives which emphasise this decision-making process. They can be summarised as follows:

- to provide information, through financial statements, for the making of economic decisions
- to provide information for predicting, comparing and evaluating the effectiveness of management's use of scarce resources
- to provide information to predict and evaluate the going concern of an entity
- to provide information on earnings, cash flows, profitability and the financial position of the entity.

The usefulness of accounting information for decision making is reinforced by accounting concepts (known as the conceptual framework or the *Framework*), discussed in more detail in Chapter 2.

This gives us a clue to the fact that accounting is closely related to other disciplines (we are recording economic data), and it also gives us some clue as to the uses of accounting information; that is, for reporting on what has happened and as an aid to decision making and control of the entity.

A definition from the *Macmillan Dictionary of Accounting* (Parker 1986) states:

> accounting, in broad terms, is the preparation and communication to users of financial and economic information. The information ideally possesses certain qualitative characteristics. Accounting involves the measurement, usually in monetary terms, of transactions and other events pertaining to accounting entities. Accounting information is used for stewardship, control and decision making.

This suggests that the role of accounting information within an organisation is at the very core of running a successful organisation.

The use of accounting information for business decision making is also brought out clearly in the definition given by the American Accounting Principles Board in 1970:

> Accounting is a service activity. Its function is to provide quantitative information, primarily financial in nature, about economic entities that is intended to be useful in making economic decisions, in making reasoned choices among alternative courses of action. *(APB 4)*

The fact that accounting is described as a service activity reinforces the point made earlier: in order to understand the usefulness of accounting, we need to know who uses it and for what purpose.

KEY CONCEPT 1.1

ACCOUNTING

Important points made in these definitions are that:
- accounting is about quantitative information
- the information is likely to be financial in nature
- it should be useful for decision making in the allocation of scarce resources.

Explain the difference between management accounting and financial accounting

For what purpose is accounting information used?

This question can be answered on at least two levels: that of the individual and that of the entity. At the individual level, people can use accounting information to help them control the level of their expenditure, to assist in planning future levels of expenditure, to help them raise additional finance (through, for example, mortgages or hire-purchase) and decide the best way to spend their money. Thus, we see that for the individual, accounting can have three functions: planning, controlling and decision support.

At the level of the entity, accounting is used to control the activities of the organisation, to plan future activities, to assist in raising finance, and to report upon the activities and success of the entity to interested parties.

You will note that the major difference between the two levels is that in the case of an entity, besides its uses in planning, controlling and decision making (which are all internal activities or functions), accounting also has what we could describe as an external function; that is, providing information to people outside the entity. The latter function is usually met through the medium of annual accounts or financial reports and is often referred to as '*financial accounting*'. The external users require the information that is contained in the financial reports to use in the decision-making process, or to evaluate what management has done with the money invested in the business.

Besides meeting the needs of external users, the system that produces the financial accounting reports also meets some of the needs of internal users. One need is to analyse the results of past actions. This requires information on actual outcomes; these can then be evaluated against the projected outcomes, and reasons for differences can be identified so that appropriate actions can be taken. This is only one of a number of needs that managers have. Their other needs are met through different reports that are based upon information provided by the internal accounting system.

The internal accounting system, which may be in addition to the system which underpins the external financial reporting system, is often referred to as the '*management accounting*' function. The major difference between financial accounting and management accounting is that management accounting is primarily directed towards providing information of specific use to managers, whereas financial accounting information, which is often less detailed, has many users apart from managers. This leads us back to the question which we posed earlier regarding the users of accounting information.

Who uses accounting information?

LO 3
Identify who the main users of accounting information are, and the main purposes for which the information is used

Whether accounting information relates to the activities of an individual or to a business entity, its users can be placed in two broad categories:

- those inside the entity – the managers or, in the case of a small business, the owner
- those outside the entity, including banks, analysts, the government, tax authorities, investors, creditors and trade unions.

INTERNAL USERS

The major internal user is the management of an entity. For a small entity this is likely to be the owner, or a small number of individuals in the case of a partnership. However, many businesses are much larger and are owned by numerous individuals or groups of individuals, as is the case with large entities such as Coles Myer, Woolworths, National Australia Bank or Woodside Ltd.

Often the major investors themselves are owned by others, as is the case with the major financial institutions. In such a situation, it is extremely unlikely that the actual owners would or could take an active part in the day-to-day running of the entity. Consider the chaos if all the people who bought shares in Telstra tried to take an active part in the day-to-day running of that business. Instead, these owners or shareholders delegate the authority for the day-to-day running to a group of directors and managers.

These directors and managers are involved in the routine decision-making activities of the entity and are the equivalent of the owner in a small business in terms of their information needs. These needs are normally met by unpublished reports of various kinds, usually based on information that is provided through both the financial accounting system and the management accounting system. The exact nature of the reports varies from entity to entity. A department store may require information about the profitability of each of its departments, whereas a factory producing a small number of different products is likely to require information about the profitability of each product.

The form of each report will also vary according to its purpose. If the purpose of the report is to assist management, it needs to show the past transactions and performance, probably measured against some predetermined standard. For planning purposes, however, a forecast of what is likely to happen in the future is more important. These different forms of reports and ways of grouping information are normally referred to under the generic heading of 'management accounting' and this form of accounting is the focus of the second part of this book.

At this stage it is worth briefly summarising the different categories of management accounting reports. To do this we need to make some broad generalisations about the needs of managers and to categorise those needs. In practice, of course, there is a certain amount of overlap between the categories but we need not concern ourselves with this at present. The categories are discussed in greater detail in Chapters 15 to 21. The broad categories that we have referred to in terms of the needs of managers are as follows:

Stewardship

Managers need to protect the entity's economic resources (normally referred to as assets) from, for example, theft, fraud and wastage.

Planning

Managers need to plan activities so that finance can be raised, marketing and promotional campaigns set up and production plans made.

Control

Managers need to control the activities of the entity. This includes measures such as setting sales targets, managing human resources, ensuring that there are sufficient raw materials to meet the demands of production and sufficient goods in stock to satisfy customer demand. It will also include identifying where targets can be set.

Decision making

Managers need to make specific decisions. For example: Should we produce the item ourselves or buy it in? How much will it cost to produce a particular item? How much money will we need in order to run the entity?

A moment's reflection leads us to the conclusion that management accounting is a vast area in its own right and so, rather than getting deeply involved at this stage, let us first look at the other broad area we identified – the needs of users outside the entity: the external users. We shall be returning to the needs of internal users in more detail in Chapter 15.

Review exercise 1

What are the needs of internal users? Can you identify any other needs of internal users? If so, can you suggest how these would be met?

EXTERNAL USERS

We need to establish who the external users are. The *Framework*, to be discussed in more detail in Chapter 2, lists the primary users of financial information. These primary users can be divided into three groups, as follows:

- *resource providers*: employees, lenders (those who lend money to the entity; for example, bankers), creditors, suppliers (those who supply the entity with goods and services) and, in the case of business entities, investors (that is, shareholders – the owners of the entity)
- *recipients of goods and services*: those who benefit from the provision of goods and services by the reporting entity; that is, customers
- *parties performing a review or oversight function*: government, trade unions and special interest groups acting on behalf of the general public; for example, Greenpeace.

These groups are normally provided with information by means of published annual reports. This type of accounting is generally referred to as financial accounting. In order to decide to what extent the annual reports meet the needs of the external users and to understand more fully the importance of accounting, we shall briefly discuss the needs of the external users listed above.

Owners and shareholders

As we have said, in the case of small entities the owners are likely to be actively engaged in the day-to-day operations of the entity. In these small entities, the owners' needs are often met by the management accounting information and reports.

KEY CONCEPT 1.2

FINANCIAL ACCOUNTING

Financial accounting can be thought of broadly as that part of the accounting system that tries to meet the needs of various external user groups. It does this by means of an annual report which includes an income statement, a balance sheet, a statement of changes in equity, a cash flow statement, information required by law and any additional information which the entity wishes to supply.

As the entity grows, however, it is likely that the owners will become divorced from its immediate and routine operations and will, therefore, not have access to the management accounting information, which in any case may be too detailed for their requirements. This is the case in companies listed on a stock exchange. (A listed or quoted company is one whose shares are traded in an open market where demand and supply govern the price of the share.) It is also the case in a number of other types of entities such as public sector and not-for-profit entities where the functions of management are carried out by people on behalf of the major stakeholders/owners.

In all these cases, the major stakeholders/owners need to know:
- whether the entity has done as well as it should have done
- whether the managers have looked after, and made good use of, the resources of the entity.

In order to evaluate whether the entity has done well and whether resources have been adequately used, it is necessary to compare the results of different entities. Information of this type is normally based on past results, and under certain conditions it can be provided by financial accounts.

Owners/major stakeholders also need to know how the entity is going to fare in the future. Financial accounting is unlikely to provide this information for a variety of reasons, in particular because it is largely, if not exclusively, based on the past. Past results may be taken into account as one piece of information among many when one is trying to predict the future, but in a changing world it is unlikely that past results will be repeated because conditions will have changed.

Although there are limitations concerning the usefulness of the information in annual reports, they are often the only form of report available to an owner/major stakeholder who is not involved in the day-to-day activities of the business. Such users therefore have to base their decisions on this information, despite its inadequacies. Therefore, for example, a shareholder – who is, after all, a part-owner – may use the accounting information contained in the annual report (by comparing the results of the business with those of another business) to decide whether to sell his or her shares.

In practice, the shareholder's involvement in this process of making comparisons, in the case of a quoted company, is likely to be fairly indirect. This is because most of the information contained in the annual report has already been looked at by the owner's professional advisers – accountants, stockbrokers or financial analysts. The investor and owner are likely to base their decision on the professional advice they receive, rather than relying upon their own interpretation of the information contained in annual reports. This is not to say that they will rely exclusively on expert information or that they will not use the information provided in the annual reports to assist with their decision. The reality is likely to be a mixture, the balance of which will depend on the degree of financial sophistication of the shareholders or owners. The less sophisticated they are, the more reliance they will have to place on their expert advisers. Students can study the financial statements of various universities to see how much money they spend on resources such as the library and computing before deciding which university to choose for their courses.

Lenders

People and organisations lend money in order to earn a return on that money. They are, therefore, interested in whether the entity is making sufficient profit to provide them with their return (usually in the form of interest). This information is normally provided in the income statement (previously called the statement of financial performance). They are also interested in ensuring that the entity will be able to repay the money it has borrowed; therefore, they need to ascertain what resources an entity controls and what it owes. This information is normally provided in the balance sheet (previously called the statement of financial position).

Research has shown that, in practice, bankers use a mixture of different approaches to arrive at a lending decision. The choice of approach has been shown to be related to the size of the entity. In the case of smaller entities the security-based approach, which emphasises the availability of economic resources to meet repayments in the event of business failure, predominates and the emphasis is clearly on the balance sheet. However, with very large businesses the approach adopted is more likely to be the 'going concern' approach where the emphasis is on the profitability of the entity.

Suppliers of goods

Goods can either be supplied on the basis that they are paid for when they are supplied or that they will be paid for at some agreed date in the future. In each case the supplier will be interested to know whether the entity is likely to stay in business and whether it is likely to expand or contract. Both these needs relate to the future; therefore, they can never be adequately met by information in the annual report because this relates to the past.

Suppliers of goods who are not paid immediately will be interested in assessing the likelihood of getting paid. This assessment is partially helped by the annual report: the balance sheet shows what resources are controlled by the entity and what is owed, and also gives an indication of the liquidity of the controlled resources. However, the balance sheet has limited usefulness for predicting the future: often the information is many months out of date by the time it is made public, because in most cases it is only published annually.

Customers

Like suppliers, customers are interested in an entity's ability to survive and, therefore, carry on supplying them with goods. For example, if you are assembling cars you need to be sure that the suppliers of components are not about to go bankrupt. The importance of this has increased with the introduction of techniques such as just-in-time management. (Briefly, this means that stocks of parts at the production centre are kept to a minimum, reducing the cost of storage space and parts. Parts are delivered to the production centre just in time, before the stocks run out.) The customers in this situation need to see that the entity is profitable, that it has sufficient resources to pay what it owes, and that it is likely to remain in business and supply components efficiently and on time. Some of these information needs are met, at least partially, by the financial statements.

Employees

Employees depend on the survival of the entity for their wages and therefore are interested in whether the entity is likely to survive. In the long term, an entity needs to make a profit in order to survive. The income statement may assist the employee in assessing the future viability of the company.

The employee may also be interested in ascertaining how well the entity is doing, compared with other similar entities, for the purposes of wage negotiations – although the accounts are only useful for this purpose if certain conditions are met. The accounts can also be used internally for wage negotiations because they provide evidence of the company's level of profitability and ability to pay.

The government

The government uses accounting information for a number of purposes, the most obvious of which is the levying of taxes. For this purpose it needs to know how much profit has been made. The profit a company reports to shareholders in its income statement is based on the application of accounting standards and concepts, which we will discuss in Chapter 2. However, the profit upon which a company is assessed for tax purposes is based on the application of the tax rules and regulations. While these rules are often identical to accounting rules, there are instances where they differ. For example, a government may exempt certain income from taxation as an incentive to participants in that industry. This was the case with the gold industry in Australia for many years. Exempt income was not included in gold producers' calculations of their taxable income; however, as it obviously was still income, it was included in their income statement for reporting to shareholders. The government also uses accounting information to produce industry statistics for purposes such as regulation.

In certain cases, the government is both owner and customer (e.g. some state energy commissions) or public watchdog (e.g. the Environmental Protection Authority). It can combine any one of these roles with other roles, such as regulatory authority (e.g. Australian Securities and Investments Commission). For all these purposes the government uses accounting information.

The general public

The general public requires many different types of information about entities in both the public and private sectors. Much of this information is not supplied directly by financial statements. For example, the public might be interested in a company's environmental performance or stance on fair trade issues.

CASE STUDY 1.1

ETHICS ARE POPULAR, NOT ALWAYS PRACTISED
Leon Gettler

Corporate social responsibility [CSR] might be moving into the mainstream but businesses are still struggling to understand it, according to a KPMG global study. The report, by KPMG's global sustainability services, found that 52 per cent of the world's 250 biggest companies issued separate reports on CSR, compared with 45 per cent in 2002, suggesting that CSR was becoming a mainstream issue.

The survey, which included data from the top 100 companies in 16 countries including Australia, also found that while the majority of companies still issued separate CSR reports, more were included in annual reports. KPMG also found there had been a significant shift from focusing on the environment to overall sustainability reporting that included social, ethical, environmental and economic aspects.

However, the study also identified serious gaps in the reports suggesting corporations were having trouble matching the rhetoric. Sixty-one per cent of the reports, for example, included a section on corporate governance, and 53 per cent identified the link between corporate responsibility and corporate governance.

Most reports, however, failed to spell out exactly how governance policies were implemented. While 18 per cent of reports included policies for bribery or corruption, few elaborated on how these commitments were put into practice.

Nearly two-thirds of the companies discussed social policies and expressed their commitment to these issues, but details remained sketchy. Generally, social policy issues were confined to one or more of four areas: core labour standards, working conditions, community involvement and philanthropy.

Similarly, supply-chain issues were mentioned in 80 per cent of cases with almost 70 per cent citing a supplier declaration where, for example, the supplier had to comply with a code of conduct set down by the company.

However, the same companies seemed to have difficulty ensuring that their suppliers were actually complying. Only 16 per cent reported they conducted supplier audits to see how well the codes were being implemented.

'The results suggest that the content of supply-chain reporting is still immature ►

in terms of the depth of issues discussed,' the report said. 'The fact that a minority of companies report on supplier audit could be an indication of the difficulties companies face with accounting for supplier performance and that companies have more developmental work to do before they can prove they "walk the talk" in the supply chain.'

While more companies in the industrialised world depicted themselves as embracing corporate social responsibility, only 25 per cent could canvass the economic impact of their core business operations on society.

Fair trade was mentioned by only 6 per cent of companies. This, however, was limited mostly to initiatives aimed at promoting fair-trade awareness among employees by, for example, providing them with fair-trade-certified food in cafeterias. Little attention was paid to the difficult issues of fair competition in terms of competition issues and procedures for selecting suppliers.

The top countries in terms of CSR reporting are Japan, where 80 per cent of the top 100 report, and Britain (71 per cent). Australia came 11th with 23 per cent.

Sydney Morning Herald, 7 July 2005
© 2005 Copyright John Fairfax Holdings Limited. www.smh.com.au
Not available for re-distribution.

COMMENTARY

The article demonstrates the growing practice of companies reporting on their social and environmental performance. It points out that while the practice of providing such reports is growing, there is great scope for significant improvements in the quality of such reports.

From this brief survey of the users of accounting information and the uses to which it can be put, it is clear that it has effects both within organisations and in the wider commercial environment in which entities operate and in which we live. It should also be clear that this wider environment can use accounting as a tool for entity control. Before going on to consider in detail the impact of accounting upon the commercial environment and vice versa, we should first consider the limitations of accounting information in order to put its potential impact in context.

Review exercise 2

Explain who are the main users of accounting information, some of the main purposes for which that information may be used and which accounting reports they are likely to use.

Limits on the usefulness of accounting information

Identify the limitations of accounting information

It has to be stressed that accounting is only one of a number of sources of information available to decision makers. Other sources of information might be just as important as, if not more important than, the information contained in the accounts that are available to decision makers. You will have the opportunity to examine this in more detail in 'Problems for discussion and analysis' at the end of this chapter.

However, to give you a flavour of what we are talking about, research into bankers' lending practices (referred to earlier) shows that a banker's personal interview with a client is as important as financial information. This is probably because accounting generally reports only on financial items (i.e. those items that can be expressed in financial, or monetary, terms), whereas the information that bankers are trying to derive from the interview is more qualitative (i.e. an impression of the ability of the applicant to run a successful business). It is also possible that the information which accounting provides is only of secondary importance: this would be the case where new technology has made the precise costing of a product irrelevant because the product is obsolete.

In general, financial accounting information relates to the past, whereas the decisions that need to be taken normally relate to the future. Thus, unless the past is a reasonable predictor of the future, accounting information will have limited value for this purpose. In the real world, because of the impact of such things as changes in technology, innovations, changing fashions and inflation, the past is unlikely to be a very good predictor of the future.

Besides these problems, there is also the question of what is and what is not included in the financial accounts. For instance, some items that it is generally agreed should be included in financial reports are difficult to measure with any accuracy; therefore, the figures become subjective. A good example of this problem is an unfinished building. How do we decide on a figure to represent something that is only half complete? Another example is the problem of deciding how long something is going to last. A motor car, for instance, clearly loses value the older it gets. A business might decide that a car ceases to be useful to it after four or five years, but this is to some extent an arbitrary decision because there are many older cars that still serve a useful purpose.

In addition to the problem of deciding how long things will last or what stage of completion has been reached, certain items are difficult to quantify in terms of value and are not easily included in financial reports. For example, the value of a football club is dependent on its ability to attract supporters; this, in turn, is dependent on its ability to succeed, which is dependent on the abilities of the players, and so on. However, it is difficult to decide what value to place on a player because this value will vary according to, for example, the player's fitness. Even so, certain football clubs in the Australian Football League attempt to quantify the value of their players. In the United Kingdom and the United States, several basketball, baseball, soccer and gridiron teams also follow this practice.

In addition to the questions raised above, there are many factors concerned with the natural and commercial environment which need to be taken into account but which cannot be adequately included in accounts, although they may be quantifiable in monetary terms. Examples are the potential market for the product, tariff restrictions, export subsidies and environmental issues. If information about these factors were included in the annual reports of a business, a loss of competitive advantage could result.

Finally, we have to deal with the fact that accounting information is expressed in monetary terms and assumes that the monetary unit is stable over time. This is patently not the case. Although there has been much discussion on the problems of accounting in times of inflation, no agreed solution has yet been found.

We can conclude from this discussion that, while it is clear that accounting provides some information that is useful to decision makers, we must bear in mind the following important points:

- The information is only a part of that which is necessary to make 'effective' decisions.
- Accountancy is an inexact science and depends on a number of judgements and estimates.
- The end result of the accounting process can only be as good as the inputs, and in times of rising prices some of these inputs are of dubious value.
- Accounting systems can be counterproductive; for example, the maximisation of a division's profit may not always ensure the maximisation of the profit of the entity.

Nevertheless, it is clear that accounting is vital to the running of a healthy and prosperous entity and, arguably, it is also an essential prerequisite for a prosperous economy. It will therefore be useful to look at accounting in the wider context of an entity and its regulatory environment. We examine how the accounting function interacts with and is different from other business functions. We will also examine the various factors that influence the choice of an accounting system – including regulatory and environmental considerations.

Review exercise 3

What are the limitations of accounting information?

Accounting as a business function

Theoretically, the accounting department, like the personnel department, operates in an advisory capacity only – providing information for managers to make decisions. In practice, however, the financial elements controlled by the accounting function and the information it generates are so central to the operation of the entity that the influence of accounting is often pervasive. Although accounting is essential to the smooth running of the business, it does not have as direct an impact as, for example, the buying department or the production line. Its effects are generally subtler, although they may in certain instances be very obvious. For example, if the accounting information indicates that expenses are too high, this may have dramatic repercussions in other functional areas. Training and recruitment budgets may be immediately frozen, affecting the work of the personnel department and other operating departments, and possibly reducing both staffing and skills. Alternatively, a decision may be taken to stop expenditure on a current advertising campaign, thus having a direct effect on the work of the marketing department.

Accounting can have unintended effects too. For example, if sales representatives are judged solely on their sales this may lead them to sell goods to customers who are unlikely to pay in order to achieve the sales targets that have been set. It can also be a very dangerous tool if used in the wrong way; for example, targets could be set to achieve cost savings on a production line with no account taken of the effect on quality or employee safety. Similarly, if accounting is used by people who do not understand its limitations it can lead to wrong decisions. If, for example, a person is unaware that accounting, as generally used, takes no account of rising prices, goods could be sold at less than they cost to produce.

The importance of accounting within a business should not be underestimated. It provides the basic information by which managers and owners can judge whether the business is meeting its objectives. Its importance is shown by the high salaries that accountants can command and by the prevalence of accountants on the boards of directors of our major public companies.

Accounting is also different from other business functions in that it is not only a function but also an industry. The accounting industry sells accounting and other advisory services to other businesses and is itself a major employer of graduate labour.

Choice of accounting systems

Discuss the factors that influence the choice of accounting systems for different types of organisations

Accounting is used within business to evaluate alternative strategies – such as making a component or buying it in from a supplier. Therefore, it shapes business plans and activities. At the same time, it is itself a function of the type of activity that a business engages in and of the strategies a business adopts. In other words, the accounting system not only influences business strategies but is itself influenced by the goals, size and structure of the organisation. For example, the accounting system that is appropriate for a local builder who does one job at a time and who can clearly identify the amount of time and materials being used on that job is not appropriate for a manufacturing plant that uses one building and many machines to produce multiple products all at the same time. In the latter case, to identify the materials used and the labour inputs for a specific product requires a much more sophisticated system of accounting. Accounting systems are variable and depend on the type of activity or activities in which a business is engaged and on the levels of activity.

Clearly, the organisation's goals will have a major impact on the accounting system it uses. For example, developing an accounting system with the primary purpose of measuring profit would be wholly inappropriate for a not-for-profit entity such as a government or public sector entity. Similarly, the requirements, in terms of accounting reports, will be very different in the case of a workers' co-operative, the Department of Education and Training and a profit-oriented company. The co-operative's members are likely to be more interested in their pay and their share of the surplus generated than in the entity's profitability. Shareholders in a company, on the other hand, are likely to be more interested in judging overall profitability and comparing that with alternative investments. In the case of the Department of Education and Training it may be that the owners, that is, the general public, are primarily interested in the service they have received rather than the Department's profitability.

Furthermore, the way in which an organisation is structured determines the type of accounting system that is needed. If a brewery operates all of its hotels by putting managers into them, it will need an accounting system that allows for the payment of regular salaries and bonuses based upon achieving preset targets. These targets are normally set in terms of barrelage so it will need to know what the normal barrelage of each hotel is; it will also need to know the mark-up on items such as spirits and soft drinks, and the approximate mix of sales in order to ensure that its managers are not misappropriating the profits. If, however, it establishes its organisation so that each publican is a tenant of the brewery, a different accounting system will be required, because the publicans are not paid a salary or bonus – their remuneration comes from the profits they make from selling the beers, wines and spirits.

We have already alluded to the effect of the size of an organisation on its accounting system. The larger and more disparate the organisation, the greater the need for organisational controls. These are achieved through a system of accountability which makes managers responsible for the performance of their divisions and which provides reports that can be used by senior managers to evaluate the performance of their subordinates and of the organisation as a whole.

As we have already mentioned, it is vital that the accounting system is tailored to the needs of the organisation. If it is not, management may be unable to control the organisation and, indeed, it may have dysfunctional effects. Frequently, in the case of a small business, little accounting information is available on a day-to-day basis. This may be because the operations are sufficiently simple not to warrant much information, but is more likely to be because the owner does not have the skills to produce the information and the costs of hiring the necessary expertise are perceived as outweighing the potential benefits. It is often the case in small businesses that the only time detailed accounting reports are produced is at the end of the year to meet the needs of the tax collector and when the bank demands them as a prerequisite to granting a loan or extending an overdraft facility.

Regulatory and environmental considerations

In general, the environmental aspects of a business which interact significantly with accounting are: the state, technology and labour. Accounting is also affected by and affects the economy. For example, a country such as Brazil, which suffers from hyperinflation out of necessity, uses costs other than original costs in its accounting reports because the value of the monetary unit in which accounting information is expressed changes so quickly. We have already discussed the potential uses of accounting information by employees and their organisations, such as trade unions. We have mentioned different forms of organisation such as not-for-profit organisations. For example, in the case of most not-for-profit charitable organisations, there is no requirement for the publication of accounting information, whereas for companies, not only the form but also the content of their annual reports is laid down by legislation in the *Corporations Act 2001*. The *Corporations Act* specifies Australian Accounting Standards (referred to as AASB standards) for companies that are reporting entities; the setting of these standards is discussed in Chapter 2. All public sector reporting entities must also comply with all Australian Accounting Standards, except in cases where the Treasurer's Instructions vary or amend a standard. A similar situation prevails in most western countries, although the importance of legislation in relation to accounting standards varies from country to country. Similarly, the reporting requirements are different in non-capitalist countries where the importance afforded to the income statement is considerably less.

Technology has also had a major effect within the accounting function as accounting systems have become computerised. This has allowed accountants to free themselves from the mundane tasks of recording and to become more involved in decision support and strategic issues. At another level, however, new technology has imposed and is still imposing challenges to accounting thought. Systems that were appropriate in a labour-intensive environment are found to be lacking in the age of flexible manufacturing systems, such as just-in-time management and computer-controlled manufacturing environments.

Review exercise 4
What are the major determinants of a useful accounting system?

Economic consequences of accounting information

LO 6

Explain what is meant by the term 'economic consequences' and relate this to the choice of accounting policies

The development of accounting standards is the responsibility of the appropriate accounting standard-setting board. We discuss the development of accounting standards in Chapter 2. The selection of appropriate accounting policies for an entity is the responsibility of management. Where an accounting standard exists, the policies must comply with the standard. In some cases the standard allows a choice of policies and in other cases no standard may exist. In these instances, the management of an entity has a choice as to the appropriate accounting policy to select.

As we will see in Chapter 2, the primary objective for the standard setters in selecting particular accounting standards is to provide useful information to the users of financial statements. As preparers of financial statements incur costs in complying with accounting standards, the standard setters attempt only to impose requirements where the expected benefits exceed costs.

Managers do not necessarily adopt the same objectives in the way they select appropriate accounting policies for their entity. Accounting policies affect the numbers that appear in the financial statements and these numbers can affect the wealth of managers and firms via:

- compensation plans
- debt contracts
- political costs.

Compensation Plans

Many entities reward their managers through a fixed salary and an annual bonus. The bonus may be determined as a percentage of net profit. The bonus scheme, it is argued, provides an incentive to managers to increase net profit. Increases in net profit are in the best interests of shareholders. Therefore, the bonus scheme is intended to align the interests of managers more closely to the shareholders.

However, a consequence of the bonus scheme is that managers may also be motivated to increase reported profit by the appropriate selection of profit-increasing accounting policies. Thus, this strategy may increase reported profit when the underlying profitability of the entity has not increased. This has been described as a cosmetic increase in profits rather than a real increase in profits.

Some spectacular corporate collapses in 2001–02 such as HIH, One.Tel and Harris Scarfe in Australia and Enron and WorldCom in the USA raised considerable public outcry about many issues including the use of share options as part of the remuneration packages for corporate executives. There is a view that the use of share options creates incentives for managers to do almost anything to keep reporting large profits so that the price of the company's shares continues to rise. In turn, this increases the value of the manager's share options. Such high-profile corporate collapses led to considerable debate about the appropriateness of using share options as part of executive remuneration, given the highly publicised impact of such a policy on financial reporting.

DEBT CONTRACTS

Many lenders require a contract before lending money to a borrower. Such contracts may impose certain restrictions on the borrower. For example, a new loan contract may contain a clause which states that if the borrower's level of debt exceeds a certain level the loan must be immediately repaid in full. The measurement of the level of debt is based on the total liabilities figure as reported in the borrower's balance sheet. Another common clause in debt contracts relates to the number of times the net profit covers interest expense.

These clauses in the debt contracts are based on accounting numbers as reported in the company's financial statements. Therefore, if an entity is approaching the limits of a clause in a debt contract, there are incentives for managers to select appropriate accounting policies which allow the entity to avoid being in violation of the debt contract.

POLITICAL COSTS

Political costs refer to the costs imposed on an entity via regulation, taxation and closer public scrutiny of its affairs. Some accountants argue that bigger firms like News Corporation are subject to more political costs. Size is often measured in terms of net profit, total assets and total sales. These are all numbers determined by the application of accounting policies. Therefore, there are incentives for managers of large entities to select profit-decreasing accounting policies.

A further argument suggests that incentives exist for certain types of businesses, such as telephone or electricity organisations, to choose profit-decreasing accounting policies. This choice is made at a time when the organisation wishes to increase the charges for its service. It is politically more acceptable to increase charges when reported profits have decreased.

Therefore, political costs create incentives for managers of large organisations to select accounting policies that decrease reported profits. This is clearly the reverse of the argument under compensation plans. The argument under compensation plans is that the manager's self-interest prevails. With political costs, it is the interests of the organisation which prevail. Ultimately, if the large organisation attracts lower political costs, its managers will be rewarded.

THE DUAL REASON FOR SELECTION OF ACCOUNTING POLICIES

The selection of appropriate accounting policies may be based on the objective of providing useful information to users, or it may be based on economic consequences. These two objectives need not be mutually exclusive and, as you read the chapters which follow, you should consider the role of both these objectives. Shareholders and lenders may initiate strategies to mitigate against the incentives for managers to select accounting policies based on economic consequences.

In this event, the selection of accounting policies is more likely to be based on the objective of providing useful information to users. In the next section we discuss the important issue of ethics in business and accounting. A small ethics case study is located at the end of each chapter.

CASE STUDY 1.2

SIA PROFIT DUE TO DEPRECIATION
By Paul Thompson

I REFER to your article 'SIA hints net profit may be above $200m' by Andrea Tan (*BT*, April 20). First, may I say that, for the sake of the hardworking staff, I certainly hope it is true. They would then stand a good chance of getting previously implemented wage cuts restored. Second, may I bring to investors' attention – if they are not already aware – that SIA is engaging in earnings management, much like their peers in Europe and North America.

SIA's earnings management makes it difficult for me to get excited about the mildly bullish sentiment surrounding SIA. While things are indeed looking up for SIA, it is worth noting that the primary reason it stands any chance of making any profit at all for the year ended March 31, 2002 boils down to what some might call an accounting sleight of hand.

I hold SIA in high regard. SIA is a high-flier in the word of aviation. It offers impeccable service, far better than any other flag carrier I have flown in. It is also one of the world's most profitable airlines and, unlike many like the big US flag carriers and British Airways, it appears to have avoided a free fall into financial losses – and it has averted slashing staff numbers (the latter achievement is especially commendable).

The main reason, however, it has managed to steer clear of reporting losses for the past financial year (announcement is due in early May but SIA, for sure, already knows the score) is through a timely change in its accounting policy on the depreciation of fixed assets.

Depreciation is a major expense for airlines whose balance sheets are bulging with an expensive aircraft fleet. In its half-year report issued last October, soon after the terrorist attack on the World Trade Center, SIA said: 'Commencing this financial year, the company changed its depreciation rate for passenger aircraft, spares and spare engines from 10 years to 20 per cent residual value to 15 years to 10 per cent residual value. This is to bring it more in line with airline industry practice. Aircraft depreciation charge was $133 million lower as a result.'

In other words, SIA's policy change for the six months to Sept 30, 2001 caused expenses to be lower by $133 million and hence profit higher by the same figure. For the full year, the effect is likely to be double – that is, a boost to profits by some $266 million.

I do not doubt SIA when it says that this policy change aligns itself with industry practice. In fact, in 1999, I compared the depreciation policy of SIA with BA and found it to be more conservative. But the fact remains that had it not made this change, SIA would almost certainly be reporting a loss for the year to March 31, 2002 in the next few weeks.

Business Times Singapore, 25 April 2002

COMMENTARY

The article shows how Singapore Airlines was able to increase reported profit by a change in accounting policy. The company stated that the aim of this change was not to boost earnings for the year, but rather to align its depreciation policy with other airlines.

A recurring theme in this book is the impact of accounting rules on a company's reported results. By the time you complete the chapters on financial accounting, you should better appreciate how accounting rules impact on a company's financial statements.

You should understand that, while SIA has changed the way it accounts for the depreciation of its aircraft, the value of the aircraft has not changed. Does this change in profit, resulting from a change in an accounting rule, make SIA more valuable? The answer is 'no', and consequently there should be no change in the value of SIA's shares based on this higher reported profit.

Review exercise 5

What are the economic consequences of accounting policy choice?

Ethics in business and accounting

Figures show that corporate fraud costs billions of dollars each year, as witnessed with the collapse of companies like Enron in the US and HIH in Australia. How does a large public company like HIH collapse, resulting in the loss of billions of dollars? How do we solve problems of corporate fraud and embezzlement?

Discuss the importance of ethics in accounting, and business in general

Dr Rushworth Kidder, president of the US-based Institute for Global Ethics, argues that this will not happen if companies adopt codes of ethics and create departments responsible for monitoring these codes. Employees must receive training about the codes of ethics and should be required to follow them.

WHAT ARE ETHICS?

Much has been written on business or professional ethics (see the References section on page 28), but very few writers have attempted to define this term, perhaps believing that it needs no definition. What do we mean by ethics?

Explain what is meant by ethical behaviour

One could go back several thousand years and note that the word is derived from the Greek *ēthikos* (from ethos meaning 'custom' or 'usage'). As employed by Aristotle, the term included both the idea of 'character' and that of 'disposition'. Ethics means, according to the *Macquarie Dictionary*, 'relating to morals'. From the foregoing it would appear that ethics is concerned with moral behaviour, and by 'moral' we mean that part of human behaviour that is formed primarily by national culture, parental influence, peer groups and religion.

A review of some of the literature on ethics provides some interesting insights into the important area of ethics. Some writers refer to business ethics, which in itself suggests that a particular set of ethics exists for business. This, in fact, is totally untrue as ethics apply to all parts of life and to think that you discard one set of ethics and adopt another as you enter the office is false. Ethics are like your skin: they go everywhere with you.

While it may be difficult to define ethics, Dr Michael Josephson, in an essay entitled 'The need for ethics education in accounting' (1992), identified the following characteristics of an ethical person:

- *honesty and integrity*: honesty is obviously important but we should really be referring to complete honesty or perhaps to not being dishonest. For example, a six-year-old student, when asked by his teacher if he had eaten any of the chocolates she had left on her desk, replied 'No'. The fact was that he had taken the chocolates but had not eaten any. It could be argued that he did not actually lie, but he was still dishonest. Integrity refers to having the courage of one's convictions and acting on principle. Further, it is important that we have good principles. A serial killer who believes all prostitutes are evil is acting in accordance with his own convictions, but he is not a person of integrity
- *promise keeping*: fulfilling a commitment
- *fidelity or loyalty*: the need to be loyal. But loyal to whom or what? The problem of conflicting loyalties is often the cause of ethical problems. In a company an employee could be loyal to his immediate boss, the general manager, the board of directors or the shareholders. The company itself exists in law but it is the people within a company that give it life. In a family relationship, for example, one person can be a mother, a wife, a daughter, a sister, a daughter-in-law, a sister-in-law, an auntie, a cousin and a niece. These different roles invariably lead to situations where being loyal to one party may involve disloyalty to another
- *fairness*: again, this is a subjective term and what is fair to one party may be unfair to another. Consider an umpire in a football game. When he awards a penalty against one side, the supporters of that side often consider the decision unfair while the supporters of the side awarded the penalty consider the decision to be fair
- *caring*: caring for others is perhaps best summed up by the rule 'Do unto others as you would have them do unto you'
- *respect*: while you may not care for everyone you should give them respect
- *responsibility*: complying with the laws of the country and being part of a community
- *excellence*: we endeavour to do our job as well as we possibly can. We expect a surgeon about to remove our appendix to be competent to do this
- *accountability*: to be ethical means to be accountable for your actions.

It is probably no coincidence that Josephson has identified 10 characteristics of an ethical person in the same way as Moses descended from Mount Sinai with the Ten Commandments. Some would argue that an individual's ethical values are better taught in a church than in a business school. A survey of professional ethics was conducted for CPA Australia by Leung and Cooper in 1994. The 1500 respondents to the survey indicated that family upbringing, conduct of peers and practices in the accounting field were the most important factors affecting the ethical conduct of accountants.

WHAT CAUSES UNETHICAL BEHAVIOUR?

Why then do we have huge problems of fraud and embezzlement? Why do people not behave in an ethical manner? Josephson (1992) identified the following five reasons:

- *self-deception*: to believe somehow that because it is business it does not matter. Phrases such as 'everybody does it' or 'to get along, go along' reflect self-deception. A common example is cheating on one's income tax return on the assumption that everybody else does. Just imagine what the streets of a city would be like if everybody dumped rubbish on the street because 'everybody does it'
- *self-indulgence*: the defence for unethical behaviour is the assertion that it was done for someone else's benefit when in fact it was for the benefit of the individual who was being unethical
- *self-protection*: many examples of fraud start from one incident and grow from there. In his book, *Rogue Trader*, Nick Leeson contends that his first illegal trade was done to cover a small error by a colleague. This small error grew to a $16 billion loss
- *self-righteousness*: the assertion that one is right no matter what others think. No doubt Adolf Hitler considered he was right
- *faulty reasoning*: not correctly estimating the costs of being ethical versus unethical. Generally the costs of being ethical ('I will lose my job') are overestimated while the costs of being unethical ('I won't get caught' or 'I will repay this later') are underestimated. In his paper 'Why I compromised my professional code of ethics', McKinley L. Tabor (1992) recounts the costs to his life of unethical behaviour. The costs included imprisonment, loss of family and friends, loss of respect, and other costs, all of which were in excess of what he embezzled from his employer.

ETHICS AND ACCOUNTING

What is the relationship between business and ethics? Are ethics good for business? The answer to such a question depends on how we assess what is good for business. If we use short-term profitability then it may be that on some occasions doing what is ethical may not enhance short-term profitability. It may well improve long-term profitability, but if you are not going to be in the company in the long term, what is the incentive to be ethical? This raises issues about the objectives of business. Is there some conflict between the goal of profit maximisation and ethical behaviour? Is there a conflict between self-interest and ethical behaviour?

LO 9

Identify the factors that should help determine appropriate ethical behaviour for accountants

Two frameworks developed by ethicists which are relevant to our discussion on ethics are utilitarianism and deontology. Utilitarianism judges the moral correctness of an action based entirely on its consequences. The action that should be pursued is the one where the favourable consequences to all parties outweigh the unfavourable consequences. The consequences to all parties that will be affected must be included.

In deontology the underlying nature of the action determines its correctness. There are two types of deontologists. Some feel the action itself is the only thing to be considered, and so lying, for example, is always unacceptable. Other deontologists are of the opinion, for example, that the nature of the action and its consequences in a particular situation should be considered, and so lying in particular circumstances may be acceptable.

Given the enormous costs of fraud and embezzlement, the potential gains to society of ethical behaviour are significant. The difficulty is in developing an appropriate code of ethical behaviour which is adhered to by all people in business.

Business or professional behaviour is governed by sets of rules laid down by the controlling bodies; members of the organisation or profession are expected to follow these rules. In some professions, 'ethics' has come to mean these rules. Professional ethics should be regarded as 'standards of professional conduct (the ethics of lawyers)' (Statsky 1985).

The problems of the late 1990s and early 2000s can, in part, be attributed to some accountants substituting 'the rules' for genuine 'ethical behaviour'. For example, it was acceptable to follow the requirements of the *Corporations Act*, even when, by following the strict letter of the law, one was able to gain an unfair advantage which did not reflect the spirit of the law.

Business or professional ethics is a marrying of the rules of society with the moral principles by which a society is judged. The question of business ethics is well illustrated in this story by W. Albrecht (1992):

> There was once a very wealthy man who loved his money so much that he did not have many friends. In fact, he had only three friends. First, he had a lawyer friend who helped him structure his transactions to take advantage of other people. Second, he had an accountant friend who helped him count his money. And third, he had a minister of religion to whom he went every Sunday to confess the fact that he had taken advantage of others during the week. When he got old and was about to die, he called his three friends together and said, 'I have been wealthy all my life and I cannot stand going to the grave poor. I am going to give you each an envelope with $50 000 in it. I want you to promise me that when I die you will go to my casket and each deposit the envelope in the casket'. They all promised that they would.
>
> A short time later the rich man died. As the three friends passed by the casket, each deposited an envelope. The casket was sealed and the body was buried. Not long after, the minister developed a guilty conscience; he called the other two and said, 'We have to meet and talk about this'. When they met he said, 'You know, I thought about the poor members of my congregation. I thought about that money rotting down there in the grave and I just could not do it. I only put $25 000 in and I kept $25 000 to help the poor'. Then the lawyer said, 'If you really want to know the truth, he had asked me for free legal advice so often that I felt he owed it to me, so I kept $25 000 and only put $25 000 in'. Finally, the accountant said, 'You know I cannot believe you would do that. I cannot believe you would both be unethical. I want you to know that in my envelope was a cheque for the full $50 000'.

As this is a text about accounting, let us look at three of several choices available to the accountant:

- He could have put an empty envelope in the grave, as the deceased only asked him to deposit the envelope. This would have been following the letter of the request but not the spirit.
- He could have done what he did in the story. Here he followed the letter of the request and some would say a small measure of the spirit of the request. Of course, we know the cheque will never be cashed and that the accountant is $50 000 better off. Is the accountant guilty of stealing the money?

- He could have carried out the deceased's wishes to the full, following the letter and the spirit of the request: that is, deposited the full $50 000 in cash in the casket.

As a professional person, the accountant was obliged to carry out, in full, the wishes of his client and friend regardless of his personal feelings or beliefs. Business or professional ethics mean just that: clever or smart alternatives are not acceptable.

Remember, one of the characteristics of an ethical person referred to by Josephson (1992) was promise keeping. All three individuals should not have promised to put the envelope in the casket if, in fact, they knew they could not do it. The lawyer should have asked for his unpaid time to be paid by the wealthy friend. The minister should have asked the friend to consider donating to the church. The accountant did not comply with the spirit of his friend's request and all three acted unethically.

As noted earlier, in some way, a lack of ethics was responsible for some of the gains made by some of the high-flyers in the late 1990s and early 2000s. However, many have since paid high costs for being unethical.

Professional accountants, in the many spheres in which they are of service to the general public and business community, should always be seen to be ethically correct. To this end, each of the major professional accounting bodies in all countries has developed a code of professional ethics. The code is there to assist members in dealing with different types of situations in their professional lives. The CPA Australia survey on professional ethics asked respondents to rank various types of ethical issues. The results showed that the issues of greatest concern were:

- client proposal for tax evasion (83.3 per cent)
- client proposal to manipulate financial statements (80.2 per cent)
- conflict of interest (79.3 per cent)
- presenting financial information in the most proper manner so as not to deceive users (76.3 per cent)
- failure to maintain technical competence in the discharge of duties (71.3 per cent)
- coping with a superior's instructions to carry out unethical acts (70.6 per cent).

The rules of the professional bodies are intended not only to guide but, in some ways, to provide protection from the above types of ethical dilemmas for accountants. However, there are always some who are tempted to move around the rules for personal gain, and in the long run the profession and society are the losers. When dealing with accountants, individuals expect, and deserve to receive, conduct that will enhance the status of all who belong to that profession. Ethics in business and accounting are a matter of judgement based on rules and moral obligations. Case study 1.3 reports on the creation of a new board to be called the Accounting Professional and Ethical Standards Board (APESB). The board has been jointly established by the Institute of Chartered Accountants and CPA Australia.

CASE STUDY 1.3

BOARD OF ETHICS TO HELP ACCOUNTANTS DO RIGHT THING

Mark Fenton-Jones

A new ethics board for the accounting profession has been created to look at issues such as those raised by the Steve Vizard insider trading case.

It will be known as the Accounting Professional and Ethical Standards Board (APESB).

The Institute of Chartered Accountants and CPA Australia will let the board draft ethical standards on tax, financial planning, independence and codes of conduct, a function they now have. But they will still be involved in the drafting process.

'We will have one body that will arbitrate on what is the right standard, and the two bodies will simply make comments on the draft,' ICA chief executive Stephen Harrison said.

Both bodies have denied that the establishment of the board was a response to the controversy earlier this year surrounding Mr Vizard's accountant, Greg Lay.

Mr Lay, an Institute member and then chairman of mid-tier accountants Bentleys MRI, refused to sign a witness statement that was requested by the Australian Securities and Investments Commission.

The commission wanted the statement to use in its case against Mr Vizard for insider trading.

'It will only set standards, it won't investigate. But in circumstances like that, it would probably review what's happened and make sure the standards represent the high standards expected of the profession,' Mr Harrison said.

Accountants who don't follow the standards will be referred to their professional bodies for investigation. Mr Lay appeared before the disciplinary board last month but no decision has been announced.

Peter Lowe, the interim chief executive officer of CPA Australia, said the APESB was the result of a review of the professional bodies' self-regulatory processes following *CLERP 9*.

Both bodies hope the presence of a non-accountant on the board will lead to greater scrutiny by the public and will increase confidence in the profession's standards.

'We don't see any problems with the way we were doing it. We feel that the external environment is changing and expecting greater independence and greater public scrutiny. This was a way of achieving that,' Mr Lowe said.

While the board will ultimately have eight members drawn from the public and corporate sectors, the audit profession, academia and the general public, it will start with six.

In a letter to Roger Cotton, the chief executive officer of the National Institute of Accountants, CPA Australia and the ICA have left open the possibility of the NIA joining the board after it is appointed in January.

Australian Financial Review,
3 November 2005
© 2005 Copyright John Fairfax Holdings
Limited. www.afr.com
Not available for re-distribution.

COMMENTARY

This article reports on the establishment of a new board responsible for the development of ethical standards across a number of areas. As the board has been established by the professional accounting bodies, the success of the board will depend, in part at least, on whether it will operate independently of the professional bodies.

There are a number of good texts available on the issue of ethics and reference to them is made at the end of this chapter. Before completing this chapter we will briefly examine careers in accounting and professional membership.

Review exercise 6

How do you think you will handle your future ethical problems? Can you do anything now to make it easier to handle your future concerns?

Careers in accounting

Accountants are employed in many different areas in both the private and public sectors. This section provides only a brief overview of the different careers for accountants.

L○ 10

Identify career opportunities for accountants

ACCOUNTING FIRMS

Most accounting firms operate as a sole proprietorship or a partnership. The most significant firms are large firms like PricewaterhouseCoopers and Ernst & Young. Large firms provide services in the areas of auditing and assurance services, tax, management consulting, and insolvency and administration.

Accountants in accounting firms work in public accounting. They are members of either the Institute of Chartered Accountants in Australia or CPA Australia.

INDUSTRY AND COMMERCE

All companies, both large and small, employ accountants to perform many different duties. These duties include the preparation of financial statements for external reporting purposes. Large and medium-sized companies also employ accountants in internal auditing. The internal auditor's role is to ensure that the internal controls in the company are adequate to safeguard the company's assets. Large and medium-sized companies also often employ tax accountants to do all the work involved with income tax, payroll tax, Goods and Services Tax and other indirect taxes. They also employ cost accountants, whose job is to generate information about the behaviour of costs, help establish budgets and generally assist management in controlling costs and establishing appropriate prices for the company's products.

NOT-FOR-PROFIT ENTITIES

The not-for-profit (NFP) sector includes all levels of government, health, education, social services, culture and recreation, business and professional associations and others such as religious groups.

Excluding the government sector, the NFP sector represented $20.8 billion or 3.3 per cent of gross domestic product (GDP) in 2000. As a result of its size, this sector employs many accounting graduates. Accounting for profit and NFP entities is very similar, although the absence of a profit motive may result in some differences.

The government employs many accountants, who work in all areas at the local, state and federal levels. Accountants can be found doing similar work to their private sector counterparts: preparing financial reports, auditing, tax work and cost accounting. Departments such as the Treasury and the Auditor-General's Office obviously employ many accountants. Other departments – such as Health, Housing and Local Government; Employment, Education and Training; and Tourism – also employ accountants to carry out all types of accounting work.

Professional membership

The two major professional accounting bodies in Australia are the Institute of Chartered Accountants in Australia (ICAA) and CPA Australia (CPAA). The National Institute of Accountants (NIA) is another professional organisation in Australia for accountants 'recognised for their practical, hands-on skills and a broad understanding of the total business environment' www.nia.com.au.

The ICAA and CPAA have different categories of membership. University graduates are initially admitted as associates. They must then complete a postgraduate program and have three years' practical experience before advancing in their membership. Finally, a public practice certificate is required for all principals in public accounting firms.

SUMMARY

LO 1 **LEARNING OBJECTIVE 1**
Understand what is meant by the term 'accounting'
In this chapter we have tried to give an idea of what accounting is and how it pervades both the internal workings of organisations and the external commercial environment. It can be seen at one level as a functional area of business and at an external level as an important determinant of business survival through its effect on groups such as shareholders, lenders and employees.

LO 2 **LEARNING OBJECTIVE 2**
Explain the difference between management accounting and financial accounting
Management accounting is prepared for internal users and is unregulated. Financial accounting is prepared for external users and is subject to regulations.

LO 3 **LEARNING OBJECTIVE 3**
Identify who the main users of accounting information are, and the main purposes for which the information is used
There are many users of accounting information and they include internal users (managers) and external users (shareholders, lenders, suppliers, customers, employees, government and the general public). We have shown that there is no perfect accounting report that will meet the needs of all users, and that the needs of users vary. For example, in the case of a small business the owner may wish to show a low profit to reduce the potential tax bill, but may need to show a high profit in order to persuade a banker to lend their business money.

LO 4 **LEARNING OBJECTIVE 4**
Identify the limitations of accounting information
We have shown that accounting will be useful only if it is used correctly and if its limitations are understood. Accounting is based on past information and only includes those elements that meet the definition and recognition criteria for assets, liabilities, income, expenses and equity, as outlined in the *Framework* (covered in Chapter 2). In addition, such elements must also fulfil qualitative characteristics – such as reliability, relevance, understandability and comparability.

LO 5 **LEARNING OBJECTIVE 5**
Discuss the factors that influence the choice of accounting systems for different types of organisations
The factors that influence the choice of an accounting system include the size of the organisation, the type of business activity being undertaken and whether it is simple or complex, the structure of the organisation and whether the organisation is for-profit or not-for-profit.

A failing business will still fail even though it has an excellent accounting system; on the other hand, potentially successful businesses have been allowed to go bankrupt because the accounting system did not give any warning signs or gave them too late to allow management to take action to rectify the situation.

LO 6 **LEARNING OBJECTIVE 6**
Explain what is meant by the term 'economic consequences' and relate this to the choice of accounting policies
The economic consequences of accounting policies can influence a manager's choice of accounting policies. Accounting numbers are used in various contracts and this, it is argued, creates incentives for managers to choose accounting policies based on their impact on the numbers in the contracts.

Managerial compensation and debt contracts create incentives for managers to favour profit-increasing accounting policies. Political costs create incentives for managers of large companies to favour profit-decreasing accounting policies.

LO ⑦ LEARNING OBJECTIVE 7
Discuss the importance of ethics in accounting, and business in general
There are many examples of large company failures (like HIH), and many of these failures involved fraudulent activities where the costs were in the public domain. In addition to these high-profile failures, there are many other cases of fraud each year and the cost to the economy is enormous.

LO ⑧ LEARNING OBJECTIVE 8
Explain what is meant by ethical behaviour
The issue of ethics in accounting and business is an extremely important one. It is difficult to define ethics, but 10 characteristics of ethical behaviour have been identified. Ethics are like your skin, they go everywhere with you. It is not something you adopt just for the workplace. The important principle is that business and professional people should act in an ethical manner.

LO ⑨ LEARNING OBJECTIVE 9
Identify the factors that should help determine appropriate ethical behaviour for accountants
Accountants have a professional code of ethics, and this should help them deal with ethical dilemmas and guide them with regard to what is appropriate ethical behaviour.

LO ⑩ LEARNING OBJECTIVE 10
Identify career opportunities for accountants
Accountants work in many areas and in many types of organisations. Accountants work in public accounting firms providing various services including audit and assurance, taxation, an advisory service, and insolvency and administration. Accountants work in large, medium and small organisations preparing financial statements and all types of information for internal decision making by managers. Accountants also work in not-for-profit entities which include all levels of government and other areas such as health, education and social services.

REFERENCES

Albrecht, W.S. (ed.), 1992. *Ethical Issues in the Practice of Accounting*, South-Western.

American Accounting Association, 1966. *A Statement of Basic Accounting Theory*.

American Accounting Principles Board, 1970. *Statement No. 4: Basic Concepts and Accounting Principles Underlying Financial Statements of Business Enterprises*, AICPA.

American Institute of Certified Public Accountants, 1973. *Objectives of Financial Statements*.

Josephson, M.S., 1992. 'The need for ethics education in accounting' in *Ethical Issues in the Practice of Accounting*, Albrecht, W.S. (ed.), South-Western.

Leung, P., & Cooper, B.J., 1994. *Professional Ethics: A Survey of Australian Accountants*, Ethics Centre of Excellence, Australian Society of CPAs publication.

Parker, R.H., 1986. *Macmillan Dictionary of Accounting*, Macmillan.

Statsky, W.P., 1985. *West's Legal Thesaurus/Dictionary: A Resource for the Writer and the Computer Researcher*, West Publishing Company.

Tabor, M.L., 1992. 'Why I compromised my professional code of ethics', in *Ethical Issues in the Practice of Accounting*, Albrecht, W.S. (ed.), South-Western.

FURTHER READING

Trotman, K. & Gibbins, M., 2006. *Financial Accounting: An Integrated Approach*, 3rd edn, Thomson.

REVIEW QUESTIONS

1   For what purposes is accounting information used:
    a   by the individual?
    b   by the entity?

2   Examples were given of certain limitations of accounting information. Can you give examples of your own?

3   What are the challenges for ethics in business? Are they different for accountants?

4   Is there a conflict between self-interest and ethical behaviour?

5   If you work for an accounting firm, whose perspective should you take – the firm's, the client's, the user's or your own?

PROBLEMS FOR DISCUSSION AND ANALYSIS

1   Refer to the 2005 consolidated figures in the Woodside financial statements in Appendix 1.
    a   What is the name of the auditing firm?
    b   Does Woodside include shares as part of the remuneration for employees?
    c   Do these shares affect the determination of profit for Woodside?

2   Discuss what information you believe would be useful to the following groups of report users:
    a   employees
    b   investors
    c   regulators
    d   suppliers of goods and services
    e   customers.

3   In fewer than 100 words, detail your understanding of the word 'ethics'.

4   Corporate fraud is estimated at $16 billion per annum in Australia. Is it possible to regulate against fraud?

5   You own and run a small supermarket. What accounting information do you need, and how often?

6   You are the manager of a small local band. You are offered $1000 for a three-hour performance. What financial (accounting) issues do you have to consider before accepting or rejecting the offer?

7   It was pointed out that accounting information is only a part of the input to the decision-making process. In order to expand your understanding of the role of accounting information, for the situation outlined below, identify:
    a   the accounting information that would be relevant
    b   any other information that would be relevant.
        Head & Co. is in the business of making navigation equipment and wishes to diversify into the production of hang gliders. The business is based in Sydney but the owners may be willing to move. The owners have little knowledge about the market for hang gliders but feel that there is money to be made in that field.

8 You are considering buying a small retail store selling electrical equipment. The selling agent is very enthusiastic. What non-financial information should you be requesting?

9 Tom was left some money in his mother's will and decided that he should give up his job and go into business for himself. While the lawyers were still sorting out his mother's estate, he started looking round for a suitable business. After a short time, he identified a small boat-building business that he felt was worth investing in. He was still uncertain about how much his mother had left him but thought that it was probably between $80 000 and $100 000. The boat-building business was for sale for $200 000 and so, assuming that he could finance the remainder, he engaged an accountant to check the books of the business and report back to him. As proof of his good faith, he deposited $2000, which he had in savings, with the business agents.

The report from the accountant confirmed his initial impression that the business was worth investing in, so he paid the accountant's modest fee of $1000 in full. At this stage he discussed his plans more fully with his bank manager, who was duly impressed with the professional approach taken by Tom.

The bank manager pointed out that Tom had no business experience and, therefore, was a high risk from the bank's point of view. However, in view of their long-standing relationship, the bank was prepared to take a chance and said that it would lend Tom 40 per cent of the purchase price.

On the basis of this, Tom signed a conditional agreement to buy the boat-building business. A short time after this he received a letter from his lawyers stating that his inheritance from his mother amounted to only $60 000. He could not raise the additional finance to purchase the boat-building business and so withdrew from the agreement, recovered his $2000 deposit, and purchased a yacht with the intention of doing charter work to the Caribbean.

Required

Discuss the point at which, in your opinion, the accounting process should begin, giving reasons for your point of view. Pay particular attention to the dual needs of Tom as an owner and as a manager.

Note to instructors: *The following problems are considered more suitable for use in MBA courses. However, undergraduate courses may also find them useful.*

10 The No-Returns Rubber Company is considering setting up a new manufacturing plant which will produce rubber arbuthnots to be used in the manufacture of nuclear-powered Frisbees. Discuss what information the managers are likely to require in order to make an informed decision about the viability of this project. Factors to be taken into account should include financial issues, health and safety considerations, and also the possible social and legal issues which may arise from the manufacture of non-biodegradable substances, such as rubber arbuthnots and nuclear items. Discuss how you think these considerations can be incorporated into a costing of the project.

11 Scasboro Beach is a beautiful beach in Bondavia. The surrounding residential area is very attractive because of the beach and the lovely views out to the ocean. After a great deal of negotiation, the Coastal Development Company obtained a permit from the local shire council to erect a 12-storey five-star hotel, which would encroach onto the lovely beach and sand dune area. Prior to this approval, the highest building permitted at Scasboro Beach was three storeys.

Construction began immediately. At this time a legal challenge to the hotel was lodged by a local ratepayers' association and environmental groups. They wanted the permit declared void because the planned structure would obstruct the views of existing property owners and cause damage to sand dunes in the area.

After the Coastal Development Company had invested $500 000 in the Scasboro Hotel project, a court held with the plaintiffs and ordered demolition of the site, as well as total restoration of the area. This would cost approximately $200 000. The company lost an appeal to a higher court.

Required

a   Discuss how you might measure the economic value (using your understanding of what economic value means) of the project before the decision of:
    i   the lower court
    ii the higher court.
b   What problems do you envisage in making such measurements?
c   What losses were sustained and who sustained the losses in this case?

(Adapted from R.G. May, G. Mueller and T.H. Williams, *A New Introduction to Financial Accounting*, Prentice-Hall, 1975, Chapter 1, Exercise 1–2.)

12 At the beginning of time there was a small dwelling of cave men and women who elected themselves a leader called Ugg. Ugg's responsibilities were to restore peace and order in the dwelling, which had become unsettled due to a recent outbreak of stealing.

Ugg was a very intelligent cave man and he began thinking that if every cave person accounted for their belongings, then less stealing would happen. Furthermore, if cave people paid him some kind of 'due' in respect of their belongings, thieves would be deterred because the more belongings a cave person had, the more in dues he or she would have to give Ugg. Ugg decided to call this due the 'rock tax'.

The next day Ugg announced the rock tax to the dwelling. He explained to the cave people his thoughts from the previous day and asked for grunts of approval for the rock tax. These outweighed the grunts of disapproval so he then proceeded to outline the rock tax guidelines. These were:

1   one large brown fur equalled 50 morsels of meat
2   one small brown fur equalled 30 morsels of meat
3   one large black fur equalled two large brown furs
4   one small black fur equalled three small brown furs
5   for every 10 morsels of meat, one large rock had to be given to Ugg, which would help to build a wall around the whole dwelling. The tax would be paid once every 300 days commencing from the next day.

Ugg also said that he would personally check every cave person's rock-cave to make sure truthful accounts were given.

Two of the oldest members of the dwelling, Thug and Olga, thought Ugg's rock tax was the best announcement they had ever heard and proceeded to add up their furs and morsels. Thug calculated he had six large brown furs, two small brown furs and five small black furs in addition to the 34 morsels of meat he had stored in his rock-fridge. Thug had exchanged three small brown furs for his rock-fridge some 400 days ago. Olga counted two large brown furs, 10 large black furs and nine small black furs in her rock-cabin. She also counted 22 meat morsels in her rock-fridge. Olga had exchanged one large black fur for the rock-fridge 200 days ago.

Required

Imagining you lived in this dwelling, calculate:
a   the amount of tax that Thug and Olga should give Ugg
b   how Thug and Olga would pay their tax to Ugg.

Ethics case study

You have been hired by Jim's Towing Service, a sole proprietorship, to prepare the tax return for the business. Upon checking the bank statements and the cash books of the business you discover that Jim has not included in the revenue any cash received when customers paid cash. Only the amounts received from insurance companies have been included in the revenue.

Discuss what you should do.

Answers to review exercises

1   Needs that are identified in the text are the need for information to enable management to carry out its duties and responsibilities in terms of stewardship, planning, control and decision making. The second part of the question should provoke a number of different answers, perhaps related to the market for the internal user's product, competition or the economic situation. We have found that by encouraging the students to think about the alternative information needs, and the sources from which information can be derived, they are better able to see accounting in a wider context.

2   In general, for external users, the accounting reports that are normally used are the annual report or statements. Where specific reports, such as the balance sheet or income statement, are mentioned in the body of the text, these are shown below.

Management	Various reports including specialist reports to help run the business profitably
Owners	Annual report to help assess if management is doing a good job and protecting their investment
Lenders	Income statement and balance sheet to assess if the loan can be repaid and, in the event of loan repayment problems, if there is adequate security
Suppliers	Income statement and balance sheet because they are interested in issues that are similar to those of lenders
Customers	Income statement and balance sheet to determine if the entity will continue to operate – particularly if the customer has a long-term contract
Employees	Profitability, therefore income statement to help assess ability of the entity to continue to operate
Government	Income statement to assess payment of taxes
The public	Annual report to assess the entity's impact on areas like the environment and to assess the entity's social policies and so on.

3   The limitations are as follows:
   a   The information is only a part of that which is necessary to make 'effective decisions'.
   b   Accountancy is, as yet, an inexact science and depends on a number of judgements, estimates, etc.
   c   The end result of the accounting process can only be as good as the inputs, and in times of rising prices some of these inputs are of dubious value.
   d   Accounting systems can be counterproductive; for example, the maximisation of a division's profit may not always ensure the maximisation of entity profit.

4   Once again, a number of alternative answers are acceptable here. However, the final summary should include the following in relation to the major determinants of a useful accounting system: the provision of information that is useful in terms of meeting the needs of users, and information that is presented in a timely manner and in a format that is appropriate and understandable. Discussion could cover the terms 'appropriate' and 'understandable' in more detail.

5   Economic consequences refer to the financial impact on a company from a particular accounting policy. For example, an accounting policy that requires all mining companies to expense all exploration and development expenditure as incurred would result in large losses for companies not yet in production. Hence, this may make it difficult to attract investors to buy the company's shares, despite its future prospects.

6   Students should demonstrate an understanding of the issues involved with ethics and appreciate the real costs of being unethical.

THE FINANCIAL REPORTING FRAMEWORK
CHAPTER TWO

2

LEARNING OBJECTIVES

At the end of this chapter, you should be able to:

1 identify the factors that influence the preparation of financial statements

2 explain the current arrangements for standard setting in Australia

3 explain what is meant by the term 'due process'

4 explain the influence of accounting standards, the *Corporations Act 2001* and the Australian Stock Exchange Listing Rules on financial reporting requirements

5 explain what is meant by a conceptual framework

6 understand the role of a conceptual framework

7 explain the terms 'reporting entity', 'general-purpose financial report' and 'qualitative characteristics', and explain the objective of financial reporting

8 explain the terms 'assets', 'liabilities', 'equity', 'income' and 'expenses'

9 identify the role of the audit and the auditor in financial reporting

10 explain what is meant by the term 'expectation gap'

11 explain the concept of audit independence and why it is so important.

Note to instructors: Instructors who defer consideration of this chapter until later in the course should be aware that the following terms, defined in this chapter, are used throughout the text: 'assets', 'liabilities', 'expenses', 'income', 'revenue' and 'equity'. These terms are restated in Chapters 4 and 5.

Introduction

In Chapter 1 we discussed the objectives of accounting and the influences of users on financial reporting. We also discussed the limitations of accounting information and the role of accounting in business, its effect on business and some of the factors which influence accounting. Mentioned also was the impact of accounting policies on management compensation and debt contracts.

LO 1

Identify the factors that influence the preparation of financial statements

The purpose of this chapter is to examine the financial reporting framework that influences the preparation of financial statements for different types of entities. The most extensive regulations exist for companies – in particular for listed public companies. Their financial reports must comply with various professional, statutory and stock exchange requirements. Other types of business organisations – such as not-for-profit and public sector entities – may be subject to various regulatory requirements, and in some cases must also comply with accounting standards. Organisations such as small private companies, partnerships or sole proprietorships are subject to much less regulation.

We also examine the process used for the establishment of accounting standards and the parties involved in the standard-setting process. The objective of financial reporting and the qualitative characteristics of financial information are also considered in this chapter. The definitions of key terms such as 'assets', 'liabilities', 'equity', 'income' and 'expenses' from the International Accounting Standards Board (IASB) *Framework* are explained and are used in this book. Finally the role of the external auditor in financial reporting is discussed.

Types of organisations

Organisations can be classified as either profit-making entities or not-for-profit entities. Common types of profit-making entities are sole proprietorships, partnerships and companies. These forms of business organisations are discussed in detail in Chapter 11. A sole proprietorship (or sole trader business) is simple to establish and allows for control of the business by the individual. Many tradespeople, such as plumbers, carpenters and bricklayers, often operate as sole traders. A partnership is where two or more individuals form a partnership to conduct a business with a view to profit. It is often used in professional practices for accountants, doctors and lawyers. A company is a third type of organisation that is commonly used in business. Unlike a sole proprietorship or a partnership, a company exists as a separate legal entity from its owners – who are referred to as shareholders.

Not-for-profit entities (NFPEs) operate in many areas in our society including education, health, community services, leisure, religion and charities. The aim of a NFPE is to use its resources in an efficient manner to best achieve the objectives for which it was formed, rather than pursuing a profit for its owner(s).

In this book we concentrate on accounting from the viewpoint of private sector, for-profit companies. However, much of what is covered in the book is also relevant for entities in the not-for-profit (NFP) sector. In some chapters we also include examples from the NFP and public sector. The remainder of this chapter examines the various influences that affect the preparation of financial reports for companies. The factors that may influence and regulate the preparation of the financial statements for most companies are Accounting Standards, Accounting Concepts and the *Corporations Act*. The Stock Exchange Listing Rules impose additional reporting obligations for listed public companies.

The framework for setting accounting standards

LO ②

Explain the current arrangements for standard setting in Australia

One of the main factors that influences the financial statements that companies must prepare is accounting standards. The Australian Accounting Standards Board (AASB) sets accounting standards for both the private and public sectors in Australia. Prior to 2000, Australian Accounting Standards (AAS) were set by the Public Sector Accounting Standards Board (PSASB) and AASB standards were set by the AASB. The AAS applied to public sector (government) reporting entities and private sector reporting entities other than companies, while the AASB standards applied only to companies that were reporting entities. The AASB now sets accounting standards for all reporting entities in Australia. A reporting entity is an entity for which there are users who rely on the financial statements as their major source of financial information about the entity to assist them with making decisions. Australia has sector-neutral accounting standards which means that there is only one set of accounting standards for both the profit and not-for-profit sectors. We will talk more about this later.

FINANCIAL REPORTING COUNCIL

The standard-setting arrangements also involve a Financial Reporting Council (FRC) which has oversight responsibility for the AASB and the AUASB (Auditing and Assurance Standards Board). There are 13 members of the FRC (plus the chairperson) who comprise key stakeholders from professional accounting bodies, the business community, government and regulatory agencies like the Australian Securities and Investments Commission. Members are appointed by the Treasurer.

The FRC is responsible for the priorities, business plan, budget and staffing arrangements of the AASB (and the AUASB) but it is not able to influence the AASB's technical deliberations. In theory, this means that the FRC cannot determine the content of accounting standards. However, given its control of the budget and priorities of the AASB, it has the potential, in practice, to influence the setting of accounting standards. This was made very evident through the decision by the FRC in June 2002 that from 1 January 2005 Australia was to adopt International Accounting Standards (now called International Financial Reporting Standards – IFRS) set by the International Accounting Standards Board (IASB). The FRC is also responsible for advising the government on the process of setting accounting standards.

AUSTRALIAN ACCOUNTING STANDARDS BOARD

There are 13 members of the AASB, including a full-time chairperson. Its responsibilities, as specified in section 227(1) of the *Australian Securities and Investments Commission Act 2001*, include the following:

- develop a conceptual framework, not having the force of an accounting standard, for the purpose of evaluating proposed accounting standards
- develop and issue accounting standards which have the force of law
- formulate accounting standards for other purposes
- participate and contribute to the development of a single set of accounting standards for worldwide use.

The AASB follows due process (as described later in this chapter) in the development of accounting standards and holds all meetings in public that relate to technical matters. The AASB has its own dedicated technical staff responsible for the preparation of various papers for the AASB to consider as it develops accounting standards.

URGENT ISSUES GROUP

The Urgent Issues Group (UIG) has 15 members and is a subcommittee of the AASB. The chairperson of the AASB also chairs the UIG. The role of the UIG is to review diverse accounting practices as they relate to the application of accounting standards and issue an Interpretation, if deemed appropriate. The AASB must then vote to approve the Interpretation. The UIG is able to respond in a more timely fashion than the AASB, but it is not empowered to issue accounting standards and the AASB must approve all UIG Interpretations. The role of the UIG is being reviewed by the AASB in 2006 and it is likely it will be dismantled, with Interpretations taken on by the AASB. The review has arisen as a result of the adoption of International Financial Reporting Standards in Australia. The standard-setting structure is represented in Figure 2.1.

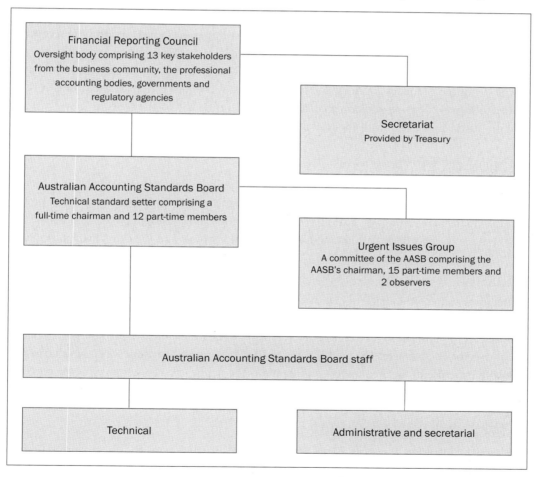

Adapted from AASB website www.aasb.com.au

Figure 2.1 Australian accounting standard setting: structure of institutional arrangements

COMPLIANCE WITH ACCOUNTING STANDARDS

In accordance with the *Corporations Act*, compliance with the accounting standards and UIG Interpretations issued by the AASB is mandatory for all companies that are reporting entities. Other jurisdictions such as state governments may also adopt AASB standards and make compliance with such standards mandatory. The Australian Securities and Investments Commission (ASIC) is responsible for enforcing compliance with the *Corporations Act*.

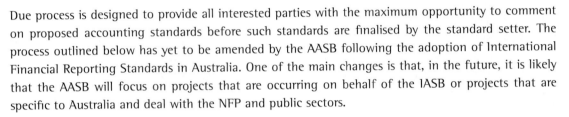

Review exercise 1

Discuss the arrangements in Australia for setting standards for the accounting profession.

Due process

Explain what is meant by the term 'due process'

Due process is designed to provide all interested parties with the maximum opportunity to comment on proposed accounting standards before such standards are finalised by the standard setter. The process outlined below has yet to be amended by the AASB following the adoption of International Financial Reporting Standards in Australia. One of the main changes is that, in the future, it is likely that the AASB will focus on projects that are occurring on behalf of the IASB or projects that are specific to Australia and deal with the NFP and public sectors.

SELECTION OF TOPICS

Projects are selected by the AASB or are allocated to the AASB by the IASB, presumably in response to emerging issues, although some would argue that the topics are selected following particular problems or crises in financial reporting. In 2005, the AASB, undertook three research projects on behalf of the IASB. The three projects dealt with intangible assets, joint ventures and the extractive industries.

DISCUSSION PAPER OR THEORY MONOGRAPH

A contractor is appointed initially to investigate all relevant aspects of a topic and prepare a discussion paper or an accounting theory monograph which is designed to inform readers in an unbiased manner. The contractor can be a staff member from the AASB, or can be from industry, the profession, academia, the public sector or elsewhere. The contractor is assisted by a project advisory panel, which consists of people with expertise in the area under consideration. The panel acts as a resource for the contractor, in addition to reviewing draft copies of the paper.

KEY DECISIONS QUESTIONNAIRE

This document identifies the main issues to be resolved in relation to the topic, and is based on the discussion paper or accounting theory monograph. The board discusses the issues raised in the questionnaire and makes tentative decisions. These decisions form the basis for a draft exposure draft which is prepared by staff from the AASB.

Draft exposure draft

The draft exposure draft is circulated to parties with an interest and knowledge in the area. Their comments are used by the board to refine the exposure draft before it is released.

Exposure draft

The exposure draft is distributed to all registrants on the AASB mailing list and to any other interested parties, with an invitation to comment on the proposed accounting standard. Following the review period, additional opportunities, such as a public hearing, are provided if the board deem it appropriate.

Draft standard

A draft statement of the accounting standard is prepared after comments have been received on the exposure draft. The draft may be given additional public exposure or it may be forwarded direct to ASIC and the Commonwealth Treasurer. These parties then have 30 days in which to comment.

Final standard

Comments received from ASIC or the Commonwealth Treasurer are incorporated into a final standard which is then issued by the AASB. Federal parliament has a 15-day veto period.

This completes the due process. Once the veto period has passed, the standards are issued for application from a specified date.

The political nature of accounting standard setting

In Chapter 1 we discussed the choice of accounting policies and their economic consequences. The standard-setting body selects accounting standards based on the objective of providing useful information to the users of financial statements. Managers, however, may choose accounting policies based on the economic consequences to themselves and their organisations.

LO 4

Explain the influence of accounting standards, the *Corporations Act* and the Australian Stock Exchange Listing Rules on financial reporting requirements

The due process employed by the standard setters provides managers with an opportunity to lobby the standard setters. They attempt to influence their deliberations, particularly with reference to standards that are relevant to their company. The 'Group of 100' is an association of the chief financial managers from Australia's 100 largest companies. The group is very active in making submissions to the standard setters. The decision by the FRC that forced the AASB to adopt International Accounting Standards from 1 January 2005 means that if Australians are to influence the standard-setting process they will now need to influence the deliberations of the IASB. Given the size of the Australian capital market, this will be a difficult task.

The Group of 100's agenda for lobbying the standard setters may be to ensure that financial statements provide useful information. Alternatively, their reasons may well be more in their own self-interest, and that of the companies for which they work.

In any event, the impact of this interest in the standard-setting process is that it is recognised as a political process. Therefore, the standard-setting bodies have to try and achieve their stated objective within a process that is quite political.

International Accounting Standards

The International Accounting Standards Board (IASB) consists of members from a number of countries. It is based in London and began operations in January 2002, replacing the International Accounting Standards Committee (IASC). All standards issued by this board prior to 2002 are referred to as International Accounting Standards (IAS). All new standards issued by the IASB from January 2002 are called International Financial Reporting Standards (IFRS).

The term 'International Financial Reporting Standards' includes:

• International Financial Reporting Standards
• International Accounting Standards
and
• Interpretations issued by the International Financial Reporting Interpretations Committee or the former Standing Interpretations Committee.

The IASB mission statement sets out that it:

> is an independent, privately-funded accounting standard-setter based in London, UK. The Board Members come from nine countries and have a variety of functional backgrounds. The IASB is committed to developing, in the public interest, a single set of high quality, understandable and enforceable global accounting standards that require transparent and comparable information in general purpose financial statements. In addition, the IASB co-operates with national accounting standard-setters to achieve convergence in accounting standards around the world.
> (IASB 2006)

Although such standards do not override national standards, the IASB hopes that its activities will result in more uniform worldwide accounting standards. Where a country does not have a standard-setting authority, it can adopt the IAS (IFRS). From 1 January 2005, Australia adopted the IFRS. As a result, Australia has now issued all the standards issued by the IASB as Australian Equivalents to IFRS (AIFRS), but only after subjecting the standards to due process. The approach taken by the AASB in adopting IFRS has been to issue all the existing IAS and new IFRS for comment before adoption. Application of these standards is now mandatory for all reporting entities in Australia for reporting periods beginning from 1 January 2005. The half-yearly report for Woodside included in Appendix 1 is the first general-purpose financial report prepared using AIFRS.

To allow users to distinguish the previous IAS from new IFRS, the following numbering system has been adopted by the AASB.

AASB 1= IFRS 1, AASB 2= IFRS 2, so the same number applies to the new standards issued by the IASB.

AASB 101= IAS 1, AASB 102 = IAS 2, so the original number of the IAS plus 100 allows users to identify AASB standards that are equivalent to the standards issued by the IASC.

In addition, there will be a few original Australian accounting standards like AASB 1031 *Materiality* retained for use beyond 2005 because there is no equivalent IFRS or IAS. These standards are identified with numbering from 1000.

The UIG has adopted the same numbering policy with respect to the adoption of Interpretations of IFRS and IAS for application in Australia.

A unpublished survey on the use and application of IASs by Hancock in 1998 showed that they were only directly applied in seven countries in 1996. A further 12 countries applied IASs with some slight modifications. Developments in the early part of the twenty-first century indicate that the goal of the IASs may indeed be achievable within the next five to 10 years. The spectacular corporate collapses of companies like Enron and Worldcom and the associated criticism of financial reporting in the USA have added impetus to this movement. The European Union required all EU listed companies to use IAS (IFRS) from 1 January 2005 and the USA standard setter is working very closely with the IASB in an effort to converge US Accounting Standards with the IAS (IFRS). There is a view that international harmonisation of accounting standards will facilitate the flow of capital across country borders. This has potential benefits to investors and for companies wishing to list their shares in other countries.

CASE STUDY 2.1

COMING TO GRIPS WITH THE IFRS
Mark Fenton-Jones

Stakeholders are yet to agree on the role of Australia's accounting standards board under the new international reporting regime, reports Mark Fenton-Jones.

Although the start of the International Financial Reporting System earlier this year fixed the pre-eminence of the London-based International Accounting Standards Board in formulating global standards, it has not completely displaced the Australian Accounting Standards Board.

David Boymal, chairman of the AASB, acknowledges that the role of the local standards setting body has changed. But that hasn't slowed the pace of its activity.

'There is no doubt the role has changed and that's basically because the standards are produced by another body, the IASB', Boymal says from AASB's Melbourne offices, which are provided by the Australian Stock Exchange as its contribution to the global standards setting process.

'In actual fact, my people are busier at the moment than they ever have been.'

In the light of this activity, Boymal has rejected the view that as standards have gone international, the AASB does not need as much government funding. The Federal Government is the main financial supporter of the AASB, through the Financial Reporting Council.

Other financial contributors include the professional accounting bodies and the ASX. Business was always seen as the logical third leg of financial support, but despite requests, and the threat of mandatory levies, funds have not been forthcoming from this sector. Funding remains an issue for the AASB.

'The system failed because the idea of voluntary contributions didn't work,' Boymal says.

According to Boymal, the accounting bodies originally wrote to the FRC stating that they would progressively reduce their contributions starting in the year ended June 2006.

But at the FRC's request, the reduction will be delayed for a year. Starting in the 2007 financial year, the professional accounting organisations will progressively reduce their contributions over three years to a total of $1 million from $1.75 million this financial year.

That will result in the three bodies – The Institute of Chartered Accountants, CPA Australia and the National Institute of Accountants – making equal payments, with the latter increasing its contribution this financial year to $275 0000 from $250 000 in line with the decrease from the two other organisations.

'They are really saying to the government, "You're running the show now so you are going to have to pay for it",' Boymal says.

'At one stage they attributed that reduction to the AASB not having as much to do as before. I think that is more an excuse than a reality.

'The reality is that because the accounting bodies have lost the level of influence they had over the process, they believe they shouldn't be contributing so much cash to the process.'

But Sepi Roshan, a policy adviser in CPA Australia's financial reporting and governance area, believes all those who benefit should underwrite the standards-setting process.

'It's really a shared responsibility now,' Roshan says. 'Not only the profession but government and business also need to be involved.

'Putting the burden on one sector is a little bit unfair given that it is there to benefit everybody.'

Boymal is concerned that any cut in government funding could restrict the AASB's activities.

'We'd be quite desperate because we've just got so much to do and that has come about for a number of different reasons,' he says.

Those reasons include the unchanged statutory role of the AASB which still has to convert international standards into Australian law and judge if they ought to be converted.

'It's really within our right if a situation arose to say, "Well, we are not going to make that into Australian law because it is not going to be in the interest of the Australian economy",' Boymal says.

The AASB is also responsible for writing standards for the public sector and not-for-profit organisations. Although the international standards were devised for with-profit entities, the AASB will amend both existing and future standards for public and not-for-profit sectors, rather than have a completely different suite of standards.

The AASB's third major activity is monitoring the IASB's projects.

'You've got to participate in what they are doing and help them with the research and you've got to let your views be known loudly and clearly whenever you don't agree,' says Boymal, who views this activity as the AASB's biggest job.

'The majority of my staff are engaged in monitoring what the IASB is up to.'

The AASB has 18 technical and six administrative staff.

Jan McCahey, PricewaterhouseCoopers' lead partner for professional standards, agrees Australia needs to maintain its influence in standards setting, although she sees a changed role for the AASB.

'There is no doubt in my mind the standard setter for the corporate sector in Australia is the IASB,' says McCahey.

'So I don't see any point in the AASB replicating those processes.'

But McCahey still sees a role for the AASB. 'The role needs to be carefully thought through so Australia can be influential in accounting standard setting,' she says.

The AASB recently came under pressure from accounting bodies and practices to avoid creating standards that have different interpretations from the intent of the original global standards.

Tom Ravlic, the National Institute of Accountants policy adviser on financial reporting and governance, says his organisation is receiving feedback from accounting practitioners that domestic guidance is leading to differences in interpretation of some standards.

'In others, the AASB has clarified guidance with the IASB but that has not happened in very single instance.'

Big four firm PricewaterhouseCoopers raised the same issue in its 'AIFRS and IFRS similar but not the same' paper released in early September.

It aims to help entities determine where those differences may result in non-compliance with IFRS due to divergence between financial reports prepared under each of the standards.

'People thought we had adopted IFRS as they were written by the IASB and were thinking all they need to worry about was applying IFRS. Actually, that is not what happened,' McCahey says.

While McCahey commends the AASB for its achievements in producing a set of international standards for Australia, she suggests that as additional local disclosure requirements and rewordings have led to some differences, the standards should be reviewed again.

'Now is a good time to take stock,' McCahey says.

Australian Financial Review, 23 September 2005

© 2005 Copyright John Fairfax Holdings Limited. www.afr.com
Not available for re-distribution.

COMMENTARY

The article discusses the role of the AASB now that Australia is adopting IFRS as Australian equivalents of IFRS. One of the touted reasons for Australia's move to IFRS was cost savings. However, according to the Chair of the AASB, the savings may not arise given the three areas of responsibilities he outlines in the article.

The *Corporations Act*

It is not our intention in this section to cover the requirements of the *Corporations Act* in detail. They are dealt with in courses on company law and company accounting.

Most companies are required to prepare balance sheets, income statements and cash flow statements in accordance with applicable accounting standards so as to show a true and fair view of the company's financial position and results for the period. Compliance with applicable accounting standards issued by the AASB is mandatory for all companies that are reporting entities under section 298 of the *Corporations Act*.

The *Corporations Act* also requires the following to be included with a company's financial statements:

- the directors' report
- the directors' statement
- the auditor's report.

THE DIRECTORS' REPORT

The directors' report is required to give certain information, including directors' names, activities of the company, profit or loss for the year, amount of dividends, review of operations and many other matters in relation to the company.

THE DIRECTORS' STATEMENT

The directors' statement/declaration states whether, in their opinion, the income statement and the balance sheet present a true and fair view, whether the company will be able to pay its debts as they fall due, and whether the financial statements comply with accounting standards.

You should now read the directors' statement in the Woodside financial report in Appendix 1 and note that it complies with the *Corporations Act*. The reference to the ability of the company to pay its debts is an important statement about the solvency of the company and is clearly intended to reassure users such as employees, shareholders, creditors and lenders. There have been cases where directors of companies have been found guilty of making this statement when the company could not in fact pay its debts. You can also view the directors' statement for Woolworths which is available at this book's website at http://www.thomsonlearning.com.au/higher/accounting/bazley/index.asp.

THE AUDITOR'S REPORT

The auditor's report is prepared by an external auditor and is meant to reassure the shareholders that they can rely on the financial statements prepared by the company. The auditor is required to form an opinion about the financial statements. The auditor's report must state whether the financial statements comply with the requirements of the *Corporations Act*, whether they provide a true and fair view of the state of affairs of the company, and whether they are in accordance with applicable accounting standards. This is discussed in more detail later in this chapter.

ANNUAL, HALF-YEARLY AND CONCISE FINANCIAL REPORTS

An annual report prepared by a reporting entity is also referred to as a general-purpose financial report (GPFR) and must contain:

- an income statement
- a balance sheet
- a statement of changes in equity
- a statement of cash flows
- notes to the financial statements.

In addition, the GPFR must comply with all applicable accounting standards and accounting concepts. Therefore, a GPFR is a product with certain qualities that a user can rely on if it is accompanied by an unqualified audit opinion (we discuss audit opinions later in this chapter).

In December 1998, the AASB issued AASB 1039 *Concise Financial Reports*. The Standard was reissued in April 2005 to reflect the changes arising from the adoption of AIFRS and the *CLERP 9* (the Corporations Law Economic Reform Program, or *CLERP 9*, contains a number of changes to the *Corporations Act*).

A concise financial report must contain:

- an income statement
- a balance sheet
- a statement of changes in equity
- a cash flow statement
- a discussion and analysis of the operations.

A concise financial report does not contain the detailed notes that are included in the annual report and is intended for users who do not want, and do not use, the more detailed annual report. Of course, users must understand that detailed information (like that found in an annual report) cannot be extracted from a concise report. Companies give shareholders the choice of receiving the full annual report or a concise financial report. The concise financial report must include a statement by the auditor that the financial report has been audited and whether, in the auditor's opinion, the financial report complies with relevant accounting standards.

The requirements for half-yearly reports are specified in AASB 134 *Interim Financial Reporting*. The *Corporate Law Reform Act 1994* requires all disclosing entities to prepare half-yearly accounts. Generally, a disclosing entity is an entity which issues securities that are listed or traded on a stock market, or those for which a prospectus has been lodged, or those offered under a takeover offer. Therefore, all companies listed on the Australian Stock Exchange (ASX) are disclosing entities. A disclosing entity could also be a non-corporate entity, such as a charity, but it is still required to comply with these requirements.

Essentially, the half-year accounts required by disclosing entities provide information to users on a more timely basis. This is despite the fact that the half-year accounts need not be as detailed as the annual accounts.

The half-year accounts consist of:

- an income statement
- a balance sheet
- cash flow statement
- a statement of changes in equity
- a directors' statement
- a modified directors' report
- either an audit report or an audit review, in which the auditor states whether he or she is aware of anything to indicate that the financial statements do not comply with the law.

The accounts for Woodside in Appendix 1 are half-yearly financial statements and, as you can see, do not contain the detailed notes that accompany the Woolworths accounts available at www.thomsonlearning.com.au/higher/accounting/bazley/index.asp.

Stock exchange influence on financial reporting

Public companies in Australia that have their shares listed on a stock exchange must comply with the listing requirements of the ASX.

The Listing Rules impose additional requirements on listed companies. These Rules require companies to provide:

- half-yearly reports
- a preliminary final statement
- additional details to the annual report
- additional details for mining exploration companies.

If companies do not comply with these Listing Rules, they are likely to be delisted, so that their shares can no longer be traded on a stock exchange.

Accounting concepts

LO 5

Explain what is meant by a conceptual framework

Accounting standards, the *Corporations Act* and the Australian Stock Exchange Listing Rules impose certain requirements on, and provide guidance for, companies as they prepare their financial statements. Public sector and NFP entities may also have legislative requirements or Treasurer's Instructions to comply with. However, not all accounting transactions can be specifically dealt with in an accounting standard or the law, or in the Listing Rules. Accounting standards establish procedures on how to account for certain transactions and events, as well as providing detailed disclosure requirements. For example, cash flow statements must be prepared in accordance with AASB 107 *Cash Flow Statements.*

The role of accounting concepts is to provide general guidance on issues, such as the definition of assets, liabilities, income, expenses and equity, in order to help accountants resolve particular problems as they arise.

In Australia, accounting concepts were developed using the same due process as is used for the development of accounting standards. Four Statements of Accounting Concepts (SACs) were issued in Australia from 1990 to 1995. Now that Australia issues accounting standards based on the IFRSs, the AASB has also adopted the IASB *Framework* but has retained SAC 1 *Definition of the Reporting Entity* and SAC 2 *Objective of General Purpose Financial Reporting* as the IASB *Framework* does not deal in adequate detail with the 'objective of financial reporting' or the 'reporting entity'.

Accounting standards must be complied with by members of the accounting profession in Australia, under the Miscellaneous Professional Statement (APS 1) *Conformity with Statements of Accounting Standards* and UIG Consensus views. APS 1 states that Statements of Accounting Concepts should be used by members as guidance.

What is a conceptual framework?

A conceptual framework is an attempt to develop some basic concepts of accounting in order to assist accountants in determining how a particular transaction ought to be accounted for. As we indicated in Chapter 1, the preparation of financial statements involves many decisions about how to record certain transactions. To assist accountants in making these decisions, certain rule-making bodies (we refer to these as standard-setting bodies) have been established in most western countries. In Australia we have the AASB. Standard-setting bodies are responsible for developing standards (rules) to assist accountants in recording certain difficult types of transactions.

We would expect standards to be developed from some underlying theory, but in practice until the late 1980s they were determined on an ad hoc basis. In recent years, standard-setting bodies have been concerned with developing a conceptual framework to provide the theory from which accounting standards can then be developed. For example, in 1978 the Financial Accounting Standards Board (FASB) in the US defined the conceptual framework as:

> a coherent system of interrelated objectives and fundamentals that is expected to lead to consistent standards and that prescribes the nature, function and limits of financial accounting and reporting.

In Australia, the purpose of the conceptual framework is similar, according to the statement in *ED42 Guide to Proposed Statements of Accounting Concepts*:

> The Conceptual Framework is a set of interrelated concepts which will define the nature, subject, purpose and broad content of financial reporting. It will be an explicit rendition of the thinking which is governing the decision making of the Accounting Standards Board (AcSB) and Public Sector Accounting Standards Board (PSASB) when they set down requirements, including accounting standards. The issuance of Statements of Accounting Concepts will fundamentally alter the nature of accounting requirements in this country. (AARF 1987)

The IASB developed the IASB *Framework*, which:

> [s]ets out the concepts that underlie the preparation and presentation of financial statements for external users. (IASB 2001)

As we have already noted, Australia has adopted the IASB *Framework* but retained SACs 1 and 2. Therefore, we use the term '*Framework*' in this book and only make mention of any significant differences (if any) from the previous Australian conceptual framework.

KEY CONCEPT 2.1

THE *FRAMEWORK*

The *Framework* sets out the concepts that underlie the preparation and presentation of financial statements for external users.

KEY CONCEPT 2.2

A GENERAL-PURPOSE FINANCIAL REPORT

A general-purpose financial report is a financial report prepared and presented at least annually and is directed towards the common information needs of a wide range of users. (AASB *Framework* para. 7) The content of a GPFR is as follows:

- an income statement
- a balance sheet
- a statement of changes in equity
- a cash flow statement
- notes to the financial statements.

Therefore, the *Framework* attempts to establish concepts or ideas which determine how financial reports are prepared for general users. It is an attempt to establish the foundations for the preparation of general-purpose financial reports. It addresses basic questions like: What entities should prepare general-purpose financial reports? Who are the users of general-purpose financial reports? What are assets, liabilities, income, expenses and equity? How should these items be measured and displayed?

In the following sections of this chapter we will examine the *Framework* and its development. The definitions of 'assets', 'liabilities', 'income', 'expenses' and 'equity' will also be explained. These are the definitions that are used throughout this book.

Objectives of a conceptual framework

Understand the role of a conceptual framework

What are the reasons behind the development of a conceptual framework? In this section we briefly discuss some of the possible reasons why standard-setting bodies have expended considerable time and resources in developing a conceptual framework.

FEWER ACCOUNTING STANDARDS

A conceptual framework will enable the resolution of accounting problems without the need to issue an accounting standard on every occasion. This should result in fewer accounting standards and help to minimise what some see as the problem of 'standards overload'. This problem is concerned with the time and costs involved in preparing general-purpose financial reports that must comply with a large number of accounting standards.

MORE CONSISTENT ACCOUNTING STANDARDS

Some accounting standards will still be required; however, because they conform to the appropriate framework, they will be more consistent with each other.

IMPROVED COMMUNICATION

There is already improved communication among accountants and between the standard-setting bodies and their constituents as a result of the various conceptual framework projects. All parties are now using common definitions for items such as assets, liabilities, income, expenses and equity.

DEFENCE AGAINST POLITICISATION

A set of concise and well-defined concepts should enhance the credibility of financial reporting and enable the standard-setting bodies to defend particular accounting standards on the basis that they are consistent with the appropriate framework. The setting of accounting standards will always be a political process, to some extent. However, a conceptual framework should serve to reduce the ability of lobby groups to influence the standard-setting process to achieve their own self-serving objectives which are not in the public interest.

Review exercise 2

Discuss the reasons why it is desirable to have a conceptual framework.

The *Framework*

In the next few sections we will highlight the major concepts from the *Framework* with regard to private-sector entities. However, you should be aware that these concepts are also applicable to public sector and not-for-profit entities. We will be using many of these concepts throughout this book.

LO 7

Explain the terms 'reporting entity', 'general-purpose financial report' and 'qualitative characteristics', and explain the objective of financial reporting

DEFINITION OF THE REPORTING ENTITY

In Australia, SAC 1 dealt with the issue of defining a reporting entity. As previously mentioned, the AASB is retaining SAC 1 until the IASB issues more detailed guidance concerning the determination of a reporting entity. Which entities should be preparing and issuing general-purpose financial reports? The definition in the Australian *Framework for the Preparation and Presentation of Financial Statements* is very similar to that in the *Framework*. Both definitions revolve around the concept that a reporting entity is an entity which has users who rely on its financial statements to help them make decisions about the entity such as: Should I sell my shares? Should I lend money to this entity?

KEY CONCEPT 2.3

REPORTING ENTITY

A reporting entity is an entity for which there are users who rely on the financial statements as their major source of financial information about the entity. (AASB *Framework*, para. 8)

In Australia the definition, which is very similar, is:

> Reporting entities are entities (including economic entities) in respect of which it is reasonable to expect the existence of users dependent on general-purpose financial reports for information which will be useful to them for making and evaluating decisions about the allocation of scarce resources. (SAC 1, para. 40)

From the above definition we note that for an entity to be a reporting entity, there must be a demand from users (other than those users who receive special-purpose financial reports, such as a bank) for general-purpose financial reports. We have already looked at who the users of financial statements are in Chapter 1. The identification of users is critical and is considered in paragraph 9 of the AASB *Framework* (SAC 2 in Australia).

Once an entity is identified as a reporting entity, it is required to prepare general-purpose financial reports in accordance with accounting standards. If an entity is deemed not to be a reporting entity, then normally, unless it is a disclosing entity, it need not comply with accounting standards in preparing financial reports. A small family company is not likely to be a reporting entity and is therefore not required to incur the large costs involved in preparing detailed general-purpose financial reports. If Mum and Dad run the family company, they normally know how the business is performing and do not require general-purpose financial reports.

Review exercise 3

What is the importance of the reporting entity concept?

THE OBJECTIVE OF GENERAL-PURPOSE FINANCIAL REPORTING

In Chapter 1 we discussed the importance of providing information that assists users in making decisions. Paragraph 9 of the AASB *Framework* lists the primary users of external financial reports as:

- investors and their advisers
- employees
- lenders
- suppliers and other trade creditors
- customers
- governments and their agencies
- the public, including groups such as the media and special interest groups like Greenpeace.

While the needs of these different groups vary, there are needs which are common to all users (i.e. all users are interested in whether the entity is operating efficiently and achieving its objectives). General-purpose financial reports should provide sufficient information to enable users to assess the performance, financial position, and financing and investing of the reporting entity. This is the objective as stated in paragraph 12 of the AASB *Framework*. We consider the analysis of financial statements in Chapter 14.

KEY CONCEPT 2.4

OBJECTIVE

The objective of financial statements is to provide information about the financial position, performance and changes in financial position of an entity to a wide range of users in making economic decisions. (AASB *Framework*, para. 12)

In order to achieve the objective, the financial statements must be prepared on an accruals basis and not a cash basis. The accruals basis is when transactions are recognised when they occur and not when cash is paid or received.

KEY CONCEPT 2.5

ACCRUAL ACCOUNTING

The method of accounting whereby revenues and expenses are identified within a specified period of time and are recorded as incurred, along with acquired assets, without regard to the date of receipt or payment of cash.

The financial statements are normally prepared on the basis of a 'going concern' which is the assumption is that the entity will continue to operate into the foreseeable future and is not in the process of liquidation.

KEY CONCEPT 2.6

GOING CONCERN

The financial statements are prepared on the basis that the entity will continue to operate into the foreseeable future. If the entity intends or needs to liquidate then the financial statements may have to be prepared on a different basis.

QUALITATIVE CHARACTERISTICS OF FINANCIAL INFORMATION

What are the qualities that financial information should possess to be included in general-purpose financial reports? Paragraph 24 of the AASB *Framework* states that the four principal qualitative characteristics are *relevance*, *reliability*, *understandability* and *comparability*. Information is relevant when it influences investors' decisions about the allocation of scarce resources. Information is reliable when the information can be depended on to represent faithfully, without bias and with minimal error, the transactions it is supposed to represent. Some information, such as forecasts of future profits, may be relevant but cannot be measured with an acceptable degree of reliability to be included in general-purpose financial reports. Conversely, some information may be reliable, such as the historical cost of an asset 20 years ago, but is it of relevance to users? We look at different measurement attributes in Chapter 3 and should keep in mind the qualitative characteristics when considering the advantages and disadvantages of each attribute.

In addition to being relevant and reliable, information must also pass the materiality test. This essentially means that if the information is not likely to affect the user's decision adversely, the information is immaterial and need not be separately disclosed in the general-purpose financial report. In other words, we can ignore it for decision-making purposes.

Paragraph 35 of the AASB *Framework* deals with the concept of *substance over form*. Financial statements should report the substance and economic reality of a transaction and not merely its legal form. For example, A purports to sell an item to B but at the same time enters an arrangement with B whereby A guarantees to purchase the item back from B in one month. Furthermore, A continues to use and enjoy the benefits from the item. The form of the transaction suggests a sale, but the substance of the arrangement is that A is borrowing money from B and using the item as collateral and no sale should be recognised by A. The objective of companies that enter into transactions of this type may be to increase reported profits and so mask the underlying problems.

Traditionally, accountants have tended to overstate liabilities, understate assets, recognise unrealised losses and defer unrealised gains. This approach is known as conservatism and the AASB *Framework* does not regard conservatism as an appropriate qualitative characteristic in deciding the type of information to be disclosed in general-purpose financial reports. However, paragraph 37 of the AASB *Framework* does require preparers to exercise prudence in the preparation of financial statements. This means that in dealing with the inevitable uncertainties that entities are confronted with in some transactions, caution must be exercised so that assets or income are not overstated and expenses or liabilities are not understated. This is supposedly different from conservatism in that there should be no deliberate overstatement of assets or income nor understatement of expenses or liabilities.

The AASB *Framework* also requires that the relevant and reliable information be presented in such a way that it is both comparable and understandable to the users of general-purpose financial reports. As we will see in Chapter 14, when analysing financial statements, it is important for users to be able to compare the general-purpose financial reports of different entities. The information should be understandable to users who have a reasonable knowledge of accounting and who are prepared to diligently study the information in financial statements. Such a user is sometimes described as a sophisticated user.

KEY CONCEPT 2.7

QUALITATIVE CHARACTERISTICS
General-purpose financial reports should provide all the financial information that satisfies the four principal characteristics of relevance, reliability, understandability and comparability.

The AASB *Framework* states that the provision of relevant and reliable information is subject to the constraints of timeliness and a balance between benefit and cost. General-purpose financial reports should be prepared on a timely basis. It is of no use to a punter in 2007 to be told which horse won the 2006 Melbourne Cup. The same applies to financial information about a reporting entity. However, for large organisations there is inevitably a delay of two to three months from the balance date until the release of the general-purpose financial reports.

The balance between benefits and costs is difficult and requires the exercise of judgement. The intent is that entities should not be required to provide information if the costs of providing the information are expected to exceed any benefits that may flow from the provision of such information. One of the problems is that often those who enjoy the benefits do not incur the costs. However, it is a general guide to standard setters that they should consider the costs and benefits to entities before imposing additional reporting obligations on them.

LO 8
Explain the terms 'assets', 'liabilities', 'equity', 'income' and 'expenses'

DEFINITION AND RECOGNITION OF THE ELEMENTS OF FINANCIAL STATEMENTS
Paragraphs 47 to 98 of the AASB *Framework* establish the definitions and recognition criteria for assets, liabilities, income, expenses and equity. Each of these elements is discussed in turn and the definitions are identified as key concepts to be used in later chapters.

Assets

Before an item qualifies for inclusion in the financial statements (in this case the balance sheet), it must not only meet the definition of an asset, it must also pass certain recognition criteria. First, it must be *probable* that the future economic benefits will eventuate and it must be possible to *reliably measure* the cost or some other value of the asset. Only when an item satisfies the definition and meets both recognition criteria will it qualify for inclusion on the balance sheet.

KEY CONCEPT 2.8

ASSETS

An asset is a resource controlled by the entity as a result of past events and from which future economic benefits are expected to flow to the entity. (AASB *Framework*, para. 49a) An asset is recognised in the balance sheet only when it is probable that the future economic benefits will flow to the entity and it must be possible to reliably measure the cost or other value of such benefits.

The essential characteristics of an asset from the above definition are as follows:

- *Future economic benefits.* This is the essence of assets and relates to the scarce capacity to provide benefits to the entities that use them. It does not depend on physical form.
- *Control.* The entity must have the capacity to control the future economic benefits. Many earlier definitions of assets used the words 'legally owned' instead of 'controlled'. While control often arises from legally enforceable rights, the absence of legal ownership does not automatically deny the existence of control. An example of this is a non-cancellable lease, where the lessee has control over the economic benefits embodied in the goods but the lessor maintains legal title to the goods. Thus, the lessor can resume possession of the goods, but only if the lessee is unable to meet the lease payments.
- *Past events.* Only present abilities to control future economic benefits are assets. A decision at balance date to buy a new machine next year does not itself create an asset. However, if the entity has entered into an irrevocable contract to acquire the machine then a right might have been obtained and an asset created as a result of the contract. The signing of the contract is, in effect, the past event.

CASE STUDY 2.2

MAN UTD TAKES A BEATING
by James Doran

MORE than £25 million was cut from the market value of Manchester United yesterday as the row over the abolition of transfer fees continues to dog the world's biggest football club.

Shares in the club tumbled 9.75 p to 392 p, one of the biggest losers in the FTSE 250 index, as European Commission plans to scrap lucrative transfer fees were digested by the market.   ⅠⅠⅠ➡

Manchester United is worth £750 million on the stock market with an estimated £200 million attributed to the value of players. If the new rules are enforced it is feared that the club could lose all of that value.

United shares are now well adrift of a record 412.5 p, struck in April, when the company was dubbed the world's first £1 billion football club.

Yesterday Manchester United opened its first merchandising store in Singapore – operated by FJ Benjamin Holdings, a luxury brands and retail firm – and outlined plans to open other stores across South-East Asia.

The Times, 2 September 2000

COMMENTARY

The article raises the interesting question of whether a football player is an asset. The £200 million attributed to the value of Manchester United's players is based on transfer payments. Consider whether, in this case, the definition of an asset is satisfied. Manchester United controls the services of a player because of the contract it has with him. The future economic benefits relate to the value of the player's services and his resale value by way of the transfer payment when he moves to another club. If transfer payments are outlawed by the European Commission, then a significant component of the future economic benefits is removed. Of course, the value of the playing services remains. The past event would be the signing of the contract.

Before being recorded on the balance sheet, an item that meets the definition of an asset must also satisfy the recognition criteria. It must be probable that the future economic benefits will flow to the entity and there must be a cost or other value that can be reliably measured. The transfer payment would be an amount that could be used to report the value of the player. This would decline to zero if the system of transfer payments were outlawed. The probability of the economic benefits flowing to the club depends on a number of issues, including a player's age, risk of injury, performance on the field, and so on.

While it is common practice for some sporting clubs to report players on balance sheets, it is not common practice with most entities to report their staff. Study the Woodside balance sheet in Appendix 1 to see if you can locate any value for employees.

Liabilities

As is the case with assets, an item that meets the definition of a liability must also satisfy the criteria for recognition before being admitted to the balance sheet. It must be probable that settlement of the liability will be required and the amount required can be reliably measured.

KEY CONCEPT 2.9

LIABILITIES

Liabilities are defined as a present obligation of the entity arising from past events, the settlement of which is expected to result in an outflow from the entity of resources embodying economic benefits. (AASB *Framework*, para. 49b) A liability is recognised in the balance sheet only when it is probable that settlement of the liability will be required and it is possible to reliably measure the amount required.

The essential characteristics of a liability from the above definition are as follows:

- *Present obligation*. This means that a transaction or event in the past has created an obligation which has not yet been satisfied. As with assets, the word 'legal' is not used in the definition of a liability. The view adopted is that legal obligations alone do not give rise to liabilities. There may be other social or moral reasons that create a present obligation. For example, an entity may decide to rectify faults in one of its products, even though the warranty period has expired. The entity is not legally obliged to rectify the faults, but the decision to do so imposes an obligation on the entity and the sacrifices required to honour the obligation constitute a liability.
- *Outflow of economic benefits*. The obligation must result in the entity having to sacrifice economic benefits in the future to discharge the obligation.
- *Past events*. Only present obligations to sacrifice economic benefits in the future are liabilities. An obligation that may arise in the future is not a liability.

Equity

The definition of equity within the AASB *Framework* is similar to that adopted by the Financial Accounting Standards Board in the USA. It is a residual definition whereby the identification of equity is dependent on the recognition of assets and liabilities. Consequently, unlike the other four elements of financial statements, the definition of equity does not require recognition criteria.

KEY CONCEPT 2.10

EQUITY

Equity is the residual interest in the assets of the entity after deducting all its liabilities. (AASB *Framework*, para. 49c)

Expenses

Before expenses are recognised in the income statement, it must be probable that the decrease in economic benefits has occurred and that the amount can be reliably measured.

KEY CONCEPT 2.11

EXPENSES

Expenses are decreases in economic benefits during the accounting period in the form of outflows or depletions of assets or incurrence of liabilities that result in decreases in equity other than those relating to distributions to equity participants. (AASB *Framework*, para. 70b) An expense is recognised in the income statement only when it is probable the decrease in economic benefits has occurred and the amount can be reliably measured.

Income

As with the other elements, income is recognised in the financial statements only when it is probable that the inflow, or other enhancement, or decrease in liabilities has occurred and can be reliably measured.

KEY CONCEPT 2.12

INCOME

Income is increases in economic benefits during the accounting period in the form of inflows or enhancements of assets or decreases of liabilities that result in increases in equity, other than those relating to contributions from equity participants. (AASB *Framework*, para. 70a) Income is recognised in the income statement only when it is probable the inflow or other enhancement has occurred and the amount can be reliably measured.

The definition of income is consistent with that of expenses, and does not differentiate gains from other revenues. In Australia we previously used the term 'revenue' for what the IASB calls 'income'.

The IASB uses the term 'revenue' in International Accounting Standard (IAS) 18 *Revenue*, as defined in Key concept 2.13, and, because of the adoption of IFRS in Australia, we now use the same definition. Revenue is, in fact, a subset of income.

KEY CONCEPT 2.13

REVENUE

Revenue is the gross inflows of economic benefits during the period arising in the course of the *ordinary activities* of an entity when those inflows result in increases in equity, other than those relating to contributions from equity participants. (AASB 118, para. 7)

KEY CONCEPT 2.14

THE INTERRELATIONSHIP BETWEEN INCOME, REVENUE AND GAINS

In accordance with IASB definitions and terminology:
- income = revenue + gains
- revenue = inflows from ordinary activities
- gains = all other inflows.

Measurement of the elements of financial statements

One of the recognition criteria that is outlined in the *Framework* is that an element must have a cost or other value that can be reliably measured. It is probably the most difficult area and yet it is very significant to the accounting process. The AASB *Framework* deals with measurement in paragraphs 99 to 101.

There are four bases of measurement outlined in paragraph 100 of the AASB *Framework* and these are:
- historic cost
- current cost

- realisable (settlement) value
- present value.

Each of these methods is discussed in detail in Chapter 3. We also add fair value to this list as it is a method of measurement that is now used in many accounting standards. The *Framework* states that while historic cost is the most common measurement method, it is normally used in combination with other measurement bases.

External audits

Users of general-purpose financial reports wish to be assured that the information contained in these reports represents a true and fair assessment of the economic activities of the entity being reviewed. The person who audits these general-purpose financial reports, as mentioned earlier in this chapter, is the auditor. They are seen as an *independent* external observer who is called upon, in the case of a company, to express an opinion that the reports provide a 'true and fair' representation of the company's financial status.

LO 9

Identify the role of the audit and the auditor in financial reporting

It is important to stress here that it is the directors of public companies, not the auditor, who are responsible for the preparation and presentation of the general-purpose financial reports of the company. The purpose of an external audit is to add credibility to the reports presented by the directors. Most large companies also have an *internal auditor* who is responsible for monitoring the processes a company uses, making sure that correct processes are being applied. An efficient internal audit process can reduce the time required by the external auditor and hence help reduce the cost of the external audit.

KEY CONCEPT 2.15

EXTERNAL AUDIT

The external audit aims to provide assurance to absentee owners that the financial statements of the company provide a true and fair view of the company's financial position, performance and cash flows.

All companies, except small private companies and some large private companies, must have their accounts audited as required by the *Corporations Act*. Other entities, such as banks, insurance companies, credit unions, building societies and some unions, are also required to be audited under separate legislation. In fact, many not-for-profit organisations, for whom there is no statutory requirement to do so, choose to present audited accounts to show users that their accounts can be relied upon. Examples of not-for-profit organisations include sporting organisations, clubs and societies. All public sector entities have their financial statements audited by the Auditor-General's office.

The external auditor, as noted above, does not prepare the general-purpose financial reports; this is the responsibility of the company's directors. The auditor's task is to review the accounting systems used to prepare the reports, check on the accuracy of certain transactions (particularly those involving large dollar amounts), and state that the accounts have been prepared in accordance with the *Corporations Act* and applicable accounting standards and that they provide a true and fair view. For annual reports, all reporting entities are required to obtain an audit opinion as to the truth and fairness of the GPFR. For interim reports, entities have a choice as to whether they provide a full audit opinion or an audit review. An audit review does not involve a detailed audit by the auditor and so the auditor is not able to express an audit opinion but is able to express a statement about the GPFR.

You should now read the independent audit review prepared by Ernst & Young for the Woodside 2005 interim financial report. You can compare this with the audit opinion from the Woodside 2004 annual report which you can locate at investor relations at the Woodside website www.woodside.com.au. Note the differences between the two reports.

THE AUDITOR
A person who is appointed as a company auditor is required, under the *Corporations Act*, to meet certain requirements. Briefly, the auditor must:
- have the appropriate tertiary qualifications and have completed a prescribed course in auditing or have other qualifications or experience that ASIC considers equivalent to both requirements; and
- meet one of the following practical experience requirements
    - satisfy all the components of an ASIC-approved competency standard; or
    - have the level of practical experience that is prescribed in the Corporations Regulations or experience that ASIC considers equivalent; and
- satisfy ASIC that you are capable of performing the duties of an auditor and are otherwise a fit and proper person to be registered as an auditor.

The shareholders at an annual general meeting appoint the auditor, though in practice management usually provides the name of an auditor for approval by the shareholders.

The auditor is required to form an opinion on the general-purpose financial reports of a company, to determine whether proper records have been kept, and to report to shareholders. The auditor must also inform ASIC of any suspected wrongdoing by management or any non-compliance with applicable accounting standards.

The auditor can be removed only by special notice, given at the annual general meeting, and the commission must be informed. The commission has the power to stop an auditor from resigning or being removed from office.

Besides the statutory requirements noted above, the auditor is bound by professional obligations, which cover:
- independence, integrity, confidentiality and ethical considerations
- conformity with accounting and auditing standards, auditing guidelines and statements of auditing practice.

THE EXPECTATION GAP
As discussed previously, the directors of a company are responsible for preparing the accounts, and the auditors are responsible for seeing that those accounts have been prepared according to statutory and

LO 10
Explain what is meant by the term 'expectation gap'

professional requirements. Are auditors responsible for detecting fraud and/or illegal acts? The law requires auditors to exercise due care when forming their opinion; it does not require them to detect fraud, though if a suspicion is aroused it must be acted upon.

During the past decade the auditing profession has been criticised for not fulfilling what is seen as its role. This criticism has arisen, in part at least, because a number of companies have failed after being given an unqualified opinion by an auditor. The difference between what an auditor is required to do and what is expected by users is known as the expectation gap.

The reporting of fraud and illegal acts, whether actual or suspected, is a requirement of the *Corporations Act*. The problem the auditor faces is that it is often extremely difficult to detect a well-organised fraud, particularly where more than one party is involved. An auditor does not check every transaction of a business, but instead selects a sample to test. While the sampling methods are based on statistical methodologies, the reality is that the auditor does not check every transaction. For this to happen, the cost of an audit would be prohibitively high.

Therefore, the auditor uses a sampling method to test certain transactions so that he or she can be reasonably assured that the financial statements provide a true and fair view of the entity. This is not a guarantee that every error in the financial statements of a business has been detected. This in part explains why there is an expectation gap. The audit profession continues to grapple with the problem of fraud and illegal acts and professional pronouncements continue to be updated.

KEY CONCEPT 2.16

EXPECTATION GAP

The expectation gap describes the difference between the role performed by the auditor and the role that shareholders expect of the auditor.

Review exercise 4
Are auditors required to check the accuracy of the financial statements? Should they be?

INDEPENDENCE

CLERP 9 included a number of changes to the *Corporations Act* and one change related to the relationship between an auditor and his/her client and the independence of the auditor. These amendments resulted from concerns about the lack of audit independence in high-profile company failures like Enron.

Explain the concept of audit independence and why it is so important

The auditor in Enron was not just providing audit services to the client but was providing other services which included tax services, corporate finance, accounting, IT and an internal audit. In many cases like Enron, the fees received for the non-audit services far exceeded the audit fee. The concern about this is that the auditor may be reluctant to be critical of the company when they rely on the other fees they receive. Consequently, companies in Australia are now required to disclose the fees that they pay to auditors for all the services carried out in addition to the audit and provide a statement as to why any additional fees have not impaired the independence of the audit relationship. Auditors must make a declaration about their independence (see Note 1 in the Woodside half-year report in Appendix 1).

One of the other issues in the Enron case involved the appropriateness of ex-partners of Arthur Andersen (Enron's auditor) serving as directors on the Enron board. It was felt that such persons would not be truly independent directors. This also had the potential to impact on the independence of the auditor because the former audit partner's firm was still engaged to do the audit. Hence, one of the CLERP 9 amendments involves a two-year ban on former audit partners taking up positions as directors on the boards of former clients.

Another CLERP 9 amendment requires an automatic rotation of an audit partner after five years. The reason behind this amendment again relates to audit independence. It was felt that after being in charge of an audit for five years, the partner would be very familiar with the client and this might potentially impair his/her independence.

The professional accounting bodies have a professional standard which deals with Professional Independence. This provides a guide to issues associated with independence. This professional standard has also been revised and reissued in response to events like the failure of Enron.

KEY CONCEPT 2.17

AUDITOR INDEPENDENCE
The auditor must be independent of the client for whom the audit is conducted so that he/she is able to express a truly objective opinion about the financial statements.

It is essential that external auditors maintain independence from audit clients so that they can properly fulfil their duties and give unbiased opinions about firms' financial statements. Failure to maintain this independence, whether real or perceived, will only harm the image of the profession. It will also serve to reinforce the expectation gap as a non-independent auditor is more likely to overlook events/transactions, as was the case in Enron. Moreover, when a company fails, shareholders have the right to ask, 'how could the auditor not see that something was seriously wrong?'.

CASE STUDY 2.3

AUDIT IS THE POT OF GOLD
By Kath Walters

While the accounting firms struggle to find new markets for their non-audit services, such as legal and tax advice, the bright light on the horizon for the firms is, paradoxically, their audit divisions. PricewaterhouseCoopers' chief executive, Tony Harrington, says: 'I think the next decade has the potential to be the decade of the auditor. The fundamental scope of

audit needs to be expanded, particularly in areas of . . . internal controls . . . so it is more effective for the board to fulfil its obligations.' All the firms say they have been able to lift the price of their audit services. Ernst & Young's chief executive, Brian Schwartz, says: 'The price discussions with clients have become easier.' The firms now claim that audit, on average, is as profitable as non-audit services. A study last year by the research company Institutional Analysis revealed that the audit fees paid by big Australian companies grew, on average, by 27%, from $1.47 million to $1.87 million.

Schwartz and Harrington deny claims that accounting firms have underpriced audits. However, KPMG's chief executive, Lindsay Maxsted, says such practices existed until recently. 'You would have been tempted 12 months ago to quote a lower price on the audit if you knew that you would have the opportunity to deliver other, non-audit, services,' Maxsted says. 'That doesn't mean, ever, that the audit would be compromised. We never compromise the service delivery.' The big firms are also more picky about who they audit. The chief executive of Deloitte Touche Tohmatsu, Lynn Odland, says: 'For every prospective audit client, [Deloitte] will determine which way is the best way to service that company. Do our other services lines offer the best way, or can we best help them by becoming their auditor? We won't do both.' Lindsey Maxsted says: 'Now we have a considered position. We say, 'We have spent 10 years building up all our other advisory services to this client . . . do we want to put some or all of these at risk by being the auditor?' We have turned down tenders on that basis.'

Business Review Weekly, 10 April 2003

COMMENTARY

This article raises the interesting question about the possible cross-subsidy of audit costs from other services provided to the audit client. It also predicts an increase in audit fees given the increase in risk management procedures and increases in audit testing.

Review exercise 5

Should auditors be allowed to provide non-audit services to an audit client?

SUMMARY

LEARNING OBJECTIVE 1
Identify the factors that influence the preparation of financial statements

While the emphasis was on companies in the private sector, much of what was discussed in the chapter also applies to the public and not-for-profit sectors. As the financial reports of companies are the most regulated, most of the discussion related to issues affecting companies. The major influences on financial reporting for companies in Australia are:

- the AASB *Framework*
- accounting standards
- UIG Interpretations
- the *Corporations Act*
- stock exchange listing requirements.

  For public sector and NFP entities there will be other factors like the relevant state legislation.

LEARNING OBJECTIVE 2
Explain the current arrangements for standard setting in Australia

The FRC has oversight responsibility for both accounting and auditing standards in Australia. It is responsible for the appointment of all members (except the chairperson) to the AASB and the AUASB. The AASB is responsible for establishing accounting standards in Australia. The UIG is responsible for developing Interpretations of accounting standards in cases where there is diversity of practice. The AUASB is responsible for establishing auditing standards.

LEARNING OBJECTIVE 3
Explain what is meant by the term 'due process'

Due process is the name given to the development of an accounting standard. This procedure involves a number of steps that are designed to allow interested parties, and the public, to provide input into the process before a final standard is issued.

LEARNING OBJECTIVE 4
Explain the influence of accounting standards, the Corporations Act and the Australian Stock Exchange Listing Rules on financial reporting requirements

The government-appointed AASB produces accounting standards which, under the *Corporations Act*, are mandatory for all companies that are reporting entities. The AASB sets accounting standards for all entities in both the private and public sectors. These standards are now the equivalent of IFRSs. The AASB has a full-time chair and employs a number of technical staff.

In addition to accounting standards, UIG Interpretations and accounting concepts also influence the preparation of external financial reports. The external financial reports prepared by companies are also influenced by certain requirements within the *Corporations Act*. In particular, the requirements of AASB standards, the directors' report, the directors' statement and the auditor's report influence the external financial reports prepared by companies. For this reason, a number of companies expend considerable resources to provide input to the standards-setting process.

For listed public companies, the Listing Rules of the Australian Stock Exchange require companies to present half-yearly reports, preliminary final statements and additional details in their annual report. Under the *Corporate Law Reform Act 1994*, disclosing entities are also required to prepare yearly and half-yearly accounts and comply with continuous disclosure requirements.

LEARNING OBJECTIVE 5

Explain what is meant by a conceptual framework

The nature of a conceptual framework was discussed in detail and we identified what is meant by a conceptual framework of accounting. It is a series of statements which will assist all parties involved in the preparation of general-purpose financial reports.

LEARNING OBJECTIVE 6

Understand the role of a conceptual framework

The proposed benefits of having a conceptual framework include:

- a reduction in the number of accounting standards required
- more consistency in accounting standards
- improved communication among parties involved in the preparation of general-purpose financial reports
- the provision of a defence against the actions of lobby groups.

LEARNING OBJECTIVE 7

Explain the terms 'reporting entity', 'general-purpose financial report' and 'qualitative characteristics', and explain the objective of financial reporting

A reporting entity is an entity where there are dependent users who rely upon a general-purpose financial report to assist in economic decision making. A GPFR is a financial report and must include:

- an income statement
- a balance sheet
- a statement of changes in equity
- a cash flow statement
- notes to the financial statements.

The four principal qualitative characteristics of relevance, reliability, understandability and comparability were identified.

The objective of financial reporting was defined as providing information to assist decision making.

LEARNING OBJECTIVE 8

Explain the terms 'assets', 'liabilities', 'equity', 'income' and 'expenses'

An asset is a resource that is controlled by the entity as a result of past events and from which future economic benefits are expected to flow to the entity. A liability is defined as a present obligation of the entity arising from past events, the settlement of which is expected to result in an outflow from the entity of resources embodying economic benefits. Assets and liabilities are only recognised in the balance sheet when it is probable that the future benefits will flow to the entity (asset) or resources will flow out of the entity (liability) and the amount can be reliably measured. Equity is the residual interest in the assets of the entity after deducting all its liabilities

Income is increases in economic benefits during the accounting period in the form of inflows or enhancements of assets or decreases in liabilities that result in increases in equity (other than those relating to contributions from equity participants). Revenue is defined in AASB 118 as the same as income except the inflows are from an entity's ordinary operations. Thus, income includes revenues and other gains.

Expenses are decreases in economic benefits during the accounting period in the form of outflows or depletions of assets or the incurrence of liabilities that result in decreases in equity (other than those relating to distributions to equity participants).

L **9**

LEARNING OBJECTIVE 9
Identify the role of the audit and the auditor in financial reporting
Auditors are there to give some assurance as to the truth and fairness of financial statements but can not guarantee that they are absolutely correct and free of errors. They provide an audit opinion in the case of annual reports or an audit review in the case of half-yearly reports.

L **10**

LEARNING OBJECTIVE 10
Explain what is meant by the term 'expectation gap'
The expectation gap describes the difference between the actual role and the perceived role of the auditor and the audit process.

L **11**

LEARNING OBJECTIVE 11
Explain the concept of audit independence and why it is so important
Audit independence is concerned with ensuring that auditors are able to give an independent opinion with regard to the financial statements of an audit client. The concern is that the auditor may be reluctant to be critical of the client when they rely on other fees that are received from the client or they have a close relationship with the client's management.

REFERENCES

Accounting Standards Review Board and Public Sector Accounting Standards Board. Statement of Accounting Concept No. 1 *Definition of the Reporting Entity*, August, 1990.

Accounting Standards Review Board and Public Sector Accounting Standards Board. Statement of Accounting Concept No. 2 *Objective of General Purpose Financial Reporting*, August, 1990.

Australian Accounting Research Foundation. *Exposure Draft 42: Guide to Proposed Statement of Accounting Concepts*, December, 1987.

Australian Accounting Standards Board. *Framework for the Preparation and Presentation of Financial Statements*, July 2004.

Australian Securities and Investments Commission Act 2001.

Financial Accounting Standards Board. Statement of Financial Accounting Concepts No. 1 *Objectives of Financial Reporting by Business Enterprises*, November, 1978.

International Accounting Standards Board. International Accounting Standard 18 *Revenue*, March, 2004.

International Accounting Standards Board. *Framework for the Preparation and Presentation of Financial Statements*, April, 2001.

International Accounting Standards Board. 2006. International Accounting Standards Board, viewed 8 February 2006, http://www.iasb.org/about/index.asp.

REVIEW QUESTIONS

1   What is meant by the term 'due process' in relation to the setting of accounting standards?

2   Discuss the various influences on external financial reporting for companies in Australia.

3   What is a conceptual framework of accounting?

4   In your own words, define a reporting entity.

5   Discuss who uses general-purpose financial reports and why they require such reports.

6   Discuss the difference between control and ownership in terms of the definition of an asset.

7 'The conceptual framework approach to setting accounting standards is not about defining ideal accounting practices but about legitimising current practice, maintaining social and economic status and staving off attempts by the government to control standard setting.' Discuss.

8 What is your understanding of the term 'conservatism'?

9 Give some examples, other than those in the text, of reliable and irrelevant financial information and of unreliable and relevant financial information.

10 What is the purpose of an external audit?

11 What is meant by the expectation gap in relation to auditing?

12 Do you think that public financial statements would present a 'true and fair' view if they were not audited?

13 You are considering investing in two similar types of private companies. One has an unqualified audit report and the other has no audit report. How important is this to you in making your decision?

Problems for discussion and analysis

1 You are asked to explain the following terms to a friend. In doing so, do not refer to the definition in your answer. Use your own words to express your understanding of the terms:
a an asset
b a liability
c equity
d an expense
e income.

2 Refer to the Woodside half-yearly report for 30 June 2005 in Appendix 1.
a On what basis are the accounts prepared?
b What are the three main segments of the business? Which of the three segments provides the greatest income?

3 Give three examples of a liability. How do your examples meet the criteria listed in Key concept 2.9? Do not use examples from the text.

4 Give three examples of an asset. How do your examples meet the criteria listed in Key concept 2.8? Do not use examples from the text.

5 ABC Ltd is being sued by a client for $100 000. The company's legal advisers say that there is only a 35 per cent chance of an unfavourable outcome. At the end of the financial year, the case has still to go to court. Should the $100 000 be reported as a liability?

6 Refer to Case study 2.2. Do you believe a soccer player should be recognised as an asset on Manchester United's balance sheet? What about a player who plays for the local community soccer club?

7 With increased competition in the airline industry, most of the major airlines are offering 'frequent traveller' specials where travellers can receive free flights, upgrades from economy to first or business class, or free accommodation packages. Some airlines have been trying to gain more market share by giving double-kilometres credit for each flight. How should the airlines account for frequent flyer points that have been issued to travellers but not, as yet, redeemed? Are they a liability?

8 Why do you think companies take an active interest in the standard-setting process of the accounting profession?

9 Given that general-purpose financial reports are aimed at providing 'information useful to users for making and evaluating decisions about the allocation of scarce resources', discuss to what extent these users are represented in the due process.

10 Discuss and explain the different reporting requirements for public and private companies. Why do you think some private companies are exempted from regulatory standards?

11 You are discussing the financial position of a company with a friend. The friend is considering buying shares in the company and he comments, 'I can't rely on the audit report as it does not guarantee the financial statements are correct'. Your friend knows you have just completed an accounting subject and he asks you for your opinion about the value of the audit report. What would you say to your friend?

12 Roy Dorro is running a small accounting practice with annual fees of $100 000. He is approached by the CEO of a company which has just established premises in Roy's area. The CEO wants Roy to conduct the annual audit for the company and has indicated that a fee of $50 000 would be provided for the audit. Should Roy have any concerns about audit independence if he were to accept the engagement?

13 Examine the following cases for Ruliable Ltd and indicate whether you believe the company should recognise a liability.
   a Potential costs due to the discovery of a possible defect related to one of its products. It is probable that claims will be made and the costs can be reliably estimated.
   b There is a potential claim for damages to be received from a lawsuit filed this year against another company. It is probable that the proceeds from the claim will be received by Ruliable next year.
   c The company has a policy whereby they overhaul their major machinery every five years. This has been their practice for the last 25 years. At the balance date, the machinery had been overhauled three years previously.

ETHICS CASE STUDIES

1 Tom has been employed at New Incentives Ltd for six months, after recently graduating from university with a degree in accounting. It is his first job after trying to find employment for six months. Tom's boss has asked him for a favour in preparing the income statement for the year. She wants Tom to include in income cash received for services to be provided next year. She also wants him to record as an asset cash paid for advertisements which were screened on television two weeks before the end of the accounting period. Tom is aware that management is to be paid bonuses based on the net profit for the period.

Discuss

   a how the transactions should be reported according to your understanding of the AASB *Framework*
   b what Tom should do.

2 Michael P. Cockley is a young accountant who has just commenced practising in the Perth suburb of Nedlands. He is, at present, trying to build up his practice which specialises in giving taxation advice and preparing clients' taxation returns.

   One of Michael's clients is Leslie Raby, a rather testy ex-navy officer. Captain Raby has only just come to Michael after falling out with another accountant. Amanda Trefrey, the former accountant, merely mentioned that there had been 'personality clashes and communication problems'.

Michael, in perusing Raby's taxation assessment, notices that it differs materially from his estimate and the difference is very much in his client's favour. In checking Raby's file, it becomes clear to Michael that the Taxation Office has made an error. Further, there is a strong likelihood that this error will result in a permanent advantage to his client. Raby's tax return was a full and proper disclosure and has been correctly prepared. An error has been made by the Taxation Office and it is unlikely that the error will ever be discovered. In discussions with his client, it becomes apparent to Michael that Raby is aware of the error and the monetary gains that will accrue to him if this error is overlooked.

Discuss

a   what Michael should do under the circumstances
b   whether the 'oversight' is any different from stealing if nothing is said about the client standing to benefit from the error made by the government department and keeping the money
c   what responsibility Michael has. Should he act independently of the captain's wishes?

(Adapted from Paul H. Northcott, *Ethics and the Practising Accountant: Case Studies*, Australian Society of Certified Practising Accountants, 1993.)

ANSWERS TO REVIEW EXERCISES

1   Accounting standards (AAS) are prepared and issued by the Australian Accounting Standards Board (AASB). These standards are legal standards and must be followed by all corporate reporting entities and disclosing entities pursuant with the *Corporations Act*. Members of the accounting bodies in Australia must also follow these standards when preparing accounts for other types of entities. AASB standards must be approved by federal parliament, which has veto power. From 1 January 2005 the standards issued by the AASB became equivalent to the IFRSs, as issued by the IASB.

2   • There will be less of a need to develop accounting standards on every issue; hence, there should be fewer accounting standards.
   • Those accounting standards still required should be more consistent than is the case at present.
   • Using the same definitions for basic concepts such as assets and liabilities should improve communication among accountants, the standard setters and the constituents.
   • Standard-setting bodies should develop standards which are consistent with the conceptual framework. Hence, standard setters will be more accountable. At the same time they will be able to better resist the lobbying efforts of parties with vested interests on certain issues.

3   The reporting entity concept allows entities that do not have users which are dependent on general-purpose financial reports to avoid the unnecessary costs that are involved in the preparation of such reports. These costs are incurred in complying with all accounting standards and concept statements. An example might be a family company where the family members do not need general-purpose financial reports to tell them how their business is performing because of their close involvement in its running.

4   Auditors are required to give an opinion as to the truth and fairness of financial statements, and whether they comply with accounting standards and the *Corporations Act*. In so doing, they give some assurance that there are no material errors. However, immaterial errors can slip through the audit. It is the director's responsibility to prepare the financial statements; therefore, the auditors should not be expected to guarantee that they are 100 per cent accurate.

5   This is a difficult and controversial question. In the USA the Sarbanes-Oxley Act 2002 places restrictions on the type of services, other than auditing, that an audit firm can provide to an audit client. The approach in Australia through *CLERP 9* involves some restrictions and more disclosure about the fees an auditor derives from the provision of other services to an audit client. The real issue is auditor independence, and some argue that an auditor can provide other services and still be independent due to professionalism. Others disagree and, partially as a result of what happened with Enron, argue for restrictions on the amount and type of other services an auditor can provide to audit clients.

3

LEARNING OBJECTIVES

At the end of this chapter, you should be able to:

1   identify what is meant by the terms 'wealth' and 'profit'

2   explain the meaning of historic cost

3   explain the replacement cost method of measurement

4   explain the economic value method of measurement

5   explain the net realisable value method of measurement

6   explain the fair value method of measurement

Introduction

In Chapter 1 we established that there are a number of different users of accounting information, each of whom requires different information for different purposes. However, there are some items of information that are required by most users. They want to know what an entity controls, what it owes and how it is performing.

An asset was defined in Chapter 2 as an economic resource controlled – but not necessarily owned – by an entity. The information about what an entity controls and what it owes could be termed the worth of the entity, or its wealth. This measure of wealth or worth relates to a point in time. The other information that is required by most users concerns the way in which the entity has performed over a period of time. This performance during a period can be measured as a change in wealth over time. If you increase your wealth you have performed better, in financial terms, than someone whose wealth has decreased over the same period of time. The measurement of the change in wealth over time is referred to in accounting terminology as 'profit measurement'. Profit is sometimes referred to as 'income'. We use the term 'profit' in this chapter to represent the 'increase in wealth', as the term 'income' was used in Chapter 2 to represent the 'sum of revenues and gains'.

In this chapter we will look at the ways in which accountants can measure wealth and profit, and discuss the merits of the alternatives available. We also examine, in some detail, the way in which the choice of a measurement system affects the resultant profit and wealth measures. To do this we need to start by defining profit and wealth, because these two ideas are directly linked.

Profit and wealth

Identify what is meant by the terms 'wealth' and 'profit'

A definition of profit that is widely accepted by accountants is based on the definition of an individual's income (profit) put forward by the economist Sir John Hicks (1946), who stated:

> Income [profit] is that amount which an individual can consume and still be as
> well off at the end of the period as he or she was at the start of the period.

This definition is shown in Figure 3.1.

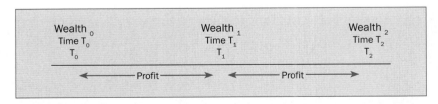

Figure 3.1 Profit or loss is determined by measuring wealth at different points in time

By referring to the diagram, we can arrive at the profit or loss for period 1 by measuring wealth at the start of the period, at time T_0, and subtracting that figure from our measurement of wealth at the end of the period, at time T_1. Similarly, the profit or loss for the second period can be measured by subtracting the wealth at time T_1 from the wealth at time T_2.

It should also be clear from Figure 3.1 that wealth is static and represents a stock at a particular point in time. Thus, $wealth_0$ is the stock of wealth at time T_0, $wealth_1$ is the stock of wealth at time T_1 and $wealth_2$ is the stock of wealth at time T_2.

KEY CONCEPT 3.1

WEALTH

Wealth is a static measure and represents a stock at a particular point in time. This stock can change over time. Thus, the wealth measured at the start of a period will not necessarily be equal to the wealth measured at the end of the period. The difference between the two is the profit or loss for that period of time.

If we look at the way in which profit is depicted in Figure 3.1, it is apparent that profit is a flow over time. To measure the profit earned over a period of time, it is necessary to measure the stock of wealth at the start and end of that period.

KEY CONCEPT 3.2

PROFIT

Profit represents the difference between the wealth at the start of the period and at the end of the period. Unlike wealth, which is essentially a static measure, profit is a measure of flow which summarises activity over a period.

To summarise, we have shown that we can express the profit for the first period, from time T_0 to time T_1, as:

$$\text{profit for period}_1 = \text{wealth}_1 - \text{wealth}_0$$

Similarly, we can express the profit for the second period, the period between time T_1 and time T_2, as:

$$\text{profit for period}_2 = \text{wealth}_2 - \text{wealth}_1$$

We have also established that the profit or loss is derived by measuring the wealth of an individual, or an entity, at two points in time. This is straightforward, but let us look in more detail at what we are trying to measure and how we can measure it.

We will start by examining the case of an individual because this is simpler and more in line with your own experience. The underlying arguments and principles are just the same for an entity but the degree of complexity increases. Let us suppose that we asked an individual to measure his or her wealth; that is, the sum of possessions less debts.

Example 3.1: Alexia

Alexia came up with the following list of assets and told us that she owed nothing.

At the start of the year: T_0	At the end of the year: T_1
A new Ford Laser	A one-year-old Ford Laser
One new dress	The same dress
Five shirts	The same five shirts
Four pairs of jeans	Five pairs of jeans
One surfboard	One surfboard
$400 cash	$500 cash

While the lists above might accurately reflect the assets Alexia controls and what she owes, we cannot easily see whether she is better or worse off at the end of the year than she was at the start. We could perhaps say, with the benefit of our own knowledge of the world, that she must be worse off because everything is one year older; this, however, assumes that the value of her possessions decreases with time. In many cases that is a reasonable assumption, but clearly there are some cases where their value increases. For example, would our attitudes towards the value of her possessions change if the car was a 1957 FJ Holden? Leaving that question aside for a moment, you will have noticed that once we started to discuss the measurement of wealth we also started talking of the more abstract concept of value.

This raises two questions: one relates to value, which we shall discuss in more detail later; the other relates to the way in which we assign value. In the case of the lists of possessions in our example, the easiest item to deal with in terms of value is the cash. This is because it has already had a value assigned to it with which we are all familiar: a monetary value. On the face of it, therefore, it seems that if we assigned a monetary value to each of the items in the list we would have solved part of our problem. In fact, it is not as easy as that because we all know that the value of money is not stable; we only have to listen to our grandparents or even our parents talking about what money used to buy to realise that the value of money has decreased over time.

If we leave the problem of the changing value of money aside and use money as a measure of value, then we have no problem with the value of the cash in the bank, but what of the other items? What is the value of the car, for example? Is it worth less because it is one year older, and, if so, how much less? The same line of argument can be applied to the dress, shirts and surfboard. However, in the case of the jeans we do not even know whether they are the same jeans; clearly, there must be at least one pair that has been acquired during the year, since Alexia had five pairs at the end of the year compared with four at the beginning. In addition we have yet to establish whether the age of the items is important for the purposes of arriving at a value. In order to decide on that question, we first need to look at the possibilities available to us.

Although numerous alternatives are put forward, many are combinations of those dealt with here. We shall limit our discussion to the most common possibilities. The terms are defined, where appropriate, later in this chapter. The important point to note at this time is the relationship between wealth and profit and the way in which a change in the measurement of one affects the other. This will be explored in more detail later, using our example of Alexia.

Alternative systems of valuation

For convenience, we will first deal with those alternatives that relate to cost and then discuss those that are based on some concept of value. We start with historic cost and after that discuss replacement cost.

HISTORIC COST

Historic cost is the cost incurred by the individual or entity in acquiring an item measured at the time of the originating transaction. It is extremely important because it underpins most current accounting practice. For example, we know that the historic cost of this textbook to you will be different from the historic cost to the bookshop. This difference is what keeps the bookshop in business. But let us take our example a stage further. Let us assume that at the end of the year you no longer need this textbook and decide to sell it. In this situation you will probably find that the book is no longer worth what you paid for it and, therefore, the historic cost is no longer a fair representation of the book's worth or your wealth. In order to tackle this problem, when measuring your wealth at the end of the year you could write the historic cost down to some lower figure to represent the amount of use you have had from the book. Accounting follows a similar process and the resulting figure is known as the written-down cost. It can be described as the historic cost after an adjustment for use. The adjustment for use is commonly referred to as depreciation, and there are several ways to arrive at a depreciation figure. This concept will be discussed in Chapter 9.

LO 2

Explain the meaning of historic cost

KEY CONCEPT 3.3

HISTORIC COST

The historic cost is the cost incurred by the individual or entity in acquiring an item – measured at the time of the originating transaction.

The problem with historic cost and written-down historic cost is that, as the value of money and goods changes over time, they are likely to be only a fair representation of value at a particular point in time; that is, at the point of the original transaction. At any other time, the historic cost of an item is a fair representation of its worth only if the world is static; that is, with no innovation, for example. Clearly this is not the case and so we should look for alternative measures. One such alternative to the historic cost of an item is its replacement cost. This is certainly more up to date and allows for the changes that take place in a non-static world.

Review exercise 1

In your own words, explain the meaning of 'historic cost'.

REPLACEMENT COST

Explain the replacement cost method of measurement

The replacement cost (also known as 'current cost' in the IASB *Framework* discussed in Chapter 2) of an item is the amount that would have to be paid at today's prices to purchase a similar item. It is often very relevant, as those who have had cars written off will know. In those cases, the amount that the insurance company pays you often bears no relationship to what it would cost to replace your car, perhaps because yours was better than average or had just had a new engine installed. The first problem that arises in using replacement cost is that you have to want to replace the item. You might not want to replace a textbook that you used at school because it is no longer of use to you. Even if you do want to replace the item, you may find that it is difficult to identify the replacement cost. Think of a unique item such as Leonardo da Vinci's *Mona Lisa*!

KEY CONCEPT 3.4

REPLACEMENT COST

The replacement cost is the amount that would have to be paid at today's prices to purchase an item similar to the existing item.

Even if you could replace an item with an exact replica, you might not wish to do so. You might wish to obtain a newer version or one with extra functions. The most obvious example of this kind is the replacement of computer equipment, which is constantly expanding in power while its size and its price are generally decreasing. This leads us to the same problem that we had with historic cost: the replacement cost of a computer does not take into account the age of the machine that we actually own. The solution is the same as for historic cost: estimate the effect of usage and arrive at a written-down replacement cost.

As we can see, there are distinct problems in using either historic cost or replacement cost. In a number of situations these two types of costs are unlikely to be useful measures of value or wealth. Historic cost is unlikely to be useful when prices change, whatever the reason for that change. Replacement cost, while overcoming that problem by using up-to-date costs, is itself irrelevant if there is no intention of replacing the item.

Before reading the next sections on measurement methods other than cost, it is worth spending a few minutes thinking of the situations in which historic cost and replacement cost are appropriate and those situations when they are unlikely to be suitable. Any measure is useful only if it is appropriate.

For example, while the acceleration of a car may be important in certain circumstances, it is irrelevant for an emergency stop. Similarly, the historic cost or replacement cost of a motor car is unlikely to be useful if we wish to sell the car, because the selling price will be governed by other factors. The alternatives to these cost-based measures are measures which are related to worth. However, as we will see, these measures also have their own set of problems.

Economic value

The economic value (referred to as 'present value' in the IASB *Framework* discussed in Chapter 2) of an item is the value of the expected earnings from using the item discounted at an appropriate rate to give a present-day value. For an example of what is meant by the terms 'present value' and 'discount rate', consider the following: a person deposits $100 in a bank at a fixed interest rate of 10 per cent compounded annually for five years. At the end of five years the $100 would have grown to $161.51 (assuming no taxes or charges). The present value of $161.51 discounted at 10 per cent per annum produces a figure of $100. Discounting is the opposite of compounding. Compounding asks: how much will I have after *x* periods at *y* interest rate? Discounting asks: what is the present value of a sum to be received in *x* periods given *y* interest rate? Chapter 16 has more detailed information on the time value of money and capital investment decisions.

LO **4**

Explain the economic value method of measurement

KEY CONCEPT 3.5

ECONOMIC VALUE

Economic value is, or would be, an ideal measure of value and wealth. Economic value is the value of the expected future earnings from using the item in question discounted at an appropriate rate to give a present-day value.

The problem is not in defining the measure of economic value but in actually estimating future earnings. This implies a knowledge of what is going to happen; problems to do with foreseeing technological change, fashion changes and so on make the estimation of future earnings problematical. Even if we assume that we can make reliable forecasts, we are left with the question of finding an appropriate rate at which to discount the estimated future earnings. The trouble here is that each individual might wish to use a different rate depending on his or her circumstances. For example, a millionaire might not worry very much if money is available in a year rather than immediately, but if you have no money to buy your next meal the situation is entirely different. We should not reject this measure because of these problems, since, with the use of mathematical techniques relating to probability, it is still a useful tool in decision making. In fact, it is the underlying techniques such as net present value (see Chapter 16) which are often used in investment appraisal decisions.

Net realisable value

The net realisable value is the estimated proceeds of sale less, where applicable, all further costs to the stage of completion and less all costs to be incurred in marketing, selling and distribution to customers. On the face of it, such a measure should be easily obtainable, but in practice the amount for which an item can be sold varies with the circumstances of the sale. These circumstances are not always connected with the item for sale but can depend on such things as the location of the property: for example, an ice works would have more value in the tropics than in Antarctica, all other things being equal. The problems of arriving at the net realisable value are apparent in the second-hand car market where there is a trade price and a range of retail prices. Another good example is the

LO **5**

Explain the net realisable value method of measurement

housing market, where independent valuations can differ by as much as $40000 on a property worth between $110000 and $150000.

KEY CONCEPT 3.6

NET REALISABLE VALUE

The net realisable value is an alternative measure of value to economic value. The net realisable value is defined as the estimated proceeds of sale, less (where applicable) all further costs to the stage of completion and less all costs to be incurred in marketing, selling and distribution to customers.

Besides the problem of arriving at a value, other factors affect the net realisable value. For example, if you are in financial difficulties you may be prepared to accept less than the market value in order to get a quick sale. The value in the latter situation is known as the forced sale value and is the most likely value where circumstances are unfavourable to the seller. Further, one is assuming that there is a buyer who is willing to buy, otherwise the property is valueless relative to converting it into cash. If, on the other hand, the market conditions are neutral between buyer and seller, then the net realisable value is likely to be the open market value.

Review exercise 2

In your own words, explain what is meant by the net realisable value method of measurement.

Example 3.1 continued

It should be clear from the preceding sections that plenty of alternative measurement methods are available, each of which has its own problems. If you remember, the starting point for this discussion was that we wished to establish whether Alexia was better off at the end of the period than she was at the start. Had she made a profit? The problem is not one of finding a concept of profit, the problem is, in fact, one of measurement: most of these concepts rely either on a measurement of a future amount or on the measurement of wealth.

We have already pointed out that to measure a future amount is extremely difficult in the real world because of the effects of uncertainty. This leaves us with the alternative of measuring wealth and leads to the problem of finding the most appropriate measure. As we have seen, all the measures put forward so far have inherent difficulties, and it may be that the solution lies in combining two or more of these to obtain the best measure. For the purposes of this introductory text it is unnecessary to probe this area in greater depth but further reading is given at the end of the chapter to provide additional background for those interested in pursuing the topic. Before leaving this area, let us reconsider the example based on the wealth of Alexia and assign some values to see what effect the choice of measure will have.

Description	Year T_0		
	Replacement cost	Historic cost	Net realisable value
	$	$	$
Ford Laser	13 500	13 500	10 500
Dress	200	210	30
Shirts	75	75	10
Surfboard	180	180	100
Jeans	400	400	60
Cash	400	400	400

If you study the figures carefully you will notice that the only figure common to all three columns is the cash figure. Apart from the cost of the dress, the replacement cost and the historic cost for all the other items are also identical. In reality this will always be the case at the time when the goods are bought, but it is unlikely to be so at any other time. In this example, the fact that the replacement cost of the dress is different from the historic cost indicates that the dress was bought when the price of dresses was higher than it was at the start of the year in question. In other words, the point in time at which we are measuring is different from the date of acquisition and, as we said, in these circumstances the replacement cost is likely to differ from the historic cost.

You will also notice that the net realisable value is lower than the historic cost and replacement cost, even though some of the items were clearly new at the start of the year. Once again, this is obviously the case in most situations because personal goods that are being resold are effectively second-hand goods, even if they have not been used. The situation for a business entity is not necessarily the same because sometimes the goods are bought not for use but for resale; for example, by a retailer or wholesaler. In these cases the net realisable value of the goods bought for resale should be higher than the cost – otherwise the retailer would not stay in business very long.

Let us now look at Alexia's situation at the end of the year and assign some values to the items owned at that time. We will then be in a position to measure the increase in wealth, or profit, and to use this as a basis for discussion of some of the problems of measurement which we referred to earlier.

Description	Year T_1		
	Replacement cost	Historic cost	Net realisable value
	$	$	$
Ford Laser	10 000	13 500	8 000
Dress	270	210	27
Shirts	80	75	5
Surfboard	180	180	90
Jeans	400	400	30
Cash	500	500	500

You will notice that (disregarding the cash) the figures have changed in all cases, except for historic cost where they are the same as at the start of the year. This highlights one of the problems with this measure: it tells us only what an item costs, not necessarily what it is worth today.

Let us look more closely at the car. As you can see, the replacement cost is lower than at the start of the year. This is because the car we are replacing at the end of the year is a one-year-old model rather than a new model. There is also a problem in using replacement cost for such items as the dress. It may be unlikely that you would try or wish to purchase a year-old dress, whereas there is a ready market for second-hand cars. You will also see that the replacement cost is higher than the net realisable value. This is because costs would be incurred in selling the car, and the amount that you would receive would be reduced by these costs.

Let us now look at what we get in terms of our measures of wealth and profit, starting with historic cost.

	Historic cost	
Description	Year T_0	Year T_1
	$	$
Ford Laser	13 500	13 500
Dress	210	210
Shirts	75	75
Surfboard	180	180
Jeans	400	400
Cash	400	500
	14 765	14 865

We can now measure the profit under historic cost as we have a figure for wealth at the start and end of the year. Thus, using the formula:

$$\text{wealth at } T_1 - \text{wealth at } T_0 = \text{profit}$$

we get:

$$\$14\,865 - \$14\,765 = \$100$$

The figures at T_1, and therefore the profit, would be different if we used written-down cost. Remember, written-down cost is the reduction in the cost of an asset to reflect the use of the asset.

Let us look at what would happen if we used replacement cost rather than historic cost.

	Replacement cost	
Description	Year T_0	Year T_1
	$	$
Ford Laser	13 500	10 000
Dress	200	270
Shirts	75	80
Surfboard	180	180
Jeans	400	400
Cash	400	500
	14 755	11 430

We can now measure the profit under replacement cost as we have a figure for wealth at the start and end of the year. Thus, using the formula:

$$\text{wealth at } T_1 - \text{wealth at } T_0 = \text{profit}$$

we get:

$$\$11\,430 - \$14\,755 = \$3325 \text{ loss}$$

In other words, according to the replacement cost figures, Alexia is $3325 worse off at the end of the year than she was at the start.

Finally, let us see what the situation would be if we were using the net realisable value to arrive at our measures of wealth.

Description	Net realisable value	
	Year T_0 $	Year T_1 $
Ford Laser	10 500	8 000
Dress	30	27
Shirts	10	5
Surfboard	100	90
Jeans	60	30
Cash	400	500
	11 100	8 652

We can now measure the profit under net realisable value as we have a figure for wealth at the start and end of the year. Thus, using the formula:

$$\text{wealth at } T_1 - \text{wealth at } T_0 = \text{profit}$$

we get:

$$\$8652 - \$11\,100 = \$2448 \text{ loss}$$

Once again, using net realisable value as the basis of measuring wealth we find that Alexia is worse off at the end of the year than she was at the start.

You might well be wondering at this point which is the correct answer. This takes us back to the question of who is to use the information and for what purpose it is to be used. Clearly this varies from case to case; however, it is more important, at the present time, that you understand that differences arise depending on the valuation method adopted. Alexia is clearly worse off at the end of the year than she was at the start since she no longer has a brand-new car, so you may feel that replacement cost or net realisable value are the better alternatives. However, you must bear in mind that we are trying to measure the amount that can be spent while maintaining wealth; there is a hidden assumption that Alexia wants to maintain the wealth she had at the start.

This might not, in fact, be the case. Alexia might, for example, have been banned from driving, which could mean that she does not want to replace her car. The net realisable value would be more useful in this case, because she would probably want to sell the car. However, although she has lost her driving licence she will still need to go out – even if only to buy food – and will need to wear some clothes, so to value these on the assumption that they are going to be sold is not a defensible position.

Current accounting practice

The historic cost method is the common measurement method adopted in most countries. This is specifically stated in paragraph 101 of the IASB *Framework*, as mentioned in Chapter 2. However, the *Framework* also acknowledges that other bases of measurement like net realisable value, present value and current cost are also used for certain types of assets in certain cases. Accounting standards like AASB 116 *Property, Plant and Equipment* require all items of property, plant and equipment to be initially recognised at cost. However, AASB 116 allows entities to choose cost or fair value subsequent to the date of acquisition if they so choose. Other accounting standards like AASB 139 *Financial Instruments: Recognition and Measurement* require the use of fair value for most types of financial assets. The use of fair value allows entities to report the changes in the value of non-current assets since the date of acquisition. AASB 102 *Inventories* requires inventories to be valued at the lower of cost and net realisable value for profit-making entities. NFP entities are permitted to use the lower of replacement cost and net realisable value for donated inventory as there is no cost.

FAIR VALUE

6

Explain the fair value method of measurement

The fair value is the amount that a willing buyer and seller are prepared to exchange for an item in an arm's length transaction. This means that it is a genuine transaction and that the two parties are in no way related. The market value of an asset traded in a liquid market such as Telstra shares is its fair value. However, where there is no liquid market (such as for the shares of an unlisted company), then the fair value needs to be derived in some other way. This could be the market value of a similar item. For example, the fair value of a house could be based on recent selling prices for houses of a similar size and condition in your area.

KEY CONCEPT 3.7

FAIR VALUE

The fair value is the amount that a willing buyer is prepared to exchange to a willing seller for an asset in an arm's length transaction.

Review exercise 3

What is the difference between fair value and net realisable value?

You should now read the Woodside financial report in Appendix 1 and observe that Note 1(A) states that the company uses the historic cost basis except for derivative financial instruments and available-for-sale financial assets which have been measured at fair value.

CASE STUDY 3.1

COCA-COLA BITES THE BULLET
By Andrew Heathcote

The new international reporting standards are about to take some of the fizz out of one softdrink maker's balance sheet. For a chief financial officer who is about to lose $1.9 billion from his company's balance sheet, John Wartig seems remarkably calm. Wartig is the CFO of Coca-Cola Amatil, and few companies will be more affected by the international financial reporting standards (IFRS) than the Australian softdrink company. Under the new standards, intangible assets must be recorded at historic cost – not fair value. For Coca-Cola Amatil this means that $1.9 billion in asset restatements made to its bottling agreements will have to go. This represents 32% of Coca-Cola Amatil's total assets and 52% of its revenue in 2004.

Coca-Cola Amatil is one of the first companies to bear the brunt of the new standards because it reports on a calendar-year basis. Australian companies must comply with the standards for financial years beginning on or after January 1, 2005. Wartig says the intangible asset restatement will appear in Coca-Cola's half-year report to June 30, 2005, which will be released in August. He says that in the notes to the report, the company will explain what the carrying value of the assets would have been under the old standards.

Coca-Cola Amatil first informed the market of the $1.9-billion restatement in August last year. When revaluing intangible assets to achieve IFRS compliance, the book entry is treated as a restatement and not a write-down. This is important because it leads to a reduction in retained earnings, not profit.

Wartig says Coca-Cola Amatil's decision to get in early and explain the consequences will minimise the backlash from investors. 'We are very satisfied with the way our transition has been received by the market. Other [companies] who are not as prepared or have not sufficiently thought through the issues may not get the same warm reception.'

Although Wartig is confident the new standard will not hurt Coca-Cola Amatil's earnings or cash flow, he remains a supporter of fair-value reporting of intangibles. 'There seems to be a lack of symmetry,' he says. 'You might have bought an asset for $1 million, which you impair and write down to $800 000. Two years later, it may be worth $1 million again but you can't write it back up.'

Extract from article in the
Business Review Weekly, 26 May 2005

COMMENTARY

The article reports on the impact of the move to IFRS for Coca-Cola Amatil. Under IFRS, intangible assets are reported at historic cost and cannot be revalued upwards unless there is an active market for the intangible asset. The $1.9 billion dollars is the difference between the fair value as determined by Coca-Cola and the historic cost. How reliable is a fair value for an intangible asset? This is one of the reasons the IFRS do not allow revaluation of intangible assets – except in very specific situations and even then only for certain types of intangible assets. The measurement of assets has had a significant impact for Coca-Cola Amatil. We discuss intangible assets in Chapter 9.

Conclusion

We have seen that there are a number of alternative ways of measuring a person's wealth and that each has its own problems. One common objection to both replacement cost and net realisable value is that they are subjective, which is true in many cases. This is one reason why accounts are still prepared using historic costs or modified historic costs, even though, as we have seen in the simple example of Alexia, this can lead to irrelevant information being produced and wrong decisions being taken. Another reason that is often cited for retaining historic cost in the accounts is that it is a system which is based on what was actually spent, and owners of entities need to know what the money has been spent on. But to what extent can the advantage of historic cost make up for its deficiencies as a measure of wealth and, therefore, as the basis of the profit measure? This question is and has been the subject of much debate which will continue for many years to come. For our purposes we need to be aware of the problems associated with using each of the alternatives, because they might well result in different decisions being taken.

SUMMARY

LO 1

LEARNING OBJECTIVE 1

Identify what is meant by the terms 'wealth' and 'profit'

Wealth is a static measure and represents a stock at a particular point in time. This stock can change over time. Thus, the wealth measured at the start of a period will not necessarily be equal to the wealth measured at the end of the period. The difference between the two is the profit or loss for that period of time.

Profit represents the difference between the wealth at the start of a period and at the end of the period. Unlike wealth, which is essentially a static measure, profit is a measure of flow which summarises activity over a period.

LO 2

LEARNING OBJECTIVE 2

Explain the meaning of historic cost

The historic cost is the cost incurred by the individual or entity in acquiring an item – measured at the time of the originating transaction.

LO 3

LEARNING OBJECTIVE 3

Explain the replacement cost method of measurement

The replacement cost is the amount that would have to be paid at today's prices to purchase an item similar to the existing item.

LO 4

LEARNING OBJECTIVE 4

Explain the economic value method of measurement

Economic value is, or would be, an ideal measure of value and wealth. The economic value is the value of the expected future earnings from using the item in question discounted at an appropriate rate to give a present-day value.

LO 5

LEARNING OBJECTIVE 5

Explain the net realisable value method of measurement

The net realisable value is an alternative measure of value to economic value. The net realisable value is defined as the estimated proceeds of sale, less (where applicable) all further costs to the stage of completion and less all costs to be incurred in marketing, selling and distribution to the customer.

LO 6

LEARNING OBJECTIVE 6

Explain the fair value method of measurement

The fair value is the amount that a willing buyer is prepared to exchange to a willing seller for an asset in an arm's length transaction

REFERENCES

Hicks, Sir John, 1946. *Value and Capital*, Clarendon Press, Oxford.

FURTHER READING

Australian Accounting Research Foundation, 1998. *Measurement in Financial Accounting*, Accounting Theory Monograph No. 10.

Australian Accounting Standards Board. *Framework for the Preparation and Presentation of Financial Statements*, July, 2004.

Belkaoui, A.R. & Jones, S., 2001. *Accounting Theory*, 2nd edn, Thomson, Melbourne.

International Accounting Standards Board. *Framework for the Preparation and Presentation of Financial Statements*, April, 2001.

REVIEW QUESTIONS

1   Profit is normally seen as a flow over time, whereas wealth can be described as a stock at a point in time. Explain in your own words what is meant by the terms 'wealth' and 'profit' and the difference between a stock and a flow.

2   There are a number of different ways in which we can measure wealth. List the options discussed in this chapter, together with any drawbacks or problems that were identified with their use.

3   In certain situations we said that written-down costs could be used as an alternative measure. Explain in your own words the difference between cost and written-down cost and suggest when the latter would be more appropriate.

4   What effects, if any, do rapid changes in technology have on the appropriateness of each of the different ways of assigning a cost or a value to an item?

PROBLEMS FOR DISCUSSION AND ANALYSIS

1   Refer to the Woodside 2005 half-year financial report in Appendix 1.
   a   How does Woodside measure oil and gas properties?
   b   How does Woodside measure other plant and equipment?
   c   Note 2(g) refers to the 'Impairment of Assets'. What does this mean?.

2   a   If $100 is deposited in a 5 per cent per annum account, and the interest compounded, what is the future value after three years? (Show workings.)
   b   If $250 is deposited in a 6.5 per cent per annum account, and the interest compounded, what is the sum that is realised after three years? (Show workings.)

3   a   You are to receive a sum of $115.76 in three years. This amount has just been invested at 5 per cent per annum compound. What is the present value? (Show workings.)
   b   You are to receive a sum of $133.10 in three years. This amount has been invested at x per cent per annum compound. If the original sum was $100 what is the annual interest rate? (Show workings.)

4   Make a list of all your possessions and all your debts (that is, all your assets and liabilities) so that you can determine your own wealth. What values did you use for your possessions? Explain why you selected these values. You may also like to calculate your wealth one year ago. Did your wealth increase or decrease in the past year?

5   One reads of large sums of money being exchanged between soccer clubs in Europe. How do you think a club arrives at a figure of, say, $10 million for a player?

6 A Ford Laser was purchased by Totem Ford for $10 000 and later sold in new condition to Spike Buzley for $12 000. One year later, Spike crashed the car and was told by the Royal Automobile Club it would cost $4000 to repair. Spike was advised that his car would be worth $1000 if repairs were not made, and could be sold for $7000 if the repairs were made. Spike was alarmed to hear this because Totem Ford were now selling new Ford Lasers for $13 000.

   At the time Spike decides to have his car repaired, what would be:
   a the historic cost
   b the replacement cost
   c the net realisable value?

7 Two sisters decided to go into business buying and selling beds. Details of their transactions are as follows.

   They initially bought 400 beds at $200 each. At the end of six months they had sold 300 of the 400 beds for $300 each. Unfortunately, during that time the bed manufacturer, who was their only source of supply, had increased the price of each bed to $240. To make matters worse, a discount store had opened in the area and it was selling the same beds for $280 each. The sisters found that, on average, over the six months they had incurred costs for advertising and so on which amounted to $20 for each bed that was sold.

   a On the basis of the information provided, calculate what the sisters' wealth was at the start of the six months and at the end of the six months, and what profit had been made. Calculations should be made using historic cost, replacement cost and net realisable value.
   b Having calculated the profit for the first six months, discuss whether the profit figure is a useful benchmark for measuring the performance of the business, and also whether it is useful as a guide to future profitability.

8 Jean owns a shop which used to sell clothes but she has now decided that, given the location, she would make more money running a restaurant on the same premises. She has obtained planning permission for the change of use and has bought some of the equipment needed, but has not yet started trading. She has made a list of the items that the business owns:
   • freehold shop
   • hanging display rail for clothes
   • a two-year-old car which is essential for the business
   • new restaurant tables and chairs
   • cash register
   • a quantity of fashion garments that were not sold in the closing-down sale.

   Under certain circumstances, only one of the various methods of valuation is appropriate. Giving brief reasons for your choice, suggest the most appropriate value to be placed on each of the above items.

   You may find that you need more information or have to make some assumptions. This is normal, but you should state any assumptions that you are making.

9 If the persons/things listed below were crucial to your entity and had to be insured:
   a How would you initially value them?
   b How would you value them 12 months after the initial date of acquisition (or accession)?
      i   An elite football player
      ii A 2001 Holden Commodore car
      iii A building of heritage value – for example, the Sydney Opera House
      iv The Prime Minister
      v   A block of land
      vi The trademark 'Coca-Cola'.
   Note: Assumptions may need to be made; please state any assumptions that you make.

10 On 1 July 20X1, the KLT Company purchased a very specialised item of machinery. KLT is the only company in Australia producing a special instrument used in the medical industry; hence, the new machinery has no resale value other than its scrap value. The following is a list of various values at 30 June 20X2 for the machine under different valuation methods discussed in this chapter.

	$
Historic cost	1 000 000
Net realisable value	10 000
Replacement cost	1 250 000

Required

From the values listed (or any other value you believe is relevant), discuss which one the following users would consider as most relevant for their purposes:
a   a banker considering lending funds to KLT with the specialised machinery providing the security
b   a shareholder in assessing the value of the company's shares
c   management in assessing the performance of the company.

Note to instructors: *The following problems are considered more suitable for use in MBA courses. However, undergraduate courses may also find them useful.*

11 Michelle Computers Ltd has had a difficult year owing to increasing costs associated with keeping its hardware and software up to date in the face of rapidly improving technology. As company accountant, you are aware that the company is overstocked with out-of-date virus software which the board of directors wishes to have valued at cost. 'After all', the managing director tells you, 'you accountants follow the historic cost convention'.
a   Should the software be valued at cost? If not, what value should be placed on it?
b   The directors are responsible for the final accounts. What action, if any, should you take?
c   If historic cost is used, will it affect the income statement?

12 Merlin's Magic Supply Company Ltd lists the following assets and liabilities at time periods T_0 and T_1:

	Historic cost		Replacement cost		Net realisable value	
	T_0	T_1	T_0	T_1	T_0	T_1
Cash	1 000	2 000	1 000	2 000	1 000	2 000
Land	10 000	10 000	12 000	14 000	12 000	14 000
Inventory	1 500	2 250	1 500	2 500	1 500	2 500
Trade creditors	1 000	1 500	1 000	1 500	1 000	1 500
Trade debtors	1 200	1 750	1 250	1 750	1 150	1 650

a   From the different valuation methods discussed in this chapter calculate the most appropriate change in net worth of the company, with supporting arguments for your decision, if it is:
  i   a small trading company
  ii a superannuation plan.
b   If you were liquidating this company at time T_1, what value would you place on it? Explain your assumptions.

13 The article 'Asset claims shrugged off' (see below) indicates that Southcorp will report a lower profit due to a low valuation of grape assets and the revaluation amount is included in the bottom line profits. This is because Southcorp was required by AASB 1037 *Self-generating and Regenerating Assets* to value its grapes at net market value (net realisable value) and include increases and decreases of this value in profit.

After reading the article, answer the following questions:

a   Do you think the change in the value of Southcorp's grape assets should be included in its profit? Give reasons.

b   Why do you think the standard setters have required net market value (fair value in IFRS) to be used for assets like grapes and sheep instead of historic cost?

ASSET CLAIMS SHRUGGED OFF

WINEMAKER Southcorp yesterday stood by its earlier forecasts after a major investment bank warned earnings would suffer from a flat asset revaluation.

Deutsche Bank issued a research note flagging a $20 million reduction in Southcorp's 2001–02 net profit to $161 million, citing a low valuation of the winemaker's grape assets.

The revaluation, which winemakers include in bottom line profits each year as an accounting standard, was now likely to be an increase of $1 million, compared with the $30 million forecast increase, Deutsche said.

Other efficiencies would cushion the bottom line from a full $29 million decline.

As well, the investment bank said a reduction in grape intake in 2001–02, compared with 2000–01, would drag down the winemaker's net profits by $5 million in 2002–03 and by $14 million in 2003–04.

It also lowered its share price target to $5.60, from $6.00.

The shares rose 18c to close at $5.55 yesterday.

Daily Telegraph, 10 July 2002

ETHICS CASE STUDY

Jane is the accountant for Salisbury Ltd and has received the following memo from her boss concerning a machine recently purchased from a competitor.

Dear Jane,

Due to the problems faced by our competitor, I have negotiated to purchase their plant and equipment, which is only 12 months old, for $500 000. The plant and equipment is worth at least $1 000 000. Therefore, I want you to record the plant and equipment at $1 000 000 and the difference between this and the cash paid should be included in profit for the period.

Signed Ted Johnson

Jane is aware that it has been a difficult year for Salisbury Ltd and it is likely to report a loss for the period. If the company reports a loss it will be in default of a contract with the bank and there is a risk the bank will stop the company's overdraft facility. Accounting standards require that assets be initially recorded at cost. Salisbury Ltd intends to use the plant and equipment, and has no intention of selling it.

Discuss

a   the appropriate way to record the transaction
b   what Jane should do.

ANSWERS TO REVIEW EXERCISES

1   Your answer should relate to what was paid for an item at the date of acquisition.

2   Your answer should include what an item can be sold for less the costs of selling it.

3   A major difference between fair value and net realisable value is that the expected costs to sell an item are deducted to determine NRV but are not deducted for fair value. Also, fair value requires knowledgeable and willing parties to the transaction whereas the NRV does not.

THE BALANCE SHEET
CHAPTER FOUR

4

LEARNING OBJECTIVES

At the end of this chapter, you should be able to:

1. explain the meaning and purpose of the balance sheet

2. identify the requirements an item must satisfy to be recognised as an asset on a balance sheet

3. explain the distinction between current and non-current assets

4. identify the requirements an item must satisfy to be recognised as a liability on a balance sheet

5. explain the distinction between current and non-current liabilities

6. explain the meaning of 'equity'

7. explain and apply the balance sheet equation

8. identify the limitations of a balance sheet

9. discuss the factors that influence the format of a balance sheet.

Note: In this chapter we refer to a balance sheet. This is the name used under Australian Equivalents to IFRS (AIFRS) for what was previously called a 'statement of financial position' in Australia.

Introduction

In Chapter 1 we discussed the objectives of accounting reports and the influences of users on financial reporting. We also discussed the limitations of accounting information and the role of accounting in business, its effect on business and some of the factors influencing accounting. In Chapter 3 we examined some possible approaches to measuring profit from the point of view of both the economist and the accountant. We now look more specifically at the ways in which accountants measure wealth and profit.

We suggested that the problem facing accountants is that of finding an appropriate basis for the measurement of wealth. There is also the additional problem that in the real world a system that only measures wealth and derives profit from it cannot cope with the complexity of present-day entities. Consider a large retailing group such as Woolworths: should they have to carry out a valuation of everything owned by the business – for example, all their premises, vehicles and stocks – on one day of the year? The costs of such an operation would make it prohibitively expensive, even if it were logistically possible. For companies such as BHP Billiton, where operations are carried out on a worldwide basis, these logistical problems would be even greater. Such a system would also make it very difficult for the managers or the owners to make decisions on a day-to-day basis because they would have information at hand only once a year. Because of these problems with annual valuation systems, we need to find separate ways of measuring wealth and profit.

The measurement of profit will be dealt with in detail in Chapter 5. In this chapter we concentrate on the problem of measuring wealth, and the way in which accounting approaches it. We look in some detail at the use of the balance sheet as the measurement of wealth, its component parts, such as assets and liabilities, and finally the format in which this statement is presented and the way in which that is influenced by the type of organisation, regulations and the needs of users.

Definition of the balance sheet

LO 1

Explain the meaning and purpose of the balance sheet

In the case of an individual, we have said that their wealth can be measured by simply listing the economic resources they control – assuming, of course, that they do not owe anybody money. To some extent the same can be said for an entity, although the level of complexity is greater. The way in which this listing is achieved is similar to that for an individual, and the resulting statement is called a balance sheet. You should note that the balance sheet relates to a position at a point in time. It is because of this that the analogy with a snapshot is often found in accounting textbooks.

KEY CONCEPT 4.1

THE BALANCE SHEET

The balance sheet is a statement, at one point in time, which shows all the resources controlled by the entity and all the obligations due by the entity.

This definition of a balance sheet is not intended to be comprehensive; it merely provides us with an outline of what we are referring to. Although an entity does not exist in the same way as a person, for accounting purposes (and for some legal purposes) an entity is presumed to exist in its own right and is treated as a separate entity from the person or persons who own or operate it. In broad terms, it is possible to account for any unit which has a separate and distinct existence. It may be that this is a hotel, for example, or a group of hotels, or a more complex organisation such as Hilton International Hotels. This idea of a separate entity is often referred to in accounting literature as 'the business entity principle'. It applies equally to organisations that are not commonly referred to as businesses, such as charitable organisations, clubs and societies. The question of whether the entity should be accounted for separately relates not only to the legal situation but also to whether it can be seen to have a separate existence.

KEY CONCEPT 4.2

THE BUSINESS ENTITY PRINCIPLE

The business entity principle states that transactions, assets and liabilities that relate to the entity are accounted for separately. It applies to all types of entities, irrespective of the fact that the entity may not be recognised as a separate legal or taxable entity.

While the application of this principle and the reasons for it are self-evident when we are looking at large public companies such as Telstra or Shell, they are less clear with smaller entities such as the corner newsagent or a second-hand car business. If, for example, you decided to set yourself up as a car dealer, for accounting purposes the cars purchased by you as a car dealer and the money earned as a result of that activity would be treated separately from your own personal car and money. This allows the tax authority to tax you separately on the profits from your business and it also helps you to determine the value of your business should you wish to sell it or take in a partner. The important point to remember is that for each business entity it is possible to account separately and, therefore, to draw up a balance sheet at a point in time. We now examine the balance sheet in more detail.

The purpose of the balance sheet

The purpose of a balance sheet is to communicate information about the financial position of an entity at a particular point in time. It summarises information contained in the accounting records in a clear and intelligible form. If the items contained in it are summarised and classified in an appropriate manner it can give information about the financial strength of the entity and indicate the relative liquidity of its assets. It also gives information about the liabilities of the entity; that is, what economic resources the entity is obliged to provide to other entities as a result of past transactions. The combination of this information can assist the user to evaluate the financial position of the entity.

It is an important statement when assessing the going concern of an entity which we discussed in Chapter 2 (see Key concept 2.6). It should be remembered, however, that financial statements are only one part of the information needed by users; therefore, the importance of this accounting statement should not be overemphasised.

KEY CONCEPT 4.3

LIQUIDITY

Liquidity refers to the ease with which assets can be converted to cash in the normal course of business.

In most entities, a balance sheet is prepared at least once a year. It can be done more frequently of course, or, indeed, less frequently. It is convention that dictates that a normal accounting period is a year, and tax laws and other legislation are set up on that basis. Because the balance sheet represents the position at one point in time, its usefulness is limited: the situation may have changed since the last statement was prepared. For example, if you prepare a balance sheet in December and consult it in October it will be 10 months out of date. To extend our snapshot analogy, we can picture a business as a movie and a balance sheet as a still from that movie. Clearly, in the case of a movie, the still does not give a complete picture, and the same can be said for the balance sheet.

Elements of the balance sheet

We need to know what a balance sheet contains. We have already said that it is similar to an individual's own measurement of wealth. If you think how you would measure your own wealth, you will realise that you need to make a list of the economic resources you control (assets) and take away the economic resources due to other entities (liabilities). For an entity, this listing of assets and liabilities at a particular point in time is the entity's balance sheet.

Given this information about the contents of a balance sheet, let us look in more detail at what is meant by assets and liabilities. We consider assets by looking at what constitutes an asset and how they are classified into subcategories. Definitions of assets and liabilities were given in Chapter 2. We restate these definitions and discuss each in turn.

ASSETS

Explain the requirements an item must satisfy to be recognised as an asset on a balance sheet

Although we can find many definitions of assets, most of them refer to legal ownership rights, and so do not accord with contemporary accounting thought. Most definitions contain some of the vital elements of a useful description, but a clear working explanation is needed. Assets are not defined in the *Corporations Act*; therefore, we turn to the definition provided by paragraph 49 of the AASB *Framework for the Preparation and Presentation of Financial Statements* (AASB 2004), already defined in Key concept 2.8 and restated in Key concept 4.4. This definition is in line with contemporary accounting thought and similar to that adopted by other standard-setting bodies.

Before an item can be considered as an asset for inclusion in the balance sheet it must not only meet the definition of an asset, it must also pass certain recognition criteria. First, it must be probable that the future economic benefits will eventuate and second, the asset must possess a cost or other value that can be measured reliably. Only when an item satisfies the definition and meets both recognition criteria will it qualify for inclusion on the balance sheet.

KEY CONCEPT 4.4

ASSETS

An asset is a resource controlled by the entity as a result of past events and from which future economic benefits are expected to flow to the entity. (AASB *Framework*, para. 49a) An asset is recognised in the balance sheet only when it is probable that the future economic benefits will flow to the entity and it must be possible to reliably measure the cost or other value of such benefits.

Future economic benefits

The clear implication in the term 'future economic benefits' is that for an item to be an asset there must be some clear expectation that some benefit will be derived from the item by the entity, either now or in the future, and that that benefit does not depend on physical form. This implies that the item must have some specific usefulness to the entity. An item that has no specific usefulness to the entity is not an asset. This is particularly important in times of rapidly changing technology as it suggests that the question of what is and what is not an asset can only be decided on the basis of its usefulness to the entity. For example, it is fairly obvious that a gold mine full of unmined gold is an asset for a mining business. However, there will come a point when all the gold has been removed and all that is left is a hole in the ground. The hole in the ground is no longer useful to the mining entity and it ceases to be an asset. On the other hand, a hole in the ground could have future economic benefits for a different entity; for example, a rubbish disposal business.

Measurement

One of the recognition criteria is that an asset must be capable of reliable measurement. The normal measure that is used is the dollar (a monetary unit). The problem, as discussed earlier, is: on what basis do we measure? Some items which may give future economic benefits are extremely difficult to measure. For example, the Sarich orbital engine, while still in the design stage, was able to raise millions of dollars in funds from investors. Alternatively, consider the worth of a trade name such as 'Coca-Cola', which obviously has future economic value to the entity. The problem facing accountants, once they have decided that there is a future benefit, is how to measure that benefit in monetary terms. In the above examples it would be impossible to isolate the effect these 'items' have in monetary terms. Therefore, we do not include them in the balance sheet as assets, even though the business is clearly getting a benefit from them. (As soon as the Sarich company had an orbital engine running that was able to demonstrate its potential, it was possible to assign a monetary figure to this asset.) Other examples of items which are clearly of benefit, but which are not included for accounting purposes, are a good location, a highly motivated workforce or a reputation for excellent service. You will remember from Chapter 1 that we discussed this problem in the context of the limitations of accounting information. Intangible assets present particular measurement problems and we discuss intangible assets in Chapter 9.

Legal ownership and control

Many definitions of assets imply that in order to be an asset something must be owned. In reality, most assets are owned, but the assertion that ownership is a precondition for the recognition of an asset by an entity is not correct. The entity must have the capacity to control the future economic benefits. While control often arises from legally enforceable rights, the absence of legal ownership does not automatically deny the existence of control. For example, a rental agreement for a house that entitles you to occupy it at a rent of $100 a week obviously confers a benefit if the market rental is, say, $200 a week, and thus may be seen as an asset. On the other hand, the fact that an individual or entity owns an item does not necessarily mean that there is any future benefit to be obtained. For example, an old motor car that has been ordered off the road by the police may cease to be an asset, and, in fact, unless it can be driven to the salvage yard it may become a liability.

Past events

A decision to expand a business next year is not an asset and would not show up in the accounting records. However, if an irrevocable contract was signed committing the entity to use economic resources which would give it future economic benefits, then the signing of that contract is the past event and the commitment could be seen as an asset.

Control by the entity

While it may seem patently obvious that the benefits of assets should accrue to the entity – that is, be received by the entity at some point in time – it is vital in many cases to be able to separate the assets of the entity from those of the owner, for reasons referred to earlier. For example, a factory building is likely to be an asset to an entity because the benefits from its use are likely to accrue to the entity. However, if the entity is a corner shop with residential accommodation, it is somewhat less clear which part of the building is an asset of the business and which is not. In practice it may well be that some of the goods held for resale are physically stored in part of the residential accommodation. There is unfortunately no general rule which can be applied and each case must be considered on its merits. The process of distinguishing between the assets of the owner and those of the business is merely an application of the business entity principle, referred to earlier, which states that the business should be viewed as separate from the owner and, therefore, accounted for separately.

Review exercise 1

What are the deficiencies, if any, in the following definition of an asset? 'Assets are the things a business owns.'

CATEGORIES OF ASSETS

For accounting purposes, assets are normally separated (as far as possible) into subcategories. The reasoning behind this is that accounting statements should provide information that is useful in making economic decisions. This is the objective of financial reporting, as stated in Key concept 2.4. These decisions can be made more precisely if some indication is given regarding the nature of the assets of the entity. The categories used in Australia are current and non-current assets. In some countries the terms 'fixed assets' or 'long-term assets' are used instead of 'non-current assets'.

LO 3

Explain the distinction between current and non-current assets

Current assets

Some accounting texts suggest that current assets are those which are part of the entity's operating cycle; they are also known as circulating assets. Other texts suggest that current assets are those which are converted into cash within an accounting period.

Before continuing on with our discussion, we need to know what is meant by the term 'operating cycle'.

The operating cycle

It is easier to understand the term 'operating cycle' if we look at one or two examples. In the case of a shop selling clothes, the operating cycle consists of buying garments and selling them for cash. In the case of an assembly business, the operating cycle involves more processes such as buying components, and then going through the process of assembly, selling and the collection of cash from a sale. Thus, the operating cycle has no fixed time period but depends on the nature of the business. It may, in fact, extend over a number of years. This is the case with property development, shipbuilding and heavy construction industries. The fact that the operating cycles are of different lengths is not vital because, in general terms, those assets that are part of the operating cycle are similar and are likely to be items such as stock, cash in the bank, and so on. This means that, in general terms, these assets are likely to be liquid (refer to Key concept 4.3).

KEY CONCEPT 4.5

OPERATING CYCLE

Operating cycle is defined as the time between the acquisition of materials entering into a process and its realisation in cash or an instrument that is readily convertible into cash. (AASB 101, para. 59)

The realisation period

As mentioned earlier, some other accounting texts suggest that what distinguishes current assets from other assets is whether or not they will be realised in the form of cash in the current accounting period. By convention, accounting periods are normally one year, though they can cover any period we care to use. If we applied this test strictly we would find that in certain cases, such as that of a shipbuilder, something that is part of the operating cycle will not in fact be realised in the form of cash within a year.

In Australia, the realisation period is normally one year, unless the operating cycle is longer, in which case the operating cycle is used.

KEY CONCEPT 4.6

CURRENT ASSETS

Current asset means an asset that:
- is expected to be realised, or is held for sale or consumption, in the normal course of the entity's operating cycle

  or
- is held primarily for trading purposes or for the short term and is expected to be realised within 12 months of the reporting date

  or
- is cash or a cash-equivalent asset unless it is restricted from being exchanged or used to settle a liability for at least 12 moths after the reporting date.

(AASB 101, para. 57)

Classification of current assets

Examples of current assets include cash, accounts receivable, short-term investments, inventories and prepaid expenses. These assets should be classified according to either their nature (such as accounts receivable which represent amounts owing from third parties) or their function (such as short-term investments which represent assets being held for sale).

Non-current assets

Most texts refer to non-current assets as fixed assets. The term 'fixed assets' has been in use, in accounting literature, for decades and is still in use in a number of countries. Non-current assets generally include those assets which were acquired with the intention of retaining them for the purpose of generating income over a number of years. Items that meet this classification include land and buildings, machinery, vehicles, plant and equipment.

The term 'non-current asset' is now applicable in Australia as it is used in the International Financial Reporting Standards. Although the term is not defined in the *Corporations Act*, it is required to be used as a heading in the balance sheet to signify all assets other than current assets. The definition given in Key concept 4.7, which fits intuitively with the requirements of the *Corporations Act*, is used in accounting standards. As you can see, it is all-encompassing.

KEY CONCEPT 4.7

NON-CURRENT ASSETS

Non-current assets are all assets other than current assets. (AASB 101, para. 57)

Other items could be classed as either non-current or current assets – depending on their nature. Examples are loans made to others over a period of years, a mortgage or a long-term investment in the shares of another entity. All these could be classed as current assets if they met the definition within the time constraint. For example, a long-term loan, which had only 12 months left of its life, would be reclassified from a non-current asset to a current asset.

Examples of non-current assets include plant and equipment, furniture and fixtures, motor vehicles, land and buildings, long-term receivables and intangibles. As with current assets, non-current assets are also classified according to their nature or function.

Having looked at what constitutes an asset, and at the way in which assets are divided into the two classes on the balance sheet, we can now turn to the other part of the statement – what economic resources are owed to other entities. In accounting terminology, these are the liabilities.

Review exercise 2

Explain, in your own words, the difference between non-current assets and current assets and why it is important to classify assets into subgroups.

LIABILITIES

As with the general term 'assets', there are several definitions of liabilities, most of which refer to amounts owed by an entity. The term 'liabilities' is not defined in the *Corporations Act*. To be consistent with our approach to assets, we will use the definition already cited in Key concept 2.9 (provided by paragraph 49 of the AASB *Framework*) and revisited here.

LO 4

Identify the requirements an item must satisfy to be recognised as a liability on a balance sheet

KEY CONCEPT 4.8

LIABILITIES

Liabilities are defined as a present obligation of the entity arising from past events, the settlement of which is expected to result in an outflow from the entity of resources embodying economic benefits. (AASB *Framework*, para. 49b) A liability is recognised in the balance sheet only when it is probable that settlement of the liability will be required and it is possible to reliably measure the amount required.

As with assets, for an item to meet the definition of a liability and be recognised on the balance sheet, it must satisfy the recognition criteria. It must be probable that settlement of the liability will be required, and the amount must be capable of being measured reliably.

From the definition given, we can see that there has to be an existence of a present obligation, in economic terms, and this obligation must result in an outflow of economic benefits from the entity at some future date. Further, these obligations must have arisen because of past events.

As is the case with assets, liabilities are divided into two classes: current and non-current.

LO 5

Explain the distinction between current and non-current liabilities

Current liabilities

The definition of current liabilities is similar to that of current assets. That is, these liabilities become due either in the operating cycle or within an accounting period normally defined as one year. As with assets, we will follow the realisation concept and use the definition given in AASB 101 *Presentation of Financial Statements*.

KEY CONCEPT 4.9

CURRENT LIABILITY

A current liability is a liability that satifies any of the following criteria:

- is expected to be settled in the normal course of the entity's operating cycle

    or

- is primarily held for trading

    or

- is due to be settled within 12 months of the balance sheet date

    or

- the entity does not have an unconditional right to defer settlement of the liability for at least 12 months after the reporting date. (AASB 101, para. 60)

Some examples of current liabilities are: amounts owed to creditors – entities from whom we have purchased items on credit; short-term loans such as bank overdrafts, which are normally repayable on demand; and other short-term loans, such as promissory notes which have a life of 90 to 180 days.

Non-current liabilities

Clearly there are other types of liabilities which do not have to be repaid in full in one year. An everyday example of this type of liability is a mortgage on a house. In the case of a business, this type of liability may take a number of forms, such as a bank loan repayable in, say, three years or five years. Liabilities of this sort are longer-term liabilities and are normally put under the heading of non-current liabilities. Some texts refer to non-current liabilities as long-term liabilities, though this term is being used less and less in Australia.

When an item that has been classified as a non-current liability becomes due for settlement within 12 months it should be reclassified as a current liability. This is important information for users. The reclassification of the item may reveal that the entity has a possible liquidity and solvency problem, and may fail the going concern test if it doesn't have the capacity to meet the repayment. Imagine that an entity has a 10-year bank loan that was issued nine years ago. The entity may expect that the bank will renew the loan and, therefore, it may continue to classify the loan as a non-current liability. Accounting standards require that such a loan must be reclassified as a current liability unless firm arrangements in writing have been completed for the loan to be extended beyond 12 months (i.e. before the end of the accounting period). It is important for users to be fully informed of the amount and timing of an entity's obligations so that they can properly assess the entity's capacity to continue as a going concern. Non-current liabilities, like non-current assets, are not defined in the *Corporations Act* – although the term is used. The following definition is taken from approved AASB 101, paragraph 60.

KEY CONCEPT 4.10

NON-CURRENT LIABILITIES

A non-current liability means a liability which is not a current liability.

Review exercise 3

List two current liabilities and two non-current liabilities, other than those mentioned in the text.

Assets and liabilities

It can be seen that there is a thread which is common to both assets and liabilities: both are concerned with the accounting period (current) and a time span greater than the accounting period (non-current). The difference between the definitions of assets and liabilities, in general terms, centres on who controls the economic resources. Assets are resources controlled by the entity, and liabilities are economic resources owed to another entity; that is, claims against those resources. It should be seen that if the claims against an entity exceed the resources controlled, then the entity will no longer be a going concern. Conversely, if assets exceed liabilities the excess will accrue to the owners of the entity.

Owners' equity

The owners' equity, or share of the capital of the business, can be viewed in a number of ways. In a sense it is a liability of the business in so far as it is a claim on the assets. However, it differs from other liabilities which have definite dates by which they are to be paid and are fixed in amount. The owners' equity is normally left in the business as long as it is required. Another way of viewing the owners' equity is as a residual claim on the assets of the business after all the other liabilities have been settled.

In general, the owners' equity is normally shown under two headings: that which is put into the business and that which is earned by and left in the business. The latter category we will refer to as retained profits. The total of the figures under these two headings, in the case of an individual, is analogous with wealth, whereas when the owner is in a business it is often referred to as capital. As we showed in Chapter 3, the amount of this wealth or capital is dependent upon the measure used; that is, replacement cost, net realisable value, and so on. It is therefore better to view owners' equity as a residual claim rather than as capital or wealth because those expressions imply that an absolute measure of owners' equity is possible. Equity is not defined in the *Corporations Act* although an acceptable definition is given in paragraph 49 of the AASB *Framework* and was stated as Key concept 2.10 in Chapter 2, and revisited here.

LO **6**

Explain the meaning of 'equity'

KEY CONCEPT 4.11

EQUITY

Equity is the residual interest in the assets of the entity after deducting all its liabilities. (AASB *Framework*, para. 49c)

Equity can be seen as the residual interest due to the owners of the entity; hence, the often-used term 'owners' equity'. We will use this term until we come to Chapter 11, which discusses final accounts, partnerships and companies.

CASE STUDY 4.1

BALANCE SHEETS ARE NOT INFALLIBLE
It's all a matter of judgement
by Joe Rock, KPMG, Thailand

THE BALANCE SHEET is supposed to present a snapshot of a company's financial position at a given date. If accurate, it should provide valuable information to readers about the company's assets and liabilities, its liquidity and its leverage.

There is, however, an inherent flaw in the balance sheet, one that is often misunderstood or underappreciated. The inherent flaw of the balance sheet is that it requires a considerable amount of management's judgement – and that could prove to be erroneous.

Preparing a balance sheet is not just an exercise of a company's accounting department lifting numbers from its accounting system's ledgers.

Management's judgement is required to determine the appropriate balances of numerous accounts. Working through some balance sheets, let's see where that judgement comes into play and what you, the financial statement reader, can do to get a feel for their assessment.

- Receivables: The gross accounts receivable balance is most often a systems-generated figure, but generally accepted accounting principles require receivables to be reported at net realisable value. That means management has to estimate just how many current receivables will eventually turn 'bad' or be uncollectible. A reserve or provision is made for the uncollectibles and it is deducted

from the gross receivables balance in order to present receivables at their estimated net realisable value.

For some industries, commercial banking being one example, this balance is perhaps the most important on the balance sheet. Management must spend a tremendous amount of time calculating the provision in line with local banking regulations and assessing how much of the current loan portfolio is expected to go bad. Their judgement is critical in determining the appropriate net receivable balance.

- Inventory: The gross inventory balance is also a systems-calculated figure that may need to be adjusted to net realisable value in line with generally accepted accounting principles.

In the case of inventory, management will need to determine how much, if any, of its inventory is overvalued due to obsolescence. Once estimated, this obsolescence reserve is deducted from the gross inventory balance to present inventory at its estimated net realisable value.

In manufacturing and retail companies, inventory is often the largest current asset. Companies are constantly monitoring inventory levels in order to limit the costs of carrying large stocks.

Yet, as we are seeing in the United States, inventories can be extremely sensitive to ⅢⅢ➡

economic fluctuations and even a slight dip in demand can lead to stockpiles and obsolescence. Management needs to exercise judgement on appropriate inventory levels in line with market demand in order to properly state inventory on the balance sheet.

- Fixed assets: Fixed assets are generally based on historical cost, though in Thailand they can be revalued based on appraised values. Still, management must estimate the useful lives of its fixed assets for depreciation purposes and evaluate whether or not these assets are impaired and therefore need to be written down. As a relatively new accounting standard in Thailand, the impairment standard has caused considerable pain in accounting departments and on balance sheets. Without appraisals, companies losing money need to prove that their operations will eventually make sufficient profit to justify the values of their fixed assets. This exercise demands a considerable amount of judgement as it relies on projected cash flows and discount rates.

- Intangibles: Intangible assets, such as goodwill and franchise rights, are generally based on the price paid when one company acquires another.
Once acquired, the accounting treatment of intangibles is similar to that of fixed assets, so judgement is required on the points of

estimating depreciable lives and determining if assets are impaired. Again, if the company isn't making any profits, how can it justify the values of such assets?

- Liabilities: Contingent liabilities are obligations that are dependent on uncertain outcomes, such as litigation claims, tax audits and warranty or product guarantee liabilities. It is management's responsibility to assess the likelihood of liabilities occurring from such contingencies in order to properly state the balance sheet.

What are some basic things that you, the financial statement reader, can do to be fairly sure that the balance sheet is a reasonable estimation of a company's financial position? First is to read the audit opinion. If the financial statements have been audited, an opinion should be attached. It should tell you whether or not the auditor has taken serious issue with any managerial judgements.

If the auditor believes that the balance sheet is materially misstated or for some reason cannot determine whether or not that is the case, the opinion should say so. Read the footnotes. They make up an integral part of the financial statements and should provide a wealth of information about a company's accounting policies and treatment of the areas mentioned.

Bangkok Post, 27 June 2001

COMMENTARY

The article highlights the fact that the balance sheet contains many estimates, and needs to be used with this knowledge. It should be read in conjunction with all the notes that accompany financial statements. We say more about some of the specific parts of the balance sheet in some of the following chapters in this book.

The balance sheet equation

LO 7

Explain and apply
the balance sheet
equation

As we have already shown, the balance sheet of an entity is a statement of its assets and liabilities at a particular point in time. Because the business is an artificial entity, by definition all the benefits arising from its assets belong to someone else. This is summed up in the balance sheet equation:

$$\text{assets} = \text{liabilities}$$

The equation describes the balance sheet in its simplest form; it must always hold true. However, it uses a very loose definition of liabilities. It can be refined to highlight the differences between pure liabilities and owners' equity, as follows.

$$\text{assets} = \text{liabilities} + \text{owners' equity}$$

This form of the equation will be used in our worksheet in Chapter 6. The equation can be rewritten to highlight the fact that owners' equity is a residual claim on the assets.

$$\text{assets} - \text{liabilities} = \text{owners' equity}$$

A simple balance sheet

To illustrate the equation, a simple balance sheet can be constructed, using the information contained in Example 4.1.

Example 4.1: Keelsafe

Susan Keel had been made redundant and she decided to start up a small business making safety harnesses which she called Keelsafe Safety Harnesses. For this purpose she purchased:

	$
One industrial sewing machine	1 100
A quantity of heavy duty webbing material	600
A quantity of sewing materials	200
A second-hand typewriter	100
A supply of office stationery and letterheads	100
One cutting machine	800

The remaining $100 of her redundancy money was put into a business bank account.

At this stage we could draw up a list of assets of the business as follows:

Assets	$
Sewing machine	1 100
Webbing	600
Sewing materials	200
Typewriter	100
Stationery	100
Cutting machine	800
Cash at bank	100
	3 000

We could also identify the owners' equity in the business as being $3000; that is, the amount Susan Keel put in. Thus, the other side of the balance sheet – and, indeed, of the equation – would be:

Owners' equity	3 000
	$3 000

Before moving on, it is worth thinking about how we obtained the figure for the owners' equity. All we did was to list what economic resources Susan Keel's business controlled and then, as there were no outside claims against the business, we balanced the balance sheet by recording the amount of residual interest in the assets to the owners' equity.

Let us take this example further.

Because she was just starting out, Susan decided that, until the business got off the ground, she would operate from home by using the garage to manufacture the safety harnesses and the front room of her house as an office. The house had cost her $20 000 in 1979.

This additional information presents us with a problem: we do not know how much of the $20 000 relates to the garage and how much to the front room. We know that the business uses some of the house and that the house is an asset. But is it an asset of Susan herself or of the business? If it is the latter, how should we record it and at what amount? To answer these questions we need to go back to our definition of an asset, which was:

> An asset is a resource controlled by the entity as a result of past events
> and from which future economic benefits are expected to flow to the
> entity. (AASB *Framework*, para. 49a)

Bearing in mind the business entity principle, we can see from the definition that the garage is not an asset of the business – where the business is viewed as a separate entity from the owner. It is Susan Keel herself who owns both the house and the garage, and she also retains the legal right to enjoy the benefits from their use. The garage is not an asset of the business because the business has no legal right to use the garage, and has no control over it. Therefore, it does not need to be included in the balance sheet of the business. A similar argument can be applied to the front room, which is being used as an office.

However, suppose Susan entered into a long-term lease of the garage, whereby the business rented the garage from her, and this lease was secure, even if Susan sold the business to another person. In this case the lease would be an asset of the business because the use of the garage would now come under the control of the business and not Susan. If you are unsure of the argument, return to the discussion on the business entity and the definition of an asset.

When Susan starts to make the harnesses, she realises that she needs to buy some fasteners. She approaches her bank which agrees to give her a loan of $1000. She pays this sum into the business bank account and then buys the fasteners with a cheque for $600 drawn on that account.

We will look at this transaction and then draw up a new balance sheet. A new one is needed because we are now at a different point in time: you will remember that a balance sheet shows the position at one point in time only. The actual transaction on its own can be looked at in two stages:

Stage 1

The first stage occurred when Susan borrowed the money from the bank. This had two effects: it increased the business's assets, because the business will get a future benefit from the use of that money; and it also increased the business's liabilities, because the business now owes the bank $1000. This viewed on its own can be depicted as:

$$\text{assets} = \text{liabilities} + \text{owners' equity}$$
$$\text{in bank (\$1000)} = \text{loan (\$1000)}$$

Stage 2

In the second stage, $600 of the money in the bank is used to buy the fasteners. We can now extend Stage 1 and depict this as follows:

$$\text{assets} = \text{liabilities} + \text{owners' equity}$$
$$\text{cash in bank (\$1000)} = \text{loan (\$1000)}$$
$$\text{fasteners} + \$600 - \$600 \text{ cash in bank} = 0$$

All that has happened is that we have exchanged one asset for another, and the totals on either side of the equation remain the same.

Before going on to draw up a new balance sheet, you should note the important principle that we have just illustrated: there are two sides to every transaction. In Stage 1, the two sides of the transaction were an increase in assets with a corresponding increase in liabilities; in Stage 2, there was a decrease in one asset with a corresponding increase in another asset. This is often referred to as the principle of duality, which is simply a grand-sounding title for the rule that all transactions have two sides.

KEY CONCEPT 4.12

THE PRINCIPLE OF DUALITY

The principle of duality is the basis of the double-entry bookkeeping system on which accounting is based. It states that:

- every transaction has two opposite and equal components.

Having established this principle, we can now draw up the new balance sheet of Keelsafe Safety Harnesses. We use the following balance sheet format:

$$\text{assets} - \text{liabilities} = \text{owners' equity}$$

The previous balance sheet was a very simple one; this time we will classify the assets into current and non-current, and group them together to make the statement more informative.

Another way in which we can make the balance sheet more informative is to list the assets in order of liquidity. Liquid assets are those that can readily be converted into cash: the more difficult the item is to turn into cash, the less liquid it is. (The liquidity concept was stated in Key concept 4.3.) The sewing machine, as a non-current asset, is less liquid than the stocks of fasteners. Similarly, these are shown as less liquid than the cash at the bank.

You will also note that each of the groups of assets is subtotalled and the subtotal is shown separately. The total of all the assets is then shown. It is conventional to use single underlining for subtotals and double underlining to denote final totals.

Having classified and listed the assets of Keelsafe, we then show the claims against the business, subclassified into current and non-current liabilities. The total liabilities are deducted from the total assets to give a figure for the residual assets. The residual assets amount is called the 'net assets'. This is the value of the business after all external liabilities have been met. It has double underlining to show that it is a final total. The amount of the owners' equity, which we have said comprises capital put into the business as well as residual profits, should balance against the net assets figure.

This is shown by our balance sheet equation:

$$\text{assets} - \text{liabilities} = \text{owners' equity}$$

Keelsafe Safety Harnesses
Balance sheet at 31 May 2002

	$	$	$	$
Assets				
Current assets				
Cash at bank	500			
Fasteners	600			
Sewing material	200			
Webbing material	600			
Office stationery	100			
Total current assets		2 000		
Non-current assets				
Typewriter	100			
One cutting machine	800			
One sewing machine	1 100			
Total non-current assets		2 000		
Total assets			4 000	
Liabilities				
Current liabilities				
Bank loan	1 000			
Total liabilities			1 000	
Net assets				3 000
Owners' equity				3 000

The balance sheet has been rearranged to emphasise the differences between the various types of assets and Susan Keel's residual claim on the assets after any liabilities have been paid. Note that the statement is headed with the name of the business and the date on which it was drawn up.

Before you proceed any further, re-examine the definitions of current and non-current assets and ensure that you understand why the items in this balance sheet have been classified as they have.

It is worth examining the balance sheet for Woodside. Note the classification of assets and liabilities into current and non-current categories. As a mining company, Woodside has some non-current assets like exploration and evaluation, which are specific to the mining industry, as well as more common types of assets like plant and equipment.

After studying the balance sheet for Woodside you should be aware that it is not possible to obtain a complete understanding of all the elements on the statement as they represent an aggregated statement of all the assets, liabilities and equity for Woodside. However, the Woodside statement is only a half-yearly report. As mentioned in Chapter 2, half-yearly reports are not required to be as comprehensive as an annual report. The annual financial statements of Woodside contain detailed notes which are like the table of contents in a book. Without reading the book, you cannot know the full story; similarly, without reading the notes accompanying the financial statements, it is not possible to fully understand an entity's position. Hence, it is important to read a half-yearly report in conjunction with the most recent annual report to get a more complete picture of the entity's balance sheet. The 2005 annual report for Woodside is available at the company's web address: www.woodside.com.au.

We can now proceed to examine the limitations of the balance sheet, together with the factors that influence the format of the balance sheet.

Limitations of the balance sheet

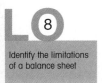

LO 8

Identify the limitations of a balance sheet

We now examine the limitations of the balance sheet.

The fact that a balance sheet represents the position of an entity at one point in time is a limitation, because it is relevant only at that point in time. At any other time, as we have seen in the case of Keelsafe, a new balance sheet has to be prepared. For the statement to be useful, it should be as up to date as possible; its utility diminishes as time passes. Similarly, for the balance sheet to provide a relevant measure of the assets and liabilities of an entity, the values assigned to those assets and liabilities should be as recent as possible, and herein lies another limitation.

As we saw in Chapter 3, there are a number of ways in which assets can be valued, some of which are more subjective than others. The right value to choose depends on the purpose for which the balance sheet is to be used. For example, if we want to know how much each item costs, then the historic cost would be appropriate. If, on the other hand, we wanted to know how much each item could be sold for, then the net realisable value would be appropriate. If we wanted to know how much the business as a whole was worth, it is likely that neither of these would be appropriate. Partly because of the difficulties involved in choosing an appropriate valuation method, and partly because of convention, accountants have traditionally used the historic cost as the basis of the valuation of assets in the balance sheet.

Clearly, in certain cases this has led to assets being stated at a figure which bears little, if any, relation to their current value. AASB 116 *Property, Plant and Equipment* allows entities to measure assets on either the cost basis or the fair value basis. If an entity chooses fair value, then any changes in the fair value are reported as an asset revaluation reserve and form part of the equity in the balance sheet. In addition, if an entity uses fair value then it must ensure that the fair value on the balance sheet is not materially different to its fair value at that point in time. If, as a result of this requirement in AASB 116, an entity is forced to revalue land and buildings on an annual basis, the entity may incur significant costs from obtaining valuations of property every year.

Allied to the problem of fluctuations in the prices of specific assets is the fact that the unit of measurement, the dollar (or other unit of currency), does not itself represent a constant value over time. You cannot buy as many goods with a dollar today as you could 10 years ago. Once again, this limits the usefulness of the information contained in the balance sheet.

CASE STUDY 4.2

BEYOND THE BALANCE SHEET: FINDING A COMPANY'S VALUE
by Mark Fenton-Jones

MEASURING the real worth of a big unlisted family company is predicted to be a major challenge for this sector over the next decade.

'It will be one of the major business issues over the next 10 years, given that balance sheets don't measure the wealth of a company,' said Neville Christie who runs the CEO mentor round table of 18 chief executives of family companies.

The round table, which meets 10 times a year, brings together heads of small to medium businesses, usually family companies with a turnover up to $50 million.

Mr Christie said that over the past 15 years, the percentage of hard tangibles on companies' balance sheets had fallen to 15 to 20 per cent from 80 per cent as companies became more knowledge- or service-based. 'There is now a mismatch between the real value of a company and what is shown on the balance sheet,' he said.

To address the problem, the round table is working with US academic and businessman Ken Standfield who specialises in intangibles management.

Another major concern that has emerged at this year's talks is improving the productivity of a knowledge- or service-based company. The question reflects the strong representation of round table members who are in the services industry.

Australian Financial Review,
24 September 2002

COMMENTARY

The article highlights the problems that entities whose main assets are intangible experience with the traditional balance sheet. In the industrial revolution, the major assets were tangible and physical, but in the knowledge revolution, the major assets are intangible and non-physical. This problem challenges the accounting profession to establish a methodology for the reliable measurement of intangibles. If the accounting profession fails to do this, the balance sheet will become less useful, and users will seek other means of obtaining the information they require to assist in their decision making.

We have illustrated with the example of a gold mine that something which is a worthless asset for one business can be a valuable asset for another business undertaking a different activity. This case is reasonably clear-cut, but consider, for example, the problems of a football club trying to account for star players, or of a high-technology business trying to decide whether the cost of the patent on a new product is going to yield any future benefit when technology is changing so rapidly.

There are also issues relating to the ways in which a business is perceived and the ways in which management wishes the business to be perceived. Research has shown that managers, especially the managers of smaller organisations, perceive that bankers are interested in the amount of assets available as security for a loan or overdraft. There is therefore a temptation to try to enhance the value of assets, perhaps by revaluing land and buildings, before applying for a loan. Similarly, in a number of cases where a business is in trouble, the assets have been revalued in order to bolster the image of the business and to promote the impression of a 'sound asset base'.

In Australia there are severe penalties for directors of public companies or other organisations who attempt fraudulently to inflate assets or decrease liabilities.

Review exercise 4

What are the main limitations of a balance sheet? Does this mean a balance sheet is useless?

We will now examine the various influences on the balance sheet and then look at the needs of users; no discussion of financial statements would be complete without some reference to their needs.

Influences on the format of the balance sheet

LO 9

Discuss the factors that influence the format of a balance sheet

TYPES OF BUSINESS

One of the prime determinants of the content and format of the balance sheet is the structure of the organisation. For example, an incorporated business (that is, a company) is subject to certain rules and regulations imposed by the state, whereas a partnership or sole proprietorship has no such restrictions. A company has to produce annual accounts, as laid out in the *Corporations Act*, and file a copy with the Australian Securities and Investments Commission (ASIC), whereas, in the case of a partnership, there is no such requirement. A business that is part of a larger organisation may have to comply with the rules and form of accounts that suit that organisation as a whole.

The need to comply with organisational requirements may also be affected by who owns the business. For example, a US-owned company operating in Australia would have to comply with Australian regulations, but would also report to the US parent company in a form that complies with US regulations. In contrast, there are no restrictions or rules imposed on a business that is owned by two partners, other than the *Partnership Act 1891*; the partners can decide for themselves what form the balance sheet should take. However, other bodies can affect the frequency and format of the balance sheet. For example, the tax office needs to know how much income the partners have earned, and if the accounts are drawn up by a professional accountant then that person is required to follow the accounting standards and rules of the profession.

Another factor affecting the format of the balance sheet is the size of the organisation. We have used a very small operation in our sample balance sheet on page 110 (Fig. 4.1), in which all the assets could be individually listed. In the case of a larger, more complex organisation, assets will need to be summarised under broad headings; otherwise the amount of detail would be so great that the user of the statement would find it impossible to get an overall picture.

Finally, we should mention the influence of organisational goals. Consider, for example, an organisation set up for charitable purposes (which may or may not be incorporated): of what relevance to that organisation is a classification such as owners' equity? Similarly, if you looked at the accounts of your municipal council you would not expect to see a heading for owners' equity or retained profits.

USERS OF ACCOUNTS

As we discussed in Chapter 1, there are a number of different users who may have conflicting needs for information. To some extent, the rules and regulations laid down by the state could be said to encompass some of these needs. However, these rules give only a minimum requirement. For example, while the *Corporations Act* requires that loans and overdrafts should be shown, research shows that bankers would like to see details of the repayment dates of those loans in the accounts. On the other hand, the owners of the company may not wish to have that information made public. A similar conflict arises between the needs of managers who wish to know what it will cost to replace an asset (rather than what the asset cost when they bought it), and the needs of the owners who wish to know what the management has spent their money on and how much each item cost.

Suggested format for a balance sheet

In this chapter we have defined the nature, purpose and content of balance sheets and have highlighted some of the problems with such a statement. We have also introduced you to the wider context in which accounting reports can be viewed. Before proceeding further, it is important that you make sure that you understand the definitions involved and can apply them to real problems. As you have seen, a balance sheet can take many forms and in a book of this nature there is no need to cover all of them. For simplicity, therefore, we will use one format throughout the book. A sample is given in Figure 4.1, followed by an explanation for the choice of this format. It is important that you understand the reasons for the choice of the suggested format because this will aid you in interpreting accounting information at a later stage.

The format of the balance sheet is determined by the needs of the organisation. We have chosen a format appropriate to an introductory text. Before following a different format, ensure that you understand the reasons behind it and consider whether the information is as clear as in the format given in Figure 4.1.

Simple Ltd
Balance sheet at 31 December 20X1

	$	$	$	$
Assets				
Current assets				
Cash at bank	40			
Finished goods inventory	1 220			
Raw materials inventory	1 400			
Total current assets		2 660		
Non-current assets				
Motor vehicles	10 100			
Machinery	5 000			
Land and buildings	100 000			
Total non-current assets		115 100		
Total assets			117 760	
Liabilities				
Current liabilities				
Bank overdraft	2 000			
Total current liabilities		2 000		
Non-current liabilities				
Bank loan, due 1 January 20X6	50 000			
Total non-current liabilities		50 000		
Total liabilities			52 000	
Net assets				65 760
Owners' equity				
Capital	50 000			
Retained earnings	15 760			
Total owners' equity				65 760

Figure 4.1 Suggested format for a balance sheet

The format chosen is that which was previously required under the *Corporations Act* and it appears that many companies still use this format in Australia.

The balance sheet is headed with the name of the organisation and the date to which the statement relates. As has already been explained, a balance sheet relates to one point in time and that date needs to be clearly stated in the heading.

Finally, we emphasise again that a balance sheet's format may differ due to the requirements of the users or owners. For example, it is unlikely that a corner store would be part of a public company: a more appropriate format, in this case, may be to list the current assets less the current liabilities. If the current assets are more than the current liabilities, this would indicate that the business should be able to meet its short-term commitments when they became due.

SUMMARY

LEARNING OBJECTIVE 1
Explain the meaning and purpose of the balance sheet
The balance sheet is the financial statement that reports all the assets, liabilities and equity of an entity at one point in time. It is an important statement for assessing the financial position of an entity, and enables its user to answer various questions such as: Does the entity have enough assets to meet its liabilities and therefore pass the going concern test?

LEARNING OBJECTIVE 2
Identify the requirements an item must satisfy to be recognised as an asset on a balance sheet
To be recognised as an asset on the balance sheet, an item must satisfy the definition of an asset, which includes the following criteria:
- inflow of future economic benefits
- control by the entity
  and
- resulting from a past event or transaction.
  In addition, the asset must meet the following two recognition criteria:
- it is probable that the benefits will flow into the entity
  and
- there is a cost or other value that can be reliably measured

LEARNING OBJECTIVE 3
Explain the distinction between current and non-current assets
Current assets include cash and assets that are to be consumed or converted into cash within 12 months of reporting date (or by the end of the operating cycle if this is greater than 12 months). Non-current assets are all other assets.

LEARNING OBJECTIVE 4
Identify the requirements an item must satisfy to be recognised as a liability on a balance sheet
To be recognised as a liability on the balance sheet, an item must satisfy the definition of a liability which includes the following criteria:
- there is an outflow of future economic benefits
- there is a present obligation for the entity
  and
- the liability arises as a result of a past event or transaction.
  In addition, the liability must meet the following two recognition criteria:
- it is probable that benefits will flow from the entity
  and
- there is a cost or other value that can be reliably measured.

LEARNING OBJECTIVE 5
5

Explain the distinction between current and non-current liabilities

Current liabilities include all liabilities that are expected to be settled or expire within 12 months of reporting date (or by the end of the operating cycle where this is greater than 12 months). It also includes those liabilities where the entity does not have an unconditional right to defer settlement of the liability for at least 12 months after the reporting date. Non-current liabilities are all other liabilities.

LEARNING OBJECTIVE 6
6

Explain the meaning of 'equity'

Equity is the residual interest in the assets of an entity, and is measured as assets less all liabilities.

LEARNING OBJECTIVE 7
7

Explain and apply the balance sheet equation

The balance sheet equation is assets = liabilities + equity. It can also be expressed as assets − liabilities = equity. The balance sheet equation can be used to analyse all accounting transactions for recording into the accounting records.

LEARNING OBJECTIVE 8
8

Identify the limitations of a balance sheet

The following are some of the limitations of a balance sheet:

- it is only concerned with at one point in time
- it only provides past information
- some items, like research and development, may not be recognised as an asset because they fail the definition or recognition criteria
- if the cost method of asset measurement is used it may mean some asset values are reliable but less relevant.

LEARNING OBJECTIVE 9
9

Discuss the factors that influence the format of a balance sheet

There are various factors that influence the format for a balance sheet. This format is not mandated by accounting standards. Factors that influence the format of a balance sheet include:

- the type of business (e.g. company or unincorporated association, for profit versus not-for-profit)
- the size of the entity
- the organisational goals of the entity
- the needs of users.

REFERENCES

Australian Accounting Standards Board. AASB 101 *Presentation of Financial Statements*, July, 2004.
Australian Accounting Standards Board. *Framework for the Presentation and Preparation of Financial Statements*, July, 2004.
The Corporations Law, 1992. CCH, Sydney.

REVIEW QUESTIONS

1   What is the purpose of a balance sheet and what information does it contain?

2   What are the essential elements of a useful definition of an asset?

3   Explain, in your own words, what a liability is and the differences between liabilities and owners' equity.

4   List three current assets and three non-current assets other than those mentioned in the text.

PROBLEMS FOR DISCUSSION AND ANALYSIS

1   Refer to the Woodside 2005 half-yearly financial report in Appendix 1.
    a   What is the amount of total assets? current assets? non-current assets?
    b   Which class of non-current assets has the greatest value?
    c   What is the amount of total liabilities? current liabilities? non-current liabilities?
    d   Which class of non-current liabilities has the greatest value?

2   In 20X6, XYZ Ltd had total assets of $200 000 and total liabilities of $250 000. Non-current assets and non-current liabilities were $50 000 and $25 000 respectively. What were the current assets, current liabilities and owners' equity for 20X6?

3   In 20X6, ABC Ltd had total assets of $100 000 and owners' equity of $50 000. In 20X7, total liabilities were $50 000 more than in 20X6, and the owners' equity was $60 000. Calculate:
    a   the total assets figure for 20X7
    b   the total liabilities figure for 20X6.

4   Given the following information, supply the missing figures. *Note*: Total assets were $10 000 less in 20X8 than in 20X9.

	PQR Ltd 20X8	PQR Ltd 20X9
Current assets	74 000	?
Non-current assets	112 000	86 000
Total assets	?	?
Current liabilities	23 000	?
Non-current liabilities	?	100 000
Total liabilities	?	100 000
Owners' equity	60 000	?

5   Prepare a balance sheet from the following information and comment on the financial position of the business. *Note*: The business had been experiencing a downturn in sales over the past three months due to the economic recession.

	$
Owners' equity	?
Cash	1 700
Accounts payable	42 250
Inventory	30 125
Motor vehicles	17 200
Bank overdraft	32 500
Accounts receivable	1 250
Office equipment	3 600
Low-interest loan to director	21 000

6   Prepare a balance sheet from the following information and comment on the position of the business as shown by the balance sheet.

	$
Stock of goods held for resale	13 000
Freehold land and building	64 000
Mortgage on land and building	58 000
Cash	1 000
Fixtures and fittings	15 200
Office furniture	4 600
Bank overdraft	20 700
Delivery van	3 200
Owners' equity	?

7   Prepare a balance sheet from the following information and comment on the financial position of the business.

	$
Cash	3 000
Inventory	8 000
Accounts payable	12 000
Salaries payable	?
Accounts receivable	16 000
Land and buildings	20 000
Plant and equipment	7 000
Furnishings and fittings	2 500
Owners' equity	13 900
Bank loan	30 000

8   The final account balances (after all adjustments) of Debbie Ltd for the year ending 30 June 20X1 are listed below. From the information given, prepare a balance sheet, in good form, and list the accounts that would not be included in the balance sheet.

	$
Bank overdraft	11 900
Salaries payable	1 000
Salaries expense	1 000
Sales	137 250
Inventory	13 100
Accounts receivable	17 300
Owners' equity	?
Interest expense	330
Land and buildings (net)	110 000
Long-term loan (due19 December 20X9)	100 000
Accounts payable	45 600
Plant and equipment (net)	22 000
Cost of goods sold	110 000

9   Below are the final account balances (after all adjustments) of ABC Ltd for the year ending 30 June 20X1. From these balances prepare a balance sheet, in good form, and list the accounts that would not be included in the balance sheet.

	$
Cash	126 000
Sales discount	5 000
Accounts receivable	50 000
Inventory	88 000
Land	364 000
Plant and equipment	234 000
Accounts payable	26 000
Ninety-day bank bill payable	80 000
Long-term loan payable	45 000
Tax payable	10 000
Vehicle expenses	10 000
Cost of goods sold	40 000
Owners' equity	701 000
Tax expense	10 000

10 In each of the following situations, identify whether the item should be included in the balance sheet of Transom Trading as at 31 December 20X1, and, if so, at what amount and under which heading. Transom Trading is a retailer of motor parts and accessories. In all cases, reasons for your decision must be given.

   a   A freehold shop bought in August 20X1 for $176 000. A mortgage of $60 000 taken out to buy the shop in August 20X1 and balance paid in cash.

   b   Goods on the shelves at the end of the day on 31 December 20X1. These goods had a resale value of $24 000 and had been purchased by Transom Trading for $16 000 cash.

   c   A delivery van, costing $12 000, that Transom Trading ordered on 20 December 20X1 but was finally delivered and paid for by cash on 12 January 20X2.

   d   Shop fittings which were worth $6000 and had been bought at an auction by Transom Trading for only $3000 cash prior to opening the shop in August 20X1.

   e   A Ford Falcon costing $7000 which the owner of Transom Trading had bought through the business in November 20X1 for his wife to use. He had found that the Ford Escort which he had bought privately second-hand in September for $8000 was being used exclusively for collecting and delivering goods for Transom Trading and not as a family car, as originally intended.

   f   One cash register which was rented from Equipment Supplies at an annual rental of $400.

   g   One cash register which Transom Trading had bought in November 20X1 for $1200 cash.

   h   A bank overdraft which had been drawn down to $13 000 on 31 December 20X1.

   i   A supply of seat belts which the owner of Transom Trading had bought for $12 000 in September from a market trader in good faith and which were subsequently found to be defective and worthless.

11 Using the information in Problem 10, calculate the owners' equity and draw up the balance sheet of Transom Trading as at 31 December 20X1.

12 Fred owns a garage and has tried to get everything together ready for the business accounts to be prepared. He has drawn up the list of items below. You are required to identify, with reasons, the balance sheet heading under which each item should be classified, and the amount which should be included.

   a   A motor car bought for resale at a cost of $7000; the retail price was $10 000.

   b   Various loose tools for car repairs which cost $1400.

   c   Two hydraulic jacks which had each cost $240.

   d   Freehold premises which had cost $80 000.

   e   The cost of $1200 for digging and finishing a pit for repairs.

   f   Spare parts held as general stock, originally costing $1580.

   g   Spare parts bought from the previous owner when the garage was bought. At that time, a value $12 000 was agreed upon but it was subsequently discovered that only $400 of these spares were of any use.

   h   Breakdown truck which cost $6000 for the basic truck and $1200 to have the crane fitted.

   i   A customer's car worth $3000 which was being held because the customer had not paid an outstanding bill of $600.

   j   Fred's own car – which cost $8000. This is used mainly for business but Fred also uses it in the evenings and at weekends for the family.

   k   Customer goodwill which Fred reckons he has built up. He thinks this would be worth at least $14 000 if he sold the garage tomorrow.

   l   A bank loan for $48 000 repayable within three months.

   m   A 20-year mortgage on the property amounting to $48 000 which has not been fully repaid. The amount still outstanding is $36 000.

13 Month-end balance sheet amounts (for three consecutive months) for the dental practice of Dr Fang, a local dentist, are presented below. The information is complete except for the balance in the owners' equity account.

	31 October	30 November	31 December
	$	$	$
Cash	9 100	3 900	3 000
Accounts receivable	16 100	16 500	8 050
Prepaid insurance	700	800	600
Surgery equipment	29 800	29 700	38 300
Building	81 000	80 800	80 600
Land	33 000	33 000	33 000
Accounts payable	10 100	3 100	3 000
Wages payable	5 100	4 100	4 800
Mortgage payable	34 700	34 300	33 900
Owners' equity	?	?	?

a Determine the balance in Dr Fang's equity account at the end of each month.

b Assuming that Dr Fang made no additional investments, determine his drawings for the months of November and December.

c Prepare a balance sheet for the business at the end of December.

14 The ledger accounts of Mickey Ltd as at 30 June 20X1 are listed below. Prepare a balance sheet in good form and insert the missing amounts.

	$		$
Total owners' equity	?	Other current assets	?
Total non-current assets	?	Total assets	?
Tax payable	?	Loan payable (31/12/20X3)	?
Total liabilities	?	Net assets	27 400
Bank	10 000	Loan receivable (30/6/20X3)	100 000
Accounts receivable	15 700	Total non-current assets	?
Accounts payable	10 300	Debentures payable (30/6/20X9)	137 000
Inventory	27 200	Loan receivable (1/7/20X1)	10 000
Fixtures/fittings (net)	7 200	Plant and equipment (net)	3 600
Salaries payable	6 200	Other current liabilities	1 200
Land and buildings	120 000	Total current assets	63 600
Total current liabilities	30 000		

15 The accounting department of ABC Co. Ltd was struck by lightning and some of the accounting records were destroyed. The senior accountant managed to salvage some records and requires you to prepare a balance sheet, in good form, from the information given overleaf.

Accounts receivable $10 000, bank overdraft $12 000, motor vehicles $20 000, net assets $115 000, total assets $217 000, inventory $20 000, land $50 000, capital $80 000, total non-current assets $185 000, plant and equipment $15 000, prepaid rent ? (note: the rent is paid monthly in advance), total current assets ?, buildings ?, accounts payable ?, total current liabilities ?, retained earnings ?, total owners' equity ?

16 A fire partially destroyed the offices of the Firesafe Company on 30 May 20X1. Some accounting records were retrieved. From the following information, prepare a balance sheet in good form. *Note*: One account does not belong in the balance sheet.

	$
Cash	200
Plant	30 000
Incendiary chemicals	17 500
Salary expenses	2 300
Accounts payable	?
Incendiary plastic containers	?
Total current assets	?
Equipment	7 000
Loan payable 29 May 20X2	17 000
Motor vehicles	?
Accounts receivable	17 800
Land	50 000
Buildings	12 500
Owners' equity	?
Total non-current assets	118 000
Total assets	156 000
Total current liabilities	47 300
Loan payable 30 June 20X0	?
Bank overdraft	7 300
Total non-current liabilities	50 000
Total liabilities	?

Note to instructors: *The following problems are considered more suitable for use in MBA courses. However, undergraduate courses may also find them useful.*

17 ABC Company and XYZ Company conduct the same type of business. Both are recently formed entities; thus the balance sheet figures for assets can be assumed to be at current market valuation. The balance sheets of the two companies as at 30 June 20X0 are as follows:

ABC Company
Balance sheet at 30 June 20X0

	$	$	$	$
Assets				
Current assets				
Cash at bank	2 400			
Accounts receivable	4 800			
Total current assets		7 200		
Non-current assets				
Office equipment	6 000			
Land	18 000			
Building	30 000			
Total non-current assets		54 000		
Total assets			61 200	
Liabilities				
Current liabilities				
Accounts payable	21 600			
Unsecured loan payable, due 30 September 20X0	31 200			
Total current liabilities		52 800		
Total liabilities			52 800	
Net assets				8 400
Owners' equity				
T. Edwards capital	8 400			
Total owners' equity				8 400

XYZ Company
Balance sheet at 30 June 20X0

	$	$	$	$
Assets				
Current assets				
Cash at bank	12 000			
Accounts receivable	24 000			
Total current assets		36 000		
Non-current assets				
Office equipment	600			
Land	3 600			
Building	6 000			
Total non-current assets		10 200		
Total assets			46 200	

	$	$	$	$
Liabilities				
Current liabilities				
Accounts payable	4 800			
Unsecured loan payable, due 30 September 20X0	7 200			
Total current liabilities		12 000		
Total liabilities			12 000	
Net assets				34 200
Owners' equity				
S. Allen capital	34 200			
Total owners' equity				34 200

Required

a Assuming that you are a banker and that the owner of each business has applied for a short-term loan of $6000 (repayable in six months), which application would you select as being the more favourable? Why?

b Assuming that you are a businessperson interested in buying one or both companies, and both owners have indicated their intentions to sell, for which business would you be willing to pay the higher price, assuming you will be taking over the existing liabilities of the company? Explain.

c If the existing owners agreed to be accountable for all the existing liabilities, how would this change your decision in (b), if at all?

(Adapted from B. Colditz and R. Gibbins, *Australian Accounting*, 3rd edn, McGraw-Hill, 1976, p. 45, business decision problem 2.)

18 For a period of years, the Remote Shire Council controlled a very large rubbish site in the southern area of Western Australia. Unfortunately, the site was nearly full and the council had to search for a new location. One of the preferred locations was an area that had previously been an open-cut coal mine. It was owned and controlled by the No More Coal Mining Venture, and the Remote Shire Council offered $4 per cubic metre to lease the quarry for a period of 10 years. This amounted to a total lease payment of $8.8 million. After this, the local paper reported the following:

This has the appearance of something for nothing but, to some experts in private enterprise, it appeared more like nothing for something. One private company, Environmental Disposals, had previously tendered $5.00 per cubic metre for the same mine site for disposal purposes, a total of $11 million.

Using the above information, explain how an asset can consist of 'nothing', and, taking into account the amounts mentioned above, illustrate your understanding of the concept of asset valuation.

Using this information, discuss whether the No More Coal Mining Venture should recognise an asset for the abandoned coal mine.

19 Read the article 'The SEC: no more hiding games' and answer the following questions:

a What do you believe is meant by the term 'off balance sheet'?

b Why do companies want items 'off balance sheet'?

c Discuss the damage that is done to the credibility of the balance sheet and the accounting profession from events such as the collapse of Enron.

THE SEC: NO MORE HIDING GAMES

edited by Robin Ajello

ENRON made famous the corporate tactic of hiding debt in off-balance-sheet partnerships. Now, the Securities & Exchange Commission aims to put a stop to such practices. On Oct. 30, the SEC proposed rules requiring public companies to disclose most such arrangements in their financial reports. The proposed rules would lower the threshold for disclosure, requiring companies to reveal off-balance-sheet transactions if there is more than a remote chance they'll have a material effect on the company. The SEC will issue final rules by Jan. 26.

BusinessWeek, 11 November 2002

20 Jill Wright, head of the Green Trees Playgroup, wanted to know how well the business was performing after six months of activity. To do this she needed to know what position the company was in at 30 June 20X1 and what the future outlook for the business was.

Mrs Wright founded the Green Trees Playgroup in January 20X1 to provide children of working parents with a specially supervised preschool education. Capital for the playgroup was raised by Mrs Wright who took out a personal loan for $26 250 of which she invested $22 500 in ordinary shares of the company. A further $11 250 in cash was invested by local business and a one-year loan of $7455 was made to the company by the local shire council.

With this capital, Mrs Wright purchased, on behalf of the playgroup, premises for $42 000, of which $8400 was for land and $33 600 for a building on the land. This was financed, in part, by a $28 350 mortgage, the remainder being paid in cash. Interest on the mortgage was to be paid in instalments every three months – though no repayment of the principal was required until the business had become established. Furniture and equipment were also purchased for $14 625 in cash.

During the first six months of operations, which ended June 20X1, the following additional amounts were paid by the business, in cash:

	$
Salary to Mrs Wright	8 250
Salaries of part-time employees	5 526
Insurance (one-year policy)	1 650
Electricity	1 070
Food and supplies	4 590
Interest and miscellaneous	3 594
Total paid out	24 680

Other events which took place included the following:
- Student fees of $17 724 were received in cash. A further $690 for fees was owed to the playgroup by parents. This amount was to be received in the period ending 31 December 20X1.
- Mrs Wright estimated that $412 worth of supplies were still on hand at 30 June 20X1, and estimated that the same amount would be on hand at 31 December 20X1. The playgroup owed $712 to food suppliers at 30 June 20X1. This amount was to be paid in the period ending 31 December 20X1.

- Mrs Wright estimated that for the next six months, to 31 December 20X1, student fees received would total $26 880.
- She estimated that, for the next six months to 31 December 20X1, the following expenditures would occur: salaries of $13 768 would be paid by the playgroup, $1344 for the electricity bill, $5880 for additional food and supplies, and $2850 for interest and miscellaneous items. The loan from the council was also expected to be paid in this period.
- No depreciation was recorded on the company's assets (buildings, furniture or equipment) as Mrs Wright has been offered $58 875 in cash for these assets from someone wanting to buy the business and she had thought it would not be appropriate to record any.

Required

a   Prepare a balance sheet for the Green Trees Playgroup as at 30 June 20X1. To minimise errors, treat each event separately. For events affecting owners' equity, other than the initial investment, record the transaction in the Retained profits account. Show negative amounts in parentheses. Show non-current assets at their original cost.
b   Prepare an estimated balance sheet as at 31 December 20X1.
c   Should the non-current assets be reported on the 30 June 20X1 balance sheets at their cost, at $58 875, or at some other amount? (This amount need not be calculated.) If they were reported at some amount other than cost, how would the balance sheet prepared in (a) change?
d   Does it appear likely that the Green Trees Playgroup will become a viable business, assuming that Mrs Wright's estimations prove correct?

ETHICS CASE STUDY

The manager of Centura Ltd has asked you to classify a $500 000 loan due for repayment in nine months as a non-current liability in the balance sheet. The company's total assets are $2 million.

Discuss

a   the impact of this classification
b   what the reasons might be for the request
c   whether any party is likely to suffer from this treatment
d   what you would do.

ANSWERS TO REVIEW EXERCISES

1   The following could be labelled as deficiencies: there is no mention of future benefits; this means an obsolete item of equipment would be classified as an asset. In addition, the concept of legal ownership is in itself too narrow because the AASB *Framework* defines assets in terms of an entity's capacity to control them.

2   Current assets are cash or other assets that are consumed or converted into cash within 12 months whereas non-current assets are used or consumed over periods of greater than 12 months. The essential difference is therefore the length of the realisation period – which is important to the liquidity of the business.

3   Current: Unearned income, tax payable, dividends payable, wages payable, etc.

Non-current: Long-term loans, employee benefits for long service leave, deferred taxes, etc.

4   The following are some of the limitations of a balance sheet:
   • it only documents one point in time
   • it provides past information
   • some items like research and development may not be recognised as an asset because they fail the definition or recognition criteria
   • if the cost method of asset measurement is used, it may mean some asset values are reliable but less relevant.

These limitations do not render the balance sheet useless; rather, they reinforce the notion that users need to be aware of a balance sheet's limitations. They should not, for example, use a balance sheet that is two years old. The most recent balance sheet should always be the one used for decision-making purposes. Furthermore, users should not ignore items such as contingent liabilities just because they are not recognised on the balance sheet.

THE INCOME STATEMENT AND STATEMENT OF CHANGES IN EQUITY
CHAPTER FIVE

5

LEARNING OBJECTIVES

At the end of this chapter, you should be able to:

1 explain the importance of the income statement

2 define and explain the terms 'income' and 'revenue'

3 explain and apply the principles involved in the recognition of revenue

4 give examples of revenue recognition

5 define and explain the term 'expense'

6 identify the recognition criteria for expenses

7 explain the process for deciding when business costs should be recognised as expenses

8 prepare a simplified income statement

9 explain the factors that influence the format of the income statement

10 explain the concept of earnings (or profit) management

11 explain the purpose of the statement of changes in equity

12 identify the main elements of the statement of changes in equity.

Note: In this chapter we use the term 'income statement'.
This is the name used within AIFRS for what was previously
called a 'statement of financial performance'.

Introduction

We have already seen that we can measure profit by comparing wealth at two points in time. We have also shown that the way in which wealth is measured in accounting terms can be roughly equated with balance sheets, and we have looked at some of the issues arising from the choices with respect to assigning monetary values to wealth measurement.

In this chapter we consider an alternative way of measuring profit – using an income statement. We look at what an income statement is, why it is important, why it is produced and what it contains. We then consider what determines the content of an income statement and some of the issues that have to be dealt with when preparing one.

Under International Financial Reporting Standards (IFRSs), a number of gains and losses are recognised directly in equity. Some gains and losses are recycled through the income statement at a later date while some are not. Therefore, in order to allow users to consider all the revenue, expenses, gains and losses for a reporting entity for a period, a statement of changes in equity must be presented. We consider the content and purpose of the statement of changes in equity at the end of this chapter.

The importance of the income statement

Unlike a balance sheet, which communicates information about a point in time, the income statement relates to a period of time. It summarises certain transactions that take place during that period. In terms of published reports, the period is normally one year, although most businesses of any size produce an income statement more regularly – usually quarterly and often monthly. The regular production of an income statement allows managers to compare actual performance against the budget. This is important as it enables managers to identify any problem areas and implement remedial action. For example, if advertising expenses are too high, management may reduce future advertising expenditure or change advertising agents.

LO 1
Explain the importance of the income statement

These statements are normally for internal consumption only, although often banks request copies or make the production of such statements a condition of lending money. The reason that the banks require these statements on a regular basis is that they need to monitor the health of the business they are lending to. They want to be confident that the managers of the business are aware of what is happening and taking action to rectify the situation if the business is making losses.

For owners and managers, there is little point in finding out at the end of the year that the price at which goods or services were sold did not cover what it cost to buy those goods or provide those services. By that stage it is too late to do anything about it. However, if a problem is identified at the end of the first month, it can be dealt with immediately by raising prices, buying at a lower price, or whatever is appropriate to the particular business.

Clearly, the income statement is very important because it tells you whether a business is profitable or not. We have all heard the expression, 'What is the bottom line?'. The bottom line is the amount of profit made by a project or business. By comparing that profit with how much wealth is needed to produce it, you can decide whether or not to invest in a business. Other factors that also need to be taken into account are the risks involved and your own judgement of future prospects in order to decide whether the return, as measured by the income statement, is adequate. Therefore, it can be argued that the income statement provides some of the basic financial information for a rational decision to be made. Managers may receive a bonus based on profitability, as discussed in Chapter 1, and share markets generally reward companies that achieve profits above what is expected and penalise companies that underperform.

However, although most of us think of business as being primarily motivated by profits, this is not always the case. Many small businesses make profits which are unsatisfactory from the point of view of a rational economic assessment, but the owner's motivation may not be solely for profit. They may simply hate working for any boss, or they may value leisure more than they do additional profits. Then there are the many not-for-profit entities operating in Australia that exist to primarily deliver services or achieve a particular outcome for society. These NFP entities require funds to operate, but their primary purpose is not the generation of a profit for a return to the owners of the entity.

Having considered why an income statement is important, let us now look at what it is and what it contains. We have said that it is a statement covering a period of time, normally one year, and that its purpose is to measure profit; that is, to measure the increase in wealth. It does this by summarising the income for that period and deducting the expenses incurred in earning that income. The process is simple, but to be able to do it we need to look at the definitions of income and expenses.

Income

LO 2

Define and explain the terms 'income' and 'revenue'

Paragraph 70 of the AASB *Framework* (2004) defines income and we used this definition in Key concept 2.12. It is given again as Key concept 5.1.

> ## KEY CONCEPT 5.1
>
> ### INCOME
> Income is increases in economic benefits during the accounting period in the form of inflows or enhancements of assets or decreases of liabilities that result in increases in equity, other than those relating to contributions from equity participants. (AASB *Framework*, para. 70a)

This definition seems complex because it attempts to cover all possible outcomes. For our purposes we can substitute 'owners' equity' for 'equity participants'. As with the other elements, income is recognised in the financial statements only when it is probable that the inflow, or other enhancement of assets, or decreases in liabilities, has occurred and can be reliably measured.

From Key concept 5.1 it can be seen that there are two main elements (besides contributions by owners) which result in increases in owners' equity. These are increases in assets and decreases in liabilities, and we discuss each of them in turn.

INCREASES IN ASSETS

In most cases, income recognition is fairly simple and does not need a detailed discussion. For example, we would all agree that a greengrocer's income is the amount that the fruit and vegetables were sold for, and in most cases that amount is in cash, which we know is a current asset. However, if we suppose that our greengrocer supplies fruit and vegetables to a couple of local restaurants who settle their bills every month, we find that in order to define income we have to include not only cash sales but also the other sales for which we have not been paid. The latter amounts are referred to as 'receivables' or as 'debtors'. Both these terms are used in Australia, although in large public companies debtors are often a subsection of receivables. (Other receivables, for example, are interest and short-term loans.) Debtors are shown in our balance sheet as assets because they meet our definition of an asset. (If you are not certain of this point, check the definition contained in Key concept 4.4.) We discuss the treatment of debtors in more detail in Chapter 8.

At this stage we should look at our balance sheet equation in the light of the two examples above. If the greengrocer has sold $100 worth of goods, either for cash or credit, and this we know has met our definition of an asset, then our balance sheet equation will be as follows:

$$\text{assets (\$100)} = \text{liabilities} + \text{owners' equity}$$

From our discussion of duality in Chapter 4, there must be another equal component to make the equation balance. (At this stage we are not discussing a reduction in an asset account through the goods being sold, but are only concerned with the cash received or the promise to pay.) It is obvious that another asset account has not decreased, nor has a liability increased; therefore, to balance the equation the owners' equity account must have increased. This has intuitive appeal because with the receipt of cash, for example, and with no other changes to the balance sheet, our wealth must have increased.

$$\text{assets (\$100)} = \text{income (\$100)}$$

At this stage we might believe that we have a fair idea of what income is: it relates to goods and services sold. This view is not necessarily correct: income can come in various forms, as can be seen from our definition of income, which was fairly broad. However, we need to be careful to ensure that we distinguish sales that are part of our normal business activity from other items of income.

To illustrate, let us assume that the greengrocer sells one of her two shops: should this be seen as income or is it different from selling fruit and vegetables? Clearly it is different, because the selling of the fruit and vegetables relates to the business of the entity while business profit relies on the success of the trading venture. The sale of the shop should be treated differently and shown separately in financial statements from the income earned through greengrocery sales. If, for example, the business was trading at a loss but a gain was made on the sale of the shop, and the gain was greater than the trading loss, this information would be lost if the two items were merged.

For this reason, AASB 18 *Revenue* deals with that component of income which arises from the ordinary activities of the entity. It is more common to talk about an entity's revenue rather than income as it is the major source of income for nearly all entities in a normal operating year. In Chapter 2 we mentioned that income includes revenue, which arises from the entity's ordinary operations, and other gains. In Chapter 2 we provided a definition of revenue as Key concept 2.13 and it is repeated here as Key concept 5.2. We will return to the concept of revenue a little later in the chapter.

KEY CONCEPT 5.2

REVENUE

Revenue is the gross inflows of economic benefits during the period arising in the course of the *ordinary activities* of an entity when those inflows result in increases in equity, other than those relating to contributions from equity participants. (AASB 118, para. 7)

Remember: Income = revenue + gains Revenue = inflows from ordinary activities

Gains   = all other inflows

Finally, before leaving the greengrocer illustration let us assume that, having sold one of the shops, the greengrocer decides to invest the money in some shares or in a building society until such time as a new shop can be found. In this situation the money invested, which is effectively surplus to immediate requirements, will generate additional income in the form of interest or dividends. This is a form of income which is different from our main source of income – which we report as revenue. It would, in this case, be shown separately but included in the total income for the period. In certain cases, however, the interest may be the major source of income. If, for example, the main activity of a business is lending money, then interest may be the major source of income and, in this instance, this is disclosed as revenue. Similarly, dividends may be the main source of income for an investment trust.

From this discussion, we can see that, although broadly speaking revenue is synonymous in many cases with sales, the actual revenue of a business is dependent on the type of business and the particular activity giving rise to the revenue. In the example we have used, we saw that in its simplest form revenue is equal to cash sales. However, for some business activities the distinctions are not so clear and this leads to problems in deciding what revenue relates to a particular period. This, of course, would not be a problem if accounting periods were the same as the period of a business cycle. For example, if a builder takes 18 months to build and sell a house there is no problem in finding the revenue for the 18 months. Unfortunately, the normal accounting period is 12 months and, as we pointed out earlier, management and other users need information on a more frequent basis than that. What then is the revenue of the house builder for the first six months, or for the first year?

The definition of revenue requires that there be an increase in equity. The borrowing of money therefore increases an asset (cash), but the transaction also creates a liability of an equivalent amount (loan payable). As we would expect, an entity does not create revenue by borrowing money.

DECREASES IN LIABILITIES

Although it is unlikely that this part of the definition of income will apply to a situation in this level of textbook, an example will be given.

Using the example of the greengrocer again, let us assume that she holds a staff party at one of the restaurants supplied by the greengrocer, and that the cost of staff parties is always met by the business. After the function the restaurant sends an account for payment to the greengrocer. This account represents a liability incurred by the business. If it is agreed between the two parties that the greengrocer will supply vegetables up to the value of the debt, in settlement of the liability, then the extinguishment of the debt, in effect, represents an increase in owners' equity (remember our balance sheet equation). This increase in equity represents income (revenue). Note that we have not yet addressed the cost of the transaction to the greengrocer; that is, the cost of the goods supplied.

We discuss this transaction in more detail on pages 133–4 when we examine the relationship between expenses and increases in liabilities.

EXCLUDING CONTRIBUTIONS BY OWNERS

Certain increases in owners' equity do not qualify as income. For example, the owners of a business may invest more capital in the entity. This transaction does not meet our definition of income because the definition precludes contributions by owners that result in an increase of equity during the reporting period. This contribution of additional capital by the owners is an investment decision, possibly with a view to generating future income.

Review exercise 1
In your own words, define income and revenue.

REVENUE RECOGNITION

In the following sections about income, we will be dealing specifically with the component of income described as revenue – that is, inflows from ordinary activities.

When does revenue arise and when should it be recognised? To help us answer this question we follow what is known as the recognition principle.

LO 3

Explain and apply the principles involved in the recognition of revenue

The recognition principle

The recognition principle is defined in Key concept 5.3. You will notice that, unlike our other definitions which are precise and all-inclusive, this simplified principle is carefully worded to avoid too much precision. It provides some basic criteria which can be applied to the particular circumstances. The final decision on whether revenue is recognised is, in practice, often a matter of judgement rather than fact. Before considering an example, look at the wording used in the simplified version of Key concept 5.3. First, you will see that it mentions the word 'process', which implies a period rather than a point in time. It also uses the term 'substantially complete', which raises the question of what is 'substantial': is it two-thirds or 90 per cent or what? The principle also says that payment should be reasonably certain. Once again this leaves room for the exercise of judgement and raises the question of what is 'reasonable certainty' in an uncertain world.

Obviously, if we sell goods to a reputable customer of long standing we are reasonably certain that we will be paid. Rather than looking at numerous examples of this type, we will start by looking in general terms at a production and selling process and examine the possible points at which we could recognise revenue in accordance with the recognition principle:

- point 1: inputs
- point 2: production
- point 3: finished goods

- point 4: sale of goods
- point 5: receipt of cash.

KEY CONCEPT 5.3

THE RECOGNITION PRINCIPLE

From the definition of revenue, the recognition principle states that revenue should be recognised only:
- when the increases in assets or reduction of liabilities have probably resulted from inflows of economic benefits

  and
- these movements can be reliably measured.

This can be simplified to:
- when the earning process is substantially complete and measurable

  and
- when the receipt of payment for the goods and services is reasonably certain.

(*Note:* Where something is simplified its meaning is often broadened and some precision is lost.)

Clearly, it is unlikely that revenue would ever be recognised at point 1 but, as we will see, all the other points could be appropriate in different circumstances. The end of the process, point 5, seems to be a safe place to recognise revenue, because the earnings process is likely to be complete and payment is certain because the cash has been received. In many cases point 5 is the appropriate point – as in the case of our greengrocer. However, she also had some other sales which were paid for monthly in arrears, so those may have to be recognised at point 4, as at that point the earning process is complete and payment is reasonably certain. On the other hand, if we take the example of the builder and use either of these points, we would have a situation where there was no revenue for the first 17 months but a lot in the 18th month. Of course, in practice, in the case of the builder, if there was a contract to build the house for someone, then some cash would have been paid in advance. The point we are making here is that points 4 and 5 are not necessarily appropriate in all cases.

One could argue that for a shipbuilder, points 4 and 5 are inappropriate because cash is received throughout a contract and the point of sale is, in fact, before the production process starts. In this case, because a ship takes a number of years to build, it is also inappropriate to choose point 3 as this would lead to all the revenue arising in one year. Therefore, it may be that point 2 is appropriate if the earning process is 'substantially' complete and it is likely that payments on account will have been received. A similar argument applies to the cases of a property developer and a building subcontractor.

4

Give examples of
revenue recognition

EXAMPLES OF REVENUE RECOGNITION

From this discussion, each case obviously needs to be judged on its merits. Consider when the appropriate time for revenue recognition would be for the following businesses:

- a local newsagent
- a supplier of components to Ford Motors
- a gold mine where all output is bought by the government at a fixed price
- an aircraft manufacturer.

Applying the recognition principle, the first example is straightforward; the others are more problematic.

A local newsagent

The business is likely to be mainly cash, so point 5 is probably most appropriate, although this will depend, for example, upon how many customers buy their newspapers on account.

Supplier of components

Clearly point 5 is too late, because even at point 4 the earnings process is complete and payment is reasonably certain. However, it could be argued that if the component supplier has a fixed contract with Ford, an earlier point, such as the point at which the goods are ready to be delivered, might be appropriate. This will come closer to the norm if more large firms adopt just-in-time principles in which designated stocks are held by their suppliers rather than by them.

A gold mine

An argument similar to that for the component supplier could be applied here because the earnings process is substantially complete at the point of production and payment is certain because the government buys all output.

An aircraft manufacturer

Your answer here will depend on the assumptions you have made. If, for example, you assumed that the aircraft manufacturer was making to order, then your judgement of certainty of payment would be different from that made if you assumed that it produced aircraft and then tried to sell them. Similarly, if you thought of an aircraft producer which made Boeing 747s, you might have thought of the production process as spreading over a number of years, in which case point 2 might have been your choice. If, on the other hand, you thought of the manufacture of light aircraft such as Piper Cubs, you would have assumed a shorter production cycle, in which case point 2 would not be appropriate.

The problem of when to recognise revenue is very important because the income statement is based upon the revenue, and other gains, for a period and the expenses for that period.

CASE STUDY 5.1

MOWLEM MOVES TO CLEAR REVENUE RECOGNITION CHAOS
Nicholas Neveling

Analysts have warned that troubled construction group Mowlem still has plenty of work to do to resolve its accounting problems, after the company announced it was undertaking a complete overhaul of its policy for revenue recognition on contracts.

The group said it would be writing down the carrying value of contracts on its 2004 balance sheet by £70m following a detailed review undertaken by new finance director Paul Mainwaring, adding that it would be adopting 'more prudent and consistent accounting rules for recognising income on contracts'.

Mowlem has issued four profit warnings in just over a year and undertaken millions of pounds in writedowns as a direct result of recognising project revenues too early.

Construction analyst at Arbuthnot Securities Andy Brown said he was yet to be convinced that an accounting revamp signalled a turnaround at the embattled company.

'I am not convinced, after what we've been through over the past two to three years,' Brown said. 'The group has obviously inherited some historical issues and with the new CEO coming in before the FD it has been difficult to clear the problems up, but at £70m the scale of the writedown is disappointing.'

Brown said it would only be possible to tell if the accounting changes were successful in six months' time. 'The group said the order book was strong and trading expectations were in line, but if you are a sub-contractor or want to go into a contract with the group you will have to think hard,' Brown said.

Accountancy Age, 22 September 2005
Copyright 2005 VNU Business Publications.
All Rights Reserved.

COMMENTARY

The article discusses problems with the revenue recognition policies used by Mowlem. The adjustments amount to approximately $170 million and so it is a significant amount. Note the reference to the problem of recognising revenues too early and the new policy being more prudent. Prudence was discussed in Chapter 2.

Review exercise 2

When should revenue be recognised? Why not only recognise revenue when cash is received?

5

Define and explain the term 'expense'

Expenses

An expense, previously defined in Key concept 2.11, is restated in Key concept 5.4, which is taken from paragraph 70 of the AASB *Framework*. The definition is straightforward and similar to that for income in that it relates to changes in assets, liabilities and owners' equity. In this case assets are reduced or liabilities increased, with a resulting reduction in equity. You should note that the reduction in equity does not include dividends paid to, or withdrawals by, the owners of the business. Further, it must be probable that decreases in economic benefits have occurred and that the amount can be reliably measured. Put simply, an expense means a money sacrifice or the incurring of a liability in pursuit of business objectives.

KEY CONCEPT 5.4

EXPENSES

Expenses are decreases in economic benefits during the accounting period, in the form of outflows or depletions of assets or incurrences of liabilities, that result in decreases in equity other than those relating to distributions to equity participants. (AASB *Framework*, para. 70b)

For our purposes we can substitute 'owners' equity' for 'equity participants'.

As with income, we will discuss each aspect of the definition in turn: assets, liabilities and owners' equity.

REDUCTIONS IN ASSETS

The definition notes that 'expenses are decreases in future economic benefits in the form of outflows or depletions of assets'. Using this part of the definition and applying it to the greengrocer mentioned earlier, we can see that when she sells goods for cash or credit, the cost of those goods is an expense. This expense results in a reduction of the asset account covering the greengrocery stock and a corresponding reduction in the equity account.

The stock of the greengrocer meets our asset definition: title to the goods passes to the purchaser, which results in an economic loss; the cost can be reliably measured; it is probable that the loss has occurred; the loss of this asset results in a reduction in wealth which reduces the equity balance. Note that the same reasoning applies whether the transaction is for cash or to a reliable debtor.

Turning to the second scenario, where the greengrocer sells one of her shops, whatever value is placed on the shop, and is disclosed in our balance sheet, would meet the definition of an expense. For example, if the net value of the shop in the balance sheet is $30 000 and the shop sells for $40 000, assuming no transactions costs, then there would be a net addition to equity of $10 000. If the reverse is true – shop value $40 000 and sale price $30 000 – there would be a net reduction in equity of $10 000. As noted in the discussion on income, this information needs to be disclosed separately.

INCREASES IN LIABILITIES

As we can see from our definition, an increase in a liability due to a decrease in economic benefits qualifies as an expense. Borrowing money creates a liability and an asset, but not an expense as there has been no consumption of economic benefit at this stage.

Using the same example as we did for income (of the greengrocer's staff party on pages 128–9), the cost of goods supplied to the restaurant owner as settlement of the liability is an expense. To explain this in more detail: the original transaction, the staff party, gives rise to an expense; that is, the increase of the liability results in the reduction of the wealth of the greengrocer. If the greengrocer paid cash to settle this liability we would have a reduction in an asset and liability account. The restaurant owner exchanges the debt for goods, which reduces the liability and increases the wealth of the greengrocer; this meets our income definition. The final part of the transaction, the supply of goods, results in a decrease in the asset account and a corresponding decrease in the equity account. Put simply, the cost of the goods supplied to the restaurant in settlement is the cost of the staff party. There were three parts to this transaction, two of which were expenses and one of which was income (a revenue):

- expenses of the staff party
- expenses of the cost of goods supplied to the restaurant
- income (revenue) of the goods supplied to the restaurant.

EXCLUDING DISTRIBUTIONS TO OWNERS

When an owner withdraws goods, services or cash from the business, this is not an expense of the business but a withdrawal of capital by the owner. These withdrawals are often referred to in the accounting literature as drawings. We could provide numerous examples of these, some of which are less obvious than others. For example, is the tax and insurance on the car a business expense if the car is also used for family transportation? The guiding principle in making a judgement is whether or not the cost has been incurred in pursuit of the objectives of the business.

Owners who believe that they are entitled to be remunerated for the work they do should pay themselves a wage or salary which equates to the effort expended. This is a legitimate business expense.

THE RECOGNITION PRINCIPLE

Identify the recognition criteria for expenses

The criteria for the recognition of expenses are the same as for revenue. Therefore, an expense should be recognised in the current period when:

- it is probable that the decrease in economic benefits has occurred
  and
- the amount can be reliably measured.

The application of the recognition criteria should help preparers of financial statements to decide when to recognise a cost incurred as an expense. However, while some costs, such as rent payments, are straightforward, others, such as research and development expenditure, present difficulties. The following examples illustrate some of the different types of costs incurred by organisations.

EXAMPLES OF EXPENSES

It is worthwhile looking at some examples of expenses, such as the:

- payment of wages, which normally involves a monetary sacrifice
- use of electricity, which normally involves incurring a liability to pay at the end of a quarter
- purchase of a machine, which normally incurs a money sacrifice or a liability
- purchase of goods for resale, which normally incurs a money sacrifice or a liability.

Although all the examples can be seen to fit our definition of expenses, they are not necessarily expenses of the period. For example, the machinery is likely to last more than one period so it cannot be seen as an expired cost. Similarly, the goods bought for resale may not be sold during the period and they, therefore, cannot be seen as an expense of the period. The benefit has not expired because we will be able to sell those goods at some time in the future. There are other situations where the point at which a cost is incurred and the point at which the benefit arises do not coincide. We will discuss this in more detail shortly.

Before we do that, it is worth emphasising once again that we are dealing with a separate business entity and only costs relating to the business's objectives can ever become expenses. This is very important as in many cases, especially with small businesses, the owner and the business are to all intents and purposes the same; however, we are preparing accounts for the business only. Thus, if we find that a bill has been paid to buy a new lounge suite for the owner of a newsagency, this cost is not an expense of the business because it relates to the owner personally, not the business. Such items often go through a business bank account but need to be separated and shown as withdrawals of the owner's capital rather than business expenses.

We will return to the discussion of drawings later, but let us now consider some possible situations in which we have to decide whether a cost, which is clearly a business cost, is an expense of the period. There are three possible situations that we need to discuss. These are where:

- costs of this year are expenses of this year
- costs of earlier years are expenses of this year
- costs of this year are expenses of subsequent years.

Costs of this year are expenses of this year

This is the usual situation and is also the simplest to deal with. It occurs when an item or service is acquired during a year and consumed during that same year. That is, costs of this accounting period are expenses of this accounting period. Where the accounting period is less than one year – for example, one month – then the discussion applies to this shorter accounting period.

No reference is made as to whether the item acquired has been paid for. It may be that it has still not been paid for, even though it has been acquired and used. A common example is telephone calls, which are only paid for at the end of the quarter. The question of the timing of payment is not relevant to the process of recognising an expense.

LO 7

Explain the process for deciding when business costs should be recognised as expenses

Costs of earlier years are expenses of this year

These can be divided into those costs that are wholly used up in the current period and those costs that are partly used up in the current period.

Wholly expenses of this year

The most obvious example of this is the stock of goods in a shop at the end of the year. The cost of buying those goods has been incurred in the year just ended, but the economic benefit has not expired; they are, therefore, assets at the year end. However, in the next year they will be sold and thus will become expenses of the next year. The process that has occurred can be illustrated as follows:

We buy goods in June 20X7 but do not sell them until July. If our accounting period ends on 30 June, then the goods are an asset at that date – 30 June 20X7 – because the economic benefit is not used up. The cost, however, has been incurred in that year. In July, the goods are sold; therefore, the benefit is used up and there is an expense for the year ended 30 June 20X8, although the cost was incurred in the previous year. This can be seen in Figure 5.1.

Figure 5.1 Costs incurred last year which are expenses of this year

A similar situation arises when services are paid for in advance and are not fully used up at the end of the accounting period. For example, if the rent is payable quarterly in advance on 31 March, 30 June, 30 September and 31 December, and the entity ends its year on 30 June, then the rent will be paid on 30 June in year 1 for the quarter to 30 September, year 2. However, the economic benefit will be used up in the first quarter of year 2 and, thus, the expense belongs to year 2.

These expenses are normally referred to as 'prepaid expenses' and frequently arise in respect of rent and water rates. For an individual, the most obvious examples of this type of expense are annual subscriptions to clubs and societies, car insurance, driving licence fees, and so on. For a business, other situations where a cost may relate to more than one period arise frequently. For example, if the car insurance of the business was payable on 1 January 20X7, then half of that cost would be used up and become an expense for year ending 30 June 20X7, and half would be used up and be an expense for year ending 30 June 20X8. The crucial test is whether the economic benefit has been used up at the year-end. If not, there is a future economic benefit and we therefore have an asset.

All these examples refer to costs incurred in the past which are expenses of the current year. Another category that needs to be considered is where costs have been incurred in the past and only part of the benefit is used up in the current year.

Part expenses of current year

An everyday example of this is any consumer durable such as a car, washing machine or TV set. In all these cases, the costs are incurred at a point in time but the economic benefits are expected to accrue over a number of years. In a business entity, the equivalents of our consumer durables are non-current assets such as machinery and office equipment. The allocation of the cost of these items to subsequent accounting periods is called depreciation, and will be dealt with in more detail in Chapter 9.

Costs incurred this year which are expenses of later years

Just as some of the costs incurred in previous years are expenses of the current accounting period, costs incurred in the current period may be expenses of future periods.

Examples that spring to mind are car registration, insurance, rates, and so on. The due date for payment of these is unlikely to coincide with the end of the accounting period, nor would we want it to because this would lead to an uneven cash flow. Other examples are goods held in stock at the year end and non-current assets bought during the year.

If we take the example of annual car insurance, we can see that, if we pay for it in the current year 20X7 on 1 January, then half of that cost will relate to the current year ending 30 June 20X7 and the other half to next year ending 30 June 20X8.

Review exercise 3

Describe the difference between an expense and an asset.

CASE STUDY 5.2

ACCOUNTANTS WARY OF EXPENSE CHESTNUTS
by Fiona Buffini

BOOKING EXPENSES as assets to boost profit and cash flow is not a new accounting trick or one unknown to corporate Australia.

Calling expenses assets and putting them on the balance sheet was an 'old chestnut', accountants said yesterday, in light of the $US3.8 billion ($6.6 billion) restatement by US telco giant *WorldCom*.

Even without the fraud alleged in the case, classifying assets required everyday judgements and could be problematic, compounded by the absence of an Australian accounting standard on intangible assets. While most accounting calls do not result in a scandal, there have been recent differences of opinion.

Failed telco One.Tel capitalised $110 million in advertising and staff costs until the Australian Securities and Investments Commission objected, citing the company for breaches of the accounting standards and corporations law.

In April 2000, One.Tel agreed to write off the amounts and ASIC said it would closely examine accounting treatments for the capitalisation of expenses by so-called new economy companies.

The issue of subscriber acquisition costs in the telco industry was referred to the Australian Accounting Standards Board's Urgent Issues Group, which released a nine-page abstract last October.

Bruce Porter, UIG member and Deloitte technical partner, said calling expenses assets when they were really expenses was an 'old chestnut'.

'It's a basic accounting matter; you have assets, liabilities, expenses and revenues and you need to make appropriate decisions about where they lie.'

John Shanahan of Spencer & Co. said asset recognition was based on concepts requiring future economic benefit, control and measurement.

The concepts have not stopped companies trying to capitalise advertising, training, fireworks, roadshows and dubious management ideas as assets in the past.

Other controversial areas were mining exploration and research and development, Mr Shanahan said.

'R&D is a major area and the basic rule is you can't capitalise research but you can capitalise development costs, if recoverable beyond any reasonable doubt that's a tough call. [sic]

'A lot of people capitalising development costs probably aren't sure they're beyond doubt.'

Asset recognition would become increasingly controversial with growth of intangible assets common in service industries.

'It's harder to determine what is the asset when you can't see it churning out widgets,' Mr Porter said.

While there is an international accounting rule on intangibles, Australia has yet to adopt it, despite the push for global standards.

Australian Financial Review,
27 June 2002

COMMENTARY

The article demonstrates the impact of classifying items as assets instead of expenses. The article indicates that, even without the WorldCom example with alleged deliberate falsification of items, the classification of costs as either assets or expenses has been a difficult issue for accountants for many years. Problems with One.Tel are also discussed in the article.

The income statement

8

Prepare a simplified income statement

Having looked at income and expenses, we now examine how these fit together in the income statement before looking at a simple numerical example. The purpose of this statement is to measure the profit or loss for the period. It does this by summarising the income for the period, and subtracting the expenses from the income to arrive at the profit or loss. This could be depicted as:

$$\text{income} - \text{expenses} = \text{profit}$$

Let us see how this fits with the measurement of wealth described in Chapter 3. We said that profit is the difference between wealth at the start of the year and the end of the year:

$$\text{wealth at } T_1 - \text{wealth at } T_0 = \text{profit at } T_1$$

The alternative way of measuring profit was to subtract expenses from income. We also said in Chapter 4 that wealth in accounting terms was measured by assets minus liabilities. The resultant figure, the residual, was referred to as the owners' equity. Thus, we said that at time T_0, the owners' equity is:

$$\text{assets at } T_0 - \text{liabilities at } T_0 = \text{owners' equity at } T_0$$

If we add to the owners' equity at T_0 the profit for the period T_0 to T_1, the resultant figure will be our wealth at T_1. This will equal our assets minus liabilities at T_1 (provided we have not changed our valuation method from one period to another). In other words:

$$\text{assets at } T_1 - \text{liabilities at } T_1 = \text{owners' equity at } T_0 + \text{profit at } T_1$$
$$= \text{owners' equity at } T_0 \pm (\text{income} - \text{expenses}) \text{ at } T_1$$

This shows us that there is a relationship between the income statement and the balance sheet; the nature of that relationship will become clearer in Chapter 6. Let us now look at an example of an income statement and then consider what it is used for, its format and its limitations. In Example 5.1 we use the transactions of Blake's Enterprises, a paint shop, and see what should go into the income statement for the year to 31 December 20X1.

Example 5.1: Blake's Enterprises

Blake's Enterprises is a new retail paint outlet set up at the start of the year. Its transactions for 20X1, its first year, are summarised as follows:

Date	Description	$
1 January	Purchase of freehold shop	120 000
1 January	Rates for the year	4 000
1 April	Purchase of van	16 000
1 April	Van registration and insurance for a year	1 200
1 July	Purchase of washing machine	600
Various	Wages to shop assistant for year	12 000
Various	Goods bought and resold	36 000
Various	Goods bought but unsold	8 000
Various	Motor expenses and petrol	2 400
Various	Cash from sales	90 000
Various	Money withdrawn by Blake	12 000

Purchase of freehold shop

The economic benefit arising from this cost has clearly not expired during the period, although some part of the economic benefit may have been used up. At this stage we will not try to measure the part that has been used up, but we should bear in mind that at a later stage we will need to make such allocations.

Rates for the year

This is clearly a cost and expense of the year in question and should be included in the income statement.

Purchase of van

As with the freehold shop, the economic benefit from the van is likely to be available over many periods and we should, theoretically, allocate to the income statement for the year the amount of the benefit used up. The allocation is made by means of a depreciation charge, which we will discuss in Chapter 9. At this stage we will only note that an allocation should be made.

Van registration and insurance

This was paid for in advance on 1 April for a full year. At the end of our accounting period (i.e. 31 December), we have used nine months' insurance and registration; that is, nine-twelfths of the total. The expense for the period, therefore, is $9/12 \times \$1200$; that is, \$900. The remaining \$300 relates to the next year (next accounting period) and is an asset at the end of the year as the business will receive some future economic benefit.

Purchase of washing machine

We know that Blake's Enterprises is a retail shop selling paint. It is highly unlikely that the washing machine was bought for use by the business, although it has been paid for out of the business bank account. Therefore, this is not an expense of the business; nor is it an asset of the business as the business will not get any future economic benefit from it. It is, in effect, a withdrawal of capital by the owner and should be treated as drawings.

Wages for year

This is clearly a business expense as the wages are paid to the shop assistant and the economic benefit has been used up. From the information we have, the whole \$12000 relates to the accounting period, and therefore the expense charged to the income statement should be \$12000.

Goods bought and resold

These goods have been sold to customers. The business no longer owns them and is not entitled to any future economic benefit. The whole of the \$36000 is an expired economic benefit and, as such, should be charged as an expense in the current year's income statement.

Goods bought but unsold

These goods are still held by the business at the end of the year. The economic benefit from the goods is still to come, in the form of cash or credit, when they are sold. Thus, goods held in stock are an asset rather than an expense of the period we are dealing with.

Motor expenses and petrol

Once again, the economic benefit from these has expired. The whole of the \$2400 should therefore be charged as an expense in this accounting period.

Cash from sales

This is the revenue of the business for the year and, as far as we can tell, it is the only revenue. The full amount of \$90000 should be shown as sales revenue in the income statement.

Money withdrawn by Blake

Given the present information, we cannot categorically say whether this is a business expense or not. If it is, in effect, wages for Blake's work, then it could be argued that it is a genuine business expense. If, on the other hand, it has simply been withdrawn for personal use it is clearly drawings, and for the purposes of this example this is how we will classify it.

Preparing the income statement

We can now draw up the income statement of Blake's Enterprises for the year ended 31 December 20X1.

Blake's Enterprises
Income statement for the year ended 31 December 20X1

	$	$
Sales revenue		90 000
Less Cost of goods sold		36 000
Gross profit		54 000
Rates	4 000	
Van registration and insurance	900	
Wages	12 000	
Motor expenses	2 400	
		19 300
Net profit		34 700

You will notice that we have shown a gross profit and a net profit. Gross profit can be defined as sales less cost of goods sold. Net profit can be broadly defined as gross profit less operating and administrative expenses and other charges.

The reason for showing the gross profit is to enable Blake to see whether the business is doing as well as it should. Most retail businesses know what percentage of selling price is profit and what is cost. Blake, for example, has costs of 40 per cent of the selling price and would expect a gross profit margin of 60 per cent of the selling price. If these figures alter, Blake would need to know why, particularly if the gross profit figure was less than expected. This information would allow Blake to take corrective action, particularly if the accounting period was, for example, one month.

The net profit figure can be affected by numerous expenses. It is the figure often referred to as 'the bottom line'. Depending on the size of the business (usually for an owner–manager) you may deduct the drawings from this net profit figure to arrive at a figure of profit retained in the business. If the drawings were subtracted in the expense section of the income statement, this would distort the ratio of net profit to sales (because the drawings figure may bear no relationship to the sales of the business). As with the gross profit percentages, managers often try to keep costs within certain percentage points.

Review exercise 4

'As long as we are making profits, however small, we can always pay our debts as they fall due.'
Discuss the truth (or otherwise) of this statement.

Factors affecting the format of the income statement

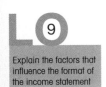

LO 9

Explain the factors that influence the format of the income statement

As is the case with the balance sheet, there are a number of factors that influence the format of the income statement, including the organisation's structure, the organisation's size and the type of user who will be utilising the statement.

TYPES OF BUSINESS

To a limited extent the type of business activity will determine the presentation and context of the income statement. In the case of a retail business, such as Blake's Enterprises, a gross profit figure may be useful, but in a service business such as a hotel, which is labour intensive, the revenue earned may bear little, if any, relationship to the inputs of physical goods. Therefore, the type of activity has an effect on what is being reported and how it should be reported.

As with the balance sheet, another prime determinant of the content and format of the income statement is the type of organisational structure involved. The content and format of the income statement for a company is influenced by the regulations imposed by the professional accounting bodies. The latter regulations are contained in Australian Accounting Standards which are now based on the IFRSs. Another important determinant is ownership. A company may have to produce statements that comply with both Australian and US regulations; for example, if it is owned by a US parent.

Refer now to Woodsides' income statement in Appendix 1. The statement reports total revenue from oil and gas operations in one line. Therefore, it is essential to study the notes following the statement while you look at the figures. Note 4(a) shows a breakdown of the various sources of the revenue.

For other types of organisational structure, such as sole proprietorships and partnerships, there are virtually no regulations covering format. Because the income statement is being prepared for owners who are also managers, it is normally the case that for these organisations the amount of detail in the income statement is greater. The reason for this is that the annual report, as well as being a report on performance, acts as a basis for management decisions about the organisation.

The size and complexity of an organisation determines the level of detail contained in statements prepared for external consumption. These statements for external consumption are only one form of statement. As we have said, regular income statements are normally prepared for internal use by the managers of an organisation and these internal reports are generally more detailed than the reports produced for external users.

Finally, it is important to remind ourselves that the type of organisation and its goals can make an income statement less relevant and in some cases irrelevant. Should charitable organisations make profits, or is the prime interest how any surplus monies have been used to further the aims of the charity? Clearly, different statements are appropriate to the needs and aims of different organisations.

Users of accounts

The users of accounts often have different requirements from each other. As we have said, owner–managers normally require detailed information. The tax authorities often require specific information to decide whether a particular expense is allowable for tax purposes. Apart from these influences, there is also confidentiality: a business does not necessarily want its competitors, or indeed its customers, to know how much profit it is making.

Earnings (or profit) management

Earnings management occurs when management's judgement in relation to financial reporting, and structuring transactions, is used to achieve particular financial outcomes. The objective may be to influence the perceptions of stakeholders about the underlying economic performance of a company and/or influence outcomes that depend on reported accounting numbers.

Explain the concept of earnings (or profit) management

It may be done so that a company reports a smooth income stream rather than a volatile number stream, because share markets generally don't like volatile earnings (profits). However, if the accounts are being prepared for tax purposes, the owner may wish to reduce profit, or defer it to the next year if at all possible. Conversely, if the accounts are to be used to borrow money, the owner may want to portray a healthy profit. While we should not give the impression that profit can be manipulated at will, it is clear from our discussion that there are areas of judgement which allow slightly different results to be obtained from the same basic data.

The practice of earnings management may potentially affect the transparency of the underlying economic reality of a client's financial performance or position to such an extent that decisions with respect to the allocation of resources may alter in the absence of such a practice (i.e. if earnings management wasn't undertaken and the economic reality of an entity was clearer, decisions about the allocation of resources may be different/unfavourable). Earnings management may also be practised in order for companies to meet earnings estimates which otherwise would be missed because the stock market penalises companies who fail to meet earnings estimates.

The extent to which the 'management' of profit is done within the scope of the accounting standards, rather than as a fraudulent abuse of the rules, is often limited by the fact that there are several conflicting requirements which mean that manipulation of profit for one purpose can prove detrimental to other purposes. It should also be borne in mind that the income statement can only be as good as the information on which it is based. Therefore, if a fish and chip shop owner only records every second sale through the till, obviously the accounts will record only those transactions that go through the till.

CASE STUDY 5.3

COMPANIES JUGGLE EARNINGS
by Fiona Buffini

MANY Australian companies manage their earnings to avoid losses and to beat the previous year's results, the first Australian research into the controversial issue has found.

A cross section of 480 public companies over the last 10 years by researchers at Melbourne's Monash University has found evidence of earnings management by ASX-listed companies.

The research comes as the Australian Securities and Investments Commission targets accounting treatments in company accounts, including the manipulation of earnings and their presentation in 2002 financial statements.

Although preliminary, the Monash research is in line with US studies, which have found companies manage their earnings to report positive profits, sustain profit levels and meet analyst expectations.

'Some companies that make a small loss or fall just below last year's earnings will manage earnings to make a small profit or just beat last year's profit,' said Monash lecturer and PhD student David Holland.

However, Mr Holland said the research was exploratory and it was difficult to quantify how many Australian companies engaged in earnings management.

He also questioned whether this earnings management was a deliberate attempt to mislead investors about the true financial position of the company or to signal directors' inside knowledge about the future profitability of the company.

He also said US statistical evidence was stronger, possibly due to the larger sample sizes or to the large numbers of stock analysts following US stocks, which could mean incentives to manage earnings in the US is higher.

'Analyst following in Australia falls away sharply outside the top 100–200 firms. Given the lower level of scrutiny, it is not clear that Australian firms (especially small Australian firms) have the same incentives to meet earnings thresholds as those in the US.'

While company earnings are subjective and readily influenced by management, investors, analysts and company managers have intensified their focus on short-term earnings benchmarks in recent years.

The number of accounting scandals and earnings restatements has risen sharply and in recent major cases of accounting fraud, executive options linked to earnings targets have been denounced for increasing incentives to improperly manage earnings and boost profits.

Researchers at Monash are extending their analysis to look at whether Australian companies manage earnings to meet analysts' forecasts and the share market reaction to just meeting or failing to meet these targets.

Australian Financial Review,
26 July 2002

COMMENTARY

The article discusses the concept of earnings management. Many companies prefer to report accounting numbers such as earnings (profit) which are not too volatile. When confronted with a choice between a stream of profit figures that swing widely up and down *or* a stream that shows a steady upward movement, managers would normally select the latter. This is due to a higher perceived risk associated with the more volatile numbers. Earnings management, or income smoothing, allows companies to avoid reporting volatile profit figures and to meet market expectations. Hence the article illustrates that accounting numbers must be viewed together with the information contained in the notes that accompany the statements, as these notes help explain how the numbers were derived.

Future changes

The IASB and the FASB (the US standard setter) have established a joint project on performance reporting. The objective of the project is to consider revisions to the presentation of the income statement. This has been done with a view to increasing the consistency and comparability of the form and content of financial statements across countries.

The project's description states that its aim is to ensure that entities 'categorise and display all income and expenses for the period in a way that enhances users' understanding of the entity's financial results and that assists users in forming expectations of future income, expenses and profit or loss' (IASB 2003, p. 2). The project has established the matrix format which is a three-column income statement that includes all items of profit or loss for the period (that is, all revenue, expenses, gains and losses) and shows, separately, items that arise due to re-measurement of financial statement elements (IASB 2005).

The three-column presentation of the matrix format would be a radical departure from the current income statement as it is outlined in this chapter. The format allows all revenues, gains, expenses and losses to be presented in one statement rather than two statements – as is currently the approach in many countries. In the US, there is a statement of comprehensive income, in the UK a statement of recognised gains and losses and the IFRSs require a statement of changes in equity (as explained in the next section). The matrix format may provide greater clarity as re-measurements are separately shown, thus assisting users to more efficiently analyse performance and predict future earnings.

To assist the standard setters with their deliberations concerning the performance reporting project, the International Association for Accounting Education and Research (IAAER), in collaboration with KPMG and the University of Illinois, awarded five Reporting Financial Performance Research Program grants. The program supports scholarly research directed at informing the IASB's decision process for the board's project on reporting financial performance. Of the five research grants awarded, three went to teams from the US, one to a team from Hong Kong, and one to a team from Australia and New Zealand. This team is comprised of Ann Tarca, Philip Brown, David Woodliff and Phil Hancock from the University of Western Australia, Mike Bradbury form Unitec and Tony van Zijl from Victoria University of Wellington. The study is 'An Experimental Study of the Decision Usefulness of the IASB's Proposed Comprehensive Income Statement' and involves testing the proposed matrix format with users including MBA students, accountants and analysts.

The statement of changes in equity

Explain the purpose of the statement of changes in equity

One of the important changes as a result of the adoption of IFRSs in Australia is the requirement for all reporting entities to now present a statement of changes in equity (SOCE). This means that all reporting entities are now required to prepare four financial statements as part of a GPFR. In this section we outline the content and elements of the SOCE, as set out in AASB 101 *Presentation of Financial Statements*.

The income statement reports all revenue and expense items for an entity. However, there are some gains and losses that occur during a period that are not recognised in the income statement. For example, in Chapter 3 we discussed the revaluation of property, plant and equipment. We noted that when such assets are revalued the changes in value are reported directly in the equity section of the balance sheet. There are also transactions with shareholders – including the payment of dividends.

The purpose of the SOCE is to report all changes to equity that are taken directly to the equity section of the balance sheet, together with the profit or loss for the period. This, therefore, gives the total changes to the equity for the period. It enables users to observe the overall change in equity during a period.

In addition to the revaluation of assets, there are other gains and losses (in relation to other assets and liabilities) that AIFRSs require be recognised directly in equity and not in the income statement. Examples include particular foreign exchange differences, gains or losses on remeasuring available-for-sale financial assets and cash flow hedging instruments. Some gains and losses are recycled at a later date through the income statement. Examples include the gains and losses on available-for-sale financial assets which are recognised in the income statement when such financial assets are sold by the entity. Some gains and losses, such as those arising from the revaluation of land, are never recycled through the income statement.

It is essential when assessing the changes in assets and liabilities that have occurred between two balance dates that users are aware of all the items of income and expense, irrespective of whether they are recognised in the income statement. The SOCE highlights an entity's total income and expenses, including those that are recognised directly in equity.

Identify the main elements of the statement of changes in equity

The requirements for what must be reported in the SOCE are specified in paragraph 96 of AASB 101. This requires that a SOCE will show the following items on the face of the statement:

    (a)   profit or loss for the period [from the income statement];

    (b)   each item of income and expense for the period that, as required by other Australian Accounting Standards, is recognised directly in equity, and the total of these items [e.g. revaluation of land];

    (c)   total income and expense for the period (calculated as the sum of (a) and (b)), showing separately the total amounts attributable to equity holders of the parent and to minority interest [we discuss this term in Chapter 12]; and

    (d)   for each component of equity, the effects of changes in accounting policies and corrections of errors recognised in accordance with AASB 108 [e.g. a change in depreciation policy which we discuss in Chapter 9].

If an entity only reports these items, the name of the statement will be a statement of recognised income and expense. However, most entities will have other items like payment of dividends or new share issues and will have to report the following items, as required by paragraph 97 of AASB 101, in addition to the above four items:

(a) the amounts of transactions with equity holders [ordinary shareholders] acting in their capacity as equity holders, showing separately distributions [e.g. dividends] to equity holders;

(b) the balance of retained earnings (i.e. accumulated profit or loss) at the beginning of the period and at the reporting date, and the changes during the period; and

(c) a reconciliation between the carrying amount of each class of contributed equity and each reserve at the beginning and the end of the period, separately disclosing each change.

KEY CONCEPT 5.5

STATEMENT OF CHANGES IN EQUITY

The purpose of the statement of changes in equity is to report all changes to equity that are taken directly to the equity section of the balance sheet, together with the profit or loss for the period. This, therefore, shows the total changes to the equity for the period. It enables users to observe the overall change in equity during a period.

Example 5.2: ABC Ltd

The following example illustrates a statement of changes in equity for a company (not a sole proprietorship-type business like the one used in Example 5.1).

ABC Ltd
Statement of changes in equity
for the year ended 30 June 20X9

	Share capital $m	Reserves $m	Retained earnings $m	Total $m
Balance at 1 July 20X7	200	80	185	465
Gain on land revaluation		75		75
Available-for-sale financial assets:				
Unrealised gain		5		5
Foreign currency cash flow hedges:				
Gains on current hedges (net of tax)		30		30
Total income and expense recognised directly in equity				110

⫸

	Share capital $m	Reserves $m	Retained earnings $m	Total $m
Profit or loss for the year (from the income statement)			125	125
Total recognised income and expense for the period				235
Dividends			(100)	(100)
Issue of share capital	100			100
Balance at 30 June 20X8	300	190	210	700
Balance at 1 July 20X8	300	190	210	700
Available-for-sale financial assets:				
Unrealised gains transferred to income statement as assets sold		(5)		(5)
Foreign currency cash flow hedges:				
Unrealised gains transferred to income statement as hedge instrument now sold		(30)		(30)
Total income and expense recognised directly in equity				(35)
Profit or loss for the year (from the income statement)			100	100
Total recognised income and expense for the period				65
Dividends			(110)	(110)
Balance at 30 June 20X9	300	155	200	655

We will now discuss each of the columns in turn.

- Share capital – in this column the opening balance at 1 July 20X7 is $200m. During the year ending 30 June 20X8 there is $100m of new shares issued but no change in the following year.
- Reserves – only one column is used for reserves in this example but in practice it is likely that a separate column would be used for each major reserve (study the SOCE in the Woodside 2005 half-year report). The opening balance at 1 July 20X7 is $80m and the closing balance at 30 June 20X8 is $190m due to the following changes reported for the year ended 30 June 20X8:
  - The fair value of land has increased by $75m, but this change is not recognised in the income statement
  - The fair value of available-for-sale financial assets on the balance sheet has increased by $5m; this is not recognised in the income statement, but is reported here
  - The fair value of cash flow hedge instruments has increased by $30m net of tax. AASB 139 *Financial Instruments: Recognition and Measurement* requires gains on cash flow hedging instruments (e.g. a forward exchange contract to hedge the price of a highly probable sale to a customer in the US) to be initially recognised in equity. This amount is then recycled to the income statement when the event occurs (e.g. the sale to the US customer) or the event is no longer likely to occur.

- Reserves – The opening balance at 1 July 20X8 is $190m and the closing balance is $155m, due to the following changes reported for the year ended 30 June 20X9:
  - The available-for-sale financial assets that resulted in the recognition of the $5m gain for the previous year were sold in the year ending 30 June 20X9 so the $5m gain is now removed from the reserves and recognised as a gain in the income statement for the year ending 30 June 20X9
  - The sale to the US customer occurred during the year ending 30 June 20X9 and, as a result, the cash flow hedge instruments were sold. Therefore, the $30m gain recognised in the previous year has been recycled to the income statement.
- Retained earnings –This column shows the opening balance at 1 July 20X7 of $185m. The profit of $125m for the year ending 30 June 20X8 is added. The dividends of $100m paid to shareholders are deducted to give an ending balance of $210m at 30 June 20X8. For the year ended 30 June 20X9, the profit for the year of $100m is added. The dividends of $110m paid to shareholders are deducted to give an ending balance of $200m at 30 June 20X9.
- Total column – this column shows the total of all three columns.

The statement also reports three important items with respect to changes for the period. These are as follows:

- total income and expense recognised directly in equity equalling $110m for the year ended 30 June 20X8 and ($35m) for the year ended 30 June 20X9
- profit of $125m for the year ended 30 June 20X8 and profit of $100m for the year ended 30 June 20X9
- total recognised income and expense of $235m for the year ended 30 June 20X8 and $65m for the year ended 30 June 20X9.

Review exercise 5

Explain the difference between profit as reported in the income statement and the total income and expense recognised directly in equity.

SUMMARY

LO 1

LEARNING OBJECTIVE 1

Explain the importance of the income statement

The income statement is important for many reasons, some of which are as follows:

- It determines the efficiency of an entity
- It compares performance with budgets
- It allows the performance of managers to be assessed
- It may provide a basis to reward managers and employees
- It determines dividends.

LO 2

LEARNING OBJECTIVE 2

Define and explain the terms 'income' and 'revenue'

Income is defined as the increases in economic benefits during the accounting period in the form of inflows or enhancements of assets or decreases of liabilities that result in increases in equity, other than those relating to contributions from equity participants.

Revenue is similar except that it only includes inflows from the ordinary operations of the entity.

LO 3

LEARNING OBJECTIVE 3

Explain and apply the principles involved in the recognition of revenue

Revenue is only recognised when:

- the increase in assets or reduction of liabilities has probably resulted from inflows of economic benefits
- these movements can be reliably measured.

LO 4

LEARNING OBJECTIVE 4

Give examples of revenue recognition

We looked at the revenue recognition for a local newsagent, a supplier of component parts to Ford Motors, a gold mine and an aircraft manufacturer.

LO 5

LEARNING OBJECTIVE 5

Define and explain the term 'expense'

Expenses are decreases in economic benefits during the accounting period that result in decreases in equity, other than those relating to distributions to equity participants. Expenses take the form of outflows or depletions of assets or the incurrence of liabilities.

LO 6

LEARNING OBJECTIVE 6

Identify the recognition criteria for expenses

Expenses should be recognised in the period in which:

- it is probable that there has been a consumption of economic benefits
- the amount can be reliably measured.

LO 7

LEARNING OBJECTIVE 7

Explain the process for deciding when business costs should be recognised as expenses

The process involves deciding when the recognition criteria for expenses are satisfied. The following situations were used to illustrate this process:

- costs of this year are expenses of this year
- costs of earlier years are expenses of this year
- costs of this year are expenses of subsequent years.

The following decision tree (Fig. 5.2) is also useful in the classification of costs to expenses.

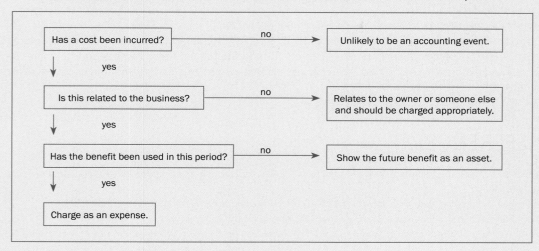

Figure 5.2 Decision tree for classifying assets and expenses

LO8
LEARNING OBJECTIVE 8
Prepare a simplified income statement
A simple income statement for one year was prepared for Blake's Enterprises, a new retail paint outlet.

LO9
LEARNING OBJECTIVE 9
Explain the factors that influence the format of the income statement
The format of an income statement is not mandated by accounting standards. Therefore, there are various factors that will influence its format. These factors include:

- the type of business (e.g. company or unincorporated association, for profit vs not-for-profit)
- the size of the entity
- organisational goals
- the needs of users.

LO10
LEARNING OBJECTIVE 10
Explain the concept of earnings (or profit) management
Earnings management occurs when people use their judgements relating to financial reporting, and the structuring of transactions, to achieve particular financial outcomes. The objective may be to influence the perceptions of stakeholders about the underlying economic performance of the company and/or influence outcomes that depend on reported accounting numbers.

LO11
LEARNING OBJECTIVE 11
Explain the purpose of the statement of changes in equity
The purpose of the SOCE is to report all changes to equity that are taken directly to equity, together with the profit or loss for the period, showing the total changes to the equity for the period. It enables users

to observe the overall change in equity during a period represented by the total amount of income and expenses, including gains and losses, generated by the entity's activities during that period irrespective of whether those items of income and expenses are recognised in the income statement or directly as changes in equity.

LEARNING OBJECTIVE 12

L 12

Identify the main elements of the statement of changes in equity

The main elements of the SOCE are the profit or loss for the period, plus each item of income and expense for the period recognised directly in equity, and the total of these items reported as the total income and expense for the period. The changes in retained earnings and contributed equity must also be reported.

REFERENCES

Australian Accounting Standards Board. *Framework for the Presentation and Preparation of Financial Statements*, July, 2004.

Australian Accounting Standards Board. AASB 101 *Presentation of Financial Statements*, July 2004.

Australian Accounting Standards Board. AASB 118 *Revenue*, July, 2004.

Australian Accounting Standards Board. AASB 139 *Financial Instruments: Recognition and Measurement,* July 2004

International Accounting Standards Board (IASB). 2003. *Performance Reporting Project: Summary Information for Field Visit Participants*, London: IASB.

International Accounting Standards Board (IASB). 2005. *Performance Reporting (Reporting Comprehensive Income)*, IASB, viewed 17 June 2004, http://www.iasb.org/current/iasb.asp?showPageContent5no&utility_catID50&recordCount53

REVIEW QUESTIONS

1 In your own words, define an expense.

2 How does an expense differ from a cost?

3 'Expenses are always the same as costs for a period.' Discuss the truth of this statement, using examples to illustrate your argument.

4 What is the purpose of an income statement, and who would use it?

5 In what circumstances would it be inappropriate to recognise a cost as either an expense or an asset?

6 Which is more important, the balance sheet or the income statement?

7 Which accounts would you expect to be changed by the following transactions?
   a cash invested in the business
   b cash received from a cash sale
   c supplies purchased on credit
   d paid electricity account
   e land purchased for $100 000 and paid for by $40 000 in cash and a $60 000 mortgage from the bank.

PROBLEMS FOR DISCUSSION AND ANALYSIS

1   Refer to the Woodside financial report in Appendix 1.
    a   What is the revenue from operations for the half-year to 30 June 2005?
    b   What is the gross profit from ordinary activities before tax for the half-year ended 30 June 2005?
        For 2004? How much did this increase by?
    c   What is the profit from ordinary activities before tax for the half-year ended 30 June 2005? For
        2004? How much did this decrease by? Why?
    d   What was the amount recorded in the statement of changes in equity for cash flow hedges in 2005?
    e   What was the total income and expense recognised directly in equity in 2005?

2   From the information in the table below calculate:
    a   owners' equity as at 1 January 20X0
    b   owners' equity as at 31 December 20X0
    c   profit earned for the 12 months ending 31 December, assuming there were no inputs or withdrawals
        of equity by the owner.

	Total assets ($)	Total liabilities ($)
As at 1 January 20X0	132 400	68 300
As at 31 December 20X0	333 000	128 300

3   Calculate the missing amounts for each independent case in the following table. Assume in case (d) that
    the assets are twice the amount of the liabilities and the expenses are 80 per cent of revenue.

Case	Total assets ($)	Total liabilities ($)	Owners' equity ($)	Total revenue ($)	Total expenses ($)	Net profit (Loss) ($)
a	100 000	?	50 000	32 000	?	6 000
b	?	27 000	(100)	7 000	8 000	?
c	32 000	16 000	?	?	10 000	3 000
d	50 000	?	?	?	?	3 000

4   Study the figures below. Calculate the missing amounts for each independent case. Assume in case (f)
    that net profit is 25 per cent of revenue.

Case	Current assets ($)	Non-current assets ($)	Total assets ($)	Current liabilities ($)	Non-current liabilities ($)	Total liabilities ($)	Owners' equity ($)	Total revenue ($)	Total expenses ($)	Net profit (Loss) ($)
a	20 000	?	140 000	30 000	?	?	20 000	112 500	?	200
b	18 200	?	?	?	110 000	132 000	33 300	86 200	?	(7300)
c	?	86 300	103 700	12 800	80 000	?	?	17 350	17 300	?
d	21 270	?	86 350	3 200	?	43 580	?	158 600	?	3 200
e	?	110 200	?	?	98 300	110 260	23 400	?	33 000	7 800
f	?	36 400	?	10 400	NIL	?	27 300	133 800	?	?

5   There are two partners in AB & Co., an electrical retailer. They have each withdrawn $10 000 in cash from the business during the year. B has also taken from the business, for personal use, a washing machine that cost $400 and had a selling price of $560. A has been paid wages of $24 000 and B has been paid $12 000 in wages.

    Discuss how each of the above should be dealt with in the accounts, giving reasons for your decisions.

6   J. Blemish's financial year ends on 30 June. However, he pays his annual insurance premium in advance on 1 January each year. How should he record the unused premium in the balance sheet on 30 June?

7   J. Blemish's balance sheet at 30 June 20X0 showed net assets of $134 645. During the year ending 30 June 20X1 an additional $5000 of capital was put into the business and the owner withdrew $56 737. The income statement for the 12 months showed a surplus of $34 692. What was the figure for owners' equity for the year ending 30 June 20X1?

8   J. Blemish's income statement for the month ending 31 March 20X1 showed a surplus of $2231. During the same month, the owner withdrew $2500 from the business. Would it be correct to say that the business incurred a loss of $269 during the month? Discuss.

9   Your friend, James Smith, knowing that you are a 'top gun' accounting student, has asked you to prepare a balance sheet and an income statement from the following information. He does not know the owners' equity figure as he has not been able to calculate the profit for the period. Provide the statements that James has requested.

	$		$
Salaries expense	1 236	Accounts payable	14 020
Cash sales	132 000	Bank overdraft	2 300
Insurance expense	932	Wages expense	38 900
Cost of supplies used to make cash sales	32 400	Land and buildings	125 000
Equipment	3 200	Vehicles	23 230
Electricity and telephone expense	9 560	Mortgage on land	23 000

10   Jimmy Jones receives a $200 000 legacy from his great-aunt. As he has some knowledge of the textile industry he decides to go into business manufacturing garments. He commences trading on 1 July 20X1 and uses all of the $200 000 as capital. Unfortunately, because he does not have an accounting background, he does not keep adequate records. At the end of the financial year, he realises that he will have to prepare financial accounts so he can ascertain whether or not he has made a profit, and whether he is liable for tax on any such profit. From the information given below, prepare, in good form, an income statement for the year and a balance sheet as at 30 June 20X2. Note that all figures given are for a full year and the owner, Jimmy Jones, withdraws amounts periodically from the business to cover his expenses.

    Debtors $50 000, inventory $100 000, bank loan (due 1 January 20X6) $80 000, machinery $80 000, total current assets $160 000, sales $127 800, rent $5000, motor vehicles $40 000, wages $42 100, motor vehicle expenses $8230, total non-current assets $132 500, electricity expense $2500, council rates $2500, total liabilities $117 600, advertising expense $2022, cost of goods sold $84 070, cash at bank ?, office equipment ?, selling expense ?, total assets ?, net assets ?, creditors ?, gross profit ?, capital ?, retained earnings ?, total owner's equity?

11   In each of the following situations, discuss whether the item would be included in the income statement for the year to 31 December 20X1 and at what amount. The business is that of a builder and builder's trader.

a   Sales of general building materials by the builder's trader to third parties amounted to $52 000 of which $48 000 was received in cash by 31 December 20X1 and the remainder was received in January 20X2.

b   Three house conversions were started and completed during the year at a price of $48 000 each. These amounts were received in full by 31 December 20X1.

c   One office conversion, which was 60 per cent complete at the end of 20X0, was completed in 20X1 at a price of $80 000. Invoices on account amounting to $48 000 had been sent out in 20X0.

d   The building materials sold to third parties during the year cost $28 000, of which all but $2000 had been paid by December 20X1.

e   The building materials used on the three houses referred to in item (b) had cost $36 000 and had all been paid for by December 20X1.

f   Wages paid in respect of the houses mentioned in item (b) amounted to $40 000 for the year.

g   The costs relating to the office mentioned in item (c) were as follows:

	$
Wages paid in 20X0	16 000
Wages paid in 20X1	12 000
Materials used in 20X0	16 000
Materials used in 20X1	14 000

h   The storeworkers' wages in the yard amounted to $16 000 for the year.

i   The owner, who worked full time in the business, paid himself a salary of $18 000 and also withdrew $2000 cash from the business to pay a pressing personal debt.

j   The motor expenses paid in the year were broken down as follows (assume the owner uses his car 80 per cent for business):

		$
Annual registration on three vans paid	1 April 20X1	600*
Annual insurance on vans paid	1 April 20X1	960*
Repairs and petrol for vans		1 200
Annual registration on owner's car paid	1 June 20X1	200*
Annual registration on owner's wife's car paid	1 June 20X1	200*
Annual insurance on owner's car paid	1 June 20X1	240*
Annual insurance on owner's wife's car paid	1 June 20X1	240*
Repairs and petrol for the two cars (50 per cent for each car)		1 600

* The charge for registration went up by $40 per vehicle and insurance premiums have risen by 20 per cent. All these charges are paid annually in advance.

k   The following bills were also paid during the year:

		$
Electricity (payable at end of each quarter)	1 February	108
	1 May	90
	1 August	90
	1 November	120
Rent for one year to 1 April 20X2	1 April 19X1	800*
TV rental to 1 April 20X2	1 April 19X1	120*

* The rent had remained the same as in 2000 but the TV rental had gone up from $100 to $120.

12 Based on your decisions, draw up an income statement for 20X1 using the information in Problem 11.

13

WATERLOO LTD
Statement of changes in equity
for the year ended 30 June 20X5

	Share capital $m	Reserves $m	Retained earnings $m	Total $m
Balance at 1 July 20X3	500	400	100	1000
Gain on land revaluation		50		50
Available-for-sale financial assets:				
Unrealised gain (loss)		?		?
Foreign currency cash flow hedges:				
Gains on current hedges (net of tax)		50		50
Net income recognised directly in equity				?
Profit or loss for the year (from the income statement)			200	200
Total recognised income and expense for the period				?
Dividends			(100)	(100)
Balance at 30 June 20X4	500	460	200	1160

Required

a   Determine the missing figures.
b   Explain the importance of the total recognised income and expense for the period.

14 Using the information from the previous question, prepare a statement of changes in equity for
Waterloo Ltd for the year ended 30 June 20X5, given the following information:
a   Net profit for the period $130m
b   Dividends of $110m
c   All available-for-sale investments were sold during the period for $150m. The carrying value in the
accounts at the time of sale was $140m
d   The fair value of the cash flow hedges declined by $15m (resultant tax savings $5m)
e   Land was revalued by $25m.

15 When a CitiPower customer uses electricity, the commission has earned revenue. It is impossible, however, to read all the customers' meters on the last day of its financial year. How does CitiPower determine its revenue for a given year?

16 The R & I Bank charges a 5 per cent service fee when issuing traveller's cheques to customers. Recently, a customer bought $1000 Diners Club International traveller's cheques, for which the bank received a fee of $50. How would the bank record this transaction, and how would the Diners Club International balance sheet be affected?

17 During November 20X0, ABC Ltd sold goods for $50 000 to XYZ Ltd, who used them as security for a hire-purchase agreement and sent the $50 000 to ABC Ltd. ABC Ltd agreed to repurchase the merchandise on or before 30 June 20X1 for $52 000, the difference being interest on the hire-purchase agreement and payment for XYZ Ltd's services. Will ABC Ltd have revenue in 20X0?

18 Swallow Ltd is a statewide real-estate brokerage company which is well known for selling small businesses through local real-estate brokers. A local broker joining the group pays Swallow Ltd an initial contract fee of $8000 plus 5 per cent of all future revenue as a service fee. In return, Swallow Ltd allows use of its well-known name, arranges various seminars throughout the year and provides a statewide referral system for the brokers. The initial contract fee currently accounts for 30 per cent of Swallow Ltd's revenues, but it anticipates that the WA market will become flooded with competitors over the next two years, from which time the company will have to rely on the service fees and any new sources of revenue. Should each $8000 be recorded as revenue by Swallow Ltd in the year in which the contract agreement is signed? If so, what will be the effect on its profits after the market has become flooded with competitors?

Note to instructors: The following problems are considered more suitable for use in MBA courses. However, undergraduate courses may also find them useful.

19 The recognition of revenue by real-estate developers is an area where diverse practices exist. Some entities recognise revenue using the percentage of completion method, as used for long-term construction projects, while others do not recognise revenue until the unit is completed and title of the unit has passed to the purchaser.

    Developers plan to construct a block of units. They attempt to pre-sell the units before commencing construction. Normally, a minimum of 70 to 80 per cent of units must be pre-sold before construction commences. Purchasers normally pay a 10 per cent deposit and the balance is paid upon completion, provided it is within the required time. Those who use the percentage of completion method argue that they are providing a service so the Accounting Standard on construction contracts applies and revenue should accrue throughout the construction period. Those who use the recognition upon completion of construction method argue that they are providing a product (the unit to a developer is like a car to Toyota) and so the normal criteria of delivery must occur before any revenue is recognised.

Required

  a Discuss the impact on the profit and loss for developers under each of the two methods of revenue recognition.

  b Discuss the factors which are important in deciding which method is appropriate.

20 You are the chief accountant of Elphick & Company, a firm of chartered accountants. Paul Cruit and his wife Debbie have asked for your advice regarding the following business proposition.

    At present, Paul earns $30 000 per annum and Debbie has a part-time job in which she earns $7000 per annum. Their eldest son is a third-year apprentice and gives his mother $50 a week towards household expenses.

Paul has been left a legacy of $250 000 by his great-aunt. This money can be invested in a bank deposit, earning 6 per cent per annum. However, Paul and Debbie favour buying a newsagency costing $370 000 (including stock, plant, equipment, a vehicle and goodwill).

The business broker selling the business states that Bankeast would be prepared to grant them a loan of $200 000 at 10 per cent per annum, repayable over 20 years.

At present, the business is operated by a husband and wife, plus one other staff member who earns $550 per week. This figure includes all employee outgoings such as payroll tax, insurance superannuation, and so on.

Additional information:

Sales for the previous 12 months:

	$
Newspapers and periodicals	780 000
Books	60 000
Stationery	87 500
Confectionery	27 600
Sundry sales	10 000

Gross profit on:

	%
Newspapers and periodicals	15
Books	40
Confectionery	50
Stationery	40
Sundry sales	30

The previous year's expenses were:

	$		$
Telephone	3 000	Wages and associated costs	28 820
Rent of premises	4 000	Rates	15 000
Insurance	12 750	Electricity and gas	7 300
Security	2 700	Advertising	3 450
Accountant's fees	3 620	Trade subscriptions	1 500
Vehicle expenses	2 300	Depreciation expense	3 820

Required

a   What would your advice be?

b   It was suggested by the business broker that the son work in the business, at a reduced wage, instead of the present employee. This would increase profits.
What points need to be considered if this course of action is to be taken?

c   What other factors should the Cruits consider before making a decision?

21 The Northshore Sailing Association (NSA) is a not-for-profit association with 1875 members.
The association represents the interests of its members through a management committee, which
organises the publication of a quarterly newsletter, and holds an annual meeting; it has subcommittees
which create various competitions and outings for the members, as well as getting involved in
community-care programs.

Every June, the newly appointed management committee meets with the old committee to discuss
whether the general policy of the NSA has been adhered to over the 12-month period. The financial
policy of the association for each year focuses on matching expenses with revenues; in other words,
the expenses of the year should approximately equal the income of the year.

At the annual meeting on 30 June 20X2, the executive secretary presented an estimated income
statement for the past financial year to the new management committee. Even though some of the
June transactions had been estimated, the executive secretary assured the committee that these figures
were carefully arrived at and should approximate the actual totals for the month.

NSA
Estimated income statement for the period 1 July 20X1 – 30 June 20X2

	$
Revenues	
Membership fees	76 680
Newsletter subscriptions	8 668
Publication sales	3 168
Government grant	14 400
Annual national sailing championship, 20X1 profit	908
Total revenues	103 824
Expenses	
Printing and mailing publications	24 640
Committee meeting expense	13 120
Annual national sailing championship advance	2 880
IBM publishing system	7 200
Administrative salaries and expenses	45 724
Miscellaneous	6 680
Total expenses	100 244
Excess of revenues over expenses	3 580

A question raised by one of the new committee members was whether a grant of $14 400 from the
government should be included as income. If it was not, a deficit would show; this would mean that
the association's reserves had been touched and, therefore, that the 20X1–X2 board had not adhered
to the general financial policy of the NSA.

This resulted in further questioning about certain items on the income statement, and led to the
disclosure of the following information by the executive secretary:
• In March 20X2, the NSA received a $14 400 grant from the government to finance a clean-up and
  erosion prevention operation along the Swanlee River, to commence in August of the same year.

Up to 30 June 20X2, $720 had been spent in preparations for the operation and was included in Committee Meeting Expenses. When asked to explain why the $14 400 had been recorded in the 20X1–X2 financial year instead of 20X2–X3, the executive secretary explained that the grant had been obtained as a result of the persuasiveness of the 20X1–X2 committee and, therefore, it should receive the credit for securing the grant.

- In early June 20X2 the association had fully installed and paid for an IBM publishing system which cost $7200. This system would dramatically reduce the hours involved in preparing membership lists, correspondence and manuscripts for publication. All of the other equipment in the association office was old.
- Members normally paid their fees during the first two months of the financial year. Due to the need to raise finance for the new IBM system, the association announced to members in April 20X2 that anyone paying their fees before 20 June 20X2 would receive a free T-shirt which would be on sale when the Swanlee River clean-up and erosion prevention operation commenced later in the year. The approximate cost of producing this T-shirt was expected to be $7.20, and it was expected to sell for $15. As a result, $8640 of fees for 20X2–X3 was received by 20 June 20X2.
- In May 20X2, the association sent a membership directory to each member; such a directory was published and sent out to members once every two years. The preparation and printing costs totalled $5760. Of the 2000 copies printed, 1875 were posted to members while the remaining 125 were held until new members joined the NSA, upon which time a directory would be sent to them free of charge.
- One of the entitlements of being an NSA member was the receipt of the association newsletter free of charge. The $8668 reported as subscription revenue was the cash received from non-members, such as libraries and interest groups, in the 20X1–X2 financial period, of which $2160 was for newsletters that would be delivered during the next financial period, 20X2–X3. Offsetting this was $1440 of subscription revenue received in 20X0–X1 for newsletters delivered in 200X–X2.
- The association had advanced $2880 for preliminary expenses to the committee responsible for planning the 20X2 annual national sailing championship held in late May. Entrance fees at the competition were set at a price to cover all of the championship costs, so it was expected that the $2880, plus any profit, would be returned to the NSA after the committee had paid the championship bill. The 20X1 championship led to a $908 profit; the 20X2 results were not known, although the anticipated attendance was about the same.

Use generally accepted accounting principles to determine if the Northshore Sailing Association had an excess or deficit for 20X1–X2.

ETHICS CASE STUDY

The sales staffs at Ellenmere are paid a bonus each year provided they sell a certain number of cars. One of your best friends, James, works as a salesperson, and you work in the accounting department. In reviewing the sales records for James, you discover that his last sale for the period was large enough for him to qualify for the bonus. All that remained was for you to approve the sale. You tell James the good news and he is elated as he will now be able to pay for his daughter to receive special medical treatment for a rare disease she suffers from.

Before the bonus can be paid, it is your job to check that the customer meets the company's credit rating requirements so that the sale can be approved. As it happens, you know the customer and you notice that his profits, as stated on the company form, are about 30 per cent overstated. If you adjust the profits, the customer does not meet the company's requirements and James will lose the sale and the bonus.

Discuss what you would do in this situation.

ANSWERS TO REVIEW EXERCISES

1   Income includes gross inflows to an entity while revenue only includes inflows to an entity that result from its ordinary activities. Therefore, for a company like Woodside, revenue arises from oil sales. If the company sells some plant and equipment, any gain would be regarded as income and not revenue.

2   In essence, the recognition principle allows for revenue to be recognised when it is probable that the inflow, or other enhancement or saving in the outflow of future economic benefits, has occurred and can be reliably measured. If revenue was only recognised when cash was received, this would be called cash accounting and not accrual accounting. The framework states that, in order for relevant information to be provided to assist users, the accrual basis of accounting should be used.

3   An asset provides a future benefit whereas, with an expense, the benefit has already been consumed. However, in some cases, there are activities (like research and development, exploration and evaluation activities) which will provide future economic benefits. However, the likelihood of such benefits flowing to the entity may be too vague to pass the probable test, or it may be too difficult to reliably measure them.

4   Profits are based on accrual accounting; therefore, it is possible to have a profit and yet have no cash. Profit means that the assets have increased by more than the liabilities – but the assets don't have in the form of cash.

5   The profit as reported in the income statement is determined after all revenues, other income and expenses for the period have been recognised, in accordance with accounting standards. The total income and expense that is recognised directly in equity is the sum of all the gains and losses that are either never recognised in the income statement or are initially recognised directly to equity and later recycled to the income statement.

6

LEARNING OBJECTIVES

At the end of this chapter, you should be able to:

1   explain the format and purpose of the worksheet

2   explain common errors in single and double-entry bookkeeping

3   explain how to identify addition, subtraction and transposition errors

4   analyse and classify transactions onto a worksheet.

Introduction

In Chapter 4 we discussed the question of how we measure what a business is worth at a particular point in time by using the balance sheet, while in Chapter 5 we discussed the measurement of the profit for a period of time through the use of the income statement. We also indicated that the profit could be measured either by using the income statement or by noting the increase in wealth over a period of time.

Because of the complexity of most business organisations, and the number of transactions involved, we need to have a system from which the details for inclusion in the balance sheet and income statement can be drawn. This system also needs to have some built-in checks and balances to ensure, as far as possible, that no transactions are omitted and any errors are identified. To cope with these and other demands, a form of recording known as double-entry bookkeeping was developed. This system is based on a rule known as the 'principle of duality' (see Key concept 4.12). This principle was discussed in some detail in Chapter 4, and it was further exemplified in our discussion of the balance sheet equation which we defined as:

$$\text{assets} = \text{liabilities} + \text{owners' equity}$$

We also showed that the owners' equity was increased by the profits made by the business, and we defined profit as:

$$\text{profit} = \text{income} - \text{expenses}$$

We can therefore see that if the balance sheet at the start of the period is stated as:

$$\text{assets at } T_0 = \text{liabilities at } T_0 + \text{owners' equity at } T_0$$

then the balance sheet at the end of the period can be depicted as:

$$\text{assets at } T_1 = \text{liabilities at } T_1 + \text{owners' equity at } T_0 + (\text{income} - \text{expenses}) \text{ at } T_1$$

From these equations it is clear that there is a relationship between assets, liabilities, owners' equity, income and expenses, and that with every transaction recorded we must ensure that there are two effects so that the equation remains true. This may seem complicated but it will become much clearer when you see how the double-entry system of recording works.

KEY CONCEPT 6.1

APPLICATION OF THE PRINCIPLE OF DUALITY

Applying the principle of duality to our equation we find that if we increase our assets we must have either:

- increased our liabilities

  or
- decreased another asset

  or
- increased our owners' equity.

In other words, the principle of duality, when applied to the balance sheet equation, holds that both sides of the equation must always be equal.

In this chapter we will use simple examples to illustrate the principles involved. These principles are the same – no matter how complex the business is. It is normally the number of transactions that is the problem rather than their complexity; most large businesses, and some fairly small businesses, require sophisticated recording systems to deal with the thousands of transactions that take place during the year. This is one of the major uses of computers in business today. Computers not only provide a vehicle for recording the accounting transactions, but the more sophisticated systems also analyse the data and produce reports such as balance sheets, income statements and other reports tailored to meet the particular needs of the users or managers of the business. For our purposes, however, we do not need to introduce a high level of sophistication to understand the principles involved. We can set up a perfectly adequate double-entry bookkeeping system using a spreadsheet. We refer to our manually-produced spreadsheet as a worksheet and we use it to illustrate the basics of double-entry bookkeeping. The worksheet is set out in the form of the balance sheet equation with the columns headed as appropriate. We use the following simple data to illustrate the worksheet.

Example 6.1: Beetle

LO 1

Explain the format and purpose of the worksheet

Beetle started up a small business selling pet food and the first transactions were as follows:

1   Open a business bank account and deposit $10 000 of Beetle's own money.
2   Buy a van for $4000 cash.
3   Buy some inventory for $7000 cash.
4   Get a bank loan of $12 000. (For the purpose of this example we will assume the loan will be a current liability.)
5   Buy some equipment for $8000 cash.

Each of these transactions has been entered on the worksheet (version 1) and you should look at it while reading the description of what has been done.

Before looking at the transactions in detail, let us briefly discuss the way in which the worksheet has been set up. There is a column in which the transaction is identified and described. In our case, this identification and description consists of the number of the transaction taking place. You could include a fuller description: the date, the invoice number, the name of the suppliers involved or whatever is appropriate.

Beetle worksheet: version 1

Transaction	Assets				= Liabilities +	Equity
	Cash	Van	Inventory	Equipment	Loans	Capital
1	10 000					10 000
2	−4 000	4 000				
3	−7 000		7 000			
4	12 000				12 000	
5	−8 000			8 000		
Balance	3 000	+ 4 000	+ 7 000	+ 8 000	= 12 000	+ 10 000

After the column containing the description, there are columns for each asset purchased and these are followed by columns for the liabilities and owners' equity. Thus, in effect, we have across the top of our worksheet the balance sheet equation:

$$\text{assets} = \text{liabilities} + \text{owners' equity (or equity)}$$

Let us now examine each of the transactions in turn and see how they have been entered into our double-entry worksheet:

Transaction 1

In the case of this transaction, Beetle expects to get a future benefit; therefore, we have an asset. So we have made a column for cash and entered the amount paid into the bank account. On the other side of our worksheet we have made a column entitled 'Capital' (part of equity) and have entered in that column the amount that the owner has put into the business. It should be noted that if we were to total up our worksheet we would have the figures for the balance sheet at that point in time, and this is true at every stage, as long as all transactions up to the statement date have been recorded.

Transaction 2

For this transaction we have opened another column in which we have recorded the van as an asset because it will give a future benefit. We have also deducted the amount paid for the van from the cash column – in other words, Beetle has exchanged one asset (cash) for another (a van). The worksheet, if totalled now, would still balance and would correctly record that the business owns a van which cost $4000 and has $6000 in the bank.

Transaction 3

Next, Beetle used some of his cash to purchase some pet food. We therefore need to record that the asset 'Cash' is reduced by $7000 and that there is a new asset, 'Inventory', which cost $7000. We have classified the inventory as an asset because we have assumed that Beetle will get a future benefit from it.

Transaction 4

In this transaction Beetle borrowed some money and put it in the bank. The amount in the bank is therefore increased by the amount of the loan ($12 000), and on the other side of the worksheet we open a column in which we record the fact that the business has a liability; that is, it has an obligation to another entity to pay cash (in this case, $12 000). Once again, if we were to total up our worksheet at this point we would find that it balanced.

Transaction 5

This transaction involves using one asset, our cash, to purchase another, equipment. Once again, the equipment can be viewed as an asset of the business as the business is going to get some future benefit. All that is needed is to open a column for the new asset and show that it cost $8000 and reduced the amount Beetle has in the bank by the same amount.

From the worksheet it should be obvious that every transaction involves two entries. For example, when the owner pays in the money an entry is made in the cash column and one is made in the owners' equity column. If all the columns are totalled, the worksheet will always balance. If either of these points is not clear to you it is important that you look again at what has been done so that you understand both these points before moving on.

You might have noticed that in the worksheet all the transactions are ones that only affect the balance sheet. In order to provide a clearer understanding of the way in which the worksheet is used and how income statement transactions are recorded we will extend our example by adding another transaction to the list at the beginning of the example:

6 Beetle sold the pet food for $10000.

From transaction 6, we see that we have some sales revenue so we can open a new column entitled 'Profit and loss' (see version 2 of the worksheet, below) and in this we enter sales of $10000. We also need to enter the increase in cash of $10000 in the cash column.

If, at this stage, we were to draw up a balance sheet, it would balance and shows us that a profit of $10000 has been made. However, that is incorrect because we have not shown any expenses incurred in producing the sales of $10000. We can try to identify these expenses directly, as we know they consist of the amount in the inventory column. An alternative is to look at each of our assets and ask ourselves the question: is there a future benefit to be obtained or has the benefit expired? If there is a future benefit, then we have an asset; if the benefit has been consumed, then we have an expense. If we did this, we would conclude that, because we sold the goods represented by the figure of $7000 in the inventory column and received the benefit from selling them in the form of $10000 in cash, then these are clearly not assets any longer and should be charged as an expense of the period. Therefore, we have to make a further adjustment to our worksheet which we will call transaction 6a. Our new worksheet will now be that shown in version 2 below.

Beetle worksheet: version 2

Transaction	Assets				= Liabilities	+ Equity	
	Cash	Van	Inventory	Equipment	Loans	Capital	Profit and loss
1	10000					10000	
2	−4000	4000					
3	−7000		7000				
4	12000				12000		
5	−8000			8000			
Balance	3000	+ 4000	+ 7000	+8000	= 12000	+ 10000	
6	10000						10000
6a			−7000				−7000
Balance	13000	+ 4000	+ 0	+ 8000	= 12000	+ 10000	+ 3000

Before leaving this simple example, let us extract from the worksheet a balance sheet at the end of the period in question and an income statement for the period.

Beetle
Balance sheet at the end of the period

	$	$	$	$
Assets				
Current assets				
Cash	13 000			
Total current assets		13 000		
Non-current assets				
Van	4 000			
Equipment	8 000			
Total non-current assets		12 000		
Total assets			25 000	
Liabilities				
Current liabilities				
Loan	12 000			
Total current liabilities		12 000		
Total liabilities			12 000	
Net assets				13 000
Owners' equity				
Capital	10 000			
Profit	3 000			
Total owners' equity				13 000

You will notice that the income statement (below) is simply a summary of the profit and loss column in the worksheet. The profit is part of the owners' equity.

Beetle
Income statement for the period

	$
Sales revenue	10 000
Less Cost of goods sold	7 000
Profit for the period	3 000

A careful study of the figures in the balance sheet and a comparison with the last line of the worksheet will make it clear that the balance sheet is in fact the bottom line of the worksheet after appropriate classifications have been made.

Review exercise 1

Explain, in your own words, the purpose of the worksheet.

Common errors in bookkeeping

Explain common errors in single and double-entry bookkeeping

Example 6.1 shows that the system of double-entry bookkeeping is a convenient way of recording transactions in a logical manner. The system is not complex – all it requires is an understanding of addition and subtraction, together with the knowledge that the equation must always be in balance. It also requires the application of our definitions to classify a particular transaction correctly, so if you have had problems in understanding why a transaction is dealt with in a particular way you should return to Chapters 3, 4 and 5 and reread the definitions of elements of financial statements.

Before trying an example yourself, it is worth spending some time reflecting on the last example. If we look at any of the columns we can see that there is simply addition and subtraction taking place; a good example is the cash column where we make additions as money comes into the business and make deductions as money is spent. Another feature of the system is not so obvious: if we make mistakes there is an automatic check because in the end the worksheet will not balance. If this turns out to be the case, we have two ways of finding the error: we can either do a line-by-line check to ensure that each of our lines has balanced, or we can total the columns at various stages to see where the error is likely to be. For example, if we had an error in the worksheet we have just done, we could look at the totals after entering transaction 4 or transaction 5 or whatever. Quite often the error is reasonably obvious because the amount involved gives us a clue. The easy way to illustrate this is to put some deliberate errors into the context of the worksheet we have just completed.

SINGLE-ENTRY ERROR

Let us assume that we forgot the basic rule that each transaction has two sides and when we received the $10 000 sales we simply added the $10 000 to the cash column. Our worksheet would appear as in version 3 of the worksheet.

Beetle worksheet: version 3

Transaction	Assets				= Liabilities	+ Equity	
	Cash	Van	Inventory	Equipment	Loans	Capital	Profit and loss
	3 000	4 000	7 000	8 000	12 000	10 000	
6	10 000						
7a			−7 000				−7 000
Balance	13 000	+ 4 000	+ 0	+ 8 000	= 12 000	+ 10 000	−7 000

You will notice that, because we did not record the other side of the sales transaction, there is no addition of any amount in the profit and loss column and so this column shows a loss of $7000. If we now add up the two sides of our worksheet we find that the assets side totals $25 000 (i.e. $13000 + $4000 + $8000) whereas the liability and equity side totals $15000 (i.e. $12000 + $10000 − $7000). The difference between the two is $10000 which should direct us to the sales as the likely cause of the problem.

DOUBLE-ENTRY ERROR

Another common cause of errors is incorrect double entry. In this case two sides are recorded but they do not leave the equation in balance. Let us assume, for example, that we had incorrectly classified the $10000 which Beetle obtained from selling the goods as an increase in cash and an increase in inventory rather than as sales revenue. The resultant worksheet would then be as shown in version 4 below.

You will notice from this version of the worksheet that we no longer have a cost of goods sold which is logical because, as a result of our error, we no longer have any goods sold. What we have instead is a worksheet which shows assets that total $42000 while the liability and equity totals $22000. The difference in this case is $20000, which is twice the amount involved in the error.

Beetle worksheet: version 4

Transaction	Assets				= Liabilities	+ Equity	
	Cash	Van	Inventory	Equipment	Loans	Capital	Profit and loss
	3000	8000	7000	8000	12000	10000	
7	10000		10000				
Balance	13000	+ 4000	+ 17000	+ 8000	= 12000	+ 10000	

ADDITION, SUBTRACTION AND TRANSPOSITION ERRORS

Another common cause of errors is that we have simply failed to add or subtract correctly. The only way to fix this problem is to recheck all our totals – and the addition and subtraction. We can reduce the size of that task by balancing our worksheet on a regular basis so that we know where the error is likely to be. A similar problem is a transposition error where, for example, we recorded the total of our cash column as $10300 instead of $13000; that is, we transposed the order of the '3' and the '0'. This is a common error and happens to all of us. In this case we can identify that it may be a transposition error because the difference of $2700 is divisible by 9. This will always be the case if we simply transpose two figures; for example, 45 as 54 or 97 as 79. Notice that the difference is divisible by 9 but it does not necessarily have the number 9 in the difference. The difference between 97 and 79 is 18 which is divisible by 9.

Explain how to identify addition, subtraction and transposition errors

Review exercise 2

In each of the following cases, describe the entries required on the worksheet.

a   The owner takes $100 worth of inventory for his personal use.

b   The bank advises that the month's transaction charges are $30.

c   The manager of the business is advised that the cost of a new piece of equipment is $27 500.

d   A cheque for $400 is received in full payment for goods sold on account.

e   Plant, with a cost of $10 000, is received and paid for.

f   The owner consults an architect on whether building extensions can be made. The architect has not submitted an account and the owner does not know the amount he will have to pay for this service.

Example 6.2: Mary's Second-hand Cars

Analyse and classify transactions onto a worksheet

Before moving on, we suggest that you draw up your own worksheet for the following set of transactions and extract a balance sheet and an income statement, comparing them with the answer. If your answer varies from the one given, try to identify what you have done; for example, classified an item as the purchase of an asset. When you have done this, compare your explanation with our explanation of that item. Your entries do not necessarily have to be identical with ours as there are many different ways of setting up the worksheet and arriving at the correct answer to show the position at the end of the month. We can illustrate this by reference to the example based on Mary's business which is set out below.

Mary decided to start a business selling second-hand cars. She had saved up some money of her own but this was not enough to get started so she obtained an interest-free loan for the business from her parents. The transactions of the business for the first month were as follows. All transactions were cash.

Day 1   Opened a business bank account and paid in $1000 of her own money.

Day 2   Paid into the bank $4000 that she had borrowed from her parents for use by the business. (*Note*: as she will repay some of this loan within this trading month we will treat the loan as a current liability.)

Day 3   Found a suitable showroom and paid a fortnight's rent of $200.

Day 4   Went to a car auction and bought the following cars for cash:
  –   1998 Ford Fiesta for $2000
  –   1993 Ford Escort for $1000
  –   1995 Volkswagen Beetle for $600.

Day 5   Bought some office furniture for $240.

Day 6   Employed a teenager (who was on social security benefits) to clean cars for her at the rate of $20 per car. Paid out $60.

Day 8   Placed advertisements for all three cars in the local paper. The cost of advertising was $40 per day for each car. She decided that all three should be advertised for two days, and so the total cost was $240.

Day 9   Sold the Ford Fiesta for $3000 cash.

Day 10   Sold the Ford Escort for $1400 cash.

Day 11   Returned to the car auction and bought a Gemini for $3000.

Day 12   Employed her teenage friend to clean the Gemini for $20.

Day 15   Re-advertised the Volkswagen for three days at $40 per day, total cost $120.

Day 17   Advertised the Gemini using a special block advertisement which cost $150 in total.

Day 18   Paid rent for showroom for the next fortnight, amounting to $200.

Day 19   Was offered $800 for the Volkswagen.

Day 20   Accepted the offer for the Volkswagen and was paid $800.

Day 22   Sold the Gemini for $3600.

Day 23   Went to the car auction and bought a Datsun 270 for $4600.

Day 24   Had the Datsun professionally cleaned at a cost of $80.

Day 25   Advertised the Datsun using the special block advertisement at a cost of $150.

Day 26   Decided that as things were going so well she would repay her parents $400.

Day 27   Took the Datsun on a test-drive with a customer, during which the engine seized.

Day 29   Had the Datsun repaired at a cost of $600.

Day 30   Sold the Datsun for $5400.

Day 31   Paid electricity bill of $80 for the month.

To illustrate the different treatments that are possible, let us consider the transaction on day 3 where Mary paid a fortnight's rent in advance. The question arises whether this is an expense or an asset. Let us consider the alternatives.

On day 3 it is reasonably clear that we have an asset in that we will get a future benefit in the form of the use of the showroom for two weeks. On the other hand, if we are recording the transaction for the first time at the end of the month we can then argue that the transaction is an expense because by then the benefit has expired. Thus, we could record, on day 3, the payment as an asset and then re-evaluate all assets at the end of the month – as we have done on our worksheet. Conversely, we could wait until the end of the month and just record an expense. We would recommend at this stage that you adopt the former treatment for two reasons: first it ensures that you re-evaluate all your assets at the end of the month, and second, shortcuts often cause more problems than they are worth if you are unfamiliar with the territory.

Another transaction that should be mentioned is the advertisements on days 8, 15, 17 and 25. In these cases there exists a similar dilemma to that of the rent. However, there is an added problem in that, although with the rent we knew that there was going to be a future benefit, with the advertising it is far from certain that there will be a future benefit. In other words, we do not know when we place the advertisement whether anyone will reply to it and, even if they do, whether they will buy the car. To answer this point we can look at our asset definition which includes the words 'that it is probable that the future economic benefits will eventuate'. In this case, as we are not certain that the advertisement will attract a buyer, we cannot classify this cost as an asset.

As you are probably beginning to recognise, accounting is not just about recording; it is also about exercising judgement within a framework of broad and often very general principles. The important factor to remember as you work through the example above is that you are making judgements and applying the definitions set out in the previous two chapters, and that you are aware of what you are doing and why you are doing it.

If your worksheet is correct, the balances on the bottom line of your worksheet should be those in the balance sheet set out below. The income statement follows the balance sheet and is merely a summary of the profit and loss column on the worksheet.

Even if you find that your answer is correct, before proceeding to the next chapter you should read the explanations for the treatment of the transactions on days 3, 6, 18, 19, 26, 27 and 29 as these are of particular interest and will assist you in the future. If your answer disagrees with ours, check the full worksheet on pages 173–4 and the explanations which follow.

Mary's Second-hand Cars
Balance sheet

	$	$	$	$
Assets				
Current assets				
Cash	5 460			
Total current assets		5 460		
Non-current assets				
Furniture	240			
Total non-current assets		240		
Total assets			5 700	
Liabilities				
Current liabilities				
Loan	3 600			
Total current liabilities		3 600		
Total liabilities			3 600	
Net assets				2 100
Owners' equity				
Capital	1 000			
Profit	1 100			
Total owners' equity				2 100

Mary's Second-hand Cars
Income statement

	$	$
Sales revenue		14 200
Less Cost of cars sold		11 200
Gross profit		3 000
Expenses		
Rent	400	
Cleaning	160	
Advertising	660	
Repairs	600	
Electricity	80	
		1 900
Net profit		1 100

Prepare your own worksheet before you read on.

Mary's Second-hand Cars
Worksheet

Day	Assets				= Liabilities	+ Equity	
	Cash	Cars	Prepaid rent	Furniture	Loans	Capital	Profit and loss
1	1 000					1 000	
2	4 000				4 000		
3	−200		200				
4	−3 600	3 600					
5	−240			240			
6	−60						−60
8	−240						−240
9	3 000						3 000
9*		−2 000					−2 000
10	1 400						1 400
10*		−1 000					−1 000
11	−3 000	3 000					
12	−20						−20
15	−120						−120
17	−150						−150
18	−200		200				
20	800						800
20*		−600					−600
22	3 600						3 600

▐▐▐➡

| Day | Assets | | | | = Liabilities | + Equity | |
	Cash	Cars	Prepaid rent	Furniture	Loans	Capital	Profit and loss
22*		−3 000					−3 000
23	−4 600	4 600					
24	−80						−80
25	−150						−150
26	−400				−400		
29	−600						−600
30	5 400						+5 400
30*		−4 600					−4 600
31	−80						−80
Balance	5 460	0	400	240	3 600	1 000	1 500
31†			−400				−400
Balance	5 460	+ 0	+ 0	+ 240	= 3 600	+ 1 000	+ 1 100

* You will notice that every time we sold a car (on days 9, 10, 20, 22 and 30) we immediately transferred the cost of that car from our cars column to the profit and loss column as an expense. This transfer was carried out because, having sold the car, we no longer expected a future benefit and, therefore, we no longer had an asset. An alternative treatment would be to do this exercise at the end of the month.

† When we complete our worksheet it is important to review our assets and ask ourselves: are these still assets? If (as in this case) the answer is no, then we need to transfer their cost to the income statement as an expense of the period.

Transaction summary

We have set out the transactions that took place, together with the treatment of those transactions on the worksheet and, where appropriate, explanations of that treatment and acceptable alternatives. If there are any items that you still do not understand, you should try to examine them in terms of the basic definitions referred to in Chapters 4 and 5.

Day 1   Opened a business bank account and paid in $1000 of her own money.

Here we have created a business asset in the form of cash and have also opened an account to show the owner's stake in the business under the heading of owners' equity.

Day 2   Paid into the bank $4000 that she had borrowed from her parents for use by the business.

Once again, the business has acquired an asset because it will get a future benefit from the cash. It has also acquired an obligation to pay somebody some money and, therefore, has a liability for the amount borrowed.

Day 3   Found a suitable showroom and paid a fortnight's rent of $200.

We discussed this transaction on page 171. Our treatment has been to reduce our asset 'cash in the bank' and record an asset of the prepaid rent from which the business will derive a benefit in the future.

Day 4   Went to a car auction and bought the following cars for cash:
- 1998 Ford Fiesta for $2000
- 1993 Ford Escort for $1000
- 1995 Volkswagen Beetle for $600.

Clearly, by paying out $3600 Mary has reduced cash at the bank, so this is one side of the entry. The other side is to record the cars as an asset because Mary will get a future benefit from them.

> Day 5   Bought some office furniture for $240.

This is exactly the same as the previous transaction. Mary has merely exchanged one asset, cash, for another, furniture.

> Day 6   Employed a teenager (who was on social security benefits) to clean cars for her at the rate of $20 per car. Paid out $60.

In this case, one side of the transaction is clear, inasmuch as the cash has clearly been reduced by $60. The question which then arises is whether there is an asset or an expense. We have shown the cost of the car-cleaning as an expense because we are uncertain that any future benefit will arise from this particular expenditure. The fact that a car is cleaned does not add any intrinsic value and, in fact, it is probably necessary to clean all the cars in the showroom regularly because customers expect to buy clean cars.

> Day 8   Placed advertisements for all three cars in the local paper. The cost of advertising was $40 per day for each car. She decided that all three should be advertised for two days, and so the total cost was $240.

Refer back to page 171 for a detailed discussion of the reasons for our treatment of this item. What we have done is assume that there is no future benefit and treated the item as an expense, charging the item to the income statement at the same time as we reduced our cash by $240.

> Day 9   Sold the Ford Fiesta for $3000 cash.

Clearly, the business has another $3000 in the bank and so we increased the amount in the cash column. The sale accords with our definition of revenue, and so we bring that revenue into the profit and loss column.

> Day 9*

Here, Mary has reduced her assets by the cost of the car she sold; we have charged that cost, that is, the cost of the expired benefit, to the profit and loss column.

> Day 10   Sold the Ford Escort for $1400.

See the explanations for day 9 above. If you have got these wrong make sure you understand why, and then correct your worksheet for all similar items before reading on.

> Day 11   Returned to the car auction and bought a Gemini for $3000.

This is, in essence, the same as the transaction on day 4. If you have made an error, you should reread that explanation and check that your treatment of the transaction on day 23 is correct before moving on.

> Day 12   Employed her teenage friend to clean the Gemini for $20.

This is, in essence, the same as the transaction on day 6. If you have made an error, you should reread that explanation and check that your treatment of the transaction on day 24 is correct before moving on.

> Day 15   Re-advertised the Volkswagen for three days at $40 per day, total cost $120.

See the explanation for day 8 above.

> Day 17   Advertised the Gemini using a special block advertisement which cost $150 in total.

See the explanation for day 8 above.

Day 18   Paid rent of showroom for the next fortnight amounting to $200.

This is, in essence, the same situation as day 3. The entry should therefore be the same. At this stage you could also reduce the amount in the rent column by the rent for the first two weeks and charge this to the profit and loss column because the benefit has now expired. We have not done this because we wished to illustrate the importance of the final review before a balance sheet and an income statement are finally drawn up.

Day 19   Was offered $800 for the Volkswagen.

Day 20   Was paid $800 for the Volkswagen.

Now we have a sale, and revenue can be recognised (as for day 9).

Day 22   Sold the Gemini for $3600.

Once again, we have a sale and revenue can be recognised.

Day 23   Went to the car auction and bought a Datsun 270 for $4600.

See day 4 for explanation of the treatment applying to this transaction.

Day 24   Had the Datsun professionally cleaned at a cost of $80.

This is the same as the cleaning for day 6. The fact that it was done professionally does not alter the argument set out there.

Day 25   Advertised the Datsun using the special block advertisement at a cost of $150.

This should be treated in the same way as previous advertisements – for the same reasons.

Day 26   Decided that, as things were going so well, she would repay her parents $400.

This is a different transaction from any of the ones we have dealt with so far. Those transactions dealt with the expenditure of cash for either a past or a future benefit. In this case we have reduced our cash in order to pay back an amount that the business owes; that is, we have used some cash to reduce our liability. Thus, we reduce the amount shown as owing in the loan column by the $400 and we reduce the amount of cash by $400.

Day 27   Took the Datsun on a test-drive with a customer, during which the engine seized.

Although an economic event has happened, we cannot account for it because, at this stage, the effect of that event cannot be adequately expressed in monetary terms.

Day 29   Had the Datsun repaired at a cost of $600.

We are now in a position to account for the event because we know its effect in monetary terms. However, we are left with the question of whether the expenditure is going to provide a future benefit or whether it is an expense. We need to decide whether the expenditure has increased the value of the asset. If it has, there is no problem in recognising the transaction as one which creates an asset. If, however, the expenditure has merely restored the asset to the state that it was in previously, then it is doubtful that it relates to an asset. We would be safer to charge it to the profit and loss column as an expense, which is what we have done.

In essence, this is a shorthand way of recording two events. The first is that the engine blew up, therefore reducing the future benefit we could expect from the asset. If we knew the extent of this reduction relating to this future benefit, we could have charged that as a past benefit. If we had done that, then the repairs could legitimately be viewed as enhancing the future benefit to be obtained in respect of the reduced asset. This whole process is, in fact, a shortcut because we do not know what the loss in value of future benefits was; we are therefore, in effect, using the cost of repairs as a surrogate for that loss in value.

Day 30   Sold Datsun for $5400.

See previous transactions of this type on, for example, days 9 and 10.

Day 31   Paid electricity bill of $80 for the month.

Here we have a reduction of the cash with respect to the use of electricity over the past month. The benefit has clearly expired and we therefore have an expense.

Day 31†

The prepaid rent has been consumed; therefore, the asset is reduced and an expense is recorded.

Review exercise 3

In each of the following cases, describe the two entries that are required on the worksheet.
  a   The owner pays $1000 into the business bank account.
  b   A desk is bought for $200 for the business, paid for from the bank account.
  c   The business buys goods for $400.
  d   The rent of the premises ($100) is paid for the first week.
  e   A potential customer makes an offer for the goods of $500.
  f   The wages of the employee, amounting to $120, are paid.
  g   The firm receives another offer of $700 for the goods, accepts this offer and is paid immediately.

Electronic spreadsheets

In this chapter we have demonstrated the use of a manual worksheet. In today's computerised world, spreadsheets in programs such as Excel or Lotus simplify the recording process. The principles are the same, but the software does have the capacity to store more data and eliminate errors in addition and subtraction. Of course, errors from incorrect recording remain. If you are familiar with the use of a spreadsheet program such as Excel, then you can use this to complete the worksheet questions at the end of this chapter.

SUMMARY

LO 1

LEARNING OBJECTIVE 1
Explain the format and purpose of the worksheet

The worksheet is a method of recording and collecting data. It is a simple vehicle for recording and checking transactions and extracting a balance sheet and an income statement.

LO 2

LEARNING OBJECTIVE 2
Explain common errors in single and double-entry bookkeeping

A single-entry error occurs when only one side of a transaction is recorded in the worksheet. It is detected by the amount of the transaction equalling the difference in the balances between the two sides of the worksheet. A double-entry error occurs when a transaction is recorded twice on the same side of the worksheet. It is detected by the amount of the transaction equalling one-half of the difference in the balances between the two sides of the worksheet.

LO 3

LEARNING OBJECTIVE 3
Explain how to identify addition, subtraction and transposition errors

Addition and subtraction errors are detected when the column totals are rechecked. This is less of a problem now because most entities now use some form of electronic spreadsheet. A transposition error can be detected when the difference in balances between both sides of the worksheet is exactly divisible by 9.

LO 4

LEARNING OBJECTIVE 4
Analyse and classify transactions onto a worksheet

Mary's Second-hand Car business was used to demonstrate that the worksheet is a simple vehicle for recording, checking and extracting a balance sheet and an income statement. We have shown that the basis of accounting is very simple if you follow the basic principles. Furthermore, for those times when you do lapse, the system used on the worksheet provides a simple and effective check.

FURTHER READING

Flanders, D. & Gourlay, D., 2004. *MYOB14 Comprehensive Edition*, Thomson.

REVIEW QUESTIONS

1 Describe, in your own words, what is meant by the concept of duality.

2 How would you identify a transposition error?

3 In each of the following cases, describe the two entries required on the worksheet.
   a The owner withdraws $200.
   b The business buys a vehicle for $27 500.
   c The business begins negotiations with a real-estate agent for the purchase of shop premises for $156 500.
   d Salaries of $1760 are paid.

    e   The business hires a consultant for $1000. This amount is paid on hiring.

    f   The business receives an electricity account for $100, payable within 14 days.

    g   The firm receives an order of $200 for merchandise.

4   In situations where doubt exists as to whether a transaction has resulted in an asset or expense, what questions should be posed?

5   If some doubt still remains, how should a choice be made? Explain any principles involved.

PROBLEMS FOR DISCUSSION AND ANALYSIS

1   In each of the following situations, discuss the potential effect on the business and suggest possible ways in which those effects could be reflected on the worksheet.

    a   The owner starts up a new business and pays $2000 into the business bank account. In addition, it is decided that the owner's car will be used exclusively for the business. The car was purchased last year at a cost of $10 000 but a similar one-year-old car could be bought for $9000.

    b   Goods previously bought by the business for $1000 were sold to a customer who then changed his mind and decided that he did not want the goods after all.

    c   Another batch of goods, bought for $800 and sold for $1200, was subsequently found to be faulty. The options available are as follows:

       •   Give the customer a rebate on the purchase price of $200.

       •   Refund the full selling price to the customer and reclaim the goods. If this course of action is followed, a further $280 will need to be spent to rectify the faults.

2   In each of the following cases, describe the two entries required on the worksheet.

    a   The owner pays $769 cash for a desk and chair.

    b   The insurance premium of $549 for one year is paid by cash.

    c   The business checks the price of widgets from a supplier and is told the price is $650 per tonne.

    d   A computer is purchased for $4999 and payment is made by cash. It is subsequently found that the computer is faulty and it is returned to the supplier for a full refund. (Treat this as two separate transactions.)

    e   An owner withdraws $100 from the business for his personal use.

    f   The owner offers to pay $5999 for a new computer.

    g   The purchase price of a Mazda De-Luxe is $48 999. A buyer offers $48 000 cash. The offer is accepted.

3   I. Cover decided to open Re-cover Upholstery Repairs on 1 January 20X4. She contributed office equipment valued at $20 000 and a van valued at $24 000. She also opened a new business account with a bank and deposited $10 000 cash. Transactions during January were:

January   4   Signed a three-year lease on a shop and paid first month's rent of $350.

              4   Purchased office supplies for $850, and paid $100 with a cheque and the balance on credit.

              6   Cash received for small repairs to chairs, $500.

              6   Revenue earned for repair work for Shipshape Ltd on credit, $1000.

              7   Purchased a special machine for sewing upholstery for $5000 paying $1000 cash and the balance was payable in 90 days.

              8   Cash revenue earned $600.

           11   Engaged an upholsterer at an agreed wage of $550 per week.

12   Paid cash for petrol $60, postage $10 and electricity $130.

13   Cash of $700 received for immediate repairs.

13   Revenue of $1200 earned from credit sales to Jon Abbott.

14   Paid for office supplies purchased on credit on 4 March.

15   Withdrew $300 for personal use.

16   Purchased office supplies for $300 on credit.

17   Cash received for minor restoration work $700.

18   Paid weekly wages to the upholsterer.

21   Revenue earned for repairs: cash $400, on account $1200.

23   Shipshape Ltd paid the amount owing from 6 January services.

24   Petrol expenses paid $70.

25   Paid weekly wages to the upholsterer.

28   Revenue earned for repair work $600, receiving $100 in cash and the remainder on credit.

31   Office supplies used $850.

Required

Complete a worksheet for the month of January using the above data. Also, prepare an income statement for the period and a balance sheet as at 31 January.

4   Joe decided to start a business selling second-hand boats. He had some money of his own, but this was not enough so he borrowed money (on interest-free terms) from a rich uncle. The transactions of the business during March were all cash transactions as follows:

March   1   Opened a bank account for the business and deposited $10 000 of his own money.

2   Deposited $20 000 (borrowed from his rich uncle) in the business bank account.

3   Paid a fortnight's rent ($500) on a yard suitable for use as a boat saleyard.

4   Went to an auction and was able to purchase the following boats (including trailers) for cash:

Thunderbird $4000

Chivers $2500

Swiftcraft $900

5   Furnished the yard office with second-hand furniture costing $2900.

6   Employed a young nephew to clean the boats.

8   Advertising for all three boats in the local paper over two days cost $300, which included photos of the boats.

9   Sold the Thunderbird for $5500 cash.

10   Sold the Chivers for $3200 cash.

11   Attended another auction and bought a Bertram for $15 000.

12   Paid his nephew $20 to clean the new boat.

15   Re-advertised the Swiftcraft for three days at a total cost of $300.

17   Advertised the Bertram in a boating magazine at a cost of $800.

18   Paid rent for the yard for the next fortnight ($500).

19   Was offered $1200 for the Swiftcraft.

20   Accepted the offer for the Swiftcraft and was paid $1200.

22   Sold the Bertram for $19 000.

23   Went to another auction and bought a Sports Fisherman for $8000.

24   Had the Sports Fisherman professionally cleaned at a cost of $180.
25   Advertised the Sports Fisherman in a fishing feature in the newspaper at a cost of $300.
26   Decided things were going so well he would repay his rich uncle $3000.
27   Took the Sports Fisherman on a test-run with a customer and damaged the hull on a
     submerged reef.
29   Had the Sports Fisherman repaired at a cost of $900.
30   Sold the Sports Fisherman for $9300.
31   Paid the electricity bill of $180 for the month.

Required

a   Complete a worksheet for the month using the provided data.
b   Prepare an income statement for the accounting period from the worksheet.
c   Prepare a balance sheet for the accounting period.

5   K. Kitten was made redundant from his job as a senior civil servant and was paid a $150 000
    redundancy fee. With this money, he invested in a toy business. Transactions during June were
    as follows:

June   1   Deposited the $150 000 into a business account and signed a seven-year lease on
             premises paying one month's rent in advance of $600.
         2   Purchased shop fittings for $27 000 on 30-day credit. Purchased stock from
             Whoopee Doo wholesalers for $58 000, paying $30 000 cash with the balance to
             be paid in 14 days.
         3   Employed Jill Smith on a casual basis for three days to help with stocking the shop.
             Payment was $100 per day paid at the end of the three days.
         4   Paid for installation of phone, fax and internet services from Telstra. As he was a new
             business customer, with no business credit history, Telstra required immediate payment
             of the connection fees of $750 and a deposit of $500 against future charges.
         5   Purchased office equipment from Charge It for $5600, payment due in seven days.
         6   Hired caterers for an opening party, paying $3100 cash, and advertised in the local
             newspaper for the next three weeks, on seven days' credit, for $500.
         7   Hired two salespersons at a weekly wage, including outgoings, of $500 each per week.
             Paid Jill Smith $300.
      7–12   Took $3456 in cash sales.
        12   A bicycle sold to R. Wobbly on 8 June, for $375, was returned due to a faulty frame. The
             customer was told that it would be repaired at the shop's expense or he could have a
             refund. R. Wobbly said he would give a decision on the following Monday, 14 June, after
             discussing it with his wife.
        12   Paid Charge It.
             Paid local newspaper.
             Paid wages $1000.
        14   R. Wobbly decided to have a refund for the faulty bike.
     14–19   Took $6320 in cash sales.
        15   One salesperson resigned, paid two days wages.
        16   Paid Whoopee Doo.
     21–26   Took $5321 in cash sales.
        21   Hired new salesperson at $450 per week. Paid the other salesperson $500 plus an
             additional $275 overtime.

23 Purchased additional stock of $23 000 from Whoopee Doo on 14 days' credit.

28–30 Took $1289 in cash sales.

28 Realised that the property and stock were not insured and took out a year's contract at an annual cost of $14 400. The first month was paid in advance.

Paid wages $950.

30 Counted stock and found that $16 300 wholesale value must have been sold.

Required

a Complete a worksheet for the month of June using the data provided.

b Prepare an income statement for the month of June and a balance sheet as at 30 June.

Note to instructors: *The following problems are considered more suitable for use in MBA courses. However, undergraduate courses may also find them useful.*

6 Mandy Plover has recently completed her professional accounting qualification and has registered as a tax agent. During the three years in which she was fulfilling the work requirement for her professional status she managed to save $30 000. As she had always wanted to run her own practice, she rented premises and opened for business. She decided the best time of year to commence her business was on 1 July, as this coincided with the beginning of the tax year.

During the month of July the following transactions took place.

July 1 Deposited $30 000 in a business bank account. Paid three months' rent in advance on premises, $3000. Placed an order with Quick Printers for stationery, business cards and letterheads. The stationery is expected to last for one year.

Paid Telstra a connection fee of $275 for the telephone and fax.

Paid the electricity company a meter rental fee of $50.

Signed a three-year lease with Office Supplies Pty Ltd at a rent of $475 per month, payable in advance, for office equipment, telephones and fax.

2 Paid Super Signs $1000 for a sign advertising her accounting services to be placed outside the premises.

3 Purchased a computer from Wizard Computers for $17 500, with payment due in 15 days.

4 Received the order from Quick Printers – payment of $1380 due on receipt of goods.

4–15 Completed a number of tax returns for clients with a total billing of $2750. Clients given 30 days' credit.

15 Signed a contract with the Widget company for bookkeeping services. The terms of the contract were that Mandy would spend one day a week at the Widget factory and be paid a weekly fee of $300.

15 Paid herself a fortnightly salary of $750.

16 Received payment from one of the tax clients (listed above: 4–15 July) of $225.

16 Signed a three-year lease on a BMW at $2000 per month, payable in advance.

18 Paid for the computer.

22 Received $300 weekly fee from the Widget company.

23 The liquidator of Jimmy Jones Holdings has informed Mandy that one of her clients who took tax advice (period: 4–15 July) has no assets and will be unable to pay the credit account of $780.

29 Paid herself a fortnightly salary of $750.

29 Received $300 weekly fee from the Widget company.

16–31   Completed work for additional clients amounting to $3450. One of these clients paid $340 in cash; the rest were given 30 days' credit.

Required

a   Prepare a worksheet for the month of July.
b   From your worksheet prepare an income statement and a balance sheet.
c   Comment on the financial position of the business.

7   Jill has recently gone into business selling office chairs. Details of her transactions for the first month are given below.

Day   1   Opened a bank account and paid in $10 000 of her own money. Transferred the ownership of her car to the business at an agreed price of $4000. Rented an office-showroom at a rental of $240 per month and paid one month's rent. Bought a desk, typewriter, answering-machine and sundry office equipment at a cost of $1600.

Day   2   Bought 100 chairs at $70 per chair and paid for them immediately.

Day   3   Received delivery of the chairs.

Day   5   Placed an advertisement in a trade paper offering the chairs for sale on the following terms: Single chairs, $100 per chair including delivery; 10 or more chairs, $90 per chair including delivery. The advertisement cost $400 and was paid for immediately.

Day   8   Received separate orders for 12 chairs at $100 each, together with accompanying cheques.

Day   9   Paid the cheques into the bank and despatched the chairs. The delivery costs were $144 in total and were paid straight away.

Day 11   Received six orders for 10 chairs each at a price of $90 per chair, together with six cheques for $900.
Banked the cheques and despatched the orders. The delivery charges were $100 for each order, making a total of $600 which was paid immediately.

Day 14   Jill paid herself two weeks wages from the business, amounting to $300 in total.

Day 16   Bought another 20 chairs for $70 each and paid for them immediately.

Day 21   Paid $300 for car repairs.

Day 23   Received an order for 20 chairs at $90 each; banked the cheque and arranged delivery for $80 which was paid immediately.

Day 24   Placed a further advertisement in the trade paper at a cost of $400, which was paid immediately.

Day 27   Received one order for 15 chairs at a price of $90 each (this order totalled $1350) and another order for seven chairs at a price of $100 each (a total of $700). The cheques were banked and the chairs were despatched at a total cost of $200 which was paid immediately.

Day 28   Drew another $300 from the bank for her own wages.
Sold the remaining six chairs at a price of $500 for all six to a customer who walked into the showroom. The customer paid the $500 in cash and this money was banked. No delivery costs were incurred because the customer took the chairs away.
Paid the telephone bill of $60 and the electricity bill, $80.

Required

a   In each situation where there are two possible treatments, discuss the arguments for and against each alternative.
b   Based on the outcome of your discussions, draw up a worksheet and enter the transactions for the month.

c   Extract a balance sheet at the end of the month and an income statement for the month.
d   Discuss the performance of the business for the period, as revealed by the accounts you have prepared, paying particular attention to its cash position and its profitability.

ETHICS CASE STUDY

Sam is an employee in the accounting department and his boss has asked him to copy the worksheet he has prepared for a meeting that afternoon in order to finalise the company's financial statements for the period. As Sam is copying the worksheet, he notices that a sale on account has not been correctly recorded. The amount has been transposed from the ledger – it was recorded as $54 000 instead of $45 000. Sam remembers the transaction as the sale was to one of his friends. If Sam says nothing, he will receive a higher bonus because the company pays a bonus to all its employees according to their total sales. The bonus will be very useful as Sam is leaving the company at the end of next week to go on an extended working holiday in Europe.

Discuss what you would do if you were Sam.

ANSWERS TO REVIEW EXERCISES

1   The worksheet is a working paper which facilitates the recording and gathering of information about transactions without the need for debits and credits. The information from the worksheet can then be used to prepare the income statement and the balance sheet.

2   a   Decrease the inventory column by $100 and increase the owners' capital column by $100.
    b   Reduce the bank column by $30 and charge an expense of $30 in the profit and loss column.
    c   No entry required.
    d   Increase the cash at bank column by $400 and decrease the accounts receivable column by $400.
    e   Increase the plant and machinery column by $10 000 and decrease the cash at bank column by $10 000.
    f   No entry required.

3   a   Increase the bank column by $1000 and increase the owners' equity column by $1000.
    b   Reduce the bank column by $200 and open up a new asset column for the new asset, a desk, and put $200 in that column.
    c   Here we have to assume that the goods have been paid for. In this case, we decrease cash by $400 and open a new asset column for the goods bought and put $400 in there.
    d   If we assume the rent is paid in arrears then the entries would be to reduce cash and charge an expense of $100 in the profit and loss column. If the assumption is that the rent is paid in advance, then the entry would be to reduce cash and open an asset account for a prepayment. As students have not been introduced to prepayment at this stage in any detail it is better if the former assumption is made.
    e   No entry is required as the earning process is not substantially complete.
    f   Reduce bank column by $120 and charge $120 as an expense in the profit and loss column.
    g   Increase the bank column by $700 and increase the profit and loss column by $700 for sales as, in this case, the earnings process is complete and receipt of money is certain.

7

LEARNING OBJECTIVES

At the end of this chapter, you should be able to:

1. discuss the importance of inventory management

2. explain what is meant by raw materials, work in progress and finished goods

3. discuss the nature of inventory that is held by different types of businesses

4. explain the periodic and perpetual methods of recording inventories

5. calculate cost of goods sold using the periodic inventory method

6. identify and apply the valuation rule for inventory

7. explain and apply the principles used to determine the cost of inventory

8. explain and apply the first in, first out (FIFO), last in, first out (LIFO) and average cost methods of determining the cost of ending inventory and cost of goods sold

9. identify the implications of the accounting policy choice used for determining inventory costing methods.

Introduction

In the examples so far, we have made some simplifying assumptions in relation to the goods purchased; that is, the inventory (or stock) of the business. The first assumption was that no inventories were held at the end of the period, so we had no problem in identifying what inventory had been sold or what it cost. This also avoided the question of whether the goods held in inventory at the end of the period were still worth what we had paid for them. Moreover, we dealt only with single-product businesses which had fairly straightforward processes for converting the goods purchased into saleable commodities. Finally, our examples dealt only with businesses in their first year, avoiding the question of how to deal with the inventory held at the beginning of the year.

Clearly the real world is more complex than this. Businesses have multiple processes or multiple inventory lines, or both. In this chapter, we relax all these assumptions and discuss the effects on the balance sheet and income statement. We also consider:

- the nature of inventories in different types of business
- the determination of the cost of inventory sold during a period
- the accounting entries needed to record inventory on the worksheet
- the issue of valuation and how a change in the basis of valuation will affect the balance sheet and income statement.

Inventory management

Discuss the importance of inventory management

In this section we discuss the important issue of managing inventories. The 2005 balance sheet for Woolworths (which can be accessed at <www.woolworths.com.au> at investor relations) shows that for the consolidated entity, inventories represent $1977.3 million of total assets (which are worth $8957.9 million); that is, inventories represent 22 per cent of total assets. This is a significant amount and indicates that Woolworths should strive to have an efficient process in place for the management of its inventories. (Later in this chapter we deal with the valuation of inventories for recording the amount unsold on the balance sheet as a current asset and the amount sold as cost of goods sold in the income statement.)

The management of inventories involves achieving a balance between holding excessive and insufficient amounts. There are costs associated with holding excessive amounts of inventories and these will vary depending on the type of business. Large items of inventory such as motor vehicles and rolls of carpet require large storage space which adds to the costs of the business. To keep costs down, storage space is kept to a minimum, but if the entity holds too few items of inventory then it risks losing profitable sales opportunities as customers will visit a competitor for their needs. How many times have you visited a supermarket looking for an item, not been able to find it and gone to the supermarket over the road to find the item you were looking for?

In addition to the costs of storage space, there is the possible loss from wastage for certain types of inventory. The fresh food sold at Woolworths has a certain use-by date and as this date approaches it is often necessary to mark down such items to increase the probability of selling them. Losses are therefore incurred, either in terms of a lower than normal price for an item or, in some cases, having to dispose of an item for no return. In some industries, like electronics and computers, obsolescence results in losses when an entity has items in inventory which are no longer in demand due to changes in technology. In the fashion industry items not sold at the end of one season are normally sold at a heavily discounted price, resulting in losses.

The more inventory an entity holds, the greater will be the amount of debt that is required to finance it. The balance sheet equation tells us that an increase in assets must be balanced by an equal increase in liabilities and/or equity. Increases in the amount of liabilities normally result in higher interest costs for the entity.

Many businesses have reappraised the way in which they operate and adopted techniques such as just-in-time management which can reduce the costs of holding high levels of inventories. The adoption of just-in-time techniques requires a reappraisal of the production process and demand cycle in order to reduce inventories to a minimum. This has caused large manufacturing firms which have adopted the technique to assess their suppliers' capability to provide supplies regularly and on time. In some cases, inventories previously held by the manufacturer are now being held by the components supplier, thus shifting the cost of holding inventory. Given the significance of inventory management, some entities now also outsource this function and pay other entities to specifically carry out this task.

Inventory turnover ratio

A tool that we can use to assess the efficiency of inventory management is the inventory turnover ratio. The ratio is measured by the following formula:

$$\frac{\text{Cost of goods sold}}{\text{Average inventory}}$$

This ratio calculates the number of times during a period the entity has turned over its inventory.

Let us look at this ratio for Woolworths in 2005. The cost of goods sold is \$24 150.8 million. To get the average inventory balance we add the balances at the end of 2004 (\$1847 million) and 2005 (\$1977.3 million) and then divide by 2 to get \$1912.15 million.

The inventory ratio for 2005 is:

$$\frac{24\ 150.15}{1912.15}$$

$$= 12.6$$

This means that, in 2005, Woolworths turned over its inventory 12.6 times. We can now take this number and divide it into 365 to convert the number to days.

The inventory ratio in days is:

$$\frac{365}{12.6}$$

$$= 29\ \text{days}$$

This seems reasonable, but we need to compare this result with some other number (which could be the number of days it takes Coles Myer to turn over its inventory) before we can evaluate the performance of Woolworths. We discuss this issue in much more detail in Chapter 14. A much lower ratio for competitors may mean that Woolworths is holding too much inventory and is therefore risking losses from storage and wastage. A much higher ratio may mean that Woolworths is holding too little inventory and is risking lost profitable sales opportunities.

Review exercise 1

Inventory management is a key tool of business. Loss of inventory (e.g. through theft) and spoilage of inventory (e.g. through poor storage) can be costly for a business. Discuss any steps that could be taken by a supermarket to minimise theft by customers and staff.

Definitions

Explain what is meant by raw materials, work in progress and finished goods

In this section we consider what we mean by the terms 'inventory', 'work in progress' and 'finished goods'. We look at examples of inventory, work in progress and finished goods, as this will lead to a better understanding of these terms.

Inventory can be said to comprise:

- goods purchased for resale. For example, cans of baked beans are purchased by a supermarket to sell to their customers; cars are purchased by used-car dealers to sell to their customers
- raw materials purchased for incorporation into the product or products being manufactured or assembled for sale. Examples are wood purchased by a furniture manufacturer or steel purchased by a car manufacturer
- consumable goods, which are bought not for resale but for use within the business operation. These consist of such things as supplies of grease for machine maintenance, supplies of stationery and cleaning materials.

You might have noticed from the examples above that the inventories are related to the type of business they are associated with. For example, cars owned by a furniture manufacturer are not classified as inventory because they are held for use in the business and not for resale. The last category, consumable goods, is different from the others because it is not held for resale. It is, in fact, another form of current asset which is called inventory only because it is an inventory of items which are held by the business and we have no other suitable term.

KEY CONCEPT 7.1

INVENTORIES

Inventories are assets:
- held for sale in the ordinary course of business
- in the process of production for such sale
  or
- in the form of materials or supplies to be consumed in the production process or in the rendering of services. (AASB 102, para. 4)

Having looked at some examples of inventory, let us now look at work in progress and finished goods. These are both different types of inventory – the difference lies in the fact that they have normally gone through some production or assembly process.

In general, all these forms of inventory and work in progress fall within the definition of current assets which we defined as Key concept 4.6 (you may wish to refer back to this key concept).

You will notice, if you consider the examples given, that it is expected the goods will be realised within the year, as in the case of the baked beans for the supermarket and the cars for the used-car dealer.

KEY CONCEPT 7.2

WORK IN PROGRESS

'Work in progress' is the term applied to products and services that are at an intermediate stage of completion; for example, if you envisage an assembly line for personal computers, at any point in time there will be some partly assembled machines somewhere on that production line. An even more obvious example, which we can observe by walking round any town centre, is partially completed buildings which are work in progress for some building contractor. A less obvious but equally valid example of work in progress is the time spent to date by an architect on a half-finished drawing.

FINISHED GOODS

Finished goods are goods that have been through the complete production or assembly cycle and are ready for resale to the customer. Examples are cars for Holden, computers for Apple or IBM, and videos for Philips.

The nature of the business is a major determinant of what is classified as inventory or work in progress. We will now explore this aspect of inventory and the question of inventory valuation in more detail.

The nature of the business and inventory valuation

We would expect the type of inventory held by a greengrocer to be different from that of a company like Woolworths. What might be less obvious is the way in which the nature of the business affects the question of inventory valuation. To illustrate this, let us first look at a retailer and a manufacturer, and then compare the latter with a provider of services, such as a firm of architects.

Discuss the nature of inventory that is held by different types of businesses

In the case of a retail business, the inventories held are those goods purchased for resale; because of the nature of the business there is generally little, if any, change between the goods bought by the business and the goods it sells. Its operating cycle could be seen as:

$$\text{Purchases} \longrightarrow \text{inventory} \longrightarrow \text{sales}$$
$$\text{(input)} \qquad\qquad\qquad\qquad\qquad \text{(output)}$$

If we can establish what the goods cost, we can arrive at a valuation of inventory, because the operating cycle is very simple.

If we now examine the situation of a manufacturing company, we find that, in order to manufacture goods, we need inputs of raw materials, of labour and of other items such as the nuts and bolts needed to assemble a car, and paint to protect and colour it. These inputs often occur at multiple points in the production process. For our purposes, a simplified version of the manufacturing process, shown in Figure 7.1, illustrates the points being made.

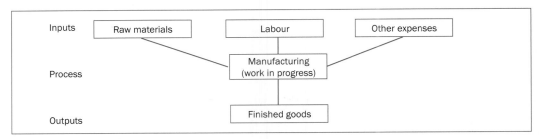

Figure 7.1 The manufacturing process

A business with a process similar to that shown in Figure 7.1 is likely, at any point in time, to have an inventory of raw materials, an inventory of goods in the process of completion (its work in progress) and an inventory of finished goods. This is illustrated in Figure 7.2.

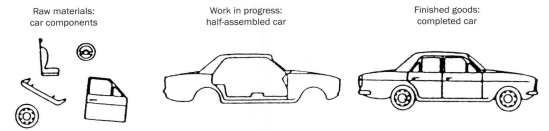

Figure 7.2 Raw materials, work in progress and finished goods

In the case of the raw materials, the question of inventory valuation is similar to that faced by a retailer. For the other categories, however, the question of valuation is often more complex. Do we include the cost of labour in the value of partially completed goods and, if so, which labour? One possible answer would be to include labour involved in the production process and exclude other labour. This is easy in theory, but in practice it is not so clear. For example, are the supervisor and production manager involved in the production process and, if so, what part of their labour cost is attributable to a particular product?

The whole question of what should and should not be included is vital because it has a direct effect on profit. In some industries where pricing is on a 'cost plus' basis, it could be the difference between survival and bankruptcy. If, for example, we quote a selling price that does not cover all our costs we could enter into a contract which leads to the downfall of the business. The collapse of Ansett in 2001 was probably caused, at least in part, by their being tied into an unprofitable pricing war with Qantas.

The discussion so far has emphasised the manufacturing sector, which we consider in more detail in the second part of this book when we look at accounting for internal users. What of the service sector? In this sector, the question of inventory valuation can be straightforward (as in the case of a newspaper vendor), or more complex (as in the case of a solicitor, architect or accountant). If we consider the case of a firm of architects, the inputs are not raw materials but labour and expenses – such as travelling expenses to see the client, to see local councils, and so on. However, it is quite likely that some proportion of the work handled by architects will take a considerable amount of time between inception and completion. Thus, for this particular service industry there will be a problem of valuing the work in progress every time the annual accounts are prepared, as was the case for our manufacturing firm.

Review exercise 2

In arriving at a figure for inventory in a business that manufactures and assembles furniture, what questions would need to be considered?

Methods for recording inventory

PERIODIC METHOD

In practice, even in simple businesses it is doubtful whether it would be possible to physically identify the goods actually sold. Even if it were possible, we would need to consider whether doing so was cost-effective. Because of the difficulties of recording every item sold and the questionable cost-effectiveness of such an exercise, some smaller businesses have few, if any, formal inventory records. Instead, they keep accurate records of purchases, and make an annual inventory count (or stocktake) to establish the amount of goods sold during a period. This annual inventory count is carried out at the balance sheet date, and so the inventory figure in the balance sheet represents a snapshot of the inventory level at that particular point in time. This is known as the *periodic method* of accounting for inventory.

You will notice that, in essence, what happens here is what we described in Chapter 3. Wealth (in the form of inventory) is measured at two points in time to establish the change over the period. While, at first sight, this might seem to be an odd way to run a business, it is in fact quite sensible when you consider the impossible job a confectionery manufacturer would have in trying to keep track of every Mars Bar, KitKat or Milky Way. If you talk to owners of small businesses you might be surprised at how accurately they can value their inventory simply by looking at what they have in the shop and on the shelves of their storerooms.

PERPETUAL METHOD

What we have just said should not be taken to imply that all retailers have poor inventory records. Some of the major retail chains have very sophisticated inventory record systems that operate at the point of sale: every time the cashier enters the sale of a tin of baked beans, the inventory records for

LO
4

Explain the periodic and perpetual methods of recording inventories

that store are updated via a computer link from the tills to the inventory recording system. This is known as the *perpetual method* of accounting for inventory. With the perpetual inventory system, the quantity of goods sold is directly measured from the computer records. Under this system an entity knows the amount of opening inventory, plus the amount purchased during the period. Therefore, by deducting the amount sold an entity can determine the amount it should have in ending inventory. A comparison of this amount with the actual inventory on hand allows an entity to measure the amount of losses from shrinkage, wastage and theft. This is a significant benefit from using the perpetual method.

In addition to entities with sophisticated computer systems, the perpetual method is also appropriate for certain types of businesses whose inventory is easy to keep track of; for example, Boeing, which manufactures and sells planes, or a jewellery store which sells items with a large dollar value. Perhaps you can add other examples. However, while such a large investment for tracking inventory might be necessary and cost-effective for large entities and for certain types of businesses, it is, at present, outside the grasp of smaller retailers and is probably more sophisticated than they need.

Review exercise 3

Explain the differences between the periodic and perpetual methods of recording inventory.

CASE STUDY 7.1

BIG SAVING FROM SYSTEMS TO REPLENISH THE SHELVES
Sue Mitchell

Woolworths' ability to achieve almost 14 per cent earnings growth on sales growth of 7.6 per cent reflects the benefits of five years of business re-engineering. Cost savings arising from Project Refresh exceeded $500 million in the latest half-year. They represented the savings generated from previous-year initiatives combined with the latest cost-cutting and efficiency measures.

Cumulative savings from the program, which was implemented in 1999, now total $1.5 billion and are forecast to reach $6.9 billion over the nine-year life of the program. However, only 12 per cent of these savings have been allowed to fall to the bottom line in the form of fatter earnings margins. The bulk of the savings 88 per cent have been reinvested back into the business in the form of reduced selling prices.

Considering the high level of price inflation in fresh food over the last two years, it's no wonder some investors and analysts are sceptical about these price reductions. The impact of the retained savings on Woolworths business is more apparent. The cost of doing business in the supermarkets division fell by 0.52 per cent of sales, offsetting a decline in gross margins and enabling EBIT margins to swell from 3.85 per cent to 4.06 per cent.

Woolworths' new automated replenishment and perpetual inventory systems, StockSmart and AutoStockR, helped to reduce inventory levels, with days inventory in supermarkets down three days on last year's levels. Group inventories at the end of the half-year were down $21 million and days inventory by 2.8 days to 35.4 days, ⟶

representing a cash-flow benefit of about $162 million.

Days stock on hand has now fallen from 44.6 in 2000 to 38.2 in 2003 and is tipped to reach 35.4 by the end of this financial year, a cash-flow benefit of $515 million. Woolworths has fully implemented the StockSmart replenishment system in all its distribution centres and there are plans to complete the roll-out of the store-based AutoStockR replenishment system this financial year.

'The successful installation of these systems is a prerequisite to realising the range of benefits available to Woolworths through its supply-chain improvement program,' the company said. Further savings would be achieved in the present half and in the 2005 financial year as distribution centres were rationalised, cross-docking in warehouses was introduced and new transport arrangements were finalised.

Australian Financial Review,
24 February 2004
© 2004 Copyright John Fairfax Holdings
Limited. www.afr.com
Not available for re-distribution.

COMMENTARY

The article demonstrates the huge benefit enjoyed by Woolworths as a result of its new inventory management system. This was one of the major reasons why Woolworths has been able to outperform Coles Myer, in terms of share market performance, in recent years.

Determining the cost of goods sold – periodic method

In previous chapters we assumed that all goods bought in the period were sold in the period and that we could clearly identify the actual goods we sold during the period. This is not the case in practice. Businesses that have been in existence for more than one year commence the year with some inventory on hand. During the year additional goods are purchased and some (we hope!) are sold. Therefore, at the end of the period it is necessary to determine:

- the cost of goods sold, which is the expense for the income statement
- the cost of goods unsold, which is the ending inventory figure and is an asset for the balance sheet.
  We can look at the problem in terms of Figure 7.3 (overleaf).

Clearly, for a business that uses the perpetual method of recording inventories, it is reasonably simple to arrive at the value of ending inventory and the cost of goods sold. Therefore, let us look at the situation where detailed inventory movement records are not kept and see how we can arrive at the cost of the goods sold and the cost of those goods still in inventory at the end of the year. In this case we need to count the inventory at the start of the year and at the end of the year. From these two figures and the figure for goods purchased during the year we can derive the cost of the goods sold during the year. In other words, if we add the purchases to the inventory of goods we had at

5

Calculate cost of goods sold using the periodic inventory method the start of the year, that will tell us the total of the goods we have held during the year. If we then subtract what we have left at the end of the year the resultant figure must be the cost of the goods we have sold during the year, assuming of course that we have allowed for any taken by the owner for personal use, and so on. Figure 7.3 will help you to understand the relationship, which can also be shown in the form of an equation:

opening inventory + purchases − closing inventory = cost of goods sold

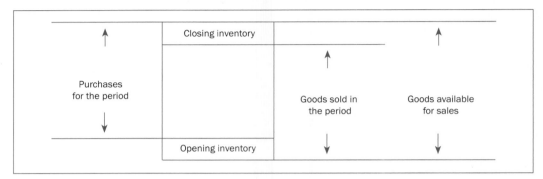

Figure 7.3 Determining the cost of goods sold

The information to solve the equation can be derived as follows:
- opening inventory, from the balance sheet at the start of the year
- purchases, from the suppliers' invoices
- closing inventory, from a physical inventory count at the end of the year.

The importance of determining inventory level is examined in Key concept 7.3.

KEY CONCEPT 7.3

THE IMPORTANCE OF DETERMINING INVENTORY LEVELS

Because with the periodic method the cost of goods sold is calculated by combining the purchases with the inventory figures, the opening and closing inventory levels are vital in determining the cost of goods sold. They therefore have a dual role: in the balance sheet in determining wealth, and, through the cost of goods sold, in determining profit.

Let us look at a simple example to illustrate the process referred to in the equation above and see how it is entered on the worksheet.

Example 7.1: Leighroy

The summarised transactions of Leighroy during the year are as follows:

	$
Sales	20 000
Purchases	12 000
Other expenses	6 000

The inventories at the end of the period have been counted and valued at $7000. The balance sheet of Leighroy at the start of the period is as follows:

Leighroy
Balance sheet at start of period

	$	$	$	$
Assets				
Current assets				
Inventories	5 000			
Cash	11 000			
Total current assets		16 000		
Non-current assets				
Premises	20 000			
Total non-current assets		20 000		
Total assets			36 000	
Net assets				36 000
Owners' equity				36 000

We start by entering the opening balances on our worksheet which now appears as follows:

Leighroy worksheet: version 1

	Assets			=	Liabilities	+	Equity
	Cash	Inventory	Premises				Capital
Balance	11 000 +	5 000 +	20 000 =				36 000

If we now enter the transactions for the year and draw up a preliminary total, our worksheet looks like this:

Leighroy worksheet: version 2

	Assets			= Liabilities	+	Equity	
	Cash	Inventory	Premises			Capital	Profit and loss
Balance	11 000	5 000	20 000			36 000	
Purchases	−12 000	12 000					
Sales	20 000						20 000
Expenses	− 6 000						− 6 000
Balance	13 000	+ 17 000	+ 20 000	=		36 000	+ 14 000

The worksheet at this stage shows that we have an inventory of goods of $17 000, whereas we know from our inventory count that what we actually have is $7000. In other words, the asset at the end of the year (i.e. the part that will provide a future benefit) is only $7000. Using our equation, we can establish that the cost of goods sold during the year was $10 000. This is, of course, an expense because the benefit is in the past.

The figure of $10 000 was arrived at as follows:

opening inventory	+	purchases	–	closing inventory	=	cost of goods sold
$5000	+	$12 000	–	$7000	=	$10 000

Having found that the cost of goods sold is $10 000, we can now enter this on our worksheet and draw up our balance at the end of the year. This is done as follows:

Leighroy worksheet: version 3

	Assets			= Liabilities +	Equity	
	Cash	Inventory	Premises		Capital	Profit and loss
Balance	11 000	5 000	20 000		36 000	
Purchases	–12 000	12 000				
Sales	20 000					20 000
Expenses	– 6 000					– 6 000
Subtotal	13 000	+ 17 000	+ 20 000		= 36 000	+ 14 000
Cost of sales		–10 000				–10 000
Balance	13 000	+ 7 000	+ 20 000		= 36 000	+ 4 000

Although the profit and loss column in the worksheet is part of equity, it is included to allow easier preparation of the income statement.

We show the calculations included in the worksheet above on an income statement as follows:

Leighroy
Income statement for the year ended 30 June 20X7

	$	$
Sales		20 000
Opening inventory	5 000	
Purchases	12 000	
	17 000	
Less Closing inventory	7 000	
Cost of sales		10 000
Gross profit		10 000
Other expenses		6 000
Net profit		4 000

A simplified presentation would be as follows:

Leighroy
Income statement for the year ended 30 June 20X7

	$
Sales	20 000
Cost of sales	10 000
Gross profit	10 000
Other expenses	6 000
Net profit	4 000

The latter format, which does not show how the cost of goods sold is calculated, is closer to what you are likely to see in the published accounts of listed companies. It should be noted that, because of the relationship between the balance sheet and the income statement, an error in the opening inventory figure, the purchases figure or the closing inventory figure not only changes the profit but also changes the balance sheet.

Review exercise 4

What would be the effect on profit if goods costing $6000 were excluded from the opening inventory figure?

Valuing inventory

In general, if the prices of goods stayed constant over time, tastes did not change and there were no changes in technology, then we would have no problem with inventory valuation. However, the real world fortunately is not like that; this has the advantage that civilisation can progress but it creates some problems for accountants. The question of how changes in prices can affect inventory valuation is wide-ranging, and is allied to the question of how the cost of inventory is arrived at. We therefore first consider the effects of changes in taste and technology; then we look at how cost is arrived at and finally consider the effects of price changes.

LO 6

Identify and apply the valuation rule for inventory

We have grouped technology and taste together because, although the causes are different, the effects on inventory valuation are the same. Let us consider the effect of changes in technology, of which there are hundreds of everyday examples such as the use of microcomputers instead of mainframe machines and the advances in microcomputer technology. An example of this effect was the introduction of the IBM personal computer, which made a number of other machines seem heavily overpriced. In turn, when other manufacturers had caught up with the technology, the IBM was overpriced and IBM had to reduce the retail price of its personal computers significantly. For the purposes of illustration, let us assume that a retailer has an inventory of 10 IBM computers bought at a cost of $3000 each. Due to competition, IBM has since decreased the price to $2000. If the retailer values its closing inventory on the basis of cost, then the asset would be reported as $30 000.

However, we said in Chapter 4 that an asset is the right to a future benefit. In the retailer's situation, the future benefit that can be obtained is only $2000 per machine, the new retail price. Thus, in this case the cost does not reflect the future benefit that the retailer is likely to get. A fairer reflection would be the amount the computers could be sold for. However, even the $2000 is probably overstating the benefit because there will undoubtedly be some costs incurred in selling the computers. If these costs were estimated to be $100 per machine, then the amount of the future benefit would in fact be $1900. This is referred to as the net realisable value of the goods.

KEY CONCEPT 7.4

NET REALISABLE VALUE

Net realisable value is defined as the estimated selling price in the ordinary course of business less the estimated costs of completion and the estimated costs necessary to make the sale. (AASB 102, para. 4)

A similar effect would have arisen if the goods could be sold only at a reduced price or for scrap because of changes in people's tastes. In each of these cases, the cost paid for the goods is not relevant to the future benefit: a better valuation would be the net realisable value. This leads us to the idea that we should compare the cost of an item with what we can get for it and, if the latter figure is lower, use that figure to value our inventory. Expressed in more formal terms, this is the valuation rule.

You might well wonder why, if the net realisable value is higher than the cost, that higher value is not used. The reason for this, it is argued, is that the attainment of the higher value is uncertain as tastes, for example, might change.

KEY CONCEPT 7.5

THE VALUATION RULE

The valuation rule states that inventory should be valued at the lower of cost and net realisable value. (AASB 102, para. 6)

In the case of a not-for-profit entity which holds goods for distribution at zero or minimal cost, the valuation rule is the lower of cost and current replacement cost.

Having established the general rule for inventory valuation and seen the reasons for the rule, the next question that we need to address is how to establish the cost that is referred to in the rule.

ESTABLISHING THE COST OF INVENTORIES

As we have already indicated, the more complex the process, the more difficult it is to establish the cost of the inventory. The problem is to decide what to include and what to leave out. The debate on this subject has been going on for some time in the literature relating to management accounting and will be explored in more detail later in this book when we discuss the alternative methods that can

Explain and apply the principles used to determine the cost of inventory

be used to arrive at cost. Fortunately, we need only be aware in general terms of what the alternative methods are because the choice between the methods has, to some extent, been made for us through custom, practice and the rules laid down for entities in AASB 102 *Inventories*. This standard deals with the question of inventories and work in progress. Before looking at that standard, let us briefly consider the alternatives by means of a simple example.

Example 7.2: Spanners

A business produces spanners. Each spanner requires $0.30 of steel and takes 15 minutes of labour to produce. The business employs 10 people to make spanners and they each produce 160 spanners per week and are paid $400 each per week. A supervisor oversees the workers and is paid $600 per week. At the end of the year we have one week's production (i.e. 1600 spanners) in inventory. The question that we have to answer is what the cost of the 1600 spanners we have in inventory is at the end of the year.

One solution is to establish how much it would cost to produce one extra spanner. Clearly, one spanner would cost $0.30 for materials and 15 minutes for the worker to produce it. The labour cost would be $2.50; that is, $400 per week divided by the number of spanners produced, which was 160. Thus, the variable cost of producing one spanner is $2.80. If we then applied this cost to our inventory we would value our inventory at 1600 × $2.80 = $4480. This would be the cost using a variable cost basis.

On the other hand, it could legitimately be argued that the cost of producing 1600 spanners (that is, one week's production) is made up as follows:

	$
Steel (1600 @ $0.30)	480
Direct labour, 10 staff at $400	4 000
Supervisor's wages	600
Total cost	5 080

This method of arriving at the cost is known as absorption costing.

You will note that the difference between the two is $600: the supervisor's wages are not included on a variable cost basis.

AASB 102 *Inventories*

As we have said, to some extent the choice between the two costing methods in Example 7.2 has been made for us by the requirements of AASB 102 which states (paragraph 7) that cost consists of:

- the cost of purchase
- the cost of conversion

  and

- other costs incurred in bringing the inventories to their present location and condition.

The costs of conversion that are referred to include direct labour and other production costs (such as the supervisor's wages) ascertained in accordance with the absorption costing method. An example of these would be the cost to Toyota of transporting engines from its production plant to the assembly line factory.

To summarise, we can say that costs will normally include the:
- cost of purchase
- cost to transport goods to a location for sale or conversion
- cost of import duty or other taxes incurred prior to sale
- cost of conversion or repackaging to make goods ready for sale.

Review exercise 5

a   Which of the following costs would be appropriate to include in a variable costing system?
   i   director's salary
   ii supervisor's wages
   iii machine operators' wages
   iv cost of raw materials.
b   Of the costs listed above, which would be appropriate to include when trying to arrive at costs under an absorption costing system?

Example 7.3: Washing machines

A Perth appliance dealer orders 10 washing machines from a manufacturer in Adelaide. The washing machines have a list price of $1000. The retailer buys on terms 2/10, Net/30. This means that they can deduct 2 per cent ($20) off the list price and pay only $980 if they pay within 10 days. If they pay after 10 days, they should pay $1000 within 30 days. Transport charges paid by the retailer are $50 per machine. Sales tax is 15 per cent of list price. The retailer incurs handling charges of $20 per unit to get the machines onto the showroom floor. The sales staff who sell the machines are paid a bonus of $50 per machine. What is the cost per machine, assuming that the retailer pays in eight days?

	$
List price	1 000
Less Discount	20
	980
Plus	
Sales tax	150
Transport	50
Handling	20
	1 200

The bonus for the sales staff is a selling expense and is not part of the cost. We deal with more complex examples on cost determination in the chapters relating to management accounting.

EFFECTS OF PRICE CHANGES

It is a reality of life that prices for goods and services do not remain static through time. Many prices increase through time – although there are some items, such as electronic goods, that actually decline in price. As we have said, there would be no problem if all sales could be identified with the actual goods sold. In practice, however, a builder's merchant, for instance, has a pile of bricks and sells them in any order depending on the ease of access. We cannot, therefore, know whether a given brick that has been sold was bought by the builder's merchant when the price of bricks was 30 cents or whether it was bought after the price had gone up to 33 cents. It is not cost-effective to trace each brick through the process. We have to find some system that will give a reasonable approximation of the cost of the goods we have sold and the cost of the inventory that is remaining. There are many possible methods with various levels of complexity. For our purposes we will concentrate on three which exemplify the problem and show that solutions tend to be arbitrary.

In order to illustrate the differences between the methods, let us take some simple data.

Example 7.4: Jackie

Jackie started the year with some goods in inventory and bought additional goods as required during the year. The price of the goods she bought rose steadily during the year. The summarised data for her transactions are as follows:

	Units	Cost per unit
Goods in stock at the start of the year	400	$1.00
Purchases, quarter 1	500	$1.10
Purchases, quarter 2	400	$1.20
Purchases, quarter 3	400	$1.25
Purchases, quarter 4	300	$1.40
Goods sold during the year	1800 units for a total of $2400	

Using these data, and the periodic method, we illustrate how the adoption of different valuation rules not only affects the inventory value at the end of the year, but also affects the cost of sales and, therefore, the profit. We start by considering a method of valuation called first in, first out (FIFO).

First in, first out

The FIFO method is based on the assumption that the first goods bought are the first sold. In effect, the inventory held at the end of the period is assumed to be that purchased most recently. There are many situations when it is the obvious choice, as for any industry or business dealing in consumables. It should be pointed out that, surprisingly, the choice of method for arriving at the cost of inventory generally has little, if anything, to do with actual inventory movements.

With this method, all of the opening inventory, together with that purchased in the first three quarters, is assumed to have been sold, together with 100 units bought in the fourth quarter. This leaves a closing inventory of 200 units which were bought in the fourth quarter.

LO 8

Explain and apply the first in, first out (FIFO), last in, first out (LIFO) and average cost methods of determining the cost of ending inventory and cost of goods sold

		$	$		$
Opening inventory	400	1.00	400.00	Sales	2 400.00
Quarter 1	500	1.10	550.00		
Quarter 2	400	1.20	480.00		
Quarter 3	400	1.25	500.00		
Quarter 4	100	1.40	140.00		
Cost of goods sold			2 070.00		2 070.00
Closing inventory	**200**	**1.40**	**280.00**	**Profit**	**330.00**

Last in, first out

The last in, first out (LIFO) method is based on the assumption that the last goods bought are the first sold. It therefore charges the latest price from suppliers against the revenue, and leaves the closing inventory at a value based on outdated prices. In industries where prices are rising steadily this is more likely to give a profit figure that can be maintained in the future. Its effect on the income statement is similar to what would occur if we had used replacement cost.

With this method, all the inventory purchased in the year, together with 200 units of the opening inventory, is assumed to have been sold. This leaves a closing inventory of 200 units which were in inventory at the start of the year. These are included at the original price and, thus, the balance sheet value is deliberately understated.

		$	$		$
Quarter 4	300	1.40	420.00	Sales	2 400.00
Quarter 3	400	1.25	500.00		
Quarter 2	400	1.20	480.00		
Quarter 1	500	1.10	550.00		
Opening inventory	200	1.00	200.00		
			2 150.00		2 150.00
Closing inventory	**200**	**1.00**	**200.00**	**Profit**	**250.00**

Weighted average cost

The weighted average cost method is a compromise between the two methods we have already discussed. It makes no assumptions about the way in which goods flow through the business.

For the purposes of arriving at the profit and loss charges, all that is needed is to work out the weighted average cost per unit of inventory and multiply that by the number of units sold. Similarly, the closing inventory is arrived at by taking the number of units left in inventory and multiplying it by the weighted average cost per unit. This leads to profit and inventory figures which, in our example, are between the figures produced by the FIFO and LIFO methods. It is calculated as shown over:

		$	$		$
Opening inventory	400	1.00	400.00	Sales	2 400.00
Quarter 1	500	1.10	550.00		
Quarter 2	400	1.20	480.00		
Quarter 3	400	1.25	500.00		
Quarter 4	300	1.40	420.00		
	2 000		**2 350.00**		
Weighted average cost	2 350 ÷ 2 000	= 1.18			
Cost of goods sold	1 800	1.18	2 115.00		2 115.00
Closing inventory	**200**	**1.18**	**235.00**	**Profit**	**285.00**

Review exercise 6

If the price of goods in inventory was falling over the year, which of the three methods, LIFO, FIFO or average cost, would give:

    a the highest cost at year-end? *LIFO*
    b the lowest cost a year-end? *FIFO*
    c the highest gross profit at year-end? *LIFO*
    d the lowest gross profit at year-end? *AVE*

Accounting policies for inventories and implications for users

AASB 102 permits the use of either FIFO or average cost but does not permit the use of LIFO. The USA is one of only a few countries that allows the use of LIFO, and this is only on the condition that companies use LIFO in both the tax return and the financial statements prepared for shareholders. It is important when comparing the financial statements of entities to know how the financial statements were prepared. Did the companies use average cost or FIFO? For example, Woolworths uses average cost to determine the cost of its inventory. If we were to compare Woolworths' financial statements with Coles' financial statements, and Coles uses FIFO, then this fact must be allowed for when comparing the results of both companies. In times of rising prices, Coles' profits would generally be higher than Woolworths', based on the use of FIFO. Thus, the difference in profits between the two companies is partly due to the accounting rules. This difference should be distinguished from differences in profits due to higher sales or lower operating costs.

Identify the implications of the accounting policy choice used for determining inventory costing methods

CASE STUDY 7.2

INVENTIVENESS IN INVENTORIES
by Elizabeth Knight

. . .

HARRIS SCARFE has demonstrated the extreme and indeed illegal side of playing around with inventories. It seems that it actually just wrote up the value of inventories to manipulate profits. In some cases there are suggestions it created inventory that didn't even exist.

It's easy enough to see how this can be achieved (and even got away with) over a couple of years, but how such subterfuge can be sustained over six years which is what receivers at Ferrier Hodgson are now suggesting is almost impossible to imagine.

A former chief financial officer at Harris Scarfe, Alan Hodgson, suggested that over the past couple of years he saw adjustments to the accounts as being just an issue of timing. I guess he believed that having written up the value of inventory in one year he could write it down in the next presumably if financial targets were being met. Seems that never happened.

But the outrageous behaviour of this Adelaide establishment retailer should send a sobering message to plenty of our large retailers. It's not that they are falsifying their inventory levels and they are certainly not doing anything illegal. But how many times have various large retailers written down big licks of inventory?

Only a few weeks ago Coles Myer announced $85 million in post-tax write-downs, a large portion of which related to inventory write-downs. And this is not an irregular feature of the market. It has taken place several times over the years at David Jones.

But if inventories were being realistically accounted for at the end of each financial year, a backlog of inventories should never be able to accumulate. Or more to the point, if inventories were being properly adjusted to their realisable values, then the build-up shouldn't happen.

The accounting standard says that inventories can be valued at the amount reasonably approximating the lower of cost and net realisable value. It also requires slow-moving or sale items to be valued at less than cost if that's what they will be sold for. There are retail experts that claim that in order to do this, all inventory has to be assessed and counted at the end of each season.

But the whole system allows the retailer to use a large amount of discretion in what it believes will be the ultimate value of particular stock that hasn't sold. And it seems that potential problems with the valuations of inventories and the trouble with auditors closing off on accounts has now come into the view of the Australian Companies and Securities Commission which has been watching its US counterpart, the Securities and Exchange Commission, also asking a lot of questions about why there are such large inventory write-downs. It's having a look at the two standards that deal with statements of financial performance and inventories.

Included in this study will be an examination of whether there is adequate disclosure on inventories, and how the value of the inventory has been established and audited. Of course, this does not just apply to retailers but also to many manufacturing companies.

But the scope for variation in the value of retail inventory is far greater. As one retail expert pointed out yesterday, CSR's plasterboard inventory valuation doesn't change if it's not sold this season.

So, how can this be rectified? Indeed, how can a more scientific approach be applied to inventory levels within the retail sector? How long is the realistic shelf life of branded apparel, or any other fashion item? It could be argued that a more accurate assessment of profit could be made by assuming a certain level of unsold goods each year and a certain level of discounting or stock loss in the same way that banks undertake dynamic provisioning.

This would involve adjustments, but it might just focus the minds of retail buyers on better targeting their markets.

Extract from article in the *Sydney Morning Herald*,
9 August 2001

COMMENTARY

The article demonstrates how the valuation of inventories impacts on both the net profit and the amount reported in the balance sheet as a current asset. The article highlights the irregularities in respect of the valuation of inventories in the books of the failed retailer Harris Scarfe. The argument is that, if the lower of cost and net realisable value rule is applied consistently, then there should not be a need for large write-downs of the value of inventories for retailers like Harris Scarfe. You should study the annual report of Woolworths (<www.woolworths.com.au> at investor relations) to see if it has recorded any large write-down of inventories.

Summary

LO 1 LEARNING OBJECTIVE 1

Discuss the importance of inventory management

For many entities, inventory can be a significant investment and it is important that the costs of holding excessive inventory are weighed carefully against the opportunity costs of lost sales when inventory is not available.

LO 2 LEARNING OBJECTIVE 2

Explain what is meant by raw materials, work in progress and finished goods

Raw materials are the inputs into a productive process while work in progress is goods in the productive process that have not yet been completed. Finished goods are items that have completed the productive process and are ready for immediate sale.

LO 3 LEARNING OBJECTIVE 3

Discuss the nature of inventory that is held by different types of businesses

Retailers acquire goods that are ready for resale while a manufacturer takes raw materials and converts them into finished goods which can then be sold. Service industries like accountants and architects also have inventory at year-end in the form of partially completed jobs.

LO 4 LEARNING OBJECTIVE 4

Explain the periodic and perpetual methods of recording inventories

The periodic inventory method relies upon a physical counting of inventory to determine ending inventory. Once determined, it is possible to derive the cost of goods sold.

The perpetual inventory method records changes to inventory levels and the cost of goods sold after every sale. It is then possible to physically count inventory at the end of a period and compare this with what the system states should be on hand. Any differences are due to spoilage, wastage and, possibly, theft.

LO 5 LEARNING OBJECTIVE 5

Calculate cost of goods sold using the periodic inventory method

The balance of opening inventory and purchases during the period are available from the accounting records. The ending inventory is determined by a physical count.

Cost of goods sold = opening inventory + purchases − ending inventory

LO 6 LEARNING OBJECTIVE 6

Identify and apply the valuation rule for inventory

AASB 102 requires that inventory be measured at the lower of cost and net realisable value. Not-for-profit entities where inventory is held for distribution at no cost measure inventory at the lower of cost and current replacement cost.

LO 7 LEARNING OBJECTIVE 7

Explain and apply the principles used to determine the cost of inventory

This was illustrated with the use of spanners and washing machines. The principle is that the term 'cost' includes all reasonable and necessary costs incurred to get the inventory ready for sale and to the location where it will be sold.

LEARNING OBJECTVE 8

Explain and apply the first in, first out (FIFO), last in, first out (LIFO) and average cost methods of determining the cost of ending inventory and cost of goods sold

FIFO assigns costs that occurred earlier in the period to goods sold while LIFO assigns costs that have occurred later in the period. Weighted average applies the average prices, and in times of rising prices will result in a cost of goods sold that sits between FIFO and LIFO.

LEARNING OBJECTIVE 9

Identify the implications of the accounting policy choice used for determining inventory costing methods

AASB 102 allows entities to use either weighted average or FIFO to assign costs to inventory. In times of rising prices, FIFO profits will generally be higher than profits determined using the weighted average method. Therefore, the difference in profits between two companies may be due, at least partly, to the choice of inventory costing method each company has used. This difference should be distinguished from differences in profits due to higher sales or lower operating costs.

REFERENCES

Australian Accounting Standards Board. AASB 102 *Inventories*, July, 2004.

FURTHER READING

Trotman, K. & Gibbins, M. 2006. *Financial Accounting: An Integrated Approach*, 3rd edn, Thomson.

REVIEW QUESTIONS

1   Explain what is included in inventory.

2   What main categories of inventory are likely to be held by a manufacturing business?

3   What are the effects of omitting goods costing $500 from the year-end inventory figure?

4   Why is it important to occasionally take a physical inventory when a perpetual system is used?

5   Why is it necessary to value inventory at the lower of cost and net realisable value?

6   Explain, in your own words, the difference between absorption costing and variable costing.

7   Name three methods of inventory valuation, and describe the differences between them and the effects of those differences.

8   Give examples of the types of business where a particular method of inventory valuation is appropriate.

PROBLEMS FOR DISCUSSION AND ANALYSIS

1   In your own words, state what you understand by the phrase 'net realisable value'. Is this concept valid? Why?

2   To reduce expenses in preparing monthly financial statements, Pamic Company decided to estimate monthly inventories. Goods are sold at cost plus 25 per cent.

   Use the following data to estimate the inventory at the end of December:

Inventory 1 December	$50 650
Net purchases for December	$146 000
Net sales for December	$220 000

3   XYZ company adds 25 per cent to the cost of the purchase price of goods in order to arrive at a retail price. The following information was available: opening inventory $10 000, ending inventory $27 000 and sales $786 000. What was the purchase price the company paid for the goods?

4   The Ready retail store prices its goods to sell at 150 per cent on cost. Records for one accounting period reveal the following information:

	Cost	Retail
Purchase returns	8 000	12 000
Purchases	100 000	150 000
Opening inventory	60 000	90 000
Sales (net)		198 000

   What was the ending inventory for the accounting period?

5   A fire destroyed all the inventory of Furnishings Ltd at the end of their financial year. The company, in making an insurance claim, was required to confirm the value of the inventory that was lost. Some accounting records were destroyed in the fire. The company has a practice of adding 30 per cent to the cost of purchases.

   Purchases in the year were $376 000, opening inventory was $27 400 and sales were $490 000. What was the closing inventory figure?

6   One of the items sold by Bodybuild, a sporting goods company, is cricket bats. One such bat, 'the humdinger', sells well. Beginning inventory, purchases and sales for this item for the month of December were as follows:

December	1	Beginning inventory 4 bats @ $56 each
	3	Purchased 6 bats @ $58 each
	6	Sales of 3 bats
	8	Purchased 6 bats @ $44 each
	10	Sales of 5 bats
	13	Sales of 6 bats
	18	Purchased 12 bats @ $50 each
	20	Sales 3 bats
	24	Sales 5 bats
25–31		Closed

   Calculate, using FIFO, periodic method, the total cost of sales for each sale day and the inventory balance after each sale day.

7   The following information has been extracted from the records of Able Biscuits Co. Ltd.

Opening inventory: 750 tins of biscuits at $8 per tin. During the month of May, the company manufactured biscuits and placed them in inventory, after calculating the cost of manufacture:

Date 20X1	Tins manufactured	Cost per tin ($)	Tins sold
May 3	400	8.10	–
4	–	–	600
7	200	7.90	700
12	1000	8.05	–
14	–	–	600
16	300	8.20	–
18	–	–	700
20	800	8.00	–
23	–	–	600
25	300	8.50	–
27	–	–	450
30	100	8.00	–

Rounding to the nearest cent, calculate the closing inventory balance using:
a   FIFO, periodic and perpetual
b   LIFO, periodic and perpetual
c   weighted average periodic and perpetual.

8   Phijen are manufacturers of widgets which are on-sold to Mipam who uses them in the manufacture of boat anchors. Phijen buys the raw materials on the world market, but during the past year prices have been erratic. Mipam has a firm contract price from Phijen for one year from 1 January 20X0. During the year ending 31 December 20X0, Phijen sold 160 000 widgets to Mipam at $1.90 each. Phijen's beginning inventory on 1 January 20X0 was 77 000 kilograms of raw materials at a cost of $7700. It takes 10 kilograms of raw material to make one widget.

Purchases of raw materials during the year ending 31 December 20X0 were as follows:

7 January	200 000 kg @ 9 cents per kg
2 February	180 000 kg @ 15 cents per kg
4 April	250 000 kg @ 6 cents per kg
26 May	250 000 kg @ 7 cents per kg
17 August	200 000 kg @ 9 cents per kg
19 September	350 000 kg @ 12 cents per kg
10 October	100 000 kg @ 17 cents per kg
11 December	175 000 kg @ 20 cents per kg

Required

Calculate Phijen's closing inventory (based on the periodic method), using the following cost methods. Then, calculate the cost of raw materials sold for each method.
a   FIFO
b   LIFO
c   weighted average.

9 During 20X0, Swimworld sold $23 440 worth of snorkel sets at $80 each. Beginning inventory on 1 January 20X0 was 26 snorkel sets at a cost of $1040. Purchases during the year were as follows:

26 sets at $42

76 sets at $38

102 sets at $36

98 sets at $43

Required

a   Compute the 31 December inventory using the following assumptions regarding the flow of costs:
   i   FIFO, periodic method
   ii LIFO, periodic method
   iii weighted average, periodic method.
b   Prepare income statements for each method to the gross profit stage.
Note: Round to the nearest dollar.

10 During 20X0, Rubber Balls Pty Ltd sold $42 400 worth of balls at $8 each. Beginning inventory on 1 January 20X0 amounted to 605 balls at a cost of $3600. Purchases during the year occurred as follows:

1596 units @ $4.00

2508 units @ $4.23

1748 units @ $4.40

730 units @ $4.55

Required

a   Compute the 31 December 20X0 inventory using the following assumptions regarding the flow of costs:
   i   FIFO, periodic method
   ii LIFO, periodic method
   iii weighted average, periodic method.
b   Prepare income statements for each method to the gross profit stage.

11 The following information is taken from the records of the Ready retail store:

Merchandise account

Date	Purchase	Sold	Unit price $
May 3	200	–	2.00
4	–	150	–
5	300	–	2.20
6	–	150	–
6	50	–	2.30
7	–	150	–

Using the data in the table, answer the following questions:

a   If inventory is based on FIFO, periodic method, the closing inventory balance is:

   i $200

   ii $230

   iii $225

   iv none of the above.

b   If LIFO, periodic method, was used, the closing inventory balance is:

   i $200

   ii $230

   iii $225

   iv none of the above.

c   Assuming inflationary trends in the economy, the inventory amount shown in the balance sheet, if based on LIFO, would be:

   i   lower than FIFO value

   ii equal to weighted average

   iii equal to current market value

   iv higher than FIFO value

   v   higher than current market value

   vi an extremely conservative value.

12 At the end of its financial year (i.e. 30 June 20X0), Bodybuild's inventory was incorrectly counted as being worth $135 678 as against the correct figure of $145 678.

a   What effect would this error have on the balance sheet as at 30 June 20X0?

b   What would be the effect on the income statement for the year ending 30 June 20X0?

13 On 31 December 20X1, goods costing $1250 were received by Judy's Cake Shop and were included in the 31 December listing of all inventory items on hand. The invoice for these items, however, was not received until 7 January 20X2, whereupon the purchase was recorded for the first time in the accounts as a 20X2 purchase and as an account payable. The purchase should have been recorded in the 20X1 financial accounts. Assuming that the error was never discovered and that Judy's Cake Shop uses a periodic inventory system, indicate the effect (overstatement, understatement or none) on each of the following:

a   Inventory, 31 December 20X1

b   Inventory, 31 December 20X2

c   Cost of goods sold, 20X1

d   Cost of goods sold, 20X2

e   Net profit, 20X1

f   Net profit, 20X2

g   Accounts payable, 20X1

h   Accounts payable, 20X2

i   Retained earnings, 20X2.

14 On 24 December 20X0, Bodybuild purchased 40 snorkel sets costing $1640. However, the invoice for these items was not received until 7 January 20X1. These items were counted in the annual year-end physical stock take on 31 December 20X0. When the invoice was received, a trainee bookkeeper added them to purchases and they were included in the 20X1 inventory. (The purchase should have been recorded in the 20X0 accounts.)

Assuming the error was not discovered, what effect would this error have (overstatement, understatement or none) on the following?

a   Inventory, 31 December 20X0
b   Inventory, 31 December 20X1
c   Cost of goods sold, 20X0
d   Cost of goods sold, 20X1
e   Net profit, 20X0
f   Net profit, 20X1
g   Accounts payable, 20X0
h   Accounts payable, 20X1
i   Equity, 20X0
j   Equity, 20X1.

15 The perpetual inventory control system identifies the amount of inventory loss resulting from theft, damage and so forth – an amount which is not revealed by the periodic inventory system. How should this amount be recorded in the financial statements?

16 The LIFO method of inventory valuation assumes that the last goods purchased are the first that are sold. Since companies normally sell the oldest goods in their inventory first, the LIFO assumption is unrealistic. Comment on whether you think the LIFO method can be justified.

17 The following is an excerpt from a conversation between Joanne Docker, the warehouse manager for Fresh Food Wholesale Co., and its accountant, Chris Anchor. Fresh Food Wholesale operates a large regional warehouse that supplies fresh grocery products to stores in smaller communities.

Joanne: Chris, can you explain what's going on here with these monthly statements?

Chris: Sure, Joanne. How can I help you?

Joanne: I don't understand this last in, first out inventory procedure. It just doesn't make sense.

Chris: Well, what it means is that we assume that the last goods we receive are the first ones sold. So the inventory is made up of the items we purchased first.

Joanne: Yes, but that's my problem. It doesn't work that way! We always distribute the oldest produce first. Most of our products are perishable! We can't keep any of it very long or it'll spoil.

Chris: Joanne, you don't understand. We only *assume* that the products we distribute are the last ones received. We don't actually have to distribute the goods in this way.

Joanne: I always thought that accounting was supposed to show what really happened. It all sounds like 'make believe' to me! Why not report what really happens?

Required

Respond to Joanne's concerns.

(Adapted from C.S. Warren, J.M. Reeve and P.E. Fess, *Accounting*, 20th edn, South-Western, Mason, Ohio, 2002, Chapter 9, Activity 9.3.)

18 A motorbike dealer uses the original cost of each motorbike as the basis for setting the selling price. The original cost for a certain model can increase during a financial year as a result of increased assembly costs. Would it be appropriate for the motorbike dealer to use the LIFO method of inventory valuation? In contrast, a car-parts dealer changes the selling price of her goods to reflect changing wholesale prices. Would it be appropriate for the car-parts dealer to use the FIFO method of inventory valuation?

Note to instructors: *The following problems are considered more suitable for use in MBA courses. However, undergraduate courses may also find them useful.*

19 For the following example discuss which costs, if any, should be included in the inventory valuation, and at what point in time they should be included.

Hank is in the business of manufacturing sails. The sail material is purchased in 100-metre lengths and these are delivered to the storeworker who sorts the materials according to quality and width. The material is then issued to the cutting room where five people are employed, one of whom is the cutting-room supervisor. After being cut, the material is passed through to the machining room where the sails are sewn up and the hanks, and so on, are put on. The machining room has seven staff employed full time, including a supervisor. From the machining room the sails go to the packaging department and then the despatch department or are put into stock. The packaging department and the despatch department each employ one member of staff working on a part-time basis. The whole operation is under the control of a production manager who also has responsibility for quality control.

20 Marx Pty Ltd has traditionally used the FIFO, periodic method, of inventory valuation. Information on transactions affecting Marx's accounts is provided below:

20X0		20X2	
Beginning balance	2 300 units @ $24.06	Beginning balance	1 300 units
Purchases	750 units @ $24.38	Purchases	1 250 units @ $26.56
	1 000 units @ $25.00		875 units @ $26.88
	500 units @ $25.31		875 units @ $26.88
	250 units @ $25.62		875 units @ $26.88
Sales	3 525 units @ $40.62	Sales	3 688 units @ $42.50

20X1	
Beginning balance	1 275 units
Purchases	875 units @ $25.62
	875 units @ $25.62
	875 units @ $26.26
	1 250 units @ $26.56
Sales	3 850 units @ $42.50

Required

a Calculate the cost of goods sold and ending inventory amounts for 20X0, 20X1, 20X2 using:
  i FIFO
  ii LIFO
  iii weighted average cost.

b Sales for 20X2 are expected to drop by an estimated 11 per cent as a worldwide recession is expected to continue for the next nine months. Total sales are estimated to be 3375 units. Marx Pty Ltd will be unable to increase its 20X1 selling price of $42.50, even though it is expected the costs will increase to $27.19 per unit for the entire year. As a result of these pressures, the company wishes to decrease its investment in inventory by keeping only 500 units of inventory on hand at any particular time during the year. What are the effects of LIFO and FIFO inventory valuation methods under these circumstances?

(Adapted from R. Anthony and J. Reece, *Accounting: Text and Cases*, 8th edn, Richard D. Irwin Inc., 1988, Chapter 6, Case 6–3.)

21 Joan Robbins, the owner of Joan's Fishing Tackle Shop, marks up the goods in her shop by 30 per cent. Figures for the past financial year, 20X0, are outlined below:

	$	$
Sales		1 550 000
Less Cost of goods sold		
Opening inventory	168 000	
Purchases	1 218 000	
	1 386 000	
Closing inventory	178 500	1 207 500
Gross profit		342 500
Less Operating expenses		340 000
Net profit		2 500

Joan has given no discounts during the 20X0 period and has kept turnover constant so her inventories have moved quickly. Nevertheless, she is unhappy with the year's results and asks you for your advice on the following:

a   Is it possible to determine from the figures whether there has been any theft by staff and/or customers?

b   On the assumption that theft has occurred, can it be determined from the figures whether it was cash or inventory that was taken?

c   A perpetual inventory control system could be established at a cost of $21 000 per year to monitor the more expensive goods in the shop. Would you recommend such a measure?

d   On the assumption that Joan is able to deter future theft, would you advise her to embark on a $21 000 advertising campaign if sales would rise by $210 000, leaving all other expenses unchanged?

(Adapted from B. Colditz and R. Gibbins, *Australian Accounting*, 3rd edn, McGraw-Hill, 1976.)

22 Elvin Company has began operations in 20X2 by selling a single product. Data on purchases and sales for the year are as follows:

Purchases:

Date	Units purchased	Unit cost ($)	Total cost ($)
April 8	3 875	12.20	47 275
May 10	4 125	13.00	53 625
June 4	5 000	13.20	66 000
July 10	5 000	14.00	70 000
August 3	3 400	14.25	48 450
October 5	1 600	14.50	23 200
November 1	1 000	14.95	14 950
December 10	1 000	16.00	16 000
	25 000		$339 500

Sales:

	Units sold
April	2 000
May	2 000
June	2 500
July	3 000
August	3 500
September	3 500
October	2 250
November	1 250
December	1 000
Total units	21 000
Total sales	$552 000

On 3 January 20X3 the president of the company, Robert Bilbo, asks for your advice on costing the 4000-unit physical inventory that was taken on 31 December 20X2. Moreover, since the firm plans to expand its product line, he has asked for your advice on the use of a perpetual inventory system in the future.

a   Determine the cost of the 31 December 20X2 inventory under the periodic system, using:
   i   first in, first out method
   ii   last in, first out method
   iii   average cost method.
b   Determine the gross profit for the year under each of the three methods in (a).
c   i   What argument can be used to justify why each of the three inventory costing methods may best reflect the results of operations for 20X2?
   ii   Which of the three inventory costing methods may best reflect the replacement cost of the inventory on the balance sheet as of 31 December 20X2?
   iii   Discuss the advantages and disadvantages of using a perpetual inventory system. From the data presented in this case, is there any indication of the adequacy of inventory levels during the year?

(Adapted from C.S. Warren, J.M. Reeve and P.E. Fess, *Accounting*, 20th edn, South-Western, Mason, Ohio, 2002, Chapter 9, Activity 9.5.)

ETHICS CASE STUDY

Troy Harvey is the financial controller of Elsi Mate Ltd. In reviewing the operations of Elsi Mate Ltd, Troy has become concerned about the continued weak profit performance of the company. The chairman of the board stresses the need for the company to improve its profits if it is to maintain the confidence of its shareholders and the bankers. Troy is concerned that, with only two weeks of the year remaining, the company is destined to record another low profit. Therefore, it will have difficulty in refinancing some loans due next year and will be forced to pay higher interest rates.

While it is too late for operations to increase profits, Troy has developed the following plan. The company will purchase large amounts of inventory in the remaining two weeks of the year. This addition of large amounts of inventory will result in increased reported profit for the following reasons:

• Prices of inventory have been falling in recent weeks.

• The company uses the LIFO method for inventories.

Discuss

a   whether Troy's plan will increase net profit for the year
b   what the positive and negative consequences of the proposed plan are for the company and the shareholders
c   whether, in your opinion, the plan is ethical.

ANSWERS TO REVIEW EXERCISES

1   The following could be undertaken to minimise theft by customers and staff:
   • Use a perpetual inventory system.
   • Employ shop detectives posing as shoppers.
   • Check customers' bags as they leave.
   • Randomly check employees as they leave work.

2   What is the inventory of raw materials? What work is in progress; what stage of completion is it at? What finished goods are in inventory? What costs and overheads should be included in the work in progress and the finished goods?

3   The periodic system relies on the stocktake to count the items in inventory and then work out the number of units sold. The perpetual system keeps a continuous record of goods acquired and sold; therefore, the number of units sold is always available and the number of units in inventory can be deduced from this. The intermittent counting of units in inventory under the perpetual system allows for a comparison of the number of units that should be in inventory with the number of units that are actually in inventory. Any discrepancy is then evidence of losses from possible theft.

4   As the cost of goods sold, especially with a small business, is often calculated by using the opening inventory plus purchases less closing inventory, the effect would be to reduce the cost of sales figure and, thereby, increase profit.

5   a   Machine operators' wages and cost of raw materials as these are the only ones which are likely to vary directly with production.
   b   The discussion should focus around the inclusion of the supervisor's wages and whether the director's salary should be included and whether the answer to the latter will be affected by the job description (e.g. production director vs sales director) and by the size of firm (e.g. BHP vs a company with five employees).

6   a   LIFO
   b   FIFO
   c   LIFO
   d   FIFO

DEBTORS, CREDITORS, ACCRUALS AND PREPAYMENTS

CHAPTER EIGHT

8

LEARNING OBJECTIVES

At the end of this chapter, you should be able to:

1 explain what is meant by the terms 'prepayments' and 'debtors'

2 illustrate the importance of the efficient management of debtors

3 explain what is meant by bad debts

4 explain and apply the direct write-off method for handling bad debts

5 explain and apply the provision method for handling doubtful (bad) debts

6 identify the term 'creditors' and explain the importance of trade credit

7 identify what is meant by the term 'accruals'

8 apply transactions involving debtors, prepayments, provision for doubtful debts, creditors and accruals to a worksheet.

Introduction

In our discussion so far, we have assumed that all transactions are on a cash basis. As we pointed out in Chapter 4, this is unlikely to be the case. Therefore, we need to consider how to deal with the situation in which a business buys goods from its suppliers on credit terms and also supplies goods to customers on credit terms. Similarly, we need to consider the situation in which a business has to pay for goods or services in advance, for example rent, or when it pays after receiving the goods or services, as is the case with most raw materials and with services such as electricity and telephones.

As these transactions directly affect both the balance sheet and the income statement, we need a system that ensures that expenses and revenues are recognised in the appropriate period and that the balance sheet reflects the position of the entity at the statement date. In other words, the system must ensure that the balance sheet shows the assets held at the statement date and the amounts owed at that date. The income statement must also record the actual sales for the period and the expenses incurred in the period. If it did not, the accounts would reflect the timing of cash receipts and payments rather than the economic substance of the transactions that the business had engaged in during the period. Such a system of accounting is known as *accrual accounting*, a concept which was introduced in Chapter 2. In this chapter we examine situations in which the economic substance of the transaction does not occur at the same time as the cash flow and show how accrual accounting deals with these situations. In particular, we look at debtors, prepayments, bad debts, creditors and accruals.

Prepayments

Explain what is meant by the terms 'prepayments' and 'debtors'

Prepayments, as the name implies, are payments in advance. They often arise in respect of such services as insurance and rent. The payments must relate to the use of such services by the business and not by the owner in a personal capacity, a distinction sometimes difficult to establish in the case of small businesses. The proportion of the payment that relates to benefits still unexpired at the end of the year is shown as a current asset in the balance sheet of the business. Prepayments therefore differ from debtors in that they relate to payments made by the business rather than to sales. Also, the future benefit will be in a form other than cash receipts; for instance, prepaid rent entitles the entity to use the facilities for which the rent was paid.

KEY CONCEPT 8.1

PREPAYMENTS: ASSETS OR EXPENSES?

When recording prepayments on a balance sheet, the question that must be considered is whether the benefit has been consumed or whether there is still some future benefit to be obtained. If there is a future benefit accruing to the business we have an asset; if there is no future benefit we have an expense.

Debtors

Debtors are often referred to as 'accounts receivable'. You might find that this term is easier to remember as it is more descriptive than the term 'debtors'.

KEY CONCEPT 8.2

DEBTORS

Debtors arise when a business sells goods or services to a third party on credit terms; that is, when the goods or services are sold on the understanding that payment will be received at a later date.

Key concept 8.2 discusses debts that are created when a business sells goods during the year for which payment is not received at the point of sale. We need to recognise the revenue from the sales even though the cash has not yet been received. We discussed the recognition of revenue in Chapter 5. However, if we simply entered the sales on the worksheet, the accounts would not balance because there would be only one side to the entry. This is in conflict with the principle of duality. We cannot use the cash account for the other side of the transaction because no cash has been received. However, we do have an asset: a right to a future benefit in the form of cash. The way in which accrual accounting solves the problem is to open a column, or account, for this asset which is called 'Debtors'. Normally, debtors pay within a year (in fact in 30 days in many industries) so debtors are generally classified under current assets.

Review exercise 1

Why are debtors and prepayments classified as current assets?

Management of debtors

In the previous chapter we discussed the importance of the efficient management of inventories for a business. Inventories and debtors represent a significant part of working capital, which are the current assets minus the current liabilities of a business. The management of debtors is also extremely important for a business. Allowing no customers to purchase goods on credit would result in a loss of profitable sales opportunities. However, if a business allows all customers to purchase goods on credit it risks the problem of bad debts, because some customers will be unable to pay. Therefore, as with inventory management, a business must develop a policy on credit sales.

Entities want to benefit from selling goods on credit but at the same time ensure that losses from bad debts are kept within an acceptable range. Some bad debts are inevitable when an entity sells goods on credit. In fact, if the level of bad debts is very low, it may signal to management that its credit policy is too strict and it is losing potential profits by denying credit to low-risk customers. Conversely, it is important to extend credit to customers only where there are reasonable prospects of the debt being paid.

LO 2

Illustrate the importance of the efficient management of debtors

Incentives are often used by businesses to encourage debtors to pay the amount owing before the due date. When a business has a large number of debtors, and significant amounts of inventories, it has to have the capital to allow it to continue operating while it collects the amounts owing from debtors and attempts to sell its inventories. The higher the number of debtors and the amount of inventories, the greater the working capital requirements. Working capital has to be financed by either equity or debt funds. This is discussed in more detail in Chapter 10.

Therefore, incentives are used to encourage early payment by debtors. These include discounts for early payment; for example, if the amount owing by a debtor is due to be paid in 30 days, the entity may offer a discount of 2 per cent if payment is made in 10 days. If the debtor forgoes this offer, the debtor is electing to pay the extra 2 per cent for the right to another 20 days before paying the original amount. A rate of 2 per cent for 20 days is equivalent to approximately 36 per cent per annum, and this is a high cost for any business to pay for the use of credit. Hence, most businesses, when presented with such an offer, would do everything possible to take advantage of the 2 per cent discount.

CASE STUDY 8.1

GOOD CREDIT PROCESS VITAL IN CASH FLOW MANAGEMENT
By Steve Dunbar

One significant reason why businesses fail is poor management of cash flow. While cash flow is affected by a number of factors, the full and timely collection of debtors will be a significant contributor to excellent cash flow. In this article we consider the phases in the credit process and what businesses can do to better manage this important area. The main cause of poor debtor collection is the lack of a defined credit process. The old adage 'A sale is not a sale until it is paid for' rings true. Businesses can suffer from poor cash flow because they simply do not have a defined credit process.

There are three distinct phases in the credit process which, if appropriately managed, will improve debtor collection and therefore cash flow.

The extension of credit
The first phase is the extension of credit. This phase is all about prevention of potential bad debts. It is seen as the fence at the top of the cliff. How well do you know your customers? Would you give a complete stranger you met in the street $1000 out of your own pocket? No? So why are we so relaxed about extending credit to complete strangers in business? A credit application is an excellent place to learn more about a potential client, including seeking a credit reference from other suppliers. Also, the terms of trade agreement should cover debt collection costs.

It is common practice for some debtors with devious intent who may be refused credit by one supplier to pop down the road and try their luck with another supplier. The processes around the extension of credit need to protect you from extending credit to these high-risk individuals.

Management of the credit function
Management of the credit function within your organisation is the second phase. Well-defined

credit procedures are essential to ensure that you get your money in on time and retain your good clients.

This revolves around three key areas: 1. Sound policy which encapsulates every aspect of the credit function. 2. Robust systems and processes. 3. Well-trained personnel. A well-defined credit process will involve agreed follow-up procedures which need to be strictly adhered to. It is, of course, your money and you are perfectly entitled to ask for it. Timely follow-up will also allow you to ascertain early if there are any problems with the account which is delaying payment.

Collection of debts

The third phase is collection of outstanding monies. Historically, businesses have often put more focus on the collection phase than the other two phases. However, because of the high degree of interdependence of the three phases, the incurring of overdue accounts will inevitably be minimised by focusing on the extension phase and the management phase. Because of the nature of credit you cannot completely eliminate the risk, but there are many things that organisations can do to avoid the self-inflicted injury.

How well you are doing in these three areas will determine whether or not your debtors are using you as a bank. A simple formula to determine how long your customers are taking to pay their accounts (and therefore if this is impacting on your poor cash flow) is: Debtors/annual sales × 365.

Ideally, this figure should be as low as possible. You might like to do this simple calculation for yourselves and compare it to the 'norm' for your industry to see how you are performing. Do not allow your organisation to become a victim of slow payers and bad debtors. Take a look at your credit practices and ask yourself 'How effective are we at managing credit?'. If you need help in establishing if your debtors are inappropriately using you as a bank, your chartered accountant will be able to establish the industry norms and assess how your business is performing against those.

If you need hands-on assistance in improving any of these areas of your business, your accountant, together with one of the specialist debt collectors' organisations, can assist you to improve these areas of your business.

Otago Daily Times, 24 October 2005
©Copyright 2005 Allied Press Limited.
All Rights Reserved.

COMMENTARY

The article discusses the three phases associated with the management of debtors. It highlights the importance of all three phases if a business is to effectively use and manage debtors.

We can now look at an example of debtors and prepayments.

Example 8.1: Pamjen

A business, Pamjen, has the following transactions for the period from 1 January to 31 March 20X7:

	$
Sales for cash	6 000
Sales on credit	4 000
Cash received from credit sales	3 000
Rent for the quarter, paid 1 January	500
Insurance, year to 31 December 20X7, paid 1 January 20X7	1 200

We can see that the revenue consists of the sales for cash and the sales on credit. With reference to the latter, we can see that there is still $1000 which has not been received; that is, $4000 less the $3000 received. This $1000 should be shown as a debtor at 31 March. As far as the payments are concerned, the rent is clearly an expense of the quarter as all the benefit from using the premises for the quarter has expired. The insurance premiums paid are for the whole year and so we have to decide how much benefit has been used up and what is a future benefit. In this case, we have used up three out of the 12 months' benefit and so we have an expense of $300 and a prepayment of $900.

Going back to our example, if we put this information onto a worksheet it appears as follows:

Pamjen worksheet: version 1

	Assets			=	Liabilities	+	Equity
	Cash	Debtors	Prepaid assets				Profit and loss
Cash sales	6 000						6 000
Credit sales		4 000					4 000
Cash from sales	3 000	−3 000					
Rent	−500						−500
Insurance	−1 200		900				−300
Balance	7 300	+ 1 000	+ 900		=		9 200

Note that, in our worksheet, we have shown the credit sales in the profit and loss column which is part of equity and recorded, at the same time, an asset of $4000. This asset was subsequently reduced by the cash received of $3000. You can also see that we charged the rent immediately as an expense and split the insurance premium paid between the prepaid assets column and the expenses.

An alternative approach would have been to enter both the rent and the insurance as prepayments when they were paid on 1 January and then consider, at 31 March, whether they were still assets. This we would do by answering the question: has the benefit been used up? If we had adopted that approach our worksheet would appear as follows:

Pamjen worksheet: version 2

	Assets			= Liabilities	+ Equity
	Cash	Debtors	Prepaid assets		Profit and loss
Cash sales	6 000				6 000
Credit sales		4 000			4 000
Cash from sales	3 000	−3 000			
Rent	−500		500		
Insurance	−1 200		1 200		
Balance	7 300	+ 1 000	+ 1 700	=	10 000
Rent expense			−500		−500
Insurance expense			−300		−300
Balance	7 300	+ 1 000	+ 900	=	9 200

As you can see, the result is the same. The advantage of the second presentation is that it shows clearly what we have done, which always helps when an error is made. The choice of which presentation to use is personal but we recommend that you use the latter and that you get into the habit of reviewing all the balances, to see whether they are still assets or liabilities, before finally extracting a balance sheet and an income statement. The advantages of this approach become more obvious as we proceed through this chapter and the next.

Bad debts

So far we have recorded all the credit sales as revenue for the period. If the business eventually collects all the amounts owing, this treatment would be correct. However, it is unlikely that the business will collect all monies owing because some debtors will not pay. When a debtor does not pay the amount owing, the business has incurred a 'bad debt'. This could be due to the debtor's bankruptcy, death, disappearance, and so on. There are two ways in which we can account for this non-payment:

- direct write-off
- provision for doubtful debts.
  We look at them each in turn.

LO 3
Explain what is meant by bad debts

Review exercise 2
Explain what a bad debt is and give examples.

DIRECT WRITE-OFF
Under this approach, the amount owing by the debtor is eliminated when it is determined that the debtor will not pay. We reduce the debtor's balance, and the other side of the transaction is the recognition of an expense: the loss of future economic benefits has caused a reduction in equity.

LO 4
Explain and apply the direct write-off method for handling bad debts

To return to our example: of the $1000 Pamjen is showing as debtors, it is likely to receive only $800 because a customer who owed $200 has left the country and is unlikely to pay. In this situation, the $200 is not an asset because any future benefit expired when our customer left the country.

The first question that arises is whether it was a genuine sale. In other words, at the time of making the sale were we reasonably certain that we would receive payment? If the answer is yes, then we have correctly recognised the revenue and the debtor. If this is not the case, we should ask why the sale was made in the first place. It is now necessary to deal with the situation that has arisen as a result of later events. We need to reduce the amount shown as debtors by $200 and charge the $200 as an expense of the period. The worksheet now appears as follows. It should be noted that the last row of the assets column now represents assets which have a future benefit at least equal to the amount shown.

Pamjen worksheet: version 3

	Assets			=	Liabilities	+	Equity
	Cash	Debtors	Prepaid assets				Profit and loss
Cash sales	6 000						6 000
Credit sales		4 000					4 000
Cash from sales	3 000	−3 000					
Rent	−500		500				
Insurance	−1 200		1 200				
Balance	7 300	+ 1 000	+ 1 700	=			10 000
Rent expense			−500				−500
Insurance expense			−300				−300
Bad debts		−200					−200
Balance	7 300	+ 800	+ 900	=			9 000

PROVISION FOR DOUBTFUL DEBTS

Explain and apply the provision method for handling doubtful (bad) debts

The business might not determine that a debtor is unable to pay until the next period following the credit sales. Therefore, if we use the direct write-off method the revenue (and therefore the profit) and assets will be overstated in the year of sale and understated the following year when it is determined the debtor will not pay. To overcome this problem, the common method of accounting for bad debts is to create a provision at balance date for the amount that we expect debtors will be unable to pay. The accountant has techniques for estimating the amount of expected uncollectable accounts, even though it is not possible to determine which debtors will not pay. For example, the accountant might determine that, of the debtors' balance of $100 000, at balance date, an amount of $8000 should be allowed for expected uncollectable accounts. At balance date we do not know which debtors will not pay, but we are able to estimate the dollar amount we do not expect to receive.

Accountants use a number of methods to estimate the amount expected for bad debts:

- taking a percentage of credit sales based on previous years
- analysing all debtors at balance date according to the length of time amounts have been owing – allowances for bad debts increasing the longer the debt has been owing (this is known as an ageing of the debtors).

Returning to the example of Pamjen, we assume that the accountant has determined that $200 of the debtors' accounts at balance date will be uncollectable. As we do not know the identity of debtors who will not eventually pay, we cannot reduce individual debtor's balances as we did in the direct write-off method. To overcome this problem, accountants create another account generally referred to as the 'provision for doubtful debts'. The word 'doubtful' is more appropriate than 'bad' because at balance date no debtor has actually defaulted. The provision account does not represent a liability: it is not a future disposition of economic benefits the business is obliged to make. It is, in fact, a negative or contra asset because the amount of the provision for doubtful debts should be deducted from the debtors (just as we did in the direct write-off method) to provide us with the net amount of future economic benefits we expect to obtain from our debtors.

KEY CONCEPT 8.3

PROVISION FOR DOUBTFUL DEBTS

The provision for doubtful debts is a contra debtors account and it shows the estimated total of future bad debts.

Review exercise 3

Why does an entity that is entirely a cash business make no provision for bad debts?

Let us now examine the worksheet for Pamjen which appears below. The provision for doubtful debts has a negative balance because it is a negative asset. The asset 'debtors' has a positive balance and, therefore, if the provision account is to be deducted from the debtors it must have a negative balance. The two accounts would be reported in the balance sheet as follows:

	$
Debtors (Gross)	1000
Less Provision for doubtful debts	−200
Balance	800

The provision for doubtful debts account has allowed us to record our assets and profit in the year of the credit sales, at amounts which are not overstated, if our estimate is reliable. While the estimation of the provision for doubtful debts involves uncertainties, fortunately such estimates are normally reliable.

Pamjen worksheet: version 4

	Assets				= Liabilities +	Equity
	Cash	Debtors	Provision for doubtful debts	Prepaid assets		Profit and loss
Cash sales	6 000					6 000
Credit sales		4 000				4 000
Cash from sales	3 000	−3 000				
Rent	−500			500		
Insurance	−1 200			1 200		
Balance	7 300	+ 1 000	+	1 700	=	10 000
Rent expense				−500		−500
Insurance expense				−300		−300
Doubtful debts expense			−200			−200
Balance	7 300	+ 1 000	− 200	+ 900	=	9 000

In the following year, when we discover that certain debts are uncollectable, we reduce both the provision account and the debtors account by the same amount. Remember we recorded the expense in the previous year and this resulted in a better measure of profit in that year, together with a more reliable estimate of the amount expected to be collected from debtors.

For example, let us now assume that in the following period Pamjen determines that Bill Bear is not likely to pay the $100 he owes because he has been declared bankrupt. We would record a +$100 in the provision for doubtful debts column and a −$100 in the debtors column. With the total debtors and provision account change, the net amount remains the same, as shown in version 5 of the worksheet.

	$
Debtors (Gross)	900
Less Provision for doubtful debts	−100
Balance	800

Pamjen worksheet: version 5

	Assets				= Liabilities +	Equity
	Cash	Debtors	Provision for doubtful debts	Prepaid assets		Profit and loss
Cash sales	6 000					6 000
Credit sales		4 000				4 000
Cash from sales	3 000	−3 000				
Rent	−500			500		
Insurance	−1 200			1 200		
Balance	7 300	+ 1 000	+	1 700	=	10 000

	Assets				= Liabilities +	Equity
	Cash	Debtors	Provision for doubtful debts	Prepaid assets		Profit and loss
Rent expense				−500		−500
Insurance expense				−300		−300
Bad debts			−200			−200
Balance	7 300	+ 1 000	− 200	+ 900	=	9 000
Next period Bill Bear unable to pay		− 100	+ 100			
Balance	7 300	+ 900	− 100	+ 900	=	9 000

ACCOUNTING POLICIES FOR DOUBTFUL DEBTS AND IMPLICATIONS FOR USERS

As is the case with inventories, it is important when comparing the financial statements of two entities to evaluate the provisioning for doubtful debts. If two entities are in the same industry and operate in similar locations, you would expect similar amounts of provisioning for doubtful debts. If this is not the case, and unless there is an explanation for the difference, some adjustment for this difference is necessary before a proper comparison can be made of the financial statements. In Chapter 5, the practice of earnings management was discussed. The provision for doubtful debts is another opportunity for earnings management by adding more to the provision in good years and less in poor years.

CASE STUDY 8.2

BAD DEBTS SLOW CBA RECORD OF $1.204B
by Matthew Hart

COMMONWEALTH Bank of Australia Ltd has unveiled a record first-half profit, marred by a bad debts blow-out after a string of high-profile corporate collapses.

CBA shares jumped 70 [cents], or 2.18 per cent, to $32.84 on the back of the $1.204 billion net profit for the December 31 half.

The result was 6 per cent up on the $1.135 billion net profit in the previous first half. However, growth slowed from the 35 per cent surge seen in the first-half profit last year following the CBA's $9.4 billion acquisition of Colonial.

The latest interim profit was fuelled by double-digit earnings growth in the CBA's banking and funds management businesses in the December 31 half last year.

The overall performance was marred by a 22 per cent profit drop in its life insurance arm on the back of weaker performances in Asia and New Zealand.

CBA's bad debt charges also rose 59 per cent to $290 million, from $108 million, due to the bank's exposure to the past year's corporate collapses, particularly failed zinc miner Pasminco and US energy group Enron.

CBA has exposures to Pasminco of $347 million and $100 million to Enron.

The United States energy trader's collapse was an unexpectedly harsh blow.

While bad debts typically run at about 30 per cent of an anticipated exposure, for Enron, it is likely to be more than 80 per cent.

Managing director David Murray said he believed it was 'extremely unlikely' that Australia would suffer a credit squeeze as a result of rising bad debts at the big four banks in 2001.

He believed the bad debt cycle had now peaked and that CBA was on track to deliver double-digit earnings a share growth this year.

'The bank expects to achieve double-digit earnings a share growth for the 2001–2002 financial year, subject to current trends in bad debt expense and life business investment earnings being maintained,' he said.

. . .

Extract from article in *The Courier-Mail*, 14 February 2002

COMMENTARY

The article highlights the impact of bad debts on the profits for the Commonwealth Bank. Banks are in the business of lending money and when borrowers of the size of Enron default, the impact on a bank's profits can be significant. Banks also suffer higher bad debts when economic conditions deteriorate as more borrowers experience difficulties in meeting repayments.

Management of creditors

LO 6

Identify the term 'creditors' and explain the importance of trade credit

When an established business buys goods it rarely pays cash. Only when a business is just starting, or in exceptional cases, is trade credit not given.

The question we have to address is how a business deals with goods supplied on credit which might have been used or sold before payment is made to the supplier. However, before we deal with that question we need to explain the difference between creditors and accruals.

Creditors arise when goods or services are supplied to an entity for which an invoice is subsequently received and for which no payment has been made at the date of receipt of the goods or services. As we have already said, established businesses receive most of their raw materials and components on the basis that payment is due within a certain period after delivery. At the date at which we prepare a balance sheet, therefore, we need to acknowledge that there are amounts owing (liabilities) in respect of these supplies. These are referred to as 'creditors' in Australia and the UK and as 'accounts payable' in the USA.

KEY CONCEPT 8.4

CREDITORS

Creditors are amounts owing at a point in time, the amounts of which are known.

Normally, a supplier will allow business customers a period of time after goods have been delivered before requiring payment. The period of time and the amount of credit a business gets from its suppliers is dependent on a number of factors. These include the 'normal' terms of trade of that industry, the creditworthiness of the business and its importance to the supplier. Thus, for example, a small clothing retailer is likely to get less favourable terms than a major group such as Woolworths.

Creditors are one source of funds for a business, and this is generally called trade credit. We discuss trade credit in Chapter 10. In a small business setting, effective management requires that a balance be struck between taking advantage of trade credit and not being perceived as a slow payer. If too long a period is taken to pay, the supplier may subsequently impose less favourable terms. The temptation to extend the repayment date can lead to the withdrawal of any period of credit, which means that all supplies have either to be paid for in advance or on a cash on delivery basis. Ultimately, relying too heavily on trade credit can leave a business vulnerable to the supplier petitioning for bankruptcy or liquidation. Although suppliers are generally reluctant to take such steps, they will do so if they believe that they are more likely to recover their money by such a course of action.

Accruals

Accruals are in some ways similar to creditors in that they relate to amounts due for goods or services already supplied to the entity. They differ not because of the nature of the transaction but because, at the time of preparing the balance sheet, the amounts involved are not known with certainty. This is usually because the invoice for the goods *has not been received*. A common example of such a situation is telephone accounts, which are always issued in arrears; other examples are electricity and gas accounts. In these situations, all we can do is estimate what we think is owed for the service which the business has used during the accounting period. This estimate is based on the last quarter of the previous year or on some other basis which the business considers more accurate. Example 8.2 will clarify the treatment of creditors and accruals and the differences between the two.

LO 7

Identify what is meant by the term 'accruals'

KEY CONCEPT 8.5

ACCRUALS

Accruals are amounts owing at a point in time, the amounts of which are not known with any certainty.

Review exercise 4

Explain the difference between creditors and accruals.

Example 8.2: Mike & Co.

LO 8

Apply transactions
involving debtors,
prepayments,
provision for doubtful
debts, creditors
and accruals to a
worksheet

For the year to 31 December 20X7 Mike & Co. had the following transactions.

1   Paid $6000 of Mike's own money into a business bank account, together with $5000 borrowed from a friend for the business.
2   Bought 1000 items from a supplier at $12 per unit.
3   Paid the electricity accounts for lighting and heating for three quarters, amounting to $1500.
4   Paid a supplier $9000 for items purchased.

If we enter these transactions on a worksheet and explain how they are dealt with, we can then deal with the other transactions of Mike's business. Our worksheet for the first transactions looks like this:

Mike & Co. worksheet: version 1

	Assets		= Liabilities		+ Equity	
Transaction	Bank	Inventory	Loan	Creditors	Profit and loss	Capital
1	6 000					6 000
1	5 000		5 000			
2		12 000		12 000		
3	−1 500				−1 500	
4	−9 000			−9 000		
Balance	500	+ 12 000	= 5 000	+ 3 000	− 1 500	+ 6 000

Let us examine each of the transactions in turn.

Transaction 1

By now we are familiar with transactions of this type which create an asset and a corresponding liability in the form of money owing either to the owner or to some other party.

Transaction 2

This is slightly different from the previous transactions that have dealt with the purchase of inventory. Up until now, we have assumed that the inventory was paid for when we received it. In this case, however, we are only told that during the year Mike bought items for $12 000. We have no idea, at present, how much was actually paid out in respect of these items or how much is still owing. Therefore, we show that Mike is owing money for all the items: we open a column for creditors and show $12 000 in that column.

Transaction 3

Once again, this is a familiar item because we received an account which was paid for in cash. However, we have in fact paid for only three quarters, whereas we have consumed a year's supply of electricity. We therefore need to make some provision for the other quarter. A reasonable estimate is that the fourth quarter's account will be the same as the other quarters; that is, approximately $500. It might, of course, turn out to be more or less. We are not attempting 100 per cent accuracy; we just need to give a reasonable picture of the situation.

Transaction 4

We now know that, of the $12 000 which Mike owes to suppliers, $9000 was paid in the year. We therefore reduce our cash by that amount and reduce the creditors by the same amount.

Treatment of accrual amount

Let us now return to the question of the electricity account. We said that we need to make an accrual which we estimated to be $500. Let us see how this affects our worksheet, using the balances from version 1 of the worksheet. As we can see in version 2, the worksheet still balances and it now gives a more accurate picture of the goods Mike controls and the amounts Mike owes.

Mike & Co. worksheet: version 2

| Transaction | Assets | | = Liabilities | | | + | Equity | |
	Bank	Inventory	Loan	Creditors	Accruals		Profit and loss	Capital
1	6 000							6 000
2	5 000		5 000					
2		12 000		12 000				
3	−1 500						−1 500	
4	−9 000			−9 000				
Balance	500	+ 12 000	= 5 000	+ 3 000	− 1 500		+ 6 000	
Accrual					+ 500		− 500	
Balance	500	+ 12 000	= 5 000	+ 3 000	+ 500		− 2 000	+ 6 000

Further transactions

Before we leave the subject of debtors and creditors, here are some more transactions for Mike & Co. which you should try to work through yourself. After you have done this, compare your answer with the answer shown below.

Mike & Co.'s other transactions in the year to 31 December 20X7 were as follows:

5 Paid loan interest of $300 in respect of the half-year to 30 June 20X7.
6 Sold 900 items at $50 per item, all on credit.
7 Received $40 000 from customers in respect of sales.
8 On 1 January 20X7, paid $1000 rent for five quarters, covering the period 1 January 20X7–31 March 20X8.

These appear in version 3 of the worksheet.

Mike & Co. worksheet: version 3

	Assets				= Liabilities			+ Equity	
	Bank	Inventory	Debtors	Prepaids	Creditors	Accruals	Loans	Profit and loss	Capital
Balance	500	12 000	0	0	3 000	500	5 000	−2 000	6 000
5	−300							−300	
6			45 000					45 000	
7	40 000		−40 000						
8	−1 000			1 000					
Balance	39 200 +	12 000 +	5 000 +	1 000	= 3 000	+ 500 +	5 000 +	42 700 +	6 000

If we review the position at the year-end on our worksheet, we find that the asset 'prepaids' no longer gives us a future benefit of $1000 because four quarters of the rent relates to the year just gone; therefore, the benefit has been used. We also find that the interest paid is only for the first half of the year and yet we have had the benefit of the loan for the full year; we therefore need to make a provision or accrual for a further $300. We should also realise that our inventory figure represents 1000 items at $12 each and that, of those, 900 items were sold; therefore, our cost of sales should be $10 800. Our worksheet is now as shown in version 4.

We can now extract the balance sheet and the income statement for the first year of Mike's business.

Mike & Co. worksheet: version 4

	Assets				= Liabilities			+ Equity	
	Bank	Inventory	Debtors	Prepaids	Creditors	Accruals	Loans	Profit and loss	Capital
Balance	39 200	12 000	5 000	1 000	3 000	500	5 000	42 700	6 000
Rent				−800				−800	
Interest						300		−300	
Cost of sales		−10 800						−10 800	
Balance	39 200 +	1 200 +	5 000 +	200	= 3 000	+ 800 +	5 000 +	30 800 +	6 000

Mike & Co.
Income statement for the year ended 31 December 20X7

	$	$
Sales		45 000
Cost of goods sold		10 800
Gross profit		34 200
Electricity	2 000	
Loan interest	600	
Rent	800	
		3 400
Net profit		30 800

Mike & Co.
Balance sheet at 31 December 20X7

	$	$	$	$
Assets				
Current assets				
Stocks	1 200			
Debtors	5 000			
Prepayments	200			
Cash at bank	39 200			
Total current assets		45 600		
Non-current assets				–
Total assets			45 600	
Current liabilities				
Creditors	3 000			
Accruals	800			
Loan	5 000			
Total current liabilities		8 800		
Non-current liabilities	–			–
Total liabilities			8 800	
Net assets				36 800
Equity				
Capital	6 000			
Profit for 20X7	30 800			
Total equity				36 800

Transactions in the second year

Having now established how to deal with debtors, creditors, accruals and prepayments, let us examine what happens in the second year of Mike's business.

For the year to 31 December 20X8 Mike & Co.'s transactions were as follows:

1   Bought 1000 items on credit at $12 per item.
2   Paid suppliers $14 000.
3   Paid electricity account of $2300 for the last quarter of 20X7 and three quarters of 20X8.
4   Paid loan interest of $600.
5   Sold 1000 items on credit terms at $50 per item.
6   Received $40 000 from customers.
7   Paid rent of $1000. This covered the period 1 April 20X8 to 31 March 20X9.
8   Made a provision for doubtful debts of $2000.

We will briefly discuss some of these items before we enter them on a worksheet.

Let us consider the payments to suppliers and the payment for electricity. In neither of these cases do we know exactly which parts of the payments relate to this year and which to last year. In the former case, it does not really matter, and in the latter case, it is reasonable to assume that $500 relates to last year and $1800 to the first three quarters of this year. As with last year, we have to make an estimate of the amount due in respect of the last quarter. Based on the same quarter of the previous year we would estimate $500 but this is clearly too low as, based on the three quarters this year, electricity is now costing $600 a quarter. Therefore, a reasonable estimate would be $600.

The loan interest is similar to the situation just dealt with except that, in this case, there is more certainty that $300 relates to the previous year and $300 to this year. Therefore, we need to make an adjustment in respect of the $300 which the business still owes for the current year.

As far as the cost of sales is concerned, there is no problem as prices have remained constant and Mike has bought and sold 1000 items in the year.

The situation with debtors is the same as for creditors. We cannot identify the individual payments, but in this particular example it does not make any difference.

The annual rent is $1000, payable in advance. As the first quarter was paid for last year, this payment relates to three quarters of the current year and one quarter of next year. The rent has increased from $200 to $250 per quarter.

Finally we must make a provision for expected uncollectable accounts related to sales this year. We will not know which accounts will be uncollectable until next year. After we enter these transactions, the worksheet looks like the one shown in version 5. It is possible to take some shortcuts and get the same answer, but you should bear in mind that such shortcuts can lead to errors.

Mike & Co. worksheet: version 5

Transaction	Bank	Inventory	Debtors	Provision for doubtful debts	Prepaid assets	Creditors	Accruals	Loans	Profit and loss	Capital
				Assets		**= Liabilities**			**+ Equity**	
Balance	39 200	1 200	5 000	0	200	3 000	800	5 000		36 800
1		12 000				12 000				
2	−14 000					−14 000				
3	−2 300						−500		−1 800	
4	−600						−300		−300	
5			50 000						50 000	
6	40 000		−40 000							
7	−1 000				1 000					
Balance	61 300	+ 13 200	+ 15 000	+ 0	+ 1 200	= 1 000	+ 0	+ 5 000	+ 47 900	+ 36 800
Cost of sales		−12 000							−12 000	
Rent					−950				−950	
Electricity							+600		−600	
Interest							+300		−300	
Doubtful debts				−2 000					−2 000	
Balance	61 300	+ 1 200	+ 15 000	− 2 000	+ 250	= 1 000	+ 900	+ 5 000	+ 32 050	+ 36 800

The balance sheet at the end of 20X8 and the income statement for that year can now be extracted.

Mike & Co.
Income statement for the year ended 31 December 20X8

	$	$
Sales		50 000
Less Cost of goods sold		12 000
Gross profit		38 000
Less Expenses		
Electricity	2 400	
Loan interest	600	
Rent	950	
Doubtful debts	2 000	5 950
Net profit		32 050

Mike & Co.
Balance sheet as at 31 December 20X8

	$	$	$	$	$
Assets					
Current assets					
Cash at bank		61 300			
Debtors	15 000				
Less Provision for doubtful debts	(2 000)	13 000			
Prepayments		250			
Inventory		1 200			
Total current assets			75 750		
Non-current assets		–			
Total assets				75 750	
Liabilities					
Current liabilities					
Creditors		1 000			
Accruals		900			
Loan		5 000			
Total current liabilities			6 900		
Non-current liabilities			–		
Total liabilities				6 900	
Net assets					68 850
Equity					
Capital		6 000			
Accumulated profits*		62 850			
Total equity					68 850

* Includes profits for 20X7 and 20X8.

Review exercise 5
Why is the accrual system of accounting a better guide to profitability?

Summary

LO 1

LEARNING OBJECTIVE 1
Explain what is meant by the terms 'prepayments' and 'debtors'

A prepayment occurs when an entity pays, in advance, for goods or services. When recording prepayments on a balance sheet, the question that must be considered is whether the benefit has been consumed or whether there is still some future benefit to be obtained. If there is a future benefit accruing to the business, we have an asset; if there is no future benefit, we have an expense.

Debtors arise when a business sells goods or services to a third party on credit terms; that is, when the goods or services are sold on the understanding that payment will be received at a later date.

LO 2

LEARNING OBJECTIVE 2
Illustrate the importance of the efficient management of debtors

Debtors can be a significant asset for an entity because entities want to benefit from selling goods on credit but also want to ensure that losses from bad debts are kept within an acceptable range. Unfortunately, some bad debts are inevitable when an entity sells goods on credit. In fact, if the level of bad debts is very low, it may be a signal to management that its credit policy is too strict and it is losing potential profits by denying credit to low-risk customers. Conversely, it is important to extend credit to customers only where there are reasonable prospects of the debt being paid.

LO 3

LEARNING OBJECTIVE 3
Explain what is meant by bad debts

A bad debt occurs when a debtor does not pay the amount that is owing.

LO 4

LEARNING OBJECTIVE 4
Explain and apply the direct write-off method for handling bad debts

Under this approach, the amount owing by the debtor is eliminated when it is determined that the debtor will not pay. We reduce the debtor's balance while also recognising an expense (this is the other side of the transaction). The loss of future economic benefits has caused a reduction in equity.

LO 5

LEARNING OBJECTIVE 5
Explain and apply the provision method for handling doubtful (bad) debts

The provision method involves an entity estimating the amount of bad debts it expects to incur as a result of the amount owing by debtors at balance date. This estimate is recognised as an expense prior to the debtor being classified as a bad debt. Then, when a debtor is classified as a bad debt, the debtors balance is reduced and so is the provision for doubtful debts. The provision is a negative or contra asset because the amount of the provision for doubtful debts should be deducted from the debtors to provide the net amount of future economic benefits an entity expects to obtain from debtors.

LO 6

LEARNING OBJECTIVE 6
Identify the term 'creditors' and explain the importance of trade credit

Creditors are people or entities to whom an amount is owed at a point in time, the amount of which is known.

Creditors provide entities with trade credit and are an important source of funding for businesses. In a small business setting, effective management requires that a balance be struck between taking advantage of trade credit and not being perceived as a slow payer. If too long a period is taken to pay, the supplier may subsequently impose less favourable terms.

LEARNING OBJECTIVE 7
Identify what is meant by the term 'accruals'
Accruals are amounts owing at a point in time, the amounts of which are not known with any certainty.

LEARNING OBJECTIVE 8
Apply transactions involving debtors, prepayments, provision for doubtful debts, creditors and accruals to a worksheet
Mike and Co. was used to demonstrate the recording of a number of transactions including debtors, creditors, prepayments and accruals, using the worksheet. A provision for doubtful debts was also included.

REFERENCES

Trotman, K. & Gibbins, M., 2006. *Financial Accounting: An Integrated Approach*, 3rd edn, Thomson.

REVIEW QUESTIONS

1   Why is it necessary to identify debtors and creditors?

2   In your own words, describe what a creditor is and when creditors arise.

3   Discuss the difference between the write-off method and the provision method for writing off bad debts.

4   In your own words, explain what is meant by the term 'prepayment'. Give three examples.

5   When do prepayments arise and how do they differ from accruals?

6   How do debtors affect the income statement?

7   What type of business could use a cash system of accounting? Give reasons.

PROBLEMS FOR DISCUSSION AND ANALYSIS

1   Refer to the Woodside 2005 financial report in Appendix 1.
    a   What is the value of trade and other receivables?
    b   What is the value of trade and other payables?

2   Accruals are sums owing at a point of time, the amounts of which are not known with certainty. How would you estimate the following, and what points need to be considered?
    a   electricity account
    b   council rates
    c   telephone account
    d   water rates
    e   income taxes.

3   ABC Ltd makes all its sales on credit. For customers who pay within 10 days of purchase, ABC gives a discount of 5 per cent. (Assume all sales are made evenly over the month and there are 30 working days in every month.) ABC knows that, on average, 50 per cent of its customers pay within the discount period, 40 per cent pay within 30 days and 8 per cent within 60 days. Two per cent are uncollectable.

Sales figures are:

Month 1	Month 2	Month 3	Month 4	Month 5
$1 200 000	$1 300 000	$880 000	$1 000 000	$1 250 000

How much cash did ABC collect in months 4 and 5?

4   Toyshop Ltd makes approximately 50 per cent of its sales on credit. Credit sales for six months are as follows. (Assume credit sales are made evenly over each month.)

January	February	March	April	May	June
$170 000	$132 000	$167 000	$149 000	$156 000	$112 000

Toyshop gives a 2 per cent discount for those debtors who pay within 15 days. On average, 45 per cent of Toyshop customers pay within the discount period, 35 per cent within one month, 16 per cent within two months and 4 per cent prove to be uncollectable.

Required

Calculate the monies collected each month, January to June inclusive. Assume each month has 30 days.

5   In each of the following situations, describe the way that the transaction would be dealt with in the accounts of the business and identify, where appropriate, the effect on the balance sheet and income statement:
a   Purchase of inventory of raw materials on credit terms.
b   Purchase of production machines for cash.
c   Receipts from customers in respect of credit sales.
d   Repayment of a loan.
e   Payment in respect of research expenditure.
f   Sale of goods on credit.
g   Payment to supplier in respect of goods already delivered.
h   Payment of wages to clerical workers.
i   Payment of wages to production workers.
j   Payment of loan interest.
k   Payment of an electricity bill from last year.
l   Payment of rent quarterly in advance.
m   Receipt of cash from the owner.
n   Withdrawal of inventory for personal use by the owner.
o   A customer going into liquidation owing money.

6   In each of the following situations, describe the way the transactions would be dealt with in the accounts of the business and identify, where appropriate, the effect on the income statement and balance sheet:
a   Applied for a bank overdraft.
b   Granted a bank overdraft of $10 000.
c   Used the overdraft to pay a creditor, the bank was overdrawn by $4563.
d   Paid annual insurance premium.
e   Paid telephone rental.
f   Advised by bank that the interest on the overdraft for the month was $100 and this amount had

been deducted from the entity's bank account.

g   Purchased land and settled cost with cash and a mortgage.

h   Payment of salaries.

i   Bought equipment on credit.

j   Sales for the day of $300 cash and $400 credit.

k   Owner withdrew cash for personal use.

l   Owner contributed a truck to the business which he had previously bought for personal use. This truck was bought before the owner commenced his business.

m   Payment of creditors.

n   Looked at new shop premises and made an offer to their owner to purchase them.

7   On 1 June 20X0 Billy Bond paid $6000 into a business bank account as capital for his new business. The business bought and sold art work from impoverished artists. Billy marked all merchandise up by 100 per cent on cost. During June, the transactions were as follows:

June	1	Bought shop equipment for $1750 on 30-day credit.
	2	Bought three paintings for $150 each, paying cash.
	4	Bought a set of pottery vases for $100, paying cash.
	6	Allowed J. Simpson to take one painting home to see if it fitted in with his lounge decor.
	9	Bought, for cash, a statue of David, paying $300.
	12	J. Simpson returned the painting as being unsuitable. However, he was taken with the vases and bought these on a 30-day credit arrangement.
	15	Sold a painting for cash.
	17	Paid phone bill of $123 and electricity account of $86.
	18	J. Simpson returned the vases saying his wife did not like them and asked for a full refund. He was told that there was no refund policy but Billy would buy them back for $150 cash. Billy put the vases back into stock.
	20	Sold a painting on a 30-day credit arrangement.
	23	Sold the statue for cash.
	25	Bought two wall hangings for $500, each on 30-day credit.
	26	Sold one wall hanging for cash and the other on 10-day credit with a 2 per cent discount if paid within three days.
	27	Bought six paintings for $150 each, paying cash.
	29	Buyer of wall hanging paid account and took discount.
	30	Paid assistant monthly salary of $600.

Required

a   Discuss how each transaction should be treated.

b   Draw up a worksheet, a balance sheet and an income statement.

8   On 1 May 20X0 Barbara paid $3000 into a business bank account as capital for her new business, which she called Barbie's Bikes. The transactions during May were as follows:

May	3	Bought van for $800 cash.
	6	Bought goods on credit from Spokes for $700.
	8	Paid rent of $120 for the quarter.
	14	Bought goods on credit from Olympic for $300.
	16	Made cash sales of $200.
	18	Made credit sales of $400 to Bill's Bikes.

21	Paid the garage account of $20 for petrol and oil.	
23	Sold more goods on credit to Wheels for $600.	
24	Paid Spokes $682.50 to take advantage of a 2.5 per cent discount for prompt payment.	
30	Received $360 from the liquidator of Bill's Bikes and was advised that no more would be forthcoming.	
31	Paid monthly salary to shop assistant of $400.	
	Received goods back from Wheels, with an invoice price of $80, which they had not ordered.	

Other information

No inventory count was done at the end of the month, but all goods were sold at a price based on the cost price plus one-third.

Required

a   Discuss how each transaction should be treated.

b   Discuss what, if any, accruals and prepayments are involved or should be treated.

c   Draw up a worksheet, a balance sheet and an income statement. (Take all figures to the nearest dollar.)

9   The Philjet company makes all its sales on 30-days credit. For the year ending 31 December 20X9, cash collections from customers amounted to $1 078 333. Net credit sales in 20X9 totalled $1 022 111 and the balance of debtors on 31 December 20X9 was $187 000. What was the balance of debtors on 31 December 20X8?

10   Big Bikes makes all bike purchases on credit. For the year ending 30 June 20X7 creditors paid amounted to $3 000 124. Net bike purchases for the year amounted to $2 975 345 and the balance of creditors on 30 June 20X7 was $200 376. What was the balance of creditors on 30 June 20X6?

11   Ace Silver runs a music school for young pianists. Beginners pay in advance for the first 52 weekly lessons at a rate of $5 per lesson, while more advanced students pay $7.50 per lesson in advance. Ace's financial year runs from 1 July to 30 June. On 30 June 20X8 Ace had 20 beginners with an average of 20 lessons each paid in advance, plus a further 30 advanced students with an average of 10 lessons paid in advance. Cash receipts for the year ended 30 June 20X9 amounted to $25 650. At 30 June 20X9, Ace had received advance payments for 500 lessons for beginners and 250 lessons for advanced students.

Given the above information, what is the revenue earned by Ace from piano lessons for the year ending June 30 20X9?

12   Alister Bondy runs a school for aspiring entrepreneurs who wish to become millionaires. All students pay their fees in advance. The fees are $100 per session (two-hour sessions) for beginners, $200 per session for intermediate students and $400 per session for advanced students. The school has a limit of 20 students for each class. The school's financial year follows the taxation year – from 1 July to 30 June each year.

Cash receipts from students for the year ended 30 June 20X8 came to $2 631 819 and unearned fees as at 30 June 20X8 amounted to $480 636. The income statement for the school (Make-a-Million Pty Ltd) showed fees earned for the year ended 30 June 20X8 as being $2 500 000.

What was the total of unearned fees reported in the balance sheet as at 30 June 20X7?

13 A lawyer received $20 000 from a client on 1 August 20X0 as a retainer; in return, the lawyer agreed to give legal advice whenever required by the client for a year. Neither the lawyer nor the client knew at this stage when such advice would be sought, if indeed it would be sought at all. Of the $20 000, how much should be recorded in 20X0? Assume the financial year ends on 31 December 20X0.

14 Alex Partridge established Flying High Financial Services on 1 January 20X3. Flying High Financial Services offers financial planning advice to its clients. The effect of each transaction and the balances after each transaction for January are as follows:

Transaction	Assets			= Liabilities	+ Equity
	Cash	Debtors	Inventory	Creditors	A. Partridge capital
1 Investment	+12 500				+12 500
2			+1 325	+1 325	
Balance	12 500		1 325	1 325	12 500
3	?			−900	
Balance	11 600		1 325	425	12 500
4 Fees earned		+8 750			+8 750
Balance	20 350		1 325	425	21 250
5 Rent expense		−2 500			?
Balance	17 850		1 325	425	18 750
6 Vehicle expense		−1 600			−1 250
Misc. expense					−350
Balance	16 250		1 325	425	17 150
7 Salaries expense		−?			−?
Balance	14 250		1 325	425	15 150
8 Cost of sales				−1 050	−1 050
Balance	14 250		275	425	14 100
9 Fees earned			?		?
Balance	14 250	4 350	275	425	18 450
10 Withdrawal		−3 000			−3 000
Balance	11 250	4 350	275	425	15 450

Required

a   Insert the missing figures in the worksheet.
b   Prepare an income statement for the month.
c   Prepare a balance sheet as at 31 January 20X3.

(Adapted from C.S. Warren, J.M. Reeve and P.E. Fess, *Accounting*, 20th edn, South-Western, Mason, Ohio, 2002, Chapter 1, Problem 1-3A.)

Note to instructors: *The following problems are considered more suitable for use in MBA courses. However, undergraduate courses may also find them useful.*

15 Fun Travel Agency chartered an aeroplane to tour the Kimberley region for the week commencing 14 February 20X1, at a cost of $150 000. The plane's owner agreed to finance the fuel and staffing costs of the tour. During December 20X0, the travel agency sold all of the seats on the plane (to passengers)

for $180 000 in cash. As an advance payment, the Fun Travel Agency paid $30 000 to the plane's owner. Of the $180 000 received by the travel agency, how much, if any, should be recorded as revenue by the firm in 20X0? Would your answer change if passengers were entitled to a refund in 20X1 if they cancelled their reservations?

16 Examine the data on loans and delinquent loans (bad debts) as a percentage of total loans for credit unions and answer the questions below:

Asset quality

Credit union size	Delinquent loans/total loans					
	20X1	20X2	20X3	20X4	20X5	20X6
Less than $5m	4.79%	3.97%	3.73%	3.76%	3.58%	3.74%
$5m to <$10m	3.27%	3.01%	3.70%	3.45%	3.29%	2.80%
$10m to <$50m	2.36%	2.15%	2.16%	2.12%	2.07%	2.32%
$50m to <$100m	2.14%	2.24%	2.63%	2.26%	2.32%	2.26%
$100m to <$200m	1.81%	1.91%	1.94%	2.12%	2.04%	2.04%
Over $200m	1.31%	1.42%	1.44%	1.48%	1.56%	1.34%
All credit unions	1.75%	1.79%	1.89%	1.88%	1.89%	1.80%

a   Which category of credit unions performs best in terms of loan delinquency rates?
b   What reasons do you think may explain this performance?
c   Is information on doubtful debts more important for financial institutions than other types of commercial entities? Explain your answer.

17 Ultra Conservative Ltd is a small credit union with total assets of $50 million, most of which is made up of loans to members amounting to $46 million. The following selected data relates to the credit union's first three years.

Selected accounts

	31 December 20X1	31 December 20X2	31 December 20X3
	$	$	$
Loans to members	40 000 000	43 000 000	46 000 000
Provision for doubtful debts	400 000	430 000	460 000
Doubtful debts expense	400 000	110 000	116 000

The credit union commenced operations on 1 November 20X1, and by 31 December 20X1 had established loans worth $40 million and incurred no bad debts. However, the board of directors wanted to be conservative and, based on other credit unions' experiences with delinquent loans, decided on establishing a provision amount of 1 per cent of loans outstanding as at each balance date (hence the figure of $400 000 at 31 December 20X1). All loans regarded as uncollectable were written off against the provision for doubtful debts account. In the time since Ultra Conservative Ltd commenced operations there have been no cases where a loan previously written off has had to be reinstated.

Required

a   Determine the amount of loans written off against the provision account in 20X2 and 20X3.

b   Given your answer to (a), evaluate the directors' policy of providing for doubtful debts at 1 per cent of loans outstanding at balance date. Evaluate the impact of this policy on the balance sheet and income statement.

c   Would you recommend any changes to the policy? If so, would adjustments be required to the provision for doubtful debts account? What would be the worksheet entries?

18   After reading the article 'Bad debt forces angry ANZ to take another $50m hit', answer the following questions:

a   Explain why the bank has stated that the bad debt 'will not affect the bottom line and reaffirmed earnings forecasts for this financial year'.

b   Would the position of the bank have been different if it only used the direct write-off method for bad debts?

BAD DEBT FORCES ANGRY ANZ TO TAKE ANOTHER $50M HIT
Geoffrey Newman

A DISAPPOINTED and angry ANZ bank yesterday confirmed it would be forced to wear another $50 million to make up for the bad loan to Telstra's Reach joint venture. But the bank said it would not affect the bottom line and reaffirmed earnings forecasts for this financial year. In a deal with a banking syndicate of which ANZ was the only Australian member, Telstra agreed to buy out a $US1.2 billion ($1.76 billion) loan facility for just $US311 million. ANZ, which had an exposure of $115 million, will recoup just 26c in the dollar. ANZ chief operating officer Bob Edgar said the loss was 'extremely disappointing'. The bank has about $600 million in provisions for bad debts each year. Dr Edgar said that even with the extra $50 million, to be booked in the second-half accounts, less would be outlayed than last year.

'The additional provision will be taken within ANZ's already strong level of provisioning,' Dr Edgar said. The bank also spread the pain of the failed loan facility by taking a $35 million charge in the first half. It still expected full-year earnings in line with market expectations of growth in cash earnings per share of about 9 per cent. Sources said ANZ's relationship with Telstra had been soured by the affair, particularly after Telstra had promised to protect the bank's exposure in letters in 2000–01. But the source said ANZ could not have secured more than 26c in the dollar because Reach's backers could have walked away from the debt. ANZ said it had substantially reduced its exposure to telcos.

The Australian, 19 June 2004

---

19   After reading the article 'Banking and finance – investors eye BankWest bad debts', answer the following questions:

a   What do you think is meant by the statement that Macquarie is factoring in a $15.6 million bad debt charge?

b   Why should the lower proportion of housing loans in its lending portfolio (compared with other regional banks) be a concern?

c   What implications does the article have for accounting policy decisions such as determining the provision for doubtful debts, particularly for listed public companies?

BANKING AND FINANCE — INVESTORS EYE BANKWEST BAD DEBTS
by Mark Drummond

BROKERS are concerned that Bank of Western Australia's bad debt problem has continued into the second half as shares in the Perth-based bank trade near 12-month lows. In a research note, Macquarie Equities said credit quality concerns left it cautious about the potential downside risk in BankWest's earnings outlook. Macquarie is factoring in a $15.6 million bad debt charge in the December half, after a similar bad debt charge crimped BankWest's earnings to a flat $79.1 million in the June half. 'Our increased [bad debt] estimates primarily reflect a concern over BankWest's business exposure, particularly on the east coast.

'Our concern lies with a number of smaller, lower quality exposures BankWest may be at risk of accumulating in its traditional corporate business loan segment. With the recent slide in BankWest's share price, a reasonable degree of concern over credit quality is now factored in.'

BankWest shares hit a 12-month low of $3.73 on Monday. Yesterday the stock closed 2 cents weaker at $3.76. In line with a weaker banking index, BankWest shares have fallen 22 per cent from a June high of $4.81.

The bad debt concerns come as BankWest continues to lose the corporate appeal that centred around the ownership intentions of its 56 per cent shareholder, HBoS, which is no longer considered a pressured seller.

Broker J.P. Morgan said BankWest had a higher loan–loss risk profile than the other regional banks because it had achieved growth in commercial lending in excess of system growth.

J.P. Morgan also pointed out that much of BankWest's commercial lending growth had been originated by third-party brokers, and that the proportion of housing loans in its lending portfolio was lower than the other regional banks.

A BankWest spokesman said it would be inappropriate for the bank to comment on the bad debt speculation. The spokesman said BankWest's calendar 2002 results would be released at the end of February.

In recent years, BankWest's aggressive expansion outside Western Australian has left the regional bank exposed to the likes of fugitive Gold Coast businessman Lux Daswani and the failed Beaconsfield gold project in Tasmania, as well as an indirect exposure to failed base metals group Pasminco.

BankWest's $25 million exposure to failed wine group Barrington Estates also saw the bank inherit outright ownership of McLaren Vale winery Haselgrove Premium Wines in August.

J.P. Morgan said the Barrington exposure had been largely responsible for the increase in BankWest's non-accrual loans without specific provisions.

Australian Financial Review, 19 December 2002

ETHICS CASE STUDY

John Jerkins is the chief executive officer of a chain of retail stores which trade as Bains Ltd in Australia and New Zealand. The company has been very successful in its 50 years of operating – until the past three years. The entry of new competition from overseas, plus a downturn in the economy, has made trading very difficult.

In reviewing the year's performance to date, John is concerned that the company's profit is down again from last year. The predicted result, if the current trends continue, will bring added pressure on the company from its bankers and the financial press.

To alleviate the problem John develops the following plan:

1   He will instruct all stores to reduce the level of income required for customers to qualify for credit. This, he reasons, will allow more families to purchase appliances such as television sets and video recorders.

2   He proposes to amend the method of providing for doubtful debts according to the following schedule:

Age category	Amount in the age category uncollectable	Original percentage expected to be uncollectable	Proposed percentage for expected uncollectable
	$	%	%
Not yet due	10 000 000	2	1.5
1–30 days past due	5 000 000	6	4
31–60 days past due	2 500 000	20	18
61–90 days past due	1 000 000	35	30
Over 90 days past due	600 000	80	60
Totals	19 100 000		

Required

a   Determine the amount of increase in profit as a result of the revised schedule for determining doubtful debts expense.
b   Discuss the effects of the revised credit policy on the company's profitability.
c   Discuss the ethical issues associated with John's plan.

ANSWERS TO REVIEW EXERCISES

1   Debtors and prepayments are classified as current assets because they will change their form in the next accounting period (in the former case to cash and in the latter, normally, to services). Hence, they meet the definition of a current asset as defined in Chapter 4.

2   A bad debt occurs when a debtor who owes you money is not expected to pay. An example would be when a debtor dies, goes bankrupt or disappears.

3   An entity that is entirely a cash business makes no provision for bad debts because, if it is a cash business, there are no credit sales and, hence, no debtors.

4   The difference between a creditor and an accrual is that, at the time of preparing a balance sheet, the amount of the former is known with certainty.

5   The accrual system is a better guide to profitability because it recognises income, revenues and expenses in the period in which the benefit is obtained or consumed irrespective of when the cash is received or paid.

9

LEARNING OBJECTIVES

At the end of this chapter, you should be able to:

1   explain and apply the criteria for determining what items are included in the cost of a non-current asset

2   explain the useful life of a non-current asset and how this is determined

3   explain the concept of depreciation

4   explain why non-current assets are depreciated

5   explain that the process of depreciation does not involve the setting aside of cash funds for asset replacement

6   summarise and apply the straight-line and reducing-balance methods of depreciation

7   identify the implications of depreciation accounting policy choices for financial reporting

8   explain what is meant by the term 'intangible assets' and identify the difference between identifiable and unidentifiable intangible assets

9   explain the accounting treatment for identifiable and unidentifiable intangible assets.

Introduction

In Chapter 4 we defined assets, and discussed non-current and current assets. The definition of an asset is restated as Key concept 9.1.

KEY CONCEPT 9.1

ASSETS

An asset is a resource controlled by the entity as a result of past events and from which future economic benefits are expected to flow to the entity. (AASB *Framework*, para. 49a)

The distinction that we made in earlier chapters between assets and expenses is that an asset relates to future benefits whereas an expense relates to past or expired benefits. Thus, inventories of goods held at the end of the year are shown as an asset, and the cost of the inventories sold during the year is charged as an expense. Some assets change form during a period, or from one period to the next. For example, debtors become cash, or they become expenses when a debt becomes uncollectable. This applies to all assets in the long run, but in the case of non-current assets it takes longer to use up the future benefits than it does with current assets. We defined non-current assets in Chapter 4, and repeat the definition here.

KEY CONCEPT 9.2

NON-CURRENT ASSETS

Non-current assets are all assets other than current assets.

The fact that these assets neither change form nor get used up in a short period poses some problems for accountants. These problems are in some ways similar to those we identified when discussing inventory valuation. We found that there was a problem in allocating costs such as the wages of a supervisor and in deciding which part of that cost should be allocated to the costs of the goods sold during the period; that is, the expired benefit. There was also the question of how much should be allocated to the inventory held at the end of the period. (This was shown as an asset because there was a future benefit to be derived.)

The problem can be looked at in a more general way. For the balance sheet (which tells us what we control at a particular point in time) we have to try to identify the amount of the future benefit left at the end of each year. On the other hand, for the income statement, we need to measure the amount of the future benefit used up during the year so that we can show it as an expense, together with the income earned in that period. Whichever way we look at the problem, we are left with the issue of how to measure the future benefit to be derived from the use of the asset. This is because the balance sheet and the income statement are linked.

It was argued in Chapter 3 that accounting generally adopts a definition of profit based on Sir John Hicks' (1946) definition.

KEY CONCEPT 9.3

PROFIT

Profit is that amount which an individual can consume and still be as well off at the end of the period as he or she was at the start of the period.

This, we said, could be illustrated (Figure 9.1).

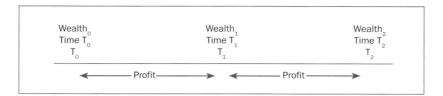

Figure 9.1 Profit or loss is determined by measuring wealth at different points in time

We can see from the diagram that wealth at T_0 plus the profit for the period will give us wealth at T_1. Thus, we can either measure the wealth in the form of future benefits at the end of each period, which brings with it the problems of valuation (as discussed in Chapter 3), or we can try to measure the profit by deducting from income the benefits used up during the period, which brings its own attendant problems (as we found with inventory and cost allocation in Chapter 7).

We first look at the idea of measuring future benefits with specific regard to non-current assets. Theoretically this might be possible. For example, we could measure the benefits to be derived from selling the products that our non-current assets help us to produce. However, in an uncertain world this process is far from straightforward. For example, what effects do technological advances have on the market for our products? How does that affect the future benefits to be derived from the use of our asset? What is the effect of competition? It might affect our market share. What is the effect of a change in production technology? It might allow competitors with newer equipment to produce the same product at a cheaper price.

In fact, it is extremely difficult to measure the future benefit in the long term because we do not know what changes the future will bring, and therefore we cannot estimate their effects. Traditionally, accounting has solved this conundrum by the simple expedient of valuing assets at cost unless there is reasonable certainty that this value is incorrect – either because it is lower, as would be the case if changes in technology made the non-current assets obsolete, or because it is clearly considerably higher. This situation generally applies only to land and buildings (although some would argue against the latter). It is difficult to measure profit by valuing assets in terms of future benefits, which leaves us with the alternative approach of measuring expired benefits and deducting these from income. The problem with this system is that if you were able to tell how much benefit had expired you would then be able to work out what the unexpired or future benefit was. This, we have just argued, is extremely difficult to do in reality because of the problems of uncertainty.

Accountants handle the difficulty by trying to take some cognisance of the fall in value of the non-current assets. This is done by means of a depreciation charge, which is a way of spreading the original cost of a non-current asset over its useful life and thereby charging the income statement with some amount relating to the use of the asset. This approach does not, in itself, solve the problem of how to deal with uncertainty because the useful life of a non-current asset is itself uncertain. Other issues also arise:

- How does a non-current asset differ from a current asset?
- What is the cost of a non-current asset?
- How should we spread the cost over the useful life?

We need to examine each of these issues if we are to understand what the figures in the income statement and the balance sheet mean.

The difference between non-current and current assets

We have already defined non-current and current assets in Chapter 4, and again at the beginning of this chapter. If you look at the definitions you will see that the difference is, in the main, related to the intention and the nature of the business. In simple terms, a car is not a non-current asset for a motor dealer because it is not the intention of the dealer to use it within the business for a considerable period of time. The problem with a definition that relies on the intentions of the business is that these change from time to time as the nature of the business changes or the product changes. An asset that was classified as a current asset might be reclassified and become subject to depreciation. As these problems rarely arise, we can ignore them in this book.

The cost of a non-current asset

1

Explain and apply the criteria for determining what items are included in the cost of a non-current asset

The question of what an asset costs should present few difficulties, but in some cases the answer is not clear. To illustrate this point, let us look at the situation in which an individual buys a house. The legal contract between the seller and the buyer states an agreed price. We could argue that the cost is that agreed price, but were you to talk to someone who has recently purchased a house you would find that there were other costs associated with the purchase, such as solicitors' and agents' fees, and stamp duty. The question is whether these should be treated as part of the cost of the asset or whether they are expenses. In this situation, an accountant might argue that the amounts involved are not material compared with the cost of the house. This is not a satisfactory solution because it avoids the question instead of answering it. Accounting does not, in fact, provide an answer to the problem. However, there are some broad guidelines which accountants use. In Chapter 7 we observed that the cost of inventories includes all costs incurred in the normal course of operations in bringing the inventories to their present location and condition ready for sale. This same principle is applied in the determination of the cost of non-current assets; that is, the cost of a non-current asset includes all the costs necessarily incurred in order to have the non-current asset ready for its intended use in the business. We will examine some examples and identify the basis of this decision. Before doing that, however, we need to explain the idea of materiality.

KEY CONCEPT 9.4

COST OF A NON-CURRENT ASSET

The cost of a non-current asset includes all reasonable and necessary costs incurred to place the asset in a position and condition ready for use.

MATERIALITY

Materiality is a concept that is often used in accounting literature and, like a number of other concepts, it provides a rule of thumb to assist in making judgements. For example, the cost of a car is likely to be material in the case of a small retailer, but in the case of the National Australia Bank the effect on the non-current assets, measured in millions of dollars, would be negligible. Thus, materiality is a relative measure and all aspects of the situation need to be looked at before a decision is made. Having introduced the idea of materiality, we can try to establish the guidelines we referred to above through a series of examples.

KEY CONCEPT 9.5

MATERIALITY

Broadly, an item can be said to be material if its omission or misstatement could influence the economic decisions of users taken on the basis of the financial statements. (AASB *Framework*, para. 30)

Example 9.1

A delivery van is purchased by a retailer of electrical goods for $40 000. The price includes number-plates and one year's registration.

Discussion

It is clear that in this example we have a non-current asset. The question is how much the non-current asset cost. Included in the $40 000 is the cost of numberplates and one year's registration. The registration can hardly be described as a non-current asset since it lasts for only one year, whereas the numberplates are clearly part of the cost of the non-current asset since they will remain with the van over its useful life.

Example 9.2

Let us now assume that, as the retailer did not have the cash to buy the van outright, it was purchased on hire-purchase. The hire-purchase contract allowed the retailer to put down a deposit of $10 000 and then make 36 monthly payments of $1000. Thus, the total cost of buying the van is $46 000, compared with the cash price of $40 000.

Discussion

The fact that the retailer has decided to finance the purchase in a different way has, on the face of it, added to the cost of purchasing the van.

However, this is somewhat misleading because the cost of the van is, in fact, the same. What has happened in this case is that the retailer has incurred an additional cost that does not relate to the van itself. This additional cost is the cost of borrowing money, which is effectively what hire-purchase is. If the retailer had borrowed money through a bank loan and then paid cash for the van, the cost of the van would have been the cash price, and the interest on the loan would be dealt with separately. Thus, in the case of hire-purchase, all that needs to be done is to identify the part of the payments that is interest and deal with it in the same way as we would deal with interest on loans. In this particular example the interest is $6000. The $6000 interest would, of course, be charged to the income statement as an expense over the 36 months it takes to pay the hire-purchase company.

Example 9.3

A manufacturer bought a second-hand machine for $10 000, which had cost $15 000 new. The cost of transporting the machine to the factory was $500 and the costs of installation were $400. When it was installed it was found that it was not working properly and it had to be repaired, which cost $300. At the same time, a modification was carried out at a cost of $500 to improve the output of the machine. After two months of production the machine broke down again and was repaired at a cost of $200.

Discussion

The starting point is the basic cost of the machine, which was $10 000. The fact that it had cost $15 000 when it was new is not relevant. What we need to bring into the accounts of our manufacturer is the cost to that business, not the original cost to the seller. With the other costs, however, the decisions are less clear. For example, should the cost of transport be included? If we apply the principle outlined in Key concept 9.4 the answer is yes, because the cost is necessary to get the machine to its place ready for use. In other words, in order to obtain the future benefits from the asset we needed to incur this cost, and so this is, in fact, a payment for those future benefits. If we followed this line of argument we would then include the costs of installation, the initial repairs and the modifications.

You will have noticed that we referred specifically to the initial repairs rather than all the repairs. Let us compare them. For the initial repairs, it could be argued that the reason the business was able to buy the machine cheaply was because it was not working properly. For the later repairs, however, the argument is less clear: the repairs might be due to normal wear and tear and should therefore be judged as part of the cost of running the machine, in the same way as the cost of car repairs is regarded as a part of the costs of running a car. If a business incurs costs which significantly improve a non-current asset, so that its ability to generate future economic benefits is enhanced, then the cost might qualify for inclusion as part of the cost of the asset.

For example, an expenditure of $2000 is incurred to install a new engine in a car with a written-down cost of $3000. This extends the life of the car by four years. This cost is properly treated as an addition to the cost of the asset rather than as an expense.

GUIDELINES FOR IDENTIFYING NON-CURRENT ASSET COSTS

We can now improve the definition of the cost of a non-current asset (previously given in Key concept 9.4).

KEY CONCEPT 9.6

COST OF A NON-CURRENT ASSET

The cost of a non-current asset includes:
- all reasonable and necessary costs incurred to place the asset in a position and condition ready for use
- all costs incurred which enhance the future economic benefits of the asset beyond those initially expected at acquisition.

We can see from these examples that there is no easy solution to the problem of what should and should not be included in the cost of non-current assets. Each case is judged upon its merits and a decision is made about whether the cost should be included in the expenses for the year or added to the cost of the asset. The rule of thumb that can be used to assist in these decisions is: has there been an enhancement of the potential future economic benefits? If there has, then the cost should be added to the asset. If, however, the effect is simply to restore the status quo, as is the case with car repairs, then it is more reasonable to treat those costs as expenses of the period in which they arise.

The classification of costs as expenses or assets was the major issue with WorldCom. Refer back to Case study 5.2.

The useful life of non-current assets

The second question posed in the introduction concerns the process of determining the useful life of a non-current asset.

A non-current asset has a number of possible lives including its:
- potential physical life
- potential technical life
- expected commercial life
- legal life.

LO 2

Explain the useful life of a non-current asset and how this is determined

An asset's potential physical life may be much longer than either its technical or commercial life. This is because the technical life of an asset is influenced by changes in technology, and these changes can render obsolete an asset that is still in working order. This is the case with assets like computers. The commercial life of an asset is a time span that is determined by the entity's belief regarding how long it is economically viable for the asset to be used within a business. For example, a business will often have a policy of replacing motor vehicles long before the expiry of their physical life. An asset may have a specific legal life, as is generally the case with assets acquired with a finance lease. The definition of 'useful life' for accounting purposes is provided in AASB 116 *Property, Plant and Equipment* (as reported in Key concept 9.7).

KEY CONCEPT 9.7

USEFUL LIFE

a   the period over which an asset is expected to be available for use; or

b   the number of production or similar units expected to be obtained from the asset by an entity (AASB 116, para. 6)

How then do we judge the useful life of an asset?

In some cases, such as with motor vehicles where the entity intends to replace them every three years, the answer is straightforward. In other cases, all we can hope for is an approximation, because of uncertainty in respect of the future. In determining the cost that we wish to spread over the useful life, we should take into account the sum that we will get for selling our asset when it is no longer viable to use in our business. This amount, the residual value, is only a guess because of the uncertainty involved. In reality, such issues are sidestepped and assets are classified into broad groups, which are then assumed to have a useful life based upon either past practice or the norm for the industry. All too often one can visit factories where a vital machine in the production process has no carrying value in the accounts because the estimate of its useful life was incorrect. Having made it clear that there is no magic formula for arriving at either the cost or the useful life, let us now examine the way in which we spread the cost over the useful life. This is done by means of depreciation.

Review exercise 1

Digger Company purchased a diamond head drill that has a manufacturer's suggested life of 15 years. The company plans to use the drill on a special project that will last 11 years. At the completion of the project, the drill will be sold. Over how many years should the drill be depreciated?

Depreciation

We have suggested some reasons for charging depreciation, which we will discuss further in the next section. What we have not done is define depreciation precisely; instead, we have tried to give a flavour of what depreciation is. The definition of depreciation is also given in AASB 116, as reported in Key concept 9.8.

Explain the concept of depreciation

KEY CONCEPT 9.8

DEPRECIATION

Depreciation is the systematic allocation of the depreciable amount of an asset over its useful life. (AASB 116, para. 6)

The definition refers to a 'systematic allocation' which means that it is not an ad hoc process but should be done on a consistent basis each year. It is also clear from the definition that depreciation is a process of allocation, not valuation. In other words, the depreciation amount is not meant to represent the decline in the value of the asset. It is meant to represent the allocation of the depreciable amount of the asset over its useful life. Therefore, the depreciable amount of the asset less the depreciation represents the unallocated amount, and not necessarily the asset's value at any point in time. We could spend some time analysing the definition, but it is more important to consider the question of why we depreciate assets and what depreciation can and cannot achieve.

WHY DEPRECIATE?

A depreciable asset is one that has a finite life extending over several accounting periods. Machinery is a depreciable asset; land is not. Depreciation is intended to show the consumption of economic benefits during an accounting period. The economic benefits associated with all depreciable assets are eventually consumed, and depreciation shows the consumption of these benefits as an expense in the income statement.

A second and more contentious reason for providing for depreciation is in order for a business to maintain the capacity to continue its production. Clearly, if a machine comes to the end of its useful life, the business will need another machine if it is to carry on producing the goods. This, of course, assumes that it wishes to replace the machine, which itself has underlying assumptions about the product still being produced, the technology in terms of production processes being the same, and so on. This question is directly related to our original problem in Chapter 3 of measuring wealth or the state of being well off. Such a measure depends on how you define wealth, and whether that changes. For example, a car might be seen as an asset until such time as the world runs out of petrol reserves. At that stage we might not want to include a car in our measurement of wealth. Therefore, to have retained profits in order to ensure that we always had a car would not have been appropriate.

The second reason for providing for depreciation is also contentious because, in fact, all accounting depreciation does is to spread the original cost and maintain the original capital. In fact, operating

Explain why non-current assets are depreciated

capacity is not maintained through depreciation, as no account is taken of changes in prices, in technology, or in consumer demand. Neither are the changes in the size of the business taken into account. This might have implications in terms of economies of scale. We cannot guarantee that we will have enough funds left in the business as a result of our depreciation charges to replace an existing machine with one of equal capacity, should we wish to.

Having made the point that there is no guarantee that the charges will equal the requirements for replacement because of changes in those requirements and the commercial environment, let us look at how depreciation would maintain capital if the requirements and the commercial environment did not change. We will start by looking at an example to see what happens if we ignore depreciation, and then how it is dealt with in terms of the accounts.

Review exercise 2
What is the purpose of depreciation?

Example 9.4: Toni's business

Explain that the process of depreciation does not involve the setting aside of cash funds for asset replacement

Toni buys a van for $40 000 and sets up a business as an ice-cream seller. In addition to the van, she puts $10 000 cash into the business, which is subsequently used to buy inventories of ice-cream.

At the end of the first year, sales have amounted to $60 000 and the total expenses, including the cost of ice-creams, van repairs and running costs, are $30 000; all the inventory has been sold so all the money is in cash. Thus, the business has $40 000 in cash – the original $10 000 plus the money from sales of $60 000 less the expenses paid of $30 000.

Toni, therefore, withdraws $30 000 on the assumption that the business is still as well off as it was at its inception. That is, at the start of the year the business had a van plus $10 000 in cash; it still has the van, so there needs to be only $10 000 left in for the status quo to be maintained. Let us assume that the situation is repeated for the next three years.

Under these assumptions, the income statement and balance sheet of the business are as follows:

Toni's business
Income statements

	Year 1	Year 2	Year 3	Year 4
	$	$	$	$
Sales revenue	60 000	60 000	60 000	60 000
Cost of sales	30 000	30 000	30 000	30 000
Profit	30 000	30 000	30 000	30 000
Withdrawal	30 000	30 000	30 000	30 000
Retained profit	0	0	0	0

Toni's business
Balance sheets

	Year 1	Year 2	Year 3	Year 4
	$	$	$	$
Current assets				
Cash	10 000	10 000	10 000	10 000
Non-current assets				
Van	40 000	40 000	40 000	40 000
Total assets	50 000	50 000	50 000	50 000
Owners' equity	50 000	50 000	50 000	50 000

If we assume that the van will last for four years and have no further useful life, we can see that, in fact, the balance sheet at the end of year 4, assuming it reflects future benefits, should be as follows:

Toni's business
Balance sheet at the end of year 4

	$
Current assets	
Cash	10 000
Non-current assets	
Van	–
Total assets	10 000
Owners' equity	10 000

As we can see, there is not enough cash left in the business to replace the van, and, in this situation, the business cannot continue. If we compare the results with our definition of profit in Chapter 3, it is clear that our profit measure must have been wrong, because Toni is not as well off at the end of year 4 as at the beginning of year 1.

The problem is that the profit has been overstated because no allowance has been made for the fact that the van has a finite useful life which is being consumed each year. If we assume that the cost should be spread evenly over the four years and call this expense, depreciation, then the income statements appear as follows:

Toni's business
Revised income statements

	Year 1	Year 2	Year 3	Year 4
	$	$	$	$
Sales revenue	60 000	60 000	60 000	60 000
Cost of sales	30 000	30 000	30 000	30 000
Gross profit	30 000	30 000	30 000	30 000
Depreciation	10 000	10 000	10 000	10 000
Net profit	20 000	20 000	20 000	20 000
Withdrawal	20 000	20 000	20 000	20 000
Retained profit	0	0	0	0

Thus, the net profit has reduced by $10 000 for depreciation each year and Toni has withdrawn only $20 000 each year. The balance sheets would now be:

Toni's business
Revised balance sheets

	Year 1	Year 2	Year 3	Year 4
	$	$	$	$
Current assets				
Cash	20 000	30 000	40 000	50 000
Non-current assets				
Van	40 000	40 000	40 000	40 000
Less Accumulated depreciation	(10 000)	(20 000)	(30 000)	(40 000)
	30 000	20 000	10 000	0
Total assets	50 000	50 000	50 000	50 000
Owners' equity	50 000	50 000	50 000	50 000

As we have seen, the effect of charging depreciation in the income statement is to reduce the net profit, which in turn has led to a reduction in the amount withdrawn each year. The reduced withdrawal has led to the cash balance increasing each year by $10 000 until, at the end of year 4, there is $50 000 in the bank and Toni is in a position to replace the van, assuming of course that the price of vans has not changed. If you compare the two sets of balance sheets there is another change – the non-current asset reduces each year by the amount of the depreciation charge. The accumulated depreciation is a contra or negative asset account. It is similar, in a way, to the provision for doubtful debts account which we discussed in Chapter 8. On the worksheet, it is shown as part of the assets with a negative balance as it is a negative asset; that is, the accumulated depreciation is deducted from the asset in the balance sheet. These two effects should not be mixed up. The increase in cash is a result of Toni withdrawing less cash, and not a result of providing for depreciation. The latter does not, in itself, affect the cash balance – as is obvious if we work through year 1 of this example on a worksheet.

Worksheet showing year 1 of Toni's business

	Assets			= Liabilities +	Equity	
	Cash	Van	(Accumulated depreciation)		Capital	Profit and loss
Balance	10 000	40 000			50 000	
Sales	60 000					60 000
Expenses	−30 000					−30 000
Depreciation			−10 000			−10 000
Withdrawal	−20 000				−20 000	
Balance	20 000	+ 40 000	− 10 000	=	30 000	+ 20 000

Accumulated depreciation does not represent cash. The only cash in the business is shown in the cash column.

An alternative way of dealing with depreciation on a worksheet is to reduce the assets column by the amount of depreciation. If we do this, our worksheet appears as shown below. However, we recommend that, wherever possible, the worksheet should include a separate column for accumulated depreciation because this adds to its clarity and allows us to identify roughly how far through its useful life the asset is at the end of the year. In our example, we can see that the van costs $40 000 and $10 000 depreciation has been charged, so we know that it is one-quarter of the way through its estimated useful life.

Toni's business: alternative worksheet for year 1

	Assets			= Liabilities +	Equity	
	Cash	Van			Capital	Profit and loss
Balance	10 000	40 000			50 000	
Sales	60 000					60 000
Expenses	−30 000					−30 000
Depreciation		−10 000				−10 000
Withdrawal	−20 000				−20 000	
Balance	20 000	+ 30 000		=	30 000	+ 20 000

In this example, we have assumed that the cost should be spread evenly over the life of the asset. This is known as straight-line depreciation and is one of a number of alternative methods that can be used as the basis for providing depreciation. Each of these alternatives gives a different figure for depreciation each year and as a result the written-down value, also referred to as the 'book value' or 'carrying value', differs. This is illustrated in more detail after our discussion of the most common methods of depreciation. Before going on to that discussion, you need to understand what written-down value means.

KEY CONCEPT 9.9

WRITTEN-DOWN VALUE (CARRYING VALUE OR BOOK VALUE)

The written-down or carrying value is normally the cost of the non-current asset less the total depreciation to date. In certain cases, usually with freehold buildings, the asset might be revalued. In these cases the written-down value is the valuation less total depreciation to date.

Review exercise 3

Why is it unlikely that depreciation will provide for the replacement of a non-current asset?

Methods of depreciation

L0
6

Summarise and apply the straight-line and reducing-balance methods of depreciation

As we have said, there are several alternative methods of depreciation; the choice of the appropriate method, at least theoretically, depends on the nature of the asset being depreciated. In practice, however, the only methods in common use are the straight-line method and the reducing-balance method. The former is used by most businesses because it is simple to calculate. In this regard, it would be useful for you to look at the accounting policies statement in published accounts to try to ascertain the reasons underlying the choice of depreciation method. As we will see in the discussion below, a case can be made for using different methods for different assets or classes of assets. In reality, it might be the fact that assets are put into broad categories that leads to the predominance of straight-line depreciation, which we now discuss more fully.

THE STRAIGHT-LINE METHOD

We have already seen that this is a simple method, which explains why so many companies use it. The assumption concerning asset life that underlies this method is that the asset is equally useful for all periods of its life. The depreciation charge is calculated by taking the cost of the asset, subtracting the estimate of any residual value at the end of its life, and dividing the resulting amount by the useful life of the asset. Therefore, a machine which costs $100 000, and has an estimated life of four years and an estimated residual value of $20 000, is depreciated by $20 000 per year. This was arrived at by using the following formula:

$$\frac{\text{cost} - \text{residual value}}{\text{useful life}}$$

In our case this works out as follows:

$$\frac{100\ 000 - 20\ 000}{4} = \$20\ 000 \text{ per annum}$$

REDUCING-BALANCE METHOD

The reducing-balance method assumes that the future benefits associated with the asset decline more in the earlier years of the asset's life than in the later years. In fact, in most cases the cost of repairs rises as the asset becomes older, and so this method, when the cost of repairs is added, produces a more even cost of using an asset over its total life. It is less frequently used than the straight-line method because it is slightly more difficult to calculate, although with the increasing use of computers this should not cause any problems. The method applies a pre-calculated percentage to the written-down value, or carrying value, to ascertain the charge for the year. In order to arrive at the percentage we use the following formula:

$$\text{Rate of depreciation} = 1 - \sqrt[\text{useful life}]{\frac{\text{residual value}}{\text{cost of asset}}}$$

Using the figures from the above example:

$$\text{Rate of depreciation} = 1 - \sqrt[4]{\frac{20\ 000}{100\ 000}}$$

$$= 1 - \sqrt[4]{0.2}$$

$$= 1 - 0.6688$$

$$= 0.33 \text{ (approximately)}$$

$$= 33\%$$

In practice, it is common to use a simpler approach to determine the percentage rate under the reducing-balance method. Often a rate of one-and-a-half times or double the straight-line rate is used. We determine the straight-line rate by dividing the expected life of the asset into 100. Hence, an asset with an expected life of 10 years has a straight-line depreciation rate of 10 per cent. In our example, the straight-line rate is 25 per cent because the life expectancy is four years. Therefore, a reducing-balance method which used one-and-a-half times the straight-line rate would result in a percentage of 37.5 per cent (25 × 1.5). Thus, in our example, we will use 37.5 per cent (and not the 33 per cent as determined by application of the formula).

Depreciation, year 1 = 37.5% of 100 000
                     = $37 500
Depreciation, year 2 = 37.5% of (100 000 – 37 500)
                     = $23 438
Depreciation, year 3 = 37.5% of (100 000 – 37 500 – 23 438)
                     = $14 648
Depreciation, year 4 = 37.5% of (100 000 – 37 500 – 23 438 – 14 648)
                     = $9255
Total depreciation   = 37 500 + 23 438 + 14 648 + 9255
                     = $84 841

COMPARISON OF THE TWO METHODS

The $4841 difference between the total depreciation after four years under the two methods is because we used a higher approximate rate of 37.5 per cent in place of the formula-based 33 per cent. It is important to understand that the calculation of depreciation is only an estimate, irrespective of which method is used.

As can be seen in the following table, the charge to the income statement in each year and the accumulated depreciation in the balance sheet are quite different with the two methods, although they both charge, in total, approximately the same amount. The difference in the total depreciation over the life of the asset is reflected in the difference of $4841 between the carrying value at the end of year 4 under both methods. This will result in a different gain or loss on the sale of the asset, as demonstrated in the next section.

COMPARISON OF TWO METHODS OF DEPRECIATION
Straight-line method

	Balance sheet		Income statement	
Year 1	Cost	100 000	Depreciation expense	20 000
	(Accumulated depreciation)	(20 000)		
	Carrying value	80 000		
Year 2	Cost	100 000	Depreciation expense	20 000
	(Accumulated depreciation)	(40 000)		
	Carrying value	60 000		
Year 3	Cost	100 000	Depreciation expense	20 000
	(Accumulated depreciation)	(60 000)		
	Carrying value	40 000		
Year 4	Cost	100 000	Depreciation expense	20 000
	(Accumulated depreciation)	(80 000)		
	Carrying value	20 000		

Reducing-balance method

	Balance sheet		Income statement	
Year 1	Cost	100 000	Depreciation expense	37 500
	(Accumulated depreciation)	(37 500)		
	Carrying value	62 500		
Year 2	Cost	100 000	Depreciation expense	23 438
	(Accumulated depreciation)	(60 938)		
	Carrying value	39 062		
Year 3	Cost	100 000	Depreciation expense	14 648
	(Accumulated depreciation)	(75 586)		
	Carrying value	24 414		
Year 4	Cost	100 000	Depreciation expense	9 255
	(Accumulated depreciation)	(84 841)		
	Carrying value	15 159		

The differences between the two methods can be summarised as follows:
- Under the straight-line method, the charge to the income statement is $20 000 each year, so the accumulated depreciation rises at a rate of $20 000 a year.

- Under the reducing-balance method, the charge to the income statement is based on 37.5 per cent of the carrying value at the end of the previous year.
- While both methods result in approximately the same amount of depreciation in total, it is the incidence of the charge to the income statement which varies, not the total charged.

While, in theory, the choice of depreciation method should be governed by the nature of the asset and the way in which the benefit is used up, in practice, little, if any, attention is paid to this. However, it is worth spending some time understanding when each method is appropriate.

We have said that the straight-line method implies that the benefit from the use of the non-current asset is used up in an even pattern over its useful life. This suggests that it is time which is the determining factor governing the life of the asset, rather than the amount of use to which it is put. In the case of a building, it is unlikely that the amount of use it gets will materially affect its life span, so straight-line depreciation is appropriate. On the other hand, the way in which a car engine, for example, wears out is likely to relate to usage; that is, the more miles the car does, the more wear and tear on the engine. In such a case, the straight-line method is unlikely to be the appropriate method. In these cases it is possible to use a method referred to as the 'units-of-output' method. This involves calculating the depreciation charge based on the kilometres travelled in each accounting period as a percentage of the total kilometres the car is expected to travel during its useful life, multiplied by the cost less residual value.

The reducing-balance method, however, has characteristics that make it a possible alternative to a direct measure related to usage: it charges the most benefit used to the early years, as would be the case if the asset were used up, for example, by the kilometres alone or by the number of hours a machine was run. It is, of course, only an approximation. However, from a cost–benefit point of view, it is not worthwhile measuring the number of hours a machine is run and calculating a precise figure, because the total life of the machine is subject to estimation errors. We can, therefore, argue that where the life of the asset relates to time, the straight-line method is likely to be appropriate; but where the asset is used up through hours run, or kilometres, or any other measure relating to usage, the reducing-balance method will give a better approximation if the benefit is used up in a period.

Refer now to the financial report of Woodside. Note 2(f) reveals that the company uses the units-of-production method for oil and gas properties (and other plant and equipment used in the production of oil and gas). Other assets are depreciated using the straight-line method.

Sale of non-current assets

Before leaving the discussion of non-current assets and depreciation, we should examine the situation that arises when we sell a non-current asset. It should be obvious from our discussion above that the carrying value (book value) of the asset – the cost less depreciation to date – is unlikely to bear any resemblance to the market price of that asset. When an asset is sold, the selling price will be either less than or more than the carrying value. If, for example, we sold the asset in the table on page 262 at the end of year 2 for $50 000, then, under the straight-line method, there would be a difference of minus $10 000: the carrying value of $60 000 compared with the $50 000 we sold it for.

However, under the reducing-balance method, the difference would be plus $10 938: the carrying value of $39 062 compared with the sale proceeds of $50 000. These differences arise because of the difference between our estimate of the future benefit being used up and the actual benefit used up. In other words, they are a measure of the error in our estimates. We now look at the way in which the sale of an asset is recorded, using a worksheet.

Example 9.5: Sale of machine

Using the preceding data, let us assume that we used the straight-line depreciation method and sold the asset at the end of year 4 for $18 000.

Worksheet: straight-line depreciation

	Assets			= Liabilities +		Equity	
	Cash	Machine	(Accumulated depreciation)			Capital	Profit and loss
Balance		100 000	−80 000			20 000	
Sale proceeds	18 000						18 000
Asset removal		−100 000	80 000				−20 000
Balance	18 000	+ 0	+ 0		=	20 000	− 2 000

Worksheet: reducing-balance depreciation

	Assets			= Liabilities +		Equity	
	Cash	Machine	(Accumulated depreciation)			Capital	Profit and loss
Balance		100 000	−84 841			15 159	
Sale proceeds	18 000						18 000
Asset removal		−100 000	84 841				−15 159
Balance	18 000	+ 0	+ 0		=	15 159	+ 2 841

In the worksheet, we record the proceeds from sale as an increase in the profit and loss column because it represents income to the business. (If you are unsure about this you should look back at Chapter 5.) We have also recorded the reduction in the carrying value of the asset as a negative amount in the profit and loss column because it represents an expense to the business. (Again, if you are unsure about this you should look back at Chapter 5.) Notice that the machine column and the accumulated depreciation column both have zero balances which, of course, is essential as the business no longer controls the asset.

Using the straight-line method would result in a loss of $2000 on disposal, while using the reducing-balance method would result in a gain of $2841 on disposal. The difference between the two methods is $4841, which is the difference in the carrying value of the asset at the end of year 4 under both methods. Only the gain or loss on the sale of a non-current asset is reported in the income statement.

Review exercise 4

What are the assumptions underlying the two main methods of depreciation?

Accounting policies for depreciation and implications for users

When comparing the financial statements of entities, it is important to be aware of how the financial statements were prepared. Did the companies both use straight-line or reducing-balance methods of depreciation? For example, Woolworths uses the straight-line method for all non-current assets. If we are comparing Woolworths with Coles Myer, and Coles Myer uses a reducing-balance method of depreciation, then Coles Myer will record higher levels of depreciation when the assets are new. Users of financial statements must adjust for this when comparing the results of both companies. Thus, as with accounting for inventories and bad debts, a component of the difference in profits between the two companies is due to the accounting rules. This difference should be distinguished from differences in profits due to higher sales or lower operating costs.

Another complication for users is the impact of different accounting rules on cash flows. If a company records a higher depreciation expense than another company, then, all other things being equal, the company with the higher depreciation expense will initially report a lower profit. However, we know depreciation is a non-cash-flow adjustment and that, over time, the differences between the two companies will not be material as a result of depreciation methods. Therefore, differences in profit due only to different depreciation policies should not result in a different valuation of either company.

However, what if the companies use the same depreciation method for both the report to shareholders and the calculation of taxable income? The company with the higher initial amount of depreciation will have greater tax deductions in earlier years than the other company. Due to the time value of money (i.e. the value of $1 today is greater than $1 in one year's time), the company with the higher initial amount of depreciation should have a higher value than the other company because it pays less tax in the earlier years of the life of the asset.

LO 7

Identify the implications of depreciation accounting policy choices for financial reporting

CASE STUDY 9.1

SIA PROFIT DUE TO DEPRECIATION

by Paul Thompson, Assistant Professor in Accounting, Nottingham University Business School

I REFER to your article 'SIA hints net profit may be above $200m' by Andrea Tan (BT, April 20).

First, may I say that, for the sake of the hardworking staff, I certainly hope it is true. They would then stand a good chance of getting previously implemented wage cuts restored.

Second, may I bring to investors' attention – ▐▐▶

if they are not already aware – that SIA is engaging in earnings management, much like their peers in Europe and North America.

SIA's earnings management makes it difficult for me to get excited about the mildly bullish sentiment surrounding SIA. While things are indeed looking up for SIA, it is worth noting that the primary reason it stands any chance of making any profit at all for the year ended March 31, 2002 boils down to what some might call an accounting sleight of hand.

I hold SIA in high regard. SIA is a high-flier in the world of aviation. It offers impeccable service, far better than any other flag carrier I have flown in. It is also one of the world's most profitable airlines and, unlike many like the big US flag carriers and British Airways, it appears to have avoided a free fall into financial losses –and it has averted slashing staff numbers (the latter achievement is especially commendable).

The main reason, however, it has managed to steer clear of reporting losses for the past financial year (announcement is due in early May but SIA, for sure, already knows the score) is through a timely change in its accounting policy on the depreciation of fixed assets.

Depreciation is a major expense for airlines whose balance sheets are bulging with an expensive aircraft fleet. In its half-year report issued last October, soon after the terrorist attack on the World Trade Center, SIA said: 'Commencing this financial year, the company changed its depreciation rate for passenger aircraft, spares and spare engines from 10 years to 20 per cent residual value to 15 years to 10 per cent residual value. This is to bring it more in line with airline industry practice. Aircraft depreciation charge was $133 million lower as a result.'

In other words, SIA's policy change for the six months to Sept 30, 2001 caused expenses to be lower by $133 million and hence profit higher by the same figure. For the full year, the effect is likely to be double – that is, a boost to profits by some $266 million.

I do not doubt SIA when it says that this policy change aligns itself with industry practice. In fact, in 1999, I compared the depreciation policy of SIA with BA and found it to be more conservative. But the fact remains that had it not made this change, SIA would almost certainly be reporting a loss for the year to March 31, 2002 in the next few weeks.

Business Times Singapore, 25 April 2002

COMMENTARY

The article discusses the impact of a change in depreciation policy on the reported profits of Singapore Airlines. The author states that this change in depreciation policy may be due to an earnings management strategy by SIA. The author suggests that the increase in profits may be due entirely to the change in depreciation rates and, therefore, may not represent a real increase in profits. An important question is whether such a strategy would mislead investors and analysts. In Chapter 14 we discuss the efficient market hypothesis. In an efficient market, sophisticated investors would not be misled by a cosmetic change in profit.

Intangible assets

Many organisations have non-current assets which lack a physical substance and are not held for investment purposes. Yet, these items still provide future economic benefits similar to plant, machinery and buildings. Such assets are described as intangible assets. Examples include trademarks, patents, intellectual property, franchises and goodwill. Assets such as accounts receivable and prepaid expenses also lack a physical substance and are not investments. However, such assets are classified as current assets and not intangible assets.

Explain what is meant by the term 'intangible assets' and identify the difference between identifiable and unidentifiable intangible assets

Intangible assets are either identifiable or unidentifiable. Identifiable intangible assets include those intangibles that have a separate existence, such as patents, trademarks, franchises and brand names. Unidentifiable intangible assets are the benefits that flow to an organisation from such things as a good location, an outstanding image in the marketplace or excellent customer relations. 'Goodwill' is the name used to describe the future economic benefits that flow from the collection of all these unidentifiable assets.

THE COST OF INTANGIBLE ASSETS

Determining the cost of intangible assets is relatively straightforward for those assets purchased externally, but far more complicated for those developed internally. For example, if Delta Company pays $200 million to acquire the patent for a new product, then the acquisition cost of the patent in Delta's accounts is $200 million. The cost of an identifiable intangible asset is the purchase price paid. Goodwill is normally purchased when one organisation acquires all or a significant portion of the net assets of another organisation. Goodwill is the excess of the amount paid for the fair value of the net assets acquired. For example, Company A pays $100 million to acquire all the assets and liabilities of Company B. The fair value of all the assets less the liabilities, once recorded in the balance sheet of company A, is $95 million. The $5 million difference is recognised as goodwill.

Many companies develop their own intangible assets, and establishing a cost for these assets is far more difficult. In the case of identifiable intangibles, the cost could include items such as the legal fees to develop the documents (e.g. patents and copyrights), the registration costs of such documents and, possibly, any legal costs incurred in successfully defending the ownership of the asset. Accounting Standard AASB 138 *Intangible Assets* prohibits the recognition of internally-developed goodwill, brands, mastheads, publishing titles and customer lists.

Companies that develop intangible assets internally are keen to recognise such assets on their balance sheets. Such companies are then not at a disadvantage when users compare their company to another which has purchased similar types of intangible assets. However, it is important that only those expenditures which provide economic benefits beyond the current period are recorded as an asset. Those expenditures where all the benefits are consumed in the current period should be recorded as an expense. Expenditures wrongly recorded as assets will overstate current profit and understate future profits.

RESEARCH AND DEVELOPMENT

Many companies spend large sums of money in the area of research and development (R&D). They may be hoping to discover a new product or process, or to improve an existing product or process.

The accounting question is whether such expenditures should be recorded as assets or expenses. In theory, the answer should be determined by applying the definition and recognition criteria for assets and expenses. Is it probable that future economic benefits will arise from the R&D expenditures? Does the company control such benefits and can the benefits be reliably measured? AASB 138 requires that all research in relation to intangible assets be expensed. Developmental costs occur when initial research evolves into a product or process that has potential commercial viability. Such costs may be carried forward as an asset, but only when they satisfy certain criteria such as probable future economic benefits and reliable measurement.

Because all research costs are expensed, does this mean that no future economic benefits will flow to the organisation? Of course the answer is no, but, in theory, the expensing of all research expenditures could be interpreted as conveying this message to users of financial statements.

PATENTS

This is a legal right granted to one person or company for the exclusive use of a certain product or manufacturing process. When a company develops a new product (through research and development) it will register a patent. The legal life of a patent is 16 years, but, of course, its useful life may be shorter as new products are developed to compete against it. A company with a patent can then sell the right to manufacture and sell the product to others. Thus, the patent can be a valuable asset. How would you like to have been the owner of the patent on products like the television, the camera or the electric shaver?

COPYRIGHT

Copyright provides protection to the creators of original work, which could be a book like this one, films, songs, music or computer games. For a small fee, a copyright can be registered. Other parties are then not permitted to copy such original work without paying a royalty to the creator. Elvis Presley's estate continues to earn millions of dollars in royalties for his music, despite Elvis having been dead for over 25 years.

TRADEMARKS OR BRAND NAMES

The costs of creating a trademark or brand name may be relatively small and may include costs paid to an artist, or advertising agency, and a small registration cost. However, the values of such trademarks and brand names can be huge. How much would you pay for the use of the name 'Coca-Cola'?

FRANCHISES

A franchise provides the franchisee with the exclusive right to sell or distribute a certain product. For example, McDonald's and Hungry Jack's are conducted through franchise arrangements. A manager of a McDonald's store pays a franchise fee. This is recognised on the balance sheet as an asset for the amount paid.

Review exercise 5

What is the difference between identifiable and unidentifiable intangible assets? Give examples.

Accounting for intangible assets

The treatment of intangible assets once they are recognised on the balance sheet is quite a controversial issue. Some argue that intangible assets are no different from tangible assets in that they have a finite life during which the economic benefits are consumed. This consumption of economic benefits should be recognised as an expense in a similar fashion to the depreciation of tangible non-current assets. Others argue that the life of some intangible assets such as brand names is extremely long, and amortisation (write-off) is not appropriate.

Traditionally, accounting standards in Australia have required that purchased goodwill be amortised over a period not exceeding 20 years. However, AASB 138 (issued in Australia as a result of the adoption of IFRSs) requires that purchased goodwill, and other intangible assets deemed to have an indefinite life, be valued at least once a year, and only where this value has declined will the difference be recognised as an impairment of the asset. This essentially means that the value of the intangible asset on the balance sheet will be reduced and an expense of the same amount recognised in the income statement.

For those intangible assets deemed to have a finite life, such as copyright and patents, a process similar to depreciation is required to amortise the cost over the life of the intangible asset. The methods available to amortise intangible assets are the same as those used for tangible non-current assets such as property, plant and equipment. The term 'amortisation' has essentially the same meaning as depreciation; that is, the systematic allocation of the cost of the intangible asset over its expected useful life. The straight-line method of amortisation is the one normally used and the formula is:

$$\text{amortisation amount} = \frac{\text{cost of intangible asset} - \text{residual value}}{\text{useful life in years}}$$

The amortisation amount is recorded as an expense in the income statement and as an increase in an accumulated amortisation account (similar to accumulated depreciation). These assets are generally not replaced at the end of their useful life and information about the estimated useful lives of intangibles is included in the notes to the accounts.

9

Explain the accounting treatment for identifiable and unidentifiable intangible assets

CASE STUDY 9.2

MEDIA TO FEEL IFRS CUT THE DEEPEST
Jane Schulze

MEDIA is expected to lose more than $1 billion of value due to massive non-cash write-downs when new accounting standards are adopted. From January 1, the new International Financial Reporting Standards was introduced, requiring intangible assets such as newspaper or magazine mastheads or TV and radio licences to be carried at cost.

That means any media company which had revalued those assets higher in recent years must reverse that book entry – a move likely to spark the large non-cash write-downs. And media groups which have issued hybrid securities (such as the Seven Network and newspaper publisher John Fairfax Holdings) must reclassify those securities as debt, which will increase their financial gearing.

While the changes will not affect companies this financial year, it is of interest now as all profit reports for 2005–06 must also restate 2004–05 results under the new guidelines.

'Media companies will be impacted in different ways depending on the history of the intangible valuation,' Macquarie Equities media analyst Alex Pollak recently wrote.

'If the intangible asset has been acquired and carried at cost then there will be no write-down. If part of the asset has been generated via internal revaluation, those amounts will have to be written down.'

In the TV world, Seven said in its annual report that it must write back the $480 million increase an independent valuer applied to its TV licences in 1998. And its debt is likely to increase by $315 million when its hybrid securities, known as TELYS, are reclassified as debt.

But the Ten Group, which is controlled by the listed company Ten Network Holdings, faces an even larger $751 million write-down of its TV licences after an independent valuation in 2002.

That will be partly offset by the reversal of a $225 million tax charge on that revaluation, taking the net write-down to $526 million. But it will have less impact on the listed company as it already values the TV licences at cost.

Publishing & Broadcasting Ltd's Nine Network must write down the value of its TV licences as they are in the books at a valuation that is $423 million above cost. PBL's annual report said its magazine mastheads were valued at cost, but it was still considering other changes to the accounting rules which could lead to some of their value being written down.

At Fairfax, publisher of *The Australian Financial Review*, the biggest change will be a $241 million increase in debt when their hybrid securities (known as PRESSES) are reclassified as debt.

Little change is expected on the valuation of Fairfax's newspaper mastheads as most were acquired after the group went into receivership in 1992. But the value of newspaper mastheads and other TV licences at News Corporation, owner of *The Australian*, will be unaffected due to its recent move to the US, where the accounting industry has decided against adopting IFRS.

The Australian, 10 January 2005
Copyright 2005 News Ltd. All Rights Reserved

COMMENTARY

The article discusses the impact of the adoption of IFRSs on the process of accounting for intangible assets. As Australia did not have an Accounting Standard on identifiable intangible assets, many companies recognised internally developed intangible brands and trademarks as well as revaluing purchased intangibles. With the adoption of IFRSs, most of this accounting has to be reversed.

SUMMARY

LO 1

LEARNING OBJECTIVE 1

Explain and apply the criteria for determining what items are included in the cost of a non-current asset

The cost of a non-current asset includes:

- all reasonable and necessary costs incurred to place the asset in a position and condition ready for use
- all costs incurred which enhance the future economic benefits of the asset beyond those initially expected at acquisition.

LO 2

LEARNING OBJECTIVE 2

Explain the useful life of a non-current asset and how this is determined

A non-current asset has a number of possible lives including its:

- potential physical life
- potential technical life
- expected commercial life
- legal life.

AASB 116, paragraph 6, defines the useful life as:

a   the period over which an asset is expected to be available for use; or

b   the number of production or similar units expected to be obtained from the asset by an entity.

LO 3

LEARNING OBJECTIVE 3

Explain the concept of depreciation

Depreciation is the systematic allocation of the cost or revalued amount of an asset over its useful life.

LO 4

LEARNING OBJECTIVE 4

Explain why non-current assets are depreciated

The future economic benefits of a non-current asset, with a finite life, are consumed over time and depreciation is meant to represent the consumption of the economic benefits of a non-current asset.

LO 5

LEARNING OBJECTIVE 5

Explain that the process of depreciation does not involve the setting aside of cash funds for asset replacement

Depreciation is a non-cash expense, and accumulated depreciation is the sum of all the depreciation expenses since the asset was first used. The only cash in a business is in the 'cash at bank' account in the current assets. By depreciating an asset, the entity reports lower profits; therefore, less is available for dividends but there is no cash in the accumulated depreciation account.

LO 6

LEARNING OBJECTIVE 6

Summarise and apply the straight-line and reducing-balance methods of depreciation

The straight-line method allocates an even amount to depreciation expense each year and the formula is:

$$\frac{\text{cost} - \text{residual value}}{\text{useful life}}$$

The reducing-balance method allocates more depreciation expense to the earlier years of an asset's life and the formula is:

$$\text{Rate of depreciation} = 1 - \sqrt[\text{useful life}]{\frac{\text{residual value}}{\text{cost of asset}}}$$

The units-of-output method involves calculating the depreciation charge based on the units extracted each year as a percentage of the total units the asset is expected to yield multiplied by the cost less residual value:

$$\frac{\text{Cost} - \text{residual value} \times \text{number of units in period}}{\text{total expected number of units}}$$

LEARNING OBJECTIVE 7

Identify the implications of depreciation accounting policy choices for financial reporting

The reported profit of an entity can vary based on its choice of depreciation policy. Moreover, even when two entities use the same policy, the depreciation expense can still vary based on the choice of variables – such as the useful life or residual value. Users need to be aware of these potential impact on reported profits.

LEARNING OBJECTIVE 8

Explain what is meant by the term 'intangible assets' and identify the difference between identifiable and unidentifiable intangible assets

Intangible assets are those items that meet the definition of an asset but lack any physical substance. Identifiable intangible assets include those intangibles that have a separate existence, such as patents, trademarks, franchises and brand names. Unidentifiable intangible assets are the benefits that flow to an organisation from such things as a good location, an outstanding image in the marketplace or excellent customer relations. 'Goodwill' is the name used to describe the future economic benefits that flow from the collection of all these unidentifiable assets.

LEARNING OBJECTIVE 9

Explain the accounting treatment for identifiable and unidentifiable intangible assets

The accounting treatment is specified by AASB 138. Goodwill is not amortised, but is assessed annually for impairment. Any impairment in the value of goodwill is recognised as an expense. An impairment loss on goodwill can never be reversed. Identifiable intangibles with an indefinite life are accounted for in the same manner as goodwill. Identifiable intangibles with a finite life are amortised over their expected life.

REFERENCES

Australian Accounting Standards Board. AASB 116 *Property, Plant and Equipment*, July, 2004.
Australian Accounting Standards Board. AASB 138 *Intangible Assets*, July, 2004.
Australian Accounting Standards Board. *Framework for the Presentation and Preparation of Financial Statements*, July, 2004.
Hicks, Sir John, 1946. *Value and Capital*, Clarendon Press, Oxford.

FURTHER READING

Trotman, K. & Gibbins, M., 2006. *Financial Accounting: An Integrated Approach*, 3rd edn, Thomson.

REVIEW QUESTIONS

1   What factors need to be taken into account in determining the useful life of an asset?

2   On what basis do we decide what should and should not be included in the cost of a non-current asset?

3   Describe what is meant by the book value, carrying value and written-down value of an asset.

4   An expense has been described as a past or expired benefit. In what way does depreciation differ from other expenses?

5   Explain what is meant by the term 'intangible asset' and give examples.

6   Discuss the concept of 'materiality'.

7   a   In what sections of the income statement are gains and losses from the disposal of non-current assets presented?
    b   When should an entry be made to remove the cost and the accumulated depreciation from the accounts?

8   Immediately after a used delivery van is acquired, a new motor is installed and the tyres are replaced at a total cost of $4750. Is this a capital expenditure, or should it be treated as an expense in the income statement?

PROBLEMS FOR DISCUSSION AND ANALYSIS

1   Refer to the Woodside 2005 financial report in Appendix 1.
    a   What is the depreciation expense for the period ended June 2005 on:
        i   land and buildings
        ii   transferred exploration and evaluation
        iii plant and equipment
        iv   marine vessels and carriers
        v   restoration assets
    b   What methods of depreciation does the company use?

2   A widget machine is purchased and expected to have a residual value of $20 000 at the end of its eight-year useful life. If the machine were depreciated on a straight-line basis, and sold at the end of four years for $88 000, giving a gain of $4000 over carrying, what was the cost of the machine?

3   A machine acquired on 2 January at a cost of $154 000 has an estimated useful life of 10 years. Assuming that it will have no residual value, determine the depreciation for each of the first two years:
    a   by the straight-line method
    b   by the reducing-balance method, using twice the straight-line rate.

4   A machine priced at $220 000 is acquired by trading in a similar machine and paying cash for the difference between the trade-in allowance and the price of the new machine.
    a   Assuming that the trade-in allowance is $35 000, what is the amount of cash given?
    b   Assuming that the carrying value of the machine that is traded in is $18 750, what is the cost of the new machine for financial reporting purposes?

5   A vehicle was purchased on 1 Jan 20X0 for $23 000. The vehicle was estimated to have a useful life of six years, after which time it could be traded in for $2000.
    a   What was the amount in accumulated depreciation at 31 December 20X5 using the straight-line method?

b   If the vehicle was traded in for a new one after three years for $11 500, was there a gain or loss on trade-in?

c   If the reducing-balance method had been used in (b) above, at a rate of one-and-a-half times the straight-line method, would your answer be different from (b) above and, if so, what would that answer be?

6   The following data relates to plant owned and operated by the Bazmic Company:

	$000
Accumulated depreciation, 31 December 20X8	750
Accumulated depreciation, 31 December 20X9	1 025
New plant acquired on 31 December 20X9	500
Gain on disposal of old plant, 31 December 20X9	50
Depreciation on plant for year ended 31 December 20X9	500
Balance in plant account 31 December 20X8	2 000
Balance in plant account 31 December 20X9	2 100

How much was the old plant sold for?

7   Anwar (Perth) Ltd purchased a machine from a company in Sydney. The machine cost $30 000, transport to Perth cost $1000, site works for the machine cost $2000 and insurance to cover damage on the trip was $500. While the machine was being installed it was damaged through careless handling. The machine cost $4000 to repair. The machine was expected to have a useful life of 10 years, with a residual value of $1000.

a   Calculate depreciation expense for the first two years using:
   i   the straight-line method
   ii   the reducing-balance method.

b   Which method would you expect to have the greatest impact on the company's profit/loss?

8   The following data relates to plant owned and operated by Philjen Ltd:

	$000
Loss on sale of old plant, 30 June 20X1	100
Balance in plant account, 30 June 20X0	37 600
Balance in plant account, 30 June 20X1	37 600
Accumulated depreciation, 30 June 20X1	12 400
Accumulated depreciation, 30 June 20X0	12 400
Depreciation on plant for year ended 30 June 20X1	1 500
New plant acquired on 30 June 20X1	2 000

Required

a   What was the carrying value of the old plant?

b   How much was the old plant sold for?

9   Bazchem bought a machine to produce widgets from Allchem in the US. The cost of the machine was US$75 000 (one Australian dollar was worth 50 US cents at the time of payment), shipping was US$5000, and insurance to cover all risks from the US factory to Sydney wharf was US$1000. Bazchem

paid for these three items before shipment. Freight from Sydney to Perth was $500 and insurance $400. Site costs were $3750, including a special transformer to supply 115 volts to the American machine. The machine was expected to have a life of 20 years and a zero residual value.

Required

Calculate the depreciation expense for the first three years using:
a   straight-line method
b   reducing-balance method at a rate of 10 per cent.

10 The Digitup Company purchased mining equipment on 3 January 20X2 for $340 000. The equipment was expected to have a useful life of three years, or 18 000 operating hours, and a residual value of $25 000. The equipment was used for 7500 hours during 20X2, 6000 hours in 20X3 and 4500 hours in 20X4.

Required

Determine the amount of depreciation expense for the years ended 31 December 20X2, 20X3 and 20X4 by:
a   the straight-line method
b   the units-of-output method
c   the reducing-balance method, using twice the straight-line rate
    and
d   determine the total depreciation expense for the three years by each method.

11 Using a worksheet, draw up the balance sheet and income statement for the business whose transactions are set out below:

Month 1   Bert put in $9000 of his own money and transferred his own car into the name of the business. At the time of the transfer, it would have cost $6000 to buy a new model of the same car, but as the car was one year old its second-hand value was only $4000. The business then bought a machine for $4000, paying cash, and, at the same time, bought a second machine on credit terms. The credit terms were a deposit of $1000 which was paid in cash and two equal instalments of $900 payable at the start of months 4 and 7 respectively. The cash price of the machine was $2500.

Month 2   Bought raw materials for $3000 cash, and made cash sales of $3000.

Month 3   Paid rent in arrears for the three months, amounting to $600 in cash. Paid wages of $1500 for the three months to date. Made cash sales of $4000 and purchased more raw materials, again for cash, amounting to $8000.

Month 4   Paid instalment on machine of $900 in cash and made cash sales of $4000.

Months 5–7   Bought raw materials for cash for $2000 and made cash sales of $5000, paid wages for three months of $1500, the rent for three months ($600) and the second and final instalment on the machine of $900.

Months 8–12   Made cash sales of $14 000, bought raw materials for cash for $6000, paid wages for six months of $3000, and paid rent for three months of $600.

At the end of the year Bert has raw materials in inventory which cost $2000. He calculates that the car will last two more years, after which he will be able to sell it for $400. The machines have useful lives estimated at three years and will then be sold for $100 each. Since Bert is not very good with figures, he opts for straight-line depreciation on all the non-current assets.

12 The Fairhead Company, owned by Gordon Fairhead, is a manufacturer of electrical equipment.
    At 31 December 20X7, the non-current assets of the business were as follows:

	Date acquired	Cost $	Residual value $	Useful life years	Accumulated depreciation $
Building A	1 July 20X3	252 000	12 000	20	54 000
Machinery	1 Jan. 20X4	29 000	1 000	7	16 000
Office equipment	1 July 20X5	14 000	1 500	5	6 250
Delivery equipment	1 Apr. 20X4	40 000	4 000	4	33 750
Land	1 July 20X5	68 000			

During 20X8, the following transactions took place:

1 Jan.   Purchased a tract of land and three buildings for $160 000. An independent appraiser's report on this property showed a total valuation of $200 000, broken down as follows: land, $100 000; building B, $40 000; building C, $50 000; and building D, $10 000. The appraisal indicated a useful life of 20 years for buildings B and C, and five years for building D, with no residual value for any of the three.

2 Jan.   Building D was demolished to make room for construction of a new storage building. The necessity of this move had been taken into consideration by management when purchasing the property. The expense was nominal.

1 Apr.   Purchased new delivery equipment with a list price of $27 000. Paid nothing initially, but signed an agreement for $28 620. This amount was payable in 12 equal monthly instalments of $2385 each. Useful life of this equipment was estimated at four years, residual value at $1800. The old delivery equipment was retained for emergency use.

1 July   Construction of a new storage building, E, was completed at a contract price of $28 000. The building was erected by the Fairhead Construction Company owned by Robert Fairhead, brother of Gordon Fairhead. Gordon Fairhead stated that other contractors had bid $50 000 or more to do the job. Payment was made by delivery of marketable securities acquired five years previously at a cost of $20 000. Stock market quotations indicated a present value of $28 000. The life of building E was estimated as 20 years, with no residual value.

1 Oct.   Purchased additional office equipment for $7500 cash. Estimated useful life, five years; residual value, $500.

Required

Prepare a depreciation schedule to compute the 20X8 depreciation expense. Use the following headings:

Type of asset	Date of acquisition	Cost	Residual value	Amount to be depreciated	Useful life	Accumulated depreciation 31 Dec. 20X7	Depreciation expense 2008

In this schedule, use a separate line for each of the four depreciable items owned at 31 December 20X7, and a separate line for each unit of plant and equipment acquired during 20X8. For assets acquired during the year, compute depreciation for an appropriate fraction of the year, including the month in which the acquisition occurred.

13 In each of the following situations, discuss the most appropriate method of depreciation, giving reasons for your choice:

a   *land and buildings.* The land was purchased for $300 000, and $400 000 was spent on the erection of the factory and office accommodation

b   *motor vehicles.* The business owns a fleet of cars and delivery vans, all of which were bought new. The owners have decided to trade in the vehicles for new models after four years or 60 000 kilometres, whichever is sooner. The anticipated kilometre figures are 12 000 kilometres per annum for the cars and 20 000 kilometres per annum for the vans

c   *plant and machinery.* The plant and machinery owned by the business can be broadly classified into three types, as follows:

   • *type 1.* Highly specialised machinery used for supplying roller bearings to Manicmotors Ltd. The contract for supply is for five years, after which it might be renewed at the option of Manicmotors. The renewal would be on an annual basis. The machinery is so specialised that it cannot be used for any other purpose. It has an expected useful life of 10 years and the residual value is likely to be negligible

   • *type 2.* Semi-specialised machinery which is expected to be productive for 10 years and have a residual value of 10 per cent of its original cost. However, other firms operating similar machines have found that, after the first three years, it becomes increasingly costly in terms of repairs and maintenance to keep them productive

   • *type 3.* General-purpose machinery which has an estimated useful life of 80 000 running hours. At present levels of production the usage is 6000 hours a year, but as from next year this is expected to rise to 8000 hours a year if the sales forecasts are correct.

Note to instructors: *The following problems are considered more suitable for use in MBA courses. However, undergraduate courses may also find them useful.*

14 Multiplex Ltd used its own construction crew to extend its existing factories. What would be the most appropriate accounting treatment for the following?

a   Architects' fees.

b   Cost of debris removed during construction, due to a storm.

c   Cash discounts received for payment of materials purchased for construction before the invoiced due date.

d   Cost of building a workshop (to assist with construction) that will be demolished once the extensions have been completed.

e   Interest on money borrowed to finance construction.

f   Government land taxes on the portion of land to be occupied by the new extensions for the period of construction.

g   The cost of major errors made during construction.

h   Overhead costs of the construction department, including supervision, depreciation on buildings and equipment of construction department, electricity, water, and allocation costs for the cafeteria, medical office and personnel department.

i   Cost of workers' compensation insurance during construction and the cost of damages on any injuries not covered by insurance.

15 Kent Pty Ltd purchased a new machine for its manufacturing plant. While it was clear that both the invoice price of the machine and the transport costs of bringing the machine to the manufacturing plant should be brought to account, there was some uncertainty surrounding the treatment of the following items:

a   Installation costs of reinforced steel to support the new machine, which is heavier than the machine it is replacing. Should this cost be charged to the building, added to the cost of the machine, or treated as an expense?

b   An outside fitter was called in to assist with the installation of the machine because the regular maintenance crew were unable to do it. Costs of the fitter included his fee, transport, accommodation and meals. The supervisor of the maintenance crew and a senior engineer both spent a considerable amount of time assisting the fitter. Before the new machine was working properly, a large quantity of materials had been ruined during trial runs. How should all of these costs be treated?

c   A state sales tax was paid when the machine was purchased. Should this be included in the machine's cost?

d   Part of the finance agreement between Kent Pty Ltd and the machine manufacturer was a trade-in on the old machine as part payment. The amount given for the trade-in exceeded the depreciated value of the old machine in the books of Kent Pty Ltd. Should the difference be treated as a reduction in the cost of the new machine or a gain on disposal of the old one?

16 A firm which manufactured office equipment sold approximately 30 per cent of its products (in dollar volume) and leased the rest. On average, the equipment was leased for five years. The initial cost of the leased equipment was recorded as an asset and was depreciated over the five years. The company assisted its customers in installing the office equipment and provided a regular maintenance service. Both these services were provided free of charge and recorded as a service expense. Service costs averaged about 7 per cent of the sales value of a piece of office equipment, but about 25 per cent of the first-year rental revenue of a leased piece of equipment.

Over the past year, the company's installation of office equipment grew rapidly, but because the service cost was such a high percentage of lease revenue, reported income showed no increase at all. Research and development costs were treated as expense as they were incurred. Should the same principle apply to service costs, or could these costs be added to the asset value of leased office equipment and amortised over the lease period? If so, should other service costs relating to leased office equipment be treated in the same manner?

(Problems 14–16 adapted from R. Anthony and J. Reece, *Accounting: Text and Cases*,
8th edn, Richard D. Irwin Inc., 1988, Chapter 7, Case 7–2.)

17 Two brothers are planning to start a bakery in Melbourne and Sydney. They are contemplating the purchase of two stores currently owned by the same company and used as retail outlets for shoes. For this reason, the buildings and fixtures for both shops have the same cost, residual value and useful lives. They also plan to purchase the same type of equipment. The following schedule provides details of the assets:

	Cost of each	Residual value	Useful life of each
	$	$	$
Building	408 000	8 000	40 years
Fixtures	40 000	5 000	5 years
Equipment	34 000	2 000	8 years

In addition, each building will need to be renovated at a cost of $40 000. The estimated income statements for the first year for the two shops have been separately determined by each brother and are shown in the schedule below.

SYDNEY			MELBOURNE		
Projected income statement for year ended 31 December 20X1			Projected income statement for year ended 31 December 20X1		
	$	$		$	$
Sales		380 000	Sales		380 000
Cost of goods sold		200 000	Cost of goods sold		200 000
Gross profit on sales		180 000	*Gross profit on sales*		180 000
Operating expenses:			Operating expenses:		
Salaries expense	60 000		Salaries expenses	60 000	
Building renovation	40 000		Other expenses	8 000	
Other expenses	8 000				
Depreciation expenses:			Depreciation expenses:		
Building	20 400		Building	11 000	
Fixtures	16 000		Fixtures	7 000	
Equipment	8 500		Equipment	4 000	
Total expenses		152 900	Total expenses		90 000
Net profit		27 100	*Net profit*		90 000

The brother who plans to open a store in Sydney does not understand how his projected profits can be so much lower than his brother's when they are projected to make the same sales, employ the same number of people, and spend about the same amount for other necessary operating items.

Required

a   Which depreciation method has each elected to use for their buildings, fixtures and equipment? Show the calculation of depreciation for each of the assets.

b   How did each brother account for the $40 000 cost of renovation? Which is correct?

c   Based on the projected income statements, which shop would you invest in? Lend money to?

18 After reading the article 'Infrastructure asset relief for industry', answer the following questions:

a   Explain how using a longer life will lower depreciation each year under the straight-line and reducing-balance methods.

b   Why would businesses such as Qantas spend resources to lobby government about the lives over which they can depreciate assets when, irrespective of the life, the total depreciation at the end will be the same?

INFRASTRUCTURE ASSET RELIEF FOR INDUSTRY
by Allesandra Fabro

IN A WIN for business, the Federal Government has stepped in to limit proposals by the Australian Taxation Office to slow the depreciation of transport and infrastructure assets by dramatically increasing their effective life.

But the new statutory limits in several cases still represent an increase from current amounts, meaning business can still expect less in annual depreciation deductions. The new caps affect aircraft, oil and gas plant, offshore rigs and distribution assets. All have been the subject of vigorous lobbying by industry groups over the past 12 months.

Estimates in last night's changes indicate the caps will limit the tax take on the depreciation changes to 'about $150 million' over the next four years, substantially smaller than originally feared. The 'effective life' of an asset is a limit set by the Commissioner of Taxation, Michael Carmody, and represents the length of time over which a taxpayer can depreciate an asset.

The ATO last year announced it was proposing to more than double the effective life of many infrastructure assets, which would have had a severe impact on the internal rate of return of investment projects around the country.

It also led to airlines, including Qantas and the now defunct Ansett, threatening to own their aircraft through corporations in countries such as Singapore, which have considerably more favourable depreciation regimes. The oil and gas industry had also threatened to pull out of new pipeline developments if the revised rates went ahead.

The Federal Government said it was introducing the caps for 'broader national interest concerns', an indication that industry lobbying has been successful.

The Minister for Revenue, Helen Coonan, yesterday said the revision of effective life rates for other asset classes would continue. 'It is important the Commissioner of Taxation continues to modernise, update and revise the effective life schedule . . . to reflect current business practices,' she said.

Australian Financial Review, 15 May 2002

ETHICS CASE STUDY

Bazley Manufacturing Company has two operating divisions, each producing different products. Company policy requires that capital expenditures of each division be approved by the company's budget committee if an expenditure exceeds $100 000. The manager of Excel Division, Adam Lake, received a memo from the budget committee in mid-April which stated that no more requests for capital expenditures above $100 000 would be considered for the remainder of that year because of the company's overall financial situation. Adam was very upset at the contents of the memo because he was about to request an approval to purchase a new machine for $200 000. He rang the chairman of the budget committee to see if an exemption could be made to allow the purchase of the new machine. The chairman said there would be no exemptions. Adam was upset because without the new machine his division would not be able to complete a large order for an important customer and the Excel Division would not meet its profit projections.

After giving some thought to the situation, Adam called in the division controller, Kylie Hansen, to find a solution. During their discussion, Adam came up with what he thought was a great idea. He told Kylie to order the new machine for delivery and installation by 1 May. Kylie would insist that the machine manufacturer charge the division for three separate components of the machine by means of three separate invoices, which should be written as if each invoice were for a different machine. He suggested that Kylie tell the machine manufacturer that Excel Division would take their business elsewhere if the manufacturer was not willing to charge with three separate invoices for the amounts of $69 000, $87 500 and $43 500. Under this plan, no one invoice would exceed $100 000, so the policy stated in the budget committee's memo would not be violated.

However, Kylie indicated some reluctance in carrying out this plan, pointing out that both she and Adam would have some serious explaining to do if the intentional deviation from company policy were discovered. As Excel Division controller, Kylie reported to Adam, the division manager, and the company controller. She realised that she could be in a difficult position if she did what Adam asked and it was later discovered that she did not inform the company controller about the situation. Despite Kylie's concerns, Adam insisted that his plan was the only solution to the Division's dilemma. He told Kylie to call in the order the next day and request the separate invoices for the three components of the machine. Kylie left Adam's office very worried and uncertain what to do.

Discuss

a   who Kylie ultimately reports to
b   whether Kylie should agree, because if Excel does not purchase the machine the customer may go elsewhere and the company could lose a substantial profit
c   what Kylie should do.

ANSWERS TO REVIEW EXERCISES

1   The drill should be depreciated over the period of use which, in this case, is 11 years.

2   Depreciation is an accounting process by which the consumption or loss of the service potential of depreciable assets is progressively brought to account by means of periodic charges against revenue.

3   Because of the effects of changes in other factors, such as the price of the asset, it is unlikely that depreciation will provide for the replacement of a non-current asset. This will mean that the cost of replacement is greater than the original cost. However, it should be borne in mind that the effects of technological advances may mitigate or even reverse this effect. The discussion should also emphasise that depreciation does not provide cash for replacement.

4   Straight-line method – asset usage and the rate at which the asset is worn out is governed by time and is equal over the asset's life.

    Reducing-balance method – asset usage and the rate at which the asset is worn out is greater in the earlier years than the later years.

5   Identifiable intangible assets relate to a special item like patents, copyright, brand names or trademarks; unidentifiable assets relate to factors (referred to as goodwill) such as a good reputation, good management and a good location.

FINANCING AND BUSINESS STRUCTURES
CHAPTER TEN

10

LEARNING OBJECTIVES

At the end of this chapter, you should be able to:

1   discuss the concept of matching the type of finance with the purpose for which it is to be used

2   explain what is meant by short-term sources of finance such as bank overdrafts, trade credit and factoring

3   explain what is meant by medium-term sources of finance such as loans, hire-purchase and leases

4   explain what is meant by long-term sources of debt finance such as long-term loans and debentures

5   explain what is meant by equity finance and how it varies according to the type of business organisation

6   explain the criteria for classifying securities as either debt or equity, and apply this to different types of preference shares

7   explain what is meant by gearing, and the effect this can have on returns to shareholders in a company.

Introduction

So far the chapters in this book have been mainly concerned with what an organisation does with an asset once it has been acquired. In this chapter we turn our attention to how the business raises the money to acquire its assets. The various types of finance available to different types of organisations are discussed, as are the effects of the finance mix on the returns to the owners.

At this point, it is important to recall that the balance sheet equation is Assets = Liabilities + Equity. This tells us that assets are financed by liabilities and equity. Liabilities are provided by the firm's creditors and are described as *debt finance*. The *equity finance* is provided, primarily, by the owners of the business; for a company, the owners are the ordinary shareholders. In this chapter we examine sources of debt finance and equity finance.

We consider the different forms of finance used by a business and the effects of the organisational structure upon the sources of finance available. We also consider the financing structure of an organisation and its effect on financial risk. For these purposes, it is necessary to differentiate between business risk and financial risk.

Broadly speaking, business risk applies equally to all firms in an industry, with some variations according to size and diversity – that is, it is industry-specific rather than firm-specific. Financial risk is more firm-specific; it relates to the financial structure of a business – that is, the way in which it finances its assets.

Before commencing our discussion of the different types of finance, it is important to appreciate that the choice of appropriate finance can be vital to the long-term success of a business. Ideally, the type of finance should match the purpose for which it is to be used. For example, using what is, essentially, short-term finance for the purchase of a building merely creates problems when the financier has to be repaid. The building is still needed, and so replacement finance has to be found. Similarly, taking out a loan repayable over 20 years to buy an asset that is only going to be needed for a few years would leave the business in the position of having to pay interest on money it no longer needs. These are, of course, extreme examples, but they do serve to illustrate the point that the finance must be matched with the purpose for which it is to be used.

LO 1

Discuss the concept of matching the type of finance with the purpose for which it is to be used

KEY CONCEPT 10.1

TYPE OF FINANCE

The finance used, and the period of that finance, should be matched to the period for which it is required and the purpose for which it is to be used.

Although any attempt to classify different types of finance is problematic, it is useful to look at some broad categories, and a division based on the period of finance is the one we have chosen to use. In considering the various forms of finance, we shall endeavour to follow a pattern that provides a general description of the source of finance as well as a discussion of its uses, limitations, costs and availability.

Review exercise 1

Why is it important to match the type of finance with the purpose of raising that finance?

Short-term finance

Explain what is meant by short-term sources of finance such as bank overdrafts, trade credit and factoring

In this section we discuss the short-term sources of finance. Conventionally, short-term finance is seen as finance for a period of less than one year. This means that the funds provided by this form of finance are repayable within 12 months from the date of accessing such finance. Therefore, according to the principle stated in Key concept 10.1, it is important that short-term finance is only used for short-term investments. The short-term investments that entities make for 12 months are what we classify as current assets and include inventories and debtors. A number of sources of short-term finance are available, the most common being trade credit, factoring and bank overdrafts.

WORKING CAPITAL

Working capital is represented by the current assets of a business minus its current liabilities. The management and funding of working capital is an important issue for all businesses. A business that fails to properly plan for its working capital requirements is likely to experience difficulties, and could ultimately fail because of it. As discussed in Chapters 7 and 8, entities need to hold certain levels of inventories and debtors. Having the appropriate amount of inventories and the appropriate number of debtors is an important management concern. In order to hold inventories and debtors, entities must be able to finance such assets. A major way to help fund the investment in debtors and inventories is to use the short-term sources of finance discussed in this section.

TRADE CREDIT

We have already come across trade credit in Chapter 8, which dealt with debtors and creditors. Normally a supplier will allow business customers a period of time after goods have been delivered before requiring payment. The period of time and the amount of credit a business gets from its suppliers is dependent on a number of factors. These include the 'normal' terms of trade of that industry, the creditworthiness of the business and its importance to the supplier. Therefore, for example, a small clothing retailer is likely to get less favourable terms than a major group such as Woolworths.

In general, trade credit, which is widely used as a source of finance, provides short-term finance. This is normally used to finance, or partially finance, debtors and inventory. As such, its importance varies from industry to industry. For example, manufacturing industries, where there is greater investment in inventory and work in progress, are more likely to rely on trade credit than are service industries. There may also be variations within an industry. For example, a restaurant is less likely to rely on trade credit than is a hotel, where a lot of money is tied up in inventories. In fact, within the licensed trade many hoteliers rely quite heavily on trade credit and this reliance makes them vulnerable if that credit is not managed effectively. Effective management in a small business setting requires a balance to be struck between taking advantage of trade credit and not being perceived as a slow payer. If too long a period is taken to pay, the supplier may subsequently impose less favourable terms. The temptation to extend the repayment date can lead to the withdrawal of any period of credit, which means that all supplies have either to be paid for in advance or on a cash on delivery basis. Ultimately, too heavy a reliance on trade credit can leave a business vulnerable to the supplier petitioning for bankruptcy or liquidation. Although suppliers are generally reluctant to take such steps, they will do so if they believe that they are more likely to recover their money by such a course of action.

Trade credit is often thought of as cost-free credit, which is not strictly true, as quite often suppliers allow a small discount for early payment. Therefore, using the full period to pay has an opportunity cost in the form of the discount forgone. This cost can be significant. For example, assume a supplier offers terms of 2/10, Net/30. This means that a 2 per cent discount is given if payment is received within 10 days of receipt of the invoice; otherwise, the net amount due is payable in 30 days. To forgo the discount means a cost of 2 per cent is paid for a further 20 days' use of the money. This equates to an approximate cost of 36 per cent per annum, which is expensive. This opportunity cost has to be weighed against the availability of funds within the business, or the cost of raising additional funds. Unlike other forms of short-term finance, there is generally no requirement for security.

KEY CONCEPT 10.2

TRADE CREDIT
Trade credit is a form of short-term finance provided to a business by suppliers. It has few costs and security is not required.

FACTORING

If a business makes sales on credit, it will have to collect payment from its debtors at some stage. Until that point, it will have to finance those debtors, either through trade credit, an overdraft, or its own capital. The costs of this finance can be very high and many small businesses will be hard up against their limits in terms of their overdraft and the amount and period of trade credit taken.

In Chapter 8 we discussed the importance of the management of debtors. Entities offer discounts for early payment as one strategy to manage the amounts owing by debtors. Another strategy used by some entities to reduce the money tied up in debtors is to approach a factoring company. A factoring company is a finance company which specialises in providing a service for the collection of payments from debtors.

Essentially, the way the system works is that the factoring organisation assesses the firm's debtors, in terms of risk and collectability. It then agrees to collect the money due on behalf of the business concerned. Once an agreement has been reached, the factoring company pays the business in respect of the invoices for the month virtually straight away. It is then the factoring organisation's responsibility to collect from the debtors as soon as possible. In this form of finance, the security provided by the business is in the form of the debts being collected. The factoring company charges for the service in the form of interest that is based on the finance provided, and by a fee for managing the collection of the debts. This form of finance is therefore more expensive than trade credit, but can be useful as it allows the business to concentrate on production and sales, and it improves the cash flow. Factoring, however, is not available to all industries. In some cases this is because it is inappropriate – as is the case in most retailing operations – while in others the factoring companies are reluctant to be involved because of a lack of clear legal definitions.

KEY CONCEPT 10.3

FACTORING

Factoring provides short-term finance. Costs include an interest charge and a debt management charge. Finance is secured on the debtors and is provided by a finance company specialising in factoring. The finance company collects payment from the debtors.

BANK OVERDRAFTS

Banks and other types of financial institutions provide short-term finance for working capital, either in the form of short-term loans or, more commonly, in the form of an overdraft. The difference is that a loan is for a fixed period of time and interest is charged on the full amount of the loan, less any agreed repayments, for that period. An overdraft, by contrast, is a facility that can be used as and when required and interest is only charged when it is used. Thus, if a business knows that it needs money for a fixed period of time then a bank loan may be appropriate. On the other hand, if the finance is only required to meet occasional short-term cash flow needs, then an overdraft would be more suitable. We discuss loans in more detail under the heading of medium-term finance.

Although many businesses use overdrafts as a semi-permanent source of finance, this is not how the banks would like to see this form of finance used. Bank managers like to see a business bank account, on which an overdraft facility has been provided, 'swinging' between having money in the bank account and using the overdraft. They do not see an overdraft as a form of permanent working capital.

A bank overdraft carries with it a charge in the form of interest and, often, a fee for setting up the facility. The bank may also charge an annual fee for the overdraft facility. As far as the interest is concerned, the rate charged is related to the risk involved and the market rates of interest for that size of business. In general, the more risk involved, the higher the rate of interest. Because they operate in a volatile market, small firms tend to be charged higher rates of interest than large firms.

In addition, banks normally require security, which can take various forms. In the case of a small business, the security could be a charge on the assets of the business. In many cases, however, the property is already subject to a charge as it is mortgaged. In these situations the bank may take a second charge on the property, or on the owner's home or homes if more than one person is involved. Alternatively, or in addition, the bank may require personal guarantees from the owner or, in the case of a limited company, the directors.

For larger companies, the security may be a fixed charge on certain assets, or a floating charge on all the assets. In the case of very large companies, the risk involved is lower and the competition between the providers of finance is greater. Because of this competition, overdrafts tend to be cheaper and more accessible for large companies; and security is less of a factor.

KEY CONCEPT 10.4

BANK OVERDRAFT

Bank overdrafts provide finance when it is needed to meet short-term cash flow needs. Costs include interest and, often, a set-up charge. In general, some form of security will be required – usually a fixed charge on certain assets or a floating charge on all assets.

Review exercise 2

What are the forms of short-term finance discussed in this chapter?

Medium-term finance

Short-term sources of finance impose certain restrictions on borrowers because the funds must be repaid reasonably quickly, otherwise the borrower risks being forced into liquidation by disgruntled creditors. Because of this, there usually is a need to access sources of finance for more medium-term or long-term, permanent, arrangements. While there is no strict definition, medium-term finance can be thought of as being for periods from one to 10 years. Medium-term finance can be used for plant and equipment, and other asset classes with useful lives of 10 years or less. There are a number of sources of medium-term finance for a business: we limit our discussion to medium-term loans, leases and hire-purchase.

Explain what is meant by medium-term sources of finance such as loans, hire-purchase and leases

LOANS

As we pointed out, bank loans are an alternative to overdraft finance for short-term finance requirements. In general, loans should only be used when finance is required for a known period of time. Ideally, that period should relate to the life of the asset or the purpose for which the finance is to be used. Loans can be obtained for short-term, medium-term or long-term finance. Compared to an overdraft facility, which can be used as and when needed, a loan is more structured and fixed. Repayment of the loan is negotiated at the time the loan is taken out, and is generally at fixed intervals. Loans are often secured in the same way as overdrafts and, if the repayment conditions are not met, the lender will take action to recover the outstanding amount.

Bank loans are often granted for a specified purpose and limitations may be imposed regarding the use of the loan and the raising of other finance while the loan is outstanding. Unlike an overdraft, the cost of this form of finance is known in advance as interest accrues from the time the business borrows the money – irrespective of the fact that it may not use it straight away. As with other forms of finance discussed so far, the rate of interest charged and the availability of this source of finance is dependent upon the size of the business and the lender's assessment of the risk involved. Thus, in general, the larger and more diversified a business, the easier it will be for it to access this form of finance.

KEY CONCEPT 10.5

LOANS

Loans are generally made for a fixed purpose and a fixed period of time. They have set repayment dates and costs include interest and set-up fees. They are normally secured on assets.

HIRE-PURCHASE

An alternative way of financing the acquisition of an asset is through the use of hire-purchase. Under a hire-purchase agreement, a finance company buys the asset and hires it to the business. Thus, a business can acquire the asset and use it, even though it has not yet paid for it in full. The finance company owns the asset during the period of the hire-purchase agreement.

The hirer has the right to use the asset and carries all the risks associated with using that asset. Thus, for example, if a car is purchased on hire purchase, the hirer would be responsible for all the repairs and costs associated with the use of the car in the same way as if they had bought the car directly. The ownership of the asset is transferred to the hirer at the end of the period of the hire-purchase agreement. A normal hire-purchase agreement consists of a deposit and a set number of payments over a number of years.

This type of finance can only be used when a specific asset is purchased; that is, the finance is for a specified asset purchase and the amount borrowed is limited by the price of the asset. Hire-purchase finance, therefore, cannot be directly used for financing working capital requirements or for any other purpose. The hire-purchase company actually pays the supplier of the asset directly and the asset belongs to the hire-purchase company. If repayments are not made in accordance with the hire-purchase agreement, the hire-purchase company has the right to repossess its property. The money borrowed is repaid by monthly instalments which include both a repayment of the capital borrowed and a charge for interest. The rate of interest charged will be dependent upon the market rate of interest, but is likely to be higher than the interest on a bank loan.

KEY CONCEPT 10.6

HIRE-PURCHASE

Hire-purchase is for a fixed period of time. Costs are in the form of interest charges. Ownership of the asset remains with the provider of the finance until all instalments are paid.

Hire-purchase is available to all businesses and individuals, subject, of course, to the hire-purchase company being satisfied as to the creditworthiness of the person or business.

LEASING

A lease is an agreement between a lessor (i.e. the person who owns the asset) and a lessee (i.e. the person who uses the asset). It conveys the right to use that asset for a stated period of time in exchange for payment, but does not normally transfer ownership at the end of the lease period. Leases can vary from very short periods to very long periods. Leasing companies often provide leases tailored to the needs of an industry. For example, in the hospitality industry it is possible to obtain lease finance for the internal telephone system or even the complete furnishing of a hotel.

In general, the cost of leasing is similar to that of hire-purchase. The major difference between the two types of finance is that, in general, leases tend to be for longer periods of time and are frequently used as sources of finance for specialised assets. In essence, there are two distinct types of leases – operating leases and finance leases. An operating lease is the same, in reality, as renting the equipment, and usually applies to items such as photocopiers, computers and cars.

KEY CONCEPT 10.7

LEASING

Leases are for a fixed period of time; the costs are in the form of interest charges. Security is related to the asset in question.

The underlying economic substance of a finance lease, on the other hand, is equivalent to borrowing money from a finance company and using that money to buy an asset. These differences are reflected in the definitions given in Key concept 10.8.

KEY CONCEPT 10.8

TYPES OF LEASE

An operating lease:
A lease where the underlying substance of the transaction is a rental agreement.
A finance lease:
A lease where the underlying substance of the transaction is a financing arrangement.

The reason for emphasising the difference between the two types of lease is that they are accorded different treatment in the accounts.

Operating leases present few accounting problems. The lessee records a lease payment as a decrease in cash and an increase in expenses. No asset or liability, other than accrual at year-end for the amount of the yearly lease payment owing as at balance date, is recorded.

The most contentious issue has been whether certain leases which are non-cancellable should result in the recognition of an asset and a liability on the balance sheet of the lessee. This is illustrated in Case study 10.1.

CASE STUDY 10.1

	Company A $	Company B $
Assets		
Current assets	100 000	100 000
Non-current assets	1 900 000	1 400 000
Total assets	2 000 000	1 500 000
Liabilities		
Current liabilities	500 000	500 000
Non-current liabilities	500 000	–
Total liabilities	1 000 000	500 000
Net assets	1 000 000	1 000 000
Shareholders' equity		
Paid up capital	500 000	500 000
Retained profits	500 000	500 000
	1 000 000	1 000 000

COMMENTARY

The only difference between the balance sheets of Company A and Company B is $500 000 in non-current assets and $500 000 in non-current liabilities. A has just borrowed $500 000 from the bank over a period of 10 years. It has purchased an item of plant which has an estimated life of 10 years with a zero residual value. B has just signed a lease agreement to acquire the use of an identical item of plant to that purchased by A. The lease agreement is for 10 years and is non-cancellable by either party. Given these facts, should the balance sheets of A and B be any different? In the balance sheet, A shows total liabilities to shareholders' equity of 100 per cent. However, for B this ratio is only 50 per cent. This suggests that B is less risky than A, but is this a fair conclusion?

Case study 10.1 demonstrates that the absence of information about the lease arrangements in the case of B could lead to an incorrect assessment of the relative risk positions of A and B. The fact that lease arrangements were traditionally not captured on the lessee's balance sheet was pushed by leasing companies as a major advantage of leasing. This advantage is normally referred to as off-balance-sheet financing. As the name implies, it refers to a method whereby an entity obtains funds but the method used does not result in the recognition of a liability on the balance sheet. Prior to the release of accounting standards on leases, entities could acquire the use of an asset via a finance lease, but were not required to recognise the liability to pay the lessor.

In response to the problem of leases, the accounting profession in Australia released AASB 1008 *Accounting for Leases* and the IASB issued IAS 17 *Leases*. With the adoption of IFRSs in Australia, the relevant standard is now AASB 117 *Leases*. This Standard requires a lessee to record a finance lease as an asset and a liability at the fair value of the leased property or, if lower, the present value of the minimum lease payments. The present value of the lease payments, when the residual value is guaranteed by the lessee, equates with the fair value of the asset at the inception of the lease. A finance lease is defined (in paragraph 4 of AASB 117) as one which:

> transfers substantially all the risks and rewards incident to ownership of an asset. Title may or may not eventually be transferred.

AASB 117 also provides criteria to assist in deciding whether substantially all the risks and rewards have been transferred from lessor to lessee. A lease will normally be a finance lease when the lease is non-cancellable and:

1 the term of the lease is for a major portion of the expected useful life of the asset being leased

or

2 the present value of the minimum lease payments amounts to at least substantially all of the fair value of the lease asset at inception of the lease

or

3 the lease transfers ownership to the lessee at the end of the lease or the lessee can purchase the asset for a bargain price.

The asset recorded in the lessee's accounts is then amortised or depreciated to the income statement over a period equal to either the lease period or the asset's useful life. Each lease payment incorporates a principal and interest component; the interest component is treated as an expense. The liability is systematically reduced in each period by the principal component of each lease payment. Therefore, each lease payment is similar to the loan repayment that A would be required to make to the bank in Case study 10.1.

Review exercise 3

What are the differences between an operating lease and a finance lease?

Long-term finance

In the previous two sections, we discussed short-term and medium-term sources of finance. We noted that short-term sources of finance are suitable for financing investments in debtors, inventories and other types of current assets. Medium-term finance is for periods from one to 10 years, and is suitable for financing investments in plant and equipment, and other asset classes with useful lives of 10 years or less. When an entity wants to invest in long-term asset classes, like land and buildings, or permanently finance the excess of current assets over current liabilities, it should use long-term sources of finance.

LO 4

Explain what is meant by long-term sources of debt finance such as long-term loans and debentures

Long-term sources of finance are generally those with maturity periods of more than one year, and normally more than 10 years. The number of alternative sources of long-term finance available is, to some extent, dependent on the type of organisation involved. We start our discussion with debt finance, such as long-term loans, which are more generally available, and then discuss equity finance. The latter discussion will be subdivided in terms of organisation types – that is, sole proprietorships, partnerships and companies – as these affect the type of equity finance available.

WORKING CAPITAL

We have previously mentioned that working capital is one of the major sources of finance for current assets (i.e. it is a short-term source of finance). However, in many entities, the amount of current assets exceeds the current liabilities, and this excess is referred to as working capital. The working capital must be financed by either medium- or long-term finance. Where it is likely that the entity will always have positive working capital, it should consider using long-term finance to fund this investment.

DEBT FINANCE

This is the term given to any source of long-term finance that is not equity finance. Often, debt finance is seen exclusively as long-term interest-bearing finance. This is, in fact, a misconception, as all the finance we have discussed so far has been debt finance. We look at two broad categories of long-term debt finance: long-term loans, which are available to all organisations, and debentures, which tend to be used by incorporated businesses.

Long-term loans

As we have said, loans can be used for short-term, medium-term or long-term finance. Interest rates are likely to be different for different loan periods as these will need to be adjusted to take into account the higher risk associated with lending money for a longer period of time. Long-term loans are often for a specific purpose, such as the purchase of property, and the time period is affected by the life of the asset, the repayments required and the willingness of the lender to lend money. For many small businesses, these loans often take the form of a commercial mortgage on property. As is the case with all the other types of finance we have discussed, the availability of this source of finance is also heavily dependent upon the lender's assessment of the creditworthiness of the prospective borrower.

In the case of large companies, international groups and, in particular, multinationals, there is also the opportunity to raise funds from other markets around the world.

Debentures

Debentures refer to particular types of long-term loans to limited companies. They basically mean the same thing and are essentially long-term loan finance. The main difference between debentures and long-term loans is that interest tends to be at a fixed rate and repayment tends to be at a fixed point in time, rather than over the period of the loan as would be the case for a commercial mortgage or other long-term loan. Debentures are issued by the company raising the finance and can usually be traded on what are known as secondary markets. The price at which they can be sold and bought on the secondary market will not be the same as the price at which they were issued. This variation is related to changes in interest rates over time. In virtually all debenture deeds, there is a right to repayment or appointment of a receiver if interest is not paid when due. The cost of this type of finance is similar to that for long-term loans and is affected by the market rate of interest, the security available and the risk involved. For this reason, they are more commonly seen in the accounts of larger companies.

Review exercise 4
Why is it important to properly fund working capital?

KEY CONCEPT 10.9

DEBT FINANCE – LONG TERM
Long-term debt finance is generally for a fixed period of time and interest rates can be higher than for short- or medium-term finance.

EQUITY FINANCE
The other major source of long-term finance is equity finance, and here we need to look at organisational types, as this can have a major effect on both the type and the amount of equity finance available.

5

Explain what is meant by equity finance and how it varies according to the type of business organisation

Sole proprietorships
In the case of a sole proprietorship, as we have seen, the only sources of equity finance are those supplied by the owner, and the retained profits. In many small businesses, the amount of funds that the owner has available to put into the business is limited. This means that the only source of equity finance is retained profits. In a fast-growing business it is unlikely that there will be sufficient retained profits to finance expansion. As such, sole proprietorships, in common with many small businesses, become very reliant on debt finance and, as we see, this exposes them to more risk, as a downturn in the market, or an increase in interest rates, could have a dramatic impact on their ability to service the debt. Unlike debt finance, equity finance has no limitations in terms of the use to which it is put.

Partnerships
Partnerships, as the name implies, are organisations that are owned, and often managed, by a number of individuals. They are most common among professionals, and so we see doctors, dentists, lawyers, architects and, of course, accountants working in partnerships. In essence, the sources of equity finance for partnerships are the same as for sole proprietorships; that is, money contributed by the owners and retained profits. There are, of course, more people involved, so more equity can be raised through contributions by the owners.

Partnerships are governed by the legislation contained in Partnership Acts, and by case law. In general, the main difference between partnerships and sole proprietorships is that, in a partnership, the partners are jointly and severally liable. This means that if a partner cannot pay his or her share of the debts, the other partners must pay. The other important difference is related to the division of profits; these must be divided among the partners in accordance with the partnership agreement.

We look at the subject of partnerships in more detail in Chapter 11. For our purposes here, we can view partnerships as having the same sources of equity finance as sole proprietorships. The only difference is that they are likely to have access to a greater supply of funds. In addition, there may be differences in relation to the availability of retained profits as some partners may leave more profits in the business than others. This will, of course, depend upon the individual partner's requirements for funds.

Limited companies

Limited companies have the advantage, from an investor's point of view, that the liability of the owners is limited to the amount they have invested in the company. As with partnerships and sole proprietorships, the major source of equity comes from the owners. However, in the case of limited companies, this is through the issue of ordinary shares.

Ordinary shares

In the case of a company, the amounts in shareholders' equity represent the shareholders' interest in the company. Some amounts have been directly contributed by the shareholders when they subscribe to shares issued by the company. This is described as issued and paid-up capital. The other amounts represent retained or undistributed profits and various reserves. Reserves can be created in a number of ways; however, one element common to all reserves is that there is *no cash* in them. Cash is an asset and appears in the current assets section of the balance sheet.

You should now study the Woodside financial statements. Look at the balance sheet and then turn to Note 5. Note 5 discloses that the company has issued 666 666 667 shares, with a collective value of $706 491 000. This is the book value of the share capital and does not represent the market value. The market value is obtained from the price of the shares on a stock exchange. The balance sheet also shows treasury shares as (148 891). This represents the amount of shares the company has repurchased from its shareholders.

The Woodside financial statements show retained profits as at 30 June 2005 of $2 676 760 000.

As with any other form of organisation, the other main source of equity capital is retained profits. Unlike a sole proprietorship or partnership, a company distributes its profits by way of dividends. The directors decide on the amount of dividend to be paid and the timing of the dividends, and until a dividend is declared by the directors, the shareholders have no *prima facie* right to a dividend. Dividends can be paid during the year and/or at the end of the year. If they are paid during the year they are referred to as interim dividends and the dividend at the end of the year is referred to as the final dividend. Dividends are treated differently from drawings which, as we have seen, are normally deducted from the owners' equity. These differences will be looked at in more detail in Chapter 11.

A company has the advantage over a sole proprietorship or a partnership in that it can issue shares to whomever it wishes in whatever proportions it wishes. The shareholders do not have to take part in the management of the company, and in most large companies the vast majority of shareholders play virtually no part in the management of the company. They merely invest their money and take the risk that they will get better returns, in the form of their share of the profits, than they would by investing in fixed interest investments. Ultimately, all the profits belong to the shareholders, so if they do not get their share of the profits in the form of dividends, because the profits are retained in the company, their share of the profits and the future profits is reflected in the price at which they could sell their shares.

Preference shares

Apart from ordinary shares, a company can also issue preference shares. Unlike ordinary shares, a preference share normally has a fixed dividend and, even if more profits are made, the preference dividend remains the same. In addition, they normally carry a right to preference in the order of payment in the event of the company going into liquidation. They are therefore less risky than ordinary shares and appeal to a different sort of investor.

Explain the criteria for classifying securities as either debt or equity, and apply this to different types of preference shares

The decision as to whether preference shares should be classified as equity or debt depends on the particular type of preference shares in question, and the rights attached to them. Remember that the definition of a liability includes a present obligation to sacrifice future economic benefits, so the existence of a present obligation is critical in this decision. The distinction between debt and equity can be clarified further by referring to the principle of substance over form. The use of the substance-over-form approach is identified in the AASB *Framework* as essential. It means that a financial instrument is not classified as an equity instrument merely because it is called a preference share or a subordinated share or, indeed, any type of share! It is the substance of the financial instrument which will determine whether it should be classified as debt or equity. This is important given the increased number of hybrid securities that are issued into the market as alluded to in Case study 10.2.

To illustrate the application of the substance-over-form principle, we examine three types of financial instruments with different characteristics:

- *Redeemable preference share with a fixed redemption date*
  This imposes a contractual obligation on the issuer to redeem the preference share at the maturity date. Such an obligation is no different to that which exists with a loan; therefore, the preference share meets the definition of a financial liability and should be presented in the liability section in the balance sheet.

- *Redeemable preference share which is redeemable on request, by the holder*
  In this case, the redemption of the share is dependent on the holder and AASB 132 *Financial Instruments: Disclosure and Presentation* requires such a share to be classified as a financial liability.

- *Redeemable preference share which is redeemable at the discretion of the issuer*
  This share would not meet the definition of a financial liability because there is no present obligation for the issuer to redeem the shares. The issuer controls when, and indeed if, redemption will take place. However, where the issuer has formally informed the holders of such shares of its intention to redeem, the shares should be classified as debt and included in financial liabilities.

Preference shares may also carry a right to dividends on a cumulative basis, meaning that, if the directors do not pay any dividends in a particular year, the preference shareholders will have a right to be paid that year's dividend and any others that have not been paid, before the ordinary shareholders can be paid any dividend. Some preference shares are participating preference shares, whereby they get a share of profits if the profit is over a certain figure.

The adoption of IFRSs in Australia means that there will need to be some reclassification of securities due to the strict definition of a financial liability under IFRS. If there is any termination or end date in a security contract then, under IFRS, it is generally classified as debt. This has been the cause of a number of concerns for Australian reporting entities. For example, many companies in Australia have issued resetting preference shares which often provide the holder with the right to convert the preference share into ordinary shares of the issuer. Most companies classified such shares as equity but, with the adoption of IFRSs, many have had to reclassify such shares as debt.

KEY CONCEPT 10.10

EQUITY FINANCE

This is long-term permanent finance and comes from three main sources: contributed capital, reserves and retained profits.

CASE STUDY 10.2

PANIC WILL RUIN GOOD PROSPECTS
John Shanahan

How well do bankers and analysts understand the effect that introducing international financial reporting standards (IFRS) will have on Australian companies? Can we trust them to have a measured and well-informed reaction to the inevitable big asset write-offs that companies will have to make under the new accounting regime, and deal promptly and rationally when gearing blows out and interest ratios drop sharply?

My guess is no. Unless we take pre-emptive action, I expect analysts to panic and make sell recommendations, and bankers to call in their loans. It's a disaster that is only seven months away for most Australian companies that have to adopt IFRS from January 1, 2005 – if the Australian Accounting Standards Board (AASB) achieves its target. Although companies won't

report under the new rules until June 2006, they must provide comparative figures from July 1, 2004, and so must keep two sets of books for the 2005 year. Australia will adopt IFRS word-for-word, including options the AASB doesn't like or disagrees with. For example, the AASB is highly critical of the proposed international standard on intangibles, which will remove some $40 billion from Australian balance sheets.

The new standard on financial instruments is also controversial. For years, Qantas has shown deferred losses on some hedges as receivables. The new rules treat these as negative equity rather than as assets. Australian balance sheets are awash with 'quasi-equity', or debt masquerading as equity. Westpac calls it 'quasi-equity', others 'resetting preference shares', 'investment notes' ▯▯▶

or 'hybrid equity'. The new rules reclassify it as debt. This will reduce equity and increase debt, increasing the debt-to-equity ratio, or gearing.

At the moment, distributions on the 'equity' are treated as dividends, with no profit effect. In future, the distributions will be treated as interest, and higher interest expenses mean lower profits. Bankers and analysts examine interest coverage: how many times profit covers the interest. With lower profit and higher interest, the interest coverage falls. With asset values falling, gearing blowing out and interest coverage dropping, alarm bells will start ringing with analysts and continuous disclosure obligations will be triggered. Reduced assets and higher liabilities – rising debt – may result in a breach of borrowing covenants and thin-capitalisation rules. Will the Australian Taxation Office and banks stand idly by in this situation?

The reality is that nothing has changed as far as these companies' performance is concerned. Companies are exactly as they were: same management, same structure, same prospects. What has changed is the accounting rules. What was a good prospect yesterday should not become bad just because accountants measure it differently. Will bankers and analysts see this purely as a cosmetic change – it's the same, it just appears differently – or will they panic?

The sensible answer is to have a global rewrite of borrowing covenants and ratio guidelines to reflect the new rules. If a company is a good economic proposition, new accounting rules should not endanger it.

Business Review Weekly, 3 November 2003
© 2003 Copyright John Fairfax Holdings Limited. www.brw.com.au Not available for re-distribution.

COMMENTARY

The article discusses the impact on gearing ratios with the adoption of IFRSs in Australia. Securities like resetting preference shares will be reclassified from equity to debt and, therefore, gearing (debt) ratios will increase. John Shanahan expresses a concern that if analysts don't properly understand the change they will make a sell recommendation, thus driving the share price down.

Review exercise 5

Preference shares, rather than ordinary shares, are often favoured by retired people. Why do you think this is?

Financing structures and financial risk

The mix of debt finance and equity finance is known as gearing, or leverage, and it affects the financial risk of an entity. Basically, the more reliant a business is on debt finance, that is, the more highly geared, the greater the risk. The risk we are referring to here is, that if interest rates go up or the profit margin comes down, the entity will not be able to pay the interest or repayments due on its debt finance. There are, of course, advantages to being highly geared as well as disadvantages, as Example 10.1 illustrates.

LO 7

Explain what is meant by gearing, and the effect this can have on returns to shareholders in a company

Example 10.1: Two companies

Ellenmere has equity capital consisting of 20 000 ordinary shares of $1 each. It has retained profits of $10 000 and $40 000 in loans on which interest at 3 per cent above bank base rate (which currently stands at 12 per cent) is due.

Roseview has equity capital consisting of 40 000 ordinary shares of $1 each. It has retained profits of $10 000 and $20 000 in loans on which interest at 3 per cent above bank base rate, that is, 15 per cent, is due.

Situation 1

Both companies make sales of $100 000, and their net profit before interest is 10 per cent on sales.
The income statements for the two companies would be as shown below:

	Ellenmere	Roseview
	$	$
Sales	100 000	100 000
Costs	90 000	90 000
Net profit	10 000	10 000
Interest	6 000	3 000
Available for equity shares	4 000	7 000
Profit per share	0.20	0.17

The profit per share, which is normally referred to as the earnings per share, is arrived at by dividing the profit by the number of shares on issue. Thus, for Ellenmere, the profit of $4000 is divided by 20 000 shares to arrive at the profit per share of 20 cents. The ordinary shareholders of Ellenmere are getting a better return (20 cents per share) than the shareholders of Roseview (17 cents per share). This is despite the fact that both companies have the same sales, costs and net profit. The differences arise as a result of the financing structure, its effect on the interest charges and the remaining profit after interest.

Situation 2 – increased costs

In this situation, instead of making a net profit before interest of 10 per cent of sales, the companies find that they can only make 8 per cent.
In this case, the income statements of the two companies would be as follows.

	Ellenmere	Roseview
	$	$
Sales	100 000	100 000
Costs	92 000	92 000
Net profit	8 000	8 000
Interest	6 000	3 000
Available for equity shares	2 000	5 000
Profit per share	0.10	0.13

The profit margin of both businesses has fallen by the same amount. As a result, the profit available for the equity shares has dropped in both cases. However, the effect on the profit per share is more dramatic in the case of Ellenmere than it is in the case of Roseview, due, once again, to the effects of the financing structure. Thus, although in Situation 1 it looked as though Ellenmere had the better financing structure, we find from a shareholder's point of view that it is more vulnerable to a reduction in the profit margin than Roseview.

Situation 3 – increased interest rates

In this situation, the facts are the same as in Situation 2 above; that is, the net profit before interest is 8 per cent on the sales. However, in addition, the bank base rate moves to 13 per cent and the interest on the loans, therefore, moves up to 16 per cent.

In this case, the income statements of the two companies would be as follows.

	Ellenmere	Roseview
	$	$
Sales	100 000	100 000
Costs	92 000	92 000
Net profit	8 000	8 000
Interest	6 400	3 200
Available for equity shares	1 600	4 800
Profit per share	0.08	0.12

Once again, both businesses are affected by the change in circumstances. However, the effect of the rise in interest rates is greater, in terms of the return to the shareholders, in Ellenmere than it is in Roseview.

EFFECTS OF HIGH GEARING

Example 10.1 illustrates the effects of high gearing, which are to increase the returns to shareholders but, at the same time, make them more vulnerable to decreases in the profit margin. In addition, their returns are also affected more by increases in interest rates than are those of a low-geared company.

On the other hand, a fall in interest rates is more beneficial to the shareholders of a highly geared company. There is therefore a trade-off between risk and return.

It is worth mentioning that the lower the share of the business that is financed by equity, the more difficult it is to raise debt finance. Banks will often include clauses in debt contracts which impose penalties on borrowers if the proportion of debt to equity increases beyond a specified level. Such clauses mean that decisions on how much profit to retain, whether to revalue land and buildings, and so on, can have a dramatic effect on a company's ability to raise finance.

Review exercise 6

What are the advantages and disadvantages of being highly geared?

CASE STUDY 10.3

BHP STEEL'S GEARING UNDER 20% 'SENSATIONAL'
by Ian Porter

BHP BILLITON has surprised analysts by establishing a balance sheet that will give its BHP Steel spin-off a gearing ratio below 20 per cent.

The balance sheet will be much stronger than that drawn up for the spin-off of OneSteel in 2000, giving BHP Steel a financial stability and flexibility the former long-products division never had.

'I think it is sensational there will be so little debt in it,' one analyst said last night.

The numbers being circulated in the market indicate that BHP Steel will have a gearing ratio of less than 20 per cent, which, the analyst said, would make the shares investment-grade securities.

The estimates suggest debt will be between $700 million and $750 million on the day BHP Steel is spun off to BHP Billiton shareholders and that cash on hand will range between $100 million and $150 million.

This will give a net debt of $600 million to $650 million and a gearing ratio (net debt to net debt plus equity) of less than 20 per cent.

That will be less than half the 42 per cent OneSteel was saddled with on its spin-out in 2000, and under even the 26 per cent ratio boasted by the world's largest steel maker, Posco of Korea.

What is not clear at present is whether these estimates are after any securitisation of receivables (debt factoring), which is a technique used widely throughout the steel industry.

For instance, at last balance date, Smorgon Steel reported receivables of $279 million, but a note to the accounts showed that this was after the securitisation of $195 million of receivables.

'It's another way of borrowing money,' the analyst said. 'You do it if the customer who owes you money has a better credit rating than you do, which gives the banks more comfort.'

The analyst said the gearing ratio had to be under 20 per cent to achieve investment grade at this time because 'banks are really gun-shy at the moment, particularly in steel. Look what's happening globally.'

However, it also gave the company some extra borrowing capacity, the analyst said.

Earlier this year, BHP Steel president Kirby Adams reported that the company had broken off talks with Amatek about the possible acquisition of the Stramit steel roofing and building products company.

A strong balance sheet may well allow Mr Adams and BHP Steel chairman Graham Kraehe to reopen talks, with the housing boom expected to ease.

The reporter holds BHP Billiton shares.

The Age, 12 April 2002

COMMENTARY

The article discusses the gearing ratio for BHP Steel and indicates that the aim is to have a ratio of 20 per cent. This means that for every $1 of net debt and equity, the net debt accounts for only 20 cents. The article suggests this would place BHP Steel in a strong position and allow it to consider possible acquisitions like Stramit Steel as it should be able to raise debt at a reasonable cost.

SUMMARY

LEARNING OBJECTIVE 1
Discuss the concept of matching the type of finance with the purpose for which it is to be used
The finance that is used, and the period of that finance, should be matched to the period for which it is required and the purpose for which it is to be used.

LEARNING OBJECTIVE 2
Explain what is meant by short-term sources of finance such as bank overdrafts, trade credit and factoring
Conventionally, short-term finance is seen as finance for a period of less than one year. It should be used to finance short-term capital requirements, such as working capital requirements.

Trade credit
Trade credit is a form of short-term finance provided to a business by its suppliers. It has few costs and security is not required.

Factoring
Factoring provides short-term finance. Costs include an interest charge and a debt management charge. Finance is secured on the debtors and provided by a finance company specialising in factoring. The finance company collects payment from the debtors.

Bank overdrafts
A bank overdraft provides finance when it is needed to meet short-term cash flow needs. Costs include interest and, often, a set-up charge. In general, some form of security will be required – usually a fixed charge on certain assets or a floating charge on all assets.

LEARNING OBJECTIVE 3
Explain what is meant by medium-term sources of finance such as loans, hire-purchase and leases
We have used medium-term finance to refer to finance for periods between one and 10 years.

Loans
Loans are generally made for a fixed purpose and a fixed period of time. They have set repayment dates, and costs include interest and set-up fees. They are normally secured on assets.

Hire-purchase
Hire-purchase is for a fixed period of time. Costs are in the form of interest charges. Ownership of the asset remains with the provider of the finance until all instalments are paid.

Leases
Leases are for a fixed period of time; the costs are in the form of interest charges. Security is related to the asset in question.

Types of leases
An operating lease: A lease where the underlying substance of the transaction is a rental agreement.
A finance lease: A lease where the underlying substance of the transaction is a financing arrangement.

LEARNING OBJECTIVE 4
Explain what is meant by long-term sources of debt finance such as long-term loans and debentures
Long-term finance is generally for periods of 10 years or more.

Debenture bonds are a security issued to raise funds for the issuer. The holder is entitled to receive interest and the face value of the bond at maturity.

Long-term loans are generally for a fixed period of time and interest rates can be higher than for short- or medium-term finance.

LEARNING OBJECTIVE 5

Explain what is meant by equity finance and how it varies according to the type of business organisation

The main source of equity finance is from ordinary shareholders. Equity finance is long-term permanent finance and comes from three main sources: contributed capital, reserves and retained profits.

Equity providers gain returns from dividends and price appreciation.

LEARNING OBJECTIVE 6

Explain the criteria for classifying securities as either debt or equity, and apply this to different types of preference shares.

The definition of a liability includes a present obligation to sacrifice future economic benefits, so the existence of a present obligation is critical in deciding if a security is a debt or equity. The distinction between debt and equity is also assisted by reference to the principle of substance over form. The use of the substance-over-form approach is identified in the AASB *Framework* as essential.

- Redeemable preference shares with a fixed redemption date – classified as debt
- Redeemable preference shares which are redeemable on request, by the holder –classified as debt
- Redeemable preference shares which are redeemable at the discretion of the issuer – classified as equity

LEARNING OBJECTIVE 7

Explain what is meant by gearing, and the effect this can have on returns to shareholders in a company

'Gearing' is the term used to describe the use of debt. Example 10.1 illustrates the effects of high gearing, which include increasing the returns to shareholders while, at the same time, making them more vulnerable to decreases in the profit margin. In addition, the returns of shareholders in a high-geared company are also affected more by increases in interest rates than are those of a low-geared company. In contrast, a fall in interest rates is more beneficial to the shareholders of a highly-geared company. There is, therefore, a trade-off between risk and return.

REFERENCES

Australian Accounting Standards Board. AASB 117 *Leases*, July, 2004.
Australian Accounting Standards Board. AASB 132 *Financial Instruments: Presentation*, September, 2005.

FURTHER READING

Peirson, G., Bird, R., Easton, S. & Howard, P., 2001. *Business Finance,* 8th edn, McGraw-Hill.

REVIEW QUESTIONS

1   What are the main differences between equity finance and debt finance?
2   What are the differences between drawings and dividends?
3   What does the term 'highly geared' refer to?

4 Which types of short-term finance require a business to provide some form of security?

5 What form of security is required for each of the forms of short-term finance discussed in this chapter?

6 What is a lease? Give an example.

7 Explain what is meant by equity finance and how it varies according to the type of business organisation using it.

8 Explain what is meant by the term 'factoring'.

9 What information is a bank likely to require before granting an overdraft to a business?

10 How does a hire-purchase agreement differ from a lease?

11 What is a debenture?

PROBLEMS FOR DISCUSSION AND ANALYSIS

1 Refer to the Woodside 2005 financial report in Appendix 1.
   a What are the total liabilities of the company in 2005?
   b What is the level of debt to total assets in 2005? In 2004?
   c What is the level of debt to equity in 2005? In 2004?

2 ABC Ltd wishes to acquire a new widget machine. The machine costs $30 000 and is expected to have a useful life of five years and no residual value. As it is short of liquid funds, the company has approached a finance broker for help. It is offered two alternatives:
   a a loan of $30 000 with an annual reducing-interest component of 20 per cent, the principal of the loan to be paid in equal annual instalments over five years at the same time the annual interest payments are made
   b a hire-purchase agreement that requires the company to pay a monthly instalment of $799 over five years.
   Given there are no other options available to the company, which proposition should it accept? Give reasons for your decision.

3 Winjet Ltd is a small coastal aircraft operator normally taking on charter work. In a bid to expand its business it wishes to purchase a second-hand Gulfstream jet for $10 000 000. Winjet does not have the funds to make a cash purchase and has approached a business broker to find the funds for the aircraft. The broker submits two alternatives:
   a a loan of $10 000 000 to be repaid over 10 equal annual repayments at the same time as the annual interest payments of 6 per cent are made on the capital sum
   b a hire-purchase agreement that requires Winjet to pay $398 000 per quarter over 10 years.
   Assuming that Winjet's only option is to use the broker, which of the two choices should the company favour? Give reasons for your decision.

4 Bettause Ltd, maker of plastic mouldings, wishes to expand its business and will need additional capital to do so. A bank has offered the following options:
   a an overdraft with an interest rate set at 4 per cent above bank rate (the present bank rate is 8 per cent)
   b a term loan with an annual interest rate of 12 per cent
   c a 50 per cent holding by the bank in the company, achieved through the company issuing shares to the bank in exchange for cash.
   Discuss the merits, or otherwise, of the three proposals.

5   Below is a brief balance sheet for ABC Ltd. You are a bank manager and ABC Ltd has approached you for a loan to expand its business. ABC Ltd makes chocolate goods and has sales of approximately $300 000 per annum. What questions need to be asked before the loan is given or refused?

ABC Ltd
Balance sheet as at 31 December 20X0

	$	$	$	$
Current assets				
Receivables		98 000		
Inventory		112 000		
Loan to supplier		50 000		
Total current assets			260 000	
Non-current assets				
Equipment	30 000			
Less Accumulated depreciation	(17 000)	13 000		
Vehicles	12 000			
Less Accumulated depreciation	(8 000)	4 000		
Total non-current assets			17 000	
Total assets				277 000
Current liabilities				
Creditors		33 000		
Taxation		5 000		
Bank overdraft		12 000		
Total current liabilities			50 000	
Total liabilities				50 000
Shareholders' equity				
Ordinary shares (88 000 shares @ $2.50)			220 000	
Retained profits			7 000	
Total shareholders' equity				227 000
Total liabilities and shareholders' equity				277 000

6   A friend has been to see the bank manager about borrowing some money to finance the acquisition of a new van and a new machine. The bank manager has said that, in view of the current financial structure of the company, the bank would not be prepared to provide funds unsecured. The latest balance sheet of the company is given below.

Balance sheet

	$	$	$	$
Current assets				
Inventory		36 000		
Cash		15 000		
Total current assets			51 000	
Non-current assets				
Equipment	60 000)			
Less Accumulated depreciation	(15 000)	45 000		
Vehicles	36 000)			
Less Accumulated depreciation	(12 000)	24 000		
Total non-current assets			69 000	
Total assets				120 000
Current liabilities				
Trade creditors		7 500		
Taxation		10 800		
Bank overdraft		12 900		
Total current liabilities			31 200	
Non-current liabilities				
Bank loan		25 000		
Total non-current liabilities			25 000	
Total liabilities				56 200
Shareholders' equity				
Ordinary shares		60 900		
Retained profits		2 900		
Total shareholders' equity				63 800
Total liabilities and shareholders' equity				120 000

a   Advise your friend what alternative sources of finance are available and which would be appropriate for the purpose of buying a van and a new machine.

b   Explain why, in your opinion, the bank manager was not prepared to lend unsecured.

7   Read the Australian Stock Exchange company announcement 'New listing statement in relation to working capital'. Discuss why the company would be requested by the ASX to give such a report. Why is working capital so important?

NEW LISTING STATEMENT IN RELATION TO WORKING CAPITAL

IN accordance with the requirements of the Australian Stock Exchange (ASX), we have been requested to provide a statement that ABB Grain Limited and its controlled entities (ABB Grain) have enough working capital to carry out its stated objectives. We have been engaged to provide an Investigating Accountant's Report for the Prospectus for ABB Grain in respect to its proposed listing on the Australian Stock Exchange. On the basis of the work we have completed as Investigating Accountant, we have not become aware of any matter that makes us believe that ABB Grain does not have enough working capital (or access to existing finance facilities to obtain further working capital) to carry out its stated objectives.

C. W. Dunsford
Arthur Andersen Chartered Accountants
Australian Stock Exchange Company Announcements, 19 July 2002
See p. xvi for © notice

8   In each of the cases below, decide whether the leases described are finance or operating leases for a lessee. Give reasons.

a

Motor vehicle leased for	3 years
Fair value (cost)	$10 000
Lease rental	$230 per month
Total lease payments	$8280
Estimated residual value	$6000 (60%)
Implicit interest rate	18%
Present value of minimum lease payments (no guaranteed residual)	$6500
Useful life	6 years
Useful life	50%
Present value of minimum lease payments	65%

b   Same particulars as above, except that this is the first time a motor vehicle has been leased. All previous vehicles have been purchased and sold three years later. (There is a union agreement that motor vehicles operated by employees must be no older than three years.)

Useful life	50% or 100%
Present value of minimum lease payments	65%

c   Same particulars as in (a), but there is a guaranteed residual value of $6000. The present value of minimum lease payments, therefore, is $10 000.

Useful life	50%
Present value of minimum lease payments	100%

d   Same particulars as in (a), but the lessee guarantees the lessor that he will make up any deficiency of the residual amount between $4000 and $6000. The maximum present value of minimum lease payments is $7700.

Useful life	50%
Present value of minimum lease payments	77%

e   As in (d), except that there is no guaranteed residual and the lessee can cancel (subject to conditions) at any time.

Useful life	50%
Present value of minimum lease payments	65%

Note to instructors: *The following problems are considered more suitable for use in MBA courses. However, undergraduate courses may also find them useful.*

9   Ben was planning to open a fish and chip shop. He has produced the following projections for the first year, based on his experience of this type of business and some careful research:

	$
Sales	36 000
Cost of 10-year lease	30 000
Refurbishment	3 000
Equipment	20 000
Rent	2 000
Electricity	900
Wages	8 000
Personal drawings	5 000

Ben estimates that the costs of fish and other purchases required to make the sales target of $36 000 will be $12 000. He says that the equipment will last for five years and have no residual value. He has $40 000 in savings but is reluctant to invest all of that amount. He has been offered a loan of $20 000 to help buy the lease, at an interest rate of 10 per cent per annum for the first year, with no repayments required during that year. After the first year, the rate will be 4 per cent above base rate. Base rate currently stands at 12 per cent. Alternatively, he can borrow money, using a bank overdraft at a rate of 17 per cent per annum.

a   Calculate what Ben's profit would be in the first year if he were to put in all his own money and use the bank overdraft to borrow anything else he needs.

Hint: The receipts and payments have to be looked at in terms of their regularity and their timing.

b   Calculate what Ben's profit would be in the first year, assuming he takes the loan.

c   Calculate what Ben's profit would be in the second year, assuming he does not take the loan and sales and costs are the same as the first year.

d   Calculate Ben's profit in the second year, assuming he takes the loan.

e   Ben has asked you to advise him on the choice between the two financing alternatives. How would you advise him, and what reasons would you give?

10 Read the article 'Calpine gets $2 billion of debt financing but must pledge nearly $4 billion in assets' and then answer the following questions:

a   What has the new debt done to the position of existing unsecured bondholders?

b   Discuss the reasons why a company would be prepared to incur $161 million in cancellation fees.

c   What is meant by refinancing risk and financial flexibility?

d   What would be the impact on Calpine if its credit rating was downgraded?

CALPINE GETS $2 BILLION OF DEBT FINANCING BUT MUST PLEDGE NEARLY $4 BILLION IN ASSETS

by Rebecca Smith

CALPINE CORP. obtained $2 billion worth of new debt financing, but on the condition it pledge nearly $4 billion in assets. Previously, it had said it was seeking $1 billion, and didn't anticipate securing borrowings with assets. The move underlines just how the power-plant operator and several other power companies have been affected by changes in energy markets in the past year. Electricity prices, at record highs in late 2000, have fallen sharply. Capital is tight. Concerns about debt levels have become intense as a result of sharply reduced power-company stock prices.

To see itself through turbulent times, Calpine, San Jose, Calif., isn't only raising new debt. It said yesterday it has restructured its turbine-delivery program, deferring or eliminating $3 billion of payments for equipment that otherwise would have come due this year and next. Calpine delayed delivery and payment on 81 General Electric Co. turbines originally slated for delivery between 2002 and 2005 at no additional cost. It also killed orders for 35 turbines, creating a pretax expense of $161 million, mostly in cancellation fees, that will be taken in the current quarter.

Chairman Peter Cartwright sought to put the best face on the steps. The company is 'doing what it takes to increase liquidity and enhance credit-worthiness while bringing new power-generation capacity on line when – and only when – power and capital-market conditions warrant,' he said.

As a result of the 'magnitude' of the collateral pledged, Fitch Ratings cut Calpine's credit rating for unsecured debt to double-B from double-B-plus. It remarked that Calpine's pledging of its equity in 10 power plants, as well as natural-gas reserves in North America, significantly reduced the pool of assets otherwise available to protect unsecured bondholders.

Standard & Poors put Calpine on CreditWatch with negative implications and warned that 'a downgrade is possible.' S&P said that while the $2 billion in commitments increases Calpine's liquidity, the arrangement adds interest expense, refinancing risk and limits financial flexibility. Calpine obtained $1.4 billion in commitments expiring May 2003 at a cost of London interbank offered rate plus two percentage points, and $600 million terminating in March 2004 at Libor plus 2.75 percentage points.

Nancy Stroker, a group managing director at Fitch, said her firm has downgraded the credit ratings of 60 companies across a broad spectrum of industries so far this year and upgraded only eight. She said it is an 'incredibly difficult credit environment'.

The Wall Street Journal, 13 March 2002

11 Ladner Pty Ltd (Leasing Brokers) is a small company with 24 employees which negotiates leasing arrangements with lessors. Its clients are small- to medium-sized businesses.

The managing director of Ladner, L. Murrish, had recently overheard, at a cocktail party, a discussion of the future prospects of leasing following the introduction of a statutory-approved Accounting Standard which requires increased disclosures of lease commitments by lessees. Concerned at what he heard at the party, Murrish invited the company accountant, A. Hill, and marketing manager, C. Raby, into the conference room to discuss the issue. The following dialogue occurred between these three.

Murrish:	This approved Accounting Standard I hear of requiring additional disclosures has me a little concerned about the industry's future prospects. How will leasing be affected by these mandatory requirements?
Raby:	Well, I am glad you have asked me that question. I am really concerned about the implications of the new requirements but I did not wish to worry you about them due to your recent poor health.
Murrish:	Forget that talk! Just level with me for once.
Raby:	All right! Look, our business is mainly in arranging finance leases. In the past, the lease costs associated with such leases were commonly left off the balance sheet. This is why leasing has become so popular over the last 20 years. In fact, I would go so far as to argue that this is the only reason why leasing has been a growth industry.
Murrish:	But surely there are other reasons, such as tax advantages, flexibility and lower costs in many cases, compared with alternative forms of finance.
Raby:	Oh yes! There are other advantages, but I believe that most of our clients leased in the past because they could keep large assets off their balance sheets, thus ensuring the apparent rate of return was higher. Of course, the commitments themselves were also not included among the liabilities, ensuring the apparent leverage level was lower. Lower leverage means . . .
Murrish:	That's enough! For a marketing manager, you are sounding a bit too pessimistic for my liking. I think finance leasing should continue to run at the same level because it's easy, quick, the price is usually right, the term of amortisation is generally the actual life of the equipment, and, very importantly, there's no other security required. We will just have to push these advantages much harder to generate the same volume of business.
Hill:	Just a moment! I think both of you have missed a very important point concerning the new disclosures. The Accounting Standard does not require those leases considered to be of an operating nature to be capitalised in the balance sheet. In other words, costs associated with operating leases may remain off the balance sheet.
Murrish:	Go on, please. This sounds interesting.
Hill:	Well, I think the company should seek out those lessors which package leases as operating leases. Operating leases are defined as those where substantially all of the risks and benefits incidental to ownership of the asset remain with the lessor. I believe a number of lessors are restructuring their leasing packages to get around the guidelines provided in the Accounting Standard. In fact, I saw an advertisement in this morning's newspaper which promoted a lease as being outside the capitalisation guidelines. We have conducted business with this lessor before and found it to be most satisfactory.
Murrish:	I am so pleased someone in the office remains up to date with trends in the industry. Now that we have a clear understanding of the issues, I want our marketing department to send out a letter to all our clients outlining the

following: 'The benefits associated with operating leases as opposed to a finance lease are now being recognised by firms as a way of assisting their balance sheet presentation due to their leverage and rate of return implications'.

Raby: Do you wish to add anything about those other advantages of leasing you mentioned earlier?

Murrish: Do you still want to be a marketing manager?

Required

a   Outline the advantages and disadvantages of leasing.

b   In your view, has Raby's argument been rightfully rejected by Murrish? Justify your opinion.

c   Is Hill's perception of changes in lease packaging by lessors supported by any available evidence?

d   How do you believe clients of Leasing Brokers would react upon receiving the letter, referred to, from the marketing department?

e   If a client of Leasing Brokers was a listed company with significant finance leases, how would you have expected the market to react to the company upon the day the accounting requirements of the Standard on leasing became known?

(Adapted from G. Carnegie, J. Gavens and R. Gibson, *Cases in Financial Accounting*, revised edn, Harcourt Brace & Company, 1991, Case 86.)

ETHICS CASE STUDY

Jack is finance director for the New Horizons Company. The company has had declining profits for the past two years, and is in serious trouble in the current year. With just two weeks before year-end, the company is set to report a loss. If this occurs, it will be in default of a loan contract with its major bank, which will result in the bank appointing an official manager to begin winding up the company. At the end of the previous year the bank had been persuaded to allow the company another year to trade out of its difficulties after reporting a small loss. This is not likely to happen this year if the company reports a larger loss.

Jack has developed the following plan: New Horizons will sell $1 million worth of goods for $2 million to Close Encounters Ltd, which is a company run by his brother-in-law. The $1 million profit on the sale will allow New Horizons to report a modest profit for the year. At the same time, a put option will be given to Close Encounters, giving that company the right to sell the goods back to New Horizons in three months for $2 100 000. The goods will actually remain in New Horizons' warehouse for the three months.

Discuss

a   how the transaction with Close Encounters should be recorded

b   whether the bank would still be able to appoint an official manager if New Horizons records the transaction as a sale and, therefore, reports a profit

c   whether Jack's plan is ethical.

ANSWERS TO REVIEW EXERCISES

1   It is important to match the type of finance with the purpose of raising that finance because this will provide the greatest benefit to the business, and the least risk. Companies should borrow short-term finance for short-term investments and long-term finance for long-term investments. For example, borrowing over the short-term for the purchase of land and buildings can be a mistake because the benefits from the land and buildings will flow to the business over the long term. Therefore, the loan would need to be renegotiated.

2   Trade credit – where the company benefits from buying goods on credit.
    Factoring – selling receivables to another company and obtaining cash now.
    Bank overdraft – short-term borrowing from a bank or other financial institution.

3   The essential differences between an operating lease and a financial lease are as follows. With an operating lease, the risks and rewards associated with ownership of the property remain with the lessor; with a finance lease, the risks and rewards of ownership move from lessor to lessee.

4   Working capital is the amount that is left when current liabilities are subtracted from current assets. In order to operate a business effectively, it is important to have adequate working capital. Many new businesses fail to properly plan for the working capital that is required to provide cash to pay bills, offer credit to customers and allow inventories to be held. It is important for businesses to have sufficient funding (whether it is equity or long-term debt) to ensure that the business can maintain its working capital at the required levels without getting into difficulties. Insufficient working capital can result in an inability to pay wages or creditors and can lead to the failure of an entity.

5   Preference shares normally offer a fixed rate of dividend and, therefore, meet the income needs of retired people. Ordinary shares do not provide for a fixed dividend.

6   The advantages of high gearing occur when the cost of interest is below the return on assets. Shareholders benefit when this is the case. Interest on debt is tax deductible while dividends are not.
    Disadvantages relate to the risk of highly-geared companies going bankrupt when interest rates increase. This happened to the Bond Corporation in the late 1980s.

FINAL ACCOUNTS, PARTNERSHIPS AND COMPANIES

11

LEARNING OBJECTIVES

At the end of this chapter, you should be able to:

1   discuss the use of debits and credits, and identify the relationship between the worksheet approach and the use of debits and credits

2   explain the role of journals, ledgers and a trial balance

3   identify three forms of business arrangement: a sole trader, a partnership and a company

4   identify the characteristics of a sole trader

5   explain the advantages and disadvantages of a partnership

6   explain the advantages and disadvantages of a company

7   identify the major differences between the financial statements of a company and a partnership or sole trader.

Introduction

The first part of this chapter has been included to assist readers who wish to continue with their studies using other textbooks, which are likely to use a more traditional approach for explaining accounting and its mechanics. It will also be helpful to readers who are familiar with that traditional approach as an aid to understanding how the exposition in this book relates to that in other texts. In the next part of the chapter we move on to look at the trial balance and the final adjustments that are required before final accounts are extracted from the worksheet. In the remainder of the chapter we consider alternative formats of final accounts and how they relate to different forms of organisation. We consider the advantages and disadvantages of the different organisational forms available, and examine the ways in which the presentation of accounting information differs. Before these new areas are discussed, however, we examine the traditional approach to accounting found in other textbooks and compare it with the worksheet approach.

The traditional approach

In the traditional approach, instead of using columns to portray the individual accounts in an organisation's accounting system, these accounts are represented by T accounts. In many basic bookkeeping courses, these T accounts form a major part of the course and students are required to spend a lot of time practising entries to these accounts. Often this is done on the basis of rote learning. It is further complicated by the terminology used: 'debits' and 'credits'.

Discuss the use of debits and credits, and identify the relationship between the worksheet approach and the use of debits and credits

For people studying accounting for the first time, the worksheet approach has been shown to be superior. Moreover, it is more in line with the increasing use of electronic spreadsheets. However, experience has shown that those who already know something of accounting often have initial problems in converting from one representation of an accounting system to another. In this chapter, we work through a simple example to illustrate that the difference between the two methods is superficial and does not, in any way, change the principles involved.

Example 11.1: Phil's business

Phil started a business, and during the first year the following transactions took place:
1 Opened a business account and paid in $10 000 of his own money.
2 Bought a van for $5000 and paid cash.
3 Bought goods for $35 000 on credit, of which $33 000 was paid for at year-end.
4 Sold goods for $45 000, all for cash.
5 Had goods in inventory at the end of the year which cost $4000.
6 Paid expenses on the van of $1000.
7 Paid rent on his premises of $1500.

Let us see what the worksheet looks like for Phil's business and we will then see how the same transactions are represented under the traditional method.

Phil's business worksheet: version 1

	Assets				= Liabilities +	Equity	
Transaction	Cash	Prepaids	Van	Inventory	Creditors	Profit and loss	Capital
1	10 000						10 000
2	−5 000		5 000				
3				35 000	35 000		
	−33 000				−33 000		
4	45 000					45 000	
5				−31 000		−31 000	
6	−1 000					−1 000	
7	−1 500	1 500					
Balance	14 500	+ 1 500	+ 5 000	+ 4 000	= 2 000	+ 13 000	+ 10 000

You should make sure that you understand the entries on the worksheet before moving on. If you do have problems, refer back to the appropriate chapters.

Now we will record the same transactions using the traditional T accounts.

Phil's business
T accounts

Cash

Transaction 1	10 000	Transaction 2	5 000
Transaction 4	45 000	Transaction 3	33 000
		Transaction 6	1 000
		Transaction 7	1 500
		Balance c/d*	14 500
	55 000		55 000
Balance b/d**	14 500		

Inventory

Transaction 3	35 000	Transaction 5	31 000
		Balance c/d	4 000
	35 000		35 000
Balance b/d	4 000		

Prepaids

Transaction 7	1 500	

Van

Transaction 2	5 000	

Capital			
		Transaction 1	10 000

Creditors			
Transaction 3	33 000	Transaction 3	35 000
Balance c/d	2 000		
	35 000		35 000
		Balance b/d	2 000

Profit and loss			
Transaction 5	31 000	Transaction 4	45 000
Transaction 6	1 000		
Balance c/d	13 000		
	45 000		45 000
		Balance b/d	13 000

* The term 'balance c/d' means the balance of the account at the end of the period carried down.

** The term 'balance b/d' means the balance of the account at the end of the period brought down.

If we examine the two systems carefully, we can see that they have recorded the same transactions. All that has changed is the way in which the recording is shown. This will be clearer if we explain some of the transactions and the ways in which they have been treated.

For example, in the worksheet, to deal with transaction 1 where Phil puts some money into the business, we opened columns headed 'Cash' and 'Capital'. We then entered the amount involved, $10 000, in each of these columns. By contrast, under the traditional approach we opened two T accounts, one for cash and the other for capital. We then entered the amount involved, $10 000, in these two accounts. All that is happening is that, in contrast with the use of T accounts to represent accounts, the worksheet uses columns.

Using T accounts, it is perhaps less clear which side of the account the entry should go on. However, we can apply some simple rules to make the transposition of entries from the worksheet to debits and credits relatively straightforward. All pluses on the left side of the worksheet are recorded as debits and all minuses are recorded as credits. A debit is placed on the left-hand side of the T account and a credit on the right-hand side. The reverse situation applies on the right side of the worksheet, where all pluses are recorded as credits and all minuses as debits. Therefore, transaction 1 is a debit for cash and a credit for capital.

KEY CONCEPT 11.1

DEBITS AND CREDITS

Under the traditional approach, assets are shown as debit balances and liabilities and equities are shown as credit balances.

We now consider the way in which transaction 2, the purchase of the non-current asset, is dealt with. In the worksheet, a new column is opened for the asset and the cash column is reduced by the amount paid for the new asset, that is, $5000. The traditional approach starts in the same way by opening a new account for the new asset, and puts the cost of $5000 on the left side because it is an asset. So far, the methods are essentially similar. The other half of the transaction is perhaps slightly more difficult to follow because we have to reduce the cash balance. This is done by putting the $5000 on the right-hand side of the cash account. This is called crediting an account – in this case we are crediting a cash account.

Even at this stage it is obvious that the worksheet is easier to follow because it relies less on jargon and rote learning than the traditional approach. Another advantage of the worksheet is that we know at the end of the exercise that the accounts are balanced; if they do not balance, the error can be found by working back through the worksheet (as described in Chapter 6). In the case of the traditional approach, we do not yet know if our accounts balance, so we have to extract what is commonly known as a trial balance. If, having extracted this trial balance, we found that it did not balance we would have to check through the entries in our accounts to find the error. It is to be hoped that that will not be the case with the trial balance for Phil's business, which is as follows:

Phil's business
Trial balance

	Debit $	Credit $
Cash	14 500	
Prepaids	1 500	
Capital		10 000
Creditors		2 000
Van	5 000	
Inventory	4 000	
Profit and loss		13 000
	25 000	25 000

We can see that the accounts do balance. You may have noticed that the columns are headed 'Debit' and 'Credit'. All the accounts from the left side of our worksheet, the asset accounts, are in the debit column and all the accounts from the right side of the worksheet, those that relate to what the business owes, are in the credit column. The accounts with a negative balance would have the opposite title to the one they would have if they had a positive balance. For example, an asset account with a negative balance would be a credit. The negative asset accounts, like provision for doubtful debts and accumulated depreciation, have a credit balance. An entity overdrawing on its bank account would have a negative (credit) balance. If an entity pays more than the amount owing to creditors, the account will have a negative (debit) balance. In this case, we assume that we have not made an error in our double entries because the trial balance balances. However, remember that we pointed out in Chapter 6 that a trial balance can balance and still be incorrect; for example, $1000 may be recorded as $10 000 on both sides of the worksheet as a debit and a credit.

KEY CONCEPT 11.2

RULES FOR DEBITS AND CREDITS

For asset accounts, increases are recorded as debits and decreases as credits. For liability and equity accounts, increases are recorded as credits and decreases as debits.

Review exercise 1

In accountancy what are debits and credits, and how do they relate to assets, liabilities and equity?

LEDGERS

Up until now we have used T accounts to demonstrate the traditional approach to accounting. In practice, the T accounts are called ledger accounts and are a means for a business to accumulate information to assist with decision making. A typical ledger account is shown below.

L ② — Explain the role of journals, ledgers and a trial balance

Title of Account							
							Account no . . .
Date	Explanation	Ref.	Amount	Date	Explanation	Ref.	Amount

As can be seen, there are two sides to this ledger, the left-hand side for debit entries and the right-hand side for credit entries. These sides are separated by the middle space between the amount and date.

The columns show the following data:

- Date: the date of the transaction
- Explanation: only recorded for unusual items; therefore, seldom used
- Ref.: the page or folio number of the journal where the transaction is recorded
- Amount: the amount of the entry.

THE JOURNAL

Transactions are normally not entered directly into a ledger account. Under the traditional approach, most businesses use a journal to initially enter a transaction into the accounting records. The journal is often called the book of original entry. It is a chronological record showing the debits and credits from transactions. At convenient intervals these transactions are transferred (posted) from the journal to the relevant ledger accounts.

Example 11.1 Phil's business (continued)

We will now record the transactions from Example 11.1 into a journal. The journal we use is called a general journal. Many businesses use a number of journals for different items. Some examples are the cash receipts journal, the cash payments journal and the purchases journal. We record all the transactions in the general journal.

General journal				Page . . .
Date (transaction)	Account titles and explanation	LP	Debit	Credit
1	Cash		10 000	
	Capital			10 000
	Invested cash in the business			
2	Van		5 000	
	Cash			5 000
	Bought a van for cash			
3	Inventory (or purchases)		35 000	
	Creditors			35 000
	Bought goods on credit			
	Creditors		33 000	
	Cash			33 000
	Paid creditors (in practice these occur throughout the year)			
4	Cash		45 000	
	Profit and loss (or sales)			45 000
	Sold goods for cash			
5	Profit and loss (or cost of goods sold)		31 000	
	Inventory			31 000
	Cost of goods sold for the period			
6	Profit and loss (or van expenses)		1 000	
	Cash			1 000
	Paid van expenses			
7	Prepaids		1 500	
	Cash			1 500
	Paid rent for the period			

The column LP is used to record the ledger account number when the entry is posted from the journal to the ledger. Until the entry is posted, no number is entered into the LP column. The number assists cross-referencing, and can help to locate errors.

All transactions which involve entries to the profit and loss account have an alternative account name in brackets. What happens in practice is that information is accumulated in various income (revenue) and expense accounts throughout the period. At the end of the period a closing entry is recorded in the journal, and these closing entries transfer the totals of the income (revenue) and expense accounts to the profit and loss account. We have recorded these amounts directly to the profit and loss account in this example.

We will move on to the next stage, where final adjustments are made for accruals, depreciation, and so on. These adjustments are often referred to as end-of-period or end-of-year adjustments.

Review exercise 2
Explain the role of ledgers and journals.

END-OF-PERIOD ADJUSTMENTS

End-of-period adjustments are required to provide for inventories, depreciation, bad debts, accruals, prepayments, and so on. These have all been covered in Chapters 7 to 9 and you should be familiar with the way in which they are dealt with in the worksheet. For the purposes of comparison, we will show again how they are dealt with in the worksheet and then look at how they are dealt with in the traditional approach.

Example 11.1 Phil's business (continued)

We continue with the example of Phil's business. At the end of the year Phil decides that the van will have no scrap value and should be depreciated at $1000 a year for five years. He also tells you that the rent is payable quarterly in advance, so that only $1200 relates to this year.

Entering these adjustments on the worksheet results in version 2 of the worksheet. You will notice that we have had to open two new accounts or columns to deal with the changes and then arrive at a new balance.

Phil's business worksheet: version 2

	Assets					= Liabilities +	Equity	
Transaction	Cash	Van	(Accum. dep.)	Inventory	Prepaids	Creditors	Profit and loss	Capital
1	10 000							10 000
2	−5 000	5 000						
3				35 000		35 000		
	−33 000					−33 000		
4	45 000						45 000	
5				−31 000			−31 000	
6	−1 000						−1 000	
7	−1 500				1 500			
Balance	14 500	+ 5 000	+	4 000	+ 1 500	= 2 000	+ 13 000	+ 10 000
Adjustment			−1 000				−1 000	
Adjustment					−1 200		−1 200	
Balance	14 500	+ 5 000	− 1 000	+ 4 000	+ 300	= 2 000	+ 10 800	+ 10 000

In the traditional approach, we also have to create the new accounts and then extract another trial balance. However, there is a shortcut which is often shown in textbooks which involves making adjustments on what is effectively a type of worksheet. The difference between that worksheet and the one we use is that the rows become columns and vice versa. This worksheet is shown below and, as you can see, it merely extends our earlier trial balance to the new trial balance.

This type of worksheet is often referred to as the extended trial balance. The main difference between the two approaches in this respect is that when using our worksheet approach the final adjustments are automatically part of the double-entry system. Under the traditional approach they can be, and often are, outside the double-entry system. This can, of course, lead to errors and omissions which might be difficult to trace. Let us look at the extended trial balance of Phil's business.

Phil's business
Extended trial balance

	Unadjusted trial balance		Adjustments		Adjusted trial balance	
	Debit	Credit	Debit	Credit	Debit	Credit
	$	$	$	$	$	$
Cash	14 500				14 500	
Capital		10 000				10 000
Creditors		2 000				2 000
Van	5 000				5 000	
Inventory	4 000				4 000	
Profit and loss		13 000	2 200			10 800
Accum. dep.				1 000		1 000
Prepaids	1 500			1 200	300	
	25 000	25 000	2 200	2 200	23 800	23 800

As can be seen, the extended trial balance has also resulted in the need to open a new account for accumulated depreciation and to make some adjustments to our existing income statement. If these adjustments were done through double-entry, in the journal, and T accounts they would be shown as follows:

General journal					Page . . .
Date	Account title and explanation	LP	Debit	Credit
Adjustment	Profit and loss (depreciation expense)		1 000	
	Accumulated depreciation			1 000
	To record depreciation for the period			
Adjustment	Profit and loss (rent expense)		1 200	
	Prepaids			1 200
	To recognise rent expense for the year			

These entries are called adjusting journal entries. Like all journal entries they are posted to the relevant ledger accounts.

Prepaids			
Transaction 7	1 500	Adjustment	1 200
		Balance c/d	300
	1 500		1 500
Balance b/d	300		

Profit and loss			
Transaction 5	31 000	Transaction 4	45 000
Transaction 6	1 000		
Balance c/d	13 000		
	45 000		45 000
Adjust	1 000	Balance b/d	13 000
Adjust	1 200		
Balance c/d	10 800		
	13 000		13 000
		Balance b/d	10 800

Accumulated depreciation			
		Adjustment	1 000

COMPARISON WITH THE WORKSHEET APPROACH

We have seen that the differences between the two approaches are not differences of principle. Rather, the two methods are alternative ways of depicting the same entries in the books of account of a firm. In the authors' opinion, the advantages of the worksheet-based approach outweigh the advantages of the alternative approach and make it easier for those coming to the subject for the first time to assimilate the main principles involved in a double-entry bookkeeping system. We now consider the way in which final accounts are produced, and the rules and regulations governing their format.

Final accounts

Before we look at the regulations and the effects of different types of organisational structures, we should remind ourselves of the way in which the final accounts, that is, the balance sheet and the income statement, are derived from the worksheet. This is readily understood if we consider the example of Phil's business. We will extract the final accounts from version 2 of Phil's business worksheet (see page 319).

Phil's business
Income statement for the year ending 30 June 20X9

	$	$
Sales		45 000
Cost of goods sold		31 000
Gross profit		14 000
Rent	1 200	
Van expenses	1 000	
Van depreciation	1 000	3 200
Net profit		10 800

You will notice that the formal income statement merely summarises what is contained in the profit and loss column of the worksheet. You will also notice that it is called the income statement for the period ended on a certain date. This emphasises that the income statement is a period statement. If we contrast its heading with the heading of the following balance sheet, we can see that the latter refers to a particular point in time; it is a snapshot of one moment in time.

Phil's business
Balance sheet as at 30 June 20X9

	$	$	$	$
Assets				
Current assets				
Cash	14 500			
Prepaids	300			
Inventory	4 000			
Total current assets		18 800		
Non-current assets				
Van (at cost)	5 000			
Less Accumulated depreciation	(1 000)			
Total non-current assets		4 000		
Total assets			22 800	
Liabilities				
Current liabilities				
Creditors	2 000			
Total current liabilities		2 000		
Non-current liabilities	NIL	NIL		
Total liabilities			2 000	
Net assets				20 800

	$	$	$	$
Equity				
Capital	10 000			
Profit and loss	10 800			
Total equity				20 800

Notice that the balance sheet merely takes the final line of the worksheet and classifies it under appropriate headings to enable the reader to interpret the information more readily. We deal with the subject of analysis in more detail in Chapter 14.

Figure 11.1 summarises the various steps involved in the recording of financial information and the preparation of financial statements.

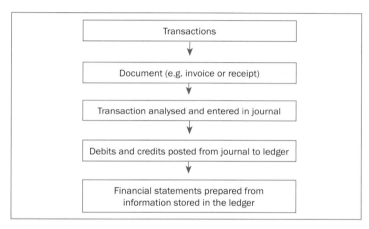

Figure 11.1 The financial recording process

Computerised accounting systems

These days most business organisations use a computerised accounting system rather than a manual one to prepare financial statements. There are a large number of computerised systems (e.g. Quicken, MYOB, AcPac, Quick Books Attaché and Microsoft Money), and the software an entity chooses depends on the size, type and complexity of its business. In all cases, however, the bookkeeping process is simplified using a computerised accounting system. For more information consult the 'Further reading' section at the end of this chapter.

Forms of organisation

At this point, we need to consider the effect of different forms of organisational structure on the presentation of final accounts. As stated in Chapters 1 and 2, there are many forms of business organisation, from sole traders, through partnerships, companies and groups of companies to multinational conglomerates. There are also not-for-profit and public sector organisations. In addition,

Identify three forms of business arrangement: a sole trader, a partnership and a company

there are other, less common, forms such as co-operatives, friendly societies and provident societies. Each of these organisational forms requires slightly different accounts. The reasons for this are because the needs of the users are slightly different or because of other factors, such as the requirements of legislation or other regulations (i.e. those imposed by a stock exchange). Rather than attempting to deal with all the different forms of organisations, we concentrate our discussion on simple forms of organisation: the sole trader, the partnership and the limited company.

There are distinct differences in the presentation of final accounts, relating to the structure, size, patterns of ownership and goals of an organisation. These influences operate at the organisational level, as explained in Chapters 1 and 2. Other influences that operate in the commercial context are legal requirements such as the reporting requirements of the *Corporations Act*, the *Partnership Act* and case law. These will be discussed in some detail here. Other influences, such as stock exchange listing requirements, are beyond the scope of an introductory text, although the influence of the ASX was briefly discussed in Chapter 2. We begin by discussing the smallest and most common form of business organisation: the sole trader.

Identify the characteristics of a sole trader

THE SOLE TRADER

The balance sheet and income statement in this case are straightforward because the business is the simplest form of organisation in accounting terms. A one-owner business is a common form of business organisation, and is simple to set up. All that is required is a business bank account. Because it is so simple and because it has no recognition in law, there are no formal guidelines for the format of the accounts, except in the situation where the sole trader is a reporting entity (refer to Chapter 2). The fact that the business and the owner are not seen as separate legal entities can be a problem if the business gets into difficulties: the owner is liable for all the debts of the business and might have to sell personal possessions, such as the family home, to meet them. In addition, this form of organisation relies heavily on the owner for finance and this can cause problems if the business expands. Owners tend to have limited funds at their disposal. These problems can be alleviated or solved by, for example, introducing a partner into the business. Alternatively, the owner may set up a company which limits his or her liability.

Explain the advantages and disadvantages of a partnership

PARTNERSHIPS

A partnership is a relationship that exists between two or more people to carry on a business in common with a view to profit. As an organisation, a partnership offers certain advantages and disadvantages compared to the sole trader. A partnership is not regarded as a legal entity separate from the partners who comprise it.

Advantages

The advantages of forming a partnership are:

- *ease of formation.* A partnership can be easily formed between two or more persons: all they have to do is agree to form a partnership. The partnership agreement is usually in writing, although a verbal agreement can be sufficient to constitute a partnership
- *limited rules and regulations.* Unlike a company, a partnership is not subject to the requirements of the *Corporations Act.* The partners are not required to prepare financial statements which comply with accounting standards unless the partnership is a reporting entity (as discussed in Chapter 2)
- *provision of capital and expertise.* A partnership is often formed to raise more capital than is possible with a sole trader. It may also be formed to bring together the different skills of the partners; for example, an accountant and an engineer
- *income tax.* There may be income tax advantages in forming a partnership since it is not a separate legal entity. A partnership is not taxed, as is the case for a company. However, the individual partners pay income tax on their share of partnership profits.

Disadvantages

Disadvantages of the partnership form of organisation include:

- *limited life.* A partnership can end at any time through, for example, the death of a partner, withdrawal of a partner, bankruptcy of a partner, incapacity of a partner, or admission of a new partner. However, the end of the partnership does not signify the end of the partnership business: it may continue under a new partnership for many years
- *unlimited liability.* As each partner is personally liable for all debts of the partnership, there is unlimited liability with all partnerships. Partners in accounting firms normally purchase professional indemnity insurance because of this risk
- *mutual agency.* As each partner is an agent of the partnership, he or she has the authority to enter contracts on behalf of the partnership provided such contracts are within the scope of normal operations.

As we have already stated, unless a partnership is a reporting entity, as discussed in Chapter 2, it is not required to prepare general-purpose financial reports which must comply with all accounting standards. As most partnerships are not reporting entities, they have a great deal of flexibility in how they prepare their financial statements. Let us now look at a set of financial statements for a partnership.

Financial statements

Price Watershed Partnership
Income statement for the year ended 30 June 20X7

	$	$
Sales		100 000
Cost of goods sold		60 000
Gross profit		40 000
Expenses		20 000
Net profit		20 000
Distributions		
Salary		
Price	6 000	
Watershed	4 000	10 000
		10 000
Profit share		
Price	5 000	
Watershed	5 000	10 000

A comparison of the income statement of the sole trader, Phil, with that of the partnership reveals that the main difference is the distribution statements for the partnership. This statement shows that Price and Watershed were each paid a salary for services provided to the partnership, and the remaining profit was then shared equally.

Price Watershed Partnership
Balance sheet at 30 June 20X7

	$	$	$	$
Assets				
Current assets				
Cash	10 000			
Inventory	10 000			
Total current assets		20 000		
Non-current assets				
Land and building	100 000			
Total non-current assets		100 000		
Total assets			120 000	
Liabilities				
Current liabilities				
Creditors	20 000			
Total current liabilities		20 000		

	$	$	$	$
Non-current liabilities	NIL	NIL		
Total liabilities			20 000	
Net assets				100 000
Partners' equity				
Capital accounts				
Price	40 000			
Watershed	40 000			
Total capital accounts		80 000		
Current accounts				
Price	11 000			
Watershed	9 000			
Total current accounts		20 000		
Total partners' equity				100 000

A comparison of the balance sheet of Phil the sole trader with that of Price Watershed reveals that the difference arises in the equity part of the statements. The balance sheet for the partnership shows a balance for each partner under the headings of capital and current accounts. The current account reveals the partners' entitlement to profit, salary, interest, drawings and other, more short-term, transactions. The capital account records the capital contributed by the partners. As current and capital items might be treated differently for legal purposes, it is useful to record them separately in the accounts.

Companies

Unlike the partnership and the sole trader, a company is recognised as a separate legal entity quite distinct from its owners. The debts incurred in the normal course of business are those of the company. In the case of a default in payment, it is the company which is sued rather than the owner. The fact that the owners might also be the managers and the only employees is irrelevant: in the eyes of the law all these roles are different.

LO 6

Explain the advantages and disadvantages of a company

Companies can be:

- private (proprietary)
  - limited by shares
  - unlimited with share capital
- public
  - limited by shares
  - limited by guarantee
  - unlimited with share capital
  - no liability.

Limited-by-shares companies

This class of company restricts the liability of members (shareholders) to a specified amount. For a limited company, the shareholders' liability is restricted to the amount paid for the share. Limited-by-shares companies include:

- *Proprietary companies or private companies.* These must have a minimum of one member and normally have a maximum of 50 members. A proprietary company must have the word 'Proprietary' or 'Pty' before the word 'Limited' or 'Ltd' as part of its name. These companies are often family companies and have fewer legal formalities than public companies, but they are unable to approach the general public to raise money.
- *Small or large proprietary companies.* A small proprietary company is one that meets at least two of the following criteria:
    - sales of less than $10 million
    - assets of less than $5 million
    - fewer than 50 employees

    A small proprietary company does not generally have to prepare audited financial statements. All other proprietary companies are large and are required to lodge audited financial statements with the Australian Securities and Investments Commission (ASIC), unless granted an exemption.
- *Public companies.* A public company must have at least one member and there is no maximum number for its members. Usually, ownership of these companies is widespread. A public company can invite the public to subscribe to its shares or debentures. A public company can be listed, which means that its shares are traded on a stock exchange, or unlisted. A public company must have the word 'Limited' or 'Ltd' as part of its name. A public company is subject to many more rules and restrictions under the *Corporations Act* than are proprietary companies.

Companies limited by guarantee

Companies that are limited by guarantee are public companies whose members undertake to provide a guaranteed amount of money in the event of the company being liquidated. This type of company does not have a share capital and, as such, it does not raise initial capital and is not, therefore, suitable for trading purposes. This form of company is often used for sporting clubs and not-for-profit charitable organisations.

Unlimited liability companies

Members of an unlimited liability company are liable for all the debts of the company. For this reason such companies are not common in Australia, although some mutual funds are organised in this way. An advantage of this type of company is that there are no restrictions on the return of capital to shareholders.

No-liability companies

This category is restricted to mining companies. The words 'No Liability' or 'NL' must be part of the company's name. Shareholders in these companies are not required to contribute the unpaid value of shares if the company is liquidated.

Advantages of companies

The advantages of the company form of organisation are:

- *separate legal entity*. Unlike a sole trader and a partnership, a company is a separate legal entity. Therefore, it can buy or sell property, sue or be sued, enter into contracts, hire and dismiss employees, be responsible for its debts and pay tax
- *limited liability*. Shareholders are liable only for the value of their shares
- *more capital*. A company has the potential to raise substantial amounts of capital, which is not possible for sole traders or partnerships
- *ease of transfer of ownership*. Shareholders can buy and sell shares without affecting the operations of the company
- *no mutual agency*. Shareholders cannot enter into contracts that would bind the company
- *professional management*. A company is managed by a board of directors and a managing director, while the shareholders maintain ownership. It is therefore possible to hire the best managerial talent available
- *continuous existence*. A company has an indefinite life and does not cease to function each time a shareholder sells shares, dies or goes bankrupt.

CASE STUDY 11.1

PROFESSIONAL INGREDIENT IN RECIPE FOR SUCCESS
by Hui Yuk-min

THE KEY for the long-term survival of Chinese family businesses is to respect and appreciate the role of professional management by outsiders.

That is the advice for longevity from the head of 121-year-old Chinese-medicine maker Eu Yan Sang International Holdings.

'The most important thing is you have to separate the ownership and the management,' said Richard Eu Yee-ming, managing director of the company formed in 1879 by Eu Kong, his flamboyant tin-miner tycoon great-grandfather.

'You have got to decide whether you want to grow the business or you just want a rice bowl for the family,' Mr Eu said.

'If you want to grow the business, you have got to look for professional management.'

He is not in favour of a family-controlled business being run by people with family ties.

His views mirrored a report issued yesterday by the Economist Intelligence Unit in co-operation with management consultancy Andersen Consulting.

It said the traditional rigid hierarchies and emphasis on personal relationships of Chinese family businesses were ill-equipped to deal with an environment of accelerating competition and increasing complexity in post-crisis Asia.

Eu Yan Sang has long been a small-size business of the Eu family, selling flagship Bak Foong pills for women and its Chinese herbs. It is one of the few traditional Chinese businesses to last four generations.

It was operated in a traditional way until Richard Eu took over 10 years ago and started a process of modernisation.

'At that time, I think the business was ⇢

not realising its full potential,' Mr Eu said. 'If we did not do something at that time the business would probably have eventually conked out.'

He brought about a major change in the organisational structure, which resulted in retirement for old people and hiring professional-trained newcomers as managers.

The company also introduced extensive staff training on product management, sales and marketing services to improve its standards – something Mr Eu believed was essential to enhance its competitiveness.

Richard Eu and his executive director cousin, Clifford Eu Yee-fong, are the only two Eu family members involved in the company's management. The rest of the staff at managerial level are professional employees.

'If you do want the right person to stay, you have to give them a career path. You cannot give them a career path if you do not grow the business,' Mr Eu said.

Mr Eu said his vision was to transform the company into a major regional and global player in the traditional Chinese-medicine business.

It seems he has succeeded, transforming the firm into a modern health-care products provider with a wider range of clients than the middle-aged women who were its staple for nearly 100 years.

Sales have risen from about S$500 000 (about HK$2.27 million) to an estimated S$70 million plus this year.

South China Morning Post, Business Post, 30 August 2000

COMMENTARY

The article discusses the importance of professional management to the success of a business. Perhaps more than any other, this is the greatest advantage of a public company structure.

Disadvantages of companies

Disadvantages of the company structure include:

- *Taxation.* A company is a separate legal entity and is required to pay company tax, which is not the case for a sole trader or partnership. However, provided shareholders receive their profits as franked dividends, the taxing of companies might not be a significant disadvantage, and, in fact, depending on income levels, may be an advantage.
- *Regulation.* A company is subject to more government intervention in the form of rules and regulations. This is particularly true for public companies. For example, they are required to produce accounts annually and to have them audited by a recognised firm of auditors, which can be expensive. A copy of the audited accounts must be lodged with ASIC, where it is available for inspection by the public. The form of these accounts is also subject to the *Corporations Act* which requires that a company's accounts should consist of the company's balance sheet, the company's income statement, the directors' report, the auditor's report and a directors' statement. In addition to these general requirements, there are detailed requirements, particularly in accounting standards, covering the content of the actual accounts. Such requirements are

more onerous for companies that are reporting entities (see Chapter 2 for a discussion of reporting entities).

- *Limited liability*. While limited liability is generally an advantage, it may be a disadvantage for a small company if its ability to borrow money is restricted by the fact that its members have limited liability.
- *Separation of ownership and control*. This can also act as an advantage or a disadvantage. Managers might have incentives to make decisions which are not in the best interests of all shareholders. The *Corporations Act* contains certain provisions that are intended to discourage managers from behaving in this manner.

Clearly, to go through these requirements in great detail is outside the scope of an introductory text. Instead we have included, in Example 11.2, a set of accounts for a private company. This example highlights areas of difference between the accounts of the limited company and those of the other forms of organisation considered (see the accounts for Phil's business on pages 322–3 and Price Watershed Partnership on pages 326–7). We consider first the income statement.

Review exercise 3

Explain the differences between a partnership and a company. Under what circumstances would you expect either to be used?

Example 11.2: Jack Pty Ltd

Jack Pty Ltd
Income statement for the year ending 30 June 20X4

	Notes	This year		Last year	
		$000	$000	$000	$000
Sales	1		60 000		45 000
Cost of sales			40 000		30 000
Gross profit			20 000		15 000
Distribution costs	2	3 000		2 500	
Administration costs	2	11 000	14 000	9 000	11 500
Net profit before taxation			6 000		3 500
Taxation	3		2 600		1 400
Profit after taxation			3 400		2 100

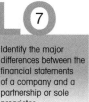

Identify the major differences between the financial statements of a company and a partnership or sole proprietor

The first difference is in the title of the income statement: the fact that Jack is a proprietary limited company must be stated, and the new title does this. In addition, the income statement contains comparative figures for the previous year, as well as references to a number of notes. These notes contain greater detail than can be shown on the face of the statement, and as such are an integral part of the analysis of the accounts of a company. This will be discussed in more detail in Chapter 14. We can see that down to 'Gross profit' the format is familiar. However, we then find that expenses are classified into broad categories. These categories are laid down in AASB 101 *Presentation of Financial Statements.*

It is from the point at which the net profit is shown that the real differences arise. The most striking of these is that taxation is included in the income statement. This is because the company is recognised as a separate entity for legal and tax purposes and its profits are liable to corporation tax. In contrast, the sole trader and the partnership are not separate legal or taxable entities: their profits are not taxed, as such, but only as they form part of the income of the owner.

We now look at the balance sheet of a proprietary limited liability company and the differences that arise therein.

Jack Pty Ltd
Balance sheet at 30 June 20X4

	Notes	This year $000		Last year $000
Assets				
Current assets				
Cash at bank		3 500		2 000
Debtors		11 000		4 000
Inventory	7	10 000		7 000
Total current assets			24 500	13 000
Non-current assets				
Equipment	5	10 000		11 000
Land and buildings	6	70 000		56 000
Total non-current assets			80 000	67 000
Total assets			104 500	80 000
Liabilities				
Current liabilities				
Creditors		4 000		3 000
Taxation	3	2 600		1 400
Dividends	4	1 600		1 100
Total current liabilities			8 200	5 500
Non-current liabilities			–	–
Total liabilities			8 200	5 500
Net assets			96 300	74 500
Capital and reserves				
Share capital	8	70 000		64 000
Retained profits	9	5 300		4 500
Reserves	10	21 000		6 000
Total capital and reserves			96 300	74 500

The format uses the current/non-current classification. AASB 101 allows companies to choose an alternative format in which assets and liabilities are listed in order of liquidity. Most banks list assets and liabilities in order of liquidity and do not use the current/non-current classification.

As you can see, the top part of the balance sheet is similar to those we have encountered before, apart from the inclusion of dividends and taxation and the fact that a lot of the detail is left to the notes to the statements. For example, Note 6 would contain details of non-current assets bought and sold during the year, as well as the depreciation to date and that charged during the year.

The lower part of the balance sheet is somewhat different: the owners' equity is referred to as share capital. This might consist of different types, each carrying different voting rights, and so on. This would only be apparent if we looked at the detail contained in the notes. Similarly, there may be a number of different types of reserves, such as a 'revaluation reserve' for revalued assets such as land and buildings. Jack has a revaluation reserve and more details are provided in the statement of changes in equity.

One of the important changes as a result of the adoption of IFRSs in Australia is the requirement for all reporting entities to now present a statement of changes in equity (SOCE). This means that all reporting entities are now required to prepare four financial statements as part of a GPFR. We now look at the SOCE, as set out in AASB 101, for Jack Pty Ltd.

Jack Pty Ltd
Statement of changes in equity as at 30 June 20X4

	Share capital	Asset revaluation reserve	Retained profits	Total
	$000	$000	$000	$000
Balance at 1 July 20X3	64 000	6 000	4 500	74 500
Gain on land revaluation		15 000		15 000
Total income and expense recognised directly in equity				15 000
Profit or loss for the year (from the income statement)			3 400	3 400
Total recognised income and expense for the period				18 400
Dividends			(2 600)	(2 600)
Issue of share capital	6 000			6 000
Balance at 30 June 20X4	70 000	21 000	5 300	96 300

The first column in the SOCE shows the contributed capital. It reveals that the company issued another $6 000 000 during the year. The second column reports on the movement in the reserves. The company revalued the land and buildings by $15 000 000 during the year and this partially explains why the land and buildings increased from $56 000 000 to $70 000 000 in the balance sheet. From the SOCE we also see that a profit (after taxation) of $3 400 000 is included and is added to the opening balance of retained profits. The company has made a dividend distribution of $2 600 000 and, as a result, the closing balance of retained profits is $5 300 000. This part of the SOCE can be seen as equivalent to the distributions in the current account section of the balance sheet in the partnership statements which we have just considered. The dividends are, in fact, a form of distribution to the owners (the shareholders) and are paid according to the number of shares held. There might be an interim and final dividend in one year but not in the next. This is not unusual: the declaration of any dividend depends upon the needs of the business and the availability of both profits and liquid funds to pay it. An interim dividend is, in fact, a payment made part way through the year and it is also dependent on both profitability and the availability of liquid funds.

Review exercise 4
Describe how the choice of organisational form determines the format of the final accounts.

FINANCIAL STATEMENTS FOR A PUBLIC COMPANY
The statements presented in Example 11.2 are for a private company and are simpler than those for a public company. Woodside is a public company and its financial statements illustrate the usual format of each statement. Refer to the Woodside financial report in Appendix 1. Many of the items in these statements should now be familiar to you.

Note that the columns relating to the figures within the statements are headed 'Consolidated'. Consolidated statements are prepared for an economic entity and will be briefly discussed in Chapter 12. The information in the Consolidated columns is for the economic entity which includes Woodside and other entities controlled by Woodside.

The notes attached to the statements provide valuable information about some of the items listed on each line on the face of the statements. As we mentioned in Chapters 4 and 5, the statements and the notes must be read together. However, as the financial statements are only half-year statements, Woodside does not have to provide detailed notes (as are required for annual financial statements). It is also not a requirement in half-year accounts to show amounts for the parent entity in addition to the economic entity. In annual financial statements, a parent entity must show four columns in the statements with two columns for the parent entity (current year and previous year) and the economic entity (current year and previous year). You can access the annual financial statements for Woodside by visiting **www.woodside.com.au**.

SUMMARY

LO 1

LEARNING OBJECTIVE 1

Discuss the use of debits and credits, and identify the relationship between the worksheet approach and the use of debits and credits

Under the traditional approach, assets are shown as debit balances and liabilities and equities are shown as credit balances.

For asset accounts, increases are recorded as debits and decreases as credits. For liability and equity accounts, increases are recorded as credits and decreases as debits.

LO 2

LEARNING OBJECTIVE 2

Explain the role of journals, ledgers and a trial balance

Transactions are normally not entered directly into a ledger account. Under the traditional approach, most businesses use a journal to initially enter a transaction into the accounting records. The journal is often called the book of original entry. It is a chronological record showing the debits and credits from transactions. At convenient intervals these transactions are transferred (posted) from the journal to the relevant ledger accounts. At the end of accounting periods, a trial balance (a listing of all ledger balances) is prepared.

LO 3

LEARNING OBJECTIVE 3

Identify three forms of business arrangement: a sole trader, a partnership and a company

A sole trader is a business run by one person and a partnership involves two or more parties. Neither of these forms of business is a separate legal entity. A company, however, is a separate legal entity.

LO 4

LEARNING OBJECTIVE 4

Identify the characteristics of a sole trader

A one-owner business is a common form of business organisation, and is simple to set up. All that is required is a business bank account. Because it is so simple and because it has no recognition in law, there are no formal guidelines for the format of the accounts, except in the situation where the sole trader is a reporting entity.

LO 5

LEARNING OBJECTIVE 5

Explain the advantages and disadvantages of a partnership

The advantages of forming a partnership are:

- ease of formation
- limited rules and regulations
- provision of capital and expertise
- more favourable tax position.

The disadvantages of a partnership, as a form of organisation, include:

- limited life
- unlimited liability
- mutual agency.

LO 6 LEARNING OBJECTIVE 6

Explain the advantages and disadvantages of a company

The advantages of companies as a form of organisation are:

- separate legal entity
- limited liability
- ease of transfer of ownership
- no mutual agency
- professional management
- continuous existence.

Disadvantages of the company structure include:

- taxation
- regulation
- limited liability
- separation of ownership and control.

LO 7 LEARNING OBJECTIVE 7

Identify the major differences between the financial statements of a company, a partnership and a sole proprietor

There are many differences between the financial statements of a company and either a partnership or a sole trader. For example, the balance sheet for a company contains shareholders' equity which includes paid-up capital, retained profits and reserves. A sole trader or partnership does not need to prepare a statement of changes in equity but a partnership may prepare a statement of partners capital accounts. In addition, unlike a partnership and a sole trader, a company is required to pay taxation.

REFERENCES

Australian Accounting Standards Board. AASB 101 *Presentation of Financial Statements*, July, 2004.

FURTHER READING

Flanders, D.D. & Gourlay, D., 2004. *MYOB14I Comprehensive Edition*, Thomson.
Trotman, K. & Gibbins, M., 2006. *Financial Accounting: An Integrated Approach*, 3rd edn, Thomson.

REVIEW QUESTIONS

1   Explain, in your own words, the meaning of the terms 'trial balance' and 'extended trial balance'.
2   Explain the meaning of the term 'final adjustments'.
3   Explain the difference between a sole trader and a partnership.
4   Why is it advantageous to set up a business as a limited company?
5   What are the differences between a sole trader and a limited liability (limited by shares) company?

6   Explain the difference between a limited liability (limited by shares), an unlimited liability and a no-liability company.

7   Why do you think that mining companies are allowed to set up as a no-liability company?

8   Discuss the advantages and disadvantages of a partnership.

9   What do you think the phrase 'it's only a $2 company' means?

PROBLEMS FOR DISCUSSION AND ANALYSIS

1   Refer to the Woodside 2005 financial report in Appendix 1.
    a   What is the basic and diluted earnings per share?
    b   What was the dividends per share in 2005? 2004?
    c   What was the value of shares issued under the Woodside employee share plan in 2005?
    d   How many fully paid ordinary shares were issued as at 30 June 2005?

2   Prepare a balance sheet from the following information:

	$
Creditors	7 500
Debtors	10 000
Equipment	137 000
Land and buildings	270 000
Inventory	7 300
Dividends	6 000
Debentures payable	250 000
Cash	6 500
Taxation	10 000
Retained profits	24 500
Paid-up capital	?

3   Prepare a balance sheet from the following information:

	$
Bank overdraft	10 000
Land and buildings	120 000
Receivables	13 450
Creditors	29 600
Inventory	63 230
Short-term loan payable	15 000
Vehicles	27 300
Equipment	7 600
Taxation	10 000

	$
General reserve	27 000
Dividends payable	13 500
50 000 $1 preference shares fully paid	50 000
Prepaid insurance	750
50 000 $1 ordinary shares fully paid	50 000
Retained earnings	?

4 Refer to Problem 7 in Chapter 6. Prepare a trial balance from your worksheet.

5 Refer to Problem 5 in Chapter 6. Record the transactions as debits and credits, and show them in the form of T accounts. Prepare a trial balance.

6 Partners Mike and Phil share profits and losses in proportion to their fixed capital balances. The following balances were taken from the partnership's books as at 30 June 20X9:

	$
Cash	3 000
Debtors	12 500
Inventory	8 400
Plant	100 000
Accumulated depreciation	3 000
Creditors	8 600
Capital: Mike	36 320
Phil	54 480
Sales	210 000
Cost of goods sold	163 000
Selling expenses	7 316
Depreciation expense	4 322
Financial expenses	1 827
General expenses	12 035

a On the basis of the above figures, calculate the profit for the period.

b What was the amount of profit/loss allocated to each partner?

7 Steve Hill and Lee Down formed a partnership, investing $250 000 and $200 000 respectively. Determine their participation in the year's net profit of $150 000 under each of the following independent assumptions:

a no agreement concerning division of net profit

b net profit to be divided in the ratio of original capital investment

c interest at the rate of 10 per cent allowed on original investments and the remainder divided in the ratio of 2:3

d salary allowances of $65 000 and $70 000 respectively, and the balance divided equally

e allowance of interest at the rate of 10 per cent on original investments, salary allowances of $65 000 and $70 000 respectively, and the remainder divided equally.

8   Andrew Glen and Norman Dale have decided to form a partnership. They have agreed that Glen is to invest $150 000 and Dale is to invest $220 000. Glen will work full time in the business, and Dale is to work half time. The following plans for the division of profit are being considered:
a   equal division
b   in the ratio of original investments
c   in the ratio of time devoted to the business
d   interest of 10 per cent on original investments and the remainder in the ratio of 5:3
e   interest of 10 per cent on original investments, salary allowances of $110 000 to Glen and $40 000 to Dale, and the remainder equally
f   plan (e) except that Glen is also to be allowed a bonus equal to 20 per cent of the amount by which net profit exceeds the salary allowances.

Required

For each plan, determine the division of the net profit under each of the following assumptions:
  i   Net profit of $276 000
  ii Net profit of $162 000.
Present the data in table form, using the following column headings:

Plan	$276 000		$162 000	
	Andrew Glen	Norman Dale	Andrew Glen	Norman Dale

9   Record the following transactions, using a worksheet, and then translate each transaction into debits and credits and show them in the form of T accounts.

Jan. 2	J. Smith paid capital into bank account	$20 000
2	Bought goods from Hall; paid cash	3 400
3	Purchased shop fittings, on credit, from Alco	1 450
3	Returned faulty shop fittings to Alco	450
3	Sold goods to Jones on credit	200
5	Paid account due to Alco	1 000
6	Received payment from Jones, less the allowed discount	190
8	Paid wages	200
9	Paid a fee to have the telephone connected	50
10	Paid the rent for January	100

10 Record the following transactions, using a worksheet, and then post each transaction into T accounts. Prepare a trial balance.

June 1	B. Bloggs deposited money in a business bank account	25 000
2	Negotiated overdraft from bank as additional capital	10 000
3	Bought inventory from A. Fiddle on credit	16 500
3	Bought equipment from T. Xerox on credit	3 000
4	Paid one month's rent in advance on shop premises	1 000
5	Sold goods on credit to I. Dunno	2 000
8	Cash sales for the week ending June 8	9 750
10	I. Dunno returned faulty goods, gave full credit	630
11	Purchased stock from B. Fawlty for cash	13 560
15	Cash sales for the week ending June 15	6 760
17	Paid A. Fiddle	16 500
18	Bought vehicle on 14 days credit	27 600
19	Paid T. Xerox	3 000
19	Paid telephone account	175
19	Paid electricity account	150
20	Bought insurance and prepaid three months	1 800
24	I. Dunno paid his account	2 000
26	Sold goods on account to M. Mouse	13 750
27	Paid bank $2000 plus interest to reduce overdraft	2 100
29	Cash sales, week ending 29 June	5 330

11 Philjen balances its books on 31 December each year. As the accountant, you are required to make adjustments to balances in the firm's accounts. Journalise, in general journal form, the following items. Each adjustment is independent of the others.

a   The next electricity account is due on 31 January the following year. Over the past three years the January quarterly account has averaged $7500.

b   The annual insurance premium was paid on 15 December and amounted to $2880.

c   Debentures to the value of $100 000 were issued on 1 August with a coupon rate of 10 per cent paid quarterly.

d   An order worth $40 000 was received by phone from Pamik to be delivered on January next. Confirmation of the order was to be sent by post but had not been received by balance date.

e   In December, Philjen ran an advertising campaign stating that cash received 28 days in advance of goods being delivered would receive a cash discount of 20 per cent. At balance date, the cash discount account had a balance of $23 000.

12 Prepare the trial balance at the end of the period, after recording the following opening balances and transactions in the appropriate accounts:

	Debit	Credit
	$	$
Cash at bank		4 000
Accounts payable		5 600
Mortgage		10 000
Capital		20 000
Accounts receivable	9 600	
Inventory	13 200	
Delivery vehicles	2 400	
Premises	14 400	
	39 600	39 600

The transactions were:
a   Purchases (on credit) amount to $2800.
b   Sales bring in $1600 cash, $800 credit.
c   Capital is increased by $8000.
d   A $2000 bill for rates and taxes is received, not yet paid.
e   Creditors are paid $2800.
f   Wages are paid, $800.

13 Prepare general journal entries to record the following transactions:
a   A building worth $100 000 is acquired and financed by paying $20 000 in cash and negotiating a mortgage for the remaining $80 000.
b   Depreciation on factory machines is estimated to be $2000.
c   A total of 100 shares in Ravan Publishing are acquired as a long-term investment for $1350 cash.
d   A partner introduces a new truck valued at $3000 as part of his partnership capital.
e   Henry Smith opens a business bank account with his own personal cheque for $4000.
f   Provided $1000 for depreciation on the factory building for this period.
g   A 10-year $100 000 debenture secured by the company's real estate is issued at a discount of 5 per cent with the balance of $95 000 received in cash.
h   A two-hectare vacant block at Welshpool is acquired for a cash payment of $50 000, to provide for future expansion.
i   Faulty goods which had cost a business $25 are returned to the supplier for a credit to the business's account.
j   Harold Black, a partner in Black, Brown, Green and White, withdraws $200 cash to meet his own personal expenses.
k   A cheque for $6000 is received for six months' interest to 30 June, on debentures held as an investment.

14 The trial balance of the Hourglass Organisation (presented below) does not balance. On examining the records, you discover the following information:

a   The purchase of supplies using $500 of cash was incorrectly recorded as a purchase on credit.

b   The debits and credits of creditors totalled $10 000 and $14 000 respectively.

c   C. Hourglass capital balance is $8500.

d   A $1000 payment for supplies was not posted to the 'cash at bank' account.

e   A payment of $500 for rent was not recorded in the 'cash at bank' account.

The Hourglass Organisation
Trial balance at 30 June 20X3

Account title	Debit $	Credit $
Cash at bank	7 620	
Debtors	3 000	
Supplies inventory	480	
Plant and equipment	10 600	
Creditors	4000	
Loan payable		6 000
G. Hourglass capital		5 800
G. Hourglass drawings	3 800	
Repairs revenues		18 000
Salary expense	6 000	
Rent expense	4 000	
Other expenses	2 500	
Totals	42 000	29 800

Required

Prepare a corrected trial balance.

Note to instructors: The following problems are considered more suitable for use in MBA courses. However, undergraduate courses may also find them useful.

15 Prepare general journal entries for the following independent transactions. You can also prepare a worksheet for the same data. *Note*: Some of the terms that are used will need to be looked up in the Glossary or an accounting dictionary.

a   Issued 5000 fully paid $1 shares for cash.

b   Exchanged a piece of equipment with a fair value of $10 000 for 5000 fully paid $2 shares in ABC Ltd.

c   The profit for the year was $12 500. The directors decided to pay a total dividend of $5000 on issued shares, the balance transferred to retained profits.

d   Transferred $6000 from retained profits to general reserve.

e   Repaid $100 000 of debentures, together with accumulated interest of $4000 from cash.

16 Prepare general journal entries for the following independent transactions. *Note*: Some of the terms that are used will need to be looked up in an accounting dictionary or text Glossary.
   a Issued 25 000 $1 ordinary shares paid to 80 cents for cash.
   b Issued 200 $2 ordinary shares to a solicitor in exchange for legal advice.
   c Profit for the year was $123 000. Directors paid the 5 per cent dividend on 100 000 $1 preference shares, and on $60 000 to ordinary shareholders and the balance was transferred to retained profits.
   d Issued $1 000 000 of 5 per cent debentures at par and for cash.
   e Exchanged 10 000 $2 fully paid ordinary shares for equipment with a fair market value of $19 500.

17 The following trial balance has been extracted from the books of the Tiger Partnership:

The Tiger Partnership
Trial balance at 30 June 20X7

	Debit	Credit
	$	$
J. Lion Capital (1 July 20X6)		25 000
K. Jaguar Capital (1 July 20X6)		31 000
Commission received		2 500
Cash at bank	22 680	
J. Lion drawings	3 700	
K. Jaguar drawings	2 100	
Rent expense	6 000	
General office expenses	3 000	
Motor vehicle expenses	4 600	
Accounts payable		23 000
Purchases	126 000	
Provision for doubtful debts		1 800
Inventories (1 July 20X6)	24 000	
Sales		165 000
Insurance expense	1 200	
Bad debt expense	1 100	
Gain on sale of van		1 200
Accounts receivable	25 000	
Motor vehicles (cost)	20 000	
Accumulated depreciation: motor vehicles		4 500
Furniture (cost)	6 000	
Accumulated depreciation: furniture		880
Salaries expense	9 500	
Totals	254 880	254 880

The following additional information is available.

a   Inventories at 30 June 20X7 are $15 000.

b   Depreciation is to be charged at the following rates:

  i   motor vehicles: four years straight-line with 10 per cent residual value

  ii furniture: 10 years straight-line with zero residual value.

c   Rent for June 20X7 ($600) is unpaid.

d   The provision for doubtful debts is to be increased to $2000.

Required

Prepare an income statement for the partnership for the year ended 30 June 20X7, and a balance sheet at that date. Use a worksheet to determine the figures for the financial statements.

18 Bev and Daniel want to buy a business of their own. Bev is a school teacher and Daniel has worked in the public service and has a degree in commerce. They decide to buy a delicatessen, and choose one close to their home. The shop has been there for several years, but has not been a great success. Bev and Daniel will have to borrow a large amount of money to finance the purchase.

Required

You have been asked to advise the following:

a   What form of organisation should they adopt for the business, a partnership or a company?

b   Will the choice of organisation affect the availability of finance for their business? Explain.

c   What skills will Bev and Daniel need to manage the business?

d   How can they raise the required finance? What security do you think they will need to provide?

(Adapted from R. Craven, I. Urquhart and R. Woolley, *Case Studies in Accounting*, 3rd edn, VCTA Publishing, 1985, Case 3–3 and p. 36.)

19 The Magic Lawn Corporation is a family-owned company that produces and sells lawn care products. The company has recently developed a new product which enhances the water retention properties of all types of lawn. The potential for this product is unlimited, but, in order to capitalise on its potential, the company needs a substantial injection of cash into the business. At present, the family owns all 10 000 shares of $1 value that have been issued. The shareholders' section of the most recent balance sheet is as follows:

	$
10 000 $1 value shares fully paid	10 000
Retained profits	2 990 000
	3 000 000

Following are the options that are being considered by the family in order to raise the additional cash:

a   five-year bank loan for $3 million – interest rate 10 per cent, payable annually in arrears; principal to be repaid at the end of five years

b   converting to a public company and issuing 600 000 shares at an estimated market price of $5. Family members will have priority in the purchase of shares

c   the issue of 600 000, 6 per cent, $5 cumulative preference shares to an investment company. The
    shares will be redeemable at the discretion of the Magic Lawn Corporation.
    There are two important issues for the company:
    i   The company has always been family owned and they are concerned about losing control of the
        company.
    ii The company has always had cash flow problems. Options (a) and (c) both involve regular cash
        payments for interest or dividends.

Required

Write a report to the family outlining the advantages and disadvantages of each option. The tax rate for
companies is 30 per cent. Interest is tax-deductible but dividends are not.

20 Bob Strongarm and Phil Hannock are partners in a consulting business. In the last three years, Bob's
    share of partnership profits has been $15 000, $20 000 and $30 000. He has been offered $80 000 for
    his share of the partnership. Bob decides that if his total share of profits over the next three years is
    less than $100 000 he will sell. The following schedule sets out some estimates of profits for the next
    three years:

Schedule

Total partnership profits		
Year 1	Year 2	Year 3
Optimistic estimate		

	Year 1	Year 2	Year 3
Optimistic estimate	75 000	85 000	95 000
Most probable estimate	55 000	65 000	75 000
Pessimistic estimate	45 000	55 000	65 000

Bob and Phil currently share profits as follows: Bob receives a salary of $20 000, Phil's salary is
$15 000, and the remainder is split in a 60 per cent/40 per cent ratio, with Bob getting the 60 per cent
side of the split.

Required

a   Calculate Bob's share of the profits over the next three years if his optimistic estimate is correct.
b   Calculate Bob's share of the profits over the next three years if his most probable estimate
    is correct.
c   Calculate Bob's share of the profits over the next three years if his pessimistic estimate is correct.
d   If the probabilities are 20 per cent that the optimistic estimate will be correct,
    60 per cent that the most probable estimate will be correct, and 20 per cent that the pessimistic
    estimate will be correct, should Bob sell for $80 000?
e   Discuss the other factors Bob should consider when deciding whether or not to sell.

Ethics case study

Jan Skully was the founder and chairperson of Extraordinary Products Ltd. The company had performed very well in the past, but over the last year the share price of Extraordinary had steadily declined. As Skully owned a majority of the shares, she decided to do something to protect her investment. She secretly channelled $200 million from other companies she owned into the purchase of additional shares in Extraordinary. These new shares were used by the other companies as security for the loans taken out to raise the necessary cash to purchase the shares in Extraordinary Ltd. After her death a year later the transactions were uncovered and revealed in the press, and the price of Extraordinary's shares plummeted.

Discuss

a   whether the transactions were unethical
b   how the scheme could have been prevented.

Answers to review exercises

1   Debits and credits are rules concerning the recording of transactions into asset, liability, income, revenue, expense and equity accounts.

2   Ledgers and journals are part of the recording process. Transactions are initially recorded in journals and then the journal entries are transferred to the relevant ledger accounts for individual accounts such as cash, debtors, and so on.

3   A company allows funds to be raised from members of the public. Therefore, it provides greater access to funds than a partnership. However, companies are subject to more rules and regulations and these rules are increasing in the wake of the collapse of companies like HIH, Enron and WorldCom. Shareholders in a limited company are only liable for the amount paid on their shares, whereas partners may be jointly and severally liable for all partners' debts. A company is a separate legal entity whereas a partnership is not.

4   An organisation's form (i.e. sole trader, partnership or company) determines the format of the final accounts in the following ways:
   • Sole traders: final accounts contain one or more owners' accounts.
   • Partnerships: final accounts contain current and capital accounts.
   • Companies: reports are governed by statutes, and subject to accounting standards and audits.

12

LEARNING OBJECTIVES

At the end of this chapter, you should be able to:

1. explain what is included in the terms 'cash' and 'cash equivalents'

2. explain internal control procedures for cash, and why they are important

3. explain the main purpose of a cash flow statement

4. discuss what is meant by the concept of cash flows of operating, investing and financing activities

5. identify cash flows from operating activities, and explain the difference between operating cash flows and net profit

6. identify cash flows from investing and financing activities

7. explain the meaning and purpose of consolidated financial statements

8. explain why it is necessary to eliminate the investment and subsidiary accounts, and transactions, between members of an economic entity

9. explain the meaning of deferred tax assets and deferred tax liabilities

10. identify the accounting that is involved for the Goods and Services Tax (GST).

Introduction

In this chapter we briefly discuss some issues that will provide a greater understanding of financial statements. We first examine the internal control of cash and the content and use of cash flow statements. Our discussion then focuses on three other important issues: consolidated financial statements, accounting for income tax, and the Goods and Services Tax (GST).

Cash and cash equivalents

Explain what is included in the terms 'cash' and 'cash equivalents'

What is cash? The cash flow statement shows the net increase or decrease in cash during the accounting period. AASB 107 *Cash Flow Statements* defines cash as 'cash on hand and cash equivalents'. Cash equivalents are highly liquid investments such as money-market accounts and government treasury bills. They can be readily converted to cash on hand by the entity, and their use is part of a cash management function. Cash equivalents also include borrowings, such as bank overdrafts; again these are used by the entity as part of its cash management function. Cash equivalents must also be subject to an insignificant risk of changes in value.

KEY CONCEPT 12.1

CASH

Cash includes cash on hand and cash equivalents, which include highly liquid investments and borrowings used as part of an entity's cash management function.

Many businesses, especially retailers, receive large amounts of cash and credit card receipts each day. Cash is the most difficult asset to control as anyone can spend cash; therefore, it is important to establish effective management procedures for cash. Such procedures are important not only to protect the cash of the business but also to:

• enable accurate reporting of cash and cash flows in the financial statements
• ensure that adequate cash is available to meet commitments as they are due
• allow idle cash to be invested so as to maximise the return to the business.

Cash budgeting is an important tool in the management of cash and we discuss the preparation of cash budgets in Chapter 20.

Internal control of cash

Explain internal control procedures for cash, and why they are important

Given the ease with which cash can be misappropriated, it is important for a business to establish effective internal control procedures to protect the cash of the business. Internal controls refer to the procedures and processes in place within a business to safeguard all assets including cash. The processes should be part of written policies within the business and, for larger businesses, an internal auditor may be employed to ensure that such processes are adequate and are being followed.

An overriding principle in internal control is to separate duties so that the same person is not responsible for receiving and recording cash. When we go to a football game we normally buy a ticket at one counter and then pass the ticket to a different person as we enter the ground. This is an internal control procedure to minimise the opportunities for employees to steal cash. One of the main reasons Barings Bank failed in the 1990s, resulting in losses of billions of dollars, was because of a failure to observe this basic internal control rule. Nick Leeson, the 'rogue trader' responsible for the large trading losses which ultimately led to the bank's failure, was in charge of trading transactions on the floor of the stock exchange and the recording of such trades in the accounting records. He was therefore able to cover up the large trading losses he was incurring as a trader, by falsifying the accounting records. In this way, he was able to escape detection for a much longer period of time than would have been the case if the duties of trading and recording had been carried out by different individuals.

Internal control procedures will vary across companies depending on their size and particular needs. However, effective internal control over cash should ideally include separation of:
- the duties of receiving and paying cash
- the duties of recording cash receipts from cash payments
- handling cash and recording cash movements in the accounting records.

In very small businesses, it may not always be possible to establish such procedures, so other security measures may be employed.

For example, a proprietor of a small corner shop employed a number of part-time staff. It came to his attention that, a few weeks after employing a new person, the cash receipts of the store were somewhat lower than normal. While there were always two or more staff working at any time, there were times when one person was alone behind the counter. The proprietor therefore called in a security firm and had a security camera installed in the roof of the store, over the cash register. The camera revealed the new employee taking money from the register and placing it in his pocket.

Effective internal control over cash should also provide for individual responsibilities that:
- require all cash receipts to be deposited with a financial institution on a daily basis
- provide for different individuals to approve a requisition to order goods and services from the individual who approves payment for the goods and services. There have been instances where a person orders goods to be delivered to his home address and then arranges for payment of the goods from the business bank account
- ensure that approval to make a cash payment and the actual signing of the cheque or electronic funds transfer are by different individuals
- require regular reconciliation of the bank statement (which is the bank's record of the business's cash position) with the accounting records of the business. This reconciliation should result in both balances being the same (after allowing for outstanding deposits and cheques not recorded on the bank statement but recorded in the accounting records of the business, and for various bank charges and fees recorded on the bank statement but not in the accounting records of the business). If this is not the case, it may signal that misappropriation of cash has occurred. Once again, the bank reconciliation should not be done by the same individual responsible

for collecting and disbursing cash in the business. To do so would allow the individual to misappropriate cash and then cover up their theft.

KEY CONCEPT 12.2

INTERNAL CONTROL

An important principle of internal control is to have separation of duties so that it requires collusion between two or more employees to misappropriate the assets of a business.

The internal control principles outlined in this section, while particularly relevant for cash, also apply to other assets such as debtors. Having briefly reviewed what we mean by cash and the importance of establishing effective internal control procedures over cash, we now examine the reporting of cash flows to external users through a cash flow statement.

The cash flow statement

In addition to the balance sheet and income statement, reporting entities are now required to prepare a cash flow statement following the release of AASB 107 *Cash Flow Statements*. In this part of the chapter, we examine the objective of cash flow statements and the relationship between the cash flow statement and the income statement. We then look at an example of a cash flow statement and how it is interpreted.

PURPOSE

Explain the main purpose of a cash flow statement

The main purpose of the cash flow statement is to provide information about the cash receipts and cash payments for an entity during its accounting period. It is cash and not profits that an entity must use to pay its bills. It is possible for a profitable firm to have insufficient cash to meet its debts and be insolvent.

The balance sheet shows the assets an entity has at a particular point in time and how these assets are financed. The income statement shows how much profit the entity has earned during the accounting period. Both these statements are based on accrual accounting and not cash accounting. These statements cannot be used to answer the following types of questions:

- Did the entity's operations produce sufficient cash to meet dividend payments?
- Did the entity issue shares or increase liabilities during the year and, if so, what happened to the proceeds?
- Did the entity purchase any new assets during the year? How did the entity pay for these new assets?

The cash flow statement is intended to provide answers to these and other questions.

WHAT DOES A CASH FLOW STATEMENT SHOW?

Having established the need for a cash flow statement, we need to look in more detail at what the statement shows. In broad terms, as we have pointed out, it tells us where we got money from, and how it was used. For the purposes of the cash flow statement, any transfers of cash between cash equivalents and cash on hand do not need to be reported as cash receipts or payments. The money coming in is referred to as cash inflows, while money going out is referred to as cash outflows. The difference between the cash inflows and the cash outflows is known as the net cash flow, which can be either a net cash inflow or a net cash outflow, depending on the magnitude of the two components. Typical cash inflows would be monies generated from trading (commonly referred to as cash flows from operations), monies from new share issues or other forms of long-term finance, and any monies received from the sale of assets. Typical outflows would be monies used to buy new non-current assets, to pay tax and dividends and to repay debenture holders or other providers of long-term capital. As we shall see, the cash flow statement separates these cash flows into various categories. The format we shall follow is the one recommended in the Accounting Standard. We shall use the example of a cash flow statement shown in Example 12.1.

LO 4

Discuss what is meant by the concept of cash flows of operating, investing and financing activities

Review exercise 1

What are the reasons for requiring a cash flow statement?

Example 12.1: Sample cash flow statement

	This year		Last year
	$000s	$000s	$000s
Cash flow from operating activities		1 800	1 400
Cash flow from investing activities			
Payments to acquire non-current assets	(900)		(200)
Payments to acquire investments			(100)
Receipts from disposal of non-current assets	50	(850)	
Cash flow from financing activities			
Dividends paid	(2 500)		(1 200)
Issue of ordinary share capital	300		
Repayment of loan	(150)	(2 350)	
Increase/decrease in cash in period		(1 400)	(100)

Example 12.1 shows that the cash flow statement not only provides the detail of the change in cash as the last figure, $1.4 million this year and $100 000 last year, but also divides the cash flows into the business and out of the business under a number of separate headings. These headings or subdivisions are intended to provide information about the source and nature of the cash flow. For

example, cash flow from operating activities tells us that the cash comes from the normal continuing operations of the business and these operations and their related cash flows are likely to continue each year. The cash flows under 'Cash flows from investing activities', on the other hand, are different as they are not likely to recur each year.

If you think of your life, you may equate these differences with the cash flows related to running a car, where expenditure on such items as petrol and insurance will recur each year and are classed as operating cash flows. The capital investment of buying another car does not occur each year and is, therefore, an investing cash flow. Finally, if you had to borrow money from the bank to finance the purchase of the new car, this would be a financing cash flow. Before we move on to looking at the subheadings and what they mean in more detail, we first need to define cash flows.

KEY CONCEPT 12.3

CASH FLOWS

Cash inflows are defined as increases in cash.
Cash outflows are decreases in cash.
Net cash flow consists of the net effect of cash inflows and cash outflows.

Review exercise 2

Explain what is meant by the cash flows of operating, investing and financing activities.

CASH FLOW FROM OPERATING ACTIVITIES

Identify cash flows from operating activities, and explain the difference between operating cash flows and net profit

The first subheading in the cash flow statement is 'Cash flow from operating activities'. If we had kept our business as the simple cash-based model we used up until Chapter 7 (before we introduced year-end inventories, debtors, creditors, non-current assets, and so on), the cash flow from operating activities would have been the same as profit. However, as we have pointed out from Chapter 7 onwards, this may reflect how the cash has been spent, but not the economic activity. This, if you remember, is because some of the spending relates to future years and some to past years, and so on. This presents us with a problem because what we have done, in effect, from Chapter 7 onwards is to adjust the cash figure to arrive at a figure for profit based upon the principles of accrual accounting. Therefore, if we start with the profit figure, we have to reverse all those adjustments in order to arrive at the cash flow from operations.

It is very important for your understanding of the cash flow statement, and its interrelationship with the income statement and balance sheet, that you understand this process and the reasons for it.

Example 12.2: Valerie's business

Valerie's business had the following balances at the start of the year.

	$
Debtors	350
Creditors	760
Bank and cash	580

At the end of the year the balances were:

	$
Debtors	210
Creditors	530
Bank and cash	1 640

If we look first at the creditors, we can see that we have used our cash to reduce the amount we owe from $760 to $530. Thus, we have used up $230. As a result, we would expect our cash balance to be reduced by $230, but, in fact, it has increased by $1060, so clearly there are other factors involved. One of these is that we sell goods for more than we buy them so we get more cash in than we pay out. Some of that cash is used to buy more stock, some is put in the bank and some is used to finance debtors.

Clearly, in order to proceed we need more information:

	$
Sales for the period	3 000
Purchases for the period	1 850
Cash received from debtors	3 140
Cash paid to creditors	2 080

From the information we have we could produce the cash flow statement very easily because we have the cash flows in (from debtors) of $3140 and the cash flows out (to creditors) of $2080, so we have a net cash flow of $1060 ($3140 – $2080) which is the difference between the opening and closing bank balance. However, as pointed out in Chapter 1, users also want to know how much profit has been made. Once again, from the information, we could produce an income statement as follows:

Income statement for Valerie's business: version 1

	$	$
Sales		3 000
Opening inventory	0	
Purchases	1 850	
Closing inventory	0	
Cost of sales		1 850
Profit for the year		1 150

The worksheet for Valerie's transactions is shown below:

Valerie's worksheet: version 1

Description	Assets			= Liabilities +	Equity	
	Bank	Inventory	Debtors	Creditors	Capital	Profit and loss
Balances	580	0	350	760	170	
Sales			3 000			3 000
Purchases		1 850		1 850		
Cash in	3 140		–3 140			
Cash paid	–2 080			–2 080		
Cost of goods sold		–1 850				–1 850
Balances	1 640	0	210	= 530	170	1 150

The difficulty we have now is that we have told the users that the cash that came in was $1060 ($3140 – $2080) more than the cash going out, and we have also told them that we have made a profit of $1150. Given this information, they might justifiably ask, why are these figures different?

Of course, by now we know that the answer is because one system is based on cash measures and the other is based on accrual accounting, which takes into account sales made that we have not yet received money for, purchases that *are* not yet paid for, changes in the levels of inventory held, and so on.

So how can we reconcile the two figures? We can start by thinking about the effect that changes in the level of debtors would have on the cash figure. If we decrease the level of debtors, we get more cash in than is shown by our sales figure. Conversely, if we increase the level of debtors, we will get less cash in than is shown by the sales figure. In the case of Valerie's business, the cash coming in was $3140 and the sales for the period were $3000. The difference between the cash received and the sales of $140 was due to the fact that at the start of the year we had $350 due to be received from our debtors and at the end of the year we only had $210 due from our debtors, a difference of $140. The general rule we have just derived is given as Key concept 12.4.

This is useful to help us on our way but is not the whole story, because our starting point is profit, not sales, and what we are trying to reconcile is net cash flow from operating activities, not cash received.

KEY CONCEPT 12.4

SALES, DEBTORS AND CASH RECEIVED

An *increase* in the debtors due over the period must be *subtracted* from the sales to arrive at the cash received.

A *decrease* in debtors due over the period must be *added* to sales to arrive at the cash received.

Profit is derived by subtracting the cost of goods sold figure from the sales figure, so it is also a net figure like the cash flow from operating activities. Thus, we are dealing with two net figures. This is a useful starting point. We now need to look at the effect that an increase in the gross figures – sales and cash received – has upon the net figures we are dealing with. In the case of goods sold there is a direct relationship between sales and profit; that is, an increase in sales leads to an increase in profit and a decrease in sales leads to a decrease in profit.

Similarly, in the case of cash received, an increase in cash received leads to an increase in the net cash flow from operating activities and a decrease in cash received leads to a decrease in net cash flow. Thus, the gross figures and net figures follow the same pattern as a result of increases or decreases: the effect on the net figures is the same as the effect on the gross figures. Consequently, we can simply restate Key concept 12.4 in terms of profit rather than sales, as shown in Key concept 12.5.

KEY CONCEPT 12.5

PROFIT, DEBTORS AND NET CASH FLOW FROM OPERATING ACTIVITY

An *increase* in the debtors due over the period must be *subtracted* from the profit to arrive at the net cash flow from operating activity.

A *decrease* in debtors due over the period must be *added* to profit to arrive at the net cash flow from operating activity.

If we now think about creditors,.we have a similar situation to that for debtors. If we increase the amount that we owe at the end of the year it means that our cash payments will be less than our purchases. If we reduce the amount that we owe, then our cash payments will be more than our purchases. In the case of Valerie's business, the cash paid and the purchases were $2080 and $1850 respectively, a difference of $230. This difference was due to the fact that, at the start of the year, we had $760 owing to our creditors and, at the end of the year, we only had $530 owing, a reduction of $230. The general rule we have just derived is given as Key concept 12.6.

KEY CONCEPT 12.6

PURCHASES, CREDITORS AND CASH PAID

An *increase* in the creditors over the period must be *subtracted* from the purchases to arrive at the cash paid.

A *decrease* in creditors over this period must be *added* to purchases to arrive at the cash paid.

At this point, we need to acknowledge an important distinction between differences in debtors and their effect on sales and profits, and differences in creditors and their effect on profits. The important point here is that, as we have already stated, the relationship between an increase in sales and an increase in cash received on the net figures is the same; that is, an increase in sales results in an increase in profit and an increase in cash received results in an increase in the net cash flow from operating activity. Therefore, the relationships are direct and in the same direction.

In the case of cash paid, the relationship between increases in cash paid and the net cash flow is an inverse relationship; that is, an increase in cash paid will have the effect of decreasing the net cash flow. Conversely, a decrease in cash paid will increase the net cash flow. Similarly, the relationship between an increase or decrease in purchases and the effect on profit is an inverse relationship. If we leave aside the effect of holding inventory for the moment, as Valerie has no opening or closing inventory, we can see that an increase in purchases would have the effect of increasing the costs and therefore reducing the profit. A decrease in purchases, on the other hand, would reduce costs and increase profits.

So, in order to adjust profit to take account of the differences between purchases and cash payments in respect of those purchases, we need to reverse the effects set out in Key concept 12.6. Key concept 12.7 sets out the relationship between profits, increases and decreases in creditors, and profits and net cash flows from operating activities.

KEY CONCEPT 12.7

PROFIT, CREDITORS AND NET CASH FLOW FROM OPERATING ACTIVITY

An *increase* in the creditors over the period must be *added* to the profit to arrive at the net cash flow from operating activity.

A *decrease* in creditors over the period must be *subtracted* from the profit to arrive at the net cash flow from operating activity.

So far, so good, hopefully! Let us see how what we have done to date works:

Reconciliation of operating profit and cash flow from operating activity: version 1

	$
Profit for the year	1 150
Less Decrease in creditors	(230)
Add Decrease in debtors	140
Increase in cash	1 060

Note: Brackets are commonly used in published accounts to denote negatives.

As you can see, we have been successful in reconciling the profit to the cash flow from operating activity.

Unfortunately, the debtors and creditors are only one part of the adjustments we made when using accrual accounting. The most common of these relate to the effect of holding inventories and the effects of having non-current assets. In general terms, these have an effect on the income statement but not on the cash flows arising out of the operating activity. In the case of non-current assets, as we discussed in relation to Example 12.1 using the example of a car, there may be an effect on cash flows in respect of capital expenditure but no effect on operating cash flows.

To understand the effects of inventory and depreciation, let us extend our Valerie example a little further by adding some inventory figures and some figures for non-current assets and depreciation.

	$
Opening inventory	420
Closing inventory	480
Non-current asset – cost	1 000
Depreciation at start	400
Depreciation for year	200
Depreciation at end	600

The new worksheet for Valerie would be as shown below:

Valerie's worksheet: version 2

		Assets				= Liabilities +	Equity	
Description	Bank	Non-current assets	Accumulated depreciation	Inventory	Debtors	Creditors	Capital	Profit and loss
Balances	580	1 000	−400	420	350	760	1 190	
Sales					3 000			3 000
Purchases				1 850		1 850		
Cash in	3 140				−3 140			
Cash paid	−2 080					−2 080		
Cost of sales		−		−1 790				−1 790
Depreciation			−200					−200
Balances	1 640	1 000	−600	480	210	= 530	1 190	1 010

If we look at the difference between the profit under version 1 and version 2 of the income statement, we can see that there are two reasons for the difference. The first is that the cost of goods sold figure has changed, due to the presence of opening and closing inventory. The second is that the resultant profit has also been reduced by the depreciation charge for the year. However, it is obvious from a quick glance at the cash column of version 2 of the worksheet that there has been no change in the cash received or paid. The double entry for both these items is between the income statement and the item concerned, and the cash column is not affected.

Income statement for Valerie's business: version 2

	$	$
Sales		3 000
Opening inventory	420	
Purchases	1 850	
	2 270	
Closing inventory	480	
Cost of goods sold		1 790
Gross profit for the year		1 210
Depreciation		200
Operating profit for the year		1 010

Looking first at the depreciation, we can see that if we charge depreciation we reduce the profit but do not affect the net cash flow. Therefore, we need to add back the depreciation charge for the year to the operating profit to arrive at the cash flow. We state this as a general rule in Key concept 12.8.

KEY CONCEPT 12.8

PROFIT, DEPRECIATION AND NET CASH FLOW FROM OPERATING ACTIVITY

Charges for depreciation and amortisation of non-current assets charged to the income statement for the period must be added back to the operating profit to arrive at the net cash flow from operating activities.

If we now turn to decreases and increases in the inventory held over the period, we can see from the Valerie example that because we held more inventory at the end than at the start this led to a decrease in cost of goods sold and an increase in profit. Similarly, a decrease in inventory would lead to an increase in cost of goods sold and a decrease in profit. Thus, we can state a general rule for inventory as shown in Key concept 12.9.

KEY CONCEPT 12.9

PROFIT, INVENTORY AND NET CASH FLOW FROM OPERATING ACTIVITY

An *increase* in the inventory held over the period must be *subtracted* from the profit to arrive at the net cash flow from operating activity.

A *decrease* in the inventory held over the period must be *added* to the profit to arrive at the net cash flow from operating activity.

It is important to note that, although the effects of an increase in inventory are the same as an increase in debtors, the relationship is different. In the case of debtors, the relationship is direct, whereas in the case of inventory, it is indirect and can be thought of as two inversions which cancel each other out.

Let us now see if we can reconcile the new profit from version 2 of Valerie's income statement with the net cash flow from operating activity.

We already have some of the figures in respect of debtors and creditors, and now need to deal with inventory and depreciation. For inventory we have an increase of $60; as this is an increase it has to be taken off the profit to arrive at cash flow from operations. In the case of depreciation, we need to add back the charge for the year, $200, to profit.

Reconciliation of operating profit and cash flow from operating activity: version 2

	$
Profit for the year	1 010
Less Decrease in creditors	(230)
Add Decrease in debtors	140
Less Increase in inventory	(60)
Add Depreciation charge	200
Increase in cash from operations	1 060

As a by-product of the explanation of how the figure for net cash flow from operating activity is arrived at and reconciled with the operating profit, we have produced a reconciliation statement. Under AASB 107, this reconciliation statement is specifically required to be disclosed in financial reports (but it is not required in IAS 7). This requirement is partially due to the fact that, in AASB 107, cash flows from operations must be determined using the direct method and not the indirect method. The direct method occurs when the gross receipts from customers and the gross payments to employees and suppliers are reported. The indirect method shows operating profit and then adds or subtracts items (as we have just done in the reconciliation) to yield operating cash flows. Users are not told the gross receipts and payments in the indirect method.

Having completed a reconciliation statement, let us now return to our example of a sample cash flow statement and look at the other headings. To remind ourselves of the format of the cash flow statement, the sample is reproduced below.

Sample cash flow statement

	2004		2003	
	$000s	$000s	$000s	$000s
Cash flow from operating activities		1 800		1400
Cash flow from investing activities				
Payments to acquire non-current assets	(900)		(200)	
Payments to acquire investments	0		(100)	
Receipts from disposal of non-current assets	50		0	
		(850)		(300)

	2004		2003	
	$000s	$000s	$000s	$000s
Cash flow from financing activities				
Dividends paid	(2 500)		(1 200)	
Issue of ordinary share capital	300		0	
Repayment of loan	(150)		0	
		(2 350)		(1 200)
Increase/(decrease) in cash in period		(1 400)		(100)

Review exercise 3

Explain the difference between cash flow and net profit.

CASE STUDY 12.1

DON'T LET CASH TAKE A HOLIDAY
Mark Fenton-Jones

In the first of a three-part series on underperforming businesses, Enterprise editor Mark Fenton-Jones shows that when a small business's capital starts walking and not working, it's time to examine the books for deficiencies. The surge in the number of retirees taking off for the wide blue yonder was proof to one fast-growing caravan manufacturer that it would have no problem succeeding. But despite the signs there would be positive demand, the company went into administration.

Insolvency practitioner Michael Jones, of Jones Condon, declined to identify the company but was more than happy to explain its demise. 'It failed to adequately capitalise the production facility. It had a lack of working capital in the first place,' Jones says. 'That boils down to improper budgeting, improper forecasting and improper cost management.'

Working capital is the financial lubricant needed to operate any business on a day-to-day basis for such things as wages, raw materials and stock. And as Nicholas Humphrey, the author of *The Penguin Small Business Guide*, says: 'A major cause of failure in small business is a lack of cash and poor management of working capital.'

The source of the caravan maker's failure was rooted in the very market that seemed to offer the chance of success. As an overheated market populated with many manufacturers, suppliers could pick and choose to whom they supplied. 'It was not a sales problem, it was a purchasing problem,' Jones says.

Suppliers would sell only to businesses they considered to be good paying customers. For the hopeful caravan manufacturer, supplies were delivered on a cash-up-front basis, not cash on delivery. The result was a two-week delay between paying for the goods and getting them, and an effective increase in the time that the caravan maker was not making any money.

'That has the net effect of increasing disproportionately the amount of working

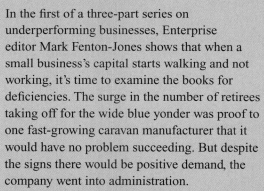

capital you need to have tied up in a company. There's a working capital deficiency right from the start, one that could easily be planned for and simply wasn't,' Jones says.

Small businesses often make the mistake of assuming that a booming market automatically means profits. That might be the case, but sometimes the profits are so late in coming, and the business lacks the working capital to span the time between delivery and payment, that a business is effectively insolvent.

An Australian company with the technology to attract United States customers expanded into the North American market, funding the growth on the basis that customers would pay within 90 days. But six months into the contract, the US customers started to slow down their payments, leaving the Australian contractor with $500 000 in outstanding debts. At that point, says Rana Pala, who works in the business advisory area of medium-sized accounting firm BDO, the alarm bells should have started ringing. 'They should have looked at the payments against their terms of trade.'

Instead, the company's owners, who he says were 'caught up in the vision of growing too quickly', pressed on with accepting more US business, while technically insolvent. Although the company does not appear to have gone bust, the lack of sufficient working capital to fund additional capacity is a critical factor that figures prominently in the minds of accountants and business advisors.

PricewaterhouseCoopers partner Gregory Will, who specialises in the operations of medium-sized companies, recounted the story of a business that almost went broke after doubling in size over two years.

During that time it had invested in a lot of stock and staff, but, as Will says, the money from sales was not coming as frequently as originally expected. 'So they had massive cash flow issues and couldn't fund their growth,' he says. Cash flow is the ultimate outcome of working capital management. Inventory, debtors and creditors all converge into cash one way or the other.

The head of the entrepreneurial growth market group at Ernst & Young, Rob Dalton, says that working capital warning signals revolve around sales. A retailer, for example, might not pick up that its core areas of business have declined because new stores are opening or new customers picked up. Consequently, inventory levels are not adjusted and the retailer is caught with working capital tied up in stock that can't be moved except at drastically discounted prices. 'The trick to being a good businessman is to be a good monitor of all of your major business functions,' Dalton says.

Australian Financial Review, 15 November 2005
2005 Copyright John Fairfax Holdings Limited.
www.afr.com Not available for re-distribution.

COMMENTARY

The article identifies problems that arise when companies don't adequately plan for their working capital requirements. This often leads to cash flow problems, and without sufficient cash flow a business can easily fail.

Identify cash flows from investing and financing activities

CASH FLOW FROM INVESTING ACTIVITIES

There are broadly two types of cash flow from investing activities: the first relates to non-current assets like property, plant and equipment, and the second to shares in other companies and similar investments. As far as non-current assets are concerned, this would involve cash outflows in relation to the purchase of non-current assets and cash inflows from the sale of non-current assets (see Figure 12.1 overleaf). Clearly, such cash flows are different from those we have discussed so far. They tend to be non-recurrent, as an individual non-current asset or investment can only be replaced or sold once. The second type is when a business purchases shares in another business or acquires a total business and this results in cash outflows. Cash inflows arise when an entity sells some of the shares or the business that has been acquired. The intention here is to differentiate the cash flows that relate to these one-off activities from the recurring cash flows.

CASH FLOW FROM FINANCING ACTIVITIES

The final heading involves the cash flows relating to the financing of the business. These include amounts received from share issues, new loans or debentures – in other words, from long-term financing. It would also show amounts paid out in respect of loans or debentures that have been repaid during the year, and in respect of any shares redeemed and dividends paid. Figure 12.1 summarises the classification of cash flows.

INCREASE (DECREASE) IN CASH IN THE PERIOD

The final figure shown on the cash flow statement is the increase or decrease in cash. This can be reconciled fairly easily with the information in the balance sheet.

INTEREST, DIVIDENDS AND INCOME TAX

The accounting standards require amounts paid and received for interest and dividends to be separately disclosed as either operating, investing or financing cash flows. As Figure 12.1 shows, the most common classification for interest paid and received and dividends received is operating cash flows. Dividends paid are normally shown as a financing cash flow. Income taxes paid must also be separately disclosed and are normally included as an operating cash flow.

NON-CASH INVESTING AND FINANCING ACTIVITIES

Sometimes an entity is involved in transactions such as acquiring land and buildings by issuing shares that do not involve cash. Such transactions, where significant, must be disclosed in a note to the cash flow statement, so that the user has a complete picture of the entity's investing and financing activities.

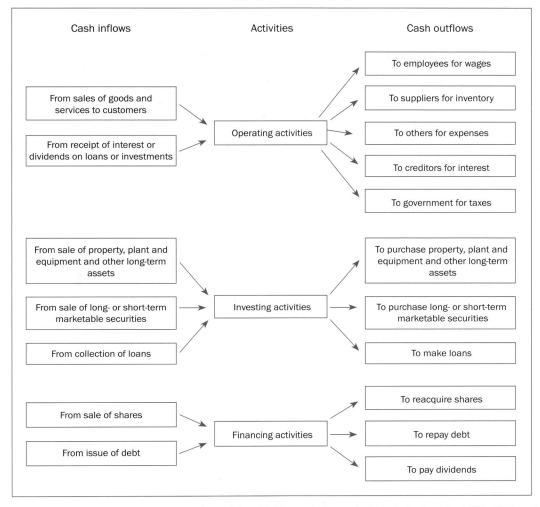

Adapted from T.D. Wise et al., *Accounting in Australia*, Houghton Mifflin, 1990, p. 714.

Figure 12.1 Classification of cash inflows and cash outflows

Review exercise 4

A company issued 200 000 $1 shares, fully paid, in exchange for land with a fair market value of $200 000. How would this transaction be reported on a cash flow statement?

Example 12.3: Woodside cash flow statement

You should now study Woodside's cash flow statement in Appendix 1. Note that the company has presented the cash flows from operating, investing and financing activities, as required by AASB 107. It does not report a reconciliation of net cash flows from operations and operating profit after income tax as this is not a requirement in half-year reports.

We now make a number of observations based on Woodside's cash flow statement.

Cash flows from operating activities

Net cash flows from operating activities were $672 673 000 for the six months ended 30 June 2005. This amount more than covers the $212 607 000 paid in dividends in the same period. This is a positive position for the company. The cash receipts from customers were $1 287 681 000 while payments to suppliers were $225 508 000 – a very healthy result for the company. The company has a very healthy cash balance as at 30 June 2005 of $617 068 000.

Cash flows from investing activities

The two major items in this section are the payment for capital and exploration expenditure of $724 113 000 and the $110 738 000 payment for interests in new joint ventures. There has been an increase in capital and exploration expenditure from the previous corresponding period. The previous period also had an inflow of $588 903 000 from the sale of exploration and evaluation.

Cash flows from financing activities

This section shows that the company paid $212 607 000 in 2005 and $166 667 000 in the previous period.

Net increase in cash

The cash on hand decreased by $189 796 000 for the period.

Consolidated accounts

LO 7

Explain the meaning and purpose of consolidated financial statements

Most major companies, such as Woodside, BHP Billiton, CSR and Woolworths, operate in a parent–subsidiary (or controlled entity) relationship for a variety of reasons. In fact, these large companies often control 100 or more companies. Since users of financial reports need to examine the performance and financial position of the parent entity on its own, and of the combination of the parent entity and the other entities it controls, group accounts are prepared. The preparation of these group accounts is called consolidation, and the terms 'group' and 'consolidated' accounts are interchangeable. In these accounts, the parent entity and its controlled entities are grouped to constitute an economic entity.

It does not have the status of being a legal entity; it does not have the legal rights and obligations of a company, which were discussed in Chapter 11.

Consolidated financial statements are useful to the management and shareholders of the parent entity in judging how well the parent has achieved its goals. They are also critical in reporting the financial position of the economic entity. For example, the collapse of Enron revealed billions of dollars in debt hidden in 'special purpose entities'. It is important that users are fully aware of all the debts of an entity when assessing issues like solvency and the going concern test. The collapse of Enron also caused losses for many employees who may have made different decisions about investing in the company they worked for, had they been aware of the true level of debts of the company.

PREPARATION OF CONSOLIDATED ACCOUNTS

Consolidated accounts are prepared in accordance with the relevant standard (AASB 127 *Consolidated and Separate Financial Statements* and AASB 3 *Business Combinations*). These standards require consolidated financial statements to be prepared for a parent entity and all other entities which it controls. Control is defined in AASB 127, paragraph 4, as:

> . . . the power to govern the financial and operating policies of an entity
> so as to obtain benefits from its activities.

The concept of control is consistent with the approach taken in the definition of assets. It is not always obvious, in practice, whether an entity controls another.

LO 8

Explain why it is necessary to eliminate the investment and subsidiary accounts, and transactions, between members of the group

CASE STUDY 12.2

The diagrams below are examples of different organisational structures which would meet the definition of an economic entity for the purpose of AASB 127.

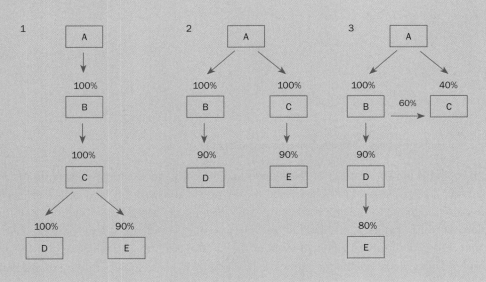

COMMENTARY

In all three cases, we have assumed that the percentage of ownership also equals the voting entitlements. Therefore, in Case 1, the economic entity consists of A, B, C, D and E, and A is the parent entity or chief entity. In Case 2, A obtains control of D indirectly through its control of B. Therefore, the economic entity in Case 2 is still A, B, C, D and E, with A still the parent or chief entity. In Case 3, A achieves control of C both through its own interest in C and through B's interest in C. Therefore, the economic entity is still A, B, C, D and E, and A is again the parent or chief entity.

In all three cases, A controls entities B, C, D and E because of the voting rights attached to its ownership interest.

The purpose of consolidated financial statements is to give a view of the parent entity and its controlled entities as if they were one entity – the economic entity – so that on the balance sheet the debtors represent the debtors of the parent entity and all its controlled entities. Similarly, the consolidated income statement shows total revenue from sales made by the parent entity and all its controlled entities. In preparing consolidated financial statements, similar accounts from the individual statements of the parent entity and its controlled entities are combined. However, some accounts result from transactions between the parent entity and a controlled entity. If consolidated financial statements are to represent the position and results of an economic entity as a whole, then any transactions between members within the economic entity must be eliminated.

If we look at Figure 12.2, we can see why it is necessary to eliminate transactions between members of the economic entity.

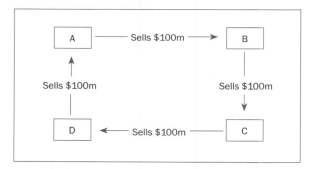

Figure 12.2 Transactions between members of an economic entity

If A, B, C and D are all members of the same economic entity, then adding sales figures together would produce $400 million of sales. However, the economic entity A, B, C and D has not sold any of this to parties external to the group. Therefore, the sales for the economic entity in relation to the transactions shown in Figure 12.2 should be zero. In preparing consolidated financial statements for A, B, C and D, it is necessary to eliminate each of the sales of $100 million which appear in each of the individual financial statements for entities A, B, C and D. This also applies to the expenses and to the profits or losses made from these sales.

It is also necessary to eliminate any amounts owing to or due from members within the economic entity. If A in Figure 12.2 was owed $100 million by B, in the consolidated financial statements it would be necessary to reduce debtors and creditors by $100 million. If this was not done, the consolidated balance sheet for the economic entity would show $100 million as owing from itself and payable to itself. Obviously this is inappropriate.

Another item which must be eliminated in the consolidated balance sheet is the 'Investment in the subsidiary' account which appears in the parent entity's balance sheet.

The 'Investment in the subsidiary' account is replaced in the consolidation process with the assets and liabilities of the controlled entity. Thus, the 'Investment' account and the shareholders' equity section of the controlled entity must be eliminated. The following example demonstrates this process:

Accounts	Company A	Company B	Elimination	Consolidation
	$	$	$	$
Assets	50 000	30 000		80 000
Investment in B				
(100% of shares in B)	10 000	_____	−10 000	_____
	60 000	30 000		80 000
Liabilities	20 000	20 000		40 000
Paid-up capital	20 000	10 000	−10 000	20 000
Retained profits	20 000	_____		20 000
	60 000	30 000		80 000

In this example, A owns all the shares of B. Therefore, the 'Investment in B' account represents A's ownership and control of the total shareholders' equity of B. The paid-up capital of B represents the ownership of the net assets of B; that is, $30 000 – $20 000. Therefore, A owns and controls the net assets of B. Thus, the elimination of the 'Investment in B' account and the shareholders' equity section of B allows the net assets of B to be added to the net assets of A. This produces the net assets of the economic entity of A + B.

The consolidated financial statements are prepared by combining similar accounts from the separate statements of the parent entity and its controlled entities after elimination of all transactions between members of the economic entity.

KEY CONCEPT 12.10

CONSOLIDATED FINANCIAL STATEMENTS

Consolidated financial statements provide information about the performance, financial position and cash flows of an economic entity.

In many cases, a parent entity owns 100 per cent of all its subsidiaries, as is the case with Woodside. However, there are also many instances when a parent entity will own enough to gain control of another entity, but not 100 per cent. Take Company E in Case 1 in Case study 12.2. Company C Ltd owns 90 per cent of E Ltd. This means that other shareholders own 10 per cent of the shares in E Ltd. Such shareholders are described as a 'minority interest' in accounting standards. Minority interests are reported in consolidated financial statements based on their interest in the relevant subsidiary. For example, in the case of E Ltd, the minority shareholders represent 10 per cent of the net assets of E Ltd at balance date. The minority interest is also entitled to 10 per cent of the net profit/loss of E Ltd for the period. Minority interest is not a liability in the consolidated statements but represents part of the equity of the net assets of the economic entity.

An examination of Woodside's financial report shows that all the statements are consolidated statements. This is because it is a half-year report and companies are only required to present consolidated statements in half-year reports. In annual financial statements companies must show parent and consolidated figures.

Taxation

Explain the meaning of deferred tax assets and deferred tax liabilities

A company's tax liability is determined by the taxable income of the company in Australia. In Chapter 1 we mentioned that accounting profit and taxable income are not necessarily the same. This is because accounting rules that are used to determine accounting profit sometimes differ from the tax rules used to determine taxable income. The example used in Chapter 1 was income that is exempt from tax but is still included as income in the determination of accounting profit. Another example is the differences that arise from the different depreciation rates used for accounting and tax purposes. These differences between taxable income and accounting profit result in the recognition of a current liability for taxes payable and, possibly, a non-current liability for deferred taxes payable. It is also possible for companies to have deferred tax assets. In this section, we attempt to explain deferred tax assets and liabilities. The approach is based on that required by AASB 112 *Income Taxes*.

TEMPORARY DIFFERENCES

The use of different rules for tax and accounting leads to temporary differences between the carrying value of an asset or liability in the balance sheet in a company's books and the balances for the same asset and liability for taxation. This is best explained with some examples.

Rent receivable

Assume Company A recognises revenue of $10 000 at 30 June 20X7 for rent it is owed but has not yet received in cash. This results in the recognition of an asset, rent receivable, of $10 000. For accounting purposes, the rent revenue increases the accounting profit by $10 000. However, the company uses the cash basis for tax purposes and is therefore not required to pay tax until the rent is received in cash. When the rent is received, the company will have to pay tax. This means the company will pay more tax in future periods; this meets the definition of a liability.

The future tax consequence for the company of receiving the rent and reducing the asset rent receivable to a zero balance is a tax liability of $10 000 × the tax rate. If we assume a tax rate of 40 per cent, this results in future tax of $4000. This will be recognised in the current year as a deferred tax liability. If we assume that the accounting profit is $100 000 for 20X7 and taxable income is $90 000, the worksheet entries involved in the current period are as follows:

Worksheet: Company A, 20X7

Assets	=	Liabilities		+	Equity
		Tax payable	Deferred tax payable		Tax expense (profit and loss)
		36 000	4 000		−40 000
		(40% × $90 000)	(40% × $10 000)		($36 000 + $4 000)

Tax expense is determined by taking the tax payable and adding (subtracting) increases (decreases) in the deferred tax payable.

In the following year, if we assume that the rent was paid to Company A, and the taxable income is $100 000 and the accounting profit $90 000, the worksheet would be as shown below:

Worksheet: Company A, 20X8

Assets	=	Liabilities		+	Equity
		Tax payable	Deferred tax payable		Tax expense (profit and loss)
		40 000	−4 000		−36 000
		(40% × $100 000)	(40% × $10 000)		($40 000 − $4 000)

The tax payable the following year is $4000 higher than the previous year and this, in effect, represents settlement of the deferred tax amount from the previous period.

The deferred tax payable arises because of the temporary difference in the balance of the asset rent receivable in the books of Company A ($10 000) and the value of the asset for tax purposes (zero).

Provision for warranty costs

Companies who provide warranties on products they sell estimate the expected costs to be incurred in future periods as a result of sales in the current period. This is based on their experience in previous years and is similar to the estimation of doubtful debts discussed in Chapter 8. This results in the recognition of an expense and a liability in the current period. However, for tax purposes, there is no deduction for any warranty costs until the actual repairs have been made and the costs incurred.

Assume Company B has estimated the liability for warranty costs at $20 000 and has created the liability 'provision for warranty costs' and recorded the expense. This results in an accounting profit of $80 000 and taxable income of $100 000 in 20X7.

The future tax consequence of creating this liability is that the liability will be reduced when the warranty repairs are provided and the company will pay less tax in future periods. The payment of less tax in the future meets the definition of an asset. Therefore, Company B must recognise a deferred tax asset of $20 000 × 40 per cent, or $8000.

This will result in a lower tax expense for the period, as illustrated in the worksheet below:

Worksheet: Company B, 20X7

Assets	=	Liabilities	+	Equity
Deferred tax asset		Tax payable		Tax expense (profit and loss)
8 000		40 000		−32 000
(40% × $20 000)		(40% × $100 000)		($40 000 − $8 000)

The deferred tax asset arises because of a temporary difference in the balance of the provision for warranty costs in the books of Company B ($20 000) and the value of the liability for tax purposes (zero). If, in 20X8, the actual warranty costs incurred total $20 000, the taxable income is $80 000, and accounting profit is $100 000, then the accounting entries would be as follows.

Worksheet: Company B, 20X8

Assets	=	Liabilities	+	Equity
Deferred tax asset		Tax payable		Tax expense (profit and loss)
−8 000		32 000		−40 000
(40% × $20 000)		(40% × $80 000)		($32 000 − $8 000)

The amount of tax payable in 20X8 is $8000 less than in 20X7. This, in effect, represents the consumption of the deferred tax asset.

Tax expense is determined by taking the tax payable and subtracting (adding) increases (decreases) in the deferred tax asset.

Tax losses

When a company incurs a loss, for tax purposes, it potentially has a deferred tax asset which it can recognise on the balance sheet. This is because the tax laws allow losses to be carried forward and used to reduce taxable income in future periods. Therefore, if a company decides that it is probable that it will earn taxable income in future periods, it can recognise a deferred tax asset in the current period.

Assume that Company C incurs a tax loss of $100 000 in the current period. The loss resulted from an unusually long and protracted strike, but the company expects to return to profitability next year. If the tax rate is 40 per cent, the company can recognise a deferred tax asset of $100 000 × 40 per cent, or $40 000. This represents future tax savings of $40 000.

Review exercise 5
What are deferred tax assets and liabilities?

KEY CONCEPT 12.11

ACCOUNTING FOR INCOME TAX

The approach adopted in accounting for income tax gives rise to deferred tax assets and liabilities which arise because of temporary differences between the tax value and carrying value (for accounting purposes) of assets and liabilities, and tax losses.

Goods and Services Tax

Income tax is a direct tax on income and this was discussed in the previous section. Goods and Services Tax (GST) is an indirect tax and is a tax on goods and services. It is a value added tax which means that the tax is levied on the amount of value added by a business at each stage of the business process. A business collects GST on behalf of the government and is required to periodically remit amounts owing to the government as determined from its Business Activity Statement (BAS). In Australia at present, the GST is levied at a rate of 10 per cent. In New Zealand the rate of GST is 12.5 per cent.

LO 10

Identify the accounting that is involved for the Goods and Services Tax (GST)

   The process of how GST works is not particularly complicated, although it is true that there is more paperwork involved for business in its role as tax collector for the government. A business has taxable supplies and creditable acquisitions. The business collects GST from the sales of taxable supplies and pays GST on its creditable acquisitions. The difference, where it has collected more than it has paid, represents a liability to the Australian Tax Office (ATO). Where the business has paid more GST than it has collected, it has an asset which is the amount it will receive from the ATO. Example 12.4 provides details of the GST paid by businesses associated with the manufacture and sale of woollen suits.

Example 12.4: GST on woollen suits

Stage 1

A manufacturer purchases $1000 of wool from a farmer and pays $100 GST, making the total cost $1100. The farmer has collected $100 GST and has not paid any GST. The farmer remits $100 GST to the ATO.

Stage 2

The manufacturer converts the wool into suits and sells the suits to a retailer for $2000 plus $200 GST. The manufacturer has collected $200 GST and paid $100 GST and so remits the difference of $100 to the ATO.

Stage 3

The retailer sells the suits to customers for $2500 plus $250 GST. The retailer has collected $250 GST and paid $200 GST and, therefore, remits the difference of $50 to the ATO.

Total GST to ATO

$100 from the farmer + $100 from the manufacturer + $50 from the retailer = $250

The $250 equals the amount of GST paid by the customers. Thus, the GST is collected at various stages by different parties but the ultimate party who bears the cost of the GST is the consumer.

ACCOUNTING FOR GST

Accounting for GST involves recording GST amounts paid and received in separate accounts with amounts paid recorded in an asset account and amounts collected in a liability account. At the end of each reporting period, either monthly, quarterly or annually, the GST asset and liability accounts are reset to a nil balance. The difference is paid to the ATO when the liability is greater than the asset; or a receivable is recognised, when the asset is greater than the liability.

CASE STUDY 12.3

TAX PENALTY PLEA
by Louise Hattam

INDUSTRY groups want GST legislation to be amended to allow small business to pass on late penalties to late debtors or extend GST payment deadlines. The Minister for Small Business Marsha Thomson has called on the Federal Government to deal with serious GST-related cash flow problems which she believes are crippling Victorian businesses.

Ms Thomson said some small and medium-sized businesses were experiencing significant cash flow disruptions because of late payments for work done and this was compounded by relatively short GST compliance periods of 28 days. 'The Federal Government's GST is still hurting some of Victoria's small business operators,' Ms Thomson said.

'All too often businesses are left waiting, sometimes for as long as 60 days for payment from recalcitrant clients. 'The GST, however, must be remitted within 28 days of the end of the BAS period even if the monies have not been received.'

Ms Thomson said this caused enormous cash flow disruption and hardship for small businesses with limited financial flexibility. 'Australia's manufacturing industry has also been hurt, with Australian Industry Group surveys reporting a cash flow tightening in small and medium firms, but not surprisingly, an improved cash flow for larger businesses,' she said.

Ms Thomson said Victoria's smash repair industry was a typical example of the problems faced by small businesses. Victorian Automobile Chamber of Commerce surveys have found that smash repair firms often face slow payments from insurance companies, with invoice payments worth tens of thousands of dollars sometimes taking up to 90 days.

The latest VACC survey of members of its body repair division shows that slow payment by some insurers is an industry-wide problem. VACC executive director David Purchase said the viability of many small businesses was being threatened because they were not being paid on time for goods sold or services rendered, and the offenders should be penalised.

'A healthy cash flow is critical to small businesses, which must meet business payments on time: rents, wages, superannuation, bills and of course quarterly GST business activity statements,' Mr Purchase said. 'Many businesses get fed up waiting for payments (from creditors) and turn to money lenders or factoring agents to survive cash-flow problems.'

He said the GST's BAS must be paid on time or businesses incur penalties of 11.28 per cent, compounding daily.

Herald-Sun, 15 July 2002

COMMENTARY

The article highlights cash flow problems associated with timing issues in respect to GST. The ATO must be paid within 28 days of the end of the reporting period and yet some businesses have longer delays in collecting amounts owing from customers which includes the GST component. It is another example of a potential cash flow threat to the existence of small businesses if it is not well managed.

SUMMARY

LO 1

LEARNING OBJECTIVE 1
Explain what is included in the terms 'cash' and 'cash equivalents'

Cash includes cash on hand and cash equivalents such as highly liquid investments and borrowings used as part of an entity's cash management function.

LO 2

LEARNING OBJECTIVE 2
Explain internal control procedures for cash, and why they are important

Effective internal control over cash is important, as cash is the most liquid asset and the one that is most easily misappropriated. The internal controls should ideally include separation of:

- the duties of receiving and paying cash
- the duties of recording cash receipts from cash payments
- handling cash and recording cash movements in the accounting records.

LO 3

LEARNING OBJECTIVE 3
Explain the main purpose of a cash flow statement

Both the balance sheet and the income statement are based on accrual accounting and not cash accounting. These statements cannot be used to answer the following types of questions:

- Did the entity's operations produce sufficient cash to meet dividend payments?
- Did the entity issue shares or increase liabilities during the year and, if so, what happened to the proceeds?
- Did the entity purchase any new assets during the year? How did the entity pay for these new assets?

The cash flow statement is intended to provide answers to these and other questions by reporting cash flows from operating, investing and financing activities.

LO 4

LEARNING OBJECTIVE 4
Discuss what is meant by the concept of cash flows of operating, investing and financing activities

Cash flow from operating activities reports cash flows from the normal continuing operations of the business. These operations, and their related cash flows, are likely to continue each year. Cash flows from investing activities are different in that they are not likely to recur each year and are related to the purchase and sale of non-current assets. Cash flows from financing activities report the cash flows associated with equity and debt providers. Financing cash flows reveal how a company has funded any large cash outflows in the operating and/or investing activities.

LO 5

LEARNING OBJECTIVE 5
Identify cash flows from operating activities, and explain the difference between operating cash flows and net profit

Cash flow from operating activities includes:

- cash receipts from customers
- cash payments to suppliers
- cash payments to employees
- interest paid and received
- dividends received.

The cash flows from operating activities are not the same as net profit (which is determined using accrual accounting). To reconcile the net profit figure to operating cash flows, adjustments have to be made for various items arising from the accruals process. This includes adding non-cash expenses (like depreciation and amortisation) back to profit. It is also necessary to adjust for changes in the balances of accounts such as debtors, creditors, accrued expenses and prepaid assets.

LEARNING OBJECTIVE 6
6
Identify cash flows from investing and financing activities

There are broadly two types of cash flow arising from investing activities. The first type relates to non-current assets like property, plant and equipment. As far as non-current assets are concerned, this involves cash outflows for their purchase and cash inflows from their sale.

The second type of cash flow arising from investing activities relates to shares in other companies and similar investments. When a business purchases shares in another business, or acquires a total business, this results in cash outflows. Cash inflows arise when an entity sells some of the shares or the business that has been acquired.

The cash flows from financing activities include amounts received from share issues, new loans or debentures – in other words, from long-term financing. Cash outflows for financing activities would include amounts paid out for loans, amounts for debentures that have been repaid during the year, and shares redeemed and dividends paid.

LEARNING OBJECTIVE 7
7
Explain the meaning and purpose of consolidated financial statements

Consolidated financial statements are prepared for an economic entity that is a group of entities with a parent and a number of subsidiaries. Consolidated financial statements are useful to the management and shareholders of the parent entity in judging how well the parent has achieved its goals. They are also critical in reporting the financial position of the economic entity.

LEARNING OBJECTIVE 8
8
Explain why it is necessary to eliminate the investment and subsidiary accounts, and transactions, between members of the group.

Transactions between members of an economic entity must be eliminated, otherwise the consolidated statements would include transactions showing the entity dealing with itself. If this process was not undertaken, a parent entity could force subsidiaries to engage in transactions with other members of the group just to improve the reported performance in the consolidated statements. The 'Investment in subsidiary' account must be eliminated otherwise the consolidated balance sheet would include, as an asset, an investment in itself.

LEARNING OBJECTIVE 9
9
Explain the meaning of deferred tax assets and deferred tax liabilities

The approach that is adopted in accounting standards concerning accounting for income tax gives rise to deferred tax assets and deferred tax liabilities. These arise because of temporary differences between the tax value and carrying value (for accounting purposes) of assets and liabilities, and tax losses.

LEARNING OBJECTIVE 10
10
Identify the accounting that is involved for the Goods and Services Tax (GST)

Accounting for GST involves recording GST amounts paid and received in separate accounts; amounts paid are recorded in an asset account and amounts collected are recorded in a liability account. At the end of each reporting period (either monthly, quarterly or annually), the GST asset and liability accounts are reset to a nil balance. The difference is paid to the ATO when the liability is greater than the asset; a receivable is recognised when the asset is greater than the liability.

REFERENCES

Australian Accounting Standards Board. AASB 3 *Business Combinations*, July, 2004.
Australian Accounting Standards Board. AASB 107 *Cash Flow Statements*, July, 2004.
Australian Accounting Standards Board. AASB 112 *Income Taxes*, July, 2004.
Australian Accounting Standards Board. AASB 127 *Consolidated and Separate Financial Statements*, July, 2004.

REVIEW QUESTIONS

1 What are the main principles of the internal control of cash?

2 What information can be obtained from a cash flow statement?

3 What are consolidated financial statements? What is their purpose?

4 Explain what is meant by the term 'subsidiary'.

5 Why might a company invest in another company?

6 Describe what is meant by the concept of control.

7 What are the three basic types of elimination that need to be made when preparing consolidated financial statements?

8 Why might accounting profit and taxable income differ?

9 Bill Smith owns and runs a supermarket. He is certain that one of the check-out staff is stealing money but, on every occasion, her till balances. If Bill is correct, how is the theft being committed and what steps can he take to overcome the problem?

10 When a business provides a service to another business, it normally does so 'on account' rather than as a cash transaction. This results in an account receivable for the business providing the service and an account payable for the business receiving the service. At some later date, the account will be paid. In contrast, when individuals conduct transactions it is usually a cash transaction.

   Why is it unusual for businesses to engage in cash transactions, while for individuals it is more common?

PROBLEMS FOR DISCUSSION AND ANALYSIS

1 Refer to the Woodside 2005 financial report in Appendix 1.
   a Did cash increase or decrease over the 26 weeks ended 30 June 2005? If so, by how much?
   b How much tax was paid in the year?
   c What amounts are reported for Deferred Tax Assets and Liabilities?

2 Explain how it is that a business which is making profits can have difficulties in meeting its debts. Perhaps you can bring to class some examples of businesses in this situation.

3 You have been appointed treasurer of your cricket club. The cricket club runs a bar and members are rostered to work on the bar. All the transactions across the bar are cash and the club uses a draw to store the cash. After reviewing the bar records, you notice a significant decline in the profits. You are concerned about the lack of control of the cash and believe this is the cause of the decrease in profits. What procedures would you recommend to improve the control of cash in the bar?

4   Explain how the following transactions would be recorded on a cash flow statement:
   a   Salaries payable were $50 000 at the beginning of the year and $45 000 at year end.
   b   Fully depreciated equipment with a cost value of $20 000 was discarded:
       i   sold to a scrap merchant for $1000
       ii given to an employee.
   c   A toy store had creditors of $23 000 at the beginning of the year and $27 000 at year-end.
   d   A company issued, for cash, 200 000 $1 shares for $1.20 per share.
   e   Bigboy Ltd reported in its annual report that it had issued 1 000 000 $1 shares, fully paid, for a company that had a net worth of $900 000.

5   Discuss the impact of each of the items below on the balance sheet, income statement and cash flow statement, giving reasons for your answer where appropriate:
   a   During the year the company sold a non-current asset with a carrying value of $5000 for $3000.
   b   The company also revalued its land from its original cost of $130 000 to $200 000.
   c   The building, which had cost $90 000, and on which depreciation of $30 000 had been provided, was revalued to $100 000.
   d   The company has also made an issue of 100 000 8 per cent $1 preference shares at a price of $1.20 per share.
   e   The company had paid back a long-term loan to the bank of $80 000.

6   Identify the type of cash flow activity for each of the following events (investing, operating, financing or non-cash transaction):
   a   Received cash from customers.
   b   Paid employees for wages.
   c   Signed a four-year lease agreement for a motor vehicle.
   d   Paid interest.
   e   Issued debentures.
   f   Issued ordinary shares.
   g   Sold long-term investments.
   h   Paid cash dividends.
   i   Redeemed debentures.
   j   Issued preference shares.
   k   Sold equipment for a gain.
   l   Purchased buildings.
   m   Purchased patents.
   n   Loss on disposal of a non-current asset.
   o   Increase in inventory.

7   Each of the transactions listed below will affect one of the four categories on the cash flow statement: cash flows from operating activities, cash flows from investing activities, cash flows from financing activities, or non-cash investing and financing activities. Analyse each transaction and state which category will be affected.
   a   Machinery to the value of $80 000 was acquired for cash.
   b   A patent that was sold for $30 000 had a carrying value of $20 000.
   c   Office supplies on-hand, valued at $2000, were exchanged for a second-hand car.
   d   Used machinery having a carrying value of $50 000 was traded for 500 shares of another company. The shares are intended to be a long-term investment.
   e   Dividends to the amount of $5000 were paid.
   f   Long-term debenture notes payable for the amount of $20 000 were paid in cash.
   g   Interest of $5000 was paid.

8   From the following information, determine the cash flows from operating activities.

	End of year	Beginning of year
	$	$
Cash	27 579	32 333
Receivables	17 632	10 849
Creditors	23 581	33 134
Salaries payable	6 373	5 687
Wages payable	11 045	11 044
Inventory	123 879	114 453
Prepaid expenses	499	1 006

9   The Royal Park Company income statement for 20X1 appears below:

Royal Park Company
Income statement for the year ended 31 December 20X1

	$000
Sales	160 000
Cost of goods sold	(96 000)
Gross profit on sales	64 000
Operating expenses:	
Rent expense	20 000
Depreciation expense	15 000
Other operating expenses	18 000
Total operating expenses	(53 000)
Net profit	11 000

The following information from Royal Park's balance sheet is available:

Account title	Balance 1 January	Balance 31 December
	$	$
Accounts receivable	10 000	12 000
Inventory	3 000	10 000
Prepaid rent	5 000	8 000
Accounts payable	26 000	28 000

Required

Determine the cash flow from operating activities for Royal Park.

10 For the current year ended 30 June, the results of operations of Hawkeye Corporation and its wholly owned subsidiary, Radar Enterprises, are as follows:

	Hawkeye Corporation		Radar Enterprises	
	$	$	$	$
Sales		8 150 000		750 000
Cost of inventory sold	5 000 000		440 000	
Selling expenses	800 000		75 000	
Administrative expenses	600 000		35 000	
Interest expense (revenue)	(30 000)	6 370 000	30 000	580 000
Net income		1 780 000		170 000

During the year, Hawkeye sold inventory to Radar for $80 000. The inventory was sold by Radar to non-affiliated companies for $120 000. Hawkeye's interest revenue was realised from a long-term loan to Radar.

a Determine the amounts to be eliminated from the following items in preparing a consolidated income statement for the current year:

  i sales

  ii cost of inventory sold.

b Determine the consolidated net profit.

11 Stephanie Flight has recently been hired as the manager of Tender Chickens. Tender Chickens is a national chain of franchised gourmet chicken retailers. During her first month as store manager, Stephanie encountered the following internal control situations:

a The store has only one cash register. Prior to Stephanie joining Tender Chickens, each employee working on a shift would take a customer order, accept payment and then prepare the order. Stephanie made one employee on each shift responsible for taking orders and accepting the customer's payment. Other employees prepared the orders.

b Since only one employee uses the cash register, that employee is responsible for counting the cash at the end of the shift and verifying that the cash in the drawer matches the amount of cash sales recorded by the cash register. Stephanie expects each cashier to balance the drawer to the cent every time – no exceptions.

c Stephanie caught an employee putting a box of chicken steaks in his car. Not wanting to create a scene, Stephanie smiled and said, 'I don't think you're putting those steaks on the right tray. Don't they belong inside the shop?' The employee returned the chicken steaks to the cooler shelf.

Required

State whether you agree or disagree with Stephanie's method of handling each situation and explain your answer.

12 Given the simplified balance sheet of Bazz Ltd & Lee Ltd, prepare a worksheet for the consolidation of the accounts of the parent company (Bazz Ltd) and its subsidiary (Lee Ltd). From your worksheet, prepare the consolidated balance sheet.

The following items need to be taken into consideration:

- Bazz Ltd acquired all the shares of Lee Ltd for $320 000 on the morning of 30 June 20X1.
- All assets and liabilities are stated at their fair values.
- Lee Ltd owed Bazz Ltd $10 000 for goods purchased on 15 June 20X1.

Bazz Ltd & Lee Ltd
Balance sheet at 30 June 20X1

	Bazz Ltd $	Lee Ltd $
Assets		
Current assets		
Bank	180 000	50 000
Accounts receivable	100 000	150 000
Total current assets	280 000	200 000
Non-current assets		
Plant and equipment (net of depreciation)	300 000	300 000
Investment in Lee Ltd	320 000	–
Total non-current assets	620 000	300 000
Total assets	900 000	500 000
Liabilities		
Current liabilities		
Accounts payable	400 000	180 000
Total liabilities	400 000	180 000
Net assets	500 000	320 000
Equity		
Paid-up capital	400 000	300 000
Retained profits	100 000	20 000
Total equity	500 000	320 000

13 Given the balance sheets for Phil Ltd and Jan Ltd, prepare a worksheet for the consolidation of the accounts of the parent company, Jan Ltd. Then, from your worksheet, prepare a consolidated balance sheet.

The following items also need to be taken into consideration:
- Jan acquired all the issued capital of Phil Ltd on 30 June 20X1 for $200 000.
- All assets and liabilities are stated at their fair values.
- Of the debentures issued by Jan Ltd, $100 000 worth are held by Phil.
- Jan owed Phil $13 000 for goods purchased in June 20X1.

Phil Ltd & Jan Ltd
Balance sheets at 30 June 20X1

		Jan Ltd		Phil Ltd
		$		$
Assets				
Bank		2 000		1 000
Debtors		33 000		27 000
Inventory		12 000		63 000
Total current assets		47 000		91 000
Non-current assets				
Plant and equipment	120 000		63 000	
CBS accumulated depreciation	73 000	47 000	6 000	57 000
Debentures investment in Phil		200 000		100 000
Total non-current assets		247 000		157 000
Total assets		294 000		248 000
Liabilities				
Current liabilities				
Creditors		36 000		53 000
Taxation		10 000		60 000
Total current Liabilities		46 000		113 000
Non-current liabilities				
Debentures	150 000		–	
Total non-current liabilities		150 000		–
Total liabilities		196 000		113 000
Net assets		98 000		135 000
Equity				
Paid-up capital	80 000		100 000	
Retained profits	18 000		35 000	
Total equity		98 000		135 000

14 ABC company depreciates its equipment at 20 per cent per annum, straight-line. The company is allowed, for tax purposes, to depreciate at 25 per cent per annum. Assume the company purchases an item of machinery for $100 000 on 1 July 20X3.

Assume a tax rate of 30 per cent and an accounting profit of $100 000 each year.

Required

Prepare a statement for this machinery for the five years under the headings of:
- Tax payable
- Deferred tax payable
- Tax expense.

15 On 1 January 20X4 the Widget Company acquires a piece of equipment which costs $40 000 and has
    an estimated life of four years with no residual value. The equipment is to be written off at 25 per cent
    per annum, straight-line. Assume the operating profit for the next four years is $100 000 per annum
    (before the deduction of depreciation and tax). For tax purposes, the company is allowed to write off the
    asset over two years at 50 per cent per annum, straight-line. The tax rate is 50 per cent.

    Set up a table with the following headings and fill in the blank spaces:

Year ending 31 December	Profit before depreciation and tax	Taxable profit after tax depreciation	Tax payable	Taxable profit after accounting depreciation	Tax expense	Differences between tax payable and tax expense
20X4						
20X5						
20X6						
20X7						
Total						

Note to instructors: *The following problems are considered more suitable for use in MBA courses.
However, undergraduate courses may also find them useful.*

16 Read the extract from the article 'Former bookkeeper charged with 170 counts of theft'. What
    procedures would have helped prevent Inaba from being able to steal successfully for eight years?

FORMER BOOKKEEPER CHARGED WITH 170 COUNTS OF THEFT
by Tracy Johnson, P-I reporter

A WOMAN who kept the books for a Bellevue produce company was charged yesterday with
170 counts of theft, accused of stealing $4.6 million in the largest embezzlement case King County
has ever prosecuted.

Police say Denise A. Inaba took tens of thousands of dollars each month while working part
time at Jaspo Inc., a business that buys local produce and sells it in Asia. She allegedly wrote
herself more than 1200 checks over a period of eight years, signing them with the owner's name.
Deputy prosecutor Scott Peterson said she made fake entries in the business's books to hide what
she was doing. 'She was the sole bookkeeper and had complete and total control,' he said.

Extract from article in *Seattle Post-Intelligencer*,
31 December 2002
© 2002 Seattle Post-Intelligencer. Reprinted with permission.

17 List the errors you find in the following cash flow statement. The cash balance at the beginning of the year was $70 700. All other figures are correct, except the cash balance at the end of the year.

The Future Zone Inc.
Cash flow statement for the year ended 31 December 20X3

	$	$	$
Cash flows from operating activities			
Net profit, per income statement		100 500	
Add: Depreciation	49 000		
Increase in accounts receivable	11 500		
Gain on sale of investments	7 000	67 500	
		168 000	
Deduct: Increase in accounts payable	4 400		
Increase in inventories	18 300		
Decrease in accrued expenses	1 600	24 300	
Net cash flow from operating activities			143 700
Cash flows from investing activities			
Cash received from sale of investments		85 000	
Less: Cash paid for purchase of land	90 000		
Cash paid for purchase of equipment	150 100	240 100	
Net cash flow used for investing activities			(155 100)
Cash flows from financing activities			
Cash received from sale of $1 ordinary shares		107 000	
Cash paid for dividends		36 800	
Net cash flow provided by financing activities			143 800
Increase in cash			132 400
Cash at the end of the year			105 300
Cash at the beginning of the year			237 700

18 The following cash flow statement is available for the Bee Pee Company:

	20X0 $m	20X1 $m
Cash flows from operating activities		
Receipts from customers	3 000	3 000
Payments to suppliers and employees	(2 500)	(2 600)
Interest received	60	35
Interest paid	(75)	(150)
Taxation paid	(17)	(13)
Net cash from operating activities	468	272

	20X0 $m	20X1 $m
Cash flows from investing activities		
Acquisition of property, plant and equipment	(250)	(1 800)
Proceeds from sale of non-current assets	50	200
Net cash from investing activities	(200)	(1 600)
Cash flows from financing activities		
Short-term borrowing – increase (decrease)		1 450
Long-term borrowing – increase (decrease)	40	
Dividends paid	(200)	(200)
Net cash from financing activities	(160)	1 250
Net increase (decrease) in cash held	108	(78)
Add opening cash brought forward	(50)	58
Closing cash carried forward	58	(20)

Required

Analyse the cash flow statement for Bee Pee. What changes to the cash management policies would you recommend to the company? Should the company continue to pay a dividend?

19 The directors of Kowloon Enterprises Ltd are concerned about the results of trading activities reported for the year ended 30 June 20X6, and failure to keep within the limit of the bank overdraft ($12 000).

Kowloon enterprises Ltd
Income statements for the years ended 30 June

	20X4 $	$	20X5 $	$	20X6 $	$
Sales		200 000		180 000		165 000
Less Cost of sales						
Opening inventory	36 000		41 000		44 000	
Purchases	95 000		87 000		80 000	
	131 000		128 000		124 000	
Less Closing inventory	41 000	90 000	44 000	84 000	49 000	75 000
Gross profit		110 000		96 000		90 000
Less:						
Selling and distribution expenses	40 000		40 000		46 000	
General and administrative expenses	20 000		20 000		18 000	
Financial expenses	15 000	75 000	16 000	76 000	20 000	84 000
Net operating profit before tax		35 000		20 000		6 000

	20X4		20X5		20X6	
	$	$	$	$	$	$
Less Taxation expense		15 000		9 000		2 500
Net operating profit after tax		20 000		11 000		3 500
Less Loss on sale of investment						1 000
Net profit for year		20 000		11 000		2 500

Kowloon Enterprises Ltd
Balance sheets at 30 June

	20X4		20X5		20X6	
	$	$	$	$	$	$
Assets						
Current assets						
Bank	1 000					
Inventory	41 000		44 000		49 000	
Trade debtors	26 000		31 000		37 000	
Less Provision						
For doubtful debts	(1 000)		(1 000)		(2 000)	
Prepayments	2 000		3 000		3 000	
Total current assets		69 000		77 000		87 000
Non-current assets						
Plant and equipment	10 000		10 000		21 000	
Less Depreciation (1000 in X3)	(2 000)		(4 000)		(7 000)	
Vehicles	80 000		80 000		114 000	
Less Depreciation (4000 in X3)	(16 000)		(32 000)		(54 000)	
Land (at valuation)	60 000		70 000		70 000	
Buildings (at cost)	40 000		56 000		56 000	
Investments (at cost)	25 000		25 000			
Total non-current assets		197 000		205 000		200 000
Total assets		266 000		282 000		287 000
Liabilities						
Current liabilities						
Bank overdraft			8 500		12 500	
Trade creditors	12 000		8 000		14 000	
Accrued wages and interest	1 000		1 500		2 000	
Provision for taxation	15 000		9 000		2 500	
Provision for dividend	13 000		15 000		3 000	
Total current liabilities		41 000		42 000		34 000

⊪➡

	20X4		20X5		20X6	
	$	$	$	$	$	$
Non-current liabilities						
Mortgage on land (due 30.6.X9)			21 000		34 500	
Term loan (due 20Y2)	75 000		75 000		75 000	
Total non-current liabilities		75 000		96 000		109 500
Total liabilities		116 000		138 000		143 500
Net assets		150 000		144 000		143 500
Shareholders' equity						
50 000 6% $1 preference shares		50 000		50 000		50 000
75 000 $1 ordinary shares		75 000		75 000		75 000
Asset revaluation reserve				10 000		10 000
General reserve		18 000		8 000		8 000
Retained profits		7 000		1 000		500
Total shareholders' equity		150 000		144 000		143 500

Kowloon Enterprises Ltd
Statements of changes in equity

	Share capital $m	Reserves $m	Retained profits $m	Total $m
Balance at 1 July 20X3	125 000	18 000	10 000	153 000
Net income recognised directly in equity				0
Profit or loss for the year (from the income statement)			20 000	20 000
Total recognised income and expense for the period				20 000
Dividends – Preference			(3 000)	(3 000)
Dividends – Ordinary			(20 000)	(20 000)
Balance at 30 June 20X4	125 000	18 000	7 000	150 000
Balance at 1 July 20X4	125 000	18 000	7 000	150 000
Land revaluation		10 000		10 000
Transfer to retained profits		(10 000)	10 000	
Net income recognised directly in equity				10 000
Profit or loss for the year (from the income statement)			11 000	11 000
Total recognised income and expense for the period				21 000
Dividends – Preference			(3 000)	(3 000)
Dividends – Ordinary			(24 000)	(24 000)
Balance at 30 June 20X5	125 000	18 000	1 000	144 000
Balance at 1 July 20X5	125 000	18 000	1 000	144 000
Net income recognised directly in equity				0

⟩⟩⟩

	Share capital $m	Reserves $m	Retained profits $m	Total $m
Profit or loss for the year (from the income statement)			2 500	2 500
Total recognised income and expense for the period				2 500
Dividends – Preference			(3 000)	(3 000)
Balance at 30 June 20X6	125 000	18 000	500	143 500

Required

a   What factors have contributed to this cash problem?

b   What steps would you recommend for Kowloon Enterprises Ltd to overcome the current cash problem?

ETHICS CASE STUDY

Jane Golly is the chief financial officer for Woppet Enterprises Ltd. She has decided to add a new ratio to the financial statements based on cash flow per share. The ratio will be reported on the cash flow statement and she believes it will provide useful information to readers of the financial statements. The cash flow per share this year will show a 25 per cent increase from last year. This will contrast with the 5 per cent decline in earnings per share.

Discuss whether there is anything unethical about Jane Golly's decision.

ANSWERS TO REVIEW EXERCISES

1   The cash flow statement is included in financial statements because it is cash, and not profits, that the entity requires in order to meet its debts. Profitability alone does not ensure that a firm has sufficient cash to be solvent.

2   The cash flow of operating activities shows the cash that is received from customers and the cash that is paid to suppliers, employees, and so on. It is the cash flow associated with the firm's operations. The cash flow related to investing activities is the cash flow from the acquisition and disposal of non-current assets such as property, plant and equipment. The cash flow of financing activities shows the cash inflows from creditors and shareholders which is used to finance the investing and operating activities. Repayments to creditors and shareholders are shown as cash outflows.

3   The cash flow statement is based on movements in cash while net profit is based on accrual accounting principles (i.e. revenues and expenses are recognised when they are earned or incurred not when the cash is received or paid).

4   This transaction would not appear in the cash flow statement as there is no cash involved. However, it would be reported as a non-cash investing transaction after the cash flow statement.

5   Deferred tax assets and deferred tax liabilities arise because of temporary differences in the carrying values of assets and liabilities for tax and accounting purposes.

13

LEARNING OBJECTIVES

At the end of this chapter, you should be able to:

1   identify the major accounting irregularities involved with the collapse of HIH, Enron and WorldCom

2   discuss the role that meeting performance targets played in the collapse of companies like Enron and WorldCom

3   explain what is meant by the term 'corporate governance'

4   identify the 10 ASX Corporate Governance Council best practice principles

5   discuss the issues associated with the role of the board of directors in corporate governance

6   discuss the issues associated with the role of the audit committee in corporate governance

7   identify the approaches to enforcing corporate governance requirements in Australia and the USA

8   identify what is meant by the term 'triple bottom line reporting'

9   summarise some of the reasons for and against the preparation of a triple bottom line report

10 identify the GRI, and explain, in broad terms, the GRI approach to triple bottom line reports.

Introduction

The early part of the twenty-first century will be remembered in the world of business for some very high-profile collapses of companies like Enron and WorldCom in the USA, Vivendi and Parmalat in Europe, and HIH, One.Tel, Ansett and Harris Scarfe in Australia. The failure of such high-profile companies raises serious concerns about financial reporting, accounting standards and corporate governance.

In this chapter, we explore the implications of these corporate failures for financial reporting and for the adequacy of accounting standards. We look at the issue of corporate governance and explain what is meant by internal and external corporate governance. We examine the issues associated with the roles of the board of directors and the audit committee as part of corporate governance. We highlight the corporate governance requirements in Australia and other countries.

As we mentioned in Chapter 1, many entities in developed countries are providing substantial information in addition to financial performance – in areas of governance, the environment and social issues. In the second part of this chapter, we examine the area of environmental and social reporting. The combination of financial, environmental and social reporting is often referred to as triple bottom line reporting.

Corporate failures

If someone had predicted that the early part of the twenty-first century would see the collapse and disappearance of one of the 'big 5' accounting firms, they would have been branded as slightly odd (if not totally insane). However, this is now a reality and the accounting firm of Arthur Andersen no longer exists. Is it a coincidence that auditors for the high-profile companies Enron, WorldCom and HIH were from Arthur Andersen, or is there some other explanation? We may never know the answer to this question, but what we can say is that the disappearance of Arthur Andersen is testimony to the enormity and significance of the issues confronting financial reporting as a result of high-profile company failures.

LO 1

Identify the major accounting irregularities involved with the collapse of HIH, Enron and WorldCom

CASE STUDY 13.1

TELCO BOSS UNFAZED BY DUD FIGURES, COURT TOLD
Paul Thomasch

FORMER WorldCom chief executive Bernard Ebbers was told that accountants would have to inflate revenue to meet profit expectations but brushed off the warning and demanded that the company hit its numbers, according to testimony from the US fraud trial's star witness on Tuesday.

Former company finance chief Scott Sullivan said he told his boss in the autumn of 2000 that revenue would have to be adjusted upward ▶

by more than $US130 million ($A170 million) to meet analysts' expectations, saying: 'This isn't right. We're doing this . . . because this is the only way I can get the numbers up to the expectations of the marketplace. Sullivan said Ebbers looked at a piece of paper with the numbers, 'studied it for a while . . . and said: "We have to hit our numbers"'.

He also said he had shown Ebbers statements showing costs were much higher than expected. US federal prosecutors claim that with telecommunications business deteriorating in 2000, Ebbers refused to admit earnings were falling short of expectations, instead arranging a massive accounting fraud. They say Ebbers told Sullivan to have his accountants puff up revenue and hide expenses, to keep Wall Street happy and keep the stock price from falling too sharply.

But investigators uncovered the 2002 accounting entries – leading to WorldCom's collapse. When it filed the largest US bankruptcy in history, calls sounded for the criminal prosecution of Ebbers. But prosecutors did not bring charges until Sullivan agreed to cooperate last year after

pleading guilty to fraud and conspiracy. He hopes his testimony will win leniency at his sentencing. Ebbers's lawyers say Sullivan was behind the accounting fraud and Ebbers stayed away from complex financial decisions.

The first witness to link Ebbers directly to the fraud, Sullivan said his accounting staff threatened to quit when they were ordered to cover up the higher than expected expenses by making adjustments to WorldCom's reserves. He told Ebbers in a handwritten note: 'We've made adjustments to this quarter to reserves that we have no support for and from here on out it was up to operations of the company to make our numbers and not the accounting department.'

Sullivan said he saw Ebbers later. 'He was very quiet and . . . said we shouldn't be making adjustments . . . We shouldn't be putting people in this position.' In all, Sullivan said, the revenue and expense adjustments for the quarter increased WorldCom's income by $US1 billion.

The Courier-Mail, 10 February 2005
Copyright 2005 News Ltd. All Rights Reserved

COMMENTARY

This article reports on the testimony of Scott Sullivan, the chief financial officer of WorldCom, against Bernard Ebbers the former CEO of WorldCom. Sullivan alleges Ebbers not only knew about the accounting fraud but, in fact, was the person responsible for it. Ebbers was convicted of fraud and, in July 2005, was sentenced to 25 years imprisonment.

The size of the debt that was left from the collapse of WorldCom is estimated as $14.6 billion. Such losses create a public perception that there is something seriously wrong with financial reporting and accounting rules. However, the real problem with WorldCom was not the accounting rules, but rather the fraudulent approach to the recording of expenditures as assets instead of expenses (with the end-result being higher reported profits).

Who is at fault when accounting rules are wrongly applied? There are some transactions which are not easily categorised, such as the cost of refurbishing a building (Is it an expense or asset?), but in the case of WorldCom, according to the testimony of Sullivan, it was simply alleged bogus accounting, and certain key players have now been convicted of criminal charges. Of course, questions can still be asked about the role of the auditor and why this alleged phoney accounting was not detected earlier. It is also now a reality that the firm Arthur Andersen has also paid dearly for its role at companies like WorldCom and Enron.

The Enron case involved different accounting irregularities (as explained in Case study 13.2) but, from all reports, the motivations of those involved in the scandal were the same – greed. These cases, and others, have raised serious concerns about the way senior executives are rewarded. Moreover, the strategy of using share options to align the interests of senior executives with shareholders has been widely criticised. Since the demise of WorldCom and Enron, a number of companies have ceased using share options as part of the remuneration package for senior managers, but many still do.

CASE STUDY 13.2

ENRON REPORT PROVIDES DETAILS OF DEALS THAT MASKED DEBT
by Mitchell Pacelle

A COURT-APPOINTED examiner has provided new details about how Enron Corp., with the help of its accountants and bankers, structured a labyrinth of complex financial vehicles that served to move debt off its balance sheet and boost the company's cash flow. In a report filed Saturday in the US Bankruptcy Court in Manhattan, Atlanta lawyer Neal Batson offered the initial instalment of what is expected to be an exhaustive attempt to dissect Enron's controversial balance sheet and eventually draw conclusions about whether any laws were broken and who might be liable. The findings could provide additional ammunition to the numerous claimants currently attempting to assign blame for the Enron debacle and to extract damages from Enron's bankers and other third parties.

A spokeswoman for Enron declined to comment on the report.

The report comes in the wake of several other official fact-finding efforts that arrived at similar conclusions following Enron's filing for Chapter 11 bankruptcy-court protection in December. A report commissioned by Enron's board identified numerous financial irregularities related to special-purpose entities, or SPEs. Earlier this year, congressional hearings raised a host of questions about the activities of Enron's executives and bankers.

The report says Mr Batson has identified at least 50 SPEs that entered into hundreds of separate financing transactions, but the report examines only six transactions involving a few SPEs. The six transactions, which occurred between 1997 and October 2001, provided Enron with $1.38 billion in cash and 'had dramatic effects on both the balance sheet and income statement portions of Enron's financial statements,' the report said.

These six deals involved numerous financial institutions, including Royal Bank of Canada and Cooperatieve Centrale Raiffeisen-Boerenleenbank BA, also known [as] Rabobank, a Dutch financial group. In the report, however, Mr Batson wrote that he had not yet drawn any final conclusions about whether the off-balance-sheet vehicles might be vulnerable to legal challenge. For example, the report drew no conclusions about whether creditors might be able to regain assets 'sold' to these entities, which are currently valued at about $500 million.

'Enron was prolific in its use of highly complex structured finance transactions using SPEs, with the result that billions of dollars of recourse obligations were not disclosed as debt in Enron's balance sheet, and the proceeds of these recourse obligations were reported as revenue and cash flow,' the report said.

The six transactions described in the report were known within Enron by the names Hawaii 125-0, Cerberus, Nikita, Backbone, SO2 and Destec. In most of these transactions, an Enron entity purported to sell an asset to the SPE in exchange for cash and other considerations, the report said. The SPE often borrowed money to pay Enron.

But unlike in most arms-length transactions, the seller, Enron, or an affiliate agreed to repay the amount borrowed by the SPE, the report said. Moreover, Enron or its affiliate would continue to control the asset and would continue to receive upside benefit from it, the report said.

The Wall Street Journal, 23 September 2002

COMMENTARY

The article explains that the real issue with Enron was that the company hid large amounts of contingent debt by using special-purpose entities which were not included in the consolidated financial statements. The article refers to recourse arrangements which, in essence, means that the issuer of loans to the SPEs could call upon Enron to repay the debt, should the SPE default. The SPE would borrow money that would eventually wind up in Enron supposedly for the sale of goods/assets to the SPE. In many cases, the goods/assets were of little value. Enron would recognise revenue and, hence, profits arising from such sales. According to the arrangements described in the article, the real debt position and financial risk of Enron was never fully disclosed to shareholders. The article mentions financial irregularities and states that conclusions about whether any laws were broken and who might be liable are yet to be finalised.

A number of persons, including Andrew Fastow, the chief financial officer at Enron, have been convicted of fraud. Ken Lay, the chairman, and Geoff Skilling, the chief operating officer, have been charged and should go to trial in 2006.

The final high-profile company failure that we examine in Australia is HIH. This case would appear to involve poor management practices and some questionable accounting practices. Case study 13.3 is a summary of the Royal Commission views as to what were the major problems at HIH.

CASE STUDY 13.3

SWALLOWED BY $5BN LIABILITIES GAP – HIH – THE FINDINGS
by David Brearley

WHO is to blame for the nation's worst ever corporate collapse? Just about everyone involved, according to counsel assisting the royal commission, who pointed the finger yesterday at weak management, a timid board, slack auditors, less-than-professional advisers and a hopelessly inept regulator.

HIH's core problem, outlined by senior commission counsel Wayne Martin QC, was the $5 billion-plus gap between the premiums it charged and the liabilities it incurred – 'hardly a blinding revelation, but it is perhaps at the broadest possible level the reason why the group collapsed'.

Mr Martin offered four 'dominant' reasons for HIH's failure: the consistent underestimation of liabilities; losses in Britain, which he pegged at $1 billion; losses in the US; and the 1999 acquisition of FAI, which had serious reserving problems of its own. He also pointed to two 'major events' which, while not directly responsible for the losses, fed into the collapse. The first was the withdrawal of Swiss insurance giant Winterthur as HIH's majority shareholder in 1998. Chief executive Ray Williams was 'instrumental' in ensuring Winterthur was replaced by many smaller interests and not the single purchaser with the deep pockets HIH needed, Mr Martin said.

The second major event was HIH's 2000 joint venture with Allianz, which only worsened the dire cash flow problems it was designed to address. All the usual mechanisms for heading off corporate collapse failed at HIH. Its senior management and directors were dominated by Mr Williams, 'whose business judgment was in the end shown to be faulty'.

Mr Williams's loyalty to lieutenants George Sturesteps and Terry Cassidy and to a lesser extent to his friend and mentor Michael Payne, was out of step with HIH's exponential growth. 'The business outgrew its management,' Mr Martin said, adding that 'executive self-indulgence' and the 'sordid saga' of Brad Cooper pointed to a corporate culture that was not responsive to shareholders.

The group's chairman, Geoffrey Cohen, was 'utterly ineffective', as were its non-executive directors and the committees on which they served. The board itself had 'no real strategy'. HIH auditors Arthur Andersen were 'misled and lied to', but yielded too easily to management and 'failed to respond with appropriate diligence and resolve'.

Mr Martin was critical of consultants engaged by HIH, especially its external actuary, David Slee, financial advisers and lawyers who had not performed up to standards expected of their professions. Finally, the Australian Prudential Regulation Authority 'lacked the expertise, the human resources and the requisite culture to undertake any effective form of regulation of HIH'.

'The group had a fundamentally flawed business,' Mr Martin concluded, 'in that it repeatedly made inadequate provision for future claims liability and made three major business decisions which proved to be disastrous: that is, in the UK, in the USA and in the acquisition of FAI.

'The lack of a major shareholder with access to substantial capital left it vulnerable and the Allianz transaction exacerbated its cash flow problems, and each and every mechanism of corporate governance and prudential regulation failed to prevent the group's slide into financial oblivion.'

The Australian, 14 January 2003

COMMENTARY

The article highlights that the main issue with HIH was a significant underestimation of its liabilities. It also discusses various events which contributed to its ultimate demise. The acquisition of FAI Insurance is seen as a major problem for HIH. During the course of the Royal Commission, there were newspaper reports of some dubious accounting transactions, the results of which were to increase reported profits of HIH or FAI. Mr Martin is also very critical of the chairman and the non-executive directors and believes they were ineffective and failed in their duty to the shareholders.

Mr Martin refers to executive 'self-indulgence' and the 'sordid saga of Brad Cooper'. This article again highlights the role of greed in this case, and it would appear to be a common factor in all three company failures that we have considered in this chapter. It is true that companies have failed in the past and there will be those that will fail in the future for reasons such as inept management, inadequate capital and for other reasons not associated with fraudulent behaviour.

In April 2005, HIH executives Rodney Adler and Ray Williams were both sentenced to jail for a period of up to four and a half years. They were found to have misused their positions to gain a personal advantage, in contravention of section 182 of the *Corporations Act*. Adler was disqualified from taking part in the management of the company for 20 years and Williams for 10 years. Adler was also ordered to pay $A900 000 as a pecuniary penalty while a penalty of $A250 000 was imposed on Williams. (Adams 2005)

Review exercise 1

Summarise the main accounting irregularities in the Enron, WorldCom and HIH failures?

Discuss the role that meeting performance targets played in the collapse of companies like Enron and WorldCom

There are some who argue that the cause of most of the problems at companies like Enron, WorldCom and HIH was the way senior executives were remunerated for their services. In particular, the use of share options has received a great deal of criticism and, as a result, many companies have moved to limit or cease their use of share options. In addition, AASB 2 *Share-based Payment* requires that any share-based remuneration which includes share options must be recognised as an expense in the income statement. Previously, this was not required so company profits were not affected by the use of share options – as would be the case if the executive were paid in cash. Therefore, part of the incentive for companies to use share options in place of a cash salary has been removed. Case study 13.4 provides one view as to the real underlying cause of debacles like Enron and WorldCom.

CASE STUDY 13.4

OBSESSION WITH PERFORMANCE LEADS TO ACCOUNTING SCANDALS
by Larry Chao

THE corporate accounting scandals currently dominating headline news are not exceptional, but rather the natural outcome of a runaway capitalist economy that demands performance at all costs. Greed seems to be the common denominator in the recent string of corporate accounting scandals. Incidents at WorldCom, Enron, Global Crossing and elsewhere show what happens when a company tampers with results to boost profits and personal gain.

Even the system's watchdogs – the Arthur Andersens of the world – have turned a blind eye to artificially-enhanced earnings, reluctant to jeopardise client fees. Indeed, finding clever loopholes in accounting rules and regulations has become the benchmark for   ⅠⅠⅠ➡

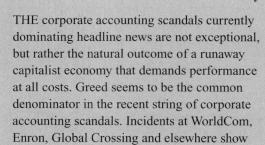

excellence. Greed is only a part of the explanation. The real problem is far more acute. It lies at the very heart of Corporation American Culture: the pressure to perform and fear of failure.

Demanding performance is nothing new. Successful companies have generally cultivated their own culture of performance. 'Managing change', 'continuous growth' and 'survival of the fittest' were mantras that guided successful companies such as General Electric through decades of economic turbulence.

Japan realised the importance of this Darwinian philosophy far too late. Only after years of flat growth has it begun to shed its grip on performance inhibitors such as lifetime employment, blanket consensus management and rigid management protocols. Even so, Japan Inc.'s reluctance to put individual and business performance ahead of traditional management practices has stifled its renewal.

The problem occurs, however, when the pressure to perform goes unchecked, fuelled by intense competition, demanding investors and, of course, huge personal incentives. Moreover, despite the rhetoric about learning from failure, in reality there is virtually no tolerance for failure to perform. Miss your quarterly budget and you're already under scrutiny. Miss your budget again and you will be lucky to get a third chance.

Ask former Xerox chief executive Richard Thomas, who was ousted after only a year of poor performance. With revenues stalling and earnings plummeting, Xerox's board did not hesitate to pressure Thomas into resigning. The company didn't care whether factors beyond Thomas' control – such as the Y2K scare or currency devaluation – contributed to the company's dismal performance. The bottom line was that Thomas did not perform.

'Very few executives refuse to accept corporate targets set for them by the head office, even if they are too much,' said one president of a multinational firm operating here in Thailand. 'If you persist in complaining that your budget is unfair and not achievable, headquarters will find somebody else to do the job.'

And so the pressure to perform mounts, as does the temptation to do what it takes to achieve objectives. WorldCom Inc., America's second largest long-distance telephone carrier, is a case in point. Through improper shifting of funds, $3.8-billion (Bt164-billion) worth of operating costs were booked as capital expenditures. Each shift enabled WorldCom to hit scheduled profit projection targets. As a result, rather than reporting negative earnings for the past year and first quarter of this year, WorldCom had a positive story to tell Wall Street.

Enron's creative accounting practices produced a similar mirage of success – erroneous earnings that painted a rosy picture not of a company going bust. Not only did it appear that Enron delivered on its financial promises, people such as former chief executive Jeffrey Skilling made huge personal profits at the expense of unsuspecting investors.

In a culture where successful performance is critical and linking performance to extraordinary personal gain provides the ultimate carrot, it is not surprising that certain individuals have tried to bend the rules and blur the distinction between right and wrong. Because it is unlikely that we will lower our performance expectations and settle for less, at the very least we need to rewrite the rules and regulations from the perspective of investors, employees, lenders and other stakeholders who stand to lose the most.

Most importantly, the fear of breaking the rules and being caught must be greater than the fear of failing to perform. Otherwise, executives will continue to risk bending the rules with the hope of escaping unscathed, rather than playing it straight and sometimes failing.

The Nation (Thailand), 23 September 2002
© 2002 Nation Multimedia Group Public Co. Ltd.

COMMENTARY

The article provides an excellent insight into the culture which is alleged to have contributed to failures of companies such as Enron, WorldCom, Vivendi, Parmalat and HIH. So, how do we prevent a repetition of events of the type that are alleged to have occurred with Enron and WorldCom? The last paragraph in Case study 13.4 suggests that part of the solution is to increase the fear of being caught if you break the rules so that this is greater than the fear of failing to perform.

Many believe that good corporate governance is one of the main ways of minimising divergent behaviour by senior executives. Better corporate governance, should (in theory, some argue) increase the fear of being caught. We discuss corporate governance in the next section.

Corporate governance

WHAT IS MEANT BY 'CORPORATE GOVERNANCE'?

There has been a huge focus on corporate governance since the company failures discussed in the last section. Regulators and governments have been reviewing the laws and regulations in respect of how corporations are governed. Corporate governance is not a new concept but it has come into prominence in the wake of the concerns about why and how the Enron and WorldCom collapses happened.

What do we mean by the term 'corporate governance'? The following definitions will assist in understanding what this means:

> The system of relations between the shareholders, Board of Directors and management of a company, as defined by the corporate charter, bylaws, formal policy and rule of law. (Investor Protection Association Executive Office 2006)

> Corporate governance is about promoting corporate fairness, transparency and accountability. [J. Wolfensohn, president of the World Bank, as quoted by an article in *Financial Times*, June 21, 1999]

In Chapter 11, we looked at different forms of business organisation including the sole trader, the partnership and the company. The company is a separate legal entity and is often managed by professionals on behalf of its owners (shareholders). Corporate governance refers to the procedures and processes put in place in recognition of the fact that the company is managed by parties, normally on behalf of the owners. This separation of owners from management gives rise to agency problems, some of which were discussed in Chapter 1 in respect of the economic consequences and the choice of accounting policies. The board of directors is part of the process of corporate governance.

Good governance is not only relevant to companies or, indeed, the for-profit sector. In fact, it is just as relevant in the not-for-profit sector where a large number of volunteers, often without management experience, find themselves sitting on management committees. Good governance is critical for such organisations. Therefore, although we use the term 'corporate governance', most of the principles can be applied to the not-for-profit sector. For example, the board of directors in a not-for-profit entity may be called the management committee.

LO 3

Explain what is meant by the term 'corporate governance'

One of the above definitions mentions fairness, transparency and accountability. All these terms are commonly used in financial reporting with accountability being an important objective of financial reporting.

KEY CONCEPT 13.1

CORPORATE GOVERNANCE

Corporate governance consists of mechanisms such as the board of directors and audit committees that exist to provide some assurance to the absentee owners that the management personnel of a company are accountable for their actions and minimise agency costs in respect of their management.

The three definitions that we have just looked at relate to what we may call internal corporate governance. External corporate governance refers to the discipline of the marketplace where a company, if it is listed on a stock exchange, is subject to the scrutiny of the share market. Companies can be taken over and managers replaced and this threat acts as an incentive for managers to behave more in a manner that is in the best interests of shareholders. We use the term 'corporate governance' as it refers to internal corporate governance.

Review exercise 2

What is meant by the term 'corporate governance'?

ISSUES IN CORPORATE GOVERNANCE

In this section we discuss the ASX Corporate Governance Council *Best Practice Principles of Corporate Governance*, published in March 2003, and we consider the role of the board of directors and the audit committee.

The ASX Corporate Governance Council

The ASX Corporate Governance Council issued the *Principles of Good Corporate Governance and Best Practice Recommendations* in March 2003, and companies have been expected to comply with them since 2005. There are 10 best practice principles, and a number of best practice recommendations accompanying each principle. Listed companies are expected to comply with the principles and recommendations, and if they don't comply they are expected to explain why (i.e. an 'if not, why not' approach').

The 10 principles are listed on page 11 of the ASX Corporate Governance Council's *Principles of Good Corporate Governance and Best Practice Recommendations* published in March 2003:

> Principle 1: Lay solid foundations for management and oversight – recognise and publish the respective roles and responsibilities of board and management.

LO 4

Identify the 10 ASX Corporate Governance Council best practice principles

Principle 2: Structure the board to add value – Have a board of an effective composition, size and commitment to adequately discharge its responsibilities and duties.

Principle 3: Promote ethical and responsible decision-making – Actively promotes ethical and responsible decision-making.

Principle 4: Safeguard integrity in financial reporting – Have a structure to independently verify and safeguard the integrity of the company's financial reporting.

Principle 5: Make timely and balanced disclosure – Promotes timely and balanced disclosure of all material matters concerning the company.

Principle 6: Respect the rights of shareholders – Respect the rights of shareholders and facilitate the effective exercise of those rights.

Principle 7: Recognise and manage risk – Establish a sound system of risk oversight and management of internal control.

Principle 8: Encourage enhanced performance – Fairly review and actively encourage enhanced board and management effectiveness.

Principle 9: Remunerate fairly and responsibly – Ensure that the level and composition of remuneration is sufficient and reasonable and that its relationship to corporate and individual performance is defined.

Principle 10: Recognise the legitimate interests of stakeholders – Recognise legal and other obligations to all legitimate stakeholders.

Some of the recommendations associated with the 10 principles include the following:

- The board should have a majority of independent directors.
- 'Independent' means a director cannot have been a substantial supplier or shareholder, or an employee of the company or its professional advisers, within the last three years.
- The CEO should not be the chairman. However, there is no restriction on the CEO being on other boards.
- No limit exists on the number of directorships.
- No limit exists on the length of service, but one-third of directors should be re-elected every three years.
- There should be an audit committee with at least one member with accounting/finance skills.
- There should be a separate nominations and remuneration committees.

For full details of the best practice principles visit: http://www.asx.com.au/supervision/governance/index.htm.

We now consider, in detail, the board of directors and the audit committee.

Discuss the issues associated with the role of the board of directors in corporate governance

Board of directors

In most countries, it is a legal requirement to have a board of directors for companies. As stated above, other types of entities, such as not-for-profit entities, also have governing bodies charged with various responsibilities. The role of the company board is to represent the interests of shareholders and its responsibility is to create value for shareholders. The board is accountable to the shareholders. It is responsible for reviewing the performance of the chief executive officer (CEO) and senior management. It is also responsible for rewarding the senior executive team. It must also ensure that the company meets all its legal and statutory obligations, and that the major risks confronting the company are managed.

KEY CONCEPT 13.2

BOARD OF DIRECTORS

The board is an important corporate governance mechanism and its role is to represent shareholders and create value for shareholders.

Some of the issues concerning company boards that have been addressed in the wake of the company collapses are the:

- *Number of independent directors on the board.* In the case of Enron, many of the directors were not really independent as some of the non-executive directors had been previous auditors of the company. The argument supporting the use of independent non-executive directors is that they are more able to defuse agency conflicts between internal managers and absentee owners. However, others disagree and argue you need directors who understand the business of the company.

- *Duality of leadership.* Should the CEO be chairman of the board or should the chairman come from the non-executive directors? If the roles are combined, some argue that the board's capacity to fulfil its duties is impaired.

- *Size of the board.* There is some research which suggests that the size of the board affects the performance of the firm.

- *Qualifications of directors.* A board should consist of directors with the appropriate skills to allow the board to discharge its duties.

- *Number of board memberships of directors.* There is a view that some directors belong to too many boards and do not have the necessary time to properly carry out their duties.

- *Length of service.* Should directors be required to step down after a certain period of time to prevent apathy, and also to prevent the director becoming too familiar with senior management?

Researchers have also been actively studying many questions concerning corporate governance. A number of studies have attempted to test if companies with good corporate governance perform better – in terms of profitability and share market performance. In a US study of 957 companies, Bhagat and Black (2002) reported that an increase in the number of outside directors results in lower financial performance. However, Brickley, Coles and Terry (1994) reported that company performance increases with effective governance and board independence. While the results of these two studies are contradictory, the majority of research studies have provided more support for the notion that having good governance does not improve performance.

Discuss the issues
associated with the
role of the audit
committee in corporate
governance

The audit committee

An audit committee is a subcommittee of the board of directors and is another important corporate governance mechanism. The audit committee may be charged with various duties and the duties may include:

- reviewing the company's financial statements and recommending them to the board for approval. The board has to sign off on the financial statements and certify that they represent a true and fair view of the company
- overseeing the appointment and relationship of the external auditor
- overseeing the appointment and relationship of the internal auditor
- reviewing matters in respect to compliance with regulations and accounting standards
- reviewing internal control procedures
- overseeing the company's risk management practices.

It is one matter to require the formation of an audit committee and another matter to specify its role and powers. The above roles are extensive and are not necessarily the roles carried out by all, or even some, audit committees. As audit committees are a relatively recent phenomenon, their roles are, in a sense, evolving. Should the committee have control over the appointment of the internal auditor? An internal auditor is responsible for assessing an organisation's internal control processes established to safeguard its assets. Should the audit committee have its own funding so it is not reliant upon management?

KEY CONCEPT 13.3

AUDIT COMMITTEE

An audit committee is a subcommittee of the board of directors and part of the corporate governance of a company. Its roles vary according to the company but, in general, the role of the audit committee is to ensure that the financial statements have been reliably prepared and verified.

The major thrust for the creation of audit committees is to add credibility to the financial reporting process. The critical issue relates to how independent the audit committee is, as this influences its effectiveness. Ian Ramsay (2001) prepared a report for the federal government of Australia following the problems with HIH, One.Tel and others. In his report, Ramsay said of audit committees:

- An effective audit committee must not only exist and be independent, it must actually meet and be active.
- Audit committee members must be independent.
- Each member should be financially literate or should, within a reasonable period of time after appointment, become financially literate.

Research on the issue of audit committees supports the notion of benefits accruing to shareholders if a company has an audit committee. Companies committing accounting fraud are less likely to have audit committees (Dechow, Sloan & Sweeney 1996). Moreover, Klein (2002) reports that there is greater incidence of accounting fraud when an audit committee's independence declines and when the financial and accounting expertise of committee is low.

CASE STUDY 13.5

GOVERNANCE COUNCIL CHIEF WARNS OF AUDIT UPHEAVAL
by Andrew Main

LIFTING audit committee independence standards would cause upheaval on the audit committees of Australia's top 500 companies, according to the chairwoman of the recently formed Corporate Governance Council. Karen Hamilton, who is also executive general manager of the Australian Stock Exchange, said yesterday that if committees were forced to have a 'majority of wholly independent' directors, as is likely, 'nearly half of all existing audit committees will require restructuring to meet any independence recommendations'.

. . .

She said the council was moving to the position, supported by the recent Higgs report in the UK, of putting the onus on non-complying companies to explain why it was not appropriate for them to follow new corporate governance 'norms'. The council appears keener on

UK-style best practice proposals than what Ms Hamilton called the 'very prescriptive reforms' now being promoted in the US. The US Sarbanes–Oxley Act, for instance, requires all members of a company's audit committee to be independent.

She said the US share market was big enough to cope with the 'costs and prescriptions' now being imposed on it in the name of good governance, but the Australian market included a lot of small companies in the early stages of growth which could not bear such costs.

Ms Hamilton conceded that one of the main areas of debate within the council was about the role of independent directors, and how company boards should be balanced between executives and non-executive directors.

Extract from article in *Australian Financial Review*, 19 February 2003

COMMENTARY

The article in Case study 13.5 raises a potential problem if, as is expected, the government enacts legislation which requires all top 500 companies to have an audit committee and the majority of its members must be independent. Given that such directors must also be financially literate, the article raises concerns that companies will not be able to recruit enough qualified directors to fill the positions. This potential problem will be exacerbated if, as is suggested by Professor Ramsay in an article by Pheasant (2003), directors on audit committees face extra legal liabilities due to their responsibilities.

Review exercise 3

What is the role of the audit committee?

LO 7

Identify the approaches to enforcing corporate governance requirements in Australia and the USA

ENFORCEMENT OF CORPORATE GOVERNANCE

The response of government to the various company failures has been somewhat different in the USA and Australia. The USA has adopted what is described as a 'black letter law' approach through the passing of the Sarbanes-Oxley Act in 2002. This is an extensive legislative response to the corporate failures and has many requirements including:

- the establishment of a Public Company Accounting Oversight Board with responsibility for overseeing the work of audit firms
- significant new rules relating to auditor independence
- a ban on the provision of many non-audit services to audit clients
- the requirement that the lead audit or coordinating partner and the reviewing partner rotate off the audit every five years
- the external auditor reporting directly to the audit committee
- the condition that the CEO, controller, CFO, chief accounting officer or person in an equivalent position cannot have been employed by the company's audit firm during the one-year period preceding the audit.

There was also a legislative response in Australia to the company failures through the federal government's Corporate Law Economic Reform Program (CLERP). *CLERP 9* (so named because it is number nine in the series) resulted in a number of changes (but nothing like the requirements of the Sarbanes-Oxley Act) including the following:

- Audit committees are now compulsory for the top 500 companies.
- Requirements have been stipulated in relation to auditor independence.
- The employment and financial relationships between an auditor and client are subject to increased restrictions.
- The provision of non-audit services is subject to increased disclosure requirements.
- There is to be automatic rotation of the audit partner every five years. This means that a partner in an accounting firm cannot be in charge of the audit of the same client for more than five years.
- Auditing standards have been made legal, similar to accounting standards.

As stated earlier in this section, the approach in Australia has been largely based on the 'best practice' approach. The 'best practice' approach really places the onus on companies to adhere to good corporate governance principles, as issued by bodies like the Australian Stock Exchange. Companies should disclose their compliance with the principles in their annual report or explain why they don't follow 'best practice' if, indeed, they don't.

While research generally does not support any strong link between corporate governance and performance, there are studies that support a link between governance practices and investment risk. The problem for investors is how to measure governance practices across a large number of companies operating in many countries in a cost-effective way. As an outcome of this demand, a number of agencies have emerged offering ratings on the corporate governance of companies in many different countries. The Institutional Shareholders Services (ISS) located in the USA, Governance Metrics International (GMI) and Reputex in Australia offer such services.

Review exercise 4

Outline the approaches that Australia has adopted in relation to corporate governance as a result of the high-profile company failures that have occurred here.

Triple bottom line reporting

Traditionally, companies and, particularly, listed companies, have pursued the maximisation of profit as their major objective. Reporting on their financial performance has been their central focus. In the previous section we considered the developments and additional reporting obligations for listed companies in relation to corporate governance. The tenth ASX best practice principle is the need to recognise the legitimate legal and other obligations to all legitimate stakeholders. It could be argued that triple bottom line reporting is one way a company can demonstrate a commitment to this principle.

LO 8

Identify what is meant by the term 'triple bottom line reporting'

In this section we examine triple bottom line (TBL) reporting – another recent development in the reporting practices of many companies. In the twenty-first century there has been a growing concern about the ability of the world's resources to be able to meet the needs of future generations, if not properly managed. Sustainability and sustainable development are now important issues on the world agenda, but what is meant by the term 'sustainable development'?

The following definition is the one used by Dantes (2005):

> The concept of meeting the needs of the present without compromising the ability of future generations to meet their needs. The terms originally applied to natural resource situations, where the long term was the focus. Today, it applies to many disciplines, including economic development, environment, food production, energy, and social organization. Basically, sustainability/sustainable development refers to doing something with the long term in mind.

Case study 1.1 in Chapter 1 (pages 10–11) provided the results of a 2005 KPMG survey concerning the corporate social reporting of the top 100 companies in 19 countries. The practice of publishing such reports is largely voluntary and has emerged with the increasing concern about sustainable development. There are a variety of names for this type of report and they include environmental report, corporate social report, sustainability report, social impact report, stakeholder impact report and triple bottom line report.

A triple bottom line report refers to the publication of economic, environmental and social information in an integrated report. The three components that are involved are the environmental, social and economic activities of the organisation. Some companies, such as mining companies, have certain mandatory reporting obligations and conditions such as restoring the land to its original condition after they have finished mining operations. However, such mandatory obligations only apply in certain industries and, in general, most companies providing information about social and environmental issues do so on a voluntary basis.

A triple bottom line report has three components, as noted below:

- *Environmental component* – this includes disclosures about many issues associated with the environment and the entity's activities within this area. These may include issues to do with air, water, land, natural resources, flora, fauna and human health (e.g. greenhouse gas emissions, water contamination and workers' safety)
- *Social component* – includes disclosures about many social issues such as the diversity of the entity's employees, treatment of minorities, employment conditions for employees and community activities (e.g. Criticism of Nike's 'sweat shop' production operations in Asian countries)
- *Economic component* – includes the more traditional financial data and, for this reason, it is likely to contain more quantitative data than the previous two components.

The three components of a triple bottom line report are often linked, and Argyle Diamonds' workforce policy for its mines workers is a good example:

> However, the percentage of mine site employees who reside in the East Kimberley region rose significantly, from 29.5% to 42.1%, reflecting a deliberate policy by Argyle to localise its mine site workforce. Approximately half of the Kimberley resident workforce are Aboriginal people, which reflects the local demographics of the East Kimberley region.
>
> Argyle has set a target of 80% of the mine site workforce being Kimberley based by the commencement of an underground operation. The target is that half of the local workforce will be Aboriginal people, again reflecting the demographics of the East Kimberley region. (Argyle Diamonds 2004)

Having a local workforce is a cheaper alternative than the 'fly-in, fly-out' workforce and has a number of social benefits for the region, including the large number of indigenous employees.

CASE STUDY 13.6

INVESTING FOR A BETTER WORLD
By Anne O'Donnell
Never doubt that a small group of thoughtful, committed citizens can change the world; indeed it is the only thing that ever has. – Margaret Mead

WHAT IS unsustainable investment? Putting your precious savings into a business or industry that consumes or contaminates natural resources (air, water, earth, plants and animals) without replacing or restoring them, or that damages the health or welfare of people as workers, consumers or passers-by. That is, when taking into account the wellbeing of society and the environment, an unsustainable investment costs more than the income it produces. Even in purely financial terms, such an investment is not sustainable because its future is threatened by public hostility, government regulation and legal compensation. Sustainable investment has a brighter future.

Based on the World Commission on

Environment and Development's definition of sustainability, the money goes into businesses and industries that meet the needs of the present without compromising the ability of future generations to meet their needs. The term sustainable investment tends to focus on the environmental implications of business activities. Socially responsible investment considers the impacts of business on society. Ethical investment covers both areas but the terms can be used interchangeably. Ethical investment began about 100 years ago when Quakers and Methodists applied their moral standards to select shares in United States companies. In the early 1970s, a group of American pacifists set up a fund that avoided investments in the Vietnam War. Since then, community groups have boycotted products from apartheid South Africa and products tested on animals.

Ethical investment has grown rapidly in Australia; the Ethical Investment Association has estimated the value of such investment in 2004 at $21.5 billion. Ethical investors have learnt that the use of capital can be a real power for social change. Many people now have access to capital markets and the influence that goes with them. Compulsory superannuation, privatisation and demutualisation have made more Australians shareholders than ever before. So they pay attention to what companies are doing. They have also realised that you can make money without exploiting resources or people. You can make money and feel good about it. This discovery has generated a lot of interest in ethical investment. Almost everyone wants to do it, but they're not always sure how to go about it.

How does ethical investment work? An ethical perspective can be applied to all sorts of assets – shares listed on the stock exchange, shares in private companies, commercial and residential property, bonds and cash. Most attention goes to listed shares, in Australia and overseas. The basic task is to find out how profits are made. One of the great challenges of ethical investment is to find and back sustainable businesses that can make a profit. This is very hard for individuals to do themselves. If you want to invest sustainably you should look for an investment that aligns with your values. You can do your own research and find the companies you like or you can go through a managed fund that suits you. If you're committed to conservation, that is the kind of fund you want. If you're more interested in social justice or deeply Christian you might want another sort of fund. Funds also differ in whether they are silent investors or active participants. Some fund managers engage in a dialogue with the management of the companies they invest in, sometimes using the fund's votes to put shareholder resolutions at annual meetings. The increasing enthusiasm of investors is encouraging even mainstream funds to take ethical stands.

At Australian Ethical we start off by screening companies according to our ethical charter. This states that we should avoid activities which are harmful to humans or the environment, such as tobacco, gambling and arms manufacture, and should support sustainable land use, the preservation of endangered ecosystems, renewable energy and the efficient use of waste. The researchers don't just read company reports; they check web sites, news reports and other external sources. They mainly look for positives. Some companies are easy to rule in or out. Others have negatives as well as positives. Some are neutral. We have to make a judgment. Then we put together a list of stocks that would be suitable in terms of the charter. Next, our investment analysts do standard financial analysis like any mainstream fund manager: profit projections, growth potential and so on. Even if we have found the most ethical company in the world, if it's never going to make any money we don't invest in it. If it's a company that is going to make a motza but is totally unethical, it wouldn't even get this far. The companies that survive the ethical and financial hurdles go to the investment committee for an investment decision. You don't have to give up returns to invest in sustainable businesses. A recent survey in the magazine *Ethical Investor* (August 2004), based on data provided by ASSIRT, showed ethical funds outstripping mainstream funds. In the five years to June 30, 2004, the Standard & Poor's/ Australian Stock Exchange 300 index returned 8.16 per cent a year. The average mainstream retail fund invested in Australian shares returned 5.7 per cent. The average ethical fund returned 11.67 per cent. These figures are net of management fees.

Of course, investments in any type of fund can go up and down and past performance is not necessarily indicative of future performance. Investors should monitor their investments wherever invested. One problem for the managers of sustainable businesses is that many of the demands on companies are short term.

Those running a business have to report every 12 months and a big business has to report every quarter. Something shareholders can do to improve sustainability is not to think, 'If my super-fund manager doesn't get the best return this year I'm walking.' That leads to a short-term approach. If a shareholder or a super-fund member is concerned about the future, they should be saying to their superannuation trustee, their fund manager or the manager of a company they have shares in, 'What are you doing about the long term? You should be thinking about sustainability. Where is your triple bottom line report?' Anyone with money to invest – and almost everyone has some super somewhere – can look at the options in ethical investment or start asking questions about the long term. People need to know that their super money is powerful. They should be putting it to use for the future of the planet. More information about ethical investment is available from the Ethical Investment Association at www.eia. org.au or from Australian Ethical Investment at www.austethical.com.au. Anne O'Donnell is the chief executive officer of Australian Ethical Investment Ltd, a Canberra-based fund manager.

Canberra Times, 19 February 2005

COMMENTARY

The article discusses ethical investments and argues that this is one way that investors can force companies to pay more attention to their social and environmental activities. By withholding funds from companies which don't have acceptable social and environmental policies, investors can influence future behaviour. Triple bottom line reporting, which is largely voluntary, is one method of reporting that companies can employ to demonstrate to investors that they do have acceptable social and environmental policies.

Review exercise 5

Explain the meaning of a triple bottom line report.

THE PROS AND CONS OF TRIPLE BOTTOM LINE REPORTING

Because the practice of providing TBL reports is largely voluntary, it is interesting to consider why companies would incur such costs. Listed below are reasons, offered in surveys, as to why entity's are, or are not, producing a TBL report.

Some of the reasons for producing a TBL report include:

- an enhanced ability to track the entity's progress against specific targets
- the fact that this type of report facilitates the implementation of an environmental strategy
- a greater awareness of broad environmental issues throughout the organisation
- the ability to clearly convey the corporate message internally and externally
- improved all-round credibility because of greater transparency
- the ability to communicate efforts and standards
- a licence to continue operating the entity's business in the community
- benefits for the company's reputation, cost savings identification, increased efficiency, enhanced business development opportunities and enhanced staff morale.

Some of the reasons for not producing a TBL report include:

- doubts about the advantages it brings to the organisation
- the fact that competitors may not be publishing TBL reports
- a belief that customers (and the general public) are not interested in it and it will not increase sales
- the company already has a good reputation for its environmental performance
- there are many other ways of providing communicating about environmental issues
- it is too expensive
- it is difficult to gather consistent data from all operations and to select correct indicators
- it could damage the reputation of the company, have legal implications or alert environmental regulators to an issue that may have otherwise gone unnoticed.

LO 9
Summarise some of the reasons for and against the preparation of a triple bottom line report

THE GLOBAL REPORTING INITIATIVE (GRI)

The most widely cited benchmark in the determination of what should be included in a TBL report is the Global Reporting Initiative (GRI) – an institution based in the Netherlands. The GRI was established through the United Nations Environment Program with the objective of enhancing the quality, rigour and utility of sustainability reporting. In 2002, the GRI released the *Sustainability Reporting Guidelines*. The GRI identified a series of trends which added momentum to the need for techniques that enhanced an organisation's ability to more consistently and comprehensively report on the economic, environmental and social dimensions of its activities, products and services. In Australia, the Department of Environment and Heritage has produced a number of publications, including *Triple Bottom Line Reporting in Australia* available at http://www.deh.gov.au/.

The GRI indicators were created through a process of stakeholder dialogue. The guidelines contain both core indicators and additional indicators. The core indicators are the more critical of the two while the additional indicators are also highly desirable. The principles upon which the GRI guidelines are based are:

LO 10
Identify the GRI, and explain, in broad terms, the GRI approach to triple bottom line reports

- transparency – how was the TBL report prepared?
- inclusiveness – engage stakeholders in the development of reports
- auditability – information should be capable of verification by an external party
- completeness – the TBL report should include all material information
- relevance – is the information significant enough to warrant reporting?
- sustainability context – the TBL report should attempt to place information in a larger context of ecological or social limits
- accuracy – there should be a low margin of error
- neutrality – the selection of what is reported should be free from bias
- comparability – maintain consistency in the preparation of the report
- clarity – make sure the report is meaningful to as wide a range of users as possible
- timeliness – should be available on a regular basis so that information is not meaningless.

In the GRI, each of the three areas (economic, environmental and social) are detailed, and if there are applicable measurement methods these are also specified. Under the environment theme, the GRI has specified, in detail, 16 core indicators and another 19 additional indicators for companies to report. The headings in the environment area are: materials; energy; water; biodiversity; emissions, effluents and waste; suppliers, products and services; compliance and transport.

In the social area, there are a total of 24 core indicators and 25 additional indicators. The headings in the social area are: employment; labour management /relations; health and safety; training and education; diversity and opportunity; strategy and management; non-discrimination; freedom of association and collective bargaining; child labour; forced and compulsory labour; disciplinary procedures; security practices; indigenous rights; community; bribery and corruption; political contributions; competition and pricing; customer health and safety; and products and services.

Finally, in the financial area there are 10 core indicators and three additional indicators. The headings in the financial area are: customers (sales); suppliers (cost of sales); employees (salaries and wages); providers of capital (dividends); public sector (taxes and subsidies); and any indirect economic benefits such as attracting investment into the region.

Review exercise 6
What is the GRI?

CASE STUDY 13.7

CORPORATE RESPONSIBILITY IN THE SPOTLIGHT
Fiona Buffini

Business can expect to hear a lot more talk about corporate responsibility, with another inquiry looking into whether business should give more consideration to stakeholders and not just shareholders. The federal parliamentary committee on corporations has announced ⅢⅢ➡

it will look into corporate responsibility and triple bottom-line reporting.

It comes at the same time as a similar inquiry by the federal Treasurer's expert committee and as the Australian Stock Exchange Corporate Governance Council reviews its principles on risk and stakeholders.

'We won't improve corporate behaviour and performance if we rely solely on regulation,' said Labor's spokeswoman on corporate governance, Penny Wong, announcing the latest inquiry last week. 'Recent regulation governing company activity has been important, but more regulation may not be the best answer.

'We need to think more strategically and more creatively about how we can maximise the likelihood of responsible corporate decision-making,' Senator Wong said. The inquiry will also look into disclosure. Only 23 per cent of the ASX 100 report on their impact on the environment, employees or the community, compared with 70 per cent in the United Kingdom and 30 per cent of the biggest companies in the US.

Ian Woods, AMP Capital Investors senior analyst for sustainable funds, said that while some Australian companies did very good sustainability reporting, particularly in the mining sector, other reports read like they came 'straight out of the PR department'.

'Much of the reporting is selective; it's only the good news. Much of it is repetitive. There's a lot of focus on systems and not performance and as a result there's a lot of motherhood statements,' Dr Woods told the annual Ratcliffe lecture on accounting by the University of NSW last week.

He said a 'responsible company' was one that did not 'rely on the externalisation of environmental, social or financial costs' an issue that a lot of companies found 'extremely difficult' to acknowledge.

AMP research finds companies that act in a socially responsible way outperform those that fail to do so by more than 3 per cent a year. Abbott Geoffrey Bazzan, a portfolio manager at Maple-Brown, said that while he would never invest in a stock where the 'ethics or integrity of management' were in question, big names such as Tabcorp and Southcorp gaming and alcohol companies that might be excluded by some ethical funds had produced strong returns for investors.

'Is a company producing alcohol any better or worse than another portfolio holding Amcor, which derives 10 per cent of its earnings from tobacco packaging?' Mr Bazzan asked.

Copenhagen Business School professor Jan Mouritsen, another Ratcliffe speaker, said European studies showed reporting on intangible assets, often ignored by accounting rules, could completely change investors' outlook.

Australian Financial Review, 28 June 2005

COMMENTARY

The article reports on the review by the federal parliamentary committee on corporations into corporate responsibility and TBL reporting. The committee has also enquired into the need to legislate with regard to whether companies should prepare a TBL report. The article also discusses what a socially responsible company is and what the benefits to companies are in reporting TBL.

The following is a quote from a joint submission on 16 September 2005 by CPA Australia and The Institute of Chartered Accountants in Australia to the Parliamentary Committee.

> The Accounting Bodies are of the view that corporations recognise that sustainable business operations and thus sustainable financial performance are dependant on building and maintaining the trust and respect of the community, and in the vast majority of cases, act accordingly. There is a growing realisation that a short term profit focus may be inconsistent with a company's long term viability – however this is culture based rather than regulation based.
>
> Regard should be given to the interests of shareholders, stakeholders and the general community to the extent that taking these interests into account add value to the business operations and evidence the corporation's 'license to operate'. In this framework it is recognised that it is likely to be those that are 'key' stakeholders rather than all and sundry to whom regard is given. In this context key stakeholders include employees, various tiers of government, suppliers and customers. Despite director's best endeavours, it is acknowledged that some people or groups will nevertheless be aggrieved by corporate actions.

It is easy to access a company's TBL report by visiting that company's website and looking for a reference to society or the environment. The rating agency Reputex assigns a grade – using its methodologies – to a number of entities in Australia and the only entity to get a AAA rating for the past three years is Westpac. You can access the Westpac report at: http://www.westpac.com.au/internet/publish.nsf/Content/WICROR+2004+Stakeholder+Impact+Report. Not all companies produce a separate report because many companies choose to disclose environmental and social information in the annual report. Of course, there are also companies that disclose very little information about social and environmental matters.

One of the principles listed in the GRI is auditability. Because TBL reports are voluntary, the provision of an external verification statement will only serve to enhance the credibility of these reports. However, the results of the 2005 KPMG International Survey of Corporate Responsibility Reporting reports that while the practice of providing an assurance statement is increasing, only about 30 per cent of the companies in the survey included an assurance statement in 2004.

SUMMARY

LEARNING OBJECTIVE 1
Identify the major accounting irregularities involved with the collapse of HIH, Enron and WorldCom
The failure of all three companies involved the following accounting irregularities:

- use of special-purpose entities to hide debt
- incorrect recognition of revenue
- incorrect classification of expenditure as assets instead of expenses
- underestimation of liabilities.

As a result of these and other company failures, there has been a review of corporate governance requirements in many countries.

LEARNING OBJECTIVE 2
Discuss the role that meeting performance targets played in the collapse of companies like Enron and WorldCom
In the USA, the practice of establishing estimates of next quarter's profit result creates pressure on companies to meet the targets or face having their share price marked down by the share market. This increases the incentive to change accounting policies or, even worse, fraudulently manufacture the results if the company is not able to meet the target through its operations.

LEARNING OBJECTIVE 3
Explain what is meant by the term 'corporate governance'
Corporate governance consists of mechanisms (such as the board of directors and audit committees) that exist to provide some assurance to the absentee owners that the management team of a company is accountable for its actions, and minimise agency costs in relation to that management.

LEARNING OBJECTIVE 4
Identify the 10 ASX Corporate Governance Council best practice principles
Principle 1: Lay solid foundations for management and oversight
Principle 2: Structure the board to add value
Principle 3: Promote ethical and responsible decision-making
Principle 4: Safeguard integrity in financial reporting
Principle 5: Make timely and balanced disclosure
Principle 6: Respect the rights of shareholders
Principle 7: Recognise and manage risk
Principle 8: Encourage enhanced performance
Principle 9: Remunerate fairly and responsibly
Principle 10: Recognise the legitimate interests of stakeholders

LEARNING OBJECTIVE 5
Discuss the issues associated with the role of the board of directors in corporate governance
The board is an important corporate governance mechanism and its role is to represent shareholders and create value for shareholders.

Some of the issues addressed in relation to boards of directors in the wake of the company collapses are the:

- number of independent directors on the board

- duality of leadership
- size of the board
- qualifications of directors
- number of board memberships of directors
- length of service.

L⊙6 LEARNING OBJECTIVE 6

Discuss the issues associated with the role of the audit committee in corporate governance

An audit committee is a subcommittee of the board of directors and is another important corporate governance mechanism. The audit committee may be charged with various duties and the duties may include:

- reviewing the company's financial statements and recommending them to the board for approval.
- overseeing the appointment and relationship of the external auditor
- overseeing the appointment and relationship of the internal auditor
- reviewing matters in respect to compliance with regulations and accounting standards
- reviewing internal control procedures
- overseeing the company's risk management practices.

L⊙7 LEARNING OBJECTIVE 7

Identify the approaches to enforcing corporate governance requirements in Australia and the USA

Government's response to the various company failures that have recently occurred has been somewhat different in the USA and Australia. The USA has adopted what is described as a 'black letter law' approach through the passing of the Sarbanes-Oxley Act in 2002. Australia made some changes in the law through *CLERP 9*. However, the main approach has been that of best practice, with the ASX Corporate Governance Council's *Principles of Good Corporate Governance and Best Practice Recommendations*.

L⊙8 LEARNING OBJECTIVE 8

Identify what is meant by the term 'triple bottom line reporting'

A triple bottom line report refers to the publication of economic, environmental and social information within an integrated report. The three components relate to the environmental, social and economic activities of the organisation.

L⊙9 LEARNING OBJECTIVE 9

Summarise some of the reasons for and against the preparation of a triple bottom line report

Many reasons are given for the production of a TBL report including benefits to a company's reputation, improved employee morale, proof of the legitimacy of the entity's operations, greater transparency, and promotion of the organisation's targets and strategies.

Many reasons are also given for not producing a TBL report including the costs versus the benefits, the creation of potential future liabilities, the fact that it won't increase sales, the fact that competitors have not prepared one and the notion that there are other ways of communicating the information.

L⊙10 LEARNING OBJECTIVE 10

Identify the GRI, and explain, in broad terms, the GRI approach to triple bottom line reports

The Global Reporting Initiative (GRI) is based in the Netherlands and was established through the United Nations Environment Program with the objective of enhancing the quality, rigour and utility of sustainability reporting. In 2002, the GRI released the Sustainability Reporting Guidelines.

The GRI guidelines contain both core indicators and additional indicators in environmental, social and financial areas. The core indicators are the more critical to include while the additional indicators are also highly desirable.

REFERENCES

Adams, M., 2005. 'Were the HIH sentences tough enough?', *Lawyers Weekly* (ABIX abstracts), 9 September.

Argyle Diamonds, 2004. *Sustainability Report*, Argyle Diamonds, viewed 11 February 2006, http://www.argylediamonds. com.au/publications/sustainability_report_2004.html, page 6.

ASX Corporate Governance Council., 2003. *Principles of Good Corporate Governance and Best Practice Recommendations*, March, Australian Stock Exchange, Sydney.

Bhagat, S. & Black, B., 2002. 'The non-correlation between board independence and long-term board performance', *Journal of Corporation Law*, vol. 27, no. 2, pp. 231–74.

Brickley, J.A., Coles, J. & Terry, R., 1994. 'Outside directors and the adoption of poison pills, *Journal of Financial Economics*, vol. 35, no. 3, pp. 371–90.

Dantes, 2005. Akzo Nobal, viewed 11 February 2006, www.dantes.info/Projectinformation/Glossary/Glossary. html.

Dechow, P.M, Sloan R.G. & Sweeney, A.P., 1996. 'Causes and consequences of earnings manipulation: An analysis of firms subject to enforcement actions by the SEC', *Contemporary Accounting Research*, vol. 13, no. 1, pp. 1–36.

Global Reporting Initiative, 2002. *Sustainability Reporting Guidelines*. Global Reporting Initiative, Boston.

Group of 100, 2003. *Sustainability: A Guide to Triple Bottom Line Reporting*, Group of 100, Melbourne, p. 12.

Institute of Chartered Accountants in Australia and CPA Australia., 2005. *Inquiry into Corporate Responsibility*, September, viewed 20 November 2005, http://www.icaa.org.au/upload/download/PJC_CSR_Submission_ (050908).pdf.

Institute of Chartered Accountants in New Zealand, 2002. *Report on the Taskforce of Sustainable Development Reporting*, Institute of Chartered Accountants in New Zealand, Wellington, p. 11.

Investor Protection Association Executive Office, 2006. viewed 11 February 2006, www.corp-gov.org/glossary. php3.

Klein, A., 2002. Audit committee, board of director characteristics and earnings management, *Journal of Accounting and Economics*, vol. 33, no. 3, pp. 375–400.

KPMG, 2005. *KPMG International Survey of Corporate Responsibility*, KPMG, Amsterdam.

MacDonald, C. & Norman, W., 2005. 'What's Wrong With the "Triple Bottom Line"?', *6 Degrees*, July 2005 newsletter, viewed 29 November 2005, http://www.6degrees.ca/newsletter_jul04.html#think.

Pheasant, B., 2003. 'Extra burden noted for auditor directors', *Australian Financial Review*, 19 February, p. 7.

Ramsay, I., 2001. *Independence of Australian Company Auditors: Review of Current Australian Requirements and Proposals for Reform*, Commonwealth of Australia.

Westpac, 2004. *Stakeholder Impact Report*, Westpac, Sydney, viewed 13 February 2006, www.westpace.com.au, p. 31.

REVIEW QUESTIONS

1   What is the role of the board of directors?

2   What are the important issues relating to the board of directors and its corporate governance role?

PROBLEMS FOR DISCUSSION AND ANALYSIS

1   Visit the Woolworths website at www.woolworths.com.au and critically review the statement on corporate governance. What are the strengths and weaknesses of corporate governance at Woolworths?

2   Case study 13.1 refers to the problems at WorldCom. Explain the accounting treatment that was used to produce the inflated profits. (You may also need to refer back to Case study 5.2.) Should the auditor have discovered this incorrect accounting practice?

3   Case study 13.2 refers to the problems at Enron. What are the reasons for trying to hide debt, as was the issue with Enron?

4   Case study 13.3 refers to the problems at HIH. Discuss how you think an insurer estimates its liabilities. At what point do you believe an insurer should recognise a liability? Before an insurable event has occurred? When an insurable event has occurred? When a claim is lodged? When a claim is settled?

5   Case study 13.4 argues that greed is a major factor behind events like Enron, WorldCom and HIH. Do you agree? In your opinion, what is the impact on financial reporting from the type of events discussed in Case studies 13.1, 2 and 3?

6   Should corporate governance practices be enshrined in legislation or is it best to allow companies to self-regulate and choose their own appropriate corporate governance structures?

7   Discuss the advantages and disadvantages of having a majority of independent directors on a board. Why do you believe a requirement for independent directors to hold separate meetings is being seriously considered?

8   Why is it important for audit committees to have their own funding independent of management? Should any members of the management team attend meetings of the audit committee? Give reasons.

9   Case study 13.6 refers to ethical investments. What would you consider ethical investments to be?

10   Should there be a legal requirement for companies to produce a TBL report or should it continue to be a voluntary practice?

11   Visit the Westpac website at www.westpac.com.au and review the 2004 *Stakeholder Impact Report* and answer the following questions.
   a   What indicators does Westpac report against?
   b   How did the bank determine the Australian Stakeholder indicators?
   c   What do Westpac mean by Socially Responsible Investment products?
   d   How does Westpac assist staff with community work and involvement?
   e   On page 31 of the 2004 report the bank states:

> Our institutional lending and investment criteria include detailed analysis of customer, industry, country and facility risk. We take into account the quality of management, including perceptions of their integrity and ethics.
>
> Critically review this claim. What additional information would you like to see to support this claim?

12   The following are two definitions of triple bottom line reporting:

> In the purest sense, the concept of TBL reporting refers to the publication of economic, environmental and social information in an integrated manner that reflects activities and outcomes across these three dimensions of a company's performance. (Group of 100 2003)

The external reporting on the economic, social and environmental performance and impacts of an entity can have four potential purposes:

1) to improve the efficient operation of entities in achieving their legal purpose, e.g. highlighting areas of an entity's negative economic, social and environmental impacts and also increasing transparency and strengthening accountability for users;

2) to help meet the preferences of present and future investors, consumers, employees, creditors, suppliers and insurers;

3) to inform stakeholders with no direct ownership, investment or consumption interests; and/or

4) as a significant public policy tool to maximise human welfare over time. (Institute of Chartered Accountants in New Zealand 2002)

Required

a   Compare and contrast the two definitions.
b   Critically evaluate both definitions.

13 The following quote is taken from the paper 'What's Wrong With the "Triple Bottom Line"?' by Chris MacDonald and Wayne Norman.

So what is the 'Triple Bottom Line'? The basic idea is that corporations should (and can) manage not just the good old-fashioned bottom line (i.e. the financial bottom line), but also their social and environmental 'bottom lines', too. On the face of it, this is an attractive idea: it is easy to agree with the idea that corporations have obligations that go beyond financial success. Unfortunately, we find that without exception the 3BL rhetoric fails to live up to its promises. Adding up the financial plusses and minuses is just a lot easier, as it turns out, than totting up, say, the ethical achievements and shortcomings of a firm. Any attempt to arrive at a calculation of a net social or environmental performance is likely to run head-on into just what it is that separates the management of finances from the management of social and environmental impacts. In the financial realm, money provides a common unit of measure that permits expenses to be subtracted from revenues. So while it makes perfect sense to take the costs of labour and materials and subtract those from sales revenues, it makes little sense to talk about (for example) taking a social 'minus' such as a sexual harassment lawsuit and subtracting that from a social 'plus', like having engaged in corporate philanthropy. How big a charitable donation do you think it takes to off-set the social 'cost' of a sexual harassment suit? Of course there's no obviously uncontroversial way to make this sort of calculation. In other words, there's no real social 'bottom line'. The kinds of issues that arise in social and environmental domains can be (and regularly are) managed, but they will never be reducible to the kind of common unit of measure that would allow for straightforward bookkeeping.

Required

a   What is meant by the financial bottom line?

b   Do you consider it possible to calculate a social and environmental bottom line?

c   In your view, does the absence of a social and environmental surplus/deficit render a TBL of little or no value, as implied in the above quote?

14 Consider the arguments for and against the two proposals to deal with environmental reporting that are discussed in the article below. Which approach do you support?

PUBLIC SHOW AND TELL IS THE WAY TO INCENTIVISE DIRECTORS AND THEIR COMPANIES TO BEHAVE NICELY

IAN RAMSAY

Two models have emerged to ensure directors are socially responsible. Disclosure of company practices is the superior option, writes Ian Ramsay.

THERE is enormous interest in the role of company directors in implementing corporate social responsibility (CSR). There are many reasons for this, including the growing power and influence of companies in our daily lives, privatisations that have led to companies taking over what were government functions, and the significant controversy created by James Hardie in its dealings with those who contracted asbestos-related diseases as a result of contact with James Hardie products.

According to commentators, companies should engage in socially responsible activities because such activity can increase sales and market share, increase appeal to investors, strengthen the brand position of the company, and increase the company's ability to attract, motivate and retain employees.

But how do we go about ensuring that company directors do engage in socially responsible activities? Two alternatives have recently been highlighted by two separate inquiries dealing with CSR and company directors. The inquiries are being conducted by the Corporations and Markets Advisory Committee (the federal government's main corporate law reform advisory body) and the parliamentary Joint Committee on Corporations and Financial Services.

The terms of reference for both inquiries focus on two approaches to directors and CSR. The first is to change the law of directors' duties to require directors to take into account the interests of stakeholders other than shareholders when making corporate decisions. The second focuses on company disclosure of CSR practices. It does not mandate that directors adopt certain practices but requires disclosure of what the company does with a view to ensuring that those practices are debated and evaluated outside the company.

A number of potential problems arise from changing the law of directors' duties to allow or require directors to prioritise non-shareholder interests over the interests of shareholders. This approach may make directors less accountable, may be inconsistent with other parts of our corporate law, and would result in vesting additional discretions and powers in the Australian Securities and Investments Commission and the courts when it is not clear they would want these additional discretions or whether it is an appropriate role for them.

The disclosure approach has grown in importance and we have seen significant changes in disclosure of CSR practices. The 2005 KPMG international survey of CSR reporting, which examined the CSR reporting of the world's largest corporations (about 1600 of them), found CSR reporting had increased steadily since 1993 and substantially in the past three years. The type of CSR reporting had also changed significantly, from purely environmental reporting until 1999 to sustainability (social, environmental and economic) reporting.

A prominent example of the disclosure approach to CSR is the recent British requirement for listed companies to publish an annual Operating and Financial Review (OFR), in which they must identify and disclose material social and environmental matters. Earlier this year, Britain's Accounting Standards Board issued a reporting standard on the OFR.

A critical issue is ensuring that any disclosure does accurately reflect the actual practices of the company. However, the approach has several advantages. Such disclosure can generate wide-ranging and important debate on the value of particular practices. It has the flexibility to promote different practices to suit the wide variety of circumstances companies operate in. Disclosure also helps shareholders and other stakeholders monitor CSR practices and can help companies build stronger relationships with stakeholders. Directors may also benefit from learning about the CSR practices of other companies and disclosure should create a climate in which directors reflect on their company's CSR practices in order to determine if they are appropriate.

The Age, Enlightened Self-Interest, 21 July 2005

ETHICS CASE STUDY

COUGH UP HARDIES OR WE'LL MAKE YOU — PREMIER SAYS THERE ARE NO OBSTACLES TO DEAL
PETER GOSNELL, JOE HILDEBRAND MATP

ALMOST a year after James Hardie agreed to spend billions compensating future asbestos victims, survivors are still enduring an agonising wait for certainty. So far, the company has still not struck a deal despite having negotiated with victims, unions, the Government and shareholders.

The NSW Government upped the pressure yesterday by threatening to change the law if James Hardie fails to strike a deal before the end of the week. The pain of those waiting was palpable outside the firm's Pitt St offices where grieving widows joined those dying – including Bernie Banton – to protest at the delays – marking the beginning of Asbestos Awareness Week.

The sticking point is not over compensation for existing sufferers, many of whom have been paid. The multi-billion dollar fund is for thousands more sufferers who are expected to develop or be diagnosed with asbestos-related diseases in the future.

With no immediate resolution in sight, Premier Morris Iemma declared that he would try to change the law to force the company's hand. 'It has gone on long enough,' Mr Iemma said. 'We've given a fair and reasonable amount of time to negotiate an outcome and the victims deserve to have a conclusion to this. 'If we can't reach an agreement we'll legislate to provide justice to the victims.'

A spokesman for Mr Iemma said he had received special counsel's advice on the matter.   ⅢⅢ➡

'The preferred option is a negotiated outcome and the legislation that would come to Parliament would give effect to that,' he said.

Last year, James Hardie moved its business offshore to Holland, meaning it is not liable for operations in Australia. But it is understood Mr Iemma has drafted legislation specific to James Hardie that would reconnect its old Australian subsidiaries with the Netherlands-based parent company – making them responsible for payouts.

Legal experts yesterday cast serious doubt on whether such a law could be enforced. 'I don't believe they can pass a law that simply says James Hardie Netherlands must return $1.9 billion to Australia. 'How do they expect to enforce that? It beggars belief,' Law Society president John McIntyre said. 'It's trying to close the gate after the horse has bolted.'

The company would almost certainly launch a lengthy and expensive legal challenge. A James Hardie spokesman said the company had 'constitutional concerns' about the proposed change.
Editorial: Page 18

The long, agonising road for sufferers

2001: James Hardie creates $293 million foundation for asbestos claims in Australia and moves to Holland. It also provides access to another $1.9 billion in case liability claims blow out.
2002: James Hardie cancels the $1.9 billion scheme.
2003: The foundation says it has insufficient funds to meet future claims. James Hardie, now legally resident in Holland, says it has no liability.
2004: In February, Government announces special inquiry into whether James Hardie met its liabilities. It finds Hardie's former CEO Peter Macdonald lied when he said the compensation scheme was fully funded.
2005: Deadlines for agreement passed in March and July.

Daily Telegraph, 22 November 2005

Required

Comment on the behaviour by James Hardie and assess how such behaviour should be reported in a TBL report. Has the company behaved in an ethical manner?

ANSWERS TO REVIEW EXERCISES

1   The three company failures involved the following accounting irregularities:
   • use of special-purpose entities to hide debt
   • incorrect recognition of revenue
   • incorrect classification of expenditure as assets instead of expenses
   • underestimation of liabilities.

2   Corporate governance refers to the rules and procedures that are adopted within a company to provide assurances to the absentee owners (shareholders) that the management of the company is accountable for the ways in which they manage the company.

3   The audit committee can have several tasks, but its main role is to ensure that the financial statements are reliable, provide a true and fair view of the company and are not biased by the company's management team.

4   Australia has made some legislative changes through *CLERP 9*, but the main approach has involved best practice regulations with the ASX Corporate Governance Council's *Principles of Good Corporate Governance and Best Practice Recommendations.*

5   A triple bottom line report refers to the publication of economic, environmental and social information in an integrated report. The three components within the TBL report relate to the environmental, social and economic activities of an organisation.

6   The GRI (Global Reporting Initiative) is based in the Netherlands and was established through the United Nations Environment Program with the objective of enhancing the quality, rigour and utility of sustainability reporting. In 2002, the GRI released the Sustainability Reporting Guidelines. The GRI guidelines contain both core and additional indicators in the environmental, social and financial areas. The core indicators are the more critical indicators to include within the report while the additional indicators are also highly desirable.

FINANCIAL STATEMENT ANALYSIS
CHAPTER FOURTEEN

14

LEARNING OBJECTIVES

At the end of this chapter, you should be able to:

1 discuss the information needs of the various users in relation to the analysis of financial statements

2 identify possible sources of external and internal information

3 explain the significance of profitability and risk in the analysis of financial statements

4 identify and apply trend analysis

5 identify and use common-size statements

6 identify the issues to be considered when choosing a benchmark for ratio analysis

7 identify and apply various ratios that can be used to assess profitability

8 identify and apply various ratios that can be used to assess efficiency

9 identify and apply various ratios that can be used to assess short-term solvency

10 identify and apply various ratios that can be used to assess long-term solvency

11 discuss the implications of the efficient markets hypothesis for financial statement analysis

12 explain the limitations involved in financial statement analysis.

Introduction

In previous chapters we considered the way in which accounting information is produced and what the components of financial statements mean. In this chapter we consider the statements themselves and, more specifically, the ways in which they can be analysed. This chapter is not intended to be comprehensive in its approach to financial analysis, but will offer some guidelines on the subject and provide the reader with some basic tools of analysis.

Users' information needs

It is important to consider the needs of the person for whom the analysis is being undertaken or, in other words, the user group. By using this approach, it is possible to establish the form of analysis that is most appropriate to these needs. The user groups were discussed in Chapter 1.

Discuss the information needs of the various users in relation to the analysis of financial statements

THE INVESTOR GROUP

Among the resource providers are the investors, who were discussed previously as if they were a homogeneous group with similar needs. However, there are, in fact, different types of investors. For sole traders and partnerships, the investor is the owner or partner. The equivalent of this type of investor in a company is the ordinary shareholder. All these investors will be referred to from now on as equity investors. We need to establish what this group has in common, and what distinguishes the equity investor in a large company from his or her equivalent in a sole trader.

In general, equity investors take on all the risks associated with ownership and are entitled to any rewards after other prior claims have been met. For a sole trader the equity investor, that is, the owner, is also likely to be heavily involved in the management and day-to-day running of the business. Where there is direct involvement, the owner's information needs are the same as those of managers (discussed on page 424). In the case of larger organisations, such as large private companies and all public companies, there is likely to be a separation of ownership and management. For large businesses, the final accounts meet the information needs of the shareholders, who are, in the main, properly characterised by the term 'absentee owners'. In general, the smaller the organisation and the greater the direct involvement of the owners in the day-to-day running of the business, the more detail that is required in the accounts. However, the information required to meet the needs of equity investors is broadly the same, irrespective of the type of ownership involved. The needs of this group of users can be met with information about the following:

- profitability, especially future profitability
- management efficiency; for example, are assets being utilised efficiently?
- return on their investment
  - within the firm
  - compared with alternatives
- risk being taken
  - financial risk
  - business risk

- returns to owners
  - dividends
  - drawings, and so on.

PREFERENCE SHAREHOLDERS

Investors in some companies are able to purchase shares known as preference shares, which were discussed in Chapter 10. These shares are generally seen as less risky than ordinary shares and, therefore, normally earn a smaller return. Although it is difficult to generalise the differences between these shares and ordinary shares (this varies from share to share), normally preference shareholders are entitled to a fixed rate of dividend and to repayment before ordinary shareholders in the event of the business being wound up. Because of the nature of these shares, these users are likely to be interested in:

- profitability, mainly future profitability
- the net realisable value of the assets
- the extent to which their dividends are covered by profit.

If we compare the needs of these two groups of investors, we see that preference shareholders are more likely to be interested in the extent to which profit is safe, rather than in the growth of the business. This is because, in most cases, only ordinary shareholders benefit from such growth. The preference shareholders' return is in the form of a dividend at a fixed rate, irrespective of the profits that are made.

Preference shares can either be in the form of equity or debt depending on their characteristics – as discussed in Chapter 10. Redeemable preference shares, which have a fixed redemption date, are regarded as debt, and dividends paid on such shares are classified as interest. Therefore, this type of preference share is similar to a long-term loan. Non-redeemable preference shares are repaid only if the business ceases to exist and sufficient funds are available. Therefore, such shares are similar to ordinary shares and are classified as equity.

We can now move on to look at other resource providers who are also users of accounting information.

LENDERS

Lenders can be conveniently subdivided into three subgroups: short-term creditors, medium-term lenders and long-term lenders. These types of debt finance were discussed in Chapter 10.

Short-term creditors are normally trade creditors; that is, creditors who supply the business with goods on credit. Their areas of interest are:

- short-term liquidity or solvency
- net realisable value of the assets
- profitability and future growth
- risk (financial and business).

Medium-term lenders are usually banks and other financial institutions. Their areas of interest are:

- profitability (future profits providing cash for repayment of loans)

- security, and the nature of the security
- financial stability.

Long-term lenders have the same needs as medium-term lenders, unless they are secured lenders. A secured lender is someone who has a legal charge over the assets of the business and can claim those assets if the business does not repay or service the loan in accordance with the lending agreement. The charge may be a fixed charge over a specific asset, such as land, or it may be a floating charge over all the assets in general but none specifically. A fixed charge gives the holder the right to seize that asset if the business defaults on its loan payments. The lender can then sell the asset to recoup the amount owed. A floating charge gives the holder a higher priority in liquidation than an unsecured creditor, but not the right to seize any specific asset. In the case of secured lenders, the areas of interest are as follows:

- risk, especially financial risk
- security: net realisable value of specific assets
- interest cover: how well their interest is covered by the profits being made.

These different types of lenders have broadly the same needs for information. It is the emphasis that changes, depending on whether the loan is short-term or long-term.

EMPLOYEES

Employees are interested in judging their job security and assessing whether their wages are relatively fair. The collapse of Ansett airlines in 2001 also highlighted the status of other employee entitlements, such as long service leave, if an entity goes into liquidation. This is another reason why employees have a vital interest in the financial health of their employer. Their areas of interest are:

- profitability: average profits per employee for the purposes of productivity bargaining
- liquidity: future trends in profit.

There has been considerable debate over the extent to which these needs are met by conventional accounts and whether a value-added statement would meet these needs better.

ANALYSTS

Many investors rely upon the advice of analysts. Analysts may be employed in a number of different types of organisations such as superannuation funds, investment bankers, stockbrokers, large companies and many others. The analysts have a wide-ranging interest in all types of information about an entity – in a similar way to the investor/ownership group.

AUDITORS

Auditors are not normally seen as users of accounting information. However, in order to carry out an audit efficiently, an analysis of accounts is frequently carried out. The audit function was discussed in Chapter 2. For the purposes of planning and carrying out their audit, the auditors are interested in:

- trends in sales, profit, costs, and so on
- variations from the norm
- accounting policies.

MANAGEMENT

It is difficult to describe the needs of managers because they vary greatly from situation to situation. They require all of the above information, because they are likely to be judged on their performance by outside investors or lenders. In addition, they require detailed information on the performance of the business as a whole, and on its parts, to enable them to manage the business on a day-to-day basis. This information includes such items as profitability by major product, costs per product, changes in sales or component mix. The information needs of management are discussed in the remaining seven chapters of this book.

Common information needs

The needs of users listed in the previous section are not intended to be comprehensive. We have tried to give the reader a flavour of the differing types of information required by the various groups, and to indicate that some of this will not be provided by the annual accounts. At this stage we need to establish what, if any, are common information needs and what other factors need to be considered.

Some common information needs which can be readily identified are profitability, liquidity and risk. The problem is how these are measured and how to judge good or bad performance. Before going on to discuss these specific issues in detail, let us first examine more closely the common information needs and look at the context in which the financial analysis is to be carried out.

The most obvious information that all these groups want is information about the profitability of the business. This can be divided into two components: past profitability and future profitability. Another factor that is common to several groups is the requirement for information about financial risk and liquidity. Another theme that emerges is the return on the investment in the business. This has associated measures such as the riskiness of the return (dividend cover or interest cover). There are also information needs that are specific to particular user groups. A good example of these is the security measures used by lenders.

We will examine how the common needs can be analysed in some detail after we have established the context in which the analysis should take place.

Review exercise 1

How do the needs of long-term lenders differ from those of equity investors?

The context for financial statement analysis

In doing an analysis, you must view it in a wide context; it is not merely a mechanical exercise using various techniques. Below, we outline some of the factors that are directly relevant to an analysis of business performance.

SIZE OF THE BUSINESS

The fact that a business is the size of BHP Billiton makes it less vulnerable to the decisions of people outside the organisation. For example, a banker might lend money to a small business at a rate of 3 or 4 per cent above base rate, whereas for BHP Billiton or CSR the rate would be much lower. Similarly, the banker is likely to ask for security from the small business whereas, with BHP Billiton, the name itself is enough security for the banker.

KEY CONCEPT 14.1

FINANCIAL ANALYSIS

Good financial analysis requires that the person for whom the analysis is being done is clearly identified, together with the purpose of the analysis. It is unlikely to be useful if it does not take into account as many relevant factors as possible.

RISKINESS OF THE BUSINESS

Besides size, the nature of the business needs to be taken into account. For example, a gold prospecting entity has a level of risk (and return) that is different from a bank. Other factors which affect the risk, known as business risk, are reliance on a small number of products, degree of technological innovation and vulnerability to competition.

ECONOMIC, SOCIAL AND POLITICAL ENVIRONMENT

Examples of the way in which the economic, social and political environment affects industry can be found in virtually any daily newspaper. For example, if the Australian dollar declines relative to the US dollar, imports and exports will be affected and firms will gain or suffer accordingly. Changes in interest rates often have sharp effects on firms that are financed by a large amount of borrowing (loans or overdrafts).

The effects of social and environmental issues have, in the past, been more subtle. However, in Chapter 13 we discussed the role of environmental and social issues, and the expanding practice of triple bottom line reporting. The impact of social and environmental issues on entities is reflected in a growing acceptance that profit is not the sole motivation for business, and must be balanced with a regard for the natural environment or ensuring full employment. These social and environmental changes frequently coincide with political changes, although the natural environment is a good example of a social concern which is likely to transcend political changes. As mentioned in Chapter 13, investors can now choose to invest in 'green' companies, and many superannuation funds now offer members this choice.

INDUSTRY TRENDS AND THE EFFECTS OF CHANGES IN TECHNOLOGY

In order to make any judgements about the performance of a business, and more especially about the future, it is vital to understand which way the industry is headed. For example, in the late 1990s many dot.com firms started and failed – reflecting a high-risk industry.

EFFECT OF PRICE CHANGES

Inflation indicators like the Consumer Price Index report movements in the general level of prices for a basket of goods and services – but the effect of price changes may be more specific. For example, the price of property in the early 2000s rose faster than the general change in prices. Over the last 50 or more years, several methods have been proposed for taking account of price changes in corporate reports, none of which has gained general acceptance. Although the perfect solution has not been found, the problem cannot be ignored. Even with a low rate of inflation of 5 per cent, what appears to be a gentle growth in sales is, in fact, a decline. It should be pointed out that, although we normally think of price changes in terms of increases, there are many examples where the effects of new technology, competition and economies of scale have led to *reductions* in price. The most obvious examples are in the electronics industries and the computer industry. For example, a calculator cost approximately $25 for the most basic model at the start of the 1970s; an equivalent today costs less than $5.

Projections and predictions

Identify possible sources of external and internal information

While we can all take a guess at the future, clearly there is a case for taking into account the opinions of those closely involved in the business and those who have expertise in the industry and in analysing likely economic trends. Financial analysis must, after all, relate not only to what has happened but also to what is going to happen.

Having looked at some of the factors that need to be considered, it should be clear that, although a set of accounts contains some of the required information, a lot more information will have to be obtained from other sources. These other sources of information can be conveniently subdivided into sources external to the business and those internal to the business. Some examples are discussed below.

SOURCES EXTERNAL TO THE BUSINESS

Sources of information external to the business include:

- *Government statistics.* These are available from the Australian Bureau of Statistics.
- *Trade journals.* These include journals specific to the trade, and more general professional or business journals such as *Business Review Weekly.*
- *Financial press.* A lot of information can be gleaned from the financial pages of quality newspapers (i.e. the *Australian Financial Review*) and from specialist publications, such as *The Professional Administrator.*
- *Databases.* There are now a number of on-line databases, which contain information about companies, industry statistics and economic indicators.
- *Specialist agencies.* These can provide an industry-wide analysis, general financial reports, credit-scoring services and many other services. Moody's Rating Agency is an example.

Most of these sources are now readily accessible in good libraries and through the use of various search engines on the Web. However, some of the more specialist sources are more difficult to access, and much more expensive.

SOURCES INTERNAL TO THE BUSINESS

Chairman's statement

In the case of public companies, a chairman's statement is included with the annual accounts. It contains summarised information for the year, as well as some predictions for the future. The information should not be taken at face value because it is likely to reflect one point of view – which may be biased. The statement often highlights the positive side of the company's operations. As a leading banker commented, 'It is as important to ascertain what is left out as it is to ascertain what has been included'.

Directors' report

This is a statutory requirement for all companies, and the information that is to be contained in it is laid down in the *Corporations Act*. The statutes, however, only lay down the *minimum* requirement so that, therefore, is normally *all* the information that is given.

Balance sheet

This gives information about the company's financial position at a point in time and is only valid at that point in time. Given that the median time for publication by large companies is over three months after the balance sheet date (and thought to be at least 10 months for small companies), the information might have little bearing on the current position. The question of how timely the information is has a major bearing on what can be concluded from an analysis of the accounting information contained in the published accounts.

Income statement

As with the balance sheet, the information in the income statement is quite old by the time it is published. A further problem is that the information is summarised: this may disguise the weak performance of parts of the business because it is offset by the strong performance of others.

Statement of changes in equity

The purpose of the statement of changes in equity is to report all changes to equity that are taken directly to the equity section of the balance sheet, together with the profit or loss for the period. This, therefore, shows the total changes to the equity for the period and enables users to observe this overall change during a period.

Cash flow statements

As discussed in Chapter 12, the requirements for the cash flow statement are set out in AASB 107 *Cash Flow Statements*. The cash flow statement shows the gross cash inflows and outflows of a business. It normally shows the cash flows associated with the business's operating, financing and investing activities.

It has been argued that this statement will allow users to assess an organisation's ability to meet its obligations and continue to operate as a going concern. Chapter 12 gave some further information on cash flow statements and we studied the cash flow statement for Woodside.

Statement of accounting policies

As we have seen, there are a number of different ways of dealing with items such as inventory. Is FIFO or average cost being used? For depreciation, is reducing-balance or straight-line being used? Many other items are subject to similar preconditions, so it is vital to understand the basis which has been adopted. This is stated in the statement of accounting policies. Unfortunately, all too often these statements are of such generality that they mean little. It is not uncommon to find a statement on depreciation which says, 'depreciation is charged on the straight-line method over the useful life of the assets'. The problem with such a statement is that different assets have different lives and residual values. In fact, it is quite likely that similar businesses have different estimates for the *same* asset. This makes it difficult to compare one company with another, because the basis adopted affects the profits, balance sheet values, and so on. The problem of comparability is explained in Key concept 14.2.

KEY CONCEPT 14.2

COMPARABILITY

It is not sufficient that financial information is relevant and reliable at a particular time, in a particular circumstance or for a particular reporting entity. The users of general-purpose financial reports need to be able to compare aspects of an entity at one time and over time, and compare entities at one time and over time.

An important implication of this concept of comparability is that users need to be informed of the policies employed in the preparation of the general-purpose financial reports, changes in those policies and the effects of those changes.

KEY CONCEPT 14.3

CONSISTENCY

Consistency implies that the measurement and display of transactions and events need to be carried out in a consistent manner throughout an entity, and over time for that entity, and that there is consistency between entities in this regard.

Within the one business, the problem of comparability is to some extent alleviated by the requirement to follow the basic accounting concept of consistency, defined in Key concept 14.3.

Notes to the accounts

These are vital to any financial analysis because they contain the detailed information. Without this information, the level of analysis is likely to be superficial, especially in complex business organisations. Looking at financial statements without studying the notes would be like only reading the table of contents of a novel. You don't get the full story until you read the novel. The same is true for the notes that accompany the annual financial statements. However, users often find that the level of detail in the notes, their complexity and their technical language make it difficult to understand the treatment of various items in the accounts. The first note to the accounts is the statement of accounting policies discussed on page 427.

Auditor's report

Every company that is a reporting entity is subject to an annual audit of its accounts. Included in the accounts is a report from the auditors stating whether, in their opinion, the accounts show a 'true and fair' view. As far as financial analysis is concerned, this report is best treated as an exception report: that is, unless it is qualified in some way no account needs to be taken of it.

It is worth mentioning that, for most bankers, an auditor's report does add credibility to the figures. It does not, however, mean that the accounts are correct in their details. Quite often, the report contains a number of disclaimers in relation to certain figures. The auditor's report was discussed in Chapter 2.

Review exercise 2

What sources of information outside the business are available to you and how would you use this information in your analysis?

The common needs explained

We have identified common needs for information about profitability, liquidity, financial risk and so on, but before we can carry out any analysis we need to know what is meant by these terms. We will therefore discuss what each term means and identify what we are trying to highlight in our analysis. For this purpose we will use the example of Jack Pty Ltd, which was introduced in Chapter 11, and is reproduced in Example 14.1.

LO **3**

Explain the significance of profitability and risk in the analysis of financial statements

Example 14.1: Jack Pty Ltd

Jack Pty Ltd
Income statement for the year ended 30 June 20X4

	Notes		This year		Last year
		$	$	$	$
Sales	1		60 000		45 000
Cost of sales			40 000		30 000
Gross profit			20 000		15 000
Distribution costs	2	3 000		2 500	
Administration costs	2	11 000	14 000	9 000	11 500
Profit before taxation			6 000		3 500
Taxation	3		2 600		1 400
Profit after taxation			3 400		2 100

PROFITABILITY

To assess profitability, it is obvious that the starting point is the income statement. It is also important to look at the statement of changes in equity in order to understand the changes during the period from all sources including the re-measurement of assets. Before looking at the information provided by the income statement, we need to establish what information is required.

We need some sort of comparison. Is the business more profitable than it was last year? Is it more profitable than a similar business, or even a dissimilar business? Each of these questions requires us to measure the profit relative to something else. The last question cannot be answered by looking at one set of statements. We need to compare a number of different businesses, and, to do this, we have to make sure that the accounts are comparable. Are assets being depreciated over the same time period? The shorter the life of the asset, the greater the charge, and the smaller the final profit figure. It is for these comparisons that the accounting policies statement is required.

We will look at comparisons over time within Jack Pty Ltd. The business made more profits this year, when it earned $6000 profit before taxation, than last year when the figure was only $3500. The question is whether it is more profitable because it is selling more – $60 000 this year compared with $45 000 last year – or whether it is more efficient, or whether it is a combination of the two.

We can go some way to answering this by working out what the increase in sales was and what the increase in profit was. In this case, the sales increased by 33 per cent, as follows:

$$\text{sales increase} = \$60\,000 - \$45\,000$$

$$\text{percentage increase} = \frac{\$15\,000}{\$45\,000} \times 100 = 33\%$$

The profit, however, increased by over 70 per cent:

$$\text{profit increase} = \$6000 - \$3500$$

$$\text{percentage increase} = \frac{\$2500}{\$3500} \times 100 = 71\%$$

Thus, we have discovered that not only is Jack making more profit by selling more items but it is also making a greater profit on each sale. However, we do not know whether this seemingly favourable change is because this year was a good year or last year was a bad year, nor do we know whether Jack has had to invest a lot of money in order to increase the profitability. The former question can only be satisfactorily answered by comparisons over a longer period than two years, and then by comparing Jack Pty Ltd with a similar business in the same industry. In the case of a small company, the question about investment can, perhaps, be answered by determining the return on investment, as represented by the profit. This then requires us to ask what is the amount invested: often in a small business the major investment made by the owner is the time spent in the business. However, for a public company, there is normally very little relationship between the amount of equity shown in the accounts and the amount you would have to pay to buy the company.

While not ignoring those problems, we can, for the present, look at the statement of changes in equity and the balance sheet, reproduced below, as a rough guide in the absence of any other information. We can see that, in this case, the investment in the form of capital and reserves has changed from $74 500 last year to $96 300 this year. These changes consist of the profit for the period, $3400, less dividends of $2600, the issue of $6000 of new share capital and an increase of $15 000 to the valuation of land – as reported in the statement of changes in equity. The change to the valuation of the land is a re-measurement of an asset rather than a profit from the operations of the business.

Jack Pty Ltd
Statement of changes in equity as at 30 June 20X4

	Share capital	Asset revaluation reserve	Retained profits	Total
	$000	$000	$000	$000
Balance at 1 July 20X3	64 000	6 000	4 500	74 500
Gain on land revaluation		15 000		15 000
Total income and expense recognised directly in equity				15 000
Profit or loss for the year (from the income statement)			3 400	3 400
Total recognised income and expense for the period				18 400
Dividends			(2 600)	(2 600)
Issue of share capital	6 000			6 000
Balance at 30 June 20X4	70 000	21 000	5 300	96 300

Jack Pty Ltd
Balance sheet at 30 June 20X4

	Notes	This year $		Last year $
		$		$
Assets				
Current assets				
Cash at bank		3 500		2 000
Debtors		11 000		4 000
Inventory	7	10 000		7 000
Total current assets			24 500	13 000
Non-current assets				
Equipment	5	10 000		11 000
Land and buildings	6	70 000		56 000
Total non-current assets			80 000	67 000
Total assets			104 500	80 000

	Notes	$	This year $	Last year $
Liabilities				
Current liabilities				
Creditors		4 000		3 000
Taxation	3	2 600		1 400
Dividends	4	1 600		1 100
Total current liabilities			8 200	5 500
Non-current liabilities			–	–
Total liabilities			8 200	5 500
Net assets			96 300	74 500
Capital and reserves				
Share capital	8	70 000		64 000
Retained profits	9	5 300		4 500
Reserves	10	21 000		6 000
Total capital and reserves			96 300	74 500

Before leaving the question of profitability, we need to discuss the future profitability of the business because this was identified as a common need for many users. The fact that a company has been profitable is comforting, but if you want to make a decision about whether to buy or sell a business you need information about the future, not the past. This information is not contained in the income statement, although it could be argued that information about the past is the best guide to the future. In practical terms, the only way you can form an opinion about the future is by using a combination of information, including past profits, knowledge of the industry, predictions about the economy and many other factors. When estimating future profits, the revaluation of land is not relevant because, as stated above, it is a re-measurement of an asset and not profit arising from the company's operations.

Summary of profitability information needs

Profitability requires comparisons:
- over time
- with other businesses.

Profitability relates to:
- the past for evaluation
- the future for prediction.

FINANCIAL RISK

The area of financial risk (or solvency) was discussed in Chapter 10. It is of vital importance: there are many cases where a business has gone bankrupt because of cash flow problems, even though it was profitable. There are also cases where two companies in the same line of business produce dramatically different results purely because of the way they are financed. For example, if a business makes a return of 15 per cent on every dollar invested and it can borrow money at 10 per cent, it is worthwhile for the business to borrow money because the excess return goes to the owners. However, there is some risk involved in such a course of action because the business will lose if the interest rate rises to, say, 17 per cent and it is still making only 15 per cent. This caused problems for many businesses in the late 1980s and early 1990s. A way of measuring the financial risk is to look at the balance sheet of a business and identify the amount of debt finance (loans, debentures, bank overdrafts and other borrowings) and compare this with the amount of equity finance (owners' capital, retained profits and reserves). The term 'leverage' is used to describe the amount of debt in a balance sheet.

In Australia, debt finance does not normally exceed equity finance, although the extent to which this generalisation holds true is dependent on the size and nature of the business. There were some notable exceptions in the late 1980s, particularly the companies of the high-flying entrepreneurs mentioned earlier. This is largely as a result of the banks' policy of lending on a dollar-for-dollar basis; that is, for each dollar of your money that you invest in the business the bank lends a dollar. While this is not a hard-and-fast rule, it is used as the benchmark by bank managers in Australia. It is interesting that other countries adopt different benchmarks. For example, banks in Germany and Japan tend to lend well above the one-for-one norm.

In the case of Jack Pty Ltd there is no long-term borrowing; there isn't even a bank overdraft. This might be a good thing as the company is making only $6000 on the shareholders' equity of $96 300 capital invested of over $75 000. This is less than 10 per cent, but it should be compared with the rate at which money could be borrowed.

Turning now to short-term solvency: a company has to maintain sufficient assets to meet its commitments as they fall due. The major area for concern is the short term, which is generally taken to be one year. This is convenient as it fits the definition used for current assets and current liabilities; therefore, we have a suitable measure which is apparent in the balance sheet. For example, Jack Pty Ltd has current assets of $24 500 and current liabilities of only $8200. It has to reserve enough funds in the next year to meet its commitments in that year.

One of the problems that arises with this measure is that 'current' can mean due tomorrow or due in 12 months. In the case of some current assets, for example inventory, the asset first has to be sold and then the money has to be collected. Another problem is the question of what is the correct level of current assets for the business. If, for example, there is a lot of cash, this is hardly an efficient use of resources. In the case of Jack, the amount of $3500 in the bank may be far in excess of its real needs. There is also the question of whether $11 000 tied up in debtors is excessive on sales of $60 000, especially if we compare this to last year where the debtors were $4000 on sales of $45 000.

Other problems with interpreting the information about short-term solvency arise if we try to compare different businesses. For example, an aircraft manufacturer has different requirements from a food wholesaler. Even within the same industrial sector, the needs differ. For example, a whisky distiller has different needs from a brewer: whisky has to be matured over years, whereas beer is produced in a few months and has a limited shelf life.

Summary of financial risk information needs

- Financial risk involves long-term and short-term solvency.
- Requirements and norms differ widely from industry to industry.

The general conclusion to be drawn is: analysis of the financial statements is only a small part of the story; that analysis needs to be put into a wider context of knowledge of the industry and the environment. The maxim that a little learning is a dangerous thing applies as much to business analysis as it does elsewhere. With this point in mind, we can now look at some of the techniques that are used to analyse financial information.

Review exercise 3

Explain, briefly, the difference between financial risk and business or commercial risk.

Techniques of analysis

Many techniques are used in financial analysis: they range from simple techniques, such as studying the financial statements (as we have just done) and forming a rough opinion of what is happening, to sophisticated statistical techniques. It should be pointed out that this rough analysis, based on 'eyeballing' the accounts, is vital: it forms the base on which the more sophisticated techniques are built. If, for example, we fail to notice that a business has made a loss for the past few years, the application of the most sophisticated techniques will not help, because we have failed to grasp an essential point.

We will examine some of the simpler techniques. The choice of technique is, once again, a function of what you are trying to do and the purpose of your analysis. For example, managers and auditors might be interested in establishing any variations from past norms and explaining these and, where necessary, taking appropriate action. For a shareholder in a large company, such an analysis, even if it were possible, would be inappropriate as no action could be taken and the level of detail is too specific.

COMPARISON OF FINANCIAL STATEMENTS OVER TIME

A simple comparison of the rate and direction of change over time can be very useful. This can be done both in terms of absolute amount and in percentage terms. Both are normally required in order to reach any conclusions. For example, a 50 per cent change on $1000 is less significant than a 50 per cent change on $50 000. If you have only $1000 to start with, a change of $500 is significant. It is not only the absolute amount, but also the amount relative to other figures, that is important.

The period of time chosen is also worth considering. Too short a period will not be informative. This was the case with Jack where we could only say that the profit had increased but had no idea whether that was part of a trend or whether it was because last year was a particularly bad year. Consider the results of companies in the early 1990s compared to the late 1990s and early 2000s; the economy in Australia changed dramatically in this period from recession to strong growth. Finally, it must be borne in mind that other changes might have affected the figures; for example, the business might have decided to depreciate its vehicles over three years instead of four. Having taken account of these warnings, let us now look at how we can make the comparisons.

TREND ANALYSIS

Trend analysis is normally used for periods of more than two or three years in order to make the results easier to understand and interpret. It involves choosing a base year and then plotting the trend in sales, profits, or whatever from then on. We will illustrate the use of trend statements with income statements, but it can apply to other statements too.

Identify and apply
trend analysis

KEY CONCEPT 14.4

TREND ANALYSIS

In trend analysis, the choice of an appropriate base year is vital. If the base year chosen is not typical the resultant analysis will be, at best, extremely difficult and, at worst, actually misleading.

Example 14.2: ABC Ltd

We will use the financial statements for ABC Ltd to illustrate the trend analysis technique.

ABC Ltd
Income statements

	20X1 $000	20X2 $000	20X3 $000	20X4 $000	20X5 $000
Sales	12 371	13 209	16 843	14 441	13 226
Cost of sales	11 276	11 896	14 818	12 595	13 017
Operating profit	1 095	1 313	2 025	1 846	209
Interest charges	215	252	460	768	676
Pre-tax profit	880	1 061	1 565	1 078	−467
Taxation	464	529	875	579	−2
Net profit after tax	416	532	690	499	−465

If we take the cost of sales, it is clear from a casual examination of the figures that it rises in 20X1 and 20X2 to a peak in 20X3, after which it falls in 20X4. This is shown as a graph in Figure 14.1 (overleaf). As you can see, the information in the graph is limited; it reflects what we have already found. To make any sensible comment, we need to see how these costs are behaving in relation to something else. This could be in relation to another item in the income statement such as sales, or in relation to the costs in a comparable company. To make the latter comparison, however, we first have to find some common means of expression because the companies being compared are unlikely to be exactly the same size. One way of doing this is to use index numbers to express the figures we are looking at and the way in which they change from year to year.

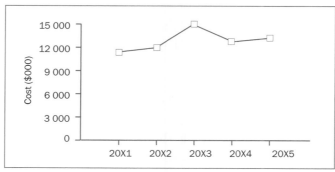

Figure 14.1 Cost of sales for ABC Ltd, 20X1–X5

ABC Ltd
Statements of changes in equity

	Share capital $000	Retained profits $000	Total $000
Balance at 1 July 20X0	1 584	1 281	2 865
Net income recognised directly in equity			0
Profit or loss for the year (from the income statement)		416	416
Total recognised income and expense for the period			416
Dividends		(164)	(164)
Balance at 30 June 20X1	1 584	1 533	3 117
Net income recognised directly in equity			0
Profit or loss for the year (from the income statement)		532	532
Total recognised income and expense for the period			532
Dividends		(185)	(185)
Issued shares	152		152
Balance at 30 June 20X2	1 736	1 880	3 616
Net income recognised directly in equity			0
Profit or loss for the year (from the income statement)		690	690
Total recognised income and expense for the period			690
Dividends		(336)	(336)
Share buy back	(243)		(243)
Balance at 30 June 20X3	1 493	2 234	3 727
Net income recognised directly in equity			0
Profit or loss for the year (from the income statement)		499	499
Total recognised income and expense for the period			499
Dividends		(387)	(387)
Shares issued	485		485
Balance at 30 June 20X4	1 978	2 346	4 324
Net income recognised directly in equity			0
Profit or loss for the year (from the income statement)		(465)	(465)
Total recognised income and expense for the period			(465)
Dividends		(123)	(123)
Balance at 30 June 20X5	1 978	1 758	3 736

Index number trends

As with other forms of trend analysis, this technique is normally used for periods of more than two or three years. It is intended to make the results easier to understand and interpret. An index number is determined by choosing a base year, setting that base year at 100 and expressing figures for all other years in terms of that index.

Using the example of the sales of ABC Ltd, if we took 20X1 as the base year and set that at 100, we would calculate the index for 20X2 as follows:

$$\frac{\text{20X2 sales}}{\text{20X1 sales}} \times 100 = \frac{13\ 209}{12\ 371} \times 100 = 107$$

For 20X3 the calculation would be:

$$\frac{\text{20X3 sales}}{\text{20X1 sales}} \times 100 = \frac{16\ 843}{12\ 371} \times 100 = 136$$

Using the same formula, we can find the index for each of the other years and then study the sales trend. In this case the figures are:

20X1, 100; 20X2, 107; 20X3, 136; 20X4, 117; 20X5, 107

We can do the same with the figures for the cost of sales and the profit and then analyse these trends. In the case of sales, we can see that they peaked in 20X3 and then declined in 20X4 and 20X5. This can be seen more easily in the following table, which reports the trend numbers for the income statement for ABC for the five years. Other numbers which are significant are the decline in sales in 20X5 by more than the decline in cost of sales; this is the main reason for the loss in 20X5. The interest charges have also risen substantially over the period.

ABC Ltd
Income statements

	20X1	20X2	20X3	20X4	20X5
	%	%	%	%	%
Sales	100	107	136	117	107
Cost of sales	100	105	131	112	115
Operating profit	100	120	185	169	19
Interest charges	100	117	214	357	314
Pre-tax profit	100	121	178	122	−53
Taxation	100	114	189	125	0
Net profit after tax	100	128	166	120	−118

Percentage changes

Another technique used in trend analysis is to identify the percentage change from year to year and then examine the trends in it. For example, if we look at the sales we find that the change from 20X1 to 20X2 was 7 per cent, while that from 20X2 to 20X3 was 29 per cent. These figures are calculated as follows:

$$\frac{\text{this year's sales}}{\text{last year's sales}} \times 100 = \frac{13\ 209}{12\ 371} \times 100 = 107\%$$

that is, an increase of 7 per cent.

Once again, it should be pointed out that these trends are of most use if they are compared with other trends, either in the business itself or in the industry. You should also bear in mind that percentage increases are often illusory because they could merely be reflecting the increase that would be expected as a result of the prevailing rate of inflation.

COMMON-SIZE STATEMENTS

Identify and use common-size statements

In examining accounts, we often encounter large numbers; these are more digestible if they are presented as 'common-size statements'. This technique, as the name implies, deals with the problem of comparing companies of different sizes. It involves expressing the items in the balance sheet, for example, as percentages of the balance sheet total.

This is illustrated by looking again at ABC Ltd, the balance sheets of which are reproduced below. We can derive some information by examining the balance sheets, but it is not easy to identify exactly what is happening. For example, why has the land and building account gone up in 20X3 by a greater amount than the other non-current assets? Where did the intangibles come from, and what are they? These questions can often be answered, in part at least, by using the detailed information contained in the notes to the accounts.

ABC Ltd
Summary balance sheets

	20X1 $000	20X2 $000	20X3 $000	20X4 $000	20X5 $000
Assets					
Current assets					
Cash	400	464	183	15	41
Debtors	2 259	2 389	3 012	2 776	2 508
Inventory	3 645	3 952	3 903	3 289	3 255
Total current assets	6 304	6 805	7 098	6 080	5 804
Non-current assets					
Plant and equipment	875	849	959	863	767
Land and buildings	639	660	682	1 070	1 103
Other non-current assets	450	554	486	663	683
Intangibles	0	0	470	451	460
Total non-current assets	1 964	2 063	2 597	3 047	3 013
Total assets	8 268	8 868	9 695	9 127	8 817

	20X1 $000	20X2 $000	20X3 $000	20X4 $000	20X5 $000
Liabilities					
Current liabilities					
Bank overdraft	0	3	86	427	663
Creditors	3 701	3 706	4 842	3 311	4 277
Taxation	110	415	196	44	48
Dividends	121	137	224	225	1
Total current liabilities	3 932	4 261	5 348	4 007	4 989
Non-current liabilities					
Deferred tax	922	843	320	400	0
Loans	297	148	300	396	92
Total non-current liabilities	1 219	991	620	796	92
Total liabilities	5 151	5 252	5 968	4 803	5 081
Net assets	3 117	3 616	3 727	4 324	3 736
Shareholders' equity					
Share capital ($1 ordinary shares)	1 584	1 736	1 493	1 978	1 978
Retained profits	1 533	1 880	2 234	2 346	1 758
Total shareholders' equity	3 117	3 616	3 727	4 324	3 736

The problem when looking at standard balance sheets is that the figures often disguise what is really happening. If we convert the statements to some common measure, the underlying trends become clearer. We could take, for example, the share capital for 20X1 and express it as a percentage of the total assets. We find that it is 19 per cent in that year compared with 20 per cent in 20X2. To calculate this we divided the share capital figure by the total assets and then multiplied the result by 100. Thus, for 20X3 we have:

$$\frac{\text{share capital}}{\text{total assets}} \times 100 = \frac{1493}{9695} \times 100 = 15\%$$

Following this procedure for all items in the balance sheets produces common-size statements as follows:

ABC Ltd
Common-size balance sheets

	20X1 %	20X2 %	20X3 %	20X4 %	20X5 %
Assets					
Current assets					
Cash	5	5	2	0	0
Debtors	27	27	31	31	29
Inventory	44	45	40	36	37
Total current assets	76	77	73	67	66

	20X1	20X2	20X3	20X4	20X5
	%	%	%	%	%
Non-current assets					
Plant and equipment	11	10	10	9	9
Land and buildings	8	7	7	12	12
Other non-current assets	5	6	5	7	8
Intangibles	0	0	5	5	5
Total non-current assets	24	23	27	33	34
Total assets	100	100	100	100	100
Liabilities					
Current liabilities					
Bank overdraft	0	0	1	5	8
Creditors	45	42	50	36	49
Taxation	1	5	2	0	0
Dividends	1	1	2	2	0
Total current liabilities	47	48	55	45	57
Non-current liabilities					
Deferred tax	11	9	3	4	0
Loans	4	2	3	4	1
Total non-current liabilities	15	11	6	8	1
Total liabilities	62	59	62	53	58
Net assets	38	41	38	47	42
Shareholders' equity					
Share capital ($1 ordinary shares)	19	20	15	21	22
Retained profits	19	21	23	26	20
Total shareholders' equity	38	41	38	47	42

One of the many things that we can see from an analysis of these statements is that the current assets declined over the period, from 76 per cent of total assets in 20X1 to only 66 per cent in 20X5, and at the same time, the current liabilities increased from 47 per cent to 57 per cent. By 20X5 the bank overdraft had risen to its highest level ever and the business had little cash. It should be noted that, with this technique, the choice of the base amount is just as important as it was with trend analysis.

Common-size statements can be applied as easily to the income statement as to the balance sheet. In the case of the income statement, it is usual to express all items as a percentage of sales, as illustrated below:

ABC Ltd
Common-size income statements

	20X1 %	20X2 %	20X3 %	20X4 %	20X5 %
Sales	100	100	100	100	100
Cost of sales	91	90	88	87	98
Operating profit	9	10	12	13	2
Interest charges	2	2	3	6	5
Pre-tax profit	7	8	9	7	−3
Taxation	4	4	5	4	0
After-tax profit	3	4	4	3	−3

This statement is self-explanatory. Note the obvious rounding errors which occur when working in whole numbers. An item that is worth highlighting is that the cost of sales in 20X5 squeezed the operating profit down to only 2 per cent return on sales in a year when the interest charges were in excess of 5 per cent of sales. This illustrates the risk of high levels of debt, which we referred to earlier in the chapter when discussing financial risk. There could be several reasons why the cost of sales as a percentage of sales has increased. Recessionary conditions in the economy could have squeezed margins; new competitors or a price-cutting war could have reduced selling prices. Consider the impact on the price of computers caused by the development of the Apple-Macintosh computer. Again, we need to consider the results for ABC Ltd together with other information.

KEY CONCEPT 14.5

COMMON-SIZE STATEMENTS
Common-size statements express all items in the financial statement as a percentage of one significant item in the relevant financial statement (such as total assets for the balance sheet). It allows for a fast review of the financial statements and fast detection of any significant changes.

We have not prepared common-size statements for the statement of changes in equity or the cash flow statement but they would be prepared using the same principles.

Common-size statements and the other techniques that we have examined so far have largely ignored the relationship between any two components of the financial statements of a business. Other techniques of analysis are available which look at the relationship between items in the balance sheet, the income statement, the statement of changes in equity and the cash flow statement. The most common of these techniques is known as ratio analysis and this is explored more fully in the following section.

RATIO ANALYSIS
Ratio analysis is explained in virtually every introductory accounting textbook, and most students have little difficulty in calculating ratios. However, many students find that they have extreme difficulty with understanding what the ratios mean once they have been calculated. Because of this, we will not

deal extensively with all the possible ratios that can be calculated; instead we will concentrate on the relationships that the ratios express. This approach will increase your understanding of the reasons for calculating these ratios and enable you to interpret the results from a knowledgeable basis.

Table 14.1 (pages 444–5) gives a list of ratios often used in analysis, together with an indication of their significance. We compute the ratios for ABC Ltd to illustrate the calculations involved. We have used 20X4 figures from ABC Ltd to illustrate the calculations involved, as 20X5 results show a loss. However, we also report the ratios for 20X5 and will comment on the comparison of 20X4 with 20X5. We assume a tax rate of 40 per cent for the calculations. You should refer to the formulas used in this book (as reported in Table 14.1) as you work your way through this section of the chapter.

Some ratios only express relationships between items in the balance sheets, while some ratios are only based upon items in the income statements. Finally, some ratios combine information from both these statements, the statement of changes in equity and the statement of cash flows – which is presented below for ABC Ltd for the years 20X4 and 20X5:

ABC Ltd
Cash flow statements

	20X4 $000s	20X4 $000s	20X5 $000s	20X5 $000s
Cash flow from operating activities		226		423
Cash flow from investing activities				
Payments to acquire non-current assets	(800)		(85)	
Payments to acquire investments	0		(10)	
Receipts from disposal of non-current assets	50		10	
		(750)		(85)
Cash flow from financing activities				
Dividends paid	(225)		(1)	
Issue of ordinary share capital	485		(11)	
Loans	96		(300)	
		356		(312)
Increase (decrease) in cash in period		(168)		26

First, we need to understand exactly what a ratio is. A ratio compares two quantities. The common mathematical notation used is A:B. For example, the ratio 3:2 ('three to two') means that for every 3 units of A, there are 2 units of B. Ratios can be expressed in a number of ways including a percentage (i.e. 10 per cent), as a decimal (i.e. 0.1) or in a ratio form (i.e. 0.1:1). Ratios are often written as simply as possible, for example, 10:4 = 5:2. It is convenient if one of the numbers in the ratio is a 1. For example, if A:B = 10:4, dividing by B gives:

$$\frac{A}{B} : 1 = \frac{10}{4} : 1 = 2.5 : 1$$

This clearly shows that A is two-and-a-half times B.

The concept of ratios, as used in accounting, is defined in Key concept 14.6.

KEY CONCEPT 14.6

RATIO

In accounting, when comparing quantity A with quantity B, the ratio R is defined by $R = A \div B$. This means that A is R times B, and may be written R:1. In essence, a ratio is merely a shorthand notation for the relationship between two or more things. It is the relationship which must be understood. Without that understanding, the ratio, no matter how precisely calculated or sophisticated, is meaningless.

For example, if we want to know how many police are needed to maintain order at a football match, we could work out a ratio of police officers to spectators. If we found that we needed 200 police for a crowd of 40 000 spectators, the ratio would be 1 to 200 or 1:200.

As well as understanding the relationship expressed by the ratio, we also need to examine ratios in a wider context. The above ratio is meaningless on its own: it does not give us any idea whether we are using the right number of police. To decide this we would need to establish whether there were problems of violence or, if not, whether we could achieve the same result with fewer police. To answer the first question we require additional information while the latter could be answered, in part at least, by looking at other football clubs and what ratio of police to spectators they use. This simple example serves to illustrate the fact that the ratio on its own cannot tell us very much. It needs to be looked at in the context of other information and experience.

Benchmarks

As we have already said, the important point to bear in mind is what the ratio is attempting to illustrate. For example, we could look at the balance sheet of ABC Ltd and calculate the ratio of plant and equipment to other non-current assets, but this would be of little use unless we knew what the relationship meant and what we expected. The calculation of ratios is not an end in itself. We could do a comparison of ratios for the same entity through time (times-series). We could also do a comparison of one entity with another entity across time (cross-sectional) or, indeed, we could do both. Therefore, it is important to choose an appropriate benchmark against which to compare the ratios of the entity you wish to analyse (i.e. the subject/entity). A number of factors are relevant in the selection of an appropriate benchmark(s), and these include:

LO 6

Identify the issues to be considered when choosing a benchmark for ratio analysis

- *Relative size of the entities.* While the benchmark(s) and the subject don't need to be of identical size, it would not make a lot of sense to compare Woolworths with the local corner store.
- *Industry.* It is important to match the benchmark(s) and the subject as closely as possible in terms of their operations.
- *Geographical location.* To minimise problems that may be specific to certain locations, it is preferable to match the location of the benchmark and the subject.
- *Similar accounting policies and periods.* It is easier to compare benchmarks and entities that have similar accounting policies. Also, while it is not essential to have the same year-end dates (such as 30 June), it is preferable.

We will now discuss some of the ratios presented in Table 14.1 in the following categories:

- profitability

(*continued on page 446*)

Table 14.1 Analysis ratios

Ratio	Components	ABC Ltd (20X4)	20X5	Use
PROFITABILITY RATIOS				
1 Net profit margin before after-tax cost of interest	$\dfrac{\text{net profit* + after-tax interest cost}}{\text{sales}}$	$\dfrac{499 + 768\,(1-0.4)}{14\,441} = \dfrac{960}{14\,441} = 6.6\%$	−0.5%	Profit produced by each dollar of sales before any payment to equity or debt providers.
2 Net profit margin	$\dfrac{\text{net profit}}{\text{sales}}$	$\dfrac{499}{14\,441} = 3.5\%$	−3.2%	Profit produced by each dollar of sales after payment of interest.
3 Gross profit margin	$\dfrac{\text{net sales} - \text{cost of goods sold}}{\text{net sales}}$	$\dfrac{14\,441 - 12\,595}{14\,441} = 12.8\%$	1.6%	Indicates the efficiency of management in turning over the company's goods at a profit.
4 Interest cost as a percentage of sales	$\dfrac{\text{interest expense}}{\text{sales}}$	$\dfrac{768}{14\,441} = 5\%$	5%	Shows the cost of interest as a percentage of sales.
5 Asset turnover	$\dfrac{\text{sales}}{\text{average total assets}}$	$\dfrac{14\,441}{(9695 + 9127) \div 2} = \dfrac{14\,441}{9411} = 1.53$	1.47	Shows how efficiently assets are used to generate sales.
6 Return on assets**	$\dfrac{\text{net profit + after-tax interest cost}}{\text{average total assets}}$	$\dfrac{499 + 768 \times (1-0.4)}{9411} = \dfrac{960}{9411} = 10.2\%$	−0.7%	Shows the overall earning power of total assets before any payments to equity or debt providers.
7 Return of ordinary shareholders' equity	$\dfrac{\text{net profit} - \text{preference dividend}}{\text{average ordinary shareholders' equity}}$	$\dfrac{499 - 0}{(3727 + 4324) \div 2} = \dfrac{499}{4026} = 12.4\%$	−11.5%	Shows the profitability of ordinary shareholders' equity.
8 Earnings per share	$\dfrac{\text{net profit} - \text{preference dividend}}{\text{weighted average number of ordinary shares issued}}$	$\dfrac{499}{1978} = 25.2 \text{ cents}$ (assume shares are $1)	−23.6 cents	To facilitate comparisons of earnings between companies.
EFFICIENCY RATIOS				
9 Debtors' turnover	$\dfrac{\text{net sales}}{\text{average debtors}}$	$\dfrac{14\,441}{(3012 + 2776) \div 2} = \dfrac{14\,441}{2894} = 5$	5	Shows the effectiveness of the collection of debtors' accounts.
10 Average days sales uncollected	$\dfrac{\text{days in year}}{\text{debtors' turnover}}$	$\dfrac{365}{5} = 73 \text{ days}$	73 days	Shows the time taken to collect debtors' accounts.
11 Inventory turnover	$\dfrac{\text{cost of goods sold}}{\text{average inventory}}$	$\dfrac{12\,595}{(3903 + 3289) \div 2} = \dfrac{12\,595}{3596} = 3.5$	4	Shows the effectiveness of investments in inventories.
12 Inventory turnover in days	$\dfrac{\text{days in year}}{\text{inventory turnover}}$	$\dfrac{365}{3.5} = 104.3 \text{ days}$	91 days	Shows the number of days to convert inventory into sales.

SHORT-TERM SOLVENCY RATIOS

	Formula	Calculation		Description
13 Current ratio	$\dfrac{\text{current assets}}{\text{current liabilities}}$	$\dfrac{6080}{4007} = 1.52$	1.2	Shows short-term debt-paying ability.
14 Quick ratio	$\dfrac{\text{quick assets}}{\text{current liabilities}}$	$\dfrac{2791}{4007} = 0.70$	0.5	Shows immediate ability to meet current debts.
15 Cash flow from operations to current liabilities	$\dfrac{\text{operating cash flows}}{\text{current liabilities}}$	$\dfrac{226}{4007} = 5.6 \text{ cents}$	8.5 cents	Shows short-term debt-paying ability based on operating cash flows.

LONG-TERM SOLVENCY RATIOS

	Formula	Calculation		Description
16 Debt to equity	$\dfrac{\text{total liabilities}}{\text{total shareholders' equity}}$	$\dfrac{4803}{4324} = 1.11$	1.36	Shows the relationship between debt financing and equity financing.
17 Debt to total assets	$\dfrac{\text{total liabilities}}{\text{total assets}}$	$\dfrac{4803}{9127} = 0.53$	0.58	Shows the proportion of total assets financed by debt.
18 Leverage ratio	$\dfrac{\text{total assets}}{\text{total shareholders' equity}}$	$\dfrac{9217}{4324} = 2.13$	2.38	Shows the use of leverage. The higher the number the greater the use of debt.
19 Interest coverage	$\dfrac{\text{net profit} + \text{income tax} + \text{interest}}{\text{interest expense}}$	$\dfrac{499 + 579 + 768}{768} = \dfrac{1846}{768} = 2.40$	0.3	Shows the protection of lenders from a default on interest payments.
20 Cash flow from operations to total liabilities	$\dfrac{\text{operating cash flows}}{\text{total liabilities}}$	$\dfrac{226}{4803} = 4.7c$	8.3c	Shows ability to pay total debt from operating cash flows.

MARKET-BASED RATIOS

	Formula	Calculation		Description
21 Price/Earnings (P/E)	$\dfrac{\text{market price per ordinary share}}{\text{earnings per share}}$	$\dfrac{\$3.30^{***}}{0.252} = 13.09$		Shows the amount the market will pay for \$1 of profit.
22 Earnings yield	$\dfrac{\text{earnings per share}}{\text{market price per ordinary share}}$	$\dfrac{0.252}{\$3.30} = 7.6\%$		Shows the earnings yield based on the current market price.
23 Dividend yield	$\dfrac{\text{dividends per ordinary share}}{\text{market price per ordinary share}}$	$\dfrac{337 \div 1978}{\$3.30} = \dfrac{0.1703}{3.30} = 5.1\%$		Shows current yield on dividends.

OTHER RATIOS

	Formula	Calculation		Description
24 Net tangible asset backing	$\dfrac{\text{net tangible assets}}{\text{number of ordinary shares issued}}$	$\dfrac{4324 - 451}{1978} = \$1.96$	\$1.85	Shows the value per ordinary share based on net tangible assets at carrying values.

NOTES TO TABLE 14.1
*   See page 446 for issues about which net profit to use.
**   The numerator in the ratio for return on assets in some books is net profit + interest + tax. Either formula is acceptable but the important requirement is to be consistent in the way you measure ratios across different firms.
*** Assume market price is \$3.30 at end of 20X4.

- efficiency
- short-term solvency
- long-term solvency
- market-based ratios.

To demonstrate the application of ratio analysis, we will compare the ratios for Coles Myer and Woolworths for the period ending 30 June 20X5. If numbers appear in brackets next to a ratio they relate to the numbers in Table 14.1 – to allow you to check the formula for that ratio.

KEY CONCEPT 14.7

RATIO ANALYSIS

The analysis of ratios involves comparison with appropriate benchmarks through time (time-series) for the same entity and across time (cross-sectional) for two or more entities.

Profitability ratios

LO
7

Identify and apply
various ratios that can
be used to assess
profitability

Most ratios that relate solely to the income statement are expressions of costs as a percentage of sales; for example, the gross profit or net profit expressed as a percentage of sales. These relationships are also made apparent with common-size statements, which we have already examined. We have also shown the various profitability ratios in Table 14.1.

Before commenting on the profitability ratios in Table 14.1, we need to consider which net profit figure is used. When analysts assess the profitability of a company and attempt to predict future profitability, they generally focus on profit from *ordinary activities*. Any unusual events which have been included in the determination of profit are generally excluded by analysts when attempting to predict future maintainable profits. AASB 108 *Accounting Policies, Changes in Accounting Estimates and Errors* requires entities to disclose the following items, if relevant, in the income statement:

- revenue or expense items which are due to a revision of an accounting estimate, such as a revision of depreciation expense
- revenue or expense items arising from an error in a prior reporting period
- impact on reported profits from a change in accounting policy.

In assessing future profitability, analysts normally use the profit figure (excluding the effects of the above items if such items do not influence the entity's future profitability). They are concerned with future maintainable profits, and any change to current profits due to irregular items, such as an error, are discounted.

From Table 14.1 we see that both the gross profit and net profit margin ratios have declined from 20X4 to 20X5. The gross profit margin decreased from 12.8 per cent to 1.6 per cent and is the major reason for the decline in profitability in 20X5. Therefore, the cost of sales in 20X5 has squeezed the operating profit down to only 1.6 per cent return on sales in a year when the interest charges were in excess of 5 per cent of sales. As stated earlier, there could be several reasons why the cost of sales as a percentage of sales has increased. Recessionary conditions in the economy could have squeezed margins; new competitors, or a price-cutting war, could have reduced selling prices.

As mentioned in the previous paragraph, the ratio of interest cost to sales has increased in 20X5 to 5 per cent. Other ratios we could calculate are the various other expenses that a business incurs as a percentage of sales, to see if these have significantly affected the change in profits. In the case of ABC Ltd, there are no other categories of expenses other than the interest costs. Therefore, the decline in the gross profit margin is the major cause of the lower profits in 20X5.

Return on assets

The return on assets declined from 10.2 per cent to –0.7 per cent. It is possible to break down or disaggregate the return on assets into its component parts to assess what is driving the change in the ratio. This is illustrated in the following equation:

Rate of return on assets (6) = net profit margin ratio (before interest expense net of tax) (1)
× total assets turnover ratio (5)

The formulas for each of these ratios can be extracted from Table 14.1 and we now insert them into the equation:

$$\frac{\text{net profit} + \text{after-tax interest cost (NPBATIC)}}{\text{average total assets (ATA)}} = \frac{\text{NPBATIC}}{\text{sales}} \times \frac{\text{sales}}{\text{ATA}}$$

We can now insert the relevant numbers for ABC for the years 20X4 and 20X5:

ABC Ltd, 20X4	ABC Ltd, 20X5
6.66 × 1.53 = 10.2%	–0.5 × 1.47 = 0.7%

The breakdown of the return on assets ratio for ABC Ltd shows that the net profit margin before the after-tax cost of interest declined significantly while the asset turnover figure remained reasonably constant. Therefore, it was the decline in the profit margin and not a lower turnover of assets which caused the loss for ABC Ltd in 20X5.

Let us now look at these ratios for Woolworths and Coles Myer for 20X5:

Woolworths (WOW) and Coles Myer (CML) for 20X5

	Return on assets	Profit margin	Asset turnover
CML	7.81%	2.02%	3.87
WOW	10.14%	2.84%	3.57

Woolworths has a higher return on assets than Coles Myer. This must be due to the higher profit margin, because Coles Myer has a higher asset turnover. Even though the profit margin differential is only 0.82 per cent, this, in effect, means that Woolworths' margin is 40 per cent higher than Coles Myer. This can be attributed, in part, to a major costcutting exercise at Woolworths called Project Refresh. Project Refresh resulted in a more efficient system for managing inventories – a very large item for the big retailers. The asset turnover is higher for Coles Myer which means that they generate more sales dollars from their assets.

Return on ordinary shareholders' equity

The return on assets ratio looks at the total return from assets before any payments of dividends or interest to equity and debt providers. The return on equity (ROE) ratio examines the return for the providers of the equity to the business. It is ratio number 14 under the 'Profitability ratios' heading in Table 14.1. The results for Woolworths and Coles Myer for 20X5 are reported here:

	ROE
CML	18.18%
WOW	36.53%

Why did Woolworths outperform Coles Myer to such a significant extent? To help us answer this question, we can dissect the ROE figure in the same as we did for the return on assets, as indicated in the following equation:

Rate of return on ordinary shareholders' equity (7) = profit margin ratio (after interest expense and preferred dividends) (2) × total assets turnover ratio (5) × leverage ratio (18)

Woolworths (WOW) and Coles Myer (CML) for 2005

	Net profit margin	Asset turnover	Financial leverage
CML	1.87%	3.87	250.57%
WOW	2.47%	3.57	407.71%

You can verify the relationship with the ROE by performing the following calculation for Coles Myer:

$$ROE = 1.87 \times 3.87 \times 2.5057$$
$$= 18.13\%$$

This is the same as the ROE of 18.18 per cent in the results table (subject to rounding differences). So, the ROE for WOW is higher than CML due to the higher profit margin, as is the case with the return on assets and the higher leverage figure.

The above relationship between the three ratios might seem to suggest that an easy way to improve ROE is to increase leverage by borrowing more money. However, by borrowing more money, the entity's cost of interest may rise thereby causing a decline in the profit margin. Also, if the entity has no use for the funds, the asset turnover figure will decline. Both of these outcomes will negatively impact the ROE.

Review exercise 4

ABC Ltd reported an increase in net profit of 20 per cent over the preceding year. Does this show an improved operating performance? Discuss.

Identify and apply various ratios that can be used to assess efficiency

Efficiency ratios

Suppose we have an increase in sales: we would expect our debtors to increase; we would probably have to buy more goods to sell, and so our creditors might rise; and in all probability our level of inventories would have to rise to cope with the increased demand. In the case of ABC Ltd, the sales have risen, as have the debtors. At this stage, we are not sure whether the increase in debtors is solely due to the increase in sales or whether it is, in part, caused by the debtors taking longer to pay. The use of a ratio that compares sales and debtors would provide the answers. The efficiency ratios show how effective an entity is in collecting monies owing and converting inventories into sales. Most businesses operate with inventories and receivables and, as stated in Chapters 7 and 8, it is important to closely monitor the amount invested in such assets. When calculating ratios that relate balance sheet items to income statement items we have to bear in mind that, if prices are changing, the relationship can be distorted. This is because the balance sheet represents prices at one point in time, whereas the income statement represents the results of operations for a period. This can be shown diagrammatically:

$$T_0 \; \underline{\hspace{2cm} \text{income statement} \hspace{3cm}} \; T_1$$
$$\text{opening balance sheet} \hspace{4cm} \text{closing balance sheet}$$

Thus, the opening inventory figure or debtors figure is expressed in beginning-of-the-year prices, the profit and loss figures in average prices, and the closing figures in end-of-year prices. In addition to the problem of changing price levels is the problem that the volume will also change. For example, as sales increase we need to hold more units of inventory in order to provide the same service. Thus, we have two problems: changes in prices and in volumes. One way to compensate for this is to use the average of the opening and closing balance sheet figures and compare that average figure for inventories, debtors, and so on, with the figure from the income statement which is already expressed in average prices. Thus, to calculate the relationship between sales for 20X5 and the debtors, we take the debtors at 20X4 and 20X5 and average the two figures. This gives us a better approximation of the true level of debtors required to sustain that volume of sales. In fact, an average based on monthly balances of debtors might be even more appropriate. However, this information is not available in annual reports.

The relationship thus calculated can be expressed either as the turnover of the balance sheet figure, that is, debtors' turnover, or as the number of days debtors take to repay. We use the latter for purposes of illustration, because experience shows it is more readily understood.

To calculate this ratio the formula we require is:

$$\text{debtor collection period (days)} = 365 \div \frac{\text{net sales}}{\text{average debtors}}$$

Thus, for 20X5 for ABC Ltd the debtor collection period is:

$$365 \div \frac{13\ 226}{1/2(2776 + 2508)} = 73 \text{ days}$$

Once again, we cannot comment on whether this is good or bad without some reference point and some more information. For example, if the sales mix had changed and ABC Ltd had moved into overseas markets, the business might need longer to collect money due to it. Knowledge about how long ABC Ltd gives its customers to pay their accounts would enable a comparison with this figure. For example, if ABC Ltd allows 60 days for customers to pay, then 73 days is reasonable. However, if ABC Ltd only allows 30 days then the current position is much worse. From Table 14.1 we can see that the ratio is the same in 20X4 for ABC Ltd. A comparison of ABC Ltd's ratios with a competitor's figures would enable further assessment of ABC Ltd's position.

Several other ratios of this type can be calculated, such as the number of days inventories are held. Table 14.1 shows this as 104 days in 20X4 and 91 days (an improvement) in 20X5. This means that ABC Ltd was able to convert its inventories into sales at a faster pace in 20X5 when compared to 20X4. This is one of the few positive signs for ABC Ltd in 20X5. It is also possible to calculate other ratios like the period taken to pay creditors, using cost of sales and purchases respectively. We will not deal with these other ratios in depth; instead we encourage you to identify the relationships which will aid your understanding, and derive your own ratios. Table 14.1 provides some for you to consider.

Woolworths (WOW) and Coles Myer (CML) for 2005

	Days inventory	Days receivables
CML	31.8	6.83
WOW	22.6	0.61

From the table, we see that Woolworths performs better than Coles Myer on both ratios because they take less time to collect debtors and less time to sell inventory. If the two companies were identical, this would mean that Woolworths is more efficient. However, the business mix of the two big retailers is somewhat different – as reported in the segment disclosures in their annual reports. The proportion of supermarket business for Woolworths is about 20 per cent higher than Coles Myer. The supermarket business is mainly cash sales for food and groceries. Hence, there will be less receivables, and food and groceries are sold quicker than clothing held in department stores such as Myer. To some extent, this explains the higher number of days in receivables and inventory for Coles Myer.

Short-term solvency ratios

Identify and apply various ratios that can be used to assess short-term solvency

Having assessed the profitability and efficiency ratios, we now turn to risk assessment and endeavour to answer such questions as:

- Does the entity have enough cash to repay the loan tomorrow?
- Will the entity have enough cash to repay the loan if it is due in six months?
- Will the entity have enough cash to repay the loan if it is due in five years?

In this section, we examine ratios that assist with short-term decisions; in the next section we examine ratios concerning long-term decisions. The balance sheet ratios that are commonly used are the relationship between current assets and current liabilities, and the relationship between current monetary assets (such as debtors and cash) and current liabilities. The current ratio, for example, is calculated by dividing the current assets figure by the current liabilities figure. Once again, on its own, the result of this calculation does not necessarily tell us very much. We need to look at trends and take into account the nature of the business. For example, we expect a greengrocer's optimum level of inventory to be different to that of, say, a car manufacturer. This is because the greengrocer's inventory, being perishable goods, has a limited shelf life. Besides the nature of the business, we also need to take into account the industry norms and the size of the business.

Turning now to the trends in ABC Ltd's short-term solvency ratios, we can see whether they give us any idea of what is happening.

$$\text{current ratio} = \frac{\text{current assets}}{\text{current liabilities}}$$

$$\text{current ratio for 20X1} = \frac{\$6\,304\,000}{\$3\,932\,000} = 1.6 \text{ or } 1.6{:}1$$

The ratios for the other years are as follows:

20X2, 1.6:1; 20X3, 1.3:1; 20X4, 1.5:1; 20X5, 1.2:1

These show that the ratio is declining, but what does this mean? To answer that, we need to think about the relationship being expressed; that is, the relationship between those assets that will be converted into cash in the short term and the amounts we potentially have to pay out in the short term. If the ratio is going down, it means that we have less cover and, therefore, there is more risk.

Review exercise 5

Taking the following ratios in isolation, list their weaknesses, if any:
   a current ratio
   b inventory turnover.

With more risk, we might wish to use a more sensitive measure. One such measure simply excludes the inventory from the current assets and compares the remaining current assets with the current liabilities. The reasoning behind the exclusion of inventory is that it will take time to turn it into cash: it first has to be sold and then the debtors have to pay before we can use the cash to pay our creditors.

This ratio – the ratio of current assets, excluding inventory, to current liabilities – is often referred to as the acid test or quick ratio and is defined as follows:

$$\text{acid test or quick ratio} = \frac{\text{current assets} - \text{inventory}}{\text{current liabilities}}$$

A modification of this ratio is to deduct prepayments from the current assets, because prepayments are not normally available to pay debts.

Calculating this ratio for ABC Ltd for 20X1 we obtain:

$$\frac{\$6\,304\,000 - \$3\,645\,000}{\$3\,932\,000} = 0.67 \text{ or } 0.67{:}1$$

The fact that the ratio is less than 1:1 tells us that we could not pay our current debts if we were called upon to do so. To put it another way, the ratio tells us that we have 67 cents to pay each $1 of current liabilities. The question is: does this matter? ABC Ltd did, after all, stay in business well after 20X1. In reality, the business on which ABC Ltd is based carried on for a further five years.

The interpretation of the information obtained from calculating this ratio, as with all the other ratios, can make sense only if it is compared to a set of industry norms. This is not as straightforward as it sounds: there are often different norms within an industry, depending on the size and relative power of the firms in that sector. Moreover, any norm based on a number of firms will be the average rather than the best, and so care has to be exercised when applying it to a particular firm. This all seems to imply that comparisons with norms are not informative. This is certainly true if the comparison is made without adequate attention to what the norms really represent.

The question of the usefulness or otherwise of an industry norm does not apply in the case of ABC Ltd as we do not have that information. However, we do have the information to calculate trends and the trend in the quick ratio for ABC Ltd is as follows:

20X2, 0.67:1; 20X3, 0.6:1; 20X4, 0.7:1; 20X5, 0.5:1

Once again, the trend shows an overall decline, with 20X4 being the odd year out. As before, we can conclude that the risk is increasing but we cannot say whether this is in line with what is happening generally because we are looking at the company in isolation. In reality, our knowledge of what was happening in the economy generally would tell us whether credit was getting tight or easing off, and this information would help us in our interpretation of the trend shown above.

As it is ultimately cash that pays debts, another ratio used to assess short-term debt-paying capacity is to examine the ratio of cash flows from operating activities to current liabilities. This ratio also has the advantage of using a figure in the numerator which is not based on year-end figures – as is the case with the current and quick ratios. Hence, it may be regarded as more representative of a firm's capacity to pay its current liabilities.

For ABC Ltd, the ratio is 0.14 in 20X4 and 0.10 in 20X5. This tells us that the operations generated cash flows in 20X4 sufficient to pay 14 per cent of the current liabilities. In 20X5 it had declined to 10 per cent. This decline in 20X5 is of concern, but we still need to compare this to other companies in the industry.

In summary, we can say that the short-term solvency of ABC Ltd has deteriorated in 20X5 and is a cause for concern. However, we still need to compare the position of ABC Ltd with some of its competitors.

Woolworths (WOW) and Coles Myer (CML) for 20X5

	WOW	CML
Current ratio (13)	0.82	1.09
Quick ratio (14)	0.28	0.29
Cash flow from operations to current liabilities ratio (15)	$0.33	$0.29

The current ratio is slightly higher for Coles Myer compared to Woolworths. However, given the size of the two companies, there is little risk of either company not meeting its short-term liabilities. The quick ratio for both companies is much lower than the current ratio which tells us that both companies have very large amounts of inventory (as it is deducted from current assets in the calculation of the quick ratio). Given the nature of the inventories held in supermarkets, the assumption that these could not be easily and quickly converted into cash is not appropriate and not relevant. This would be different for a construction company where the inventory may be a half-finished building that would not be readily and easily convertible into cash.

Review exercise 6

Based on the following information for Jaybond Corporation, it can be seen that working capital at the end of the current year is $5000 greater than the working capital at the end of the preceding year. Has the current position improved? Explain.

	Current year	Preceding year
	$	$
Current assets		
Cash	4 000	5 000
Debtors	30 000	25 000
Inventories	51 000	32 500
Total current assets	85 000	62 500
Current liabilities	42 500	25 000
Working capital	$42 500	$37 500

Long-term solvency ratios

In this section, we look at ratios that assist in answering the last of the three questions posed at the start of the previous section: will the entity have enough cash to repay a loan if it is due in five years? Therefore, will the entity be able to survive and remain a going concern? There are some relationships that are significant in answering this question. For example, earlier in this chapter we discussed the need to find out about short-term solvency and financial risk. We said that financial risk was related to the amount of debt finance compared with equity finance.

L10

Identify and apply various ratios that can be used to assess long-term solvency

To express this as a ratio, using ABC Ltd as an example, we could take the total liabilities and compare them with the equity in that same year. This ratio is referred to as the debt to equity ratio. In 20X1, the ratio was $5151/$3117 or 1.65, in 20X5 it was $5081/$3736 or 1.36. This shows that the amount of total liabilities to equity has decreased from the start of the period. However, from Table 14.1 we see that the ratio of total debt to equity was 1.11 in 20X4 and this means that ABC Ltd has increased its reliance on total debt in 20X5 compared with 20X4 – but it is still less than what it was in 20X1.

We could also look at the total liabilities to total assets ratio – which is another way of observing the amount of leverage for an entity. In order to form an opinion about whether this amount of debt is too high, one must compare the levels of debt with other benchmark entities in the same industry.

Another way to measure leverage is to measure the relationship between total assets and shareholders funds. We refer to this as the leverage ratio, as listed in Table 14.1. It shows how many dollars of assets there are for each one dollar of shareholders' funds. For example, a ratio of 10:1 means that there is $10 of assets for every $1 of shareholders' funds. This must mean that there is $10 – $1, or $9, of total liabilities because we know that the sum of liabilities and shareholders' funds must equal total assets. For ABC, the leverage ratio in 20X1 was $8268/$3117 or 2.77 and in 20X5 it was $8817/$3736 or 2.36.

It is important to note that all the ratios represent different ways of measuring the amount of leverage or gearing for an entity. The ratios do not reveal different outcomes because, if an entity is highly geared, this will be disclosed by all of the above ratios. They simply represent a different way to view an entity's use of debt. Both the debt to equity and leverage ratios report that ABC Ltd had less leverage in 20X5 when compared to 20X1.

It is also possible to look at other ratios to highlight any relationship the analyst deems important. For example, the size of the interest-bearing debt or long-term loans may be of particular interest when assessing long-term solvency. For ABC Ltd, the figure for loans for 20X4 was $396 000 and the equity figure was $4 324 000. The ratio is calculated by dividing the equity figure by the loans figure as follows: 4 324 000/396 000 = 10.91

This tells us that for every $1 of long-term loan finance there is $10.91of equity finance, or that there is 10.91 times more equity than loans. If we compare this with 20X5 we find that the ratio in that year was 3736/92 or 40.6. This tells us that ABC was in a much stronger position in terms of their long-term solvency in 20X5 as there were more dollars of equity to the loan compared with 20X4.

However, with the debt to equity ratios discussed above, we noted that the debt to equity ratio increased from 20X4 to 20X5. If the relationship between total debt to equity has increased but the ratio for long-term debt or non-current liabilities has decreased, then we know that current liabilities must have increased. In fact, we determined this in the previous section on short-term solvency ratios. The short-term debt, in the form of the bank overdraft for ABC Ltd, has increased from nil in 20X1 to $663 000 in 20X5.

Calculation of the total liabilities to equity ratio and the total non-current liabilities to equity ratio will highlight any changes in leverage, and the use of current versus non-current liabilities. Of course, the common-size statements will also reveal this information at a glance.

We have calculated the long-term loans ratio by dividing the equity figure by the loans figure but we could easily have calculated the ratio of loans to equity and the results would show the amount of loans ABC Ltd has for every $1 of shareholders' funds. **Remember, the important and essential requirement with ratios is that the same formula is used when you are calculating a ratio for different years or different entities – otherwise the ratios cannot be compared.**

Woolworths (WOW) and Coles Myer (CML) for 20X5

	Debt to equity (16)	Net interest cover (19)	Cash flow from operations to total debt (20)
CML	1.50	13.7	$0.21
WOW	3.07	7.82	$0.18

Woolworths had a debt to equity ratio of 3.07 in 20X5. This means that there were $3.07 worth of liabilities for every $1 of shareholders' equity. Coles Myer is about one-half of that figure with $1.50 of liabilities for every $1 of shareholders' equity. Coles Myer also has a much better interest coverage ratio and has less financial risk when compared with Woolworths. The result of the higher financial risk may mean that Woolworths will pay a higher rate of interest than Coles Myer. It doesn't mean that Woolworths can't service the debt. In fact, a closer analysis of the Woolworths balance sheet reveals that accounts payable represents 34.5 per cent of total liabilities. Long-term interest-bearing liabilities only account for 39 per cent of total liabilities.

In Chapter 1 we discussed the concept of the economic consequences of accounting information and debt contracts were mentioned. It is common in Australia for debt contracts to contain covenants placing limits on a borrower's debt to equity and interest coverage ratios. Where this is the case, managers must ensure that they do not default on such covenants and risk having the debt recalled by the lender.

Market-based ratios

There is a substantial amount of evidence supporting the notion that share prices adjust very quickly to the release of accounting information. This body of knowledge is called the efficient markets hypothesis (EMH). The semi-strong form of the EMH states that share prices, on average, reflect all publicly available information. As a consequence of this, it is not possible to consistently use publicly available information to generate above-average profits from trading.

If one subscribes to the EMH, then there are some interesting implications for managers and investors.

For managers, the EMH would mean that any attempt to influence share prices by choosing accounting policies which increase reported net profit will not succeed. The share market will see through the cosmetic change in reported profit and, thus, share prices will not change. Of course, if managers do not subscribe to the EMH, or if they are concerned about compensation plans and debt contracts as discussed in Chapter 1, then incentives still exist for the selection of profit-increasing accounting policies.

For investors, the EMH would suggest there is little point in spending time analysing publicly available information. Instead, they would be better served in investing in a diversified portfolio. In fact, it might seem the annual reports and financial statements have very little information for investors. However, without financial statements and published annual reports, the share market would be less efficient. Financial statements are used by analysts who diligently analyse the information as soon as it is publicly available. This ensures that share prices are efficient and enhances the efficiency of the allocation of resources.

Furthermore, the EMH applies on average; therefore, it is possible that at any time there will be individual inventories which are under- or overpriced. Some investors may see this as a worthwhile challenge.

Another important implication of the EMH for investors concerns the role of market-based ratios. Market-based ratios that are shown in Table 14.1 include the price/earnings ratio (P/E) and the earnings yield. In an efficient market, the price of any shares should represent the intrinsic value of the shares; that is, what they are worth. Therefore, a company's price/earnings ratio can be compared to other firms in the industry. A higher than normal P/E ratio could mean that either the price is too high or, as is more likely in an efficient market, the market is expecting an increase in earnings per share (EPS) in the future and is adjusting share price to reflect this. For example, ABC Ltd has a P/E ratio of 13.09. If we assume that the average in the industry is 10, then, if the EMH is valid, the price on average will not be too high because this would mean that the share is overpriced. However, this may happen in some instances for individual shares.

LO 11
Discuss the implications of the efficient markets hypothesis for financial statement analysis

In our example, the price of $3.30 for ABC Ltd is what the shares are worth. Therefore, the share market believes the current EPS of 25.2 cents is lower than what it expects the future level of EPS to be. In our example, we assumed a P/E ratio of 10 was appropriate for ABC Ltd. Therefore, the market is expecting the future EPS of ABC Ltd to be around 33 cents.

The other explanation for the difference in P/E ratios between companies could relate to the use of different accounting policies. For example, a company that uses reducing-balance depreciation methods should, other things being equal, report a lower P/E ratio than a comparable company that uses straight-line depreciation. Therefore, before comparing P/E ratios between different companies, adjustments should be made to the EPS to compensate for differences in accounting policies.

CASE STUDY 14.1

DECODING THE MUMBO JUMBO — SECRETS OF READING COMPANY REPORTS
by Joanna Tovia

THE rows of numbers in an annual report may look daunting to anyone without an economics degree. A quick look, however, at key figures is all you really need to get a good idea of how your shares are likely to perform over the coming year. Lonsdale Securities head of equity research John Watson says you do not have to be a financial whiz or carry out complex analysis to find out how things are going within a company or pick up on brewing problems.

'Many mum and dad investors feel understandably daunted by annual reports, especially if they don't have much knowledge of accounting practices,' Mr Watson says. 'But that's no excuse for filing it away unread.' Annual reports will tell you what the company does, what it owns and what it owes. It will reveal what the company has earned and how those earnings have been distributed. But it can be difficult judging the company from information released at the annual meeting, where the best spin is often put on results.

There are three main parts to an annual report: the statement of financial performance [income statement], the statement of financial position [balance sheet] and the statement of cash flows. 'These financial reports provide the nitty-gritty of a company's financial performance . . . it's worth becoming familiar with them all,' says *Share Investing for Dummies* author James Dunn.

Mr Watson recommends time-poor investors leave the financial analysis side of things well alone. He recommends this three-step approach to speed-reading an annual report:

- Step one: Read the chairman's report. This usually includes a review of the company's operating conditions and performance, details of any management changes, and expectations for future business conditions and earnings growth.

  A careful reading of the report can reveal other useful information, such as the company's business strategy and capital management (including future capital raisings, dividend policy and share-buybacks, etc.).

- Step two: Look for warning signs in the auditor's report. This is usually located towards the end of the annual report and may also be called an 'independent audit report'. Mr Watson says the thing to watch out for is any mention of a company's accounts ⫸

being qualified in some way. Likewise, make sure the auditors state the accounts fairly represent the financial position of the company as at year-end. The auditor's report should disclose any concerns regarding the company's cash position, ability to service debt, or capacity to remain as a going concern.

• Step three: Do some basic analysis of the financial statements. Unless you've studied financial analysis, Mr Watson says you probably won't have much joy interpreting the consolidated statement of financial position (balance sheet) and the consolidated statement of financial performance (income statement), as the reported numbers often need to be adjusted to make them meaningful. Mr Watson says investors should focus their attention on the consolidated statement of cash flows.

But ASIC recommends starting with the statement of financial performance [income statement], taking note of the following:

• Did the company make a profit or a loss?

• Was it better or worse than last year?

• Look for a trend, and see if any major event caused the change. Then look at the dividend:

• What is the dividend going to be and how does it compare with last year? How does it compare with the profit? ASIC says if the company is paying out nearly all or even more than its profit as dividends, then trouble could lie ahead.

Mr Dunn says the key figure in a profit and loss statement is the operating profit after tax.

This is the amount left over after all wages, operating costs, overheads, interest, taxes, and allowances for depreciation and the like have been subtracted from sales revenue.

ASIC suggests looking at the statement of cash flows which tells you about cash the company has already received and spent. The company's cash is provided from, and employed in, three areas: operations, investing and financing.

'A company doesn't have to rely on operations to generate overall positive cash flow, it can bring in cash through investing or borrowing,' Mr Dunn says. Eventually, however, a company must make a living from selling products or services. 'If operating cash flow doesn't provide enough cash, the other two wells will run dry.' If the company reports profits much higher than the cash flows from operations, then ASIC says it may be having trouble collecting its debts. Next comes the balance sheet, or statement of financial position. A quick look at this will tell you what your company owns or owes.

Compare current assets (what it owns) and current liabilities (what it owes) from this year to last year. Does the company look as though it might have trouble meeting its commitments? Check its assets for large amounts in 'intangibles', such as brands or licences.

ASIC says it is very difficult to value intangible assets accurately, and changing conditions can slash the value of even blue chip brands.

The Courier-Mail, 7 December 2002

COMMENTARY

The article provides some interesting comments and advice about analysing a company's financial statements. It is important to seek advice if you are unable to devote the time and don't have the necessary skills to read and understand financial statements. The article has some suggestions to enable you to look for important signals about the company like a qualified audit report, or a consistently poor record of cash flow from operations.

Key limitations of financial statement analysis

Explain the limitations involved in financial statement analysis

Unfortunately, there are some limitations that have to be borne in mind when discussing financial analysis. These limitations can be usefully summarised under three headings, as follows.

INFORMATION PROBLEMS

- The base information is often out of date; that is, timeliness of information leads to problems of interpretation.
- Historic cost information might not be the most appropriate information on which to base the decision for which the analysis is being undertaken.
- Information in published accounts is generally summarised; detailed information might be needed.
- Analysis of accounting information identifies only symptoms, not causes, and thus is of limited use.

COMPARISON PROBLEMS OVER TIME

- Effects of price changes make comparisons difficult unless adjustments are made.
- Changes in technology affect the price of assets, the likely return and the future markets.
- A changing commercial environment affects the results and this is reflected in the accounting information.
- Changes in accounting policies may affect the reported results.
- There are problems in establishing a normal base year with which other years can be compared.

COMPARISON PROBLEMS BETWEEN FIRMS

- The selection of industry norms and the usefulness of norms based on averages are problematic.
- It is difficult to compare the distribution of ratios for each firm without industry averages or some other appropriate benchmark such as another firm in the same industry.
- The financial risks and business risks of firms differ, and this affects the analysis.
- Firms use different accounting policies.
- The size of the business and its comparators affects risk, structure and returns.
- Environments affect results; for example, different countries, or home-based versus multinational firms.

These are the issues that you need to bear in mind when carrying out your analysis, and interpreting and reporting the results. They should not, however, be used as a reason not to attempt the analysis.

Summary

LEARNING OBJETIVE 1
Discuss the information needs of the various users in relation to the analysis of financial statements

- Investor group: interested in the return on their investment and will look at all aspects of the entity including current and future profitability, management performance, solvency and financial risk, future prospects.

- Lenders: interests will vary depending on whether they are a short-term or a long-term lender. Both want to have their funds repaid but long-term lenders will be concerned with the long-term viability of the borrower; this will be of less interest to short-term lenders.

- Employees: Employees are interested in judging their job security and assessing whether their wages are relatively fair. Their areas of interest are profitability (i.e. average profits per employee for the purposes of productivity bargaining) and liquidity (i.e. future trends in profits).

- Auditors: For the purposes of planning and carrying out their audit, auditors are interested in trends in sales, profit, costs and so on, variations from the norm and accounting policies.

- Analysts: Because they earn a living from making good decisions, analysts are, like investors, interested in all aspects of an entity including current and future profitability, management performance, solvency and financial risk, future prospects.

- Management: Managers need all the above information because they are likely to be judged on their performance by outside investors or lenders. In addition, they require detailed information on the performance of the business as a whole and on its parts to enable them to manage the business on a day-to-day basis. This information includes such items as profitability by major product, costs per product, changes in sales or component mix.

LEARNING OBJECTIVE 2
Identify possible sources of external and internal information

The following is a summary of some external sources of information:

- Government statistics available from the ABS
- Trade journals, as published by broking firms for example
- Financial press such as the *Australian Financial Review*
- Databases like Aspect Huntley Financial Analysis
- Specialist agencies like Standard and Poor's.
  The following is a summary of some internal sources of information:

- Chairman's statement
- Directors' report
- Balance sheet
- Income statement
- Statement of changes in equity
- Cash flow statement
- Accounting policies
- Notes to the accounts
- Auditor's report.

LO 3

LEARNING OBJECTIVE 3
Explain the significance of profitability and risk in the analysis of financial statements

Investors invest in order to earn a return on their investment. The return will, in part, be dependent on the risk the investor is willing to take. Any analysis of potential investments must assess the expected profitability, but the expected profitability must be assessed in terms of the risk involved. Investors who take a higher risk only do so on the basis that they expect a higher rate of return.

LO 4

LEARNING OBJECTIVE 4
Identify and apply trend analysis

Trend analysis involves choosing a base year and assigning the number 100 to all items in the base year. In periods after the base year, items are calculated on the basis of their relationship with the corresponding item in the base year. If they are above the base year figure, the number will be above 100, and if they are below the base year figure, the number is less than 100.

In trend analysis, the choice of an appropriate base year is vital. If the base year that is chosen is not typical, the resultant analysis will be, at best, extremely difficult and, at worst, actually misleading. Trend analysis allows identification of declining or increasing amounts of items.

LO 5

LEARNING OBJECTIVE 5
Identify and use common-size statements

Common-size statements express all the items in a financial statement as a percentage of one significant item in the relevant financial statement – such as total assets for the balance sheet. It allows for a fast review of the financial statements and fast detection of any significant changes.

LO 6

LEARNING OBJECTIVE 6
Identify the issues to be considered when choosing a benchmark for ratio analysis

The following are some of the items to be considered when selecting an appropriate benchmark:

- Relative size of the entities: While the benchmark(s) and subject don't need to be of an identical size, it would make little sense to compare Woolworths with the local corner store
- Industry: It is important to match the benchmark(s) and subject as closely as possible in terms of their operations
- Geographical location: To minimise problems that are specific to certain locations, it is preferable to have similar areas of location for both the benchmark and the subject
- Similar accounting policies and periods: The more closely aligned the accounting policies, the easier is the comparison. Also, while it is not essential to have the same year-end dates (such as 30 June), it is preferable.

LO 7

LEARNING OBJECTIVE 7
Identify and apply various ratios that can be used to assess profitability

There are many ratios that can be used to assess profitability. In this chapter we illustrated return on assets, return on ordinary shareholders' equity, net and gross profit margins, asset turnover and earnings per share.

LO 8

LEARNING OBJECTIVE 8
Identify and apply various ratios that can be used to assess efficiency

There are many ratios that can be used to assess efficiency. In this chapter we illustrated inventory and debtors turnover ratios; we also expressed them in days. The total asset turnover is also a measure of the efficiency with which the entity generates sales from the asset base.

L⑨ LEARNING OBJECTIVE 9
Identify and apply various ratios that can be used to assess short-term solvency
There are many ratios that can be used to assess short-term solvency. In this chapter we illustrated the current and quick ratios. We also looked at the cash flow from operating activities as a percentage of current liabilities.

L⑩ LEARNING OBJECTIVE 10
Identify and apply various ratios that can be used to assess long-term solvency
There are many ratios that can be used to assess long-term solvency. In this chapter we illustrated debt to equity, debt to total assets, leverage and the interest coverage ratio. We also looked at the cash flow from operating activities as a percentage of total liabilities.

L⑪ LEARNING OBJECTIVE 11
Discuss the implications of the efficient markets hypothesis for financial statement analysis
The efficient markets hypothesis would suggest that for investors there is little point in spending time analysing publicly available information. Instead, investors would be better served by investing in a diversified portfolio. In fact, it might seem that the annual reports and financial statements have very little information for investors. However, without financial statements and published annual reports, the share market would be less efficient. Financial statements are used by analysts who diligently analyse the information as soon as it is publicly available. This ensures that share prices are efficient and this enhances the efficiency of the allocation of resources.

L⑫ LEARNING OBJECTIVE 12
Explain the limitations involved in financial statement analysis
A range of limitations were covered and include the problems of historical information, the choice of an appropriate benchmark, changes in structures over time, changes in accounting policies, the different sizes of businesses, problems with exchange rates and the role of other factors like the entity's social and environmental policies.

FURTHER READING

Trotman, K. & Gibbins, M., 2006. *Financial Accounting: An Integrated Approach*, 3rd edn, Thomson.

REVIEW QUESTIONS

1   Identify the main user groups and their common needs in terms of financial analysis.
2   What factors do we need to take into account in order to put a financial analysis in context?
3   What information would you derive from reading the chairman's statement?
4   What other parts of the annual report would you use in your analysis?
5   How would you measure financial risk in the short and long term?
6   What are the limitations to analysis which are inherent in the accounting data we are using?
7   Explain the relevance of sources external and internal to the business in the analysis of financial statements.
8   When comparing similar firms, what steps need to be taken to make the comparisons meaningful?

PROBLEMS FOR DISCUSSION AND ANALYSIS

1 Refer to the Woodside half-yearly financial report to 30 June 2005 in Appendix 1.
   a What were the two major liabilities as at 30 June 2005?
   b What was the value of shares issued under the employee share plan in 2005?
   c Calculate the following ratios for Woodside (consolidated accounts):
      i current ratio
      ii quick ratio
      iii gross profit margin
      iv debt to equity.

2 The following information is available concerning Wuffalot Pet Foods Ltd:

Current ratio	1.5:1
Non-current liabilities to equity ratio	0.5:1
Issued capital	$150 000
Retained profits	$50 000
Total assets	$400 000

   a What is the value of Wuffalot's current assets?
   b What is the value of the non-current assets?

3 ABC Ltd has provided its bank with the following information. The bank manager did ask for a statement showing the current liabilities and assets. What are the current liabilities and assets?

Debt to total assets	0.3:1
Total assets	$300 000
Current ratio	2:1
Non-current liabilities	$40 000

4 Skippy Ltd reported the following current assets and current liabilities at the end of 20X1 and 20X2:

	20X2	20X1
	$	$
Cash	311	1 928
Marketable securities	83	955
Debtors	2 453	2 150
Inventories	1 016	732
Prepaid expenses	499	486
Short-term borrowings	3 921	–
Creditors	3 870	3 617
Income taxes payable	123	640

   a Determine, for both years, (rounding to two decimal points) the:
      i current ratio
      ii acid-test (quick) ratio.
   b What conclusions can you draw from this data?

5   Phantom Ltd reported the following information:

	20X2	20X1
	$	$
Sales	3 600 000	3 900 000
Beginning inventories	310 000	290 000
Cost of goods sold	2 010 000	2 400 000
Ending inventories	360 000	310 000

a   Determine, for each year, (rounding to two decimal points):
   i   inventory turnover
   ii   inventory turnover in days.
b   What conclusions can be drawn from this data concerning inventories?

6   Homer and Bart Ltd reported the following information for a five-year period. From the data, prepare a trend analysis and comment on the results.

	20X1	20X2	20X3	20X4	20X5
	$	$	$	$	$
Sales	400 000	425 000	450 000	525 000	650 000
Gross profit	200 000	220 000	230 000	265 000	330 000
Net profit	40 000	41 000	42 000	38 000	45 000

7   Bazz Co. has provided the following information. Prepare a trend analysis and comment on the results.

	20X2	20X3	20X4	20X5	20X6
	$	$	$	$	$
Sales	129 000	130 000	131 000	129 000	130 000
Gross profit	83 000	87 000	88 000	89 000	73 000
Net profit	13 500	12 900	12 500	11 875	8 800

8   Following is a simplified balance sheet for XYZ Ltd.

XYZ Ltd
Balance sheet at 30 June 20X1

	$
Current assets	
Bank	12 000
Inventory	7 500
Debtors	5 000
Total current assets	24 500
Non-current assets	
Land and buildings	100 000
Total non-current assets	100 000
Total assets	124 500

||▶

	$
Liabilities	
Current liabilities	
Creditors	20 000
Total liabilities	20 000
Net assets	104 500
Equity	
Share capital	100 000
Retained profits	4 500
Total equity	104 500

The present current ratio is: 1.225:1.

The company has been told by its bank to increase its current ratio to 1.5:1. Given the balance sheet, what simple step does the company have to take to achieve the required current ratio?

9   As an analyst, you have extracted the following information from the accounts of Romeo Construction Co. Ltd:

Romeo Construction Co. Ltd
Income statements for the years ended 30 June

	20X4	20X5	20X6
	$	$	$
Sales	60 000	54 000	75 000
Less Expenses			
Material	22 500	21 000	35 813
Labour	15 000	13 500	18 000
Production expenses	7 500	6 000	6 750
Administrative expenses	7 500	7 500	8 250
Finance expenses	1 500	1 500	1 500
	54 000	49 500	70 313
Net profit	6 000	4 500	4 687

Romeo Construction Co. Ltd
Balance sheets as at 30 June

	20X4	20X5	20X6
	$	$	$
Work in progress	60 000	52 500	67 500
Non-current assets	30 000	37 500	37 500
	90 000	90 000	105 000
Bank overdraft	15 000	18 000	12 000
Other current liabilities	15 000	12 000	18 000
Shareholder funds	60 000	60 000	75 000
	90 000	90 000	105 000

Required

a   Comment on the profitability of the business.

b   Comment on the financial situation of the business.

c   What action do you suggest for the forthcoming year?

10 You have been given the following financial information for Bigboy Catering Ltd:

Bigboy Catering Ltd
Income statements for years ending 31 December

	20X1	20X2	20X3	20X4
	$	$	$	$
Sales (net)	87 000	78 000	85 000	90 000
Food and beverage expenses	50 000	51 000	49 000	51 000
Wages	22 000	21 000	23 000	23 500
Finance expenses	1 000	2 000	1 500	1 000
Taxation	500	0	0	2 000
Other operating expenses	10 000	12 000	13 500	9 500

Bigboy Catering Ltd
Balance sheets as at 31 December

	20X1	20X2	20X3	20X4
	$	$	$	$
Cash at bank	500	0	0	3 000
Inventory	17 500	19 000	16 500	21 000
Non-current assets	125 000	123 000	121 000	119 000
Bank overdraft	0	1 000	13 500	0
Creditors	28 000	32 000	17 000	13 000
Issued shares	100 000	100 000	100 000	120 000
Retained profits	15 000	9 000	7 000	10 000

Required

a   Comment on the profitability of the business.

b   Comment on the financial situation of the business.

c   What would be your advice to the company after viewing the figures for 20X4?

11 The balance sheets and selected information are given on pages XXX–X for Katrina Ltd and Catherine Ltd for the year ended 30 June 20X2:

Katrina Ltd and Catherine Ltd
Balance sheets for year ended 30 June 20X2

	Katrina		Catherine	
	$	$	$	$
Assets				
Current assets				
Cash at bank	80 000		220 000	
Marketable securities	8 000		190 000	
Accounts receivable (net)	100 000		130 000	
Merchandise inventory	560 000		300 000	
Total current assets		748 000		840 000
Non-current assets				
Property, plant and equipment (net)	1 200 000		1 280 000	
Intangibles	6 000		–	
Total non-current assets		1 206 000		1 280 000
Total assets		1 954 000		2 120 000
Liabilities and shareholders' equity				
Current liabilities		180 000		310 000
Non-current liabilities		340 000		330 000
Paid-up capital ($10 value)		1 300 000		1 300 000
Retained profits		134 000		180 000
Total liabilities and shareholders' equity		1 954 000		2 120 000
Other information				
Accounts receivable, 1 July 20X1	130 000		110 000	
Merchandise inventory, 1 July 20X1	520 000		420 000	
20X1–X2 Sales:				
Cash	852 000		400 000	
Credit	1 100 000		1 500 000	
20X1–X2 Cost of goods sold	1 200 000		1 100 000	
20X1–X2 Net profit	310 000		400 000	
20X1–X2 Interest expense	60 000		40 000	
Total shareholders' equity, 1 July 20X1	1 334 000		1 380 000	
Total assets, 1 July 20X1				
Tax rate: 30%	1 854 000		2 020 000	

Required

a   Calculate the current ratio, quick ratio, inventory turnover, debtors turnover and average days sales uncollected for each company.

b   Which company do you think has a better liquid position? Why?

c Calculate, for each company, the rate of return on total assets, asset turnover and net profit margin before after-tax cost of interest. Which company has the higher ROA? Why?

d Calculate, for each company, the rate of return on ordinary shareholders' equity, asset turnover, net profit margin and financial leverage ratios. Which company has the higher ROE? Why?

e Which company is using leverage more effectively to increase the rate of return to ordinary shareholders? Explain.

f What do accountants mean by 'window dressing'? Show how Katrina Ltd and Catherine Ltd could improve their liquid ratios by window dressing.

12 Following are the summarised accounts of Apple Ltd for the past five years. These form the basis for the questions which follow.

Apple Ltd
Summarised balance sheets of Apple Ltd

	20X1 $000	20X2 $000	20X3 $000	20X4 $000	20X5 $000
Non-current assets					
Intangible non-current assets	5 247	5 220	7 305	9 969	10 674
Tangible assets	20 175	23 130	43 920	43 740	69 225
	25 422	28 350	51 225	53 709	79 929
Current assets					
Inventory	20 031	23 034	53 091	74 823	99 606
Debtors	17 589	24 693	60 270	48 987	66 768
Bank and cash	4 698	6 801	7 839	3 273	9 747
	42 318	54 528	121 200	127 083	176 121
Current liabilities					
Creditors	16 197	24 588	55 659	41 130	72 831
Taxation	459	768	4 302	2 712	3 444
Dividends	801	1 812	3 339	3 738	3 672
Bank loans and overdraft	10 581	4 026	18 180	29 316	37 638
	28 038	31 194	81 480	76 896	117 585
Net current assets	14 280	23 334	39 720	50 187	58 536
Total assets *less* current liabilities	39 702	51 684	90 945	103 896	138 465
Non-current liabilities					
Loans	14 793	15 477	35 241	35 430	67 844
	24 909	36 207	55 704	68 466	70 621
Represented by					
Ordinary share capital	5 160	10 359	17 994	18 039	19 464
Retained profits	19 749	25 848	30 975	43 692	41 734
Revaluation reserve			6 735	6 735	9 423
	24 909	36 207	55 704	68 466	70 621

NOTES

i During 20X3 and 20X5 some of the freehold properties were revalued.

ii Loans amounting to $22 million were repaid during 20X5.

iii No non-current assets were disposed of during the year.

Summarised income statements of Apple Ltd

	20X1 $000	20X2 $000	20X3 $000	20X4 $000	20X5 $000
Sales	93 930	116 232	259 470	278 340	372 753
Cost of goods sold	65 751	82 525	197 197	208 775	294 475
Gross profit	28 179	33 707	62 273	69 585	78 278
Operating expenses	17 022	21 398	36 830	35 130	59 881
Net profit before interest and tax	11 157	12 309	25 443	34 455	18 397
Interest	2 727	2 652	7 707	10 167	14 082
Net profit after interest and before tax	8 430	9 657	17 736	24 288	4 315
Taxation	2 517	1 746	9 270	7 833	2 601
Net profit after tax	5 913	7 911	8 466	16 455	1 714

Statements of changes in equity for Apple Ltd

	Share capital $000	Retained profits $000	Asset revaluation reserve	Total $000
Balance at 1 July 20X0	5 160	14 637	0	19 797
Net income recognised directly in equity				0
Profit or loss for the year (from the income statement)		5 913		5 913
Total recognised income and expense for the period				5 913
Dividends		(801)		(801)
Balance at 30 June 20X1	5160	19 749		24 909
Net income recognised directly in equity				0
Profit or loss for the year (from the income statement)		7 911		7 911
Total recognised income and expense for the period				7 911
Dividends		(1812)		(1 812)
Issued shares	5 199			5 199
Balance at 30 June 20X2	10 359	25 848		36 207
Asset revaluation			6 735	6 735
Net income recognised directly in equity				6 735
Profit or loss for the year (from the income statement)		8 466		8 466
Total recognised income and expense for the period				15 201
Dividends		(3339)		(3 339)
Issued shares	7 635			7 635
Balance at 30 June 20X3	17 994	30 975		55 704
Net income recognised directly in equity				0
Profit or loss for the year (from the income statement)		16 455		16 455
Total recognised income and expense for the period				16 455

	Share capital $000	Retained profits $000	Asset revaluation reserve	Total $000
Dividends		(3 738)		(3 738)
Issued shares	45			45
Balance at 30 June 20X4	18 039	43 692		68 466
Asset revaluation			2 688	2 688
Net income recognised directly in equity				2 688
Profit or loss for the year (from the income statement)		1 714		1 714
Total recognised income and expense for the period				4 402
Dividends		(3 672)		(3 672)
Issued shares	1 425			1 425
Balance at 30 June 20X5	19 464	41 734		70 621

Required

a   Complete the common-size income statements below for the five years and analyse these statements with particular reference to the profitability of Apple.

b   Using whatever form of analysis you consider appropriate, analyse and comment on the financial performance and financial position of Apple Ltd.

c   What are the limitations of your analysis?

Common-size income statements of Apple Ltd

	20X1 $000	20X2 $000	20X3 $000	20X4 $000	20X5 $000
Sales	100	100	100	100	100
Cost of goods sold	70	71	76		
Gross profit	30	29	24		
Operating expenses	18	18	14		
Net profit before interest and tax	12	11	10		
Interest	3	2	3		
Net profit after interest and before tax	9	8	7		
Taxation	3	2	4		
Net profit after tax	6	7	3		

Note to Instructors: *The following problems are considered more suitable for use in MBA courses. However, undergraduate courses may also find them useful.*

13 The balance sheets and additional information follow for Jayco Ltd:

Jayco Ltd
Balance sheets at 30 June

	20X4 $	20X5 $	20X6 $
Assets			
Current assets			
Cash	364 700	292 720	123 790
Inventories			
Finished products	600 000	700 000	800 000
Work in progress	245 500	258 000	342 000
Raw materials and supplies	483 050	450 000	550 000
Accounts receivable	521 000	669 280	1 184 210
Total current assets	2 214 250	2 370 000	3 000 000
Non-current assets			
Land (at cost)	600 000	816 300	1 334 104
Buildings (at cost)	1 215 500	1 323 000	2 400 000
Machinery (at cost)	1 538 980	1 500 370	3 505 640
Goodwill (at cost)	2 000 000	2 000 000	2 000 000
Total non-current assets	5 354 480	5 639 670	9 239 744
Total assets	7 568 730	8 009 670	12 239 744
Liabilities			
Current liabilities			
Accounts payable	355 700	360 000	544 620
Provision for tax	500 000	500 000	800 000
Provision for dividend	130 000	430 000	672 000
Total current liabilities	985 700	1 290 000	2 016 620
Non-current liabilities			
Debentures	683 030	903 370	2 999 020
Mortgages	500 000	400 000	1 000 000
Total non-current liabilities	1 183 030	1 303 370	3 999 020
Total liabilities	2 168 730	2 593 370	6 015 640
Net assets	5 400 000	5 416 300	6 224 104
Owners' equity			
8% preference shares	500 000	500 000	1 200 000
Ordinary shares ($1)	4 000 000	4 000 000	4 000 000
Retained profits	900 000	916 300	1 024 104
Total owners' equity	5 400 000	5 416 300	6 244 104

Additional information from Jayco Ltd's financial statements

		20X4	20X5	20X6
		$	$	$
i	Annual sales			
	Credit (terms 2/10 net 45)	2 605 000	3 011 760	4 500 000
	Cash	120 000	142 600	1 500 000
ii	Cost of goods sold	1 662 250	1 861 070	3 720 000
iii	Net profit (after tax at 50%)	463 250	473 150	789 902
iv	Interest expense	94 642	104 269	399 902
v	Share price	$1.50	$1.52	$2.08
vi	Balances as at 30 June 20X3			$
	Accounts receivable			450 000
	Total tangible assets			5 000 000
	Inventory			1 441 870
vii	Selected financial ratios			Industry
				20X6
	Current ratio			2.25
	Quick ratio			1.10
	Debtors turnover			6 x
	Inventory turnover			4 x
	Debt/Total assets			33%
	Debt/Net tangible assets			0.6
	Equity ratio			72%
	Rate of return on ordinary shareholders' funds			16%
	Gross profit margin			40%
	Net profit margin			16%
	Net operating profit rate of return			26%
	Overall interest coverage			11 x
	Return on assets			14 %

Required

Evaluate the position of Jayco Ltd. Cite specific ratio levels and trends as evidence.

14 The directors of Efficient Distributors Ltd are concerned at the results of trading activities reported for the year ended 30 June 20X6, and failure to keep within the limit of the bank overdraft ($12 000).

They request that a comprehensive survey be made of the financial state of the company, and provide the following information:

Income statements for the years ended 30 June

	20X4		20X5		20X6	
	$	$	$	$	$	$
Sales		200 000		180 000		165 000
Less Cost of sales						
Opening inventory		36 000		41 000		44 000
Purchases		95 000		87 000		80 000
		131 000		128 000		124 000
Less Closing inventory	41 000	90 000	44 000	84 000	49 000	75 000
Gross profit		110 000		96 000		90 000
Less:						
Selling and distribution expenses	40 000		40 000		46 000	
General and administration expenses	20 000		20 000		18 000	
Financial expenses	15 000	75 000	16 000	76 000	20 000	84 000
Net operating profit before tax		35 000		20 000		6 000
Less Provision for taxation		15 000		9 000		2 500
Net operating profit after tax		20 000		11 000		3 500
Less Loss on sale of investment						1 000
Net profit for year		20 000		11 000		2 500

Statements of changes in equity

	Ordinary share capital	Preference share capital	Retained profits	Reserves	Total
	$	$	$	$	$
Balance at 1 July 20X3	75 000	50 000	10 000	18 000	153 000
Net income recognised directly in equity					0
Profit or loss for the year (from the income statement)			20 000		20 000
Total recognised income and expense for the period					20 000
Dividends			(23 000)		(23 000)
Balance at 30 June 20X4	75 000	50 000	7 000	18 000	150 000
Asset revaluation				10000	10 000
Transfer to retained profits			10 000	(10 000)	
Net income recognised directly in equity					10 000
Profit or loss for the year (from the income statement)			11 000		11 000

⇢

	Ordinary share capital $	Preference share capital $	Retained profits $	Reserves $	Total $
Total recognised income and expense for the period					21 000
Dividends			(27 000)		(27 000)
Balance at 30 June 20X5	75 000	50 000	1 000	18 000	144 000
Net income recognised directly in equity					0
Profit or loss for the year (from the income statement)			2500		2500
Total recognised income and expense for the period					2500
Dividends			(3000)		(3000)
Balance at 30 June 20X6	75 000	50 000	500	18 000	143 500

Balance sheets as at 30 June

	20X4 $	$	20X5 $	$	20X6 $	$
Assets						
Current assets						
Bank	1 000					
Inventory	41 000		44 000		49 000	
Trade debtors	26 000		31 000		37 000	
Less Provision for doubtful debts	(1 000)		(1 000)		(2 000)	
Prepayments	2 000		3 000		3 000	
Total current assets		69 000		77 000		87 000
Non-current assets						
Plant and equipment	10 000		10 000		21 000	
Less Depreciation (1000 in X3)	(2 000)		(4 000)		(7 000)	
Vehicles	80 000		80 000		114 000	
Less Depreciation (4000 in X3)	(16 000)		(32 000)		(54 000)	
Land (at valuation)	60 000		70 000		70 000	
Buildings (at cost)	40 000		56 000		56 000	
Investments (at cost)	25 000		25 000		–	
Total non-current assets		197 000		205 000		200 000
Total assets		266 000		282 000		287 000
Liabilities						
Current liabilities						
Bank overdraft			8 500		12 500	
Trade creditors	12 000		8 000		14 000	

	20X4		20X5		20X6	
	$	$	$	$	$	$
Accrued wages and interest	1 000		1 500		2 000	
Provision for taxation	15 000		9 000		2 500	
Provision for dividend	13 000		15 000		3 000	
Total current liabilities		41 000		42 000		34 000
Non-current liabilities						
Mortgage on land (due 30.6.X9)			21 000		34 500	
Term loan (due 20Y2)	75 000		75 000		75 000	
Total non-current liabilities		75 000		96 000		109 500
Total liabilities		116 000		138 000		143 500
Net assets		150 000		144 000		143 500
Owners' equity						
50 000 6% $1 preference shares		50 000		50 000		50 000
75 000 ordinary shares		75 000		75 000		75 000
Asset revaluation reserve				10 000		10 000
General reserve		18 000		8 000		8 000
Retained profits		7 000		1 000		500
Total owners' equity		150 000		144 000		143 500

Required

a Analyse the company's financial position, indicating the causes of the present situation and recommending future policy. What are the implications of the continuation of the company's present practices?

b Indicate any limitations of your analysis.

c What additional information (if any) would you like to assist you with your analysis?

ETHICS CASE STUDY

Allandale Ltd is a company which builds small luxury boats and employs 500 people. The company has been operating for 10 years. Two years ago the company underwent a major expansion of its boat-building facilities because of increased demand for its boats from overseas buyers. To do this it borrowed $20 million through a mortgage loan with a major bank.

The loan agreement contains the following clauses:

i Allendale is to maintain a current ratio of at least 2:1

ii the after-tax return on assets must be at least 10 per cent.

If the company fails to meet either ratio in any year, the $20 million is immediately repayable.

Last year the government removed a 10 per cent tariff on small luxury boats and the company has had difficulty competing in overseas markets. Consequently, the company has had to reduce its profit margin in order to compete against suppliers from other countries.

Tom Lyons is the accountant of Allandale Ltd, and he has completed the preliminary financial results for the current year. Based on these results, the current ratio is 2.1:1 and the return on assets is 11 per cent. However, Tom has some concerns about the following items:

i   One boat that was still unsold at year-end is recorded in the balance sheet at $500 000. However, Tom is certain that the most it could be sold for is $350 000.

ii An overseas customer who owes the company $1 million has recently informed Allandale Ltd that they are in severe financial trouble and will only be able to pay half the amount owing. The balance in the provision for doubtful debts is only $300 000.

If Tom recognises the decline in the net realisable value of $150 000 and the $200 000 uncollectable account in excess of the provision, the company's current ratio will fall to 1.6:1 and the return on assets to 2 per cent. This would result in a call for immediate repayment of the $20 million loan. In turn, this would force the company into bankruptcy and Tom and his best friends will lose their jobs.

Discuss

a   the ethical problems faced by Tom
b   what Tom should do.

ANSWERS TO REVIEW EXERCISES

1   Both long-term lenders and equity investors have many common needs, but they differ in that long-term lenders look at interest cover rather than dividend cover or earnings per share. They are also interested in measures of security.

2   Sources are given below. Students should be encouraged to identify, for themselves, how this information would be used and what they could get out of it. External sources include government statistics, trade journals, the financial press, databases and specialist agencies. Internal sources include the chairman's statement, directors' report, balance sheets, income statements, statements of changes in equity, cash flow statements, accounting policies statement, notes to the accounts and the auditor's report.

3   Financial risk relates to the mix of owners' equity and debt financing, whereas business risk refers to the type of business or trade in which the enterprise is engaged.

4   A 20 per cent increase in net profit is, on the surface, an improvement. However, we need to consider how the company's competitors have performed so that we have a benchmark for comparison. If the average increase of other companies' net profit was 30 per cent, then the company has fallen behind. It may also be that last year's net profit was low, so achieving a 20 per cent increase may not mean much in terms of dollars.

5   a   The current ratio can be manipulated by using cash to pay creditors at year-end.
    b   The inventory turnover ratio can be manipulated by running down inventories at year-end.

6   The amount of working capital and the change in working capital are just two indicators of the strength of the current position. A comparison of the current ratio and the quick ratio, along with the amount of working capital, gives a better analysis of the current position. Such a comparison shows:

	Current year	Preceding year
Working capital	$42 500	$37 500
Current ratio	2.0	2.5
Quick ratio	0.8	1.2

It is apparent that, although working capital has increased, the current ratio has fallen from 2.5 to 2.0, and the quick ratio has fallen from 1.2 to 0.8.

INTERNAL USERS, INTERNAL INFORMATION, AND PLANNING AND CONTROL

15

LEARNING OBJECTIVES

At the end of this chapter, you should be able to:

1. explain why management's information needs are not met solely by general-purpose financial reports

2. explain which external users are likely to be able to gain access to internal company information not published in annual reports

3. explain why the size and structure of an entity influences the need for management to have access to more complex internal information

4. explain what the planning and control processes are in relation to entity objectives

5. explain what is meant by strategic and operating decisions

6. explain the concept of responsibility accounting and how it helps management to monitor and control performance within the entity

7. explain the problems entities have in contending with, establishing and implementing control systems

8. explain the potential costs and benefits of developing accounting information systems to implement monitoring and control of performance.

Introduction

In Chapter 14 we discussed external users of information, their information needs and the ways in which they use the accounting information that is available. This information is derived from the financial reports via the annual accounts of the entities being analysed. The underlying information for these financial reports comes from the organisation's accounting system. This accounting system might be very simple or extremely sophisticated, depending on the size of the business and the needs of the users of the accounting information. One of these users is management, who need not only more detailed information than that normally contained in the financial accounts, but more up-to-date information and, indeed, some different types of information. This does not mean that the information needed by management is not useful to users external to the entity; it might, in fact, be very useful to them if they had it. One reason it is not used by the external user groups discussed in Chapter 14 is that, in some cases, they do not have the power to demand access, as, for example, in the case of the larger public companies such as CSR Ltd. In other cases, the entities are too small and their internal accounting system too unsophisticated to produce any information other than that required for the annual accounts; this would be the case with, for example, your local fish-and-chip shop.

To be able to make decisions wisely, individuals and organisations need to have some vision about the future. A decision made without any thought to the future could well result in undesirable consequences. This is particularly so in the business context. Small businesses often fail despite the fact that they trade profitably. One of the main reasons for this is the lack of planning for future cash requirements. As well as the need to make plans, actual performance has to be monitored to ensure that the objectives in the plans are being attained. The latter activity is an essential part of the control that is exercised by organisations to help secure their survival and efficiency.

In this chapter, we examine the needs of management in terms of the information it requires in order to make decisions between alternative opportunities, to plan the entity's activities, and to ensure that the plans are carried out. This information is primarily prepared for internal users; it is only available to external users if they have sufficient power to obtain access to it.

We then examine the planning and control process, using a framework which not only explains the process itself but also provides an essential foundation for analysis and discussion in subsequent chapters. It is important to recognise that the planning and control process cannot be examined in isolation. There are a number of factors that influence its design and application. In this chapter, we discuss some of the more significant factors (such as technology) that influence the design of accounting information systems, in the context of the planning and control process, and consider some of the main limitations of the application of these processes.

Management's information needs

LO 1

Explain why management's information needs are not met solely by general-purpose financial reports

As a starting point we examine the situation of an existing business where management has already decided on the course of action to follow. In this situation, management is interested in the outcomes of those past decisions. The managers can obtain certain information from the annual accounts, but often this is insufficient for their purpose because, for one thing, the annual accounts contain summarised and simplified information. This summarised information might alert management to the fact that profit is lower than anticipated, but it is unlikely to be sufficiently detailed to identify the cause of this variation. Managers almost always need more detailed information about the results of their past decisions and actions than that which is contained in the annual accounts.

As the name implies, annual accounts are drawn up only once a year, and this is another reason why they are unlikely to be sufficient to meet the needs of managers, who need more regular and up-to-date information. The fact that annual accounts are produced only at the year's end means that, even if they are able to establish why the results have varied from those anticipated, it might be too late to take appropriate action. For example, if an entity has a January year-end for accounting purposes, its accounts will normally not be available until some time after the end of January. Thus, any corrective action is correspondingly delayed. Although management has access to the year's results before they are published, there might still be considerable delays. These delays will not be as great as for the published accounting information: the time span between the year's end and the actual production of the annual accounts varies from about three to four months for listed companies to periods of more than 10 months for smaller entities.

KEY CONCEPT 15.1

MANAGEMENT INFORMATION NEEDS
Managers generally need detailed information.
They need up-to-date information.
They need frequent information.
They need information suited to the decisions they are required to make.

We have established some needs of management that are not satisfied by the production of annual accounts. The reason that managers are likely to require information more frequently is so they can monitor the results of their actions and decisions, and finetune the business as required. This is not to imply that none of the needs of managers is met by the financial information system on which the annual accounts are based. For example, although the annual accounts show only one figure for debtors, the accounting records contain much more information about the individual debts making up that debtors figure. This includes information about when the sales took place and the customer's past payment record. This detailed information allows management to collect the money more quickly and to chase the slow payers. By doing this, management will be able to ensure that business does not face more problems, because of poor cash flow, than are absolutely necessary.

There are, of course, other examples of information contained within the accounting system which, if presented and used in different ways from those required for drawing up annual accounts, better meet management's needs. For example, as indicated in Chapter 7, the basic information that is required for both variable and absorption costs is available from the accounting system. In that chapter we also discussed the impact of the Accounting Standard AASB 102 on the choice of either absorption and variable costing for reporting purposes. Chapter 17 contains a fuller explanation of these alternative systems, and the problems associated with their use in practice. This provides the basis for an understanding of the relative merits and limitations of these alternatives from the point of view of management. From that discussion you will see that, depending on the decision faced by management, it might need information presented in different ways. For example, to decide whether to continue making a particular product or not, managers require forward-looking information in the form of forecasts. They might wish to know the point at which the revenue is going to be equal to the cost, that is, the break-even point, and how likely it is that such a point will be reached. Whether sales are likely to be sufficient to break even is a question for the sales and marketing department; the cost of the product at different levels of output is a question that accountants will be called upon to answer.

A full discussion of the way costs behave and how to establish the break-even position is contained in Chapter 18. An understanding of these principles is vital if appropriate decisions are to be made by management, whatever industry is being considered. For example, it can be argued that in the airline industry you need to know a break-even position that covers costs, one that covers costs plus the interest charges incurred in buying planes, and a third position at which the airline is profitable. In that case, the break-even positions could be expressed in terms of seat occupancy. Of course, this knowledge is only a portion of what is required by managers in the airline industry.

Having said that management needs other information, possibly in different forms, it is important to understand that the base information used to produce the annual accounts is also used as the source for many different reports that are provided to meet the specific needs of management. As with the other users referred to in Chapter 14, for management purposes, financial information is only one of a number of types of information needed in order to make decisions about the future direction and actions of the business. These other types of information are outside the scope of this text, but they include marketing information, employment legislation, and so on.

We will continue our discussion of management's information needs within the relatively narrow confines of financial information.

We have said that management needs frequent and detailed information in a different format from that contained in the annual accounts. This information is used to monitor progress and take appropriate actions to finetune the business. Implicit in this monitoring process is that the results are judged against some expectations. These expectations might be rough plans carried in the head of the owner of a small business, or detailed plans and budgets in the case of a larger entity.

The process of planning and control, and the ways in which the information is derived and used, are discussed in detail later in this chapter, where we look at the process of setting objectives and the problems of goal congruence. The budgeting process is discussed in Chapter 20, which contains a detailed analysis of the ways in which budgets can be used within an organisation to help planning – both as a control mechanism and as a motivator of people.

As we have said, most, if not all, of this information is also useful to users other than managers. However, some of it is commercially sensitive, and the achievement of the goals of an entity might be dependent on its plans being kept secret from competitors. Not all external users will be able to obtain access to the information: it depends not only on who they are, but also upon their importance to the entity. The information required to implement budgets and restructure is confidential to a company and, if made generally available, would be of value to its competitors.

We now consider what the external users' needs might be, who they are, and the factors (such as relative power, competition and confidentiality) that determine their access or lack of access to internal information.

Review exercise 1

What are the main reasons management requires more information than is given in the annual reports?

External users' information needs

Explain which external users are likely to be able to gain access to internal company information not published in annual reports

One group of external users who can demand access to internal accounting information is the taxation authorities. The nature of the information they require varies but is normally either more detailed breakdowns of particular expense headings or details of the timing of purchases and sale of non-current assets. The reason for this is that the taxation system is based upon a set of rules for arriving at the taxable profit which are different from those that are used to arrive at the accounting profit. The taxation authorities, which include the Australian Taxation Office (ATO), the Customs and Excise Department and state governments, have a statutory right of access to information.

Another group of external users that is often in a sufficiently powerful position to obtain further information is the entity's bankers. The information they demand will, of course, depend on the circumstances involved. If the entity is doing well, the information demanded would be quite different from that required if the entity had problems. We will discuss, at a general level, some of the additional information bankers might require and why they might require it. We will then go on to examine what determines whether or not this information is available to these external users.

In general, the information demanded by an entity's bankers can be divided into two categories: that required for routine monitoring and that required to arrive at judgements about the future needs of the entity. The former category includes regular management accounts, such as monthly profit statements, an analysis of debts in terms of how old they are (this is known as an 'aged debtors analysis') and other up-to-date information, such as the amount owed by the entity; that is, the monthly creditors' balance. All this information is required to monitor the health of their customer's business on a more regular basis than would be possible if they had to rely on the information provided by annual accounts which, as we have said, are likely to be a few months out of date when they are produced.

Bankers also require other information to make judgements about the future needs and prospects of the entity in order to ascertain whether to lend money, when it is likely to be repaid and the risk involved. The information on future prospects is normally required in the form of projected cash flow statements and income statements, but also includes information about any other loans that the entity has and their due dates for repayment. The financial information is only part of the information that the banker requires; other information could also include future orders, plans, analysis of competitors, and so on.

As we have already indicated, there are circumstances where, like other external users such as shareholders and competitors, the banker cannot get access to this additional information. We examine those circumstances in our discussion of the impact of organisational size and structure on the information produced for management purposes, which is one factor that determines what these external users have access to.

Effects of organisational size

We have discussed the needs of management in terms of information to make decisions about the future, to plan future actions and to control the business on a day-to-day basis. The more complex and sophisticated the business, the more likely it is that management will require additional information. For example, the local garage owner might be able to carry in his head all the information needed to enable the business to run effectively on a day-to-day basis. This is because the business is sufficiently small and the owner, who is also the manager, is directly involved in the running of the business and is available to take whatever action proves necessary.

Explain why the size and structure of an entity influences the need for management to have access to more complex internal information

However, in a large and complex business there is a need for a more formalised system – for a number of reasons. First, the amount of information required in, for example, a multi-product firm is such that it is unlikely that management personnel would be able to remember all the details necessary to run the business effectively. (A fuller discussion of the problems faced by multi-product firms and the techniques available to solve such problems is contained in Chapter 19, where we look at the effects of resource constraints and at make or buy decisions.) Second, the larger the business, the more distant the senior managers are from its day-to-day operations. Not only do they require information of a strategic type, they also require additional information to control the activities and actions of those below them.

Thus, the size of the organisation influences the information needs of its managers and the way in which these needs are met. More formal systems are needed as the size of the business increases. The nature of the business also has an effect on information needs: a multi-product business requires more sophisticated information systems than a single-product business. Consider, for example, the information required to run a restaurant, where the only product is food, compared with the information required to run a hotel. In the latter case, not only do you need information about the food component of the hotel, but information is also required on bed occupancy rates, the bar profit, and so on.

In discussing the information needs of managers, it has to be borne in mind that information is not free. In general, the more sophisticated the information system, the more it costs to set up and run. The need for better and more up-to-date information always has to be balanced against the costs and benefits of obtaining that information. However, as we point out later in this chapter, although there is considerable literature on cost–benefit analysis, the practical implementation of such an approach is fraught with difficulties. We should also remember that more up-to-date information is not, in itself, better: it also needs to be relevant to the use to which it is to be put. A fuller discussion of what constitutes relevant information in relation to costs and benefits, and how these relate to short-term decisions, is contained in Chapter 19.

The need to obtain relevant information at a reasonable cost partly explains why many small businesses produce little in the way of formal management information. In many of these cases the information, if it exists at all, is held in the owner–manager's head in a form that is not readily accessible to others. In these situations, bankers are often able to exercise considerable influence as a major provider of finance; however, no matter how much pressure they exert, they cannot access information that does not exist. They therefore have to rely on the annual accounts and such other information as is available.

We have shown that the information available is influenced not only by the needs of managers but also by the size and complexity of the organisation's products. We have also suggested that the nature of the product or products can influence the information systems. There are, of course, many other factors that will have an influence on what is required and what is produced. Consider several examples: the needs of high-technology industries, and the effects of flexible manufacturing systems and management techniques such as 'just-in-time'. These, like the nature of the industry, produce specific needs.

In subsequent chapters we will look at different industries in both the manufacturing and service sectors. We now consider a more general influence upon the information needs of managers: the structure of the organisation.

Effects of organisational structure

It is clear that different organisations have different structures and this means that their information needs also differ. If we consider retailing, it is obvious that a business such as Woolworths (which operates both within Australia and overseas) needs information about its New Zealand branches that differs from that about its Sydney branches, if for no other reason than the effect of different currencies. Thus, in general, an organisation that has a multinational operation has different information requirements to one which operates solely in the domestic market.

Similarly, department stores such as Myer are organised on departments as profit centres and the departments' profits are identified separately. This implies that both the cost records and the takings from sales have to be identified and recorded by the department. In such organisations, the managers may be rewarded on the basis of schemes, such as profit sharing, or by comparing profits achieved against predetermined targets. In such circumstances, the information system has to be designed to meet the structural requirements of the organisation. These and similar matters are touched on in the discussion of department and divisional accounting in Chapter 19 and the impact and uses of budgets in Chapter 20. We could, of course, find many more examples of different structures apart from those referred to above. Other structures depend on, and to some extent are determined by, the product, the market in which the business operates and the competitive environment, as well as more mundane factors such as geography and location of its branches or outlets. In general terms, the more decentralised an organisation is, the more complex its information systems are.

The planning and control process

A number of stages have been identified in the planning and control process:

- *Stage 1*: setting objectives
- *Stage 2*: making strategic decisions
- *Stage 3*: making operating decisions
- *Stage 4*: monitoring and possible corrective action.

Explain what the planning and control processes are in relation to entity objectives

We begin by considering the four stages in the planning and control process before turning to the technical aspects of this process and factors that might influence the design of the accounting system within it.

KEY CONCEPT 15.2

PLANNING AND CONTROL

Planning involves the determination of objectives and expressing how they are to be attained. The control process is the means of ensuring that the plans will be achieved.

STAGE 1: SETTING OBJECTIVES

From both a practical and a theoretical perspective, the determination and setting of objectives is probably the most complex stage of the planning and control process in a business organisation. In the absence of any explicit objectives, there is no basis for management to evaluate whether the business is succeeding, nor any criterion for choosing between alternative business opportunities.

Organisations themselves do not have objectives; the objectives of the organisation are those of the people involved in it. These individuals each have their personal goals, and it is likely that some will conflict with those of other participants. A sales manager's objective might be the maximisation of sales, in volume terms, without any strong consideration of profitability. This might conflict with the objectives of the financial management of the firm whose primary concern could be to maximise profits through the introduction of higher prices with lower volumes of sales. This conflict in objectives is commonly referred to as a lack of goal congruence. The problem of goal congruence is more acute in large business organisations because of the number of participants and their varying vested interests. In the case of a company, it is likely that employees would desire an increase in remuneration and this could be one of their personal goals. However, this might conflict with the interest of shareholders if it reduces the amount available to them for payment of dividends.

KEY CONCEPT 15.3

GOAL CONGRUENCE

Goal congruence is the alignment of organisational goals with the personal and group goals of the individuals within an organisation.

From a wider social perspective, there is a growing awareness of the need to recognise the interests of parties external to the organisation itself when it sets its objectives. In particular, customers, government and the local community all have an interest in the survival and the activities of the organisation. For example, in recent years there has been a growing public concern about environmental issues. As a result of public pressure, a number of firms have changed policies regarding their production activities. A good illustration of this is the change in policy of petrol companies to produce unleaded petrol. If a business organisation's objectives are to be effective, there must be a congruence of goals. When an organisation sets its objectives, the interests of all the participants need to be recognised and common goals identified.

Quantitative objectives such as making a profit are appealing because where markets are, by and large, unregulated and competitive, profit-making is an essential element in ensuring a firm's survival. Profits are, by nature, quantifiable and targets can readily be set in terms of formulating objectives. The quantifiable nature of profits also means that they are measurable. This attribute is very attractive to managers, as deviations from the set objectives during an accounting period can easily be identified. This feature is particularly important in the control process, which will be discussed later in the chapter. It is common, in practice, to find the profit objective stated more precisely in terms of maximisation of profits.

Qualitative objectives, in contrast with those of a quantitative nature, suffer from the problems associated with measurement. The quality of a product (in meeting its purpose and customer requirements) is far more difficult to define in measurable terms, and difficulties also arise when comparing the objective with the actual performance in the control process. Although product or service quality is often cited as a prime objective of a business, in reality it is often disregarded or assessed inappropriately through movements in sales revenue.

Due to the difficulty of setting unquantifiable goals, such as a quality definition or social responsibilities, most firms tend to compromise and take the easier option of profit-setting as the major (or sole) criterion for expressing their objectives. Although this gives a simple version of the firm's objectives, it has the disadvantage of disregarding the interactions which take place with various other interests. This can effectively undermine the firm's performance and even, paradoxically, threaten the profit which the company has put in esteem.

The problems related to unquantifiable goals are particularly pertinent to not-for-profit organisations, such as municipal councils and charities. Frequently, the objective of such organisations is expressed in terms of the amount of the service rendered and the quality of that service. These objectives are inherently difficult to express in quantitative terms. A considerable amount of research has been carried out over recent years in an attempt to overcome these problems associated with not-for-profit organisations. A detailed discussion of the potential ways in which qualitative objectives can be effectively employed in such organisations can be found in Jones and Pendlebury (1996).

Review exercise 2

There are several stages in the planning and control process. Identify these and give a brief description of each stage.

STAGE 2: MAKING STRATEGIC DECISIONS

Strategic decisions in a business organisation relate to policy changes in respect of the products or services that are currently being offered and the markets where they are sold.

LO 5

Explain what is meant by strategic and operating decisions

KEY CONCEPT 15.4

STRATEGIC DECISIONS

Strategic decisions are those that determine the long-term policies of the firm and that are necessary if the firm is to meet its objectives.

The nature of the commercial environment in which businesses operate is uncertain and outside the control of management. Some examples of the variables that can confront an organisation are changes in taste, high inflation, recession and competitiveness. If organisations remain static and do not consider alternative policies in such an environment, it is likely that their objectives will not be met, and this could threaten their survival in the long term. There are many examples of companies making strategic decisions primarily to meet their objectives. Often these decisions have been made to maintain their long-term profitability by diversifying – making them less dependent on their traditional markets. For example, Rothmans, who primarily concentrated on the tobacco market, have diversified into the confectionery industry.

In order to have effective strategic decisions, firms should be constantly searching for alternative courses and developing:

- new products for sale in existing and new markets
- new markets for existing products.

Because of the importance of strategic decisions, they tend to be taken at the higher levels of management within organisations. These decisions are of a long-term nature, and this is one of the features that differentiates them from operating decisions.

CASE STUDY 15.1

IT ALL COMES DOWN TO BANK ABILITY
by Leon Gettler
The winner THE GOOD REPUTATION INDEX

A DECADE after its near-death experience, Australia's oldest bank has bounced back by outperforming everyone else in the Good Reputation Index. Having the best reputation in a country where bank bashing is a vogue sport might be surprising in itself. But it's even more so, given Westpac's recent history. Just 10 years ago, it posted a record $1.56 billion loss, the legacy of a slew of bad management and strategic decisions following deregulation in the '80s.

Since then, however, Westpac has been ▐▐▐➡

reporting healthy profits, after a complete makeover from former chief executive officer Bob Joss and his successor Dr David Morgan. Morgan says it was a 'moment of truth' in 1999 when he had to announce a record profit while 'we never had the community more dissatisfied with us, we never had our customers more dissatisfied and staff morale was never where it should have been'.

Westpac went to work, and signs that changes were afoot emerged in 2001 when it was runner-up in the index to Australia Post, which took second place this year. One of Westpac's first decisions was to slap a moratorium on rural branch closures. This was followed by another moratorium on metropolitan branch closures 12 months ago. Westpac introduced fee-free transactions for social security recipients and low-income earners. It also tightened up on extending credit card limits for people who were likely to spend beyond their means.

This year the bank is the only Australian financial institution, and one of only five globally, to deliver a triple bottom line report conforming to the standards of the United Nations-sponsored Global Reporting Initiative. The report covers more than 70 social, environmental and economic performance indicators – some developed by the Australian Council of Social Services (ACOSS) and the Australian Council of Trade Unions (ACTU).

Just weeks ago, Westpac was ranked number one in the banking sector on the global Dow Jones Sustainability Index. Other firsts have occurred in the workplace. Four years ago, it became the first bank to introduce paid maternity leave and provide for six weeks' paid paternity leave. It is now expanding its childcare centres and has other policies aimed at making it the employer of choice for women.

Sydney Morning Herald, 28 October 2002

COMMENTARY

The article describes how Westpac initially suffered from poor strategic decisions following deregulation of the banking sector. Once the company returned to profitability, it embarked on a strategy to improve its image and the strategy included a moratorium on branch closures, fee-free transactions for disadvantaged customers, controlling the amount of credit given to customers who were likely to spend more than they could afford and improved working conditions for staff. It is essential that companies continue to address their strategic plans if they are to survive and be successful.

STAGE 3: MAKING OPERATING DECISIONS

The majority of operating decisions in an organisation are concerned with pricing and output (e.g. price-setting), and the determination of production volumes and inventory levels.

To be effective, these decisions must conform to the objectives and strategic policies of the organisation. As these decisions are made in an economic environment, often there are constraints on the levels of sales and production which prevent an organisation, in the short term, from meeting its objectives. For example, a firm might experience shortages of skilled labour which effectively constrain the level of output in the short term. If the maximisation of profits is an objective of the firm, the constraint effectively limits the extent to which the objective can be met in the short term. In the long term, these constraints can usually be relieved – more skilled labour, for example, can be trained or recruited. In circumstances where resource constraints exist, although the long-term objectives cannot be satisfied, it is still important to allocate scarce resources efficiently. Management accounting techniques have been developed to allocate scarce resources efficiently in these circumstances and they will be considered in detail in Chapter 19.

KEY CONCEPT 15.5

OPERATING DECISIONS

Operating decisions are decisions that focus on the efficient use of the resources available to the firm in the short term.

The long-term plans of an organisation, as previously mentioned, are formulated through the making of strategic decisions with reference to overall objectives. In cases where, in the short term, the targets embodied within the long-term plans cannot be met, there is a need to amend or revise these plans in the light of the current economic situation. The process of re-examining long-term plans in such circumstances is an important feature of the effective management of organisations in a dynamic economic environment.

Operating decisions are translated into a short-term plan which is referred to as a budget. Budgets are simply plans of action expressed in monetary terms. The process of aggregating operating decisions into a plan compels managers to look ahead and coordinate their activities. For example, from this aggregation process the required level of inventories for production activities over the planning period can be identified. Without forward plans that coordinate production activities, the business might drift along and encounter undesirable situations – such as not having enough inventories to meet production requirements – that should have been anticipated and avoided. The budget also provides a basis for judging performance, through comparison of actual and budgeted figures. This comparison can highlight strengths and weaknesses within the organisation. It is important that budgets should be communicated to personnel in an organisation so that they are aware of the planned (budgeted) targets. This enables them to act in accordance with the plan.

The degree of sophistication and detail of budgets depends on the size of the organisation and the needs of the internal users. Often, the budgets cover a period of one year and are broken down in monthly intervals. Monthly budgets provide control, and enable a comparison of budget and actual activity at regular intervals so that timely monitoring of the plan is facilitated.

The process of preparing budgets and the types of budgets that are commonly employed will be examined in detail in Chapter 20.

STAGE 4: MONITORING AND CORRECTIVE ACTION

Monitoring and corrective action are the major components of the control activities of any organisation. The first element is the monitoring of actual performance against budget. From this comparison, differences (commonly referred to as 'variances') are identified – it is unlikely that the actual performance will be exactly the same as the budget. The reason for this is that the operating decisions embodied in the budget are normally determined well in advance of actual performance, and the process of forecasting costs and revenues in a dynamic economic environment is surrounded by uncertainty.

KEY CONCEPT 15.6

MONITORING AND CORRECTIVE ACTION

Monitoring is the process of comparing actual performance with a predetermined target (plan). It provides the basis from which corrective action can be planned and undertaken.

3

Explain the concept of responsibility accounting and how it helps management to monitor and control performance within the entity

To monitor performance effectively, personnel in an organisation who incur expenses and generate revenues are identified and made responsible for these costs and revenues. The approach adopted is known as 'responsibility accounting'. It recognises various decision centres throughout an organisation and traces costs and revenues to individual managers who are primarily responsible for making decisions and controlling the costs and revenues of their centres. Managers' knowledge of their centres places them in an advantageous position within the organisation to ensure that budget targets are achieved. These responsibility centres are normally departments, branches or divisions of a company.

In effect, in responsibility accounting systems, managers (to some extent) participate in the preparation of their own budgets. Evidence from research suggests that participation by responsible managers in the setting of budgets enhances the probability of effective planning and control within an organisation.

KEY CONCEPT 15.7

RESPONSIBILITY ACCOUNTING

Responsibility accounting occurs when an entity's structure is divided into strategic business units and the performance of these units is measured in terms of accounting results.

To support a system of responsibility accounting, the reporting system of the organisation needs to communicate relevant information. The reports should show the actual performance, the budget and the deviations (variances) from budget. The mode in which budgeted and actual costs and revenues are collected and then reported – for example, by product, labour or material input costs – is determined by management. The major factors that influence management in deciding the extent and sophistication of the reporting system are the costs of installing and operating such a system compared with the benefits it generates.

When variances have been identified, it is necessary to determine the reason for them in order for corrective action to be taken. If deviations from budget – assuming the budget reflects realistic targets – are not corrected, it could be harmful to the company in the long run. For example, the use of materials in a production process might exceed the budget in a particular control period. This could result in losses and, consequently, threaten profitability if action is not taken.

While the methods for the identification of variances, and their causes, are outside the scope of this text, you should have some insight into the general causes of variances. Traditionally, textbooks have tended to concentrate on variances that are caused by operating problems; for example, the prices of raw materials are greater than anticipated in the budget, perhaps because of inefficient buying practices by buyers. However, there are other potential causes of variances, such as the following:

1   Operating variances can be related to human or mechanical factors (such as human error).
2   Random variances are caused by divergences between actual and planned costs that arise without any pattern; that is, they occur by chance and it is not possible to control them. For example, in some chemical processing the output can vary per unit of input because of evaporation – this variation is inherent in the process.
3   Planning variances occur if plans are not realistic at the time of actual performance, even if operations have been efficiently carried out. For example, during the planning stage, oil costs might have been set with due care, but, because of a potential war in the Middle East, the price of oil may rise and therefore the costs that have been planned for may no longer represent realistic budget targets.

Case Study 15.2 illustrates variances from budget.

CASE STUDY 15.2

VARIANCES

ABC employs a budgeting system to control costs. The original budget for 20X7 included material A, which was estimated to cost $5 per kilogram. It was anticipated that 1000 kilograms would be used during the year. Therefore, the budget in total cost terms was $5000. During the year, however, although 1000 kilograms was used, the cost was $6000.

COMMENTARY

Traditionally, the analysis of the variance between actual and budget would be presented as follows.

	Actual	Budget	Variance
	$	$	$
Material A 1000 kg	6 000	5 000	(1 000)

The negative variance of $1000 (often indicated by brackets) indicates that it is 'unfavourable'; that is, actual costs exceed budget (plan).

This analysis does not give any indication as to the cause of the variance. For example, it could be because of inefficient buying practices by the purchaser of the materials or because prices have increased through inflation during the year. In the former case, the variance is due to operating ⫸

problems, so action might be taken in the future to ensure that more efficient buying practices are used. In contrast, if the variance is caused by inflation after the price was set in the original budget, the variance arises because the plan is out of date. In this case, it is unlikely that the firm can take any action to prevent such variances occurring again.

Let us now assume that the firm has information at the end of year 20X7 indicating that a realistic planned price, taking account of inflation during the year, would be $5.50 per kilogram. The variances could then be analysed as follows.

	Actual	Budget	Variance
	$	$	$
Variance caused through inefficient operations	6 000	5 500	(500)

	Original budget	Updated budget	Variance
	$	$	$
Variance caused by the plan being out of date	5 000	5 500	(500)

In this analysis, the causes of the variance are clearly identified; that is, $500 relates to operating problems and $500 is because the original budget was out of date. The information presented in this way is more informative and useful for management purposes.

Although the analysis of operating, random and planning variances is theoretically sound, there are a number of problems which limit its use in practice. For example, in Case study 15.2 the updated budget of $5500 was established at the end of the year. In other words, this budget was established in hindsight after the purchase of the material. To establish a realistic budget reflecting recent operating conditions, these budgets, by their nature, must be determined after the event. While such budgets are useful for variance analysis purposes, they do not give any targets for management to work towards during the actual production period. This is a major deficiency in the use of these types of budgets.

Another effective limitation is the cost of investigating the causes of variances. The activity of investigation can be costly. It might not be worth the time and money to carry out an investigation for the benefits derived, particularly for variances which are seen as insignificant.

In Chapter 21 we will discuss issues relating to the assessment of individual performance.

The control system

LO 7

Explain the problems entities have in contending with, establishing and implementing control systems

The accountant's control system (i.e. the monitoring and corrective action stage of the planning and control process) is often compared with that of an engineer, using the analogy of a central heating system. Figure 15.1 (overleaf) is a diagram of a central heating system. In this system the desired temperature is set and a comparator compares this with the actual room temperature. If there is any deviation, action is automatically taken by the system to fuel the boiler to enable it to compensate. This system therefore involves the process of monitoring actual output against a desired output, and, when a variance is identified, taking corrective action automatically.

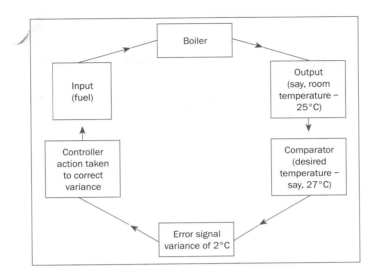

Figure 15.1 A central heating system demonstrates automatic monitoring and controls

Earlier, when examining the planning and control process, we identified and described similar stages. However, there are several interesting differences between the two systems which give us a greater insight into the limitations of the planning and control process.

An important difference is that the central heating model is a physical system where there are *automatic* responses to outputs; that is, corrective action is taken to obtain the desired temperature automatically and without any reference to operatives. In contrast, the control model within the planning and control process normally depends on humans. In this system, the response to deviations from the budget is not taken automatically. Time lags are experienced in all accounting reporting systems and people have to be motivated to respond to variances and take corrective action if it is perceived to be necessary.

The extent of these time lags in reporting depends on the sophistication of the accounting information system. Some large companies monitor performance every week and, with computerisation helping to speed up the reporting process, have the capacity to take corrective action relatively quickly. However, in most organisations control reports are produced on a monthly basis. The main restriction on implementing more timely systems is the installation and running costs. This relates back to costs and benefits: an information system should be installed only if the benefits generated from the system exceed the cost of installing and running it. The variances that are reported in an accounting information system can, of course, be used only as a guide for future operations. An organisation cannot remedy past mistakes.

It is only in recent years that the accounting function and its interaction with human behaviour have been brought to the forefront of accounting research and literature. It is now recognised that the effectiveness of accounting information systems is very much dependent upon the internal and external attitudes of individuals associated with the organisation. Attention is now correctly given to the influence of individuals on accounting information systems, but there is still considerable scope for further research into how human behaviour distorts the effectiveness of accounting systems.

In the context of control systems, the process of setting targets is influenced and affected by the behaviour of individuals. A sales manager might respond negatively if she is set a target that, in her opinion, is impossible. Another example is the action that is required to correct further undesirable variances. This action will very much depend upon the motivation of the responsible managers and their subordinates. Managers who perceive that targets are unrealistic are unlikely to be motivated to take corrective action to ensure they are met in the future. The accountant's control system is therefore limited in its application by the motivation of individuals in setting budgets and taking action on variances that have been identified.

Review exercise 3

Define responsibility accounting with reference to the planning and control process.

Explain the potential costs and benefits of developing accounting information systems to implement monitoring and control of performance

THE COSTS AND BENEFITS OF ACCOUNTING INFORMATION SYSTEMS

An accounting information system is a commodity in much the same way as household goods like detergents, soap and food. That is, there is a cost, often considerable, in installing and running the system. The benefits from employing the system should exceed the cost; otherwise it should not be installed.

The best system for an organisation is the system that generates the greatest amount of benefits net of costs. Horngren, Foster and Srikant (2000) contrast this approach with choosing a system because it is more accurate or a truer approximation of economic reality. The cost–benefit approach does not use accuracy as a criterion but focuses on the net benefits derived from alternative systems, giving preference to the system that generates the greater net benefits. The practical implementation of the cost–benefit approach, however, is rather complex. While it might be feasible to determine the cost of alternative systems, the benefits (the quality of information) are difficult to measure because they are qualitative. Although this is a problem, the cost–benefit approach is relevant in the choice of systems and is particularly relevant to the systems within the planning and control process described earlier.

THE COMMERCIAL CONTEXT

A number of writers and researchers argue that the installation of effective planning and control processes in businesses requires consideration of individual and organisational factors. We have briefly examined individual behaviour with reference to the setting of budgets and the motivation required to take corrective action to maintain control of costs and revenues within an organisation. We will now briefly consider other organisational and environmental issues.

Businesses are affected by, and dependent on, the commercial environment. Emmanuel, Otley and Merchant (1990) stress that a firm's 'ultimate survival is determined by the degree to which it adapts and accommodates itself to environmental contingencies (uncertain events)'. Therefore, the design of a planning and control system must be carefully tailored to match the environment and the organisational context in which it will be employed. This approach is not new; it has been implicitly recognised by accountants for a number of years.

Traditionally, writers of textbooks have suggested that there is one best way in which a particular task can be carried out, regardless of the environment the organisation operates in; for example, the nature of the market and the production process. Accounting information systems, as illustrated in textbooks, have adopted this approach, and have not differentiated among the needs of accounting for different organisations. This approach follows classical management and scientific management theories. The *contingency theory* of organisations, in contrast, accepts that different types of organisation require differing types of accounting information to enable them to function effectively.

Emmanuel, Otley and Merchant (1990) identify three major classes of contingent factors:
- *technological*: for example, whether the production process is labour-intensive
- *environmental*: for example, the degree of competition and the degree of predictability
- *structural*: for example, the size of the organisation and the type of organisation.

These contingent factors affect accounting information systems, and, in particular, the effectiveness of the planning and control process. For example, in the context of planning, businesses that are in a relatively risky market tend to invest more in planning in an attempt to predict outcomes and analyse alternative opportunities to reduce their risk. The design of planning and control systems should take account of these wider issues if a firm is to survive.

The needs of small business

So far we have made little reference to small businesses in the context of employing planning and control systems. Clearly, there are constraints for small businesses in their use and choice of such systems. One of the major constraints relates to the cost and benefits of installing these systems, as described earlier. Nevertheless, there is increasing evidence to suggest that there is a greater chance of survival if small firms use budgets to plan their future and employ control mechanisms to ensure that these plans are met. The reason often cited for the high failure rate of small firms in Australia is the lack of planning and control of cash resources. Much of what has been said so far regarding the need for planning and control is relevant to small businesses too.

SUMMARY

LO 1 LEARNING OBJECTIVE 1

Explain why management's information needs are not met solely by general-purpose financial reports

Annual accounts provide an overview of an entity's financial performance for the past year. They are available after the year and are of little value to management if corrective action is required during the financial year. Managers need frequent, up-to-date information tailored to their needs so that corrective decisions can be made.

LO 2 LEARNING OBJECTIVE 2

Explain which external users are likely to be able to gain access to internal company information not published in annual reports

External users who are in a position to obtain additional information occur in two groups: (1) those who have a statutory right, such as the taxation department, and (2) those who are able to exert influence on an entity, such as a lender or banker.

LO 3 LEARNING OBJECTIVE 3

Explain why the size and structure of an entity influences the need for management to have access to more complex internal information

A small business, with few employees and a restricted product or service, is unlikely to want additional information because this information is likely be known by the owner or manager anyway. On the other hand, a large company, such as Coles Myer, which has several subsidiaries (Kmart, Target and Liquorland), with many outlets, would want a breakdown of relevant information for each business and each area of operation.

LO 4 LEARNING OBJECTIVE 4

Explain what the planning and control processes are in relation to entity objectives

The planning process involves setting objectives and deciding how they will be achieved; the control process ensures that the plans will be implemented. Four stages are identified for the planning and control process. The stages are setting objectives, making strategic decisions, making operating decisions, and monitoring and taking corrective action when required. Objectives are important for the ongoing evaluation of a business. Difficulties can be experienced within an organisation due to conflicting objectives between managers. For example, a sales manager who wants additional sales may not have any regard for the costs involved, while a financial manager will be interested in costs and income. Goal congruence is the alignment of an entity's overall goals with those of the managers within the business.

LO 5 LEARNING OBJECTIVE 5

Explain what is meant by strategic and operating decisions

Strategic decisions are the long-term policies of a business. They are required if the business is to achieve its objectives.

The efficient use of a business's short-term resources is an operating decision. This type of operating decision is tied in with a budget, which can be a short- or long-term planning tool.

It is important that the strategic and operating decisions are known to managers so that the objectives can be met.

LO 6

LEARNING OBJECTIVE 6
Explain the concept of responsibility accounting and how it helps management to monitor and control performance within the entity

Responsibility accounting is a method of measuring and controlling performance through the use of accounting results. Performance and control can be met by putting monetary values on the inputs and outputs of a business cycle.

LO 7

LEARNING OBJECTIVE 7
Explain the problems entities have in contending with, establishing and implementing control systems

The control system monitors and controls performance so that appropriate corrective action can be taken. With the computerisation of systems, control can be achieved on a daily basis with the benefit of timely remedial action. On the other hand, a sophisticated computer system may cost more than the benefits obtained from it. Care needs to be taken to ensure that, in any system, the benefits outweigh the costs.

LO 8

LEARNING OBJECTIVE 8
Explain the potential costs and benefits of developing accounting information systems to implement monitoring and control of performance

Costs and benefits were mentioned above. The economic gains of implementing a system need to be borne in mind. Small business ventures may be unable to afford costly monitoring systems, and may not even have a need for one because a smaller organisational size often means fewer variables to contend with.

REFERENCES

Emmanuel, C.R., Otley, D.T., & Merchant, K., 1990. *Accounting for Management Control*, Chapman and Hall.

Horngren, C.T., Foster, G. & Srikant, M.D., 2000. *Cost Accounting: A Managerial Emphasis*, 10th edn, Prentice Hall.

Jones, R. & Pendlebury, M., 1996. *Public Sector Accounting*, 4th edn, Pitman Publishing.

FURTHER READING

Hansen, D.R. & Mowen, M.M., 2003. *Management Accounting,* 6th edn, South-Western, Mason, Ohio.

REVIEW QUESTIONS

1   One of the major improvements that bankers wish to see in respect of financial information is more timely information. Explain what this means and why it is important to bankers. How might this differ for managers?

2   What is likely to be the major impact of organisational size on the information needs of managers?

3   What useful management information is available from the accounting records from which the annual reports are produced?

4   Explain why some external users are likely to gain access to internal company information that is not published in financial reports.

5   What additional information would bankers wish to have and for what purposes would they use this?

6   In recent years, more external users of accounting information have required accounting information that is normally reserved for internal management. Explain why such information is useful to these users.

PROBLEMS FOR DISCUSSION AND ANALYSIS

1   Refer to the Woodside 2005 financial report in Appendix 1.
   a   Do you think there is more information in the accounts than is required by the average investor?
   b   Who do you consider would most likely benefit from reading the detailed accounts?

2   With regard to the information which you identified in your answer to Problem 1 above: would managers' use of this information differ from the way it is used by bankers, and if so, how would it differ?

3   In each of the situations below, identify what you believe your information needs would be:
   a   You are the manager of a local branch of a national retail organisation. All buying is done centrally and prices are fixed. You are in charge of the day-to-day management, and hiring and firing of staff. Your annual remuneration is fixed.
   b   The situation is the same as in (a), except that, in addition to your annual salary, you receive a bonus of $2 for each $200 profit made above that expected by your employer.
   c   As in (b), except that you are able to decide on selling prices yourself.
   d   You have been so successful as a branch manager that the company has promoted you to the position of regional manager in charge of 20 shops. The managers of these shops work under the conditions outlined in (c).

4   Discuss the meaning of and difference between strategic and operating decisions.

5   Discuss the main differences between the control models of accountants and engineers. Give details of any limits on the planning and control process that can be identified through this comparison.

6   Give illustrations of ways in which the behaviour of individuals can affect the planning and control process.

7   'For plans to be effective, management should consider the wider environmental factors that relate to the firm.' Discuss.

8   Describe why it is important to set objectives in a firm, and comment on the problems of setting objectives.

9   You work for an organisation primarily involved in health care, which runs a number of nursing homes for the elderly and has a head-office staff consisting of yourself and two owner–directors. Each of the nursing homes has a sister-in-charge who looks after the day-to-day running of the nursing home, but the advertising of the service, and the overall administration, is carried out by one of the directors, while the other director looks after the billing of the patients and collection of monies due. The overall profitability of your organisation has fallen drastically in the last year and you have been asked to investigate the situation.

   Identify what information you would need and what level of detail is required in order for you to start your investigation.

Note to instructors: *The following problem is considered more suitable for use in MBA courses. However, undergraduate courses may also find the problem useful.*

10 Giggling Brothers, wholesalers of fine wines, have been trading profitably for a number of years using a manual accounting system. However, they have experienced, every six months or so, severe cash-flow problems which appear to have been caused by a number of factors. These factors include the excessive purchase of 'special price' stock from vineyards, inappropriate timing of stock purchases relative to sales, inadequate control of debtors and mistimed marketing drives. Giggling Brothers believe that many of these problems are caused by inadequate and untimely feedback from the Accounting department. Purchasing department staff maintain that they are given inadequate financial information by the Accounting department, and that the Sales department consistently misrepresents expected sales. Sales department staff consider that management's expectations of their performance are unrealistic and that the Accounting department does not keep them sufficiently informed about the payment performance of customers. Additionally, Accounting department staff maintain that they are not consulted with regard to expenditure on purchases, or given sufficient information about the credit history of customers. Management believes that the implementation of a computerised accounting and reporting system would obviate most of these problems.

Required

a   What type of accounting and reporting information system should be designed for Giggling Brothers?
b   What benefits would such a system offer to the firm and how might the information produced be incorporated into the planning process?
c   Suggest how Giggling Brothers might best evaluate the cost against the benefit of implementing a new system.
d   Who do you think should be involved in the design and specifications for the new system?
e   Do you think that an examination and evaluation of the approaches used by their competitors would be of benefit to Giggling Brothers?

ETHICS CASE STUDY

John Kellog is the financial controller for Energisers Ltd. He is preparing a report for a proposed plant expansion at two possible locations – Mandurah or Rockingham. He is of the opinion that Mandurah is the better location for the new plant and he therefore intentionally excludes any reference to the fact that property taxes are 100 per cent higher in Mandurah than they are in Rockingham. Kellog owns some properties in Mandurah and if the plant is built there, property values should significantly increase.

Discuss whether John is behaving in an ethical manner.

ANSWERS TO REVIEW EXERCISES

1   Annual accounts contain summarised information – more detail may be required by management. More regular and more up-to-date information is also needed by managers to take action. The information in the annual accounts may not be suitable regarding decisions to be made in relation to planning, control or investment. There are a number of examples in the chapter but students should be encouraged to identify others.

2   Stage 1: Setting objectives – This involves detailing the objectives of the organisation in the short- and long term. Organisations do not have objectives per se; the objectives will reflect the objectives of those people involved in the organisation. These objectives can be in quantitative terms (e.g. statements about public responsibility).

    Stage 2: Making strategic decisions – Strategic decisions are those which determine the long-term policies of the firm and are necessary if the firm is to meet its objectives (e.g. policy changes relating to the range of products that are sold).

    Stage 3: Making operating decisions – Operating decisions are those that focus on the efficient use of the resources that are available to the firm in the short term. These decisions are embodied in plans that are conventionally referred to as budgets.

    Stage 4: Monitoring and possible corrective action – Monitoring is the process of comparing actual performance with a predetermined plan. It provides the basis from which corrective action can be planned and taken.

3   Responsibility accounting is a system that identifies decision centres and the managers responsible for those centres (e.g. departments). Costs and revenues are traced to these centres and compared with planned costs and revenues; therefore, the performance of managers, and their centres, can be measured.

16

LEARNING OBJECTIVES

At the end of this chapter, you should be able to:

1   explain and apply the concept of accounting rate of return (ARR)

2   explain and apply the concept of payback

3   explain and apply the concept of internal rate of return (IRR)

4   explain and apply the concept of net present value (NPV)

5   explain how to deal with mutually exclusive investments.

Before we can examine methods of evaluating capital investment decisions, it is important that you are able to identify and solve some basic financial mathematics problems. The following review exercises are intended to assess your capacity to solve three basic financial mathematics questions. If you are not able to complete the review exercises then you should study the material at the web address www.thomsonlearning.com.au/bazley/index.html.

Review exercise 1

Calculate the simple interest on $1245 at 5.6 per cent per annum from 1 June to15 December.

Review exercise 2

How long will it take $100 to accumulate to $200 at 6 per cent per annum?

Review exercise 3

A family buys a house for $12 000. It sells its old house for $7000 and uses this as a deposit. It borrows the balance at 7 per cent per annum compound interest. What amount, payable at the end of each year, would pay off the loan over 10 years?

Introduction

In this chapter we examine decisions that involve the commitment of substantial sums of money over significant periods. This is an important decision-making area for management. Capital investment decisions are difficult because they involve cash flows over time, and the time value of money must be incorporated into the decision. There is also the problem of determining the relevant future cash flows associated with an asset that may have an expected life of a number of years.

Management must make decisions such as whether to purchase machine X or Y, or whether to invest money in project A or B, and there are techniques to assist these decisions. Examples of these techniques are presented in this chapter.

Traditional methods of project evaluation

We begin the analysis of capital investment decisions by examining the traditional methods used to evaluate capital projects:
- accounting rate of return (ARR)
- payback period.

These methods are based on accounting numbers and do not consider the impact of cash flows occurring in different years. They were popular because they were simple and easily understood and used familiar terms such as 'net profit'.

Accounting rate of return (ARR)

Explain and apply the concept of accounting rate of return (ARR)

The accounting rate of return (ARR) method was widely used by businesses before the development of the discounted cash flow techniques discussed later in this chapter. The appeal of the ARR was its simplicity and the use of the familiar terms 'net profit' and 'book value of investment'. The ARR can be calculated in two ways: by using either the average value of investment or the total book value of investment in the denominator. Key concept 16.1 illustrates the two formulas for the ARR.

KEY CONCEPT 16.1

ACCOUNTING RATE OF RETURN

Formula 1

$$ARR(\%) = \frac{\text{average net profit}}{\text{average book value of investment}} \times 100$$

Formula 2

$$ARR(\%) = \frac{\text{average net profit}}{\text{total initial investment value}} \times 100$$

The ARR using formula 1 will be higher than that under formula 2. Provided the same formula is used to evaluate competing projects, a consistent approach is achieved. The net profit in the formula is after depreciation and tax expenses.

Example 16.1: Projects Alpha and Beta

The following details relate to projects Alpha and Beta. The combined initial book value for both projects is $15 000:

		Year 1 $	Year 2 $	Year 3 $	Average $
Alpha net profit (after depreciation and tax)		4 000	6 000	8 000	6 000
Beta net profit (after depreciation and tax)		8 000	6 000	4 000	6 000
Book values	1 January	15 000	10 000	5 000	–
	31 December	10 000	5 000	0	–
	Average book values	12 500	7 500	2 500	7 500

Using formula 1, the ARR for each project is:

$$ARR \text{ (Alpha)} = \frac{6000}{7500} \times 100 = 80\%$$

$$ARR \text{ (Beta)} = \frac{6000}{7500} \times 100 = 80\%$$

Using formula 2, the ARR for each project is:

$$ARR \text{ (Alpha)} = \frac{6000}{15\ 000} \times 100 = 40\%$$

$$ARR \text{ (Beta)} = \frac{6000}{15\ 000} \times 100 = 40\%$$

The decision criterion for ARR is to accept projects with a rate of return that is higher than some minimum desired rate of return. If the projects are competing or mutually exclusive, we accept the project with the highest rate of return, provided it is above the minimum desired rate of return.

From Example 16.1, projects Alpha and Beta appear equally desirable. However, Beta returns more profit in the earlier year. Would you prefer $100 today or $100 in one year's time? Of course we would all choose $100 today as the money could be invested, and in one year's time we would have $100 plus interest (this is often referred to as the time value of money). Consequently, we would value Beta more than Alpha. However, this is not the result of the application of the ARR. A major weakness of the ARR is that it ignores the time value of money.

ADVANTAGES OF ARR

The advantages of the ARR method for evaluating capital projects are:
- it is simple to calculate and easy to understand
- profit and returns on assets are used by investors as a ratio to assess the performance of management. This was discussed in Chapter 14. The ratio is familiar to managers and investors.

DISADVANTAGES OF ARR

The disadvantages of the ARR method are:
- it applies the same weighting to profits in all years and ignores the time value of money
- it uses accounting measures and not cash flows. While accounting measures are important in assessing managerial performance, cash flows are important in investment evaluations, for it is the cash flows that are used to pay wages, pay for supplies, and so on
- the two different formulas for ARR can result in different decisions.

Payback period

LO 2
Explain and apply the concept of payback

Another traditional method used to assist in decisions about capital investments is the payback period. An important issue when considering any long-term investment is how long it will take for the initial investment to be recouped. Investments are made with a view to profit, but an important component of this view to profit is the desire to avoid a loss. The payback period is the period of time within which recovery of the initial investment is expected. Other things being equal, if two competing investments offered similar expected benefits, the one with the shorter payback period would be preferred.

The payback period is used as a measure of risk: the longer the payback period, the higher the risk of the project. This is a crude measure of risk and there are certainly more sophisticated techniques available, such as sensitivity analysis, to assess risk. Nevertheless, it continues to be used in conjunction with other techniques of investment analysis, including discounted cash flow methods (discussed later in this chapter).

To determine the payback period for a project, the after-tax cash inflows are added together until the sum equals the initial investment, as shown in Example 16.2.

KEY CONCEPT 16.2

PAYBACK PERIOD FOR EQUAL CASH INFLOWS

The payback period is calculated by dividing the initial investment by the net cash inflow.

Example 16.2: Projects Z and Y

Project Z costs $15 000 and will return a net cash flow of $5000 per annum for four years.

$$\text{payback} = \frac{\text{initial investment}}{\text{net cash inflow}}$$

$$= \frac{15\,000}{5\,000}$$

$$= 3 \text{ years}$$

To determine payback when the net cash flows are uneven, we sum each year's cash inflows, until the sum equals the initial investment.

Project Y offers the following cash flows for an investment of $15 000:

	Net cash flow	Cumulated cash flow	
	$	$	$
Year 1	2 000	2 000	
Year 2	4 000	6 000	
Year 3	6 000	12 000	15 000
Year 4	6 000	18 000	
Year 5	20 000	38 000	

The payback period for project Y is three and a half years, assuming cash inflows are evenly spread over the year.

The decision criterion for the payback method would be to set a minimum period and accept only projects with a payback below this minimum. For mutually exclusive investments where only one project is required, the one with the lowest payback period would be selected, provided this was less than the minimum period.

For projects Z and Y, the payback method would favour project Z. Project Y does offer significantly higher cash flows, but these occur after the payback period. Hence, a significant deficiency with the payback method is that it ignores cash flows after the payback period.

ADVANTAGES OF THE PAYBACK PERIOD

The advantages of using the payback period to assist in decisions about capital investments are:

- it is easy to understand
- it provides some assessment of risk

- it is a simple and well-understood method. Managers are well aware that the payback period means the time required to recoup the initial investment
- it is used as a means of assessing the risk associated with a project – even though it is a crude measure of risk.

DISADVANTAGES OF THE PAYBACK PERIOD
The disadvantages of the payback period method are:
- it does not take into consideration a project's cash flows after the payback period and can therefore result in the selection of less profitable investments if used in isolation
- it ignores the time value of money and treats all cash flows as equal, irrespective of the year in which they occur. This problem can be overcome by using the discounted payback period, in which cash flows are discounted to reflect the time value of money. However, cash flows after the discounted payback period are still ignored and so the first disadvantage of payback remains.

Discounted cash-flow techniques

The most common methods for evaluating capital investment proposals involve the use of discounted cash-flow techniques. The two main methods are:
- internal rate of return
- net present value.

Both methods focus on cash flows, rather than accounting profit, and utilise the fact that the use of money has a cost. The alternative to buying a productive asset would be investing the money, which will then be compounded. With capital investments, cash is invested now with the hope of receiving a greater amount in the future.

In discussing the discounted cash-flow techniques, we use concepts from financial mathematics such as the present value of $1 per period.

Remember, the concepts of financial mathematics are explained in material available at the website for this book. The present and future value factor tables are in Appendix 2 and are used in the examples that follow.

Internal rate of return (IRR)

Explain and apply the concept of internal rate of return (IRR)

To overcome the problems associated with the traditional methods of project evaluation, the internal rate of return (IRR) method was developed and is now widely used in business. We have already discussed various rates of return in Chapter 14, and earlier in the present chapter we examined the accounting rate of return (ARR).

The IRR differs from the ARR in that it uses cash flows and adjusts for the fact that $1 today is worth more than $1 in one year's time. The IRR is that rate of return which equates the present value of the expected cash inflows with the present value of the expected cash outflows. It is, therefore, not the same as the ARR and is regarded as a superior method.

KEY CONCEPT 16.3

INTERNAL RATE OF RETURN

The internal rate of return (IRR) is the rate of return which discounts the cash flows of a project so that the present value of cash inflows equals the present value of cash outflows.

To calculate the IRR, the following formula is used. We have to solve for 'R' in the formula:

$$OC = \frac{NCF_1}{(1+R)^1} + \frac{NCF_2}{(1+R)^2} + \ldots + \frac{NCF_n}{(1+R)^n} +$$

where   OC = original cost
NCF = net cash flow (the sum of all cash flows)
R = IRR ÷ 100
n = number of periods

When the net cash flow remains the same each year, the formula becomes:

$$OC = NCF \times [\frac{1}{(1+R)^1} + \frac{1}{(1+R)^2} + \ldots + \frac{1}{(1+R)^n}]$$

$$OC = NCF \times PVF\ (IRR,n)$$

where   PVF = present value factor

Example 16.3: IRR on a machine

An amount of $17 946 was outlaid on a machine which is expected to return cash inflows of $6000 per year for five years. At that time the machine is expected to be worthless. Calculate the internal rate of return on the machine.

The investment of $17 946 produces a benefit of $6000 a year for five years. Therefore OC = 17 946, NCF = 6000 and n = 5. R is unknown.

$$OC = NCF \times PVF(IRR,n)$$
$$17\,946 = 6000 \times PVF(IRR,5)$$
$$PVF(IRR,5) = 17\,946 \div 6000$$
$$= 2.991$$

In Table 4 in Appendix 2, we can look along the n = 5 row until we find the PVF closest to 2.991. This is 2.9906, in the 20 per cent column. Hence, the IRR is 20 per cent.

This approach is possible only when the cash inflows each year are equal. In practice, this is not likely to be the case. Determining the IRR when net cash flows vary from year to year is more complicated. Consider the following data:

Net cash flow

Year 0	Year 1	Year 2	Year 3	Year 4
−5 000	1 000	1 500	2 300	2 800

In this case, OC = 5000, NCF_1 = 1000, NCF_2 = 1500, and so on. We want to find the value of R which will make OC equal to 5000; that is:

$$OC = 5000 = \frac{1000}{(1+R)^1} + \frac{1500}{(1+R)^2} + \frac{2300}{(1+R)^3} + \frac{2800}{(1+R)^4}$$

Solving such an equation algebraically would be too difficult for most people. An alternative approach is to use trial and error. We pick a value for R and substitute into the right-hand side of the equation.

Let IRR = 20 per cent, so R = 0.2.

$$OC = 5000 = \frac{1000}{(1.2)^1} + \frac{1500}{(1.2)^2} + \frac{2300}{(1.2)^3} + \frac{2800}{(1.2)^4}$$
$$= 833 + 1042 + 1331 + 1350$$
$$= 4556$$

This is too small since we want OC to equal 5000.

Try IRR = 10 per cent, so R = 0.1.

$$OC = 5000 = \frac{1000}{(1.1)^1} + \frac{1500}{(1.1)^2} + \frac{2300}{(1.1)^3} + \frac{2800}{(1.1)^4}$$
$$= 909 + 1240 + 1728 + 1912$$
$$= 5789$$

This is too large since we want OC to equal 5000.

Our next try would be a value of IRR between 10 and 20 per cent.

Try 16 per cent.

$$OC = 5000 = \frac{1000}{(1.16)^1} + \frac{1500}{(1.16)^2} + \frac{2300}{(1.16)^3} + \frac{2800}{(1.16)^4}$$
$$= 862 + 1114 + 1473 + 1546$$
$$= 4995$$

Therefore, IRR is approximately 16 per cent.

You can see how much time this trial-and-error approach could take. Fortunately, computers and certain calculators make the task of determining IRR a matter of pressing a few buttons.

The decision criterion for IRR is to accept projects which offer an IRR above a certain minimum desired rate of return. This rate of return is often called the cost of capital, which is the rate of return that equates the present value of a firm's expected future cash flows to the firm's value. For mutually exclusive investments, the project with the highest IRR is accepted, provided the IRR is above the minimum.

KEY CONCEPT 16.4

COST OF CAPITAL

The cost of capital is the rate of return that equates the present value of a firm's expected future cash flows to the value of the firm.

ADVANTAGES OF IRR

The advantages of the IRR method of project evaluation are:

- it uses the concept of a rate of return and this concept is familiar to many managers. Managers will often prefer to make decisions using concepts with which they are familiar. (Remember, this is one of the advantages of the ARR.)
- it does not treat cash received in different years as equal and thus incorporates the time value of money. It is essential that cash flows received or paid in different periods are not treated equally
- it uses cash flows and not profit figures. It is the cash inflows from a project which will be required to pay the cash outflows.

DISADVANTAGES OF IRR

The disadvantages of the IRR method are:

- some types of investment can have more than one IRR, and in some cases no IRR. These types of investment are often described as non-conventional. A conventional investment is one in which there is a cash outflow in year 1 and then a series of cash inflows during the years that follow. A non-conventional investment is one in which further cash outflows occur during the life of the investment. It is these investments which can have more than one IRR, and this complicates the decision-making process for managers
- for competing investments, where the selection of one means the rejection of the others, the IRR can provide a ranking of investments different from the net present value (discussed next). In effect, this means that the project that will not maximise the firm's value (which is one of the main objectives of a firm), may be ranked first using IRR
- it is dependent on the accuracy of the estimates of future cash flows. Consequently, the less reliable the estimates, the less reliable the IRR.

Net present value (NPV)

The second discounted cash-flow technique is the net present value (NPV) method. Unlike the IRR, which expresses a result in a percentage, the NPV expresses a result in dollars. The NPV is determined by calculating the present value of all cash inflows and outflows at a certain rate and then adding the two together to arrive at either a positive or a negative result. A positive NPV suggests that the project should be accepted, while a negative NPV suggests that the project should be rejected.

LO 4

Explain and apply the concept of net present value (NPV)

Example 16.4: NPV on investment

An investment of $100 000 is expected to yield a company $60 000 net cash inflows at the end of each year for two years, after which time it will be worthless. The company requires a rate of return of 10 per cent on such investments. To determine the NPV, we must calculate the present value at 10 per cent of a cash inflow of $60 000 each year for the next two years.

The outflow occurs immediately, so the value in today's dollars is $100 000.

The inflows occur at the end of each of the next two years and the present value is calculated by using Table 2 in Appendix 2 as:

Year 1	$60 000 × 0.90909 =	$54 594
Year 2	$60 000 × 0.82645 =	$49 587
Total		$104 181

The NPV is:

$$-\$100\ 000 + \$104\ 181 = \$4181$$

As the NPV is positive, the decision would be to accept the project, even though the amount is only small and management would have to consider other factors, like the risk associated with the investment. How certain are the cash inflows? Are there alternative uses for the money? What is the opportunity cost of investing in this project?

How did we arrive at the figure of 10 per cent as the discount rate? This is often called the cost of capital, which was defined in Key concept 16.4. It is beyond the scope of this book to discuss how this rate is determined. However, the rate should be such that acceptance of all projects with a positive NPV will result in an increase in the overall value of the firm.

KEY CONCEPT 16.5

NET PRESENT VALUE

The NPV is the figure that results from discounting all the cash flows of a project at the minimum rate of return and summing the resultant present values.

We can develop formulas for the calculation of NPV as follows:

$$NPV = -OC + \frac{NCF_1}{(1+K)^1} + \frac{NCF_2}{(1+K)^2} + \ldots + \frac{NCF_n}{(1+K)^n}$$

where
- OC = original cost
- NCF = net cash flow
- K = cost of capital ÷ 100
- n = number of periods
- NPV = net present value

For example, assuming a minimum rate of 10 per cent and the following cash flows:

Year 0	Year 1	Year 2
−10 000	7 000	5 000

$$
\begin{aligned}
NPV &= -10\ 000 + \frac{7000}{(1+0.1)^1} + \frac{5000}{(1+0.1)^2} \\
&= -10\ 000 + 6364 + 4132 \\
&= \$496
\end{aligned}
$$

When the net cash flow is the same each year, this formula becomes:

$$NPV = -OC + NCF \left[\frac{1}{(1+K)^1} + \frac{1}{(1+K)^2} + \ldots + \frac{1}{(1+K)^n} \right]$$

or $\quad NPV = -OC + NCF \times PVF(K,n)$

Using the data from Example 16.3, and assuming a minimum desired rate of return of 10 per cent, we now calculate the NPV as follows:

$$
\begin{aligned}
NPV &= -OC + NCF \times PVF(K,n) \\
&= -17\,946 + 6000 \times PVF(10,5) \\
&= -17\,946 + 6000 \times 3.7907 \text{ (from Table 4 in Appendix 2)} \\
&= -17\,946 + 22\,744 \\
&= \$4798
\end{aligned}
$$

The IRR for this investment was 16 per cent, and, as it is a conventional investment, the NPV should be positive – as indeed it is. This means that by using both the IRR and NPV methods, we arrive at the same 'accept' decision for this particular project. However, as stated earlier, the two methods can give conflicting results for projects with non-conventional cash flows and in the ranking of mutually exclusive projects. Therefore, the decision rule for NPV is to accept all projects with a positive NPV except mutually exclusive projects; for mutually exclusive projects, choose the project with the highest positive NPV.

ADVANTAGES OF NPV

The advantages of the NPV method of project evaluation are:

- it incorporates the time value of money into calculations and so does not treat as equal cash flows received or paid in different years
- once the cash flows have been discounted at the minimum rate of return, they can be added together to arrive at an amount in present-day dollars
- for mutually exclusive projects, it gives a ranking superior to IRR (this is explained in the next section)
- it uses cash flows, not profit numbers, and is a more sophisticated and less arbitrary approach to investment evaluation.

DISADVANTAGES OF NPV

The disadvantages of the NPV method are:

- if the calculation of the minimum rate of return is not accurate, then the NPV will be less reliable
- because it is dependent on the accuracy of the estimates of future cash flows, the less reliable the estimates, the less reliable the NPV.

Review exercise 4

The Bluejet Co. is looking at a capital expenditure proposal that involves an investment of $78 345 and annual net cash flows of $15 250 for each of the eight years of the useful life of the project. There is a zero scrap value.

    a   What is the internal rate of return?

    b   What is the net present value if the cost of capital is 11 per cent?

    c   What is the payback period?

Review exercise 5

The Waugh Electronics Company Ltd is thinking of buying, at a cost of $25 093, some new quality control equipment that is expected to save $5000 in cash operating costs. Its estimated useful life is 10 years, and it will have a zero disposal value. Calculate:

    a   the internal rate of return

    b   the net present value if the cost of capital is 10 per cent

    c   the payback period.

Comparison of IRR and NPV

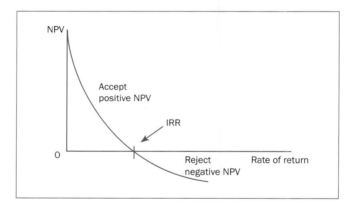

Figure 16.1 Project evaluation with IRR and NPV

The graph in Figure 16.1 shows the relationship between NPV and IRR. Remember that:

$$NPV = -OC + \frac{NCF_1}{(1+R)^1} + \frac{NCF_2}{(1+R)^2} + \ldots + \frac{NCF_n}{(1+R)^n}$$

This value will be at a maximum when the rate of return, R, is zero. This is the intercept on the vertical axis and will be a positive value if the sum of the net cash flows exceeds the original cost.

As R becomes larger, each term $\frac{NCF_1}{(1+R)^1}$, $\frac{NCF_2}{(1+R)^2}$, and so on, becomes smaller.

Hence, the NPV decreases as R increases, in a curve as shown. At some stage, the NPV becomes zero. At this point:

$$NPV = -OC + \frac{NCF_1}{(1+R)^1} + \frac{NCF_2}{(1+R)^2} + \ldots + \frac{NCF_n}{(1+R)^n} = OC$$

so

$$NPV = \frac{NCF_1}{(1+R)^1} + \frac{NCF_2}{(1+R)^2} + \ldots + \frac{NCF_n}{(1+R)^n} = OC$$

But this is the formula we use to find the IRR. Hence, the intercept on the horizontal axis is the IRR.

Do the IRR and NPV methods give the same answer for decision-making purposes? Unfortunately they do not! The answer will depend on whether the investments are *independent* (that is, the acceptance or rejection of one project has no effect on the other) or *mutually exclusive* (that is, if one project is selected, the other is automatically rejected). It will also depend on whether the cash flows associated with the project are what are described as conventional (i.e. cash outflow, followed by cash inflows) or not conventional (i.e. cash outflow, cash inflow, cash inflow, cash outflow). We only illustrate mutually exclusive projects in this book.

MUTUALLY EXCLUSIVE INVESTMENTS

Independent conventional cash-flow projects are ranked the same using both the NPV and IRR methods. For mutually exclusive projects, the IRR and NPV methods can give different rankings and therefore lead to different decisions as illustrated in Example 16.5.

LO 5

Explain how to deal with mutually exclusive investments

Example 16.5: Projects A and B

In examples 16.5 and 16.6, note that the net cash flow for year 0 is the negative of the original cost. For example, for project A in year 0 the net cash flow is –$4500; therefore, the original cost is +$4500.

The cash flows for two mutually exclusive projects are as follows:

Net cash flow (NCF)

	Year 0	Year 1	Year 2	Year 3	Year 4	Year 5
Project A	–4 500	1 350	1 350	1 350	1 350	1 350
Project B	–3 000	915	915	915	915	915

Which project should be chosen? Assuming a minimum rate of 10 per cent per annum, the NPV and IRR for both projects can be calculated. The answers are summarised and ranked in Table 16.1 on the next page.

IRR: Project A

$$OC = NCF \times PVF(IRR,n)$$
$$4500 = 1350 \times PVF(IRR,5)$$
$$3.333 = PVF(IRR,5)$$

Looking across the row n = 5 in Table 4 in Appendix 2, you will see that the PVF for 15 per cent is 3.3521. Hence, the IRR is slightly more than 15 per cent. Using a computer program gives a more accurate answer of 15.2 per cent.

IRR: Project B

$$3000 = 915 \times PVF(IRR,5)$$
$$3.2787 = PVF(IRR,5)$$

Looking once again across row n = 5, you will see that the PVF for 20 per cent is 2.9906. Therefore, the tables only tell us that the IRR is closer to 15 per cent than to 20 per cent. A sensible guess would be about 16 per cent; a computer program confirms this answer.

NPV: Project A

$$NPV = -OC + NCF \times PVF(10,5)$$
$$NPV = -4500 + 1350 \times 3.7907$$
$$= \$617.45$$

NPV: Project B

$$NPV = -3000 + 915 \times 3.7907$$
$$= \$468.49$$

Using these results, we can rank the projects:

Table 16.1 Summary of IRR and NPV results and rankings for projects A and B

	IRR	Rank	NPV	Rank
Project A	15.2%	2	$617	1
Project B	16%	1	$468	2

Table 16.1 shows that the IRR method ranks B the best while the NPV method ranks A the best. Which project should be chosen? We could answer the question by looking at the return on the extra dollars invested in project A.

The differences in net cash flow for projects A and B are shown in the following table:

	Year 0	Year 1	Year 2	Year 3	Year 4	Year 5
A–B	−1 500	435	435	435	435	435

$$OC = NCF \times PVF(IRR,n)$$
$$1500 = 435 \times PVF(IRR,5)$$
$$PVF(IRR,5) = \frac{1500}{435} = 3.448$$

From Table 4 in Appendix 2, the IRR is between 12 per cent and 15 per cent. Using a computer, we can perform the following calculation:

$$IRR (A - B) = 13.8\%$$

Therefore, the extra investment in A (the incremental IRR) provides a rate of return higher than the minimum rate of return; therefore, on this basis project A should be accepted. If we apply the NPV method, then project A should be chosen because it returns more dollars to the company and therefore increases the firm's overall value.

COMPARISON OF IRR AND NPV RANKINGS

The difference in the ranking of projects under the IRR and NPV methods arises because of the assumption on the reinvestment rates for cash flows received during the life of the project. IRR assumes reinvestment of intermediate cash flows at the IRR of the project, while NPV assumes reinvestment at the minimum rate of return. This is illustrated in Example 16.6.

Example 16.6: Projects P and Q

Net cash flows

	Year 0	Year 1	Year 2	IRR	NPV
Project P	−20 000	2 000	36 400	40%	1 190
Project Q	20 000	20 000	15 000	50%	1 059

Note that a minimum rate of return of 10 per cent was assumed. The IRRs were calculated using the trial-and-error method. The NPVs were calculated using:

$$NPV = -OC + \frac{NCF_1}{(1+1)^1} + \frac{NCF_2}{(1+1)^{2}}$$

As an exercise, you might like to check that the values in the table are correct.

Analysis of reinvestment assumptions

			Project P		Project Q
IRR	Proceeds year 1 reinvested at IRR year 2	$2 000 × 1.4 =	2 800	$20 000 × 1.5 =	30 000
			36 400		15 000
			$39 200		$45 000
NPV	Proceeds year 1 reinvested at 10% year 2	$2 000 × 1.1 =	2 200	$20 000 × 1.1 =	22 000
			36 400		15 000
			$38 600		$37 000

The above analysis illustrates that the IRR reinvestment assumption results in project Q ranking above project P. The NPV assumption results in the ranking being reversed.

If we wish to evaluate the two projects, then reinvestment should be considered at the minimum rate of return; otherwise, we are prejudging the use of available funds for other projects. A business should be able to reinvest funds at a return that is at least equal to its minimum rate of return for all projects.

The recommended rule to use is the NPV rule, although supporters of the IRR method argue that using the incremental IRR overcomes all the problems with mutually exclusive projects.

KEY CONCEPT 16.6

DECISION RULE

The net present value (NPV) method is the recommended method for evaluating capital investment decisions.

Qualitative factors and capital investment decisions

The techniques outlined in this chapter provide important quantitative information for managers to assist in their very significant and important capital investment decisions. However, it is the role of managers to take the quantitative information provided by the accountant and consider this with qualitative factors before arriving at a final decision.

Qualitative factors include considering the impact of the decision on:

- employees
- other parts of the business
- the environment
- future opportunities
- the image of the company.

Finally, managers must decide if the risk is too high, even if there is a positive NPV. In short, the financial details are only part of the puzzle; managers must bring together all the pieces of the puzzle to make the final decision.

CASE STUDY 16.1

RETAILERS REBOUND ON WOOLIES' WHOPPER
by Leonie Wood

A BUMPER profit from supermarket group Woolworths and expectation of higher dividends from other retailers helped spur a 2.3 per cent jump in the retail sector yesterday as market heavyweights regained favour among investors.

Woolworths surprised the market with a

better-than-expected 14 per cent increase in full-year net profit before abnormals to $355.6 million, and rewarded shareholders by lifting fully franked, final dividends three cents to 13 cents a share.

Woolworths' shares closed on a record high of $6.75, up 30 cents, after peaking at $6.77, as the retailer suggested the GST had not impinged on its business.

At the same time, rumours abound that Coles Myer in October will unveil a special dividend of up to 35 cents, or launch an off-market buyback, as it moves to discharge as much as $400 million of accrued franking credits.

After opening five cents above their previous close, Coles Myer shares ran as high as $7.55 and ended the day up 24 cents, or 3.3 per cent, at $7.49.

Even David Jones, which despite launching a shareholder discount card earlier this year, has struggled to find favour with investors, rose three cents, or 2.2 per cent, to $1.39 amid hopes that stronger sales across the retail sector have translated into higher profits for the department stores group.

Woolworths' solid result followed a volatile trading year for retailers, who endured hot and cold consumer sentiment, spent heavily on systems adjustments associated with the Y2K rollover for computers early in the year, and ended the financial year with massive reticketing and systems changes related to the GST.

Woolworths heralded steady trading ahead, and executives noted revenues from the Big W, Dick Smith Electronics and Powerhouse stores were already 9 per cent ahead of 1999 levels.

'We anticipate ongoing sales growth in the high single digits and profit growth in the low double digits,' said Woolworths chief executive Roger Corbett.

This year, Mr Corbett has slashed Woolworths' capital expenditure budget to $420 million from $764 million, with spending on new stores, major refurbishments and store updates all cut.

Gross abnormal charges totalled $93.9 million, including $53.2 million related to GST implementation and $68.1 million on Woolworths' long-term project to cut costs and improve its supply chain.

Woolworths expects the tighter management system will help trim annual costs by as much as $134 million within three years.

Chairman John Dahlsen said the result reflected a renewed focus on Woolworths' core stores as it improved its capital management strategies. It sold the Rockmanns fashion chain in February. The 585 Woolworths and Safeway supermarkets generated 16.8 per cent higher profit before interest and tax of $601 million as sales rose 8.3 per cent to $16.67 billion.

Profit before tax, and before paying dividends to holders of income securities, rose 20 per cent to $593.8 million, and Woolworths' underlying earnings per share climbed 18.8 per cent to 32.4 cents (before abnormals). In total, Woolworths lifted shareholder payments by five cents in 1999–2000, from 18 cents to 23 cents. It will pay final dividends on October 5 to shareholders registered by September 14.

The Age, 29 August 2000

COMMENTARY

The article describes how Woolworths has a new capital management strategy with a focus on its core stores. This has resulted in a reduction in its capital expenditure budget of some $344 million and a 20 per cent increase in profit for the year. The decision to focus on core activities is based not only on financial data but also important qualitative considerations.

SUMMARY

LO 1 LEARNING OBJECTIVE 1
Explain and apply the concept of accounting rate of return (ARR)

The accounting rate of return is a simple method of calculating return based on net profit or book value. It is not used very often today because its main disadvantage is that it does not take into account the time value of money.

LO 2 LEARNING OBJECTIVE 2
Explain and apply the concept of payback

This concept focuses on the time it takes for the cost of the initial investment to be recouped. It is simple to use and provides a low-level assessment of risk. Like the ARR method, it ignores the time value of money. This problem can be overcome by using the discounted payback period, in which cash flows are discounted to reflect the time value of money. However, cash flows after the discounted payback period are still ignored.

LO 3 LEARNING OBJECTIVE 3
Explain and apply the concept of internal rate of return (IRR)

The IRR method uses the present value of future dollars received against the present value of cash outflows. The IRR method measures projects against a rate of return and discounts the values of cash flows into and out of a business. Problems can occur when it is possible to have more than one IRR for a given project, and it can rank investments differently from the NPV method (see below).

LO 4 LEARNING OBJECTIVE 4
Explain and apply the concept of net present value (NPV)

The NPV method uses the present value of future dollars received against the future value of cash outflows. Discounted cash flows can be added and, for mutually exclusive projects, the NPV method is superior to the IRR method.

   NOTE: All methods mentioned above rely on the estimates of future returns.

LO 5 LEARNING OBJECTIVE 5
Explain how to deal with mutually exclusive investments

Problems arise when mutually exclusive investments with unequal lives are being ranked. This is mainly due to the different reinvestment assumptions for the project/investment with the shorter life under the NPV and IRR methods. The NPV method is generally regarded as the preferred method in such cases.

FURTHER READING

Hansen, D. & Mowen, M., 2003. *Management Accounting and Control*, 6th edn, South-Western, Mason, Ohio. www.thomson.com.au/bazley/index.html

REVIEW QUESTIONS

Note: *You may need to refer to 'An introduction to financial mathematics' at the web address www.thomson.com.au/bazley/index.html and also to Appendix 2: 'Present and future value factor tables' to answer the following review and problem questions.*

1 Find the simple interest on $900 at 4.5 per cent per annum from 1 April to 16 May.

2 If the following amounts are invested at compound interest, what will they amount to at the end of the following periods?
   a $1000 invested at 5 per cent for five years.
   b $200 invested at 10 per cent for 15 years.

3 If the following amounts are invested at compound interest, what will they amount to at the end of the following periods?
   a $1250 at 6.5 per cent per annum for six years, interest compounded annually.
   b $6500 at 7.75 per cent per annum for four years, interest compounded semi-annually.

4 If the cost of funds is 10 per cent, what is the present value of:
   a $1000 to be received in three years time
   b $1500 to be received in 10 years time?

5 How long will it take $125 to accumulate to $330 at 10 per cent per annum with interest compounded quarterly? Take your answer to the nearest quarter.

6 At a given annual compound rate of interest, $1000 amounts to $2100 after seven years. What is the interest rate?

7 A machine costing $100 000 has a life of 10 years and no salvage value. It will require annual maintenance expenditure of $10 000 but will save labour costs totalling $25 000 per annum. What rate of return can be expected from this machine?

8 An investment costs $75 and pays $100 after a period of 10 years. What is the effective annual compound interest rate?

9 At a given annual compound rate of interest, $1000 amounts to $1500 in 10 years. What will it amount to after six years?

10 What annual rate of interest must be earned for deposits of $400 at the start of the year for 10 years and deposits of $1000 for the following five years to accumulate a sum of $20 000 at the end of 15 years?

11 What is the purchase price of a house which can be bought for $4000 cash plus $400 at the end of each year for 20 years? (Interest 6 per cent per annum compound.)

12 If I deposit $100 in the bank now, $100 regularly at 12-month intervals for the next five years and $200 regularly at 12-month intervals for the following 10 years, what is:
   a   the accumulated value at the end of the 15 years
   b   the present value of the payments?
       (Assume 5 per cent per annum compound interest.)

13 What annual rate of interest must be earned for deposits of $500 at the start of each year to accumulate to $10 000 in 15 years?

14 A company pays $1000 each year into a bank sinking fund earning 6 per cent per annum compound interest. After five payments, the rate of interest granted by the bank on the fund is reduced to 4 per cent. The company, therefore, decides to increase its future deposits to $1200. What amount is in the fund after 15 payments altogether have been made?

15 A loan of $81 000 is to be repaid by 10 equal annual instalments of principal and interest which is at the rate of 5 per cent per annum.
   a   What is the annual instalment?
   b   Draw up a schedule showing the amount of principal and the amount of interest contained in each instalment, and the principal still outstanding after each payment.
   c   As a check, calculate, independently, the amount outstanding after the fourth and seventh payments.

16 What amount payable in 10 years time would be equivalent to $500 payable in five years time plus $1000 payable in 15 years time? (Assume 6 per cent per annum compound interest.)

17 A person owes $1000 payable in three years time and $1000 payable in 13 years time, and would like to settle the debt by making a $2000 payment. If interest is
5 per cent per annum compound, when should the payment be made?

18 A $200 refrigerator is sold 'on easy terms'. These terms are:
a   no deposit
b   simple interest of 10 per cent
c   monthly repayments over two years.
    Given such terms, what is the true rate of compound interest which the customer is paying?

PROBLEMS FOR DISCUSSION AND ANALYSIS

1   What is the present value of an annuity with payments of $1000 per year for five years if money is worth 12 per cent per annum compounded quarterly?

2   A car is priced at $27 000 cash, or a $6000 deposit and six two-monthly payments of $4200. What is the implied interest rate in the hire-purchase option?

3   A car yard is offering special terms of no repayments for two years. A down payment of $5000 is required, followed by six half-yearly payments of $2000 starting at the end of two years. If the cash value of the car is $11 000, what is the implied interest rate? (*Note:* interest is calculated from date of purchase.)

4   Bloggs Ltd has to replace its widget-making machine in five years. The company estimates the new machine will cost $30 000. It wishes to provide for this machine by putting aside a regular annual amount in a reserve. Natbank has offered the company two options:
a   Deposit five equal amounts at the beginning of each year to earn 5 per cent compound interest.
b   Deposit five equal amounts at the beginning of each year to earn an increasing compound interest rate of 2.5 per cent for the first year and increasing by 1 per cent each year after that.
    Which option allows the company to put the least annual amount into a reserve, and what is that annual amount?

5   The Fidget Co. is proposing to spend $91 280 on a seven-year project whose estimated net cash flows are $20 000 for each of the seven years.
a   Calculate the net present value using a rate of 15 per cent (use the table of present values in Appendix 2).
b   Based on the analysis prepared in (a), is the rate of return:
    i   more than 15 per cent
    ii 15 per cent
    iii less than 15 per cent?
        Explain.
c   Calculate the internal rate of return.

6   The following details are available for three projects:

Cash flow ($)

Project	Year 0 ($)	Year 1 ($)	Year 2 ($)	Year 3 ($)	Year 4 ($)	Year 5 ($)
1	−5 000	500	500	500	500	5 500
2	−5 000	1 319	1 319	1 319	1 319	1 319
3	−5 000	–	–	–	–	8 053

a   Calculate the net present value of each of these projects, and then rank them. Use discount rates of 5, 10 and 15 per cent.
b   Calculate the internal rate of return for each of the projects and then rank them.

7   Use the following data:

Project cost	$20 000
Estimated life	5 years
Estimated salvage value	$2 000
Annual net cash inflow	$6 000
Required rate of return	10%

to calculate:
a   the accounting rate of return
b   the payback period
c   the internal rate of return
d   the net present value.
e   How would your answers differ if the net cash inflows were as shown below?

	$
Year 1	6 000
Year 2	7 000
Year 3	12 000
Year 4	3 000
Year 5	10 000

8   AKP Fashion Designers are considering two investment projects. The estimated net cash flows from each project are as follows:

Year	Plant expansion ($)	Retail store expansion ($)
1	100 000	150 000
2	130 000	120 000
3	150 000	110 000
4	130 000	110 000
5	170 000	190 000
Total	680 000	680 000

Each project requires an investment of $380 000. A rate of 20 per cent has been selected for the net present value analysis.

Required

a   Compute the following for each project:
   i   cash payback period
   ii   net present value.
b   Prepare a brief report advising management on the relative merits of each of the two projects.

9   Jenny and Bill Smith wish to buy a property costing $100 000. They have a $20 000 deposit. Bankpac offers them the following alternatives:
a   a fixed interest rate of 7.5 per cent with the interest being charged on the first day of the month each year, commencing with the first day of the loan
b   a fixed interest rate of 8.5 per cent with the interest being charged from the last day of each month. The loan is to commence from the first day of the month.
   If Jenny and Bill want to pay off their loan in 10 years, which loan requires the least outlay of money? Show workings.

10   Silver Corporation is evaluating five investment opportunities. The company's cost of capital is 15 per cent. No investment is accepted if the payback period is greater than three years. The company will only accept a maximum of two investment projects. The following investments are being considered.

Investment	Initial cost ($)	Expected returns ($)
A	130 000	40 000 per year for five years
B	60 000	30 000 per year for six years
C	40 000	12 000 per year for 10 years
D	25 000	9 000 per year for six years
E	15 000	4 500 per year for three years

Required

a   Which projects would be accepted using the NPV and payback methods to screen investments?
b   Discuss the benefits of using the payback method together with NPV or IRR.

Note to instructors: *The following problems are considered more suitable for use in MBA courses. However, undergraduate courses may also find them useful.*

11   Reflex Ltd is considering the purchase of a new punch machine to produce coins. The machine would cost $11 000 cash. A service maintenance contract on the machine is essential and would cost an extra $100 per month. The expected life of the machine is four years and the expected salvage value is $200. The new machine will save $350 per month in labour costs and $40 per month in materials costs. The old machine would be sold for its book value of $500. The cost of capital for Reflex is 15 per cent. The tax rate is 40 per cent, which means depreciation tax savings of $1080 each year.

Required

a   Calculate:
   i   the payback period
   ii   the net present value.

12   The Porter Group is considering allocating a limited amount of capital investment funds among four proposals. The amount of proposed investment, estimated income from operations, and net cash flow for each proposal are as follows:

	Investment ($)	Year	Income from operations ($)	Net cash flow ($)
Proposal A:	600 000	1	40 000	160 000
		2	40 000	160 000
		3	40 000	160 000
		4	0	120 000
		5	0	120 000
Proposal B:	520 000	1	96 000	200 000
		2	56 000	160 000
		3	56 000	160 000
		4	56 000	160 000
		5	48 000	152 000
Proposal C:	180 000	1	44 000	80 000
		2	24 000	60 000
		3	24 000	60 000
		4	24 000	60 000
		5	22 500	58 500
Proposal D:	250 000	1	50 000	100 000
		2	50 000	100 000
		3	(10 000)	40 000
		4	(10 000)	40 000
		5	(10 000)	40 000

The company's capital rationing policy requires a maximum cash payback period of three years. In addition, a minimum average accounting rate of return of 10 per cent is required on all projects. If the preceding standards are met, the net present value method and present value indexes (= total present value of net cash flows divided by amount to be invested) are used to rank the remaining proposals.

Required

a   Calculate the cash payback period for each of the four proposals.

b   Assuming straight-line depreciation on the investments, and no estimated residual value; calculate the average accounting rate of return for each of the four proposals. Round to one decimal point.

c   Using the following format, summarise the results of your calculations in (a) and (b). Indicate which proposals should be accepted for further analysis and which should be rejected.

Proposal	Cash payback period	Average accounting rate of return	Accept/Reject
A			
B			
C			
D			

d   For the proposals accepted for further analysis in (c), calculate the net present value. Use a rate of 10 per cent. Round to the nearest dollar.

e   Calculate the present value index (PVI) for each of the proposals in (d). Round to two decimals points (PVI = total present value of net cash flows divided by amount to be invested).

f   Rank the proposals from the most attractive to the least attractive, based on the present values of net cash flows calculated in (d).

g   Rank the proposals from the most attractive to the least attractive, based on the present value indexes calculated in (e).

h   Based upon the analyses, comment on the relative attractiveness of the proposals ranked in (f) and (g).

(Adapted from C.S. Warren, J.M. Reeve and P.E. Fess, *Accounting*, 20th edn, South-Western, Mason, Ohio, 2002, Problem 24-6A, p. 1009).

ETHICS CASE STUDY

Newark Ltd is planning to build a new manufacturing plant. Jenny Frame is the person appointed to head the task force responsible for preparing an analysis of the options available to Newark. Frame's team completes a detailed analysis of three possible types of manufacturing facilities:

* *option 1.* This is the lowest cost option but it has a higher risk of employee injuries and a greater risk of environmental damage from toxic gases arising from poor venting

* *option 2.* This has a higher cost than option 1 but reduces the risk of injury to employees. It still has the potential for environmental damage

* *option 3.* This is the highest cost option but provides the greatest safety to workers and offers the least danger to the environment.

Jenny submits the results of the analysis to her boss and he thanks her for the fantastic job that she and her team have done. He will make special mention of her efforts in her job evaluation report this year.

Jenny is pleased with her boss's response, but a week later she is disturbed after coming across a copy of a report from her boss to the board. The report focuses on the costs associated with each option and does not mention the risks to the workers and the environment.

Jenny is unsure of what she should do. She could speak to her boss and risk losing the favourable job evaluation (or even her job). Alternatively, she could pretend she never saw the report. She is uncertain as to where her responsibilities end. She is, however, also worried about how she would feel if someone were to be hurt as a result of the company selecting option 1.

Discuss Jenny's responsibilities, after you have identified them. Suggest a possible course of action.

ANSWERS TO REVIEW EXERCISES

1   Simple interest $= \$1\ 245 \times 5.6\% \times \frac{198}{35}$

$= \$37.82$

2   We are looking for a future value factor of 2 ($200/$100) at 6 per cent in Table 1 of Appendix 2.

At different years we see:

For life = 11, factor = 1.89829

For life = 12, factor = 2.01219

Therefore, it is close to 12 years (11 years 11 months) before an annuity accumulates from $100 to $200.

3   Amount borrowed = $5000
From Table 4, Appendix 2, the present value (PV) of $1 per annum for 10 years at 7 per cent = 7.0235
PV of $1/(7.0235) per annum for 10 years at 7 per cent = $1
PV of $5000/7.0235 per annum for 10 years at 7 per cent = $5000
Therefore, an amount of $711.90 (= $5000/7.0235 for 10 years at 7 per cent) would repay the loan.

4   a   IRR

$$OC = NCF \times PVF\ (IRR, n)$$
$$78\ 345 = 15\ 250 \times PVF\ (IRR, 8)$$
$$5.13737 = PVF\ (IRR, 8)$$

from Appendix 2, Table 4, IRR is approximately 11 per cent.

b   NPV

$$NPV = -OC + NCF \times PVF\ (8,11)$$
$$NPV = -78\ 345 + 15\ 250 \times 5.13737 \text{ (Table 4, Appendix 2)}$$
$$= 0$$

c   Pay back

$$NCF = \frac{\text{Initial investment}}{}$$
$$= \frac{78\ 345}{15\ 250}$$
$$= 5.137 \text{ years}$$

5   a   IRR

$$OC = NCF \times PVF\ (IRR, n)$$
$$25\ 093 = 5\ 000 \times PVF\ (IRR, 10)$$
$$5.0186 = PVF\ (IRR, 10)$$

From Table 4, Appendix 2, IRR = 15 per cent.

b   NPV

$$NPV = -OC + NCF \times PVF\ (10,10)$$
$$NPV = -25\ 093 + 5\ 000 \times 6.1445 \text{ (Table 4, Appendix 2)}$$
$$= \$5\ 629.50$$

c   Pay back

$$NCF = \frac{\text{Initial investment}}{}$$
$$= \frac{25\ 093}{5000}$$
$$= 5.0186 \text{ years}$$

17

LEARNING OBJECTIVES

At the end of this chapter, you should be able to:

1   explain that attaching costs to a product is a problem for multi-product firms

2   explain the cost assignment process

3   explain the difference between direct and indirect costs

4   identify what is meant by product and period costs

5   identify the stages that are involved in determining the allocation of overheads to products

6   explain what is meant by predetermined overhead absorption rates

7   explain the difference between functional-based and activity-based costing methods

8   explain what is meant by the absorption-costing and variable-costing methods

9   explain the effect on inventory and net profit of using either absorption- or variable-costing methods.

Introduction

The income statement summarises all the expenses and income of an entity over a defined period. While this information is extremely useful in determining the overall profitability of the organisation, there is also a need to determine the costs and profitability of individual products, services, departments and various other cost objects. The issue of cost allocation is examined in this chapter. How are the various costs of a business allocated to its products or services? While we focus on the allocation of costs to products in this chapter, the same principles can be applied to services. We look at the allocation of both the direct and indirect costs using functional-based and activity-based costing systems. Finally, we examine the use of absorption-costing and variable-costing methods, and the impact of these methods on valuing inventory and measuring net profit.

Management's need for information about costs

Management needs information about costs for the following purposes:

- ## Control costs
  Actual product costs are compared with planned costs. If the actual costs deviate from the plan, management may need to take corrective action so that their predetermined targets are met in the future.

- ## Aid planning
  Past product costs are a useful base for estimating future product costs in the planning process. But when using past costs for this purpose, management must be careful to take account of any potential changes in the level of costs in the future, due to inflation, scarcity and so on.

- ## Value inventories
  Product costs need to be determined so that the value of products which are complete (finished goods) and products which are partially complete (work in progress) can be established at the end of each accounting period for inclusion in the balance sheet and the income statement.

- ## Aid the setting of selling prices
  The cost of products influences the setting of prices. From a marketing viewpoint it can be argued that the price is determined through market forces, that is, from consideration of what the market can bear. However, in a number of situations, particularly where there is little or no competition, prices are often set with reference to the cost.

- ## Ascertain the relative profitability of products
  In times of scarce resources, when a firm is constrained as to its level of output, it is likely that management will favour selling only its most profitable products. In these circumstances, knowledge of product costs is essential.

Costing in multi-product firms

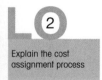

LO 1

Explain that attaching costs to a product is a problem for multi-product firms

When firms manufacture only one product, the process of product costing is relatively straightforward. All the costs of the business are directly attributable to the single product that is produced. The complexity with product costing occurs when an organisation produces more than one product. In multi-product firms, management is confronted with two main problems. First, it is necessary to set up a system to account for costs that can be directly attributed to individual products; these costs are referred to as direct costs. The second problem, which is more complicated, is to account for costs that are not directly attributed to any one product. There are two terms in accounting terminology for these types of costs: 'indirect costs' or 'overhead costs'.

The assignment of costs is an important part of the management accounting system and is discussed in the next section.

Cost assignment process

LO 2

Explain the cost assignment process

In Chapters 1 to 14 we dealt with financial accounting and the preparation of financial statements. The financial accounting system collects information to assist with the preparation of these statements. Management accounting is very much concerned with the collection of cost information and the assignment of such costs to cost objects. Accordingly, the management accounting system assists managers when they are allocating the costs of a business to various cost objects and when they are making the types of decisions outlined above. The more accurate the cost assignment process, the better the decisions that management will make about selling prices – and product mix for multi-product firms. In addition, the better the choices about prices and product mix, the higher the profits.

In Chapters 1 to 14 we examined financial accounting where it is important to classify costs as either expired (expenses) or unexpired (assets).

A cost object can be a product, service, customer, process or any other object about which management requires cost information. For example, Toyota allocates costs to the different models of cars, Westpac may allocate costs to categories of customers and a not-for-profit entity, such as the Salvation Army, may allocate costs to the various activities in which it is involved. An activity is a basic unit of work such as billing a customer, paying an invoice or approving a loan. An activity describes the process of doing something and so it always includes an action verb followed by a noun; for example, 'setting up machinery' where 'setting up' is the action verb and 'machinery' is the noun or name.

KEY CONCEPT 17.1

COST OBJECT

A cost object can be a product, service, customer, process, activity or any object for which costs are measured and assigned.

KEY CONCEPT 17.2

ACTIVITY

An activity is a cost object and involves an action verb and an object. It is the doing of something such as invoicing a customer or setting up equipment ready for production.

How does a business allocate costs to a cost object? Some costs can be easily allocated to a cost object; for example, the cost of an engine for a car. Other costs are much more difficult to allocate; for example, the electricity costs of the factory where the cars are produced. Costs are either directly or indirectly related to a cost object. Direct costs are those costs that can be easily traced to a cost object with a high degree of accuracy. Indirect costs are those that cannot be so easily traced to a cost object or where the costs of doing this outweigh any benefits to be derived. The higher the proportion of costs that can be traced and attached to a cost object, the greater the accuracy of the cost assignment process. It is possible for the same cost to be direct for one cost object and indirect for another cost object. For example, if the cost object is a factory, then electricity is a direct cost for the factory, but if the cost object is the cars produced in the factory, then the electricity is an indirect cost.

3

Explain the difference between direct and indirect costs

KEY CONCEPT 17.3

DIRECT AND INDIRECT COSTS

A direct cost is one that is easily traceable, and thus attributable, to a cost object. Indirect costs (also known as overhead costs) are those that cannot be easily and conveniently identified with a particular cost object.

The allocation of direct costs to a cost object is relatively straightforward, provided the cost accounting system is adequate to provide the necessary information. The most common direct costs are direct labour and direct material costs in a manufacturing business. These costs are sometimes referred to as *prime costs*. In practice, there are a number of different types of costing systems that are contingent on the type of technology used in the production process and the type of product being produced. Traditionally, the systems are classified into two categories: job costing and process costing.

At this stage of your studies it is not necessary to examine these two systems in detail, but a brief description will be useful. Job-costing systems are used when the costs of each unit of production, or a batch of units, can be identified at any time in the manufacturing cycle. For example, job costing is relevant for cars and aircraft. In contrast, in a system of process costing, individual products cannot be identified until the manufacturing process is complete. A number of similar products are manufactured at the same time within the process. Costs are accumulated on a process or departmental basis and are then divided by the number of units produced to obtain an average unit cost. In such cases, product costs represent the average unit costs of production. Examples of areas where process costing applies include the production of petroleum and chemicals.

In this chapter we focus on the allocation of indirect costs to a cost object. Indirect costs are also described as overheads. We examine two different systems that deal with the allocation of overheads to cost objects. The *functional-based costing* (FBC) system is the more common method, while the *activity-based costing* (ABC) system is a more recently developed system and is becoming more popular as the proportion of indirect costs compared to direct costs increases.

Before we examine these two approaches it should be stressed that the need to identify costs and revenues is not restricted to manufactured products but extends to services provided and to organisations that are purely service-oriented. An insurance broker, for example, needs to identify the costs of selling different types of policies, such as car insurance and life assurance, in order to determine the profitability of the varying policies that are sold. This information will influence what policies are sold and the mix of policies. A bank also needs to determine the costs of its various products just like a manufacturer, but for the purposes of our analysis we will focus on manufacturing organisations.

Before we begin, however, study Note 3 in Woodside's financial report (see Appendix 1). This note reports the results of the four business segments of Woodside. The North West Shelf business unit is by far the largest. Its revenue increased by approximately $272 million from 2004 to 2005, and profit for the business unit increased by almost $350 million. The Australian business unit increased revenue by about $19.5 million, but profit declined by a massive $562 million. The African business unit had a decline in revenue of about $6 million and the loss increased by almost $12 million. The Group and Unallocated unit only reports other income and not revenue, and its result for the period is an increase in the loss of about $52 million. The definition of each business unit is provided at the bottom of Note 3.

How did the North West Shelf unit manage to increase profit by $350 million on a revenue increase of only $272 million? What is the reason for the result in the Australian business unit? An inspection of the components for the Australian business unit reveals a decline of $484 million of other income by 2005. This, combined with a $57 million increase in the petroleum resource rent tax, explains most of the $562 million decline in profit for this business unit. It is important that you appreciate the usefulness of collecting costs and revenues by segments so that management can initiate policy reviews and implement strategies to control costs.

Costing methods

In the previous section we described the cost assignment process. In a manufacturing organisation, the costs incurred in producing and selling a product consist of production costs and other costs such as administration, selling and distribution expenses. The production costs are either direct or indirect costs. The costs to be included in a cost object for internal management accounting purposes will depend on the wishes of management. The two most common cost methods are described as absorption costing (sometimes called full costing) and variable costing (sometimes called direct costing). Absorption costing allocates all the direct and indirect costs of production to a product while variable costing only allocates the variable costs of production to a product. For external reporting purposes, absorption costing must be used to comply with accounting standards, as discussed in Chapter 7, but for internal purposes either method can be used. We now examine in more detail the absorption-costing method. We will return to the variable-costing method later in this chapter when we illustrate the impact of both methods on inventory valuation and profit measurement.

Review exercise 1
Define direct and indirect costs.

Absorption costing

The costs to be included under the absorption-costing method might include all costs or just some, such as the production costs. The definition of absorption costing that is adopted will depend upon the purpose for which products are being costed, and the preferences of management. As has already been emphasised, for management purposes, accounting information is not regulated by any external forces, such as the law or accounting standards set by the professional accounting bodies. Management is free to adopt definitions and use accounting data at its discretion to meet the organisation's requirements.

For the purposes of our analysis, we will adopt the definition of absorption costing that includes only production costs. This is the definition of absorption costing conventionally used for the purpose of valuing finished inventories and work in progress, as was discussed in Chapter 7. In the context of inventory valuation, it is argued that it is only appropriate to include those costs that are incurred prior to the sale of the inventory. Normally, these costs will only consist of those related to production.

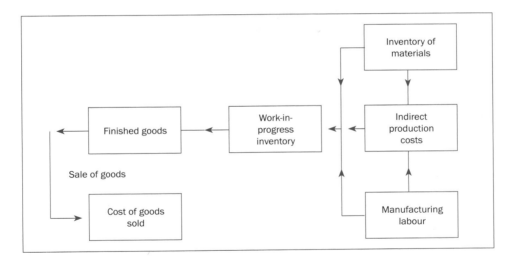

Figure 17.1 The flow of costs in a manufacturing organisation under the absorption-costing approach

Figure 17.1 shows the flow of costs associated with a manufacturing organisation when the absorption-costing method is adopted, where only those costs associated with production – whether they are direct or indirect costs – are absorbed into the product. Materials and labour are classified here as both direct and indirect costs. For example, in the case of manufacturing labour, the arrows point both to work in progress (that is, directly into the production process, thereby indicating that they are a direct cost) and to indirect production costs (indicating they are an indirect cost). The classification of these costs into direct and indirect, not surprisingly, will depend upon whether the cost can be easily identified directly with products or not.

KEY CONCEPT 17.4

ABSORPTION COSTING

Absorption costing allocates the direct and indirect costs of production to the cost object.

KEY CONCEPT 17.5

VARIABLE COSTING

Variable costing allocates only the variable costs of production to the cost object. A cost is variable if it changes in response to changes in the level of activities.

Sometimes it is more convenient to classify a cost as indirect, even though it is possible to identify it directly with a product. Consider, for example, the labour costs of a supervisor who is responsible for a group of employees working on various products. An elaborate system would have to be set up to record the time spent supervising each employee and then to relate this time (and thus costs) to particular products. In this case it may be considered more cost-effective and convenient simply to classify supervision costs as indirect.

An example of an indirect material cost is the cost of machine lubricant. Indirect costs, other than materials and labour, are typically costs that relate to heating, lighting, training and the depreciation of machinery and premises (if owned). All direct and indirect production costs are 'absorbed' into the products being produced, so that, at any point in time, the value of work in progress and finished goods consists of materials, labour and indirect costs. The cost of goods sold is matched with the revenue from the sales of these goods in the income statement. When absorption costing is applied, as in our definition, the cost of goods sold consists of both direct and indirect production costs, as shown in Figure 17.1.

PRODUCT AND PERIOD COSTS

Identify what is meant by product and period costs

Product costs include all the costs that are attached to a product; the costs that are included depend on whether the entity uses an absorption-costing or variable-costing approach. While a car is obviously a product for a car manufacturer, a variable rate home loan is also a product for a bank. The concept of a product is not restricted to a manufacturing firm. Any costs not categorised as product costs are normally classified as period costs. This means such costs are expensed to the income statement in the period they are incurred. Product costs are recognised as an expense in the income statement only when the product is sold.

Prior to the sale, the cost of products is shown as an asset (either as work in progress or finished goods) in the balance sheet, thereby indicating that these items have some future benefit to the business. The principle adopted here is the concept of accruals. Period costs, in contrast, are seen as costs that relate to the current period in question. They are therefore viewed as costs that cannot justifiably be carried forward to future periods because they do not represent future benefits, or the future benefits are so uncertain as to defy measurement. Thus, period costs are recognised in the income statement in the accounting period when they are incurred. The distinction between product and period is important in the valuation of inventory and the determination of profit.

We examine the effect of this categorisation of costs in further detail later in this chapter, when we analyse the differences between the variable-costing and absorption-costing methods.

Review exercise 2
Explain the difference between product and period costs.

Review exercise 3
Explain what is meant by the term 'absorption costing'.

ABSORBING OVERHEADS

We have already mentioned that a system has to be devised to trace costs to individual products. This process is relatively straightforward for direct costs since they can be identified precisely with a particular product. For example, when materials are obtained from inventory, their cost is recorded against the product and accounted for as a cost to the product. The complexity arises when we have to share out indirect costs to products. The objective is to share them out equitably. The method adopted should therefore take into account the amount of indirect services used to support the manufacture/development of products. The term used for the process of sharing out indirect costs to products is 'absorption of overheads'. As we have already indicated, the two main systems used to allocate the indirect costs to products are the functional-based and activity-based systems.

LO 5

Identify the stages that are involved in determining the allocation of overheads to products

Functional-based costing systems

A functional-based cost (FBC) accounting system classifies all costs as either variable or fixed in relation to changes in the volume or units produced. Variable costs are those that vary with usage or activity while fixed costs do not. We examine this aspect of cost behaviour in Chapter 18. Under an FBC system, the main drivers used to assign the overhead costs to products are volume-based, such as direct labour hours or machine hours. We now illustrate the process of allocating overhead costs in a functional-based system. Much of the process described here also applies in the activity-based (ABC) system which we describe later in this chapter.

Production overhead costs are incurred by cost centres that support the production activity. A 'goods inwards' department, whose function it is to ensure that goods and materials received from suppliers are of the standard and quantity ordered, is a typical example of a service cost centre in a manufacturing organisation. The overhead costs of both the production and service cost centres must be absorbed into the product to establish the full cost of products.

At this stage it is appropriate to summarise the stages in the absorption of overheads. Figure 17.2 shows the three stages in this process, which we go on to examine in detail.

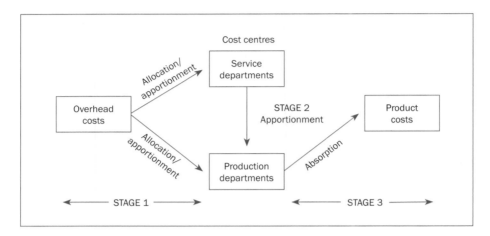

Figure 17.2 Stages in the absorption of overheads

Stage 1

The first stage in the absorption of overhead costs is to identify and collect overhead costs associated with both the production and service cost centres. Some of these costs can be relatively easily allocated to particular cost centres. The word 'allocated', in the context of product costing, means that the cost can be directly traced to a cost centre. For example, in a drawing office that has been classified as a service cost centre because it provides a service to a number of production cost centres, the salaries of draughtsmen and women can be identified with the centre by recording the salary payment from the payroll against the cost centre. In contrast, the cost of heating and lighting consumed by the drawing office may not be so easy to establish. The cost of heating and lighting is probably billed for the whole building, in which the drawing office is only one of many occupant cost centres. In such cases, because the cost is difficult, if not impossible, to identify accurately with any one cost centre, a method of apportioning these costs on a fair and equitable basis must be adopted.

The term 'apportioning' describes the sharing out of overhead costs that cannot be directly traced to a cost centre. A reasonable method of apportioning heat and lighting costs, under a functional-based system, that relate to the benefits (that is, heating and lighting) enjoyed by the drawing office is on the basis of the area that the office occupies. For example, if the total cost of heating and lighting is $15 000 and the area used by the drawing office, measured in square metres, is 6000 out of the total area of the building of 30 000 square metres, the cost apportioned to the drawing office would be $15 000 × 6000 ÷ 30 000 = $3000.

Stage 2

When all the overhead costs – allocated and apportioned – have been established for each service cost centre, it is then necessary to charge these costs to the production cost centres. Once again, some method of apportionment has to be used. The reason for this is that the service cost centres usually service several production cost centres and the costs of the service are unlikely to be easily identified with any one of them. Using the example of the drawing office again, it is likely that the service supplied by this office spreads over a number of production cost centres and it will be impractical to identify accurately the cost of this service with production departments. In these circumstances, a method of apportionment has to be adopted that fairly charges the service cost to the production cost centres. Before we move to stage 3 of the process of absorbing overhead costs into products, we will consider an example that illustrates the allocation and apportionment of costs to production cost centres.

Example 17.1: Charging costs to production cost centres

Table 17.1 Allocation and apportionment of the costs of one year

Item	Basis	Total amount	Production cost centres		Service cost centres	
			A	B	X	Y
		$000	$000	$000	$000	$000
Indirect materials	Allocated	20	8	4	5	3
Indirect labour	Allocated	30	14	6	4	6
Electricity	Machine hours	22	10	12	–	–
Rent and rates	Area	10	2	5	2	1
Insurance	Book value	8	3	2	3	–
Total overheads		90	37	29	14	10
Service X to production	Number of employees		5	9	(14)	
Service Y to production	Direct labour hours		8	2		(10)
Total overheads		90	50	40	–	–
Data used for apportioning overheads						
Item	*Quantity*					
Machine hours	110 000		50 000	60 000	–	–
Area	3 000 sq. m		600	1 500	600	300
Book value of fixed assets	$96 000		$36	$24	$36	–
No. of employees	7 000		2 500	4 500		
Direct labour hours	20 000		16 000	4 000	–	–

This example demonstrates the allocation and apportionment of overhead costs to production cost centres, as shown in Table 17.1 above. Costs for various overhead 'items' are first identified and shown under 'total amount'. The costs are then allocated or apportioned to production and service cost centres. In the case of indirect labour and materials, the costs are allocated to these cost centres because they can be directly identified with them. With reference to Table 17.1, of the total amount of indirect materials consumed ($20 000), $8000 has been directly identified with production cost centre A. In contrast, the costs related to power, rent and rates, and insurance cannot be directly identified with the cost centres. Therefore, they are apportioned to the centres, using some equitable basis reflecting the benefits the centres have enjoyed. In the case of the cost of power, for example, the number of machine hours consumed by the cost centres is considered an equitable basis for apportionment. If you refer to the information relating to the use of machine hours in Table 17.1, you will notice that machinery was used only in the two production cost centres. Of the total of 110 000 machine hours, 50 000 were consumed by production cost centre A and 60 000 hours by cost centre B. The cost of electricity for each of these centres is then calculated with reference to the consumption by the two departments as follows:

	$
Production cost centre	
A 50 000 hours ÷ 110 000 hours × $22 000 =	10 000
B 60 000 hours ÷ 110 000 hours × $22 000 =	12 000
Total cost of electricity	22 000

Therefore, the apportioned charge to production cost centre A is $10 000 and to B is $12 000.

Similar calculations, using different assumptions, are made to establish the apportioned charge to the cost centres for rent and rates, and insurance.

After allocating and apportioning the overheads to the production and service cost centres, the next stage is to apportion the service centre costs to the production cost centres. The basis of apportionment chosen in the case of service cost centre X is the number of employees in each production cost centre. The number of direct labour hours worked by the employees in the production cost centres is the basis of apportionment used for service centre Y. As previously mentioned, the basis of apportionment should reflect the benefits enjoyed by the consuming production cost centres. For example, it might be that service cost centre X is the works canteen. If so, the number of employees in each production cost centre might be a reasonable basis for calculating the amount of use made of this facility by each of the two production cost centres. The calculation of the apportioned charge to the production cost centres is very similar to the calculation for apportioning electricity costs. Thus, in the case of service cost centre X, the calculation will be as follows:

	$
Production cost centre	
A (2500 ÷ 7000) × $14 000 =	5 000
B (4500 ÷ 7000) × $14 000 =	9 000
Total cost of service cost centre X	14 000

It can be seen that the whole of the costs of service centre X are now apportioned to the two production cost centres. Similar calculations will be made to apportion the cost of service cost centre Y to the two production cost centres. Finally, the overhead costs are aggregated for each of the two production cost centres, as can be seen in the final 'Total overheads' row of Table 17.1.

Stage 3

As has been mentioned, the production cost centres are where the manufacturing activity takes place. Units of products physically pass through these cost centres in the course of the manufacturing cycle. As the products pass through the centre, a proportion of the overhead cost is charged to the product (or absorbed into the product). The objective here is to charge overheads to units of production on some equitable basis. Normally, an absorption rate is used for this purpose. The absorption rate is determined by the following formula.

$$\frac{\text{total overheads of a production cost centre}}{\text{level of activity}}$$

We discussed how the numerator in this formula is determined in stage 2 above. The denominator, the activity level, is chosen with reference to the types of products passing through the production cost centres and the main activities of these centres. If, for example, the particular products passing through the centre are homogeneous – that is, similar in construction – the appropriate activity to be chosen is likely to be the number of units worked on in the production centre. In these circumstances, the activity, units of production, should represent an equitable basis for absorbing the overheads because the benefits enjoyed by each unit from the expenditure of overheads should be equal or very similar. In Example 17.1, if it was estimated that 10 000 units were to be worked on in the year by production cost centre A, and assuming the products were homogeneous, the absorption rate would be $50 000 ÷ 10 000 units = $5 per unit. This rate would then be applied to each unit of production worked on in the cost centre and would represent a reasonable share of the overhead cost appropriate to each product.

In contrast, if the products are not homogeneous it is necessary to choose an activity measure that corresponds more closely with the overhead expenditure of each production cost centre. If, for example, overhead expenditure of a production cost centre is mainly incurred in supporting the direct labour function, the measure chosen should be based on this activity. In these circumstances, the number of direct hours would be a suitable measure.

In practice, in a functional-based cost management system, the most common activity measures used to absorb overheads into product costs are:

- direct labour hours
- direct labour costs
- machine hours
- cost of materials.

The following shows the calculation of the absorption rate with reference to the data given in Example 17.1 for production cost centre A, assuming that the number of machine hours is the appropriate activity measure.

$$\frac{\text{total overheads of cost centre A}}{\text{level of activity}} = \frac{\$50\ 000}{50\ 000\ \text{machine hours}}$$

Therefore, the absorption rate is $1 per machine hour. This rate is applied to units of product passing through cost centre A. For example, if one of the products passing through cost centre A uses up 40 machine hours in the manufacturing process, the charge to the product will be:

$$40\ \text{hours} \times \$1\ \text{per machine hour} = \$40$$

PREDETERMINED OVERHEAD ABSORPTION RATES

In practice, overhead absorption rates are normally determined once a year, before the actual cost is incurred. Thus, the two elements of the above formula will be estimates. That is, the total overheads of each production cost centre and the level of activity chosen are based on estimates rather than on actual costs. The term 'normal costing' refers to the method whereby the cost of a product is determined using the actual costs for direct costs and a predetermined rate for the allocation of indirect costs.

There are two main reasons why estimates are used rather than actual costs. First, some overhead costs are not known until some months after they have been incurred. For example, electricity costs are normally billed to consumers at the end of each three months. Therefore, an organisation would have to wait three months before it could determine this overhead cost, and only then could it charge the cost to products that have already been manufactured and sold. Clearly, such a delay in determining costs would mean that management would receive out-of-date information. Second, some overhead costs, such as heating costs, are seasonal. Seasonal variations can distort the costing of products. For example, if a product is manufactured in summer, the cost of heating absorbed into the product cost is likely to be zero, whereas if the product was manufactured in winter, the cost would include a charge for heating. Thus, the cost of a product can depend upon when it was produced. It can be argued that such circumstances distort the costing of products, and a firm would have to set up complex costing systems to reflect seasonal variations.

The use of estimates in determining the overhead absorption rate creates problems. Often, the actual overheads incurred during a period are not equal to the overheads that have been absorbed into product costs because the absorption rate is based on estimates. The amount of overheads absorbed during a period will be the same as the cost actually incurred only if the actual overhead cost of the production cost centre is equal to the estimated cost (the numerator in the formula) and the actual level of activity is equal to the estimated activity level (the denominator in the formula). Normally, any difference between the total overheads absorbed and the actual overheads incurred during a period is directly charged to the income statement for that period. These differences in costs are not allocated or apportioned to products, but are classified as a period cost. It is generally seen as impractical and too costly to identify these differences for individual products, but large differences might need to be investigated.

LO 6

Explain what is meant by predetermined overhead absorption rates

KEY CONCEPT 17.6

NORMAL COSTING

Normal costing is where the cost of a cost object is determined using the actual costs for direct costs and a predetermined rate for the allocation of indirect costs.

Example 17.2 illustrates the process of absorbing overheads into units of production where the actual overhead cost is different from the original estimates on which the absorption rate was based.

Example 17.2: Absorbing differences in overhead costs

The following are estimates relating to the manufacture of a number of similar products for the forthcoming year 20X7:

Estimated units to be produced during the year	100 000
Estimated overhead cost during the year	$150 000

Therefore, the overhead absorption rate is calculated thus:

$$\frac{\$150\ 000}{100\ 000\ \text{units}} = \$1.50\ \text{per unit}$$

The actual number of units produced in 20X7 was 110 000; thus, the charge to products passing through the cost centre is 110 000 units × $1.50 (the absorption rate) = $165 000.

However, the overheads actually incurred during 20X7 were $176 000. Thus, the difference between actual overhead costs and what was absorbed during the year is $176 000 – $165 000 = $11 000. This $11 000 is charged to the income statement as 'under-recovery of overhead' during the year; it is classified as a period cost because it is not identified with any of the units of production produced during the year.

In this example, the cost and the activity level were underestimated during the year. Differences between estimates and actual costs and activity levels often occur in practice, because it is very difficult to make accurate estimates.

Case study 17.1 illustrates a number of the procedures and principles that we have discussed regarding the absorption of overheads in a functional-based cost management accounting system.

CASE STUDY 17.1

SARICK MACHINES LTD

Sarick Machines Ltd has organised its production cost centres by the types of machines it uses to manufacture its products. There are four production cost centres, which are known by the machine type: 101, 201, 301 and 401. The company wishes to establish an overhead absorption rate for each of these cost centres, based on machine hours. The company also wishes to determine the cost per unit of one of its products, Aztec.

The management of the company has made the following estimates for the forthcoming year 20X7.

	$	$
Indirect materials		
Machine type 101	300	
Machine type 201	600	

	$	$
Machine type 301	700	
Machine type 401	400	2 000
Maintenance costs		
Machine type 101	700	
Machine type 201	800	
Machine type 301	1 200	
Machine type 401	900	3 600
Other overhead expenses		
Electricity		1 400
Rent and rates		3 200
Heat and lighting		800
Insurance of buildings		800
Insurance of machinery		1 000
Depreciation of machinery		10 000
Supervision		4 800
Total overheads		27 600

Management provides the following relevant information, based on estimates.

Machine type	Effective horsepower	Area occupied m²	Book value of machinery $	Working hours
101	10	400	5 000	2 000
201	15	300	7 500	1 000
301	45	800	22 500	3 000
401	30	500	15 000	2 000
	100	2 000	50 000	8 000

To determine the machine hour rate, we must first allocate costs that can be directly identified with the four cost centres; that is, indirect materials and maintenance costs. We then need to apportion those overheads that cannot be directly identified with a cost centre – that is, those described in the management estimates as 'other overhead expenses'. This is done by sharing out these overheads to the cost centres based on some equitable method that reflects the use made of these resources. The following table sets out the apportioning of costs to the four cost centres. The basis of apportionment is indicated in parentheses.

Machine type	101	201	301	401
	$	$	$	$
Costs allocated				
Indirect materials	300	600	700	400
Maintenance costs	700	800	1 200	900

Machine type	101	201	301	401
Costs apportioned				
Electricity				
(effective horsepower)	140	210	630	420
Rent and rates (area)	640	480	1 280	800
Light and heating (area)	160	120	320	200
Insurance on building (area)	160	120	320	200
Insurance on machines				
(book value of machine)	100	150	450	300
Depreciation of machines				
(book value of machine)	1 000	1 500	4 500	3 000
Supervision (working hours)	1 200	600	1 800	1 200
Total overheads	4 400	4 580	11 200	7 420

The calculation of the apportioned costs to the cost centres in this case study is similar to that in Example 17.1. To illustrate it further, the calculation of the apportioned costs of rent and rates to cost centres is as follows:

Machine type	Calculation	Cost $
101	(400 sq. m ÷ 2 000 sq. m) × $3 200 =	640
201	(300 sq. m ÷ 2 000 sq. m) × $3 200 =	480
301	(800 sq. m ÷ 2 000 sq. m) × $3 200 =	1 280
401	(500 sq. m ÷ 2 000 sq. m) × $3 200 =	800
Total cost of rent and rates apportioned		3 200

The basis of apportionment for each type of overhead cost, we can assume, has been chosen because it represents a reasonable method for sharing out the cost and reflects the benefits enjoyed by the cost centre from the resource. For example, the supervision cost has been apportioned on the basis of working hours and it is likely that this basis reasonably reflects the benefits enjoyed from this resource by each cost centre.

Now that the total overheads have been collected for each of the four cost centres, we can divide these costs by the estimated working hours of each machine to obtain the absorption rate:

Machine type	Calculation	Cost $
101	$4 400 ÷ 2 000 hours =	2.20
201	$4 580 ÷ 1 000 hours =	4.58
301	$11 200 ÷ 3 000 hours =	3.73
401	$7 420 ÷ 2 000 hours =	3.71

An alternative system that could be adopted by the company would be to absorb the total overhead cost by the total estimated machine hours. In this case it would not be necessary to allocate and apportion costs to individual cost centres because the same rate would be applied to all cost centres. The overhead absorption rate would therefore be

$$\text{total costs} \div \text{total hours} = \$27\ 600 \div 8\ 000 \text{ hours}$$
$$= \$3.45 \text{ per machine hour}$$

This rate is then charged to all items of production passing through all cost centres. Although this method is appealing, because far less time is spent in calculating the overhead absorption rate, it does not take account of the resources consumed by the individual cost centres in the production process. It is, therefore, likely that such a system would distort the costing of individual products.

Turning now to the product costs of Aztec, the following information is given. A total of 2000 units were produced in the year. The direct costs incurred were:

- direct material, $870
- direct labour, $940.

The machine hours actually worked in the year, producing 2000 units of Aztec, were as follows:

Machine type	Hours
101	400
201	400
401	200

To determine the cost per unit, we first need to determine the total cost associated with the manufacture of the product. The direct costs are given above. The overhead costs to be absorbed into the product are based on the overhead absorption rate, the machine hour rate and the actual hours worked in these cost centres on the product. The total cost of product Aztec is as follows:

	$
Direct material	870
Direct labour	940
Machine type 101: 400 hours × $2.20 =	880
Machine type 201: 400 hours × $4.58 =	1 832
Machine type 401: 200 hours × $3.71 =	742
Total cost	5 264

It is now necessary to divide the total cost by the number of units produced to determine the cost per unit.

$$\$5264 \div 2000 \text{ units} = \$2.63 \text{ per unit}$$

LO 7

Explain the difference between functional-based and activity-based costing methods

Activity-based costing systems

In the functional-based cost accounting system, as shown in Case study 17.1, an overhead absorption rate is determined. This rate is calculated by dividing the overhead cost of a production department by a selected volume of activity. In Case study 17.1, the activity chosen was machine hours, and the rationale for this choice was that the overhead costs have been incurred from supporting one particular activity. With advanced manufacturing technology, overhead costs tend to be predominant, and direct cost tends to be a very small proportion of cost. For example, the manufacture of motor cars is highly mechanised and much work that was previously done by humans is now performed by robotics; therefore, the cost has shifted from direct to indirect. The majority of today's overhead costs are not necessarily incurred in direct manufacturing activities but rather as a result of transactions in the service departments where the overhead is incurred.

Activity-based costing (ABC) tries to capture this change in technology by apportioning overheads into product costs on a more realistic basis that takes account of the activity and transactions that drive the cost. The focus in ABC is on managing activities instead of costs. In an ABC system, costs are assigned to cost objects using both unit- and non-unit-based activity drivers. For example, costs could be allocated to inspecting products on the basis of the number of units (unit based) or number of inspections (activity based).

The application of ABC involves the following stages:
- *Stage 1.* Identify significant activities and assign overhead costs to each activity. This is called an 'activity cost pool'
- *Stage 2.* Identify cost drivers and allocate the cost from each activity pool to each cost object.

KEY CONCEPT 17.7

ACTIVITY COST POOL
An activity cost pool is where the costs of an activity under the ABC system are accumulated.

KEY CONCEPT 17.8

DRIVER
Drivers are factors that cause changes in the use of resources.

Thus, costs are grouped according to what drives them or causes them to increase. These cost drivers are then used as the bases upon which overhead costs are absorbed into the cost object. Remember Key concept 17.2 defines an activity as one that involves an 'action verb' and an object. It is the doing of something, such as invoicing a customer or setting up equipment ready for production. Case study 17.2 illustrates the way in which ABC is used, and contrasts this method with the functional-based method.

CASE STUDY 17.2

ONYX LTD – ABC VERSUS FBC

Onyx Ltd manufactures two products, X and Y. The manufacturing process for the two products is very similar. Information about the product data for these two products for 20X7 is provided below:

	X	Y
Units produced	5 000	7 000
Direct labour hours (DLH) per unit	1	2
Labour cost per DLH	$20	$20
Direct material cost per unit	$40	$20
Number of set-ups	10	40
Number of orders	15	60
Machine hours	3	1

	$
Overhead costs:	
Cost of setting up	20 000
Cost of handling orders	45 000
Costs relating to machine activity	220 000
Total overhead costs	285 000

The company wishes to determine the cost per unit in respect of overhead costs, using:

1. a functional-based cost accounting system absorbing costs on the basis of machine hours
2. an activity-based cost accounting system using suitable cost drivers to trace overheads to cost.

1   Functional-based system

Machine hour basis

Product		Total machine hours
X	(5 000 units × 3 hours)	15 000
Y	(7 000 units × 1 hour)	7 000
Total		22 000

Total overhead costs: $285 000.

Therefore, the overhead absorption rate is:

$$\frac{\$285\ 000}{22\ 000\ \text{hours}} = \$12.95 \text{ per machine hour}$$

The overhead absorbed into each unit is as follows:

X   3 hours × $12.95 = $38.85

Y   1 hour × $12.95 = $12.95

⫸

We are now in a position to determine the total unit cost under the functional-based cost system.

Total unit cost

	X ($)	Y ($)
Overhead	38.85	12.95
Direct labour	20	40
Direct materials	40	20
Total unit cost	98.85	72.95

2 Activity-based costing

The appropriate cost drivers in this example are those which relate to the way in which overhead costs are incurred. Overhead costs are those relating to machine activity, setting up, and handling orders. The main driver of set-up costs are the number of set-ups and this is a non-unit activity measure. 'To set-up machinery' is an activity and involves 'doing something.'

The overhead costs, based on the following cost drivers, will be absorbed into products:

Machining costs	$220 000 ÷ 22 000 hours	=	$10 per machine hour
Set-up driven costs	$20 000 ÷ 50 set-ups	=	$400 per set-up
Order driven costs	$45 000 ÷ 75 orders	=	$600 per order

We can now determine the product costs for products X and Y as shown below:

Product X

			$
Overhead			
Machine costs	(15 000 hours × $10)	=	150 000
Set-up costs	(10 × $400)	=	4 000
Order costs	(15 × $600)	=	9 000
Total overheads		=	163 000
Unit costs			
Overheads	$163 000 ÷ 5 000	=	$32.60
Direct material			$40
Direct labour	1 hour @ $20		$20
Total unit cost			$92.60

Product Y

			$
Overhead			
Machine costs	(7 000 hours × $10)	=	70 000
Set-up costs	(40 × $400)	=	16 000

			$
Order costs	(60 × $600)	=	36 000
Total overheads		=	122 000
Unit costs			
Overheads	$122 000 ÷ 7 000	=	$17.43
Direct material			$20
Direct labour	2 hours @ $20		$40
Total unit cost			$77.43

COMMENTARY

The following conclusions can be drawn regarding the different methods of determining the cost per unit for overhead costs for Onyx Ltd:

- *FBC (direct labour hour basis).* None or very little of the overhead costs appear to be incurred in support of the direct labour activity as $220 000 relates to machine activity. That is, overhead costs are not driven by the direct labour activity. Using direct labour hours as the basis for apportioning overhead costs in these circumstances would distort the costs apportioned to individual products. This is because more direct labour hours are worked on Y than on X
- *FBC (machine hour basis).* Although this basis for absorbing overheads clearly takes account of the main cost driver – machine-related costs – it does ignore other cost drivers associated with overhead costs, namely handling and set-up costs
- *ABC.* A more realistic basis for absorbing costs because it takes account of all the significant cost drivers.

The difference in costs under functional-based and activity-based systems would have an impact on the selling prices for X and Y. For example, if the pricing policy was cost plus 25 per cent then the selling prices under the two systems would be:

	X ($)	Y ($)
FBC	124	91
ABC	116	97

As a result, Onyx would be overpricing X and underpricing Y when the ABC prices are compared to the functional-based system prices. Companies which have moved to ABC have found that, with better knowledge about costs, they are able to determine more appropriate selling prices for their products.

The following steps are taken when employing ABC, as shown in Case study 17.2:

Step 1: Identify major activities; for example, machining, production runs and orders.

Step 2: Collect the overhead costs in a cost pool for each major activity.

Step 3: Determine the cost drivers for each activity:
- machining – cost per machine hour
- production runs – cost per set-up
- number of orders – cost per order.

Step 4: Trace the cost of the activities to the cost object using the cost drivers as a measure of demand.

Review exercise 4

Explain why it is necessary to use estimates in determining an absorption rate for overheads.

CASE STUDY 17.3

SUNCORP MONITORS THE BOZO LAYER
by Katrina Nicholas

SUNCORP METWAY won't admit it but its new software package makes it easier to identify bozos, those below zero customers who contribute little or nothing to the bank's bottom line. Instead Cameron Trappett, Suncorp Metway's activity-based management manager, likes to call it 'getting help implementing our all-finance strategy'. Whichever way you look at it, Suncorp Metway's new Metify ABM (activity-based management) system will allow it to more thoroughly monitor its costs and better attribute worth to products and customers.

The new software, for example, will allow it to deduce how much it costs to originate a loan via the telephone versus the internet, or how much it costs to service customers face-to-face versus via a call centre. Such software is, according to John McKenzie, international business development director with Armstrong Laing, the UK group that developed Metify, becoming increasingly popular with organisations keen to do activity-based costing and improve customer service levels.

'The purpose of activity-based costing is to better understand organisational costs,' McKenzie said. 'If you can collect that information, you can work out the profitability of customers and tailor customer service. Some businesses are using it as a precursor to CRM [customer relationship management] systems.'

The software could be used to work out how much it was costing a company to chase its debtors. He said such costs were often hidden and organisations were not aware of the extent to which they were eroding profits. 'Activity-based costing software allows a company to understand what drives costs and to allocate resources or modify behaviour accordingly,' he said.

Suncorp Metway financial controller Michael Cottier denied the bank was out to highlight bozos. 'I think that's a terrible term' but said the bank 'clearly wanted to have a better understanding of where the value drivers are'. He also said the software would be used to provide detailed reports to product managers and was expected to deliver serious cost savings.

Trappett said Suncorp Metway decided to implement Metify ABM, which is distributed in Australia by Global Technology Australasia, after building a pilot software program in-house to help with its GST cost allocation processing. 'By costing out expenses by product and business line, we were able to determine the correct GST level,' he said. 'But to implement our all-finance strategy, we felt we needed commercial software with more grunt.'

Trappett said the all-finance strategy, driven by an increased focus on customer service, involved transforming the bank into a financial 'one-stop shop'.

Australian Financial Review, 17 July 2001

COMMENTARY

This article reveals that Metway Corporation will use ABC to help it distinguish the profitable from the non-profitable customers and to determine the costs of activities such as raising a loan via the internet compared with face to face. The article shows that ABC is as applicable to service organisations as it is to manufacturers. Activity-based costing is a powerful tool that more and more companies are using to properly allocate and control costs and set more appropriate prices for products and services.

Review exercise 5

Explain the term 'activity-based costing'.

Variable versus absorption costing

8

Explain what is meant by the absorption-costing and variable-costing methods

Variable costs vary in proportion to production. Under a variable-costing system, only the variable costs of production are included in a cost object and the other costs, such as the fixed overhead cost of production, are treated as period costs.

The classifications of costs that we have concentrated on in this chapter are direct and indirect costs. We have defined a direct cost as one that is traceable, and thus attributable, to a given cost object – in our case, a product. For a multi-product firm, the only direct costs that can be identified with a product are those costs that change when production increases or decreases.

When we defined product costs, we said that, in the case of absorption costing, both direct and indirect costs of production should be included in the cost. It follows that product costs, in the case of absorption costing, will include both fixed and variable costs of production. The process of absorbing overheads, and in particular the apportionment of costs, although based on clearly identified criteria, is relatively arbitrary. Often, several equally fair bases for apportioning overhead costs are available. However, the use of these different bases will result in differing amounts of costs being apportioned to products. The cost of a product often depends on the choice of the basis used to apportion costs. It is part of the job of a management accountant to examine the basis of apportioning costs.

In Chapter 19 it will be argued that fixed costs should be ignored in the decision-making process; that is, they are irrelevant to the decision. This is another argument in support of variable costing rather than absorption costing.

The use of the absorption-costing method can distort costing, and the value placed upon products. Those who oppose absorption costing argue that the only costs that should be classified as product costs are those that are direct, which, we are assuming in this analysis, are only variable costs. All other production costs – that is, fixed overheads – are classified as period costs.

Although variable costing of products is attractive and convenient, it implies that fixed costs are not incurred in the production process. This is clearly not true. Expenditure on fixed costs is just as essential in the manufacture of products as expenditure on variable costs.

In recent years the case for the inclusion of fixed costs in product costs has gained momentum as the proportion of fixed costs incurred in the manufacture of products has grown as a result of automation. Most of the costs associated with automation, such as the cost of machinery, are fixed costs. Another argument in support of absorption costing is that the omission of fixed costs causes the cost of products to be understated. For example, if the costs of a unit of production consist of $2 of variable costs and $10 of fixed costs, the value given to this product for inventory valuation purposes under the variable-costing regime will be just $2. The cost of resources employed in the production of this unit, and thus its true value, is clearly more than $2! It is therefore not surprising that, in practice, firms tend to favour absorption costing for inventory valuation.

The absorption and variable methods of costing both have their virtues, and, to some extent, the method that is preferred is dependent on its application. For example, in the case of future decision making, the arguments in favour of variable costing as the preferred method are well documented, as we will see in Chapter 19. However, the preference is not so clear when other applications are considered. The preferred method depends on individual judgements regarding the strengths and weaknesses of the two methods.

Perhaps the most controversial debate regarding the use of absorption and variable costing relates to inventory valuation and its effect on profit measurement. It is therefore appropriate to examine these two methods of product costing in more detail.

Measuring profit and valuing inventory

In Case studies 17.4 and 17.5 we consider a firm that produces only one product. In such a situation all the costs are, by definition, identifiable with the one product and therefore are classified as direct costs – whether they are fixed or variable. However, in practice, the distinction between these two classifications is still valid in this situation. The reason for this, as mentioned in the discussion on overhead absorption rates, is that many of the indirect costs are not known until some months after they have been incurred. For management purposes, it is often preferable to absorb these costs using estimates, rather than waiting until the actual cost can be determined. In Case studies 17.4 and 17.5 we treat fixed factory overheads in a similar way to their treatment in a multi-product firm.

LO 9

Explain the effect on inventory and net profit of using either absorption- or variable-costing methods

CASE STUDY 17.4

DOOR CHIME COMPANY LTD

The Door Chime Company Ltd manufactures and sells one design of door chime. The following are the costs of production for 20X7:

- variable costs (direct cost), $3.00 per unit
- fixed factory overhead absorption rate, $2.00 per unit.

The fixed factory overhead rate is based on estimates of overhead costs of $40 000 and an activity level of 20 000 units. Actual fixed overheads incurred in 20X7 were $40 000. The sales price is $8.00 per unit.

Sales and production data for 20X7 in units is as follows:

	Units
Opening inventory of finished goods	1 000
Production	20 000
Sales	20 000
Closing inventory of finished goods	1 000

During 20X7, selling expenses were $1600 and administration expenses not associated with production were $1000.

We will begin by producing an income statement for 20X7, using the absorption-costing approach, and assume that any over- or under-absorption of overheads is charged or credited to the income statement as a period cost.

Door Chime Company Ltd
Income statement for 20X7 (using absorption costing)

	$	$
Sales (20 000 @ $8)		160 000
Less Cost of goods sold		
Opening inventory of finished goods (1000 @ $5)	5 000	
Plus production (20 000 @ $5)	100 000	
Cost of goods available for sale	105 000	
Less Closing inventory of finished goods (1000 @ $5)	5 000	100 000
Gross profit		60 000
Less Period costs		
Administration	1 000	
Selling	1 600	
Over- or under-absorption of overheads	–	2 600
Net profit		57 400

The production value and the value of the opening and closing inventory of finished goods in this statement, using the absorption-costing approach, are costed at the full cost of the product; that is, the direct costs of $3 and the overheads absorbed at $2 per unit. You will also note that there are no movements in the opening and closing inventories during the year. This is because the units produced are equal to those sold.

The period costs are represented by selling and administration expenses; thus, they are not included in the production cost.

There is no over- or under-absorption of overheads. This is because the total overheads absorbed ($2 per unit multiplied by the number of units produced, 20 000, equals $40 000) are the same as the actual overheads incurred during the year.

Door Chime Company Ltd
Income statement for 20X7 (using variable costing)

	$	$
Sales		160 000
Less Cost of goods sold		
Opening inventory of finished goods (1000 @ $3)	3 000	
Production (20 000 @ $3)	60 000	
Cost of goods available for sale	63 000	
Less Closing inventory of goods sold (1000 @ $3)	3 000	
Contribution		60 000
		100 000
Less Period costs		
Fixed factory overheads	40 000	
Administration	1 000	
Selling	1 600	42 600
Net profit		57 400

Therefore, the net profit is the same in both cases.

From these income statements, it can be seen that the main differences between absorption and variable costing are as follows:

- The product costs are different. The production costs, and the values of opening and closing inventories of finished goods, consist only of the direct costs of $3 per unit under variable costing. Under absorption costing, the cost is $5 per unit as it also includes the fixed factory overhead.
- Fixed factory overheads are classified as period costs under the variable-costing approach and are not included as product costs.

Now consider Case study 17.5, where there is a movement in inventories over the two-year period. The units produced here are greater (20X8) or less (20X9) than those sold.

CASE STUDY 17.5

We assume that the costs and sales price are the same as in Case study 17.4 for the following years 20X8 and 20X9.

Sales and production data, in terms of units, for 20X8 and 20X9, are as follows:

	20X8 Units	20X9 Units
Opening inventory of finished goods	1 000	6 000
Production	22 000	16 000
Sales	17 000	21 000
Closing inventory of finished goods	6 000	1 000

We will also assume that the overhead absorption rate, actual overheads incurred, and administration and selling expenses are the same as in Case study 17.4.

We begin our analysis by considering the absorption-costing method.

Door Chime Company Ltd
Income statement (using absorption costing)

20X8	$	$	$
Sales (17 000 @ $8)		136 000	
Less Cost of goods sold			
Opening inventory of finished goods (1000 @ $5)	5 000		
Production (22 000 @ $5)	110 000		
Cost of goods available for sale	115 000		
Less Closing inventory of finished goods (6000 @ $5)	30 000	85 000	
Gross profit		51 000	
Less Period costs			
Over-absorption of overheads – see note below	(4 000)		
Administration costs	1 000		
Selling costs	1 600	(1 400)	
Net profit		52 400	
Over-absorption of overheads			
Overheads absorbed during the year (22 000 units @ $2)			44 000
Actual overheads incurred during the year			40 000
Over-absorption of overheads			4 000

Note: The $4000 represents the amount that we have overcharged to products during the period. That is, we have charged $44 000 through applying the absorption rate, which is based on estimates, while the actual overhead costs were $40 000. The difference will, therefore, be credited to the income statement.

20X9	$	$	$
Sales (21 000 @ $8)		168 000	
Less Cost of goods sold			
Opening inventory of finished goods (6000 @ $5)	30 000		
Production (16 000 @ $5)	80 000		
Cost of goods available for sale	110 000		
Less Closing inventory of finished goods (1000 @ $5)	5 000	105 000	
Gross profit		63 000	
Less Period costs			
Under-absorption of overheads – see note below	8 000		
Administration	1 000		
Selling	1 600	10 600	
Net profit		52 400	

Overheads absorbed during the year (16 000 @ $2)		32 000
Actual overheads incurred during the year		40 000
Under-absorption of overheads		8 000

Note: In this case we have absorbed less than we estimated by $8000 and this amount will, therefore, be charged to the income statement as a period cost.

Door Chime Company Ltd
Income statement (using variable costing)

20X8	$	$
Sales		136 000
Less Cost of goods sold		
Opening inventory of finished goods (1000 @ $3)	3 000	
Production (22 000 @ $3)	66 000	
Cost of goods available for sale	69 000	
Less Closing inventory of finished goods (6000 @ $3)	18 000	51 000
Contribution		85 000
Less Period costs		
Fixed factory overheads	40 000	
Administration	1 000	
Selling	1 600	42 600
Net profit		42 400

20X9	$	$
Sales		168 000
Less Cost of goods sold		
Opening inventory of finished goods (6000 @ $3)	18 000	
Production (16 000 @ $3)	48 000	
Cost of goods available for sale	66 000	
Less Closing inventory of finished goods (1000 @ $3)	3 000	63 000
Contribution		105 000
Less Period costs		
Fixed factory overheads	40 000	
Administration costs	1 000	
Selling	1 600	42 600
Net profit		62 400

The following summarises the differences between the net profits of the methods used in this case study.

	20X8	20X9
	$	$
Variable costing	42 400	62 400
Absorption costing	52 400	52 400
Net profit difference	(10 000)	10 000

The difference in the net profit over these two years is a direct result of the methods that have been used. In the case of absorption costing, fixed costs are classified as product costs and are therefore included in the valuation of inventories. When there is an increase in inventories during a period (as in 20X8), the fixed costs associated with these inventories are included in the inventory value rather than being included (recognised) as a cost in the 'cost of goods sold' computation. In contrast, when there has been a decrease in inventory during a period (as in 20X9), which means a proportion of the goods sold (5000 units) has been obtained from the opening inventory rather than production, the fixed costs related to these inventories are realised as expenses and matched against sales. In the case of the variable-costing approach, all fixed costs during a period, because they are classified as period costs, are charged in the income statement in the period in which they are incurred.

The following summarises the movement in inventories over the two-year period:

Movement in finished inventories	20X8	20X9
	Units	Units
Opening	1 000	6 000
Closing	6 000	1 000
Difference	5 000	(5000)

In 20X8 there was an increase in inventories of 5000 units. Under the absorption-costing approach, the fixed cost element of these inventories (5000 units × $2 absorption rate = $10 000) is included as an ⟶

asset in the period. But in the case of a variable-costing approach, these fixed costs ($10 000) will be charged, as period costs, to the income statement in 20X8; that is, when they were incurred. The net profit in the case of absorption costing is $10 000 more than the profit under the variable-costing approach.

The reverse situation arises in 20X9. In this year, the fixed costs associated with the decrease in inventories, under absorption costing, are released as costs and matched against the sales during the period. Thus, 5000 units × $2 absorption = $10 000 is now recognised as a cost in the cost of goods sold. These fixed costs are excluded in the case of variable costing because they were not incurred during the year: they relate to the previous year. Therefore, the net profit calculated under absorption costing is $10 000 less than the profit under the variable-costing method.

From Case studies 17.4 and 17.5 we can summarise the differences between the methods as follows:

- When sales equal production (that is, when there is no movement in inventory), variable and absorption costing yield the same profit. The amount of fixed costs charged to the income statement is the same.
- When production exceeds sales (that is, when inventories are increasing), absorption costing shows a higher profit than variable costing does. Under absorption costing, a portion of the fixed production costs is charged to inventories and thereby deferred to future periods.
- When sales exceed production, absorption costing shows a lower profit than variable costing does. This is because the fixed costs included in the inventories are charged to the period in which the inventories are sold.

In the long run, the profit figures disclosed by the two methods must even out because sales cannot continuously exceed production, nor can production continuously exceed sales.

The differences in profits derived from the application of the two methods can be reconciled by the following arithmetical expression:

fixed overhead absorption rate × the movement in inventories during a period
= difference in profits

SUMMARY

LO 1

LEARNING OBJECTIVE 1
Explain that attaching costs to a product is a problem for multi-product firms
Multi-product firms have to account for costs that can be tied to a product (direct costs). Sometimes this can be a complex problem. They also have the problem of accounting for costs that are not directly measurable in relation to a product, such as electricity charges. These costs are called indirect (overhead) costs.

LO 2

LEARNING OBJECTIVE 2
Explain the cost assignment process
A 'cost object' can be a product, service, customer process or any other item for which management requires cost information. Costs can be either direct or indirect, and the way costs are assigned depends on their nature (see learning objective 3 below).

LO 3

LEARNING OBJECTIVE 3
Explain the difference between direct and indirect costs
A direct cost is one that is easily traceable (with a high degree of accuracy) to a cost object; for example, bottles being used in a bottling factory.

Indirect costs (also known as overhead costs) are those that cannot be easily and conveniently identified with a particular object; for example, electricity charges.

LO 4

LEARNING OBJECTIVE 4
Identify what is meant by product and period costs
Product costs are those costs which can be allocated to a product. All other costs incurred during a period are period costs.

LO 5

LEARNING OBJECTIVE 5
Identify the stages that are involved in determining the allocation of overheads to products
Stage 1. Overhead costs need to be identified and collected from production and service cost centres. An example of a service cost centre could be the design department. These costs are apportioned to production departments using a predetermined formula. For example, electricity costs could be apportioned based on the square footage of space of the entity.
Stage 2. Once the production and service department overhead costs have been identified and collected, they are then allocated to production departments on some basis. For example, the percentage of square footage the production department uses could determine the percentage of electricity costs allocated to the product.
Stage 3. The allocation of these overheads to a single product can be done by dividing the number of products manufactured into the total overhead. The resulting sum can then be applied as cost to the single product.

LO 6

LEARNING OBJECTIVE 6
Explain what is meant by predetermined overhead absorption rates
Many overhead costs are estimates of future expenditure. The reasons for estimating costs are mainly two-fold. First, many costs are known after the event; for example, electricity charges are billed in arrears quarterly. Second, other costs vary over time; for example, air conditioning. Because management usually sets budgets 12 months in advance (see Chapter 20), these costs are budgeted and set at a constant rate over the year so that seasons do not influence product cost.

LO 7

LEARNING OBJECTIVE 7
Explain the difference between functional-based and activity-based costing methods
A functional-based cost accounting system classifies all costs as either variable or fixed in relation to changes in the volume of units produced. Activity-based costing (ABC) is a method that tries to capture changes in technology by apportioning overheads to product costs on a more realistic basis, taking account of the activity and transactions that drive the cost. The focus in ABC is on managing activities instead of costs.

LO 8

LEARNING OBJECTIVE 8
Explain what is meant by the absorption-costing and variable-costing methods
Absorption costing is a costing method where the cost of inventories is determined in order to include the appropriate share of both variable and fixed costs. Fixed costs are allocated on the basis of normal operating capacity. In variable costing, only the variable production costs are used.

LO 9

LEARNING OBJECTIVE 9
Explain the effect on inventory and net profit of using either absorption- or variable-costing methods
Using absorption costing, production overhead costs are included as a product cost, whereas, in variable costing, they are treated as a period cost. This leads to differing values of inventory and, subsequently, differing net profit figures.

FURTHER READING

Hansen, D.R. & Mowen, M.M., 2003. *Management Accounting and Control*, 6th edn, South-Western, Mason, Ohio.

REVIEW QUESTIONS

1   Explain why it is important to determine the cost of products.
2   Give examples of expenditure that would be classified, in a manufacturing organisation, as direct costs and indirect costs.
3   What are period costs?
4   Discuss the advantages and disadvantages of using variable costing for product costing.

PROBLEMS FOR DISCUSSION AND ANALYSIS

1   If a manager is paid a bonus based on the profit they have earned, what might be the problems, in the short run, of using absorption costing?
2   Discuss how the use of variable costing may ignore the impact of fixed costs.
3   Refer to Case study 17.3 (p. 545). How could Metway use the information about profitable and less profitable customers, as generated by the ABC system, as part of its customer relationship management system?

4   JB & Q Ltd produces electronic mapping devices for luxury cars and uses a normal costing system. The following data is available for 20X4:

Budgeted:

Overhead	$900 000
Machine hours	37 500
Direct labour hours	120 000

Actual:

Units produced	150 000
Overhead	$893 250
Prime (direct) costs	$1 350 000
Machine hours	37 575
Direct labour hours	117 000

Overhead is applied on the basis of direct labour hours.

Required

a   What is the predetermined overhead rate?
b   What is the applied overhead for 20X4?
c   Was overhead over-applied or under-applied, and by how much?
d   What is the unit cost for the year?

5   Barclay Ltd uses a predetermined overhead rate in applying overheads to product costs, using direct labour costs for cost centre X and machine hours for cost centre Y. Following are the details of the estimated forecasts for 20X1:

	X	Y
Direct labour costs	$100 000	$35 000
Production overheads	$140 000	$150 000
Direct labour hours	16 000	5 000
Machine hours	1 000	20 000

a   Calculate the predetermined overhead rate for cost centres X and Y.
b   BNH is one of the products manufactured by Barclay. The manufacturing process involves the two cost centres, X and Y. The following data relates to the resources that were used in the manufacture of the product during 20X1:

	X	Y
Direct materials	$20 000	$40 000
Direct labour	$32 000	$21 000
Direct labour hours	4 000	3 000
Machine hours	1 000	13 000

Determine the total production cost for product BNH, using absorption costing.
c   Assuming that product BNH consists of 20 000 units, what is the unit cost of BNH?

d   At the end of the year 20X1, it was found that actual production overhead costs amounted to $160 000 in cost centre X and $138 000 in cost centre Y. The total direct labour cost in cost centre X was $144 200 and the machine hours used were 18 000 in cost centre Y during the year. Calculate the over- or under-absorbed overhead for each cost centre.

6   Agent Orange Pty Ltd operates a factory with two production departments, P1 and P2, and one service department, S1. Estimates of factory overhead for the year commencing 1 July 20X3 were as follows:

	$	$
Fixed overhead		
Factory rates		7 500
Insurance (buildings)		5 200
Maintenance		14 600
Depreciation (equipment)		32 800
Variable overhead		
Electricity		12 000
Indirect labour		
P1	18 000	
P2	23 500	
S1	44 000	85 500
Indirect materials		
P1	10 000	
P2	13 000	
S1	8 000	31 000

Other information available is as follows:

	Department		
	P1	P2	S1
Floor space (m²)	800	1 400	400
Value of equipment	$180 000	$100 000	$48 000
Machine hours	4 400	1 200	500
Direct labour hours	8 800	12 500	–
Allocation basis – S1	60%	40%	

Required

a   Prepare overhead application rates for department P1 based on machine hours and for department P2 based on direct labour hours.

b   Calculate a single plant-wide overhead application rate based on direct labour hours.

7   Briefly respond to each of the following comments. Indicate how management accounting information can assist managers in doing their jobs.

a   *Division manager*: 'Our accountants perform a valuable function in providing information to the shareholders about the performance of our company, but my task is to manage this division and I can't see how they can assist me in this task.'

b   *Café proprietor*: 'I agree that management accounting is valuable in a manufacturing firm, but I manage a café. How can it help my business?'

c   *Local council recreation manager*: 'Management accounting may be significant in a for-profit entity, but my task is to provide community services, without the goal of making a profit. Why should I be concerned with costs?'

d   *Project supervisor*: 'I carefully analyse my project's performance on a regular basis and reprimand my staff whenever we spend too much money and let them know they must perform better.'

e   *Sales senior manager*: 'Pricing a product is like throwing darts at a dartboard. Pick the numbers out of the air and hope the product sells and the company makes a profit if this happens.'

f   *Civil engineering graduate*: 'I have a real desire to be in charge of and responsible for the building of bridges, airports and massive dams. Why do I need to know about management accounting?'

8   Formula 500 Cars Ltd manufactured the metal frames of a small racing car called the Formula 500. It produced two different models, and the costs of direct material and direct labour for each model in February 20X1 were:

	Model ABC	Model XYZ
Direct materials	$200 000	$250 000
Direct labour	$400 000	$450 000

Formula 500 uses an activity-based costing system to allocate the overhead costs. The following details are available about cost drivers:

Activity	Cost driver
Welding	Number of welds (W)
Assembly	Number of direct labour hours (DLH)
Inspection	Time to inspect (IH)

The following schedule shows the projected costs and the amount of each cost driver for the year 20X1:

	Estimated costs	Estimated cost driver
Welding	$1 000 000	800 000 welds
Assembly	$800 000	400 000 DLH
Inspection	$500 000	20 000 IH
	$2 300 000	

During February 20X1, the actual amounts for each cost driver were:

	ABC	XYZ
Number of welds	30 000	40 000
Direct labour hours	15 000	20 000
Hours of inspection	600	1 000

Required

a   The total costs for model ABC and model XYZ for February.

b   The cost per car for each model if, during February, 1500 of ABC and 1630 of XYZ were produced.

c   If actual overhead for February was $190 000, determine if the factory overhead was under- or over-applied in February. How does the company report this under- or over-application of overhead?

9   JayDees Boats Ltd builds custom-designed company boats. The company uses an activity-based costing system for determining the costs of each boat it produces. The following activities and cost drivers apply to the construction of boats.

Activity	Cost driver
Construction	Direct labour hours (DLH)
Inspection	Time to inspect (TTI)
Testing	Time to test (TTT)

At the beginning of 20X0, the following estimates were made for each activity and cost driver.

	Estimated costs for year	Estimated cost driver hours
	$	
Construction	3 000 000	100 000 (DLH)
Inspection	1 000 000	20 000 (TTI)
Testing	500 000	8 000 (TTT)
	4 500 000	

During March 20X0, the actual direct materials and amounts for each cost driver for two boats – Mustang and Jaguar – were:

	Mustang	Jaguar
Direct materials	$160 000	$120 000
Direct labour hours	4 000	6 000
Inspection time	800	1 200
Testing time	200	300

Required

a   Determine the total cost for Mustang and Jaguar.
b   If the actual overhead for March was $440 000, was the overhead under- or over-applied in March?

10   The Benzfor company manufactures cars. The following data covers the months of April, May and June 20X1.

	April	May	June
Car production			
Opening inventory	0	100	250
Production	600	800	650
Sales	500	650	350

	April	May	June
	$	$	$
Variable costs			
Manufacturing costs per car	10 000	10 000	10 000
Marketing and administration	1 000	1 000	1 000
Fixed costs			
Manufacturing	500 000	500 000	500 000
Administration, etc.	85 000	90 000	85 000

The retail price for each car is $27 000.

Required

a   Prepare an income statement for the three months using:
　　i   variable costing
　　ii   absorption costing.
b   Explain how, and why, the figures vary.

Note to instructors: *The following problems are considered more suitable for use in MBA courses. However, undergraduate courses may also find them useful.*

11 The managers of Absent Ltd have been studying the results for the first three years of this newly formed company and are concerned about the figures. They think of profits as being directly related to the volume of sales, and find it confusing that for one year the reported sales are higher than those of the previous year but the reported net profit is lower.
　　The following figures apply to the years under consideration.

	20X1	20X2	20X3
Actual sales (units)	36 000	50 000	60 000
Actual production (units)	58 000	35 000	53 000

In each of the three years, the estimated production volume was 45 000 units and the estimated fixed overheads were $67 500.
　　The selling price was $4 per unit and variable costs were $1.50 per unit for the three years.
　　Actual costs were equal to estimated costs in all years. Selling and administrative expenses for each year were $10 000. The company had no opening inventory. The management accountant had difficulty explaining to the managers that fluctuations in profits resulted from differences between the volume of sales and the volume of production within an accounting period, together with the system of product valuation used.

Required

a   Prepare income statements for Absent Ltd using variable costing and absorption costing for each of the three years to aid the management accountant's explanation.
b   Reconcile the net profit reported under the costing methods.
c   Which costing method would you recommend for management decision-making purposes, and why?

12 Drawrod Ltd has three manufacturing cost centres: Punching, Stamping and Assembly. In addition, the company has two service cost centres: Maintenance and Inspection.

The following table gives the estimated production overhead expenses for the year to 31 December 20X2:

	$	$
Indirect materials		
Punching	12 000	
Stamping	14 000	
Assembly	10 000	
Maintenance	8 000	
Inspection	4 000	48 000
Indirect labour		
Punching	24 000	
Stamping	30 000	
Assembly	14 000	
Maintenance	36 000	
Inspection	10 000	114 000
Other overhead expenses		
Electricity	56 000	
Rent	128 000	
Rates	32 000	
Insurance of buildings	32 000	
Insurance of machines	40 000	
Depreciation of machines	40 000	328 000
Total		490 000

The following figures are additional estimates relating to manufacturing for the year ended 31 December 20X2.

	Punching	Stamping	Assembly	Maintenance	Inspection	Total
Area occupied (m²)	18 000	12 000	24 000	3 000	3 000	60 000
Working hours	52 500	45 000	30 000	15 000	7 500	150 000
Book value of machines	200 000	140 000	60 000	–	–	400 000
Machine hours	51 200	64 000	44 800	–	–	160 000
Number of employees	180	150	240	30	60	660

The costs of the service cost centres are to be apportioned as follows:

	Maintenance	Inspection
	%	%
Punching	40	20
Stamping	30	30
Assembly	30	50
	100	100

The company's bases for the absorption of overheads are as follows:

Punching: machine hours
Stamping: machine hours
Assembly: working hours

Required

a   Calculate the absorption rates for the Punching, Stamping and Assembly cost centres (to the nearest cent).

b   Specify and explain the factors that need to be considered in determining whether to use a single factory-wide overhead absorption rate for all factory overheads or a separate rate for each manufacturing cost centre, with reference to the system applied to Drawrod Ltd.

13 ChemWise is engaged in the production of chemicals for industrial use. One plant specialises in the production of chemicals used in the nickel industry. Two compounds are produced: compound Y-5 and compound Z-9. Compound Y-5 was originally developed by ChemWise chemists and played a key role in the extraction of nickel from low-grade ore. The patent for compound Y-5 has expired, and competition in this market has become fierce. Compound Y-5 produced the highest volume of activity, and for many years was the only chemical compound the plant produced. Six years ago, Z-9 was added. Compound Z-9 was more difficult to manufacture and required special handling and set-ups. For the first four years after the addition of the new product, profits increased. In the last two years, however, the plant has faced intense competition, and its sales of Y-5 have declined. In fact, the plant reported a small loss in the most recent accounting period. The plant manager is convinced that competing producers have been guilty of selling Y-5 below the cost to produce it – perhaps with the objective of increasing their share of the market.

ChemWise has concerns about the future of the plant and its products, and has hired independent consultants to investigate its production costs and relative efficiency. After a four-month review, the consulting group has provided the following information on the plant's production activities and costs associated with the two products:

	Y-5	Z-9
Production (kilograms)	1 000 000	200 000
Selling price	$15.93	$12.00
Overhead per unit*	$ 6.41	$ 2.89
Prime (direct) cost per kilogram	$ 4.27	$ 3.13
Number of production runs	100	200
Receiving orders	400	1 000
Machine hours	125 000	60 000
Direct labour hours	250 000	22 500
Engineering hours	5 000	5 000
Material handling (number of moves)	500	400

*   Calculated using a plant-wide rate based on direct labour hours, which is the current way of assigning the plant's overhead to its products.

The consulting group has recommended switching the overhead assignment to an activity-based approach. It maintains that an activity-based costing assignment is more accurate and will provide higher-quality information for decision making. To assist with this recommendation, the plant's activities have been grouped into similar sets based on common processes, activity levels and consumption ratios. The costs of these activity pools are as follows:

	$
*Overhead pool**	
Set-up costs	240 000
Machine costs	1 750 000
Receiving costs	2 100 000
Engineering costs	2 000 000
Material-handling costs	900 000
Total	6 990 000

* The pools are named for the major activities found within them. All overhead costs within each pool can be assigned using a single driver (based on the major activity after which the pool is named).

Required

a Confirm the overhead cost per unit reported by the consulting group using direct labour hours to assign overhead. Compute the per-unit gross margin for each product.

b Recompute the unit cost of each product using activity-based costing. Calculate the per-unit gross margin for each product.

c Should the company change its emphasis from the high-volume product to the low-volume product? Comment on the validity of the plant manager's concern that competitors are selling Y-5 below its cost of production.

d Explain the apparent lack of competition for Z-9. Also, comment on the fact that customers are prepared to accept a 25 per cent increase in price for this compound.

e What steps would you take given the information provided by the activity-based unit costs?

(Adapted from D. Hansen and M. Mowen, *Management Accounting*, 6th edn, South-Western, Mason, Ohio, Problem 4-21, p. 152.)

ETHICS CASE STUDY

Digital Electronics Ltd manufactures specialised scientific instruments to customer specifications. It has contracts with government departments which are on a cost-plus basis. Under this arrangement, the costs are defined as those costs which can be directly traced to the product, plus overheads based on a predetermined overhead rate, using an appropriate application base. Digital's other customers are in the non-government sector and are on a fixed-cost basis.

During February 20X1, the company worked on two main contracts – one with the defence department and the other with the Sarich Corporation. The two contracts were quite different, with the contract for the defence department requiring a large number of direct labour hours, while the contract for Sarich was the reverse.

The financial controller of the company has recommended to the general manager of Digital that the most appropriate base for the allocation of overheads is machine hours.

The general manager, however, has decided in favour of using direct labour hours to allocate the overheads to both contracts.

Discuss

a   why you think the general manager has chosen direct labour hours for the allocation of overheads instead of the machine hours recommended by the financial controller

b   the ethical issues involved in this case. Should the financial controller take any further action?

ANSWERS TO REVIEW QUESTIONS

1   A direct cost is one that is traceable, and thus is identifiable with a product. Indirect costs (also known as overhead costs) are those costs that cannot be easily and conveniently identified with a particular product.

2   Product costs are those costs which can be allocated to a product. As in Chapter 7 – when we discussed inventory – we use the principle that product costs are all the costs that are reasonable and have, by necessity, been incurred to get a product to a condition and location ready for sale. All other costs incurred during a period are period costs.

3   Absorption costing means that it has been determined that the costs of a product include all direct (variable) and indirect (fixed) costs of production.

4   There are two main reasons why estimates are used in determining absorption rates. First, some overhead costs are only known some months after they have been incurred. For example, telephone charges are normally billed to customers every quarter in many areas. Therefore, a firm would have to wait three months before they could determine this charge – which is not timely for management purposes. Second, a number of overhead costs are seasonal (e.g. heating and lighting costs).

Seasonal variations can distort the costing of products. For example, if a product is manufactured in the summer, it is likely that heating costs would be minimal. Thus, the cost of a product could, to an extent, be dependent upon when the product was manufactured. It is argued that such variations could distort the costing of products and also require complex systems to reflect these seasonal variations.

5   Activity-based costing (ABC) is a system of costing where the costs are allocated to a cost object based on an activity measure. Therefore, this is the major influence on the costs incurred by various cost objects.

18

LEARNING OBJECTIVES

At the end of this chapter, you should be able to:

1   explain the difference between variable and fixed costs

2   explain the relationship between the fixed costs and the variable costs of production

3   explain what is meant by a linear cost function

4   identify what is meant by the relevant range of activity

5   identify what is meant by cost–volume–profit analysis

6   explain what is meant by a break-even chart

7   explain and apply the contribution margin approach to measuring break-even sales levels and other sales levels for required profits

8   discuss the limitations of using a linear cost assumption in CVP analysis.

Introduction

For managers to be able to choose among alternative business opportunities, they need information regarding future costs and revenues and the ways in which these vary at different levels of activity. In order to use this information effectively, managers also need to understand how costs are determined. In Chapter 17 we examined some basic cost concepts, such as direct and indirect costs, and we looked at two costing systems as different ways of determining the cost of products in a multi-product firm. Our main concern in Chapter 17 was with the allocation of indirect costs to products or services.

In this chapter our focus is on how costs behave and we begin by examining cost behaviour and the ways in which costs are predicted, we then consider the application of this information to decision making using cost–volume–profit (CVP) analysis. This technique, which examines the interrelationships between cost, volume and profit at differing activity levels, aids managers in their decision making. We also critically appraise the traditional methods and models that are used and their underlying assumptions.

Fixed and variable costs

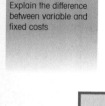

Explain the difference between variable and fixed costs

To understand how costs behave, it is first necessary to recognise the different types of costs. The concepts of fixed and variable costs were introduced in Chapter 17. Some costs are essentially fixed in nature; for example, the service and equipment charge for the domestic telephone service. Others vary with usage or activity; for example, the cost of calls made. The latter are known as variable costs. Unfortunately, not all costs fall neatly within these categories; therefore, it is necessary to make some simplifying assumptions for the purpose of decision making.

Before examining fixed and variable costs it is worthwhile to define them.

KEY CONCEPT 18.1

FIXED COSTS

A cost is fixed if it does not change in response to changes in the level of activity. (The activity level may be measured in terms of either production output or sales output. The choice will depend upon what is being measured.)

KEY CONCEPT 18.2

VARIABLE COSTS

A cost is variable if it changes in response to changes in the level of activity. For the sake of simplicity, it is assumed that the unit activity cost does not change. If the variable cost of one telephone call is 30 cents, then this cost is the same whether 100 or one million calls are made so total variable costs will increase or decrease in direct proportion to the increase or decrease in the activity level.

Cost functions

A basic notion of science is the idea that one thing may depend on another according to some mathematical relation. It is likely that in your study of economics you have also come across mathematical relations. For example, to show that the total spending (c) of a nation depends on the total income (y) of all persons in the nation, economists use the following equation:

$$c = f(y)$$

This states that consumption is a function of the level of income.

Mathematical formulas are also used in accounting to show relationships between costs and activity levels.

There are two important variables involved in the construction of cost functions. We will use the example of the cost of travelling to illustrate the nature of these variables and their interrelationship:

- The dependent variable, expressed as variable y, is the cost to be predicted – the total cost for an activity; for example, the cost of petrol for a journey.
- The independent variable x is the level of activity; for example, the number of kilometres to be travelled on the journey.

The dependent variable is expressed as a function of the independent variable:

$$y = f(x)$$

In our example, this relationship can be expressed as: 'The total cost of petrol for a journey is a function of (depends upon) the number of kilometres travelled'.

The relationship between the dependent and independent variables is illustrated in Figure 18.1, where the vertical axis shows the dependent variable – the total cost of petrol – and the horizontal axis shows the independent variable – the activity; that is, the kilometres travelled.

A cost function may be linear or non-linear. Traditionally, accountants assume cost functions to be linear, which is not necessarily a realistic assumption.

LO 2
Explain the relationship between the fixed costs and the variable costs of production

LO 3
Explain what is meant by a linear cost function

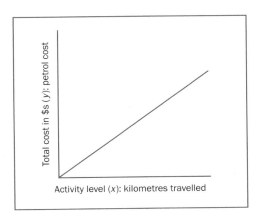

Figure 18.1 The relationship between a directly dependent variable (petrol cost) and an independent variable (kilometres travelled)

THE CHOICE OF THE INDEPENDENT VARIABLE

Often, there is more than one independent variable that affects the total cost of an activity. The speed at which the vehicle travels, as well as the distance travelled, are variables that affect the amount of petrol consumed and, thus, the total cost of a journey. However, it is usually too complex to take account of all the variables that affect total costs. The independent variable chosen should be the most influential variable in relation to the cost. In the case of petrol for a journey, this is obviously the distance travelled rather than the speed.

In some cases, the selection of the most influential variable is obvious. When it is not, past costs should be examined to establish which of the independent variables are most influential.

VARIABLE COSTS

The cost of raw material is a good example of a cost that varies directly with the level of production output. For example, if one unit of output requires 2 kilograms of material which costs $3.00 per kilogram, then the material cost for 50 units of output will be:

$$\text{2 kilograms} \times \text{\$3.00 per kilogram} \times \text{50 units} = \text{\$300}$$

Sales commission normally varies with sales output. For example, if a salesperson receives 10 per cent commission on every unit that is sold, and the selling price per unit is $40, the commission received will be $4 per unit. If the salesperson sold 3000 units during the year, the total commission received would be 4 × 3000 units = $12 000.

Labour paid on an hourly basis is conventionally classified as a cost that varies with production output. In reality, however, workers are paid a fixed wage which bears no direct relationship to output levels. There might be some output-linked incentive bonus included in the pay structure, but most of the remuneration is fixed for a set working week. Nevertheless, for decision-making purposes it is assumed that this category of labour is variable because, physically, production levels are a function of the labour input.

Figure 18.2 (opposite) illustrates a cost which varies directly with activity levels. Note that the graph goes through the origin; that is, when the activity is zero, the costs are zero. As activity increases, the variable cost increases. This can be compared with Figure 18.6 on page 571 where fixed costs are also included.

In reality, it is unlikely that costs which are traditionally classified as variable will behave strictly in a linear fashion. The variable cost function often tends to be curvilinear, or made up of several straight lines. The following examples illustrate some of the reasons why variable costs are not strictly linear:

- Manufacturers are likely to benefit from bulk discounts for the purchase of raw materials.
- Prices of resources tend to increase as a scarcity arises, due to increased demand.
- Increased activity may lead to diminishing returns. For example, attempts to sell more units of a product may entail transporting the extra units over longer distances to reach more distant

markets; therefore, distribution costs may increase at a faster rate than activity. Assuming that selling prices are constant, these greater distribution costs will result in diminishing profit margins.

Figure 18.3 shows a variable cost function with diminishing returns.

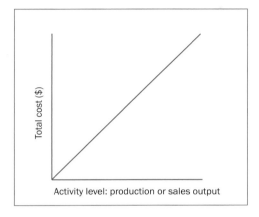

Figure 18.2 A linear cost function

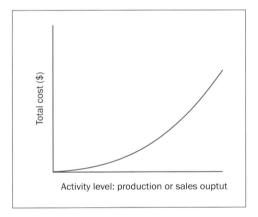

Figure 18.3 A curvilinear cost function

FIXED COSTS

Examples of costs that are normally classified as fixed are rent, rates, salaries of administrators, and the service and equipment charge for a telephone service referred to earlier. Fixed costs of this type are normally also classified as overhead costs, which were described in Chapter 17. Figure 18.4 (overleaf) shows a fixed cost function.

Figure 18.4 A fixed cost is not affected by increases in activity levels

However, the concept that fixed costs are constant over all levels of activity is often unrealistic. In reality, a fixed cost is fixed only over a limited range of output. For example, in the case of the telephone bill, the service and equipment charge is, theoretically, fixed. However, if the telephone company increases its charges, or if an extension is required, the service and equipment charge increases. Similarly, a factory has a limited capacity; if production were to exceed that capacity another factory would be required, and costs would increase. Therefore, these types of costs tend to behave in a stepped fashion. Figure 18.5 illustrates a stepped cost function in the case of renting a factory. The rent is $2000 for one factory which has a capacity, in output terms, of 1000 units. Another factory will be required for output levels exceeding 1000 units, and the total rent will increase to $4000 (assuming that the rental and the capacity are the same). This cost will remain at $4000 up to 2000 units, when another factory will be required and costs will increase in the same fashion, and so on.

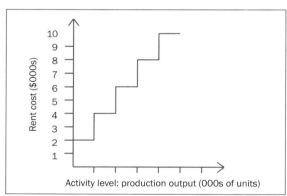

Figure 18.5 A stepped cost function: renting factory space

Review exercise 1

Variable and fixed costs are traditionally assumed to be linear. Explain why this assumption is unrealistic.

Review exercise 2

What is the difference between a linear fixed cost and a stepped fixed cost? Give examples, other than those given.

LINEAR COST FUNCTIONS

In reality, many cost functions are made up of two parts – a fixed cost and a variable cost.

KEY CONCEPT 18.3

LINEAR COST FUNCTIONS

In general, we can express a linear cost function as:

$$y = a + bx$$

where y is the total cost to be predicted; x is the level of activity measured in units of output; a is the fixed cost; and b is the variable cost.

Let us again consider a telephone bill, since this is a good example of a linear cost function. Look at the graph in Figure 18.6. Point a represents the fixed costs – the service and equipment charge – which remain the same for any level of activity. The line illustrates the variable cost (the cost of calls), rising in proportion to increases in activity x (the number of call units).

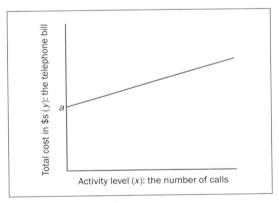

Figure 18.6 A linear cost function of a telephone bill

We can determine the total telephone bill (y) using the equation in Key concept 18.3 if we know the service and equipment charge (a), the cost per unit call (b) and the number of units registered (x).

service and equipment charge, $a = \$50$
cost per unit call, $b = 20c\ (\$0.2)$
number of unit calls made, $x = 1500$

The total cost of the bill, y, can be calculated thus:

$$y = \$50 + (\$0.2 \times 1500) = \$350$$

If the number of unit calls increased to 1800, the total cost of the bill would be:

$$y = \$50 + (\$0.2 \times 1800) = \$410$$

To help you to understand this equation and its use, examine a recent telephone bill for your household and calculate the total cost of the bill if the number of unit calls made increased by, say, 50 per cent. This exercise might also result in your spending less time on the telephone!

THE RELEVANT RANGE OF ACTIVITY

KEY CONCEPT 18.4

THE RELEVANT RANGE OF ACTIVITY

The relevant range of activity relates to the levels of activity that the firm has experienced in past periods. It is assumed that, in this range, the relationship between the independent and dependent variables will be similar to that previously experienced.

LO 4

Identify what is meant by the relevant range of activity

Assuming that an entity's intention is to operate in the relevant range of activity, we can be reasonably confident about predicting the pattern of cost behaviour. This confidence is important to managers because the information regarding the way in which costs behave is the basis for decision making about the future. If the costs do not behave as predicted, decisions could be taken that will jeopardise the organisation's future.

Outside the relevant range, we cannot be confident that the relationship between the variables will hold. Figure 18.7 shows a cost function in the relevant range of activity and other cost functions outside this range, which are not of a similar pattern.

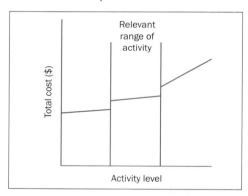

Figure 18.7 Cost functions inside and outside the relevant range of activity

If an organisation is intending to operate at an activity level not experienced previously, it must be extremely cautious in the prediction of future costs, and should rely more on forecasting methods than on predicting costs on the basis of past behaviour. The examination of forecasting methods is outside the scope of this text; you can find references to the methods in advanced management accounting texts.

Conventionally, for convenience, graphical representations of the relations between costs and volumes show cost functions that are the same for all levels of activity; that is, the same pattern of costs is shown inside and outside the relevant range of activity. This is the case in all the graphical representations showing cost functions illustrated in Figures 18.1 to 18.6.

Review exercise 3
Explain what is meant by the relevant range of activity and its significance in CVP analysis.

Cost behaviour: assumptions and limitations

As we have already mentioned, accountants conventionally employ linear cost functions for use in making operating decisions. This practice is based on a number of assumptions and we have discussed most of them. For clarity, they are summarised as follows:

- All costs can be divided into either fixed or variable costs.
- Fixed costs remain constant over different activity levels.
- Variable costs vary with activity but are constant per unit of output.
- Efficiency and productivity remain constant over all activity levels.
- Cost behaviour can be explained sufficiently by one independent variable.

From our earlier analysis, it is obvious that these assumptions are simplistic and tend to be approximations of reality. Therefore, the question arises: Are the cost functions used by accountants justified? The answer is often difficult to establish with much confidence. Primarily, this is a cost–benefit question (this approach was generally considered in Chapter 15): are the net benefits greater when accountants' linear cost functions are used compared with more sophisticated cost functions such as curvilinear functions? The non-linear functions are more costly to establish but developments in information technology have tended to reduce the cost of using these more sophisticated models.

Arnold and Turley (1996) argue that the use of a linear cost function:

> is not unreasonable as statistical studies have presented evidence which suggests that within specified output limits [the relevant range of activity], organisations do have cost functions which are approximately linear.

Figure 18.8 shows a curvilinear cost function. Look closely at the curve in the relevant range of activity. In fact, it is very close to a straight line. You might like to use a ruler to mark in such a line. Note that the curve on either side of the relevant range could be approximated with two different straight lines.

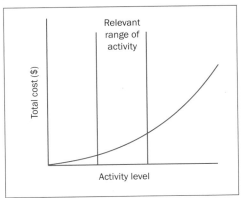

Figure 18.8 A curvilinear cost function approximates to a linear cost function within the relevant range of activity

Estimating costs

KEY CONCEPT 18.5

COST ESTIMATION

Cost estimation relates to methods that are used to measure past (historical) costs at varying activity levels. These costs are then employed as the basis for predictions of future costs that will be used in decision making.

There are many methods of cost estimation. Detailed knowledge of each of these methods is not necessary at this stage of your studies. However, it is important that you appreciate the basic principles and limitations of cost estimation. For a detailed examination of the methods see Horngren, Foster and Srikant (2000).

Methods of cost estimation range from simple to mathematically complex. The essential factor is to choose the estimation technique that generates the greatest benefits net of the costs of deriving the information. This, to a great extent, depends on the size of the organisation. The smaller the organisation, the less likely it is that a sophisticated method will be employed, because the costs will be relatively high compared to the benefits that will be generated from the use of such a method.

Cost estimates are based on historical cost accounting data; that is, on the costs of past production, service and sales activity. One of the simplest methods is the account classification method, which involves simply observing how costs behaved in a previous period and classifying these costs as fixed or variable. The method relies on subjective judgement and is therefore limited in its ability to predict the future behaviour of costs accurately.

A more sophisticated method of cost estimation is regression analysis. The linear regression model involves making a number of observations from past cost behaviour and statistically analysing the data to produce a line of best fit. Figure 18.9 shows, graphically, a number of points (past costs at varying levels of activity) and the line of best fit established using the mathematical technique of regression analysis.

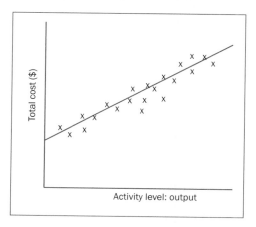

Figure 18.9 Regression analysis of past cost behaviour

A clear pattern of behaviour – where the points lie close to the line of best fit over the activity range – indicates a high correlation between cost and output (activity), while a more widely dispersed arrangement of points indicates a lower correlation. (For a more detailed explanation see a text on quantitative methods, such as Curwin and Slater, 1996, *Quantitative Methods for Business Decisions*.) In the example illustrated in Figure 18.9, there is a fairly clear pattern; therefore, we can conclude that there is a relatively high correlation between cost and output.

There are more sophisticated regression analysis techniques. These include multiple regression, which takes account of more than one independent variable, and curvilinear regression.

The use of past data to determine future costs and the way in which they behave is problematic. The following briefly summarises some of the problems:

- *Relevant range of activity.* As previously mentioned, little confidence can be placed in cost estimates beyond the range of activity from which the data has been derived. It is dangerous to extrapolate cost trends well beyond the levels of output previously experienced.
- *The number of observations.* It is important in statistical analysis to derive many observations of output and cost levels in order to be able to make accurate predictions about future behaviour. The greater the number of observations, the higher the accuracy of the estimate and therefore the better the prediction.
- *Changes in prices.* Past costs may not reflect current price levels and they will bias the estimates downwards. There is therefore a need to adjust these prices to current levels.
- *Changes in technology.* Only observations made under current production procedures should be included in the analysis. Costs of work practices using, for example, machinery that is no longer used, are irrelevant to future decisions.
- *Incorporation of past inefficiencies.* If operations were performed in an inefficient manner in the past and cost estimates are derived from this past period, they will incorporate inefficiencies.

With the development of more sophisticated techniques, there is increasing use of industrial engineering methods to predict future costs. Using time and motion studies, input and output analysis, and production control productivity surveys, it is possible to specify relatively accurately the relationship between labour time, machine time, materials and physical output. These techniques look to the future physical levels of resources and then convert them into money values instead of using past costs as the basis of estimating future costs.

Cost–volume–profit analysis

Organisations are constantly faced with decisions relating to the products and services they sell, such as the following:

- Should we change the selling price, and if so what would be the effect on profit?
- How many units must be sold to break even?
- How many units must be sold to make a specified target profit?
- Should more money be spent on advertising?

The cost data that are used in cost–volume–profit (CVP) analysis are derived from the prediction of future costs discussed earlier in this chapter.

L 5

Identify what is meant by cost–volume–profit analysis

KEY CONCEPT 18.6

COST–VOLUME–PROFIT (CVP) ANALYSIS

CVP analysis is a tool used by organisations to help them make decisions by examining the interrelationships between cost, volume and profits.

SALES REVENUE

It is normally assumed in CVP analysis that sales revenues, like costs, behave in a linear fashion for varying output levels. That is, the sales price per unit sold is the same for all levels of output. Figure 18.10 illustrates a sales revenue function; the vertical axis represents the total sales revenue and the horizontal axis is the sales output levels.

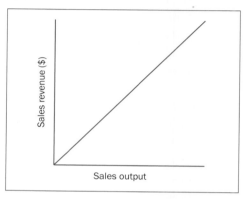

Figure 18.10 The sales revenue increases in direct proportion to sales output

It can be seen that the sales revenue function increases in direct proportion to sales output. This is because the selling price is the same for every unit that is sold.

The assumption that the selling price remains constant for all levels of sales is often unrealistic. For example, often you will find quantity discounts being offered for consumable goods at supermarkets: if you buy one cake of soap the price is 60c, whereas if you buy two cakes of soap the price is $1.00, or 50c each. This limitation on the application of CVP analysis will be considered in more detail later.

THE CVP EQUATION

CVP analysis is based on the relationship expressed by the following equation:

$$P = Sx - (FC + VCx)$$

where S = selling price per unit
   x = number of units sold
   FC = fixed cost
   VC = variable cost
   P = expected profit.

This expression can be rearranged as follows.

$$Sx = VCx + FC + P$$

This equation is similar to the cost functions considered earlier. Only one independent variable is being considered; that is, the sales activity. The fixed and variable costs together are equal to the total cost. The only additional variables are sales price, and profit, which is the difference between sales revenue and total costs.

To illustrate the application of CVP analysis in decision making, we will consider the example of Boycott Industries.

Example 18.1: Boycott Industries

Boycott Industries produces only one product. The following revenues and costs have been estimated for the forthcoming month:
- selling price, $70 per unit (S)
- variable costs, $40 per unit (VC)
- fixed cost, $2400 (FC).

The managers of the firm wish to know the following:
1 How many units must be sold to break even; that is, to make neither a profit nor a loss?
2 How many units must be sold to make a profit of $600?
3 Would it be worthwhile to introduce advertising, at a cost of $1200, if this increases sales from 520 to 600 units?
4 What should the selling price be to make a profit of $15 000 on sales of 120 units?

Solutions

1 S = 70, VC = 40, FC = 2400, break-even point, P = 0. Use the sales version of the CVP equation:

$$Sx = VCx + FC + P$$
$$70x = 40x + 2400 + 0$$
$$30x = 2400$$
$$x = 80 \text{ units}$$

We can check this in the following manner:

	$	$
Sales (80 units @ $70)		5 600
Less Costs		
Variable cost (80 units @ $40)	3 200	
Fixed costs	2 400	5 600
Profit		0

2 For this question, P = 600.
$$Sx = VCx + FC + P$$
$$70x = 40x + 2400 + 600$$
$$30x = 3000$$
$$x = 100 \text{ units}$$

3   First, determine the profit for $x = 520$ units. Use the profit version of the CVP equation:

$$P = Sx - (VCx + FC)$$
$$P = 70 \times 520 - (40 \times 520 + 2400)$$
$$P = \$13\ 200$$

Advertising costs will increase fixed costs by $1200 (FC = 3600). The profit for $x = 600$ units will be as follows:

$$P = 70 \times 600 - (40 \times 600 + 3600)$$
$$P = \$14\ 400$$

Therefore, the profit with advertising is $14 400 compared to $13 200. Presumably, the firm will go ahead and advertise the product because it will generate greater profits. However, management must decide on matters such as the probability of selling the extra units if the $1200 is paid for advertising.

4   $P = 15\ 000$, $x = 120$. Use the sales version CVP equation:

$$Sx = VCx + FC + P$$
$$S \times 120 = 40 \times 120 + 2400 + 15\ 000$$
$$120 \times S = 22\ 200$$
$$S = 185$$

THE BREAK–EVEN CHART

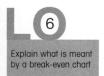

Explain what is meant by a break-even chart

A useful method of illustrating the relationships between cost, volume and profit is a break-even chart. The relationship between these variables is plotted on a graph. The cost functions and the sales revenue function, which in previous illustrations have been shown separately, are now included together in the break-even chart.

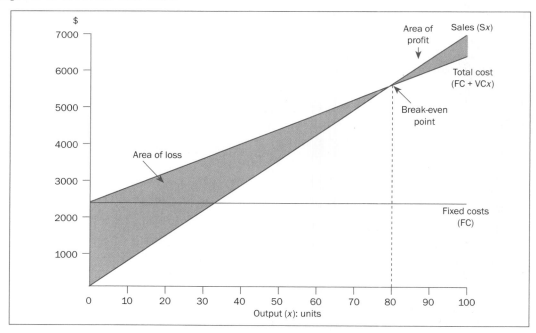

Figure 18.11 The break-even chart for Boycott Industries

Figure 18.11 shows the break-even chart for Boycott Industries, using the data given in Example 18.1. You will notice that in the construction of this chart the variable costs are plotted above the fixed costs, resulting in a total cost function that rises from the intercept at $2400 and increases at the rate of $40 per unit. (Another way of constructing the total cost function in break-even charts will be illustrated later.) The main advantage of the chart for management is that the break-even point, and the areas of loss and profit, can be clearly and quickly identified. This enables management to establish the effect of varying output levels that it wishes to consider and look at the impact on profit by referring to the chart.

CASE STUDY 18.1

DOME 'WILL NOT BREAK EVEN'
by Mark Henderson

THE MILLENNIUM DOME is unlikely to attract the 12 million paying visitors it needs to break even because of the negative critical response to its opening, according to an independent study of its prospects published yesterday.

Bad publicity about the Dome's contents, queues and cost mean that the £758 million exhibition will probably sell just over 10 million tickets this year, nearly 2 million short of its target, the report by Volterra Consulting found.

The results add to growing fears that the Dome will not prove to be popular enough to cover its costs, even though the organisers insist that tickets are selling better than expected. It must attract an average of 33 000 visitors a day, but is operating at a reduced capacity of 20 000.

Volterra's figures were compiled using an advanced computer modelling process known as complex systems analysis.

The New Millennium Experience Company said: 'Ticket sales are ahead of expectations at this stage, and well on track for what we need. Any computer model of how we are doing would need to take all sorts of things into account to be accurate – such as higher demand in the summer and even the weather.'

Better news for the Dome came from an opinion poll of 505 visitors carried out since its opening. It found that 80 per cent had enjoyed their day out.

The Times, 14 January 2000

COMMENTARY

The article discusses how the Millennium Dome in London was not expected to attract the 12 million visitors it needed to break even. Given the cost of the dome was £758 million (about $2 billion), the failure to achieve the attendance needed to break even would have been a major concern to shareholders. The article does not indicate the expected loss if only 10 million people paid to visit the Dome. The management of the Dome could have considered increasing the admission charge to reduce the numbers required to break even, but this might have discouraged even more people from visiting the Dome.

Review exercise 4

Define the term 'break-even point'.

THE CONTRIBUTION MARGIN METHOD

LO
⑦

Explain and apply
the contribution
margin approach to
measuring break-
even sales levels and
other sales levels for
required profits

The contribution margin is equal to the sales price per unit, less the variable cost per unit; that is:

$$C = S - VC$$

The contribution margin is commonly described as the contribution per unit. Using the data from Boycott Industries in Example 18.1, the contribution margin is as follows:

$$C = S - VC$$
$$= 70 - 40$$
$$= \$30$$

This means that each unit sold makes a contribution of $30. The contribution initially reduces the loss incurred by fixed costs by $30 per unit. When fixed costs have been covered at the output level of 80 units (that is, at the break-even point), every unit sold thereafter contributes $30 to profits.

Figure 18.12 is another version of the break-even chart; once again using the data relating to Boycott Industries.

Here, the total cost function is constructed by first plotting the variable costs and then adding the fixed costs. By constructing the total cost function in this way, we can identify the contribution margin; that is, the difference between the sales and variable cost functions, as shown on the chart.

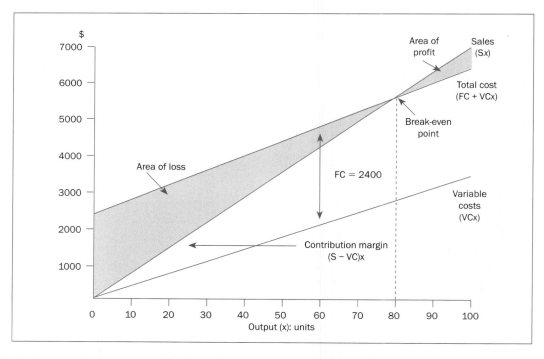

Figure 18.12 The break-even chart for Boycott Industries, showing the contribution margin

Note that at the origin (that is, no sales) a loss is made of $2400, which is the sum of the fixed costs. When one unit is sold it contributes $30, thereby reducing the loss to $2370. As sales output increases, the loss is reduced by $30 per unit up to the break-even point – where the fixed costs are totally covered. After the break-even point has been reached, each unit sold increases profit by $30 per unit; thus, if 81 units are sold, a profit of $30 would be made.

KEY CONCEPT 18.7

CONTRIBUTION MARGIN

The contribution margin is sales revenue less all variable expenses.

KEY CONCEPT 18.8

CONTRIBUTION MARGIN RATIO

The contribution margin ratio is the contribution margin divided by sales revenue. This shows the proportion of each sales dollar available to cover fixed costs and contribute to profit.

The contribution margin is an important concept and is used widely in accounting to aid managers in making decisions. We examine the concept in more detail in Chapter 19.

Using the contribution margin approach, we can answer the various questions about Boycott Industries posed earlier. First, we need to rearrange the CVP equation:

$$Sx = VCx + FC + P$$
$$Sx - VCx = FC + P$$
$$(S - VC)x = FC + P$$
$$\text{since } C = S - VC$$
$$Cx = FC + P$$

To find the break-even point, we put P = 0

$$Cx = FC$$
$$x = FC \div C$$

Using the data for Boycott Industries:

$$x = 2400 \div 30$$
$$= 80 \text{ units}$$

CASE STUDY 18.2

AMEX SOUNDS LTD

Amex Sounds Ltd is a company that specialises in the sale of domestic electronic sound equipment. The company purchases goods from manufacturers and sells them to the retail trade. A high proportion of the goods they sell is manufactured abroad and imported. Since starting five years ago, they have been very successful, in terms of sales and profit growth. The managing director has recently been offered an ⫸

exclusive contract to sell a DVD player that is manufactured in South Korea. Although this player has been sold successfully in the USA, it has yet to be sold in the Australian market.

The company is currently assessing whether or not to enter into the contract. The following information relates to the estimated costs and revenues of the contract:

- A market survey has been completed with the help of a market consultant. At a price of $40 per player, the estimated sales in the first year would be 9500 players. This is considered to be the most realistic price and volume level in the forthcoming year, taking account of competition.
- The price paid for each recorder will be $19.50. This includes the cost of packaging and shipment. The contract specifies that this price will be fixed for one year from the contract date.
- Variable costs, other than the cost of the player, are estimated to be $3.00 per player sold.
- The company is currently trading from a rented warehouse in Sydney. However, there is very little space for further expansion. After due consideration of location and costs it is decided that, if the contract is accepted, a warehouse in Parramatta will be rented and used exclusively for the sale of these recorders. Parramatta has been chosen primarily because the cost of renting premises there is relatively lower than in the inner city and the employment situation is better. The rent for the warehouse will be $46 000 per year and it is estimated that salaries will be $65 000 per year.
- Other fixed costs are anticipated to be $15 000.

The following table summarises the costs per unit that will be incurred in selling the DVD player:

	$ Costs per unit
Variable costs	
Purchase price of DVD players	19.50
Other variable costs	3.00
	22.50
Fixed costs (per year)	
Rent of warehouse	46 000
Salaries	65 000
Other fixed costs	15 000
	126 000

When deciding whether or not to accept this contract, CVP analysis will be a useful aid. We begin by determining the profit for the estimated sales of 9500, first rearranging the equation used earlier:

$$Sx = VCx + FC + P$$
$$P = x(S - VC) - FC$$
$$P = 9500(40 - 22.50) - 126\,000$$
$$= \$40\,250$$

To determine the number of units which need to be sold to break even, we find that putting $P = 0$ gives:

$$x = FC \div C$$

where
$$C = S - VC$$
$$= 40 - 22.50$$
$$= 17.50$$

so
$$x = 126\,000 \div 17.50$$
$$= 7200 \text{ units}$$

The difference between the break-even point and the estimated sales in terms of units is 9500 − 7200 = 2300 units; this would give the company a margin of safety in percentage terms of 2300 ÷ 9500 × 100 = 24 per cent, approximately.

Clearly, the information derived from our analysis is useful in the assessment of this contract. In particular, the determination of the break-even point gives the managers of the company a basis from which to evaluate the risk associated with the contract. Knowledge that there is a margin of safety of 2300 units will be useful in this assessment.

We now extend our analysis to consider advertising. It will be assumed that costs and revenues listed earlier remain constant with the exception of any effect associated with advertising.

The company consults an advertising firm regarding the sales of the players. Two separate strategies are proposed:

1   Expenditure on advertising of $16 000 will increase the sales volume in the year to 10 300 units.
2   Expenditure of $30 000 will increase the sales volume in the year to 11 500 units.
These two strategies will be considered separately and compared with the original analysis above, taking into account the profit and break-even levels.

1   Advertising costs $16 000, sales volume 10 300 units

The advertising costs are classified as fixed costs; therefore, fixed costs will now be $126 000 + $16 000 = $142 000. Using the equation, we can determine the profit:

$$P = x(S - VC) - FC$$
$$P = 10\ 300 \times 17.50 - 142\ 000$$
$$= \$38\ 250$$

The break-even point is given by:

$$x = FC \div C$$
$$= 142\ 000 \div 17.50$$
$$= 8114 \text{ units (to the nearest whole number)}.$$

This proposal, we can safely say, will not be attractive to the company because profits are $40 250 − $38 250 = $2000 lower than the original proposal, and the risk is greater because the break-even point is higher by 8114 − 7200 = 914 units.

2   Advertising costs $30 000, sales volume 11 500 units

Fixed costs increase to $126 000 + $30 000 = $156 000.

$$P = x(S - VC) - FC$$
$$P = 11\ 500 \times 17.50 - 156\ 000$$
$$= \$45\ 250$$

The break-even point is:

$$x = FC \div C$$
$$= 156\ 000 \div 17.50$$
$$= 8914 \text{ units (to the nearest whole number)}.$$

In this case, the decision as to whether to use advertising is somewhat more complex. First, the profit will increase by $45 250 − $40 250 = $5000, which presumably will be attractive to the company. However, the risk (measured in terms of break-even analysis) is greater, because the break-even point has risen from 7200 to 8914 units.

The analysis of these advertising strategies, in terms of profit and break-even points, is clearly useful in determining whether the company should use advertising. However, it is important to appreciate that this is only a part of all the information that is necessary to evaluate such a proposal. For example, it is also necessary to consider the effect on cash flow. It is likely that the company will require additional funds to support an advertising campaign and this should be taken into account.

Review exercise 5

Classify the following cost items as fixed, variable or a mix of fixed and variable.

a   power to operate a drill
b   engine in a car
c   advertising
d   sales commissions
e   fuel for a forklift
f   depreciation on a boat
g   amalgam used by a dentist
h   forms used to file insurance claims
i   printing and postage for advertising circulars

CVP analysis: assumptions and limitations

LO 8

Discuss the limitations of using a linear cost assumption in CVP analysis

The cost–volume–profit model that has been examined and illustrated in this chapter has been assumed to be linear. The assumptions and limitations of a linear cost function were described earlier in the section relating to cost behaviour, and these are relevant to the CVP model.

The sales function, as previously discussed, is also linear because it is assumed that the sales price will remain constant for all levels of activity. Empirical evidence suggests that this is unlikely for the majority of goods and services. A more realistic sales function would be represented by a curvilinear pattern. However, although the assumption of a linear function seems to be too simplistic, there is evidence that within the relevant range of activity the sales function, like cost, does approximate to a linear pattern.

The choice of employing a linear or a non-linear function to represent sales in the CVP analysis, once again, depends on the costs and benefits of the information.

In the example of the application of CVP analysis, we examined a one-product firm – Boycott Industries. In reality, most firms produce more than one type of product. There are particular problems associated with the application of CVP analysis in multi-product firms.

In many cases, there are interdependencies between the production and demand of two or more of the firm's products. For example, the demand for one product, such as butter, might be affected by the demand for another product, such as margarine. In these cases, it is necessary to examine the CVP relationships together. This will not cause a problem if the sales mix (the proportion of sales volumes of the interdependent products) and the profit margins are the same. If the mix changes, the overall volume targets might be achieved, but the effects on profits will depend on whether the product of higher or lower margin predominates in the mix.

Not all costs are fixed or variable. Some costs are *mixed costs*, having both a fixed and a variable component. For example, a computer salesperson might be paid $1000 a month, plus $100 for each computer sold.

Fixed costs represent another problem in the application of CVP analysis in multi-product firms. If the fixed cost can be identified with particular products, there is no cause for concern. But if fixed costs are of a general nature, for example, head office expenses, they will have to be apportioned or allocated on some fairly arbitrary basis. This could be misleading and lead to inaccurate decisions.

If one or more of the resources available to a firm is scarce, there will be a constraint on the potential total sales output. The problem is how the resources should be allocated among the products. This depends on how effectively each product uses the resource. We will be examining this problem in more detail in Chapter 19.

SUMMARY

LO 1

LEARNING OBJECTIVE 1
Explain the difference between variable and fixed costs

A cost is fixed if it does not change in response to changes in the level of activity within the relevant range of activity. A variable cost is the same per unit of activity within the relevant range of activity. Total variable costs increase or decrease in direct proportion to the increase and decrease in activity level whether being measured on productivity or sales output.

LO 2

LEARNING OBJECTIVE 2
Explain the relationship between the fixed costs and the variable costs of production

The total costs of production are made up of fixed and variable costs. Within the relevant range of activity, fixed costs remain static whereas variable costs move in relation to output.

LO 3

LEARNING OBJECTIVE 3
Explain what is meant by a linear cost function

A linear cost function is a straight-line cost function that can be shown mathematically as $y = a + bx$. Within this mathematical expression, y is the total cost to be predicted, a is a constant (fixed cost), b is the cost that will be the same for each unit of activity (variable cost) and x is the number of units measured in units of output or sales.

LO 4

LEARNING OBJECTIVE 4
Identify what is meant by the relevant range of activity

The relevant range of activity is the levels of activity that a firm has experienced in past periods. In this range, it is assumed that the relationship between the independent and dependent variables will be similar in a following period.

LO 5

LEARNING OBJECTIVE 5
Identify what is meant by cost–volume–profit analysis

Cost–volume–profit (CVP) analysis is a technique that is used by organisations to assist them in making decisions by examining the interrelationships between cost, volume and profit.

LO 6

LEARNING OBJECTIVE 6
Explain what is meant by a break-even chart

Break-even is a point in CVP analysis where costs are equal to revenues; therefore, at this level of activity, there is no loss or profit.

LO 7

LEARNING OBJECTIVE 7
Explain and apply the contribution margin approach to measuring break-even sales levels and other sales levels for required profits

The contribution margin is the sales revenue less all variable costs. Provided that the variable costs are less than the sales revenue, then there is a contribution towards reducing the cost of the fixed overheads. By using this approach, the break-even point can be calculated – along with a profit figure that is required above break even.

LO 8

LEARNING OBJECTIVE 8
Discuss the limitations of using a linear cost assumption in CVP analysis

CVP analysis is a useful tool, however there are certain problems associated with its use. They are as follows:

1   The assumption that all costs and revenues are linear. For example, costs may increase in order to gain extra sales (advertising), or fixed costs could change and follow a stepped path.

2   It is assumed that we are dealing with a single-product firm. Where a firm produces more than one product, allocating costs can be a problem.

3   Not all costs are fixed or variable, some may be mixed; for example, sales staff being paid a wage and a bonus on sales.

4   In a multi-product firm, fixed costs may be difficult to allocate; for example, the heating of premises. A suitable allocation method then needs to be found.

REFERENCES

Arnold, J. & Turley, S., 1996. *Accounting for Management Decisions*, 3rd edn, Prentice-Hall.

Curwin, J & Slater, R., 1996. *Quantitative Methods for Business Decisions*, 4th edn, International Thomson Business Press.

Horngren, C.T., Foster, G. & Srikant, M.D., 2000. *Cost Accounting: A Managerial Emphasis*, 10th edn, Prentice Hall.

FURTHER READING

Hansen, D.R. & Mowen, M.M., 2003. *Management Accounting and Control*, 6th edn, South-Western, Mason, Ohio.

REVIEW QUESTIONS

1   It is often assumed that there is only one independent variable in cost behaviour. Explain the nature of independent variables and why this assumption is made.

2   What is the difference between a linear fixed cost and a curvilinear variable cost? Give examples, other than those given in the text.

3   What are some of the problems in using past data to predict future cost behaviour?

4   What are the problems associated with CVP analysis in a multi-product firm?

5   Explain why the contribution margin produces profit when an entity sells goods above the break-even point.

6   Suppose a firm with a contribution margin ratio of 0.3 increased advertising expenses by $10 000 and found sales increased by $30 000. Why is this simple problem an important one?

PROBLEMS FOR DISCUSSION AND ANALYSIS

1   In the table below, fill in the blank spaces.

Sales $	Variable costs $	Fixed costs $	Total costs $	Profit $	Contribution $
2 000	1 400		2 000		
3 000		600		1 000	
	1 000		1 600	2 400	
4 000		600		400	

2   In the table below, fill in the blank spaces.

Sales $	Variable costs $	Fixed costs $	Total costs $	Profit $	Contribution $
7 249	1 436		7 250		
3 642		1 028		738	
	8 321		8 321	932	
634		236		83	

3   With a sales figure of $500 000, Fidget Ltd reaches the break-even point for widget sales. Fixed costs are $200 000.
   a   What is the contribution margin?
   b   If variable costs are $6 per widget, what is the selling price?
   c   If 55 000 widgets are sold, calculate the profit/loss.

4   Remember Enterprises manufactures miniature digital diaries. Variable costs are $30 per diary, the price is $45, and fixed costs are $90 000.

Required

   a   What is the contribution margin for one diary?
   b   How many diaries must Remember Enterprises sell to break even?
   c   If Remember Enterprises sells 6300 diaries, what is the net profit?

5   Mr Potter sells various pottery items at local markets. His fixed expenses (depreciation on the kiln, utilities, tools and portable selling booth) are $5000 per year. The average price for a piece of pottery is $5.50, and the average variable cost (e.g. clay, paints, glazes and price tags) is $3.50 per item.

Required

   a   How many pieces of pottery must Mr Potter sell to just cover his expenses?
   b   If Mr Potter wants to earn $7000 profit, how many pieces of pottery must he sell? Prepare an income statement (using variable costing) to verify your answer.

6   Hayly and Peter Brush have started their own business, Cleaner Homes, which offers cleaning services for households. The Brushes have fixed expenses of $4000 per month for office rent, advertising and a receptionist. Variable expenses for the cleaners' wages and cleaning supplies are $22 per job. Cleaner Homes charges $42 for the average job.

Required

   a   How many jobs must Cleaner Homes average each month to break even?
   b   What is the net profit for Cleaner Homes in a month with 240 jobs? With 190 jobs?
   c   Suppose that Cleaner Homes decides to increase the price to $45 per job. What is the new break-even point in the number of jobs per month?

7   Clean-it Pty Ltd makes washing machines, and with its existing plant capacity the maximum production possible is 1000 units per year. Fixed costs are estimated at $36 000 per annum and the selling price of each machine is $240. Sales for the next year are expected to drop to 800 units. The cost of each washing machine is calculated as follows:
   • direct material cost, $40
   • direct labour cost, 10 hours at $8 per hour.
   a   Calculate (i) the break-even point, (ii) the maximum profit and (iii) the profit at an estimated sales level of 800 units.
   b   Costs alter by the following proportions:
      • direct materials increase by 20 per cent
      • fixed costs come down by $12 000
      • direct labour costs increase by $2 per hour.
      What will be (i) the new break-even point and (ii) the new profit at the estimated sales level of 800 units?

8   The Green Finger Co. is considering an investment in a new compost bin. The equipment is expected to generate additional annual sales of 4000 units at $21 per unit. The cost of the equipment is $160 000 and it is expected to have a 10-year life and a zero residual value. Selling expenses related to the new product are expected to be 2 per cent of sales revenue. The variable costs to manufacture the compost bin are shown below:

	$
Cost per unit:	
Direct labour	5.00
Direct materials	8.25
Variable factory overhead	1.50
Total variable cost per unit	14.75

Determine

   a   the break-even sales per year in units for the new investment
   b   the expected profit each year from the investment
   c   whether the company should proceed with the investment. Give reasons for your recommendation.

9   You are in charge of organising a conference for a group of accounting academics. You have obtained the following details:

	$
Rental of conference venue	300
Speakers' costs	500
Notebooks and pens	100
Cost of lunch, and morning and afternoon teas (per person)	30

   The conference fee for the 45 academics is $50 per person.

Required

   a   How many academics would have to attend at $50 per person for the conference to break even?
   b   If 60 academics attend at $50 per person, what is the expected profit?
   c   The committee believes that $250 spent on promotion would attract a total of 80 academics. Should they spend this if they want to keep the fee at $50 per person?

10 The Threadbare Clothing Company has to decide whether to produce trousers or skirts. The manager knows that the demand for trousers is 1200 per month at a selling price of $45 each and the demand for skirts is 800 at $60 each. Costs of production are as follows:

	Trousers ($)	Skirts ($)
Monthly rent	550.00	550.00
Material per unit	15.00	21.00
Labour hours per unit	1.25	0.75
Selling costs per unit	0.25	0.30
Administration costs	1 000.00	1 000.00
Labour rate per hour	8.50	8.50
Depreciation on plant	120.00	120.00

Required

Advise Threadbare's management as to whether it is more profitable to produce trousers or skirts, giving the break-even points for each product, and the level of profits or losses in either event.

11 Cords Pty Ltd manufactures a style of corduroy jeans that it sold last year at $36 a pair. The cost specifications for these jeans were as follows:

Variable cost per pair of jeans	$
Materials	13
Labour	7
Fixed overheads per month	52 800

Cords Pty Ltd made a profit of $22 080 each month.
a How many pairs of jeans did Cords Pty Ltd sell each month?
b Cords Pty Ltd is now planning next year's operations. The sales director is proposing to boost sales by reducing the selling price to $34 and spending an additional $6000 per month on advertising. She estimates that these actions will enable the company to sell 5800 pairs of jeans each month. Evaluate the sales director's proposals, taking into account the expected impact on profits and the break-even point. State any assumptions you need to make.
c If the managing director of Cords Pty Ltd were to require that next year's profit shows a 15 per cent increase over last year's performance, how many pairs of jeans would have to be sold each month, (i) assuming that the sales director's policies were adopted, and (ii) assuming that they were not?

12 The Incr-Edible Pie Company Ltd has the following revenue and cost functions for 20X3:

$$\text{total revenues} = \$30x$$
$$\text{total costs} = \$150\,000 + 20x$$
$$\text{where } x = \text{number of units}$$

Required

a Prepare a break-even chart for the Incr-Edible Pie Company. Label the vertical axis in $50 000 amounts and the horizontal axis in 5000-unit amounts.
b What is the break-even point in units and dollars?
c Prove your answer in (b) by calculating the profits at the break-even level.

13 ABC Ltd produces stereos and sells these for $250 each. The company can produce a maximum of 5000 units per year. Variable costs are $185 per unit and fixed costs are $250 000 per year, regardless of production.
a Calculate the break-even point.
b What is the profit for the company if it sells 5000 units?
c The company believes it can sell more units if it leases additional equipment. The lease costs are $200 000 a year and the company has to give one year's notice to cancel the lease. Because of the increased production, variable costs are reduced to $175 per unit. If the maximum number of units the company can produce and sell with the new equipment is 8100, should the company lease the new equipment?
d What if there is a recession in the audio industry and the company can now sell only 4000 units at $240? Should the company keep producing or not? Give reasons for your answer. (Assume it did not lease additional equipment.)

Note to instructors: The following problems are considered more suitable for use in MBA courses. However, undergraduate courses may also find them useful.

14 The Gigantic DVD Store sells three categories of DVDs relating to sport, drama and comedy. Unit selling prices and variable costs for each category are as follows:

	Sport	Drama	Comedy
	$	$	$
Selling price	100	70	200
Variable cost	60	50	100

The fixed costs at Gigantic are $90 000 per year and this amount is subject to income tax at the rate of 40 per cent. The company aims to make after-tax profits of $27 000 per year. The current unit sales mix is as follows:

	Percentage of total
Sport	40
Drama	50
Comedy	10

Required

Calculate each of the following for the current sales mix:
a the break even, in units, for each category
b the average unit contribution margin
c the break-even unit sales volume in total, and for each category
d the unit sales volume required to earn the desired after-tax profits in total and for each category.

15 In 20X1, Ashfield Ltd sold 8000 car alarms at $90 each. The following details are available.

Variable costs	$	Fixed costs	$
Production	50 per unit	Production	100 000
Selling	10 per unit	Selling	80 000
	60 per unit		180 000

Ashfield can reduce its variable production costs by $10 per unit if it invests $100 000 in new equipment.

Required

a   Calculate the break-even point in units for the original and revised set of figures.

b   Calculate the profit using the original and revised set of figures for sales of 8000 units.

c   What are the sales, in units, when the profit is the same for both the original and revised set of figures?

d   If the company reduced its selling price by $10 per unit, expected sales would increase to 15 000 units. Should the company reduce its selling price under either alternative?

16 Golden Bakeries Ltd has three major product lines: bread rolls, donuts and fudge cakes. The income statement for the year ended 30 June 20X3, prepared by product line using absorption costing, is as follows:

Golden Bakeries Ltd
Income statement for the year ending 30 June 20X3

	Bread rolls	Donuts	Fudge cakes	Total
Sales in kilograms	400 000	100 000	100 000	600 000
	$000	$000	$000	$000
Revenue from sales	2000	800	400	3200
Cost of sales				
Direct materials	660	320	200	1080
Direct labour	180	80	40	300
Factory overhead	216	96	48	360
Less Total cost of sales	1056	496	288	1840
Gross profit	944	304	112	1360
Operating expenses				
Selling expenses				
Advertising	100	60	40	200
Commissions	100	80	40	220
Salaries	60	40	20	120
Total selling expenses	260	180	100	540
Administration expenses				
Royalties	100	40	30	170
Salaries	120	50	30	200
Total administration expenses	220	90	60	370
Less Total operating expenses	480	270	160	910
Net profit	464	34	(48)	450

The following additional information is available:

i   *Advertising* is considered necessary by management, despite the fact that no direct correlation between the level of sales and the amount spent on advertising has been demonstrated. As a result, an annual advertising strategy is developed for each product line. Each product is advertised separately.

ii *Sales commissions* are paid to the sales people at the rates of 5 per cent on the bread rolls and 10 per cent on the donuts and fudge cakes.

iii *Royalties* for the recipes for each product are required. These are an annual payment for each product.
iv *Salaries costs* are related to the company's overall activities rather than to any product line. Sales and administrative staff spend time and effort on each product line, and on the company as a whole. Managers estimate the amount of time spent on each product and these estimates are used to allocate the cost of salaries and wages.
v   *Cost of sales information:*
    Common facilities are used to produce all three products. The company's inventories of raw materials and finished goods are similar from year to year. The inventories at 30 June 20X3 and 20X2 were basically the same.
    The factory overhead costs for the 20X2–X3 financial year were as follows:

	$
Variable indirect labour and supplies	30 000
Variable employee benefits	60 000
Supervisory salaries	70 000
Plant occupancy costs	200 000
Total	360 000

There was no over- or under-applied overhead for the year.
Factory overhead was applied to products at the rate of 120 per cent of direct labour dollars.

Required

The financial controller of Golden Bakeries has recommended that the company do a cost–volume–profit analysis of its operations. They have also asked that you first prepare a revised income statement that utilises a product contribution margin format that will be useful in CVP analysis. The statement should show the profit contribution for each product line and the net profit (before taxes) for the company as a whole.

ETHICS CASE STUDY

Dave Johnston is analysing a request from a special customer for an order of 1000 electric kettles. The customer has proposed that he will pay an amount per unit based on the contribution margin plus 20 per cent. The customer is in Hong Kong and he wants the goods before Christmas and the date is 12 December.
    The other details of the proposal are:
i   The customer is to pay all freight costs.
ii Dave's company is to make a $5000 payment to a friend of the customer who works in the customs area in Hong Kong so that the kettles can be cleared through customs before Christmas.
    The relevant data for the kettles is as follows:

Variable unit manufacturing costs	$25
Variable unit selling and administrative costs	$12
Selling price	$50

Dave's boss has explained that the customer is a very important one and, as the order will lead to the plant operating at full capacity, workers will be able to earn a little extra for Christmas by working overtime.

Discuss

   a   the accounting and ethical issues in this case

   b   whether Dave should accept the terms proposed for the special order.

ANSWERS TO REVIEW EXERCISES

1   It is assumed that variable costs are the same per unit of activity; therefore, the variable costs will move in proportion to activity levels (i.e. in a linear fashion). In reality, variable costs do not behave strictly in this manner. For example, firms will often receive quantity discounts when they purchase large quantities of goods for manufacture or resale. In such cases, the cost per unit of material will not solely depend upon the activity but will also depend on the amount of goods that are purchased. As a result, the variable costs will not behave in a linear fashion and will tend to follow a curvilinear function.

     A fixed cost is assumed to be constant over all levels of output. Once again, in reality, these costs tend to not be strictly linear. Fixed costs will often only be fixed over a limited range of output, and will tend to behave in a stepped rather than linear function.

2   A linear fixed cost is one that remains constant for all levels of activity. A stepped fixed cost is constant for certain levels of activity but steps up to a new figure at a certain level of activity.

3   The relevant range of activity refers to the level of activity that the firm has experienced in past accounting periods. The significance of this range is that cost behaviour – the relationship between the dependent and independent variables – can be established with a certain amount of accuracy. This is because the firm has experienced cost behaviour in this range before and can observe the relationship between cost and activity levels. This information is useful in predicting future costs for decision-making purposes. Past cost behaviour is not known outside of this range and it is therefore more difficult to predict.

4   The break-even point is the point where costs are exactly covered by income and there is no profit or loss.

5   a   variable
     b   fixed
     c   variable
     d   variable
     e   variable
     f   fixed
     g   variable
     h   variable
     i   variable

19

LEARNING OBJECTIVES

At the end of this chapter, you should be able to:

1 explain what is meant by the term 'sunk costs'

2 explain what is meant by differential (incremental) costs

3 identify what is meant by avoidable and unavoidable costs

4 discuss the concept of opportunity costs, and its role in decision making

5 explain the costs and benefits that are relevant to specific decisions

6 explain and apply the contribution approach to decision making in cases where there are no resource constraints

7 apply the contribution approach to decisions concerning whether to close unprofitable sections

8 explain what is meant by decision making with constraints

9 illustrate the use of the contribution margin approach in relation to decisions with one scarce resource

10 explain what is meant by internal opportunity cost

11 evaluate problems of whether entities should make or buy a product or a service in cases where there is spare capacity and no spare capacity

12 discuss the role of qualitative factors in decision making with constraints

Introduction

Management needs to make decisions about future business opportunities to ensure that the organisation's objectives are met. Many of these decisions relate to the short term and are expressed in financial terms in the organisation's budget (see Chapter 20). Management is also required to make decisions of a more immediate nature, which relate to opportunities that were not anticipated at the planning stage. To ignore profitable opportunities because they have not been specifically included in the budget would be irresponsible in a dynamic business environment. These decisions can be categorised as follows:

- ## Decisions where there are no resource constraints
  In these circumstances, organisations are free to make a decision, knowing that it will not affect other opportunities. For instance, the introduction of a new product may not affect, in any way, the demand and production levels of other products. These decisions can also be simply described as 'accept or reject' decisions.

- ## Decisions where there are resource constraints
  This situation occurs when an organisation experiences a shortage of physical resources; for example, a particular material. In such cases, the organisation cannot accept all potentially desirable opportunities. To decide which of these opportunities to choose, it will be necessary to implement a priority (ranking) system.

- ## Mutually exclusive decisions
  These are decisions where the acceptance of one opportunity means that the others will be rejected. For instance, when management has to decide whether to make or buy a component to be embodied within one of the firm's products, the decision to make it means that the option to buy is rejected. Mutually exclusive decisions can include situations either with or without resource constraints.

In the case of decisions where there are resource constraints, we will consider situations where there is only one scarce resource. Decision making when there are two or more scarce resources is outside the scope of this introductory text. The same principles apply, but when there are two or more scarce resources, more complex mathematical skills are required in the calculation of the solution.

It is conventional to assume that short-term decisions are those that will affect the firm within a period of one year. It will also be assumed that the values of cash inflows and outflows throughout the year are of an equivalent value. This is naive, because, clearly, all individuals and firms prefer to receive, for example, cash today rather than in 11 months time. For clarity, it is convenient in our analysis to make this assumption, because complexities arise when we begin to take account of the time value of money in the decision-making process.

In our analysis of short-term decisions, we will initially assume that only quantitative factors are relevant in the decision-making process. In reality, however, qualitative factors are also influential in the decision-making process. We will conclude our examination of short-term decision making by considering the nature of qualitative factors and looking at some examples in which they influence the decision.

Costs and benefits relevant to decision making

Decisions relate to the future, and the purpose of decision making is to select courses of action that satisfy the objective of the firm. There is no opportunity to alter the past, although past experience might help us in future decisions. For example, the observation of past cost behaviour might help to determine future levels of cost.

Relevant costs and benefits can therefore be defined as those costs and benefits that result from making a specific decision. A more precise definition will be established after we have examined the underlying principles of relevant costs and benefits and considered some examples of the application of these principles.

The relevant costs for decision making are different from those used in accrual accounting. This is not surprising because the principles of traditional costing (e.g. overhead absorption methods) evolved from the need to report historical events, rather than to determine future costs and benefits. A number of methods adopted by accountants to account for decisions about the future are derived from economic theory and therefore might be familiar to you.

We now consider the principles underlying relevant costs for decision making and the application of these principles to specific types of decisions. The differences between the application of relevant costs and traditional costing methods will also be discussed.

FUTURE AND SUNK (PAST) COSTS

Costs of a historical nature, which are normally referred to as sunk costs, are incurred as a result of a past decision and are therefore irrelevant to future decisions and should be ignored.

LO 1

Explain what is meant by the term 'sunk costs'

KEY CONCEPT 19.1

SUNK COSTS

Sunk costs, or past costs, can be easily identified in that they have either been paid for, or the firm is committed and cannot avoid such payment in the future.

Example 19.1: Disposal of obsolete machine

A firm has an obsolete machine that was purchased and paid for two years ago. The net book value of the machine, as shown in the accounts of the firm, before it became obsolete, is $72 000. The alternatives now available to the firm are:

• to make alterations to the machine at an estimated cost of $20 000 and then sell it for $40 000
• to sell it for scrap, at an estimated selling price of $15 000.

The net book value of $72 000 represents the original cost of purchasing the machine less the accumulated depreciation (charge for depreciation over the two-year period). The original cost is the result of a past decision: it was incurred two years ago and therefore is a sunk cost. It is irrelevant to the future decision concerning whether to alter the machine and sell it, or sell it for scrap. The depreciation is also based on the original cost of the machine and is therefore irrelevant to this future decision. The only relevant costs and benefits in this example are those related to the future; we can analyse these as follows.

	Alter $	Scrap $
Future benefits	40 000	15 000
Future costs	20 000	–
Future income	20 000	15 000

From the analysis of relevant costs and benefits, it can be seen that the firm will be $5000 better off by altering the machine and selling it rather than selling it for scrap.

Review exercise 1

In the context of decision making, explain the meaning of a sunk cost.

DIFFERENTIAL (INCREMENTAL) COSTS

Explain what is meant by differential (incremental) costs

Another important principle in the determination of relevant costs and benefits is that only differential (incremental) costs and benefits are relevant to future decisions. The application of the principles underlying differential costing is illustrated in Case study 19.1, where a firm which has spare capacity is offered a special order. By comparing the costs and benefits that are associated with the opportunities available to the firm, we can identify differential costs and benefits. It is these costs and benefits that are relevant to decisions between competing opportunities.

KEY CONCEPT 19.2

DIFFERENTIAL COSTS

Differential (incremental) costs are the differences in costs and benefits between alternative opportunities available to an organisation. It follows that when a number of opportunities are being considered, costs and benefits that are common to these alternative opportunities are irrelevant to the decision.

CASE STUDY 19.1

KT'S INC.

KT's Inc. manufactures hats and has a current capacity of 120 000 hats per year. However, it is predicted that, in the forthcoming year, sales will be only 90 000 hats. A mail-order firm offers to buy 20 000 hats at $7.50 each. The acceptance of this special order will not affect regular sales and it will take a year to complete. The managing director is reluctant to accept the order because $7.50 is below the factory unit cost of $8 per hat.

The following gives the predicted total profit and the predicted profit per unit, in a traditional costing format, if the order were not accepted.

	Total		Per unit	
	$	$	$	$
Sales: 90 000 hats at $10 each		900 000		10.00
Less factory expenses:				
Variable	540 000		6.00	
Supervision	90 000		1.00	
Other fixed costs	90 000	720 000	1.00	8.00
Gross profit		180 000		2.00
Selling expenses:				
Variable	22 500		0.25	
Fixed	112 500	135 000	1.25	1.50
Profit		45 000		0.50

The management accountant, with the production and sales manager, is requested to review the costs of taking on the special order. These are their conclusions:

1 The variable costs of production relate to labour and materials and these will be incurred at the same rates as for the production of the normal production units.

2 There will be a need for additional supervision. However, it is anticipated that four of the current supervisors can cover this requirement if each of them works overtime of five hours per week. Supervisors are paid $10 per hour and overtime is paid at a premium of $2 per hour. There are 48 working weeks in the year. Therefore, the additional costs are:

$$5 \text{ hours} \times \$12 \text{ per hour} \times 48 \text{ weeks} \times 4 \text{ supervisors} = \$11\,520$$

3 Other fixed costs are factory rent and the depreciation of plant. It is anticipated that these will remain the same if the order is accepted.

4 There will be a need to hire an additional machine, costing $10 000, if the contract is accepted.

5 The variable sales cost relates to salespersons' commissions, and this cost will not be incurred on the special order.

6 The fixed sales expenses relate to the administering of sales. These costs will remain the same, except that a part-time clerk will be required to help with the additional workload if the special order is accepted. The salary will be $6000 per year.

⟩

Using the differential costing approach, we can compare the total profit for the year for KT's Inc. if the order is accepted or rejected:

	Accept	Reject	Differential cost and revenue
	$	$	$
Sales	1 050 000	900 000	150 000
Factory expenses:			
Variable costs	660 000	540 000	120 000
Supervision	101 520	90 000	11 520
Other fixed costs	90 000	90 000	–
Hire of plant	10 000	–	10 000
	861 520	720 000	141 520
Sales expenses:			
Variable costs	22 500	22 500	–
Fixed costs	118 500	112 500	6 000
Total costs	1 002 520	855 000	147 520
Profit	47 480	45 000	2 480

COMMENTARY

From the differential analysis, it can be seen that KT's Inc. will be $2480 better off if the special order is accepted. Also, it can be observed that a number of the costs are irrelevant in the decision analysis. That is, they are the same whether or not the order is accepted: for example, 'other fixed costs' are $90 000 for both the 'accept' and the 'reject' decisions. The analysis of data could have been simplified by considering only the differential costs and revenues related to the special order. If the differential analysis of costs and revenues results in a profit, then, from a purely quantitative perspective, the order should be accepted.

Avoidable and unavoidable costs

Identify what is meant by avoidable and unavoidable costs

There is an alternative way of determining whether a cost is relevant or irrelevant in decisions, such as the special order for the hats illustrated in Case study 19.1. Instead of using the differential analysis, we ask the question: would a cost be avoided if the company did not proceed with the special order? If the answer is yes, the cost is relevant and should be included. For example, consider this question with regard to the cost of plant hire for the special order Case study 19.1: will the cost of plant hire be avoided if the company does not proceed with the order? The answer is yes; that is, the cost is relevant to the decision because it will only be incurred if the order is accepted. A cost is described as unavoidable if it will be incurred regardless of the decision to accept or reject; that is, the cost is irrelevant to the decision.

Review exercise 2

In the context of decision making, explain the meaning of avoidable and unavoidable costs.

OPPORTUNITY COSTS

The economists' concept of opportunity cost has been adopted by accountants for decision-making purposes. This concept relates to the cost of using resources for alternative opportunities.

L O 4

Discuss the concept of opportunity costs, and its role in decision making

KEY CONCEPT 19.3

OPPORTUNITY COST

The opportunity cost of a resource is normally defined as the maximum benefit which could be obtained from that resource if it were used for some other purpose. If a firm uses a resource for alternative A rather than B, the opportunity cost is the potential benefits that are forgone by not using the resource for alternative B. Therefore, the potential benefits that are forgone – the opportunity cost – are a relevant cost in the decision to accept alternative A.

The following is an example of the concept of opportunity costs. Jeff Jones, a qualified accountant, is a sole practitioner. He works 40 hours per week and charges clients $40 per hour. Jeff is already overworked and will not work any extra hours. A circus offers Jeff $2000 per week to become a clown. In the decision to become a clown, Jeff must consider the benefits he would forgo from closing his accounting practice; that is, $40 × 40 hours = $1600 per week. This is the opportunity cost of Jeff becoming a clown. Assuming that Jeff is concerned only with financial rewards, he will accept the offer to become a clown because he will be $2000 – $1600 = $400 per week better off.

CASE STUDY 19.2

WORTHIER CAUSES OUT THERE THAN HOLDING F1 RACE HERE
by Leow Aik Kheng

HOSTING the Formula One (F1) Grand Prix Championship in Singapore is a venture worthy of consideration, but it must be an economically self-sustaining one and not a 'prestige' project that uses public resources in the interests of the middle and upper classes. Singapore Motorsports Association president Tan Teng Lip said in the article, 'A S'pore Grand Prix?' (ST, March 14), that Formula One's organising body, the Federation Internationale de l'Automobile (FIA), favoured purpose-built tracks over street circuits in new host venues. Land here is too valuable to be allocated to golf courses and racing circuits unless economically

justified. Malaysia's Sepang track takes up 400 ha, nearly as big as Sentosa.

Hundreds of millions are also required to construct and maintain the track and other facilities to meet FIA specifications. Tens of millions would have to be paid to the Formula One Constructors' Association to host the event. Singapore will likely have to pay much more than Sepang or Zhuhai in China for hosting rights in the Asian legs of the championship.

Sepang is entrenched under its existing contract, and Malaysian state and private companies are the main sponsors for two competing Formula One teams, while ⟼

advertisers are salivating at the exposure opportunities in the Chinese market. The most obvious benefit as host would be to raise Singapore's international profile. Formula One is the world's widest televised event, with cumulative viewership exceeding even the football World Cup.

But Singapore does not stand to benefit as

Malaysia has in terms of a transfer of technology to a local car-making industry. Hosting an F1 race is a nice thing to do. But resources are limited, and the move may incur substantial opportunity costs. There are other causes that are more worthy, such as education and health care.

Straits Times, 15 March 2002

COMMENTARY

The article mentions limited resources, and if Singapore were to host the Formula One race then the article is claiming that this will result in less funds being spent in areas such as health and education. In other words, the opportunity cost of hosting the race is decreased services in other areas.

REPLACEMENT COSTS

If a resource was originally purchased for some purpose other than an opportunity currently under consideration, the relevant cost of using that resource is its replacement cost. This cost has come about as a direct result of the decision to use the resource for a purpose not originally intended and the need to replace the resource. The following example will help you to understand the application of this principle.

Easy Done Ltd has been approached by a customer who would like a special job done. The job would require the use of 500 kg of material Z. Material Z is used by Easy Done for a variety of purposes.

Currently, the company holds 1000 kg in inventory which was purchased one month ago for $6 per kilogram. Since then, the price per kilogram has increased to $8. If 500 kg were used on this special job it would need to be replaced to meet the production demand from other jobs.

The relevant cost of using material Z on this special job is the replacement cost, 500 kg $\times$ $8 = $4000. This is because the material will need to be replaced as a result of its use, and the replacement will cost $4000. This cost has arisen as a direct result of accepting the special order and, therefore, it is relevant to the decision. It should be noted that the original cost of $6 per kilogram is irrelevant to the decision as it relates to a past decision and has already been incurred (that is, it is a sunk cost).

Review exercise 3

Explain the meaning of opportunity costs.

COMPARISON WITH TRADITIONAL COSTING METHODS

Case study 19.3 illustrates the application of the principles of relevant costs compared with traditional costing methods.

LO 5

Explain the costs and benefits that are relevant to specific decisions

CASE STUDY 19.3

NO PROBLEM LTD

No Problem Ltd is considering whether to accept the offer of a contract to undertake some reconstruction work at a price of $73 000. The work will begin almost immediately and will take about one year to complete. The company's accountant has submitted the following statement:

	$	$
Contract price		73 000
Less Costs		
Cost of work already incurred in drawing up detailed costings		4 700
Materials		
A	7 000	
B	8 000	15 000
Labour		
Direct	21 000	
Indirect	12 000	33 000
Machinery		
Depreciation on machines owned	4 000	
Hire of special equipment	5 000	9 000
General overheads		10 500
Total cost		72 200
Expected profit		800

The management personnel of the company doubt whether it is advisable to incur the inevitable risks involved for such a small profit margin. On making further enquiries, the following information becomes available:

1. Material A was bought two years ago for $7000. It would cost $8000 at today's prices. If not used on this contract, it could be sold for $6500. There is no alternative use for this material and no expected future use.
2. Material B was ordered for another job but will be used on this job if the contract is accepted. The replacement for the other job will cost $9000.
3. The trade union has negotiated a minimum wage agreement, as a result of which direct wages of $21 000 will be incurred whether the contract is undertaken or not. If not employed on this contract, these employees could be used to do much-needed maintenance work, which would otherwise be done by an outside contractor at an estimated cost of $18 500.
4. The indirect labour is the wage of a supervisor who will have to be taken on to supervise the contract. A suitable person is ready to take up the appointment at once.

〉〉⟶

5　The machine, which is already owned, is six years old. The final instalment of depreciation required to write off the balance on the asset account is $4000. There is no alternative use for the machine, and its scrap value is negligible, because of the high cost of dismantling and removal.

6　The general overhead absorption rate is 50 per cent of direct labour. Overheads are expected to rise by $4000 if the contract is accepted.

With reference to this information, and the principles of relevant costs, we can now consider the individual cost items that should be accounted for in the decision concerning whether to accept or reject the contract:

1　*material A*: The $7000 originally paid for the material is a sunk cost and is, therefore, irrelevant. We are told that the current replacement cost is $8000. However, the company would only obtain $6500 if it was sold; that is, the net realisable value. This is the benefit the company forgoes (the opportunity cost) by using the material on this contract. Thus, $6500 is the relevant cost.

2　*material B*: The fact that this material has already been ordered means that the company is committed to pay the supplier of the material. Thus, the cost of $8000 can also be considered as a sunk cost and is irrelevant to the decision. The only alternative is to use the material on the other job. If so, the company would have to purchase some more material at a cost of $9000. This is the opportunity cost of using the material on this contract.

3　*direct labour*: These employees will be paid whether the contract is accepted or not; therefore, this cost is unavoidable and irrelevant. However, if they were not employed on this contract the company would save $18 500 in fees to the outside contractor for maintenance. The $18 500 is therefore a relevant cost as this is the opportunity cost of using the employees on the contract.

4　*indirect labour*: The cost of $12 000 for employing the supervisor is an incremental cost; that is, it will be incurred only if the contract is accepted. Therefore, it is relevant to the contract.

5　*depreciation on the machine owned*: The cost of depreciation relates to a past cost (that is, a sunk cost) and is, therefore, irrelevant to the decision. A relevant benefit is the machine's scrap value. However, as this is negligible, it is ignored.

6　*hire of special equipment*: The cost of $5000 will be incurred only if the contract is accepted; it is an incremental cost and is relevant to the decision.

7　*general overhead*: The only cost that is relevant is the increase in cost of $4000 if the contract is accepted. This cost is incremental; hence, it is relevant to the decision. All the other costs related to general overheads are unavoidable (and irrelevant).

8　*cost of work already incurred in drawing up costings ($4700, detailed at the beginning of the schedule)*: This cost is irrelevant to the contract: it is a sunk cost and therefore should be excluded.

We are now in a position to draw up an amended statement of costs for the contract.

	Relevant costs $	Relevant benefits $
Contract price		73 000
Less Costs		
Materials		
A	6 500	
B	9 000	15 500
Labour		
Direct	18 500	

	Relevant costs	Relevant benefits
	$	$
Indirect	<u>12 000</u>	30 500
Hire of special equipment		5 000
Overheads		<u>4 000</u>
Total costs		55 000
Expected profits		<u>18 000</u>

COMMENTARY

In this case study, it is apparent that, when we consider only costs that are relevant, the contract is more attractive to the company. In the original schedule of costs and revenues, which were based on traditional costing methods, the expected profit was only $800 compared with $18 000. It should be stressed that the higher profits yielded from the analysis of relevant costs and benefits compared with the traditional analysis is not always the rule. The result depends on the particular circumstances of the firm making the decisions.

The principles underlying the relevance of costs and benefits to decisions, described and illustrated in Case study 19.3, focus on costs rather than income. However, the same principles apply to income. Only the income that will be generated as a result of the decision is relevant to the decision and should be brought into the decision model. Relevant benefits, by their nature, relate to the future. All benefits that have been received, or are due to be received from a prior commitment, are irrelevant to future decisions.

THE MEANING OF RELEVANCE

Earlier in this chapter relevant costs and benefits were defined, in general terms, as those costs and benefits that result from a specific decision. We are now in the position to derive a more precise definition.

KEY CONCEPT 19.4

RELEVANT COSTS AND BENEFITS

Relevant costs and benefits are those cost and benefits that relate to the future. They are additional costs and income that will be incurred, or result, from a decision.

Costs that are relevant to a decision might also be:

- the cost of replacing a resource that was originally purchased for some other purpose
- the opportunity cost of using a resource that could be used for some alternative purpose.

There are also costs and income that are incurred or generated by an organisation that are irrelevant to a decision; that is, are not affected by a decision. It is important to identify these costs and benefits so that we can eliminate them for our analysis.

Unfortunately, some organisations still ignore the principles of relevant costs and benefits in making future decisions. This distorts decision making and causes organisations to take wrong courses of action.

Review exercise 4

Depreciation is an important concept in the determination of profit. Discuss why it is classified as an irrelevant cost in decision making.

Fixed and variable costs and the contribution approach

Explain and apply the contribution approach to decision making in cases where there are no resource constraints

The concept of contribution was introduced in Chapter 18. The contribution is the difference between the sales revenue and the variable costs. We reintroduce the concept here in the context of relevant costs and decision making.

It is normally assumed that costs behave in a linear fashion: fixed costs are constant for all volumes and variable costs vary in direct proportion to volume. Often, fixed costs are irrelevant to decisions because they remain the same whatever the decision is; that is, they are unavoidable. When there are no scarce resources and the sales revenue exceeds the relevant variable costs, a decision to accept will be made. This rule applies to several types of decisions.

A word of caution: There are some situations when costs do not behave in a linear fashion so variations in unit variable costs or in fixed cost levels might occur. For example, the cost of new machinery that is specifically purchased for a future contract is classified as a fixed cost, but it is relevant to the contract because it is avoidable. When fixed costs are directly attributable to opportunities, they are relevant to the decision to accept or reject. However, unless you are given a clear indication to the contrary, you should always assume that costs behave in a linear fashion. It should be noted that this assumption was also adopted in Chapter 18.

The contribution approach can be applied to a number of types of decisions that management must take when running a business. Examples 19.2 and 19.3 illustrate this with respect to the range of products an organisation has and closing an unprofitable section within an organisation.

THE RANGE OF PRODUCTS

The management of an organisation is confronted with a number of opportunities each year and has to decide which to embody in their plans. In Example 19.2, the products are independent of each other. We can derive a simple rule from this example: if a product makes a positive contribution, it is worth considering for acceptance in the firm's production program. The fixed costs have been apportioned to products. This is the convention under absorption costing, described in Chapter 17, where overheads are absorbed into products using predetermined rates based on budgeted figures for overhead costs and activity levels. Normally, these overhead costs are unavoidable, and are therefore not relevant, as in this example. Overhead costs are relevant only if they are incremental in nature.

Example 19.2: Products 1, 2 and 3

A firm has the opportunity to manufacture and sell three products, 1, 2 and 3 in the forthcoming year. Here is a draft summary of the profit or loss on the products:

| | Total | 1 | 2 | 3 |
	$	$	$	$
Sales	200 000	30 000	20 000	150 000
Variable costs	136 000	21 400	13 200	101 400
Fixed costs	44 000	3 400	7 400	33 200
Total costs	180 000	24 800	20 600	134 600
Profit (loss)	20 000	5 200	(600)	15 400

The fixed costs of $44 000 represent overhead costs which have been apportioned to the products and will remain the same regardless of whether (or not) all or some of the products are sold during the year.

Because of the loss shown by product 2, the management proposes to eliminate that product from its range.

The firm would be making a profit of $20 000 if all three products were manufactured and sold. However, if only 1 and 3 were sold, as management suggests, the profit would be reduced.

| | Total | 1 | 3 |
		$	$
Sales	180 000	30 000	150 000
Variable costs	122 800	21 400	101 400
Contribution	57 200	8 600	48 600
Fixed costs	44 000		
Profit	13 200		

This reduction in profit is because product 2 makes a contribution of $6800 ($20 000 – $13 200) and the fixed costs remain the same at $44 000, regardless of whether or not 1, 2 or 3 are manufactured and sold.

CLOSING AN UNPROFITABLE SECTION

In a dynamic business environment, organisations regularly appraise the economic viability of their departments and divisions. Although a decision regarding whether or not to close a department or

7

ply the contribution
pproach to decisions
ncerning whether
close unprofitable
ctions

division is very different from that involved in the determination of the range of products to be manufactured and sold, the same principles of relevance are adopted.

Invariably, in practice, there are a number of costs that are allocated to departments which are outside their control and relate to overheads that are incurred by the firm as a whole. A typical example is head office expenses, which relate to the administrative costs of running the business. These types of costs are irrelevant because they are unavoidable.

The rule to be applied in such decisions is that if a department makes a positive contribution – that is, income exceeds variable costs – the department should remain open, and *vice versa*. However, when there are fixed costs that are directly attributable to a department, and therefore are avoidable, the rule can be amended as follows: if the income generated by a department exceeds the costs directly attributable to that department, it should remain open, and *vice versa*. Example 19.3 illustrates such a decision.

Example 19.3: Alpha, Beta and Gamma departments

The following are the costs and income of three departments, Alpha, Beta and Gamma, summarised in a traditional costing format:

	Alpha $000	Beta $000	Gamma $000	Total $000
Sales	80	40	60	180
Department costs	24	15	46	85
Apportioned costs	20	10	20	50
Total costs	44	25	66	135
Profit (loss)	36	15	(6)	45

The apportioned costs of $50 000 in total are unavoidable and relate to head office overhead costs.

From the way in which the data is presented, it could be argued that Department Gamma should be closed because it makes a loss of $6000. Currently, the total profit of all departments is $45 000. However, if Department Gamma were closed, the profit would be reduced.

	Alpha $000	Beta $000	Total $000
Sales	80	40	120
Less Department costs	24	15	39
Departmental profit	56	25	81
Less Apportioned costs			50
Profit			31

The reduction in profit to the firm as a whole of $14 000 is due to the closure of Department Gamma, which, in fact, makes a departmental profit of $14 000 ($60 000 – $46 000) which contributes to the head office overhead costs and the firm's overall profit. Thus, Department Gamma should remain open.

Decision making with constraints

In situations where there are no constraints and fixed costs are unavoidable (that is, irrelevant), we have come to the following conclusion: all opportunities should be accepted if they make a positive contribution to fixed costs and profits.

However, if the availability of one or more resources is restricted, an organisation will be unable to accept every opportunity that yields a positive contribution. It is therefore necessary to formulate a decision-making rule that takes account of these resource constraints.

Before considering the process that is used to determine the optimum output, it is appropriate to examine the nature of constraints that an organisation might be subjected to in the context of its operations.

Traditionally, in accounting textbooks, the constraints that are considered relate to shortages of manufacturing resources, such as particular types of materials, labour skills and the size of the manufacturing plant. However, organisations in the service sector can similarly be restricted in their earning capacity as a result of such constraints. For example, an accounting practice could be restricted as to the number of clients it can accept for audit work because of the shortage of qualified accounting staff available to the practice. The principles to be applied when there are constraints are the same for both manufacturing and service sectors.

The constraints described relate to the short term and can invariably be eliminated in the long term. For example, a firm has the opportunity to manufacture and sell two products, Jack and Jill, both of which yield a positive contribution per unit. However, due to a shortage of skilled machine operators, the firm cannot satisfy the demand for these products. Clearly, this constraint is only a short-term phenomenon as the firm could train machine operators now to ensure that there will not be a shortage in the long term. However, in the short term this will be an effective constraint on production and, ultimately, on income.

KEY CONCEPT 19.5

DECISION MAKING WITH CONSTRAINTS: OBJECTIVES

When there are resource constraints, the objective that should be applied is to establish the optimum output within the constraints to maximise contribution and, thus, profits.

The contribution approach with one scarce resource

In determining the optimum output, the analysis takes account only of quantitative factors. Qualitative factors often influence the final decision: for example, unprofitable products might be included in the range in order to maintain customer loyalty to all products sold by the firm. This should always be borne in mind when making such decisions.

To determine the optimum output with one constraint we must first determine the contribution. Second, we must establish the contribution per unit of the constraint for all those opportunities that

LO 8

Explain what is meant by decision making with constraints

LO 9

Illustrate the use of the contribution margin approach in relation to decisions with one scarce resource

yield a positive contribution. For example, say product Jack yields a positive contribution of $16 per unit and takes four labour hours to produce; assuming that labour is the only effective production constraint, then the contribution per labour hour in producing product Jack is $16 ÷ 4 hours = $4 per labour hour. This provides crucial information about the efficiency of the use of the constrained resource in terms of contribution and, thus, profitability.

The next stage is to rank these opportunities, preferring those that yield the highest contribution per constraint. If, for example, product Jill generates a positive contribution per labour hour of $3, product Jack will be ranked higher, in the absence of other factors, because it yields a contribution of $1 more per labour hour. The optimum plan can then be derived within the total resources available. In the example above, this will be total labour hours available to the firm in a defined period.

Case study 19.4 illustrates the stages of this process.

CASE STUDY 19.4

TROY LTD

The directors of Troy Ltd are drawing up the production plan for the forthcoming year. There are five products that are under consideration: A, B, C, D and E. The following statement regarding the contribution per unit of these opportunities has been prepared by the company's accountant:

	A	B	C	D	E
	$	$	$	$	$
Selling price	10	24	48	13	22
Variable costs					
Materials	7	3	2	3	2
Labour	4	7	10	2	5
Total variable costs	11	10	12	5	7
Contribution per unit	(1)	14	36	8	15
Estimated demand in units	800	700	800	600	400
Labour hours per unit	4	7	10	2	5

For convenience of calculation, we will assume that all labour is paid at the rate of $1 per hour. The total of fixed costs for the year is estimated to be $14 990 and will vary with the range of products actually produced and sold.

Labour is scarce, and it is expected that only 7000 hours will be available next year.

We begin our analysis to determine the optimum production plan, within the labour constraint confronted by Troy Ltd, by accepting all opportunities that yield a positive contribution and rejecting those that yield a negative contribution. All the opportunities with the exception of product A yield a positive contribution. Product A, which has a negative contribution, will therefore, at this stage, be eliminated from the company's possible future range of products.

Before we continue, it is wise to check whether the labour constraint of 7000 hours is an effective constraint on the company's activities. We do this by calculating the total labour hours required to meet the demand for the four products that yield positive contributions. We will begin with product B and follow an alphabetical order.

| Product | Demand | Labour hours | | |
	(units)	per unit	total	cumulative
B	700	7	4 900	4 900
C	800	10	8 000	12 900

It can be seen from the cumulative labour hours column that, if we satisfied the demand of only products B and C, the company would exceed the labour hours it has available (that is, 7000 hours). Thus, we can conclude that labour hours are an effective constraint on the company's level of production and that the company will be unable to accept all the opportunities available to it.

We can now calculate, for the four remaining opportunities, the contribution per labour hour by dividing the labour hours per unit into the contribution per unit and ranking the opportunities in order of the highest contribution per labour hour.

	B	C	D	E
Contribution	$14 ÷ 7 hours	$36 ÷ 10 hours	$8 ÷ 2 hours	$15 ÷ 5 hours
per labour hour	= $2	= $3.6	= $4	= $3
Ranking	4	2	1	3

Product D is ranked first because it yields the highest contribution per labour hour ($4), followed by product C with a contribution of $3.60 per hour, and then products E and B. This priority ranking can now be applied to determine the products that will be included in the optimum plan and to establish the total contribution that is generated by this plan.

| Ranking | Product | Demand units | Labour hours | | Contribution | Total |
			per unit	total	per unit	
1	D	600	2	1 200	$8	4 800
2	C	580	10	5 800	$36	20 880
				7 000		25 680

It can be seen that the company is able to satisfy the total demand for product D, which was ranked first, within the labour constraint, leaving 7000 – 1200 = 5800 hours available for the production of other products. Product C is the next product preferred within the ranking order and the total demand for C is estimated to be 800 units. However, to satisfy the demand for C will use up 800 units × 10 hours per unit = 8000 hours, and we have only 5800 hours available. Therefore, the company will be restricted to producing 5800 ÷ 10 = 580 units of product C because of the shortage of labour. Products B and E are excluded from the plan because there are no more labour hours available.

This is the optimal plan because it takes account of two important variables: contribution and the scarce resource, labour hours. If the production plan had been based on a priority ranking scheme that took account only of the contribution and ignored the labour constraint, the ranking order in terms of the highest contribution per unit would be as follows:

Ranking	Product
1	C
2	E
3	B
4	D

The total contribution that would be yielded from this ranking order would have been as follows:

Product	Demand	Labour hours		Contribution	
	units	per unit	total	per unit	total
C	700	10	7 000	$36	$25 200

It can be seen that, following this approach, only product C, which was ranked first using the ranking order based on the highest contribution per unit, would be produced and sold by the company. This is because the maximum demand for product C is 800 units and, because of the restriction on labour hours available, only 700 units can be produced (that is, 10 hours × 700 units = 7000 hours). The important point to recognise, however, is that the contribution of $25 200 generated from this ranking order is less than the contribution ($25 680) from using the order of ranking based on contribution per labour hour described earlier.

COMMENTARY

The comparison of profitability using two approaches clearly shows that if an organisation is to maximise its profits when there are resource constraints, these constraints must be taken into account in the decision process.

KEY CONCEPT 19.6

DECISION MAKING WITH CONSTRAINTS: RULE

All products should be ranked in terms of the contribution per unit of resource constraint. The decision rule is to choose to sell products with the highest positive contribution per unit of resource constraint until demand for the product is exhausted and/or the scarce resource is depleted.

Contribution per unit and opportunity cost

10

Explain what is meant by internal opportunity cost

Using the contribution per unit of a scarce resource in establishing an organisation's optimum production plan produces some interesting insights into the measurement of the opportunity cost of scarce resources. Earlier in this chapter we defined the opportunity cost of a resource as 'the maximum benefit which could be obtained from that resource if it were used for some other purpose'. Invariably, the opportunity cost of a resource that is scarce will be greater than its purchase price. This is because there will be competing opportunities for the resource within the organisation. A number of examples have been shown earlier in this chapter where the relevant cost of using a resource (the opportunity cost) exceeded the purchase price of the resource.

The concept of opportunity cost can also be applied in the selection of products to be included in an organisation's optimum production plan. We continue with the example of Troy Ltd to illustrate this application and help us understand further the role of opportunity costs in this type of decision.

In the case of Troy Ltd, labour was scarce, and there were competing alternative opportunities for this resource within the company. In particular, there were only enough labour hours to satisfy the demand for product D, and partially to satisfy the demand for C, producing 580 units out of a total demand of 800. The contribution per labour hour of product C was $3.60. Opportunities that yield a higher contribution per labour hour are preferred, and in the case of products B and E, the contribution per labour hour was less; thus C was preferred. Indeed, if any new opportunities became available to Troy Ltd they would be included in the optimum production plan only if they generated a contribution per labour hour greater than $3.60.

The following shows the increase in contribution from one more hour used in producing one-tenth of C.

	$
Selling price ($48 ÷ 10)	4.80
Less Costs	
Materials ($2 ÷ 10)	0.20
Labour ($10 ÷ 10)	1.00
Total variable costs	1.20
Increase in contribution	3.60

This computation would be the same if one less hour were available, but would result in a loss in contribution of $3.60.

At this stage, we will summarise the three main points that have been derived from our analysis so far and examine their implications.

• Implication 1

If one more labour hour becomes available, it will contribute $3.60 per hour. In the case of Troy Ltd, the contribution of $3.60 per hour will be generated from an additional 2200 hours, if these hours are available. This figure is the number of hours that would be used in making another 220 units (220 × 10 hours per unit) of product C, the unsatisfied demand for C. (Remember, the total demand was 800 units, and 580 units can be produced within the original labour constraint.) If more than 2200 hours became available, assuming there were no new opportunities, labour would then be used to produce product E, which would generate $3 per hour. The number of units of E produced would clearly depend upon how many hours became available: 2000 hours would be required to satisfy the total demand for E. If any more hours were available, these would be employed on the least preferred product, B.

This information at the planning stage is extremely useful to managers in considering scenarios. For example, management might be unsure as to the exact number of hours available, and could ask the question: if 300 additional labour hours became available in the coming year, what would be the increased contribution? This can be quickly calculated when the contribution per labour hour is known, by multiplying the contribution per labour hour by the number of hours; in this example $3.60 × 300 hours = $1080

• Implication 2

If one less hour is available, Troy Ltd would lose $3.60 per hour in contribution. The loss in contribution of $3.60 per hour would continue for every hour lost up to 5800 hours (580 × 10 hours per unit). These are the total hours that are required to satisfy the original constrained demand of 580 units of product C. This information, similarly, could be useful to management at the planning stage. For example, what would be the loss in contribution if 600 labour hours were lost due to machine breakdowns during the year? Knowing the loss in contribution for every hour lost, the calculation is simple: 600 hours × $3.60 = $2160

• Implication 3

If future opportunities became available, they would have to contribute at least $3.60 per labour hour before they would be considered for inclusion in the future production plan. It would not be necessary, in such cases, to recalculate the contribution from each product and then to rank each product in coming to this conclusion. All that is necessary is to calculate the contribution per labour hour for any additional opportunities that become available. These are then compared with the contribution per labour hour generated from the current opportunities. If these new opportunities yield a higher contribution per labour hour, they will displace those currently in the plan. Once again this information is extremely useful to management.

We can conclude that knowledge of the contribution from the use of constrained resources is extremely useful to management in making decisions to ensure the future profitability of an organisation.

INTERNAL OPPORTUNITY COST

The contribution per labour hour is also known as the internal opportunity cost of labour. The term 'internal opportunity cost' is more appropriate when it is used in examining the efficient use of resources within an organisation. In the example of Troy Ltd, labour was paid at $1 per hour, but there is the additional cost of labour (that is, the internal opportunity cost of $3.60 per hour) that relates to its use within the organisation because there are competing opportunities for the use of the scarce resource. The cost of labour per hour is therefore represented by two elements of costs:

- the cash cost of employing the labour, which can be described as the 'external opportunity cost'
- the internal opportunity cost, which reflects the cost of using the resource within the organisation itself due to competing opportunities.

These costs can be summarised as follows.

	$
Cash cost of employing labour (the external opportunity cost)	1.00
Internal opportunity cost for the use of labour in the organisation	3.60
Total cost of labour	4.60

KEY CONCEPT 19.7

INTERNAL OPPORTUNITY COST

The internal opportunity cost is the cost of using the resource within the firm itself due to competing opportunities within the firm for the use of the resource.

Determining the internal opportunity cost is extremely useful because it indicates how much Troy Ltd would be willing to pay to obtain one more labour hour. For example, to release more labour hours to produce additional units of product C, the manager decides to offer overtime to employees at a premium, but does not know what premium to offer. The total opportunity cost of $4.60 per hour is the maximum the company should be willing to pay for an additional labour hour. The payment of a higher rate will result in a loss. On the basis of this information, the company might decide to offer its employees $3 per hour (that is, a premium of $2 per hour) for any overtime worked, which is $1.60 less than the maximum they can afford to pay. The contribution generated from one hour to produce one-tenth of product C will then be as follows:

	$	$
Selling price (one-tenth of $48)		4.80
Less Costs:		
Materials ($2 ÷ 10)		0.20
Labour		
External opportunity cost	1.00	
Premium for overtime	2.00	3.00
Total costs		3.20
Contribution		1.60

If the company anticipated that employees would be willing to work 350 hours of overtime during the period, the additional total contribution will be $1.60 × 350 hours = $560.

In this analysis we have used the example of a labour constraint. The same principles apply to any situation where a resource is scarce: we must determine the opportunities that use these resources most efficiently.

Review exercise 5

Many organisations, at particular times, are subject to a shortage of resources. These shortages restrict their ability to meet the demand for their products or services. Describe four examples of these constraints, two for a manufacturing firm and two for a service firm.

Make or buy decisions

An example of a make or buy decision is a decision concerning whether an organisation should design and develop its own computer programs or whether an external software house should be hired to do the work.

LO 11

Evaluate problems of whether entities should make or buy a product or a service in cases where there is spare capacity and no spare capacity

The 'make' option gives the management of the organisation more direct control over the work. However, an external contractor often has specialist skills and expertise. As with most of the decisions considered in this chapter, make or buy decisions should not be made on the basis of cost alone. Qualitative factors will be considered in more depth at the end of this chapter.

KEY CONCEPT 19.8

MAKE OR BUY DECISIONS

A make or buy decision is one in which a firm chooses between, on the one hand, making a product or carrying out a service using its own resources, and, on the other hand, paying another external firm to make a product or carry out a service for it.

We begin our analysis by first examining whether it is more beneficial to make or buy a product or service when an organisation has spare capacity. We then consider the situation when capacity is restricted because of shortages of resources.

WHERE THERE IS SPARE CAPACITY

We assume that the organisation is not working at full capacity and, therefore, has enough resources available to make a product or component, if it so wishes, without affecting the production of other products. Case study 19.5 illustrates the principles that should be applied to make and buy decisions in these circumstances.

CASE STUDY 19.5

LEIGH LTD

Leigh Ltd is a company that is confronted with the problem of whether to make or buy three components, Bot, Lot and Tot. The respective costs are as follows:

	Bot	Lot	Tot
Production units	1 000	2 000	4 000
	$	$	$
Variable costs per unit:			
Materials	4	5	2
Labour	10	12	5
Total variable cost	14	17	7

The fixed costs per annum that are directly attributable (avoidable costs) to the manufacture of the components and are apportioned (unavoidable costs) to components are as follows:

	$
Avoidable costs:	
Bot	1 000
Lot	5 000
Tot	13 000
Apportioned fixed costs	30 000
	49 000

A subcontractor has offered to supply units of Bot, Lot and Tot for $12, $21 and $10 respectively.

The relevant costs to be taken into account in this decision are the differential costs associated with making and with buying. For this decision, the differential costs are the differences in unit variable costs and the directly attributable fixed costs. The following is a summary of the relevant costs:

	Bot	Lot	Tot
Variable cost per unit, making	$14	$17	$7
Cost per unit, buying	$12	$21	$10
Additional cost per unit of buying	$(2)	$4	$3
Production units per annum	1 000	2 000	4 000
Additional total variable cost of buying	$(2 000)	$8 000	$12 000
Fixed costs saved by buying	$1 000	$5 000	$13 000
Additional total cost of buying	$(3 000)	$3 000	$(1 000)

COMMENTARY

The organisation would save $3000 per annum by subcontracting component Bot (this is because the variable cost per unit to make the component is greater than the purchase price), and $1000 per annum by subcontracting component Tot (this is due to the saving of $13 000 of fixed costs directly attributable to making the component). In the case of component Lot, the organisation will be $3000 better off by making the component.

It should also be noted that the apportioned fixed costs are irrelevant to this decision because they are unavoidable.

In such decisions there will normally be another consideration. If components Bot and Tot are to be purchased from a subcontractor, it is likely that the organisation will have spare capacity which has some value to the organisation; for example, it might decide to let the space to an outside party, which would generate additional profit. This additional profit should be included as a relevant cost of making the components because the profit will be forgone if the component is made by the company. It is an opportunity cost.

Inevitably there will be qualitative factors that should be taken into account. Leigh Ltd, for example, might be concerned about the quality of the subcontractor's work. This factor might lead the organisation to favour making components Bot and Tot, although, in cost terms, this policy would be unprofitable.

WHERE THERE IS NO SPARE CAPACITY

A firm might be confronted with a decision about whether to make or buy a component when it is currently working at full capacity. To make the component, it will be necessary for the firm to stop or restrict its current production output. In such cases, the cost of making the component must include not only the costs directly attributed to making it but also the contribution that is lost from the production that has been displaced by the decision to make the component. This loss in contribution from the displaced production is the internal opportunity cost, which was discussed earlier.

Case study 19.6 illustrates the application of the internal opportunity cost concept in the make or buy decision when capacity is restricted.

CASE STUDY 19.6

KELLEE LTD

Kellee Ltd is in the process of deciding whether to make or buy a component of one of the products it manufactures and sells. Labour is in short supply and the factory is currently working at full capacity. The following are the estimated costs per unit to make the component. (The assumption that labour is paid $4 per hour is made for convenience of calculation.)

	Cost per unit
	$
Direct labour (5 hours @ $4 per hour)	20
Direct material	15
Fixed overheads	5
Total cost per unit	40

The fixed overhead costs are apportioned to the product and are unavoidable, whether or not the component is made, so this cost is irrelevant to the decision. All the other costs are directly attributable to the cost of producing the component and are, therefore, relevant. As a result of this, the relevant cost associated with making the component is $35.

The alternative is to buy in the component from another firm. The cost of buying the component is $38 per unit.

If labour was not in short supply, the firm would make the component rather than buy it because the relevant costs of making ($35) are less than the purchase price of buying ($38).

However, in view of the shortage of labour, we must consider the contribution that is forgone because of the decision to make. To do so, we must account for the contribution generated from the current production activity that is to be restricted if we decide to make the component. The following data relates to the income and cost per unit associated with a product that is to be displaced by producing (making) the component:

	Per unit data	
	$	$
Selling price		26
Less Costs		
Direct labour (3 hours @ $4 per hour)	12	
Direct material	8	20
Contribution per unit		6

The contribution per hour of labour generated from this product is $2 (that is, contribution $6 divided by three hours of labour). This is the internal opportunity cost of using the labour on the manufacture of this product. If the labour is to be efficiently diverted into making the component instead of this product, it must therefore yield a contribution of at least $2 per hour. We can also conclude that the effective cost of labour employed in making the component consists of two elements: the cash paid to employees for their labour of $4 per hour (that is, the external opportunity cost) plus the internal opportunity cost of $2 per hour. These two elements of cost should therefore be included in the calculation to decide whether to make or buy the component. The following summarises all the relevant costs in making the component:

	$	$
Direct labour		
Cash paid to employees (the external opportunity cost) ($4 × 5 hours)		20
Internal opportunity cost ($2 × 5 hours)	10	30
Direct materials		15
Total relevant costs		45

COMMENTARY

The inclusion of the internal opportunity cost because it is relevant to the decision to make the component has resulted in a cost of $45 for making the component. This exceeds the buying price of $38; thus, purely on financial grounds the decision should be to buy rather than to make.

The principle that the internal opportunity cost should be included in the relevant costs of a make or buy decision applies to all situations where there is no spare capacity because resources are scarce.

Qualitative factors

In our analysis of decision making in this chapter, all the decisions we have made have only been based on financial criteria. Often, qualitative factors also have an immense influence in such decisions. Indeed, on some occasions, an opportunity that would be rejected on purely quantitative (financial) criteria is accepted because of other, qualitative, reasons.

Qualitative factors are those factors which cannot be quantified in terms of costs and profit. They might stem from either non-financial objectives or factors which could be quantified in monetary terms but have not been because there is insufficient information to make a reliable estimate.

LO 12

Discuss the role of qualitative factors in decision making with constraints

The nature of these qualitative factors varies with the circumstances. The following are some examples of qualitative factors that might influence decisions.

CUSTOMERS

The inclusion or exclusion of a product from the range offered or the quality of the product and after-sales service affects demand for the product and customer loyalty. For example, the exclusion of one product from a range because it is uneconomic to produce and sell, could affect the demand for other products. Products manufactured by firms are often interdependent and this interdependence should be considered when a decision is made.

EMPLOYEES

Decisions involving the closure of part of a firm, or relocation, or changes in work procedures, require acceptance by employees. If the changes are mishandled, problems between employees and management could lead to inefficiencies and losses.

COMPETITORS

In a competitive market, decisions by one firm to enhance its competitive advantage might result in retaliation by competitors. For example, the decision to reduce selling prices in order to raise demand will not be successful if all competitors take similar action.

A firm might decide to produce an unprofitable product or offer a service at a loss because it would otherwise be leaving the market to its competitors. The firm considers that continued service to customers will eventually affect the demand for its other products.

LEGAL CONSTRAINTS

An opportunity is sometimes rejected because of doubts about pending legislation. The decision to open a hotel, for example, might be influenced by pending legislation on safety requirements that would result in additional costs which are too complex to estimate.

SUPPLIERS

A firm might rely heavily on a good relationship with a particular supplier for the prompt delivery of supplies. Some decisions might affect that relationship.

Review exercise 6

Qualitative factors are often influential in the decision-making process. Describe the nature of qualitative factors and give three examples that might influence a decision to make a component rather than buy it from another firm.

SUMMARY

LO 1 LEARNING OBJECTIVE 1
Explain what is meant by the term 'sunk costs'
Sunk costs are those costs which have been paid or are owed and committed to be paid by a firm. They are irrelevant for future decision making.

LO 2 LEARNING OBJECTIVE 2
Explain what is meant by differential (incremental) costs
Differential costs are the differences in costs and benefits between alternative opportunities available to an organisation. When a number of opportunities are being considered, costs and benefits that are common to these alternative opportunities are irrelevant to the decision.

LO 3 LEARNING OBJECTIVE 3
Identify what is meant by avoidable and unavoidable costs
An avoidable cost is one that will not have to be paid if a firm does not proceed with a decision. An unavoidable cost is one that will be incurred regardless of whether the firm has decided to accept or reject a project.

LO 4 LEARNING OBJECTIVE 4
Discuss the concept of opportunity costs, and its role in decision making
The opportunity cost of a resource is normally defined as the maximum benefits which could be obtained from that resource if it were used for some alternative purpose. If the benefits from project 'A' are $400 and the potential benefits from project 'B' are $600, the opportunity cost that is given up by taking on project 'B' is $400.

LO 5 LEARNING OBJECTIVE 5
Explain the costs and benefits that are relevant to specific decisions
Relevant costs and benefits are those costs and benefits that relate to the future. They are additional costs and income that will be incurred or result from a decision.

LO 6 LEARNING OBJECTIVE 6
Explain and apply the contribution approach to decision making in cases where there are no resource constraints
Assuming a linear cost and sales function, where there are no restraints on available resources, a firm will accept all projects that produce a positive contribution margin.

LO 7 LEARNING OBJECTIVE 7
Apply the contribution approach to decisions concerning whether to close unprofitable sections
Normally, within the contribution margin approach, if a project's income exceeds variable costs, the project should proceed. However, some fixed costs are allocated based on a predetermined ratio; for example, supervision. These allocated costs need to be taken into account when making a decision to close a project/section.

When a project has fixed costs that are directly attributable to a project and are avoidable, the approach should be: where income exceeds all costs directly attributable to a project, that project/section should be kept.

LO 8 LEARNING OBJECTIVE 8
Explain what is meant by decision making with constraints

When there are resource constraints, the objective should be to establish the optimum output within the constraints in order to maximise contribution and, therefore, profits. These resource constraints could be labour, materials or available machinery.

LO 9 LEARNING OBJECTIVE 9
Illustrate the use of the contribution margin approach in relation to decisions with one scare resource

To determine the optimum output with one constraint, we must first determine the contribution margin. Second, we must establish the contribution per unit of the constraint for all those opportunities that yield a positive contribution. Third, we rank them according to the contribution per unit of the constraint, with the highest ranked project the one that yields the highest contribution per unit of the constraint.

LO 10 LEARNING OBJECTIVE 10
Explain what is meant by internal opportunity cost

The internal opportunity cost reflects the cost of using the resource within the organisation itself due to competing opportunities.

LO 11 LERNING OBJECTIVE 11
Evaluate problems of whether entities should make or buy a product or a service in cases where there is spare capacity and no spare capacity

The make or buy decision is one that is made by an organisation when it chooses between using its own resources or purchasing a product, part product or service externally. If there is spare capacity, the firm needs to look at its variable and directly attributable fixed costs, plus any opportunity costs in relation to the spare capacity that would be available to potentially rent to others, before making a decision. If there is no spare capacity, the firm needs to look at its variable and directly attributable fixed costs plus the loss that results from losing the contribution from the product or service that has been displaced.

LO 12 LEARNING OBJECTIVE 12
Discuss the role of qualitative factors in decision making with constraints

Some decisions that need to be made may override the financial criteria involved and focus on other issues such as good customer relations, giving exceptional service and discounts, environmental issues and conditions for employees (especially changes in the work environment). There are many more and, in evaluating a financial decision, the qualitative factors might very well be the ones that change the outcome of the overall decision.

FURTHER READING

Hansen, D. & Mowen, M., 2003. *Management Accounting and Control*, 6th edn, South-Western, Mason, Ohio.

REVIEW QUESTIONS

1   Discuss the reasons why accrual accounting methods are not appropriate for decisions concerning the future.

2   In the majority of cases, fixed costs are irrelevant in decision making, but on some occasions they are relevant. Describe the circumstances when fixed costs are relevant to future decisions.

3   Explain why a shortage of resources in an organisation is a short-term phenomenon.

4   Explain what is meant by the term 'internal opportunity cost'.

5   Discuss the importance and usefulness of the concept of 'internal opportunity cost' in the making of decisions.

6   In some circumstances, the opportunity cost of a resource might be higher than the resource's purchase price. Explain why this might be the case.

PROBLEMS FOR DISCUSSION AND ANALYSIS

1   Calculators Ltd manufacture and sell pocket calculators. The price of these calculators is $22. The company's current output is 40 000 units per month, which represents 90 per cent of its productive capacity. Kodix, a chain-store customer who specialises in selling electronic goods, offers to buy 2000 calculators as a special order at $16 each. The calculators would be sold under the name of Kodix.
    The total costs per month are $800 000, of which $192 000 are fixed costs.
  a   Advise Calculators Ltd on whether it should accept the special order.
  b   Would your advice change if Kodix wanted 5000 calculators?

2   Sprinks Ltd produces three products, A, B and C. The following is an estimate of costs and revenues for the forthcoming year:

	A $	B $	C $
Sales	32 000	50 000	45 000
Total cost	36 000	38 000	34 000
Net profit (loss)	(4 000)	12 000	11 000

The total cost of each product comprises one-third fixed costs and two-thirds variable costs. Fixed costs are constant whatever the volume of sales.
    The managing director argues that because product A makes a loss, production of it should be discontinued.
    Comment on the managing director's argument.

3   Agro Company has been producing 10 000 units of part 7021 for its products. The unit cost for the part is as follows:

	$
Direct materials	5
Direct labour	10
Variable manufacturing overhead	6
Fixed manufacturing overhead	8
Total	29

Agro can purchase 10 000 units of part 7021 for $25 each. If the part is purchased, Agro can make another product and provide a contribution margin of $10 000. If the part is purchased, 75 per cent of the fixed manufacturing overhead costs will still be incurred.

Required

Should Agro make or buy the part?

4   Advance Ltd manufactures two solar powered Frisbees – Wild One and Bold One. The company has only a limited supply of skilled labour which is essential in the production process.

The following information is available:

	Wild One	Bold One
Contribution margin per unit	$15	$18
Hours to produce one unit	3	4

Anticipated sales exceed capacity for both products.

Total labour hours available: 12 000 hours.

Required

Determine which product should be produced.

5   XYZ Ltd manufactures two products. On average, it sells 40 000 units of product 1 and 60 000 units of product 2 each year. This year the company has a restricted advertising budget of $50 000, which is only enough to effectively promote one of its products. The marketing department estimates that average sales of product 1 will increase by 20 per cent if it is advertised, while product 2's average sales will increase by 15 per cent if it is advertised.

The following data is provided:

	1	2
Selling price per unit	$20	$30
Variable cost per unit	$10	$14
Fixed costs ($800 000) per unit based on average sales levels	$5	$10
Production time per unit (direct labour hours)	2	4

Required

a   Assuming unlimited direct labour hours, which product should it advertise?

b   Assuming there are only 336 000 direct labour hours, would you change your decision?

6   The ABC Company manufactures gas cylinders for use in campervans and caravans. The costs per cylinder are as follows.

	$
Direct materials	5.30
Direct labour	4.20
Variable overhead	0.35
Fixed overhead (per month)	125 000

The company manufactures and sells 20 000 cylinders per month and has the capacity, without increasing overhead costs, to manufacture 25 000.

Fixed costs are allocated on the basis of cylinders manufactured.

Avco Ltd have offered to purchase 6000 cylinders for $72 000. This is a one-off order and will not be repeated.

a   Should ABC accept the order? Why?

b   What problems might the company face if it accepts the order?

7   Gallop Corporation Ltd has two divisions, production and assembly. The cost per unit that is charged by the production division to the assembly division is set to increase from $12 to $15, which is the same price as customers pay when they purchase directly from the production division. The manager of the assembly division is extremely upset and has expressed his intentions to buy the units from an outside supplier at a cost of $12 per unit.

The following data relates to the production division:

Units produced	100 000
Variable production costs per unit	$10
Indirect fixed costs allocated to the production division	$200 000
Normal profit per unit with production division	$3

The assembly division normally purchases 50 000 units from the production division.

Required

a   What is the impact on Gallop Corporation's overall profit if the assembly division purchases units from outsiders?

b   Discuss the implications of this decision for (i) the shareholders of Gallop, (ii) the management of Gallop Corporation, and (iii) the heads of the production and assembly divisions.

8   At present, Coyle Ltd manufactures all the components that go into making up its finished products. A components supplier has offered to fulfil the firm's requirements in relation to two components, the BC100 (at $7.75 each) and the BC200 (at $2.00 each).

If the firm buys in components, the capacity that is presently utilised for these components would be unused. The firm currently manufactures 50 000 units of each component and the current costs of production are as follows:

	BC100	BC200
	$	$
Materials	2.50	1.00
Labour	3.00	1.25
Fixed overheads	3.50	1.75
Total cost per unit	9.00	4.00

a   On a quantitative basis, should the firm continue to manufacture BC100 and BC200 or should it buy in one or both of the components?

b   Discuss the qualitative factors which are likely to influence this decision.

9   Mikel Ltd manufactures components for bicycles. At the moment, sales are 100 000 units at $10 per unit. Fixed costs are $500 000 and variable costs are $5.50 per unit.

If Mikel stopped production, it would still have long-term fixed costs of $100 000.

a   Should Mikel stop production? If not, what steps could the company consider to improve profit?

b   Mikel has been offered a contract by Dell Ltd to supply 150 000 units at $9.00 per unit. Assuming Mikel has the capacity to produce these units at the same variable and fixed costs, should it accept the order?

10 Philco is a manufacturer of radios. The costs per radio, for a production run of 20 000 units, are as follows:

	$
Direct materials	27.00
Direct labour	13.00
Variable overhead	6.00
Fixed overhead	10.00

Fixed overhead is applied on a per-unit basis.

Dorro Ltd has offered to supply the circuit board with components for $20.00 per unit. This would result in a saving of $10.00 in direct materials, $3.00 in direct labour and $4.00 in variable overhead. There would be no saving in fixed overhead. If Philco were to accept this offer, it would then have the capacity to manufacture 10 000 baby transistor radios. The costs for the transistors are as follows:

	$
Direct materials	4.00
Direct labour	3.00
Fixed overhead per unit	2.00

The fixed overhead for the transistors is in addition to the fixed overhead incurred on the radios. Each transistor radio sells for $10.10.

Should Philco accept Dorro Ltd's offer, assuming that all production is sold?

11 Sory Ltd manufactures a range of television sets. At present, the company is able to sell only 80 per cent of the plant's capacity of its 20-centimetre digital sets. These sets are sold to retailers for $200 per unit. With the present production, Sory sells 100 000 sets, and has fixed costs of $7 500 000 and variable costs of $100 per unit.

a   What is the present profit?

b   If Sory reduced its price to retailers to $185 it believes it would operate at 100 per cent capacity. Should Sory take this step?

c   Low Price Stores Ltd has offered to purchase 20 000 sets at $175. If Sory accepted this offer, the variable costs on the additional sets would be $95 because there would be no marketing costs. Given that Sory is operating at 80 per cent capacity, which of the three options produces the maximum profit:

   i   the present profit

   ii   reduce the selling price to $185

       or

   iii   retain existing price of $200 and accept special offer conditions and sell 20 000 sets to Low Price Stores?

12 Pigeon Ltd proposes a production plan for 20X1, aiming to maximise profits. The following details are available:

	A	B	C	D	E	F
Labour hours per unit	6.4	7	4	9	5	12
Machine hours per unit	3	2	1	3	1	8
Maximum demand	2 500	1 200	700	1 100	900	2 900
	$	$	$	$	$	$
Selling price	20	28	8	36	16	40
Costs:						
Direct materials	4	4	1.2	2.4	2.8	1.6
Direct labour	4	6	2.4	8.8	3.6	3.2
Fixed overhead	4	6	2.4	8.8	3.6	3.2
Total cost	12	16	6.0	20.0	10.0	8.0
Profit	8	12	2.0	16.0	6.0	32.0

Fixed overhead, which is estimated to cost $10 000 irrespective of what is produced and sold, is applied at 100 per cent of direct labour cost.

A maximum of 64 000 direct labour hours is expected to be available.

a   Calculate the optimal profit-maximising production plan and explain the reasons for your choice.

b   Explain the following hypothetical internal opportunity costs:

   i   direct labour hours $2.40

   ii   machine hours $1.70

13 Tredways Shoe Company produces three different types of shoes. The condensed results for the company for the past year are as follows:

	Scout	Trouper	Hounddog
	$	$	$
Sales	250 000	150 000	320 000
Cost of goods sold	210 000	155 000	250 000
Gross profit	40 000	(5 000)	70 000
Operating expenses	55 000	20 000	35 000
Net profit	(15 000)	(25 000)	35 000

The CEO believes Tredways should stop making Scouts and Troupers. However, before making a final decision she asks the accountant to provide more details about the cost items. These details are presented below.

	Scout	Trouper	Hounddog
	$	$	$
Cost of goods sold			
Variable manufacturing costs	125 000	100 000	170 000
Fixed manufacturing costs	85 000	55 000	80 000
Operating costs			
Variable	35 000	13 000	20 000
Fixed	20 000	7 000	15 000

Required

Is the CEO correct? Should the information that is provided lead to the company stopping the manufacture of Scouts and Troupers? What additional information do you need?

Note to instructors: The following problems are considered more suitable for use in MBA courses. However, undergraduate courses may also find them useful.

14 You have recently been appointed as a consultant to the Murphy Manufacturing Company. The management of the company has prepared a report showing certain data concerning the two products Mox and Tox. The following information has been extracted from this report:

	Mox	Tox
Monthly sales in units	1 000	2 000
	$	$
Selling price	3.0	1.5
Costs		
Direct materials	0.8	0.5
Direct labour	1.0	0.2
Fixed overheads	1.4	0.5
Total cost	3.2	1.2
Profit (loss)	(0.2)	0.3

In view of the poor results shown by Mox, the following changes have been proposed by management:

* Abandon the production of Mox and buy in 1000 units per month for $2800. The quality is identical and selling price will remain unchanged.
* Use the spare capacity to make Cox. It is estimated that 1000 units could be sold at $1 each. Material costs are $0.4 per unit and labour costs $0.2.

All overheads are fixed and are not expected to change from the present cost of $2000 per month. No inventories are held.

a Comment on the suitability of management's approach to assessing product profitability, as illustrated in the report, and indicate any ways in which you think it could be improved.

b Prepare a monthly income statement for the present program and the proposed new program. Do the proposed changes appear to be profitable? Explain the reasons for your answer.

15 Burco Ltd produces and sells two products, X and Y. During the last year, 700 hours were worked and the operating results were as follows:

	X	Y	Total
Units sold	1 000	1 000	2 000
	$	$	$
Sales	1 000	2 000	3 000
Variable costs:			
Labour	200	500	700
Materials	550	900	1 450

	X	Y	Total
Total variable costs	750	1 400	2 150
Contribution	250	600	850
Fixed costs			600
Net profit			250

All variable costs are a linear function of output. The material used for X is quite different from that used for Y, but both can be produced with the same labour force.

Five units of X can be made in one labour hour, while only two units of Y can be made in one labour hour. Labour hours are expected to be limited to 800 next year.

Information about the market for X and Y for the next year is set out below:

	X	Y
Maximum quantity that can be sold (units)	1 100	1 200
Minimum quantity that must be sold to retain market (units)	600	800

a   Assuming that plant capacity is fully used, what is the optimum mix of X and Y?
b   Assuming that the price of material for Y decreases by 20 per cent, what is the optimal mix of X and Y? Assume no change in the price of X or Y.
c   Assuming that the cost of labour increases by 20 per cent, that prices can be put up by only 10 per cent without affecting sales limits and that the number of labour hours available is reduced to 600, what is the optimal mix of X and Y?
d   What is the net profit in each of these three cases?
e   Discuss the limitations of your analysis.

16 Eatinatural Ltd is a company which specialises in the manufacture and sale of health foods. The company has just completed market research on a new type of organic toothpaste called Abrasive. The budget derived from the market research for one year's production and sales, which was presented to the board by the marketing manager, is as follows:

Abrasive toothpaste

	$	$
Cost of production (100 000 kg)		
Labour		
Direct wages	50 000	
Supervisory	30 000	80 000
Raw materials		
Ingredient X	17 000	
Ingredient Y	7 000	
Ingredient P	9 000	
Ingredient Z	1 000	34 000
Other variable costs		10 000
Fixed overheads (60% of direct labour)		30 000
Research and development		20 000

⇥

	$	$
Total costs		174 000
Sales (100 000 kg at $1.60 per kg)		160 000
Loss		(14 000)

The board of directors is disappointed with this budget in view of the research and development costs of $20 000 that have already been incurred and the need to make use of the spare capacity in the factory. Fred Sharpe, the managing director, suggests bringing in a consultant to examine the costs of the new product.

The following additional information is available:

i It would be possible to transfer 60 per cent of the direct labour requirement from another department within the company. The monthly contribution of this department ($5000), subject to the introduction of a special machine into the department at a hire cost of $4000 per year, would fall by only 20 per cent of its current level as a result of the reduction in the labour force. The remainder of the direct labour requirement would have to be recruited. It is anticipated that their wages will be the same as the workers transferred from the other department. In addition, it is estimated that the costs of recruitment – for example, advertising – will be $3000.

ii Two supervisors would be required at a cost of $15 000 per year each. One would be recruited; the other, Reg Raven, would remain at work instead of retiring. The company will pay him a pension of $5000 per year on his retirement.

iii Inventories of ingredient X are currently available for a whole year's production of Abrasive, and are valued at their original cost. The price of this ingredient is subject to dramatic variations, and the current market price is double the original cost. It could be resold at the market price less 10 per cent selling expenses, or retained for use later in another new product to be manufactured by the company, by which time it is expected that the market price will have fallen by about 25 per cent.

iv Ingredient Y's price has been very stable and it is used for other products currently manufactured and sold by the company. There are no inventories available for the production of Abrasive.

v Ingredient P is another commodity with a fairly static price. Half of the annual requirement is in inventory and the other half will have to be purchased during the year at an estimated cost of $4500. The materials in inventory could be resold for $4000 less 10 per cent selling expenses, or could be used to produce another product, after some further processing. This processing, which would take 2000 hours in the Mixing Department, where labour is paid $12 per hour, would save the company additional purchasing costs of $5000. The Mixing Department only has sufficient idle capacity to do this amount of work.

vi Ingredient Z was bought well in advance and is in inventory. It has no alternative use. Fred Sharpe is beginning to regret the decision to buy this ingredient in advance because it will deteriorate in store and might become dangerous before the end of the budget period. It cannot be sold and it will cost the company $500 to dispose of it if it is not used to produce Abrasive.

vii The other variable costs can all be avoided if the contract is not accepted.

viii Fixed overheads for the company are expected to increase by $2000 per year as a result of manufacturing and selling Abrasive.

Required

As the consultant employed by the company, you are requested to re-examine this statement, taking account of the additional information, and recommend any necessary action. Clearly state any assumptions that you make.

17 As a company's secretary, you have been directed by the managing director to prepare a confidential report on the possible closure of the Hobart factory and centralisation of activities at the Perth facility. The combination of an expected increase in rent of $15 000 and the managing director's daughter's (who is married to the Hobart manager) desire to return to Perth, appear to be the major reasons behind the request for the report.

Due to the nature of the report, information for the decision is difficult to obtain. However, the following data is available from corporate budgets for the ensuing year:

  i The fixed costs of the Hobart operations are, at present, $85 000. This figure comprises the $50 000 salary of the Hobart manager (who will be transferred back to Perth), rent at $25 000 and the $10 000 salary of a part-time clerk whose services would be dispensed with.
  ii Variable costs at the Hobart factory are $125 000.
  iii You have established that the sale of plant and other assets in Hobart will be sufficient to pay the termination of all Hobart staff, including the part-time clerk.
  iv Additional space in Perth may be rented in steps of $10 000 per 10 000 units.
  v A common price policy has established the price of the sole product at $10.00. Budgeted figures call for 25 000 units to be produced at Hobart and 40 000 units to be produced at Perth. There are no inventories.
  vi Additional staff in Perth would need to be hired to meet the additional demands experienced. This cost is expected to be $17 500. The cost to service the Hobart market from Perth would be $1.10 per unit in addition to the variable costs.
  vii Variable costs at Perth have been budgeted at $160 000.
  viii The Hobart factory has been allocated $45 000 of the head office costs.
  ix A local manufacturer in Hobart can supply the Hobart region and is willing to do so, a royalty of $2.00 per unit being paid to your company.

Required

In your report, list the alternatives that are available to your company, including a full and complete cost justification to support your recommendation. What factors should be considered besides the cost factor? List such qualitative factors in your report.

ETHICS CASE STUDIES

1 Orbital Machines Ltd is a company that has been manufacturing a revolutionary new engine for motor vehicles for 10 years. It employs 1000 workers, and the economy of Winjarra is completely dependent on Orbital Machines.

On 10 July 20X0 the company won a major contract with the Ford Motor Company to provide orbital engines for all its cars from 1 January 20X1. In order to meet the production requirements, the company would need to make a significant investment in additional manufacturing equipment and employ more workers.

The costs of operating in Winjarra have increased because of higher rates and taxes, as well as wage demands flowing from a strong local trade union. The company would be reluctant to invest significant funds if increases in costs are likely to continue to be a problem.

The company has received an approach from the mayoress of a small city 500 kilometres from Winjarra. The mayoress would like Orbital to move its entire operation to her city, and she has offered the following incentives:

i   A large parcel of land with no rates and taxes for five years.
ii A work force where the average labour costs are 25 per cent lower than in Winjarra.
    In return, Orbital must employ local residents.
    This move could allow Orbital to avoid the cost pressures in Winjarra, which, in turn, would allow it to compete more effectively in foreign markets.

Discuss

a   who the stakeholders are in this decision
b   the quantitative and qualitative factors which are relevant to this decision
c   whether there are any ethical issues for the management of Orbital Machines to consider.

2   Forpark Ltd is planning to add slides to the cubby houses they produce. Joe Clark, the accountant of Forpark, has just completed an analysis to see if the company should make or buy the slides. His analysis shows that, based on the written quotations received from two suppliers of the slides, the company should purchase the slides.

The manager of Forpark agrees with Clark and they issue instructions to the purchasing department that orders should be placed for the slides, as long as the price is not greater than $35 per unit.

A couple of days later, Clark is informed by the purchasing department that both suppliers have increased their price to $40 per unit. He discusses the situation with the manager and they decide that Forpark should now manufacture the slides. Clark thinks it is odd that both suppliers have increased their prices to the same figure.

Later in the week, Joe Clark is approached by his secretary, Jane Brown. Jane informs him that a friend of hers, who works for one of the suppliers of the slides, has told her about an agreement reached between the two suppliers of the slides. Essentially, the two suppliers have agreed to raise the price of their slides to $40 per unit. Jane does not want her friend to get into trouble for disclosing this type of confidential information, but at the same time she thought she ought to tell Joe.

Discuss

a   what Joe should do with the information received from Jane, remembering his responsibilities to the accounting profession, to his company and to Jane
b   who is affected by the scheme to manipulate tenders in this manner.

ANSWERS TO REVIEW EXERCISES

1   Sunk costs are costs of an historical nature; therefore, they have been incurred as a result of a past decision. It follows that these costs are irrelevant to future decisions. Sunk costs can be easily identified because they either have been paid or are subject to legally binding contracts, so the firm is committed to paying for these contracts in the future.

2   An avoidable cost is a cost that is avoided if an opportunity is not taken up. These costs are relevant because they are directly attributable to the decision to take up an opportunity. In contrast, an unavoidable cost is one that is going to be incurred regardless of whether the decision in relation to a particular opportunity is accepted or rejected. This cost, by its nature, is irrelevant in decision making.

3   An opportunity cost is defined as the maximum benefit which could be obtained from a resource if it were used for some alternative purpose other than the opportunity under consideration. The opportunity costs of resources are, therefore, relevant costs in decision making.

4   The cost associated with the depreciation of an asset is based on the historic cost of that asset. The historic cost of an asset is the result of a past decision and is therefore a sunk cost and irrelevant in decision making. It follows then that the cost of depreciation, which is based on the asset's historic cost, is also a sunk cost and therefore an irrelevant cost.

5   a   Manufacturing – Two typical constraints that are often experienced in the manufacturing industry are shortages of particular labour skills and space for machinery. The shortage of skilled labour will often occur when there are competitive local labour markets. A lack of available space often restricts the number of machines that can be installed in a factory which thereby reduces the factory's production capacity.

     b   Service sector – For professional firms in the service sector, a typical resource constraint is a lack of the necessary professional qualified staff needed to meet client demand. Another example of resource constraints in the service sector is the shortage of trained motor mechanics required by garages. This constraint will, effectively, limit the amount of vehicles that a firm can service.

6   Qualitative factors are not capable of being quantified in terms of costs and revenue. They may stem either from non-financial objectives or from factors that might be able to be quantified in monetary terms, but have not been quantified because there is insufficient information to make reliable estimates. The nature of qualitative factors within decision making will vary with the circumstances that relate to the opportunities being considered.

     Examples of qualitative factors in the make or buy decision:

     i   *Quality.* If a firm makes a component rather than buys it from an external party it has greater control over the quality of the component. For example, the firm can implement its own quality and inspection policies and amend these as they see fit. Although this factor may be difficult to assess in monetary terms it may be influential in the make or buy decision.

     ii   *Reliability of supplies.* It is likely that a firm will have greater control over the reliability of supplies if it makes a component rather than buying it in from another firm. For example, the cost of buying a component externally may be less than the cost of making the component; however, the potential supplier may have a history of poor industrial relations which may jeopardise supplies periodically. This factor may be significant in the decision to make or buy.

     iii   *After-sales service.* When a firm sells a product that has a component purchased externally, it may find it difficult to service the product if the component is the cause of a malfunction. After-sales service may be influential in the firm's ability to sell the product, and it follows that the make or buy decision will also be influenced by this factor.

BUDGETS
CHAPTER TWENTY

20

LEARNING OBJECTIVES

At the end of this chapter, you should be able to:

1   discuss some of the reasons for producing budgets

2   explain what is meant by the budget process

3   explain the stages and parties that are typically involved in the budget process

4   identify the factors which influence the choice of the budget period

5   summarise what is normally included in the master budget

6   outline the role of sales and production budgets, and the relationship between them

7   calculate budgets for materials purchased in units and in monetary terms

8   calculate budgets for materials costs per unit manufactured and sold, and for labour costs

9   explain why, in addition to budgets for materials and labour, it may also be important to construct budgets for overhead costs.

Introduction

In Chapter 15, four stages of the planning and control process were identified. The third stage, making operating decisions, focused on the use of resources and the individual decisions necessary to use them consistently within the overall objectives of an organisation. It was also stated that, in this stage, the decisions would be translated into a short-term plan, a budget, defined as 'a plan of action expressed in monetary terms'. In this chapter, we will examine the purpose of budgets, the budgeting process and the preparation of budgets.

A budget must match the organisation's needs. In Chapter 15 we mentioned the application of contingency theory to all accounting information systems. The major contingency factors identified were technology, the commercial environment and the structure of the organisation. These factors affect the type of budget that is used by an organisation. For example, in a retail organisation the budget deals mainly with the level of consumer sales and the purchase of goods necessary to satisfy these sales. In contrast, the budget of a manufacturing organisation focuses on the sales of products and the production activity necessary to meet these sales. There are some similarities between the two types of budget, and there is a common basis for preparing the budgets of different types of organisation. We will concentrate in this chapter on large manufacturing organisations, which have relatively sophisticated budgets.

The purposes of budgets

Following are listed a number of the traditional purposes of budgets. The purpose of budgets, as we have said, depends on the type of organisation; the following are common to most organisations:

LO 1

Discuss some of the reasons for producing budgets

• Encourage planning

The introduction of budgets within an organisation forces management to look ahead and set short-term targets. By looking to the future, management can anticipate potential problems. For example, the identification of shortages of cash at particular times in the budget period gives management the opportunity to make provisions to supplement this shortage; for example, by negotiating an overdraft facility with the bank.

• Coordinate functions within an organisation

The preparation of budgets tends to increase the coordination between departments and units within an organisation because it requires that the individual plans of managers are integrated. The managers are obliged to consider the relationships between various departments. For example, it is important that a purchasing department is aware of the material requirements for manufacture so that buying and inventory (stock) levels are maintained to service the needs of the manufacturing activity during the budget period.

• A form of communication

A budget is often a useful means by which senior management can formally communicate objectives and strategies for the forthcoming period. This function is reinforced periodically through a control mechanism – referred to later – which reviews actual performance against the budget during the budget period. The extent to which lower level managers are involved in establishing a budget communicates important information about the philosophy of senior management. We also discuss this issue later in this chapter.

• Provide a basis for responsibility accounting

Individual managers are identified with their budget centres and are made responsible for achieving the budgeted targets. These targets are in terms of expenditure, income and output that are considered to be within the manager's control. Responsibility accounting was outlined in Chapter 15. Within the context of budgets, responsibility accounting represents an important feature of the delegation of responsibility within an organisation.

KEY CONCEPT 20.1

RESPONSIBILITY ACCOUNTING

Responsibility accounting is where an entity is structured into strategic business units and the performance of these units is measured in terms of accounting results.

• Provide a basis for a control mechanism

The budget provides a basis for comparing actual performance with a plan and identifying any deviation from that plan. The identification of these deviations gives management the opportunity to take corrective action so that such deviations do not persist in the future. When budgets are used as a control mechanism, it is described as 'budgetary control'.

• Authorise expenditure

The budget can act as a formal authorisation of future expenditure from senior management to the individuals who are responsible for the expenditure. If an item of expenditure is contained in the budget that has been approved by the top management of the organisation, it implies that the item has been approved, and generally no further authorisation is required.

• Motivate employees

The budget can be used as a target to motivate employees to reach certain levels of attainment. For example, if, during one budget period, a salesperson achieves sales of products to the value of $30 000, management might in the next period set a target of $40 000, believing, rightly or wrongly, that this new target will motivate the salesperson to exceed the levels of the previous period.

Budgets mean different things to different people within an organisation. For example, a budget which is introduced by management with the aim of monitoring production costs might be perceived by production managers as a device to monitor their performance. Budgets can lead to much misunderstanding, frustration and friction within an organisation.

Positive behaviour flows from budgets when the goals of the entity and the individual are aligned so that there is goal congruence (which we discussed in Chapter 15). In these cases, the manager is motivated to achieve the budget's goals. Negative or *dysfunctional* behaviour flows from budgets where the goals of the individual and the entity are different.

There is an ethical aspect to dysfunctional behaviour as it involves managers taking actions like deliberately understating sales targets or overstating costs in order to easily achieve the budget that is set out for them. This process of padding the budget (sometimes referred to as 'budgetary slack') is one of the many behavioural aspects to budgeting and it would be very easy to devote an entire chapter (or even a book!) to this subject.

Review exercise 1
What is a budget? What are the main reasons for an organisation to introduce budgets?

The budget process

The following analysis focuses on the main features of the budget process. The products that are manufactured and sold in a budget period are determined via operating decisions, as previously described in Chapter 19. These decisions are initially made separately from the functions within an organisation that are there to support the manufacture and sales of the products that have been chosen. In a manufacturing organisation, these supportive functions relate to purchasing, production, marketing, administration and finance. Each of these functions also requires investment in resources, such as personnel.

LO 2

Explain what is meant by the budget process

KEY CONCEPT 20.2

THE BUDGET PROCESS
The phrase 'the budget process' refers to the sequence of operations necessary to produce a budget for a particular organisation. The sequence of operations depends upon the type of organisation and its perceived requirements for planning and control.

It is at the beginning of the budget process that consideration is given to the operating decisions collectively and their interrelationships with these functions. At this stage, the resource implications of the decisions are analysed to determine the extent to which they will draw upon the functions that were described above. From this analysis, guidelines are formulated for the preparation of the budgets. The guidelines represent a framework for people who prepare the budgets; they identify the overall levels of activity and the organisation's policies on performance criteria, such as productivity.

At this stage, the only people involved in the process are the organisation's top-level management. They include those who have overall responsibility for the sales and production activities and those who are responsible for ensuring that the activities are coordinated; for example, an accountant who has responsibility for the coordination of the accounting information input, often referred to as the budget accountant. Thus, the vitally important management task of coordinating the various interrelated aspects of decision making begins in the budgeting process.

In a manufacturing organisation, for example, the main task of coordination is concerned with the overall policy on the level of sales and production activities. The coordination of these activities involves ensuring that the level of production is sufficient to meet the sales demand for products plus any inventory of finished goods that is required. For example, if the sales demand for a product is 150 units and the desired closing inventory of finished goods is 30 units, assuming there is no opening inventory of finished goods available, 180 units will have to be manufactured to meet the sales and inventory requirements in the budget period. The functions such as marketing and finance necessary to support these levels of output are also considered at this stage. In addition, management's policies on the levels of performance for the budget period are also formulated.

When the output levels and associated policies have been determined by top management, they must be communicated to the preparers of the budgets, along with the guidelines. Budgets are prepared for the individual responsibility centres, which have been defined by the organisation's hierarchy. These centres are managed by personnel who are responsible for particular functions within the organisation, such as generating sales, producing products, and supporting the sales and production functions.

There is some debate on the extent to which managers who are responsible for departments that spend and generate income should be involved in the preparation of their own budgets – but they usually have some influence. The extent of influence varies from organisation to organisation and depends on management style. For example, the top management of some organisations might impose rules on subordinates without any discussion. Where a manager is solely responsible for the preparation of the budget, it is likely to be biased in favour of the manager; this is not in the best interests of the organisation as a whole. For example, a manager who is responsible for the sales of a particular product range will probably set budget targets that can easily be attained, thus gaining the favour of superiors.

It is likely, however, that a manager of a responsibility centre will have a greater degree of knowledge and understanding of the operation of the centre than any other personnel within the organisation, and this knowledge is important in the formulation of budgets. There is a strong case for some involvement by the manager of a responsibility centre in the preparation of the centre's budget. Typically, in the budgeting process of an organisation, individual budgets for each responsibility centre are the subject of negotiations before they are approved and adopted by the organisation. The parties to the negotiations include the manager of the responsibility centre, the preparer of the budget (if not the manager) and the manager's superior. The accountant who is responsible for budgets within the organisation often acts as an intermediary in the negotiations. In large organisations, the negotiation process has several stages as the budget moves up the management hierarchy for approval.

Participative budgeting occurs when lower level managers are involved in the budget process rather than having the budget imposed from above. Figure 20.1 shows a two-way flow in the establishment of the budget. This process will vary across entities. In some entities, the flow will be one way down from the board while in others there will be participation by lower level managers in the process. In some entities, lower level managers will appear to be involved in the process but, ultimately, top-level managers make the decisions. This process of only appearing to involve lower level managers is referred to as '*pseudo-participation*'.

LO 3

Explain the stages and parties that are typically involved in the budget process

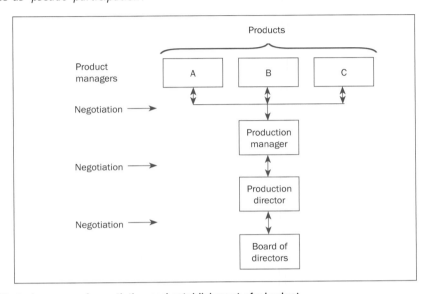

Figure 20.1 Typical process of negotiation and establishment of a budget

KEY CONCEPT 20.3

PARTICIPATIVE BUDGETING

Participative budgeting is where lower level managers are involved in the process of establishing the budget.

Figure 20.1 illustrates a typical hierarchy for the production management of an organisation and the stages of negotiation of the production budget for three groups of products. First, the production budgets (in terms of costs and output levels) are determined for products A, B and C. It has been assumed that a product manager is responsible for the production of each of the products. As mentioned, it is likely that each product manager will prepare his or her own budget – or at least influence its content. When the budgets have been prepared, the first stage in negotiation takes place between the individual product managers and the production manager who has overall responsibility for this range of products. After agreement has been reached on the individual budgets, the combined budgets for the range are then negotiated with the production director who has responsibility for all the production of the organisation. The negotiation of the production budget will occur at the board level where the budget will eventually be approved.

At each stage of the negotiation process, bargains are struck between the managers responsible for the budget and their immediate superiors. The negotiations between managers in the hierarchy of an organisation represent a bargaining process where the individual goals of managers are formulated for a forthcoming budget period.

The finetuning of the respective budgets takes place at board level. The board has the final decision on the budget. This process involves ensuring that all the budgets are consistent with each other; for example, that the required material inventory levels are sufficient to meet the production requirements throughout the year. When all the individual budgets have been finalised and approved at this level, they are summarised into what is commonly referred to as a 'master budget'. The master budget is usually in the form of a budgeted balance sheet and income statement for the budget period. The information in the master budget is, in effect, a summary of all the individual budgets, and thus represents the overall plan for an organisation. It clearly sets out the targets for the organisation in an easily understandable form and can later be compared with the actual balance sheet and income statement.

After final approval at board level, the budgets are passed down the organisation to the respective responsibility centre managers. It is these managers who carry out the plans contained within each individual budget.

Plans in the form of budgets are extremely useful to an organisation. Several of the purposes identified earlier for budgets highlight their usefulness. For example, they compel organisations to look ahead and thereby anticipate any particular problems that might arise in the future.

The nature of budgeting that has been described so far is static, in the sense that the planning process is based upon certain assumptions and events that will occur in the forthcoming budget period. However, in reality, the business environment is dynamic; therefore, events might not turn out as anticipated in the budget. Deviations from the budget might be harmful to the organisation. For example, the cost of producing a product might be greater than that anticipated in the budget, and losses might be made. It is therefore important that the 'actual' events in a budget period are monitored against the budget so that action can be taken to alleviate any undesirable situations.

When undesirable deviations from the budget are caused by events which are within the organisation's control, action can be taken to ensure that such deviations do not occur in the future. In contrast, events outside the control of the organisation, such as a downturn in the economy, could mean that the organisation has to reconsider its plans. Typically, this results in organisations 'trimming' their operations to lower levels of activity, or diversifying into other markets. The point here is that undesirable situations can be averted if an efficient system of control is imposed, and if the actual and budgeted performances are compared frequently.

Review exercise 2

What kind of human behaviour problems might one expect if budget goals have no flexibility and are set too high?

The budget period

The budget period normally employed by organisations is one year, which coincides with the periodic reporting requirements for published accounts regulated by the law. Most public companies, for example, are required by law to publish accounts annually. There is usually a link between the information in the budgets and the annual accounts: a firm's budget normally includes the planned total sales for the period while the annual accounts show the actual sales achieved in the same period. Generally, for control purposes, the budget for the year is broken down into quarterly, monthly and weekly periods, depending on the needs of the particular organisation and the state of the economy. An organisation that operates in a very competitive market will want to monitor performance on a fairly frequent basis to ensure it is maintaining its competitive position, as reflected in actual income, costs and outputs.

LO 4
Identify the factors which influence the choice of the budget period

Preparation of the master budget

KEY CONCEPT 20.4

THE MASTER BUDGET
The master budget usually consists of the budgeted income statement and balance sheet which represents a summary of the individual functional budgets of the organisation as a whole.

The master budget is defined in Key concept 20.4. As we have said, it clearly sets out the objectives and targets for the forthcoming budget period and provides a basis for coordinating individual functional budgets. In a medium-sized or large manufacturing organisation, these functional budgets usually consist of sales, production, administration, distribution and cash budgets. Sales and production budgets are discussed in the next section.

LO 5
Summarise what is normally included in the master budget

Frequently, for small organisations, the income statement, balance sheet and cash budget are sufficient for the manager's needs. The information contained in these three budgeted statements provides a reasonable base from which to analyse the forthcoming period. In particular, a number of ratios and indicators can be derived, such as those relating to profitability, liquidity and financing. The use of these ratios and indicators was discussed in Chapter 14.

In Example 20.1 we consider the preparation of an income statement, balance sheet and cash budget for a small firm just starting out.

Example 20.1: Sivraj Ltd

Sivraj Ltd was formed on 1 July 20X5 with a share capital of $40 000. Of this, $24 000 was immediately invested in non-current assets, leaving $16 000 cash.

It is estimated that the non-current assets have a 10-year life, and will have no value at the end of that time. The company has decided to depreciate these assets using the straight-line method of depreciation. Therefore, the depreciation charge per year will be $24 000 ÷ 10 years = $2400, or, expressed in monthly terms, $2400 ÷ 12 months = $200.

Business plans have been formulated for the first months of operations. The cash budget for these plans is set out on the opposite page.

Sales for the six months are estimated to be $600 000. However, the company operates in a seasonal market and will also be allowing some of its customers to take credit. The company anticipates the following receipts of cash over the six months from sales:

	Cash receipts $
July	40 000
August	50 000
September	50 000
October	70 000
November	120 000
December	170 000
	500 000

From this breakdown of the anticipated cash received over the six-month period, it is apparent that at the end of the period there will be money owing from customers (that is, debtors) of $600 000 – $500 000 = $100 000.

The materials required to meet the demand for sales are estimated to be $240 000. To enable the company to maintain an inventory (to ensure against any shortages), $260 000 worth of materials will be purchased in the period. Because of the production cycle, and the credit that the company will be obtaining from its suppliers, the pattern and amount paid to suppliers will be as follows:

	Payment to suppliers for materials $
July	60 000
August	60 000
September	20 000
October	20 000
November	20 000
December	20 000
	200 000

At the end of the six-month period, the company has purchased materials costing $260 000 but has paid only $200 000 for them; thus it owes (that is, has creditors of) $60 000 at the end of December 20X5.

The estimated labour cost that will be incurred over the six months will be $180 000. In addition, the firm anticipates that overheads (excluding depreciation) of $138 000 will also be incurred over this period. Overheads and wages will be paid evenly over the six-month period. We will assume that any cash deficits are financed by a bank overdraft.

To ensure that sufficient cash resources are available, the company wishes to calculate a cash budget (forecast), on a monthly basis, as well as a budgeted income statement for the period and a balance sheet at the end of the period.

We will begin by constructing the three budgeted statements from the information given. This will be followed by a commentary concerning the usefulness of these statements to management. The cash budget will be considered first.

Sivraj Ltd
Cash budget for six months ending 31 December 20X5

	July $	August $	September $	October $	November $	December $
Cash inflows:						
Share capital	40 000					
Sales receipts	40 000	50 000	50 000	70 000	120 000	170 000
Total cash inflows	80 000	50 000	50 000	70 000	120 000	170 000
Cash outflows:						
Materials	60 000	60 000	20 000	20 000	20 000	20 000
Wages	30 000	30 000	30 000	30 000	30 000	30 000
Overheads	23 000	23 000	23 000	23 000	23 000	23 000
Non-current assets	24 000	–	–	–	–	–
Total cash outflows	137 000	113 000	73 000	73 000	73 000	73 000
Net cash flow	(57 000)	(63 000)	(23 000)	(3 000)	47 000	97 000
Balance brought forward	–	(57 000)	(120 000)	(143 000)	(146 000)	(99 000)
Balance carried forward	(57 000)	(120 000)	(143 000)	(146 000)	(99 000)	(2 000)

It can be seen from the cash budget for Sivraj Ltd that the inflows and outflows of cash are recorded in the budget statement when the cash is actually received or paid. There are a few main points to remember when constructing a cash budget:

- The dates of receipt and payment of cash and purchases are relevant; allowance must be made for any credit period given or received. For Sivraj Ltd, the relevant sales figures are when the cash is actually received and not when the sales are earned in the period.
- Provisions should be excluded as they do not affect cash flows; for example, depreciation on non-current assets is excluded because the cash flow associated with non-current assets occurs when the asset is paid for.
- Any inflows of capital, and outflows, such as drawings, payment of tax and dividends, must be included. In the example of Sivraj Ltd, the only relevant item of this nature is the capital which was injected into the business when it began.

- The format of the cash budget is similar to the worksheets that were introduced in Chapter 6. In the case of cash budgets, the column headings relate to the time period chosen for the budget. In this example, the requirement is monthly for six months to the end of December 20X5. The company could have chosen weeks, for example. In such a case, there would be a column for each week of the six-month period. The time dimension depends upon the requirements of the managers of the organisation.

Sivraj Ltd's income statement, for convenience, has been constructed in a summary form rather than through the use of a worksheet. Unlike the cash budget, the income statement is constructed by applying the concept of accrual accounting rather than cash flow accounting. Thus, the material cost is the cost of materials included in the sales rather than the cash paid for the materials. The depreciation charge for the six months is calculated by multiplying the monthly charge of $200 by six.

Sivraj Ltd
Income statement for the six months ending 31 December 20X5

	$	$
Sales		600 000
Cost of sales:		
Materials	240 000	
Wages	180 000	420 000
Gross profit		180 000
Depreciation	1 200	
Overheads	138 000	139 200
Net profit		40 800

The balance sheet, like the income statement, has been constructed without the use of a worksheet. After the statement, we will briefly explain how the value of some of the assets and liabilities has been derived:

Sivraj Ltd
Balance sheet as at 31 December 20X5

	$	$
Assets		
Current assets		
Inventory	20 000	
Debtors	100 000	
Total current assets		120 000
Non-current assets		
Cost unspecified (at cost)	24 000	
Less Accumulated depreciation	(1 200)	
Total non-current assets		22 800
Total assets		142 800

|||➡

	$	$
Liabilities		
Current liabilities		
Bank overdraft	2 000	
Creditors	60 000	
Total current liabilities		62 000
Net assets		80 800
Equity		
Share capital		40 000
Profit and loss		40 800
Total equity		80 800

The inventory figure represents the difference between materials purchased ($260 000) and materials consumed in the sales during the six-month period ($240 000). Debtors of $100 000 is the difference between the sales in the period and the cash received. The sum of $60 000 for creditors is the difference between the materials purchased ($260 000) and the cash paid at the end of the six months ($200 000). The bank overdraft is derived from the cash budget, and is the balance at the end of December 20X5.

The use of worksheets in the construction of the income statement and the balance sheet illustrates the interrelationships between these statements. Although worksheets were not used in this example, the interrelationships between these statements should still be apparent.

From a brief glance at these three budgeted statements for Sivraj Ltd, their usefulness for planning should be apparent. For example, it is predicted that although the company anticipates making a profit of $40 800 for the six months, which appears reasonably healthy, there will be large deficits of cash during this period. The problem for Sivraj Ltd is the pattern of cash payments and receipts. High material costs are incurred in the first two months, as well as the payment for the non-current assets. In contrast, the major source of cash, sales, is greater in the latter part of the period. Identifying this situation prior to trading is extremely useful because action can be taken to reduce these cash deficits while trying to obtain some additional funding. It might be possible to get receipts from sales in earlier, either by restricting the credit given to customers or by encouraging customers to pay more quickly by offering a discount for prompt payment. This would result in cash being received earlier and would reduce the cash deficit each month.

By identifying cash shortages at this stage, Sivraj Ltd is also in a better position to finance any deficits. The bank would look more favourably on an application for an overdraft after having some insight into the future profitability of the company. This situation can be contrasted with the negative attitude of the bank when an application for funding is made after a firm has gone into debt without any prior communication with the bank. Another alternative action to relieve the cash shortage is to raise additional share capital to fund the cash deficits of the business.

In the analysis of the budgets of Sivraj Ltd, our main concern has been, not surprisingly, the cash deficits. If Sivraj Ltd had cash surpluses rather than deficits during the budget period, this information would also be useful to the business. By identifying surpluses at this early stage, the firm would be in a better position to plan the investment of such funds (e.g. in short-term deposits) to obtain the maximum amount of interest.

As mentioned, a number of other characteristics of the business can be analysed through the use of ratio analysis. In general, the major benefit of budgets of this nature to an organisation such as Sivraj Ltd is that events can be anticipated and action taken in the best interests of the organisation.

External funding organisations always require budgeted information from firms, similar to that produced for Sivraj Ltd, before they agree to lend money. This is particularly the case when small businesses, such as Sivraj Ltd, apply for funding from banks.

CASE STUDY 20.1

Willpower the key to budgeting
Kathy Bowler, CPA Australia manager of financial planning

BUDGETS are a great strategy for debt reduction but so few people muster the will or master the skill to prepare a winning budget.

That's a shame because budgets work. The secret, of course, is to reduce debt and increase savings. It sounds simple and it is. Start by allocating some time to working through your essential and discretionary spending. This will tell you if you are living beyond your means. Budgets are easier to prepare on a computer because totals are automatically calculated, regular expenses are automatically entered across months and changes can be made easily.

Budgets have many advantages. They can:

• help manage your cash flow to ensure you always have enough money for expenses

• calculate how much you can comfortably contribute to a savings plan/managed fund, which will provide better long-term returns

• work out how long it will take to save for your dream holiday or some other goal

• encourage you to work out where you really want to spend your money, such as holidays or CDs.

To make your budget a success you need goals. By having clear reasons for budgeting, saving and reducing debt, you'll be more committed.

One easy measure to kick the budget along is to consolidate your loans. If you have more than one loan, it might be worthwhile consolidating any personal loans and credit card debt into one loan on a lower interest rate.

Adelaide Advertiser, 18 November 2002

COMMENTARY

While the above article discusses personal budgeting, the same principles apply to businesses. Cash budgets are useful to help manage cash flow and allow businesses to plan to invest surplus cash at the best rates or, when cash is required, arrange borrowings at the cheapest rates. Budgets assist a business to plan where it is heading in the future and the use of budgets can help a business to get there.

Review exercise 3

What is a master budget?

Review exercise 4

Describe the main differences in the budgeting process for a small retail firm and a large manufacturing firm.

Sales and production budgets

The sales and production budgets prepared for manufacturing organisations reflect the respective targets for these functions in the forthcoming budget period. As previously mentioned, the summation of these budgets is embodied within the overall income statement and balance sheet. Since these functions involve cash payments and receipts, they are also the source for the overall cash budget.

In Example 20.2, we will concentrate on the sales and production budgets. We also emphasise the importance of coordinating these different functions within an organisation – in particular the production output level to support the sales volume and desired inventory levels.

LO 6

Outline the role of sales and production budgets, and the relationship between them

Example 20.2: Nadia Ltd

Nadia Ltd has gathered the following data about future sales and production requirements for the year 20X7:

Estimated sales

Product	Units	Price ($)	Opening inventory 1 January 20X7 Units	Desired closing inventory 31 December 20X7 Units
A	20 000	55	8 000	10 000
B	50 000	50	15 000	14 000
C	30 000	65	6 000	6 000

Materials used in manufacture

Item no.	Unit	Amount per unit A	B	C
54	component	3	–	5
32	metres	2	1	3
44	kilograms	–	2	–

Estimated purchase price of materials

Item no.	Price
54	$3 per component
32	$2 per metre
44	$4 per kilogram

Levels of inventory materials

Item no.	Opening inventory 1 January 20X7	Closing inventory 31 December 20X7
54	21 000 components	25 000 components
32	17 000 metres	23 000 metres
44	10 000 kilograms	8 000 kilograms

Labour requirements

Product	Hours per unit	Rate per hour $
A	4	7
B	5	5
C	5	6

Production overheads are estimated at $500 000 per year. For internal management purposes, Nadia Ltd adopts a variable costing system, and therefore treats these overheads as a period charge (see Chapter 17).

In this example, we presumed that the sales demand, in terms of volume, is the constraining factor. Thus, the production volume will be dependent upon the sales demand.

The management of Nadia Ltd requires the following budgetary information for the forthcoming budget period:

- sales budget in monetary terms
- production budget in units
- materials-purchased budget in units
- materials-purchased budget in monetary terms
- materials cost per unit manufactured and sold
- the total labour hours worked during the period and the cost, plus the labour cost per unit manufactured and sold
- the unit contribution for each product
- the profit and loss for the budget period
- the value of closing finished inventory at the end of the budget period.

Sales budget in monetary terms

We have been given the price per unit and the volume of units that it is estimated will be sold. To calculate the total sales revenue generated from these sales, we multiply these two variables.

Product	Unit × price ($)	Sales revenue ($000)
A	20 000 × 55	1 100
B	50 000 × 50	2 500
C	30 000 × 65	1 950
Total		5 550

Production budget in units

The production level during the budget period must not only satisfy the sales demand but must ensure that the inventory levels are sufficient for the period. In the case of Nadia Ltd, the opening and closing inventory levels have been estimated, and we have been given the sales demand; from this information, with the help of a simple equation, we can determine the production level to satisfy this demand.

The equation we use, sometimes referred to as the 'inventory formula', is as follows (measured in units):

$$\text{production} + \text{opening inventory} = \text{sales} + \text{closing inventory}$$

It states that the units produced during the budget period plus what is in inventory at the beginning of this period are equal to the units to be sold plus the units required as inventory at the end of the period.

For our purposes, as there is only one unknown quantity (production), we need to re-arrange the equation as follows:

$$\text{sales} + \text{closing inventory} - \text{opening inventory} = \text{production}$$

Applying this equation to the figures for Nadia Ltd, measured in units, we obtain the following:

Product	Sales (units)	+	Closing inventory (units)	−	Opening inventory (units)	=	Production (units)
A	20 000	+	10 000	−	8 000	=	22 000
B	50 000	+	14 000	−	15 000	=	49 000
C	30 000	+	6 000	−	6 000	=	30 000

Materials-purchased budget, measured in units

Three types of materials described by item numbers (54, 32 and 44) are used in the production of A, B and C.

LO 7

Calculate budgets for materials purchased in units and in monetary terms

Materials	Materials required per unit of product		
	Product A (units)	Product B (units)	Product C (units)
No. 54	3	–	5
No. 32	2	1	3
No. 44	–	2	–

Before determining how many units of inventory will need to be purchased in the period, we must first calculate the number of units of inventory necessary to satisfy production requirements:

Materials	Production materials (units) required for products		
	Product A: 22 000 units	Product B: 49 000 units	Product C: 30 000 units
No. 54	66 000	–	150 000
No. 32	44 000	49 000	90 000
No. 44	–	98 000	–

The purchase of materials that are required for the forthcoming budget period can now be calculated using a similar equation to that used in determining the production level:

$$\text{purchases} + \text{opening inventory} = \text{production} + \text{closing inventory}$$

Purchases and so on in this equation are measured in terms of material units; for example, components in the case of item no. 54.

The equation states that the materials required for production during the period and closing inventory at the end of the period will be met from the purchase of materials and the inventory that is available at the beginning of the period.

In this example we are told the opening and closing inventory requirements and we have calculated the materials required for production. Therefore, three of the four variables in the equation are known to us, and by rearranging the equation we can calculate the purchases figure:

$$\text{production} + \text{closing inventory} - \text{opening inventory} = \text{purchases}$$

Applying this equation to the information that has been given for the three inventory numbers, we obtain the following:

Item no.	Production	+	Closing inventory	–	Opening inventory	=	Purchases
54	216 000 components	+	25 000 components	–	21 000 components	=	220 000 components
32	183 000 metres	+	23 000 metres	–	17 000 metres	=	189 000 metres
44	98 000 kilograms	+	8 000 kilograms	–	10 000 kilograms	=	100 000 kilograms

It should be remembered that the above purchases figures represent the units for the respective materials; thus, for example, in the case of item no. 54 the purchases requirement will be 220 000 components.

Materials purchased in monetary terms

The calculation of purchases, measured in monetary terms, is straightforward. We multiply the purchases, in terms of units, by the cost per unit which was given at the beginning of the example:

Item no.	Purchases (units)	Cost per unit ($)	Total cost ($)
54	220 000	3	660 000
32	189 000	2	378 000
44	100 000	4	400 000
			1 438 000

Materials cost per unit manufactured and sold

This information might be required by management to determine the profitability of each of the products sold, and for inventory valuation purposes. All the relevant information regarding this calculation has been given and it just remains for us to perform the calculation. For each unit of product, we need to multiply the cost per unit of material by the amount of the material required to manufacture each product.

Calculate budgets for materials costs per unit manufactured and sold, and for labour costs

Item no.	Cost per unit of item ($)	Cost ($) per unit of product		
		A	B	C
54	3	9	–	15
32	2	4	2	6
44	4	–	8	–
Material cost per unit sold		13	10	21

Labour

Management needs to know the total labour worked in the period, the total cost, and the cost of labour per unit of goods manufactured and sold.

We begin by computing the labour cost per unit of goods manufactured and sold. This information will provide management with data that is useful to assess profitability, and for inventory valuation purposes. The arithmetic for the calculation is simple – to obtain the total labour cost per unit we multiply the hours per unit by the rate per hour.

Product	Hours per unit	Rate per hour $	Total labour cost per unit $
A	4	7	28
B	5	5	25
C	5	6	30

For calculation of the total labour hours, the production units are multiplied by the hours per unit. If we then multiply the total labour by the rate per unit, we can determine the total cost. It is important to appreciate why production units are used in these calculations rather than sales units. The reason is that the objective here is to determine how many hours were actually worked and the cost of those hours during the year. If sales units were used, we would be establishing the total hours that have been consumed in producing the sales. If there are changes between the opening and closing levels of finished inventory, the units produced will not equal the sales units sold. This was the case for products A and B, as can be seen when we determined the production levels for these two products earlier. In contrast, for product C the finished inventory level remained unchanged. Therefore, the production units and the sales units were the same; that is, 30 000 units.

Product	Production units	Labour hours per unit	Labour hours total	Rate ($) per hour	Total cost ($)
A	22 000	4	88 000	7	616 000
B	49 000	5	245 000	5	1 225 000
C	30 000	5	150 000	6	900 000
			483 000		2 741 000

Unit contribution of each product

We have used the concept of contribution in earlier chapters in relation to, for example, cost behaviour and cost-volume-profit analysis. The contribution per unit is equal to the sales price per unit, less variable costs per unit. The only variable costs in this example are materials and labour. These variable costs, you will remember, were determined earlier. Thus, the contribution per unit for these three products will be as follows:

	A $	A $	B $	B $	C $	C $
Sales price		55		50		65
Less Variable costs						
Material	13		10		21	
Labour	28	41	25	35	30	51
Contribution per unit		14		15		14

Profit or loss for the budget period

We begin by determining the total contribution for the three products and then deduct the overhead cost, which is the convention under the variable costing regime:

Product	Contribution per unit ($)	Units sold	$
A	14	20 000	280 000
B	15	50 000	750 000
C	14	30 000	420 000
Total contribution			1 450 000
Less Overheads			500 000
Profit			950 000

Value of finished inventory at end of budget period

Under the variable costing regime, finished inventory is valued at variable cost. From the information already obtained, we know the variable costs of each product; we multiply this cost by the number of units of finished inventory, which was given at the beginning of this example.

Product	Finished inventory in units	Variable cost ($)	Value of finished inventory ($)
A	10 000	41	410 000
B	14 000	35	490 000
C	6 000	51	306 000
	Total value of finished inventory		1 206 000

THE USES OF SALES AND PRODUCTION BUDGETS

Budgets, such as those presented for Nadia Ltd, act as a source of information in the construction of the income statement, the balance sheet and the cash budget. The figures are broken down further to provide budgets for responsible departments, enabling the management of these departments to identify clearly the plans which affect them.

The budgets prepared for Nadia Ltd are not suitable for all manufacturing organisations, but the example illustrates the main principles in the preparation of budgets for manufacturing organisations.

Review exercise 5

Why should preparers of the production budget liaise with the preparers of the sales budget?

Budgeting for overhead expenditure

In Example 20.2, Nadia Ltd's overheads were given as one figure; that is, $500 000 per year. Normally, as mentioned in the earlier section on the budgeting process, organisations also prepare detailed budgets for overhead expenditure. These represent the planned costs associated with supporting the

Explain why, in addition to budgets for materials and labour, it may also be important to construct budgets for overhead costs

manufacturing function, such as machine maintenance, administration and sales. As new technology and automation are introduced into the manufacturing environment, overhead costs are tending to grow as a proportion of the total cost of operations. Organisations should be placing more emphasis on the planning and control of such costs, but many of the systems that are in use have not been designed to cope with this phenomenon. There is considerable debate at present about the methods of costing and budgeting that should be introduced to monitor overhead costs.

Review exercise 6

What is the purpose of the cash budget?

SUMMARY

LO 1

LEARNING OBJECTIVE 1
Discuss some of the reasons for producing budgets

There are a number of reasons why firms produce a budget or budgets. Some of these reasons are:

- to encourage planning
- to provide a control mechanism
- as authorisation for expenditure
- to motivate employees
- as a form of communication
- to provide a basis for responsibility accounting.

LO 2

LEARNING OBJECTIVE 2
Explain what is meant by the budget process

The budget process is the sequence of operations that are necessary to produce a budget for a particular organisation. The operations depend upon the type of organisation and its perceived requirements for planning and control.

LO 3

LEARNING OBJECTIVE 3
Explain the stages and parties that are typically involved in the budget process

At the beginning of the budget process, consideration is given to operating decisions which involve all levels of the production cycle; for example, the manufacturing area. This can involve purchasing, production, marketing, sales, and so on. It is important that all levels of lower management are involved and consulted in this process.

LO 4

LEARNING OBJECTIVE 4
Identify the factors which influence the choice of the budget period

The timeframe of a budget is normally one year. The reason for this period is that most public entities, for example, are required, by law, to publish annual accounts. However, depending on the information that is required by a firm, the budget period can be broken down into whatever period is required for good decision making.

LO 5

LEARNING OBJECTIVE 5
Summarise what is normally included in the master budget

The master budget normally consists of the budgeted income statement and balance sheet, and represents a summary of the individual functional budgets of the organisation as a whole.

LO 6

LEARNING OBJECTIVE 6
Outline the role of sales and production budgets, and the relationship between them

The production budget prepares a production schedule to meet inventory needs, and the sales department's projected sales. It is important that there is communication between the sales and production departments so that production does not fall short of expected sales (or exceed them by too much), otherwise the firm incurs the costs of lost sales or storage, and the potential loss from obsolescence.

LEARNING OBJECTIVE 7
Calculate budgets for materials purchased in units and in monetary terms

Budgets for materials purchased in units are a useful indicator of inventory levels. This is necessary for production to continue effectively. Conversely, the calculation of materials purchased in monetary terms is required for the cash budget.

LEARNING OBJECTIVE 8
Calculate budgets for materials costs per unit manufactured and sold, and for labour costs

This information might be required by management in order for it to determine the profitability of products sold, and for inventory valuation purposes.

Both materials and labour budgets are important. In relation to materials, budgets show if prices have increased or there is wastage in the manufacturing process. In relation to labour, budgets ensure that there is not an abnormal amount of overtime worked or that labour efficiency is below what was budgeted.

LEARNING OBJECTIVE 9
Explain why, in addition to budgets for materials and labour, it may also be important to construct budgets for overhead costs

The importance of overhead budgets is to keep track of planned overhead costs that support items such as supervision, administration and advertising, to name a few.

FURTHER READING

Hansen, D. & Mowen, M., 2003. *Management Accounting*, 6th edn, South-Western, Mason, Ohio.
Hilton, R., 2002. *Managerial Accounting: Creating Value in a Dynamic Business Environment*, 5th edn, McGraw-Hill.

REVIEW QUESTIONS

1   Discuss the stages and parties that are typically involved in the budget process.
2   Explain how budgets can mean different things to different people within an organisation, giving reasons.
3   Why should all senior personnel participate in formulating and submitting budget estimates?
4   Discuss the interrelationships between the sales budget and the production budget in a manufacturing organisation.
5   Explain, giving examples, the main advantages of identifying cash surpluses and deficits in a cash budget.
6   What determines the budget time period?
7   What is a master budget? Describe its role in relation to other budgets.

PROBLEMS FOR DISCUSSION AND ANALYSIS

1   What points need to be considered before preparing a budget?
2   There are some companies, such as Volvo, that no longer prepare budgets. What are the main advantages and disadvantages of using a budget?

3 Projected sales for each of the first three months of operations for AKP Ltd are as follows:

	$
March	480 000
April	590 000
May	505 000

The company expects to sell 10 per cent of its merchandise for cash. Of sales on account, 60 per cent are expected to be collected in the month of the sale, 30 per cent in the month following the sale, and the remainder in the second month following the sale.

Required

Prepare a schedule indicating cash collections from sales for March, April and May.

4 Jenny Smith, an accountancy student, decided to prepare a cash budget on her personal finances for the months March to June inclusive. From the following information, prepare a cash budget for each month and comment on her cash position:

	$
Cash balance at 1 March	2 637
Paid guild fees, 7 March	250
Rent paid on the 1st of the month in advance	750
Monthly food bill	600
Electricity quarterly account paid, 15 May	89
Average spent monthly on entertainment	130
Part-time monthly earnings, paid on 15th of each month	850
Paid deposit on 15 June for travel during vacation	500
Purchased ticket on 10 May to Foo Fighters concert	125

5 With reference to Sivraj Ltd (Example 20.1), prepare an income statement and balance sheet from the data, using worksheets.

6 CJH Ltd is preparing its annual budget. The following data is available:

Product	Estimated sales (units)	Opening inventory (units)	Closing inventory (Units)
X	18	8	10
Y	50	15	15
Z	30	6	6

Material	Cost per unit ($)	Units of material used per unit of product			Opening inventory (units)	Closing inventory (units)
		X	Y	Z		
A	3	3	–	5	21	25
B	2	2	1	3	17	23
C	4	–	2	1	10	15

a   Prepare the production budget in units.
b   Give the total budgeted cost of materials used in the production of X, Y and Z.
c   Give the total cost of materials, A, B and C, purchased.

7   Buzzbub is preparing its quarterly production budget and the following forecast information is available:

Product	Estimated sales (units)	Opening inventory (units)	Closing inventory (units)
P	276	12	33
Q	33	7	6
R	99	12	15

Material	Cost per unit ($)	Units of material used per unit of product			Opening inventory (units)	Closing inventory (units)
		P	Q	R		
F	76	0.5	2	–	22	8
G	8	–	3	7	102	45

Required

a   Prepare the production budget in units.
b   Give the total cost of materials used in the production of P, Q and R.
c   Give the total cost of materials purchased.

8   Kanga Meat Pie Company produces two types of pie: chicken and fish. The monthly sales budget is for sales of 20 000 chicken pies and 12 000 fish pies. Pies are snap frozen after manufacture. For this month, opening inventory is 2000 chicken pies and 1500 fish pies. Kanga wishes to budget for a closing inventory of 20 per cent of production.

Direct materials	Chicken pies (grams)	Fish pies (grams)
Pastry	500	750
Chicken	100	–
Fish	–	150
Vegetables	400	600

The following information is available for each material:

	Pastry	Chicken	Fish	Vegetables
Opening inventory	745 kg	100 kg	50 kg	125 kg
Estimated closing inventory	600 kg	100 kg	90 kg	200 kg
Price per kilogram	$2.00	$7.00	$10.00	$0.90

Required

   a Prepare the (material) purchases budget for the month.

   b Prepare the production budget for the month.

9 The finance manager of Art & Craft Direct Ltd has provided the following information:

	Materials used in manufacture			
	Enamel ($)	Paint ($)	Porcelain ($)	Total ($)
Total purchases budgeted for June	28 580	5 340	96 400	130 320
Estimated inventory, 1 June	1 250	2 400	4 540	8 190
Desired inventory, 30 June	2 000	2 150	5 000	9 150

	Direct labour cost		
	Kiln department	Decorating department	Total
Total budgeted for June	$36 500	$105 800	$142 300

	Finished goods inventories ($)				Work in progress inventories ($)
	Dish	Bowl	Figurine	Total	
Estimated, 1 June	4 180	3 270	2 580	10 030	2 900
Desired, 30 June	3 250	3 940	3 100	10 290	1 350

Budgeted factory overhead costs for June

	$
Indirect factory wages	45 800
Depreciation of plant and equipment	14 600
Power and lighting	5 300
Indirect materials	3 400
Total	69 100

Required

Use the information provided to prepare a budget for the cost of sales section of the income statement for June.

10 The owner of a business that sells fitness equipment for use in homes has requested a forecast of sales from her two salespeople for the next three months. She is trying to prepare a cash budget for the first quarter of 20X1/X2. The two salespeople provide the following sales forecast:

	Joe's estimates	Debbie's estimates
	$	$
July	100 000	90 000
August	150 000	200 000
September	170 000	300 000
October	160 000	400 000

The following details are available:

a   Inventory costs average 70 per cent of sales. Purchases are enough to cover the next month's sales and all purchases are paid in the month of purchase.

b   All sales are on account. Most customers pay the total within one month of the sale. Accounts receivable at 30 June 20X1 is $80 000.

c   Fixed expenses are $30 000 per month and variable expenses are 1 per cent of sales. All operating expenses are paid in the month in which they are incurred.

d   The company has cash in bank of $5000 at 1 July 20X1. The owner wants a minimum balance of cash on hand of $5000 at the end of every month starting in July.

Required

a   Prepare two cash budgets for July to September 20X1 for the estimates provided by Joe and Debbie.

b   Discuss what the owner should do in view of the differing sales estimates from Joe and Debbie.

11   The financial controller of BBQ Essentials requests estimates of sales, production and other operating data from the various administrative units every month. Selected information concerning sales and production for May 20X3 is summarised as follows:

	Estimated sales for May	
Sales territory	Basic 'backyard' model	Deluxe 'master' model
Sydney	3 500 units @ $550 per unit	1 800 units @ $1 300 per unit
Hobart	2 800 units @ $500 per unit	1 500 units @ $1 200 per unit
Perth	4 000 units @ $600 per unit	2 900 units @ $1 500 per unit

	Estimated inventories at 1 May	Desired inventories at 31 May	Anticipated purchase price
Direct materials:			
Grates	1 000 units	800 units	$15 per unit
Stainless steel	2 500 kg	1 900 kg	$3 per kg
Burner sub-assemblies	600 units	800 units	$72 per unit
Shelves	400 units	480 units	$7 per unit
Finished products:			
Basic model	1 500 units	1 200 units	
Deluxe model	400 units	500 units	

	Direct materials used in production	
	Basic model	Deluxe model
Grates	2 units per unit of product	6 units per unit of product
Stainless steel	25 kg per unit of product	65 kg per unit of product
Burner sub-assemblies	1 unit per unit of product	4 units per unit of product
Shelves	2 units per unit of product	3 units per unit of product

Department	Direct labour requirements	
	Basic model	Deluxe model
Prefabrication	0.50 hours @ $12 per hour	0.60 hours @ $12 per hour
Forming	0.75 hours @ $10 per hour	1.50 hours @ $10 per hour
Assembly	1.50 hours @ $9 per hour	2.50 hours @ $9 per hour

Required

a Prepare a sales budget for May.
b Prepare a production budget for May.
c Prepare a direct materials purchases budget for May.
d Prepare a direct labour cost budget for May.

Note to instructors: *The following problems are considered more suitable for use in MBA courses. However, undergraduate courses may also find them useful.*

12 Borough Equipment Ltd produces two products, A and B, for sale to electrical wholesalers. The following information relates to the six months ending 31 December 20X3:

Product	Budgeted sales (units)	Price per unit ($)	Budgeted inventory (units) 1 July 20X3	Budgeted inventory (units) 31 December 20X3
A	16 200	14.35	5 100	8 100
B	11 800	12.20	2 600	6 600

Components bought in and used in manufacture:

Component	Amount used per unit of product		Price	Expected inventory 1 July 20X3	Expected inventory 31 December 20X3
	A	B	($)	(units)	(units)
X	5	3	0.68	38 000	46 000
Y	2	4	0.24	13 500	19 500

Labour:

Product	Hours per unit	Rate per hour ($)
A	2	4.50
B	1	4.00

Overheads for the six months are expected to be $25 000. The company uses a variable-costing system and treats overheads as a period cost.

a Prepare the following:
  i sales budget
  ii production budget
  iii purchases budget in terms of components
  iv purchases budget in dollars
  v the total labour hours and cost for the period
  vi the contribution per unit
  vii the profit and loss for the period.
b Comment on the budgets' usefulness for planning, decision making and control.

13 Alan Blue is considering going into business by opening a supermarket. Suitable premises have been found. Before granting him overdraft and lending facilities, his local bank has asked him to draw up a cash budget for the first three months of trading.

Alan has $100 000 of his own money, which he is willing to invest in the business. The premises will have to be leased one month before opening, and inventory and staff need to be on hand two weeks prior to trading. The following information is relevant:

a   Expected sales for each of the first three months of trading are: $75 000, $90 000 and $110 000.

b   Costs: staff costs, $1500 per week; rent, including rates, $2000 per week, payable one month in advance; utilities, $500 per week, payable a month in arrears; insurance, $10 000, payable a year in advance; administration, $200 per week; equipment, $45 000, to be bought when the premises are first rented and to be depreciated, straight line, over 10 years with no residual value.

c   Alan is allowing a 25 per cent mark-up on all goods sold. Because he is a new customer, all suppliers are insisting on being paid within seven days. Inventory is ordered three weeks before it is required and there is a weekly delivery. It is assumed that sales are even throughout the four-week period.

d   The bank is prepared, if the cash budget indicates that there has been successful trading, to grant overdraft facilities to a maximum of $10 000, with interest set at 0.5 per cent per week. Further, the bank is prepared to grant a long-term loan of $50 000 with an interest rate of 12 per cent per annum, with interest to be paid quarterly (every 13 weeks). The long-term loan, if required, must be taken in full regardless of whether or not all the $50 000 is needed.

e   Alan further estimates that his weekly turnover in 12 months time will be $175 000.

Required

a   Prepare a cash budget that covers all the operations until the end of the last week of the budget period.

b   Given that the forecasts are reasonable, will the business be successful?

c   Given that the turnover will increase, what other costs would you expect to increase?

14 The manager of a sports store wants to expand the size of her shop by renting the vacant premises next door. She approaches her bank with the following projections for the six months from 1 July 20X0:

Income statement

		$	$
Sales			400 000
Inventory costs			225 000
Profit before expenses			175 000
Purchase of shelves, counters, etc.		80 000	
Salaries and dividends		60 000	140 000
Profit after expenses			35 000

Cash in and cash out

		$	$
Cash collections			400 000
Expenditures:			
Depreciation		30 000	

	$	$
Six months rent prepaid in June	6 000	
Cost of sales	185 000	
Repayment of note and interest	60 000	
Salaries and dividends	60 000	341 000
Difference		59 000

Balance sheet

Debits	$
Cash	20 000
Furniture and fixtures	150 000
Total	170 000

Credits	$
Accounts payable	50 000
Capital	40 000
Accumulated profits	80 000
Total	170 000

Required

The manager has asked you for your opinion about these projections. What advice would you give her?

15 Faraday Ltd is a wholesaler. The management has been extremely worried about the firm's cash position over the last few years. In January 20X1, they sought your advice and asked you to prepare a cash budget for the forthcoming months of April, May and June 20X1. In addition, they asked you to write a report on the cash position over this period, and, in particular, to identify ways in which it could be improved.

The following data is made available to you regarding the firm's operations:

a   Estimated sales for the six months to June 20X1 are as follows:

Month	Credit sales $	Cash sales $
January	122 000	12 900
February	137 000	14 500
March	142 000	17 700
April	148 000	20 100
May	134 000	15 000
June	126 000	12 600

Cash is received immediately on cash sales. The firm allows customers one month's credit on sales other than those for cash.

b   Purchases of goods for resale are made on credit. The firm receives two months credit on these purchases. The purchases for the six months to June 20X1 are as follows:

Month	$
January	62 000
February	58 000
March	71 000
April	80 000
May	54 000
June	48 000

c   An inventory check at the end of last year has revealed that $45 000 of inventory, valued at cost, is considered obsolete. The firm is currently negotiating the sale of this inventory for $9500 and expects payment in May 20X1.

d   Faraday's manufacturing overheads are estimated to be $12 000 per month. This includes a charge for depreciation of $2000 per month. The company takes one month to pay these expenses.

e   Selling and distribution expenses are estimated to be $50 400 a year and are incurred evenly over the year. One month's credit is taken.

f   In June, the firm anticipates paying $3880 tax to the Australian Taxation Office.

g   The firm has agreed to purchase new inventory-handling equipment. The cost of $105 200 is payable in two equal instalments in April and May 20X1.

h   The firm expects to be able to buy adjacent property (costing $150 000) in June to expand its operation.

i   The firm is currently negotiating an advertising program with an agency. The cost will be $6300 in May and $7700 in June. Payments will be made in cash.

j   It is estimated that the cash balance at 1 April will be $16 000.

ETHICS CASE STUDY

Jetco Ltd manufactures and sells Tyrus, an automatic vacuum cleaner for swimming pools. Jetco employs 10 salespeople and pays them a commission of $50 for each Tyrus they sell. In addition, if they meet the annual budgeted sales figure of 1000 units, they receive an annual bonus of $10 000.

Sue Clean is one of the sales staff and a close friend of Roger Pool, the accountant for Jetco. One day over lunch, Sue confides in Roger about a problem that is hurting Jetco's profits. She explains that the sales target of 1000 is quite easy for the sales staff to achieve. Once achieved, there is no further financial incentive to increase sales in that year as the bonus is fixed at $10 000. Therefore, many sales staff commit customers to buy at the beginning of the following year, which may mean a delay on the delivery of the vacuum cleaners of four to eight weeks. This means that these sales are recorded next year and the salesperson is well on the way to achieving next year's target.

Discuss

a   the problems for Jetco as a result of the strategies of the salespeople

b   what Roger should do with this information. Should he tell management or keep it confidential as Sue requested? If management discovered that he knew of this practice and did not say anything, he could lose his job. However, if he does say something then Sue could lose her job, and Roger could lose a friend.

ANSWERS TO REVIEW EXERCISES

1   A budget is a defined plan of action expressed in monetary terms. However, it should be stressed that different types of organisations will require different types of budgets to enable them to function effectively. The budget must match the organisation's situation; for example, units of production in a production budget.

The following are the main reasons that organisations introduce budgets:

*   Budgets compel management to look ahead and set short-term targets. By looking ahead, management are then in a good position to anticipate potential problems.
*   The introduction of budgets encourages greater coordination of the functions within the organisation. For example, a production budget can only be constructed with knowledge of the forthcoming period's sales and desired stock levels.
*   Budgets may be introduced to force management to formally communicate their objectives and strategies in the forthcoming periods. Communications between staff are also enhanced in the organisation when budgets are compared periodically with actual expenditure. Discussions through this control mechanism will invariably occur regarding future actions.
*   Budgets provide a basis for identifying those responsible for differing functions within an organisation and provide a basis for measuring their performance.
*   If an organisation wishes to implement control mechanisms, the budget is an important part of these mechanisms. In such cases, budgets will act as a benchmark that can be compared with the actual performance of managers and operatives.
*   Budgets may be introduced as a medium through which expenditure is authorised. If expenditure is contained within a budget, it implies that it has been approved by top management and no further approval is required.
*   A reason for introducing budgets in an organisation may be to motivate employees. In this sense, the budget is once again being primarily used as a target to motivate employees to reach certain levels of attainment.

2   If budget goals have no flexibility and are set too high, employees will become de-motivated, which can result in poor quality work, absenteeism and so on.

3   The master budget will normally represent a summary of the individual functional budgets of the organisation as a whole. It conventionally consists of a budgeted income statement and a balance sheet for the organisation.

4   In the case of a small retail firm, the main emphasis of the budget will be on consumer sales and, in particular, the changing pattern of sales. In addition, attention will also be given to ensuring that there are sufficient purchases to meet the demand of customers. Typically, in a manufacturing firm, the budgets will be more complex due to the production process itself being complex. The emphasis here will be on the sales budget, and the production planning necessary to meet the sales budgets. The production plan will normally include functional budgets concerning direct and indirect labour, materials and bought-in parts, machining resources, stocks and overheads.

5   It is important that there is communication between the sales and production departments so that production levels do not fall short of expected sales, or exceed them by too much. If there is no communication, the firm may incur the costs of lost sales or storage, and potential losses from obsolescence.

6   The cash budget helps a business to plan when to invest excess cash at the highest rates and, when necessary, borrow cash at the cheapest rates. It also allows a firm to decide when it may have the cash resources to embark on equipment purchases.

PERFORMANCE MEASUREMENT AND THE BALANCED SCORECARD
CHAPTER TWENTY-ONE

21

LEARNING OBJECTIVES

At the end of this chapter, you should be able to:

1   explain the concept of responsibility accounting

2   identify cost centres, profit centres and investment centres

3   discuss the issues associated with assessing and rewarding performance

4   discuss financial and non-financial measures of performance

5   identify the strengths and weaknesses of financial and non-financial measures of performance

6   explain and apply the Economic Value Added method (EVA®) of measuring performance

7   explain what is meant by the term 'balanced scorecard'

8   identify the difference between operating and strategic key performance indicators (KPIs)

9   identify the difference between driver and outcome KPIs

10 explain the four perspectives of a balanced scorecard.

Introduction

How do we decide if an executive is worth $33 million? The notion of rewarding people based on performance is a principle most of us would support. How do we measure performance? This is the main focus of this chapter.

CASE STUDY 21.1

LEADERS — IT'S TIME TO CLOSE THE GREED GAP
Editorial opinion

WHATEVER the reasons for excessive executive payments, their effect is to be deplored.

Australia's $33 million man, Chris Cuffe, is not in the same category as the former head of BHP Billiton, Paul Anderson, who last year departed with $18.4 million, or even Mr Anderson's successor, Brian Gilbertson, who reportedly received $30 million. It is not just that Mr Cuffe's $33 million payout from the Commonwealth Bank is believed to have set an Australian record for executive payouts. Mr Cuffe was a manager of Colonial First State, a fund-management business the Commonwealth bought two years ago for $9.4 billion. Since then it has had to pay more than $50 million to former Colonial executives as a result of contracts negotiated before the takeover. So it is not as if the Commonwealth Bank just agreed to grant Mr Cuffe a glowing golden handshake; the payout has to be understood in the context of a complex web of acquired obligations, and of a $426 million write-down in the value of Colonial that the bank announced at the same time as it announced Mr Cuffe's payout. It has been speculated that the size of the payout was announced in the hope of distracting attention from the amount written off Colonial's value. If that was the Commonwealth's aim, it has succeeded.

The reality is that, whatever special circumstances may surround the payments to former Colonial executives, the payment to Mr Cuffe will only generate further — and justified — popular anger at the size of executive packages in general and departure payments in particular. Federal Treasurer Peter Costello will not be the only Australian who thinks it is impossible to imagine how any executive could be worth $33 million. This is not a matter of envying the success of others. In October last year the chief executive of the Association of Superannuation Funds of Australia, Philippa Smith, said that under the existing superannuation guarantee a worker on average earnings could expect a retirement income of only $19 000 a year. The gulf between that expectation and the payouts made to many executives is obscene. And, as Workplace Relations Minister Tony Abbott has said, corporations calling for wage restraint lose credibility when their executives do not practise what they preach.

It is sometimes argued that a company's shareholders ought to keep a tight rein on executive salaries. So they should, but not all shareholders have the same clout in annual general meetings. Large investment funds that wield the most influence over directors may be the least likely to oppose big payouts. If excessive payments to executives are to be brought under control, the government will have to take action — perhaps through the tax system — to deter companies from negotiating contracts that confer such payments. Government ministers have spoken against excessive payouts many times, but mere talk has evidently not been enough to solve the problem.

The Age, 14 February 2003

In Chapter 13, we discussed various company failures and the role of share options (which were used as part of the remuneration package for senior managers) in such failures. In this chapter we will again discuss the concept of responsibility accounting (referred to previously in Chapters 15 and 20), and look at the organisational structures that entities adopt and how this influences the assessment and rewarding of performance. We will examine the role of financial and non-financial performance indicators in a performance measurement system. Finally, we will introduce the concept of a balanced scorecard, discuss its use as a strategy tool and look at the four key components of a balanced scorecard.

Responsibility accounting

LO 1

Explain the concept of responsibility accounting

Responsibility accounting occurs when an entity is structured into strategic business units and the performance of these units is measured in terms of accounting results. It recognises various decision centres throughout an organisation and traces costs, or costs and income, to individual managers who are primarily responsible for making decisions and controlling the costs and income of their centres. Each manager's knowledge of their responsibility centre places them in an advantageous position within the organisation with regard to ensuring that their budget targets are achieved. These responsibility centres are normally departments, branches or divisions of a company. Managers are then held accountable and rewarded based on the results of their department or division. The steps involved in a responsibility accounting model are:

- assigning responsibility
- establishing performance measures or benchmarks
- evaluating performance
  and
- assigning rewards.

The more common types of centres are cost centres, profit centres and investment centres.

COST CENTRES

LO 2

Identify cost centres, profit centres and investment centres

A cost centre is a business unit; this could be a function, activity or even an item of equipment. The objective of identifying a cost centre is to enable the costs that may be attributed to that centre to be allocated to it. This, in turn, enables the managers in the cost centre to be held responsible for such costs. A cost centre is an appropriate type of business unit structure when a manager only has control over costs but not income. A research and development department is an example of a centre where the manager has control over certain costs but has no control over income. The principle is to judge performance only over the items a manager can control. In a cost centre, the costs over which a manager has control are described as 'controllable costs'.

PROFIT CENTRES

A profit centre is a business unit which is accountable for both costs and income. For example, if a business school in a university is set up to be self-funding, it can be assessed as a profit centre. The business school has control over the fees it charges and direct costs such as staff salaries, printing and stationery. However, the central administration department of the university levies a charge for the use of infrastructure: including the building, payroll, security and other services provided by the centre. Such costs are described as 'uncontrollable'. The controllable and uncontrollable costs should be separately reported in determining the net profit or loss for the business school. If the university decides to increase the infrastructure charge, this should not affect the assessment of the business school manager's performance because the manager has no control over the level of the infrastructure charge.

INVESTMENT CENTRES

An investment centre is a business unit where the manager not only has control over the profits of the unit but also has some discretion as to the amount of investment that can be undertaken by the unit. In this case, the performance assessment of the manager should not be based solely on profit but must also relate to the size of the investment available to generate profits. The return on assets ratio discussed in Chapter 14 is one relevant method of performance assessment for an investment centre manager.

KEY CONCEPT 21.1

RESPONSIBILITY ACCOUNTING

Responsibility accounting occurs when an entity is structured into strategic business units and the performance of these units is measured in terms of accounting results.

Managers of responsibility centres should, to some extent, participate in the preparation of their own budgets. Evidence from research suggests that participation by responsible managers in the setting of budgets enhances the probability of effective planning and control within an organisation. To support a system of responsibility accounting, the reporting system of the organisation needs to communicate relevant information. The reports should show the actual performance, the budget and the deviations (variances) from budget. The mode in which budgeted and actual costs and income are collected and reported – for example, by product, labour or material input costs – is determined by management. The major factors which influence management in deciding the extent and sophistication of the reporting system are the costs of installing and operating such a system compared with the benefits it generates.

Review exercise 1

Explain the terms 'cost', 'profit' and 'investment centres'.

Measuring and rewarding performance

The objective of assessing performance should be to reward managers who have performed well. In addition, the measures used to assess performance should focus on areas over which the manager has

3

Discuss the issues associated with assessing and rewarding performance

the capacity to influence the outcome. For example, a manager of a cost centre may be rewarded for achieving certain cost reductions or having certain costs come in below budget. A manager of a profit centre may be rewarded based on measures such as return on assets. It is important that the measure of performance is consistent with the goals of the entity. The measures should help the entity in the pursuit of its objectives.

The use of budgets is common in the measurement of performance; this then forms the basis for rewarding good performance. If performance is to be assessed and rewarded based on budgets, the establishment of budgets, as discussed in Chapter 20, is very important. Forecasts can be set that are easily achievable, or they can be 'stretch targets' that push the organisation and its employees in order to meet the forecasts. Setting easily achievable targets is not likely to assist the entity in achieving its strategic objectives; however, setting targets that are too difficult to achieve is likely to de-motivate staff. The measure should discourage *dysfunctional* behaviour; that is, behaviour by an individual which is inconsistent with the goals of the entity. The measure that is used to assess an individual's performance should be one that results in behaviour from the individual that is consistent with the goals of the entity.

Rewards to managers can be cash-based or share-based. The use of share options was a popular method of providing incentives to managers in the 1990s and early 2000s. The rationale behind the use of share options was that it was in the manager's interest to focus on strategies, which would result in increases in the share price of their company. The outcome meant that shareholders were better off and so too were the managers, as the value of their share options also increased. However, the wisdom of this strategy is now being questioned following the failure of high-profile companies such as those discussed in Chapter 13.

The results of performance measures, both positive and negative, should be fed back within a reasonable period of time to allow corrective action, if required. The way performance is measured and rewarded should allow all section managers to understand and accept the goals of the entity, should encourage them to behave in a manner that is consistent with those goals, and should provide regular feedback on each section's contribution to the achievement of those goals.

CASE STUDY 21.2

REAPING REWARDS
by Lauren Mulhall

TO RETAIN top performers, companies are taking the time to ensure that working conditions are attractive and that remuneration reflects performance, KPMG recruitment associate director Janine Fitzgerald said this week. Ms Fitzgerald said that, to improve overall business operations and staff retention, organisations had become increasingly focused on ensuring that employees were being rewarded fairly for individual, team and business unit performance.

'To attract the top candidates in the market place, organisations are recognising the need to have relevant remuneration packaging and incentives that reward good performance,' ▐▐▐➡

Ms Fitzgerald said. 'It's not enough to pay someone a certain amount of money and expect they'll give their best. It's more about tailoring their remuneration against the specific key performance indicators for their job role,' she said.

Ms Fitzgerald said that many companies previously had failed to properly analyse the remuneration packaging of their employees against comparative positions in the market place. 'Times are changing and the demand for organisations to research annual market trends in terms of base salaries and variable rewards is increasing,' Ms Fitzgerald said.

She said a common problem within many organisations was that the key performance indicators of some executives did not directly relate to their actual duties and responsibilities. Focus groups were taking place in certain organisations where employees could have their say about what they perceived as fair 'at risk' incentives, she said.

'It's become evident, while undertaking executive remuneration reviews, that senior managers want their incentives to include an element based on their individual performance and the impact they have on the organisation,' Ms Fitzgerald said. 'For this to happen, key performance indicators should be updated annually to ensure they remain a true reflection of organisational goals,' she said.

KPMG recruitment manager Sue Dean said that, once the organisation had the correct incentive scheme in place, it was important for employees to understand that, although they had the opportunity to earn more, they also had an increased level of responsibility and accountability. 'Employees are now less able to get themselves into comfort zones where average performance is acceptable,' Ms Dean said. 'As the demands on business grow so does the pressure on employees to perform,' she said.

The Courier-Mail, 24 August 2002

COMMENTARY

This article highlights the importance of ensuring that key performance indicators (KPIs) are measuring the results of activities, which relate to the actual duties and responsibilities of the individual being assessed. The KPIs should remain a true reflection of the goals of the organisation. Finally, the article mentions that employees should understand that the chance to earn more is accompanied by an increase in the level of responsibility and accountability they will have to accept.

In deciding on the measures to use to assess performance, entities can choose to use financial or non-financial measures – or, indeed, a combination of both. We now examine the use of both types of measures.

LO 4

Discuss financial and non-financial measures of performance

FINANCIAL MEASURES

'What gets measured gets done' is a well-known saying, and financial measures have traditionally been the most common measures used to assess and reward performance. Financial measures can be absolute measures, such as profit, or ratios such as the return on assets. Some examples of absolute measures are:

- revenue or turnover, which could be expressed as the entity's share of the market
- costs (separated into controllable and uncontrollable)
- profit, taking into consideration that this figure is very dependent on the accounting policies used.

The problem with absolute measures like profit is that it is difficult to assess what it means without knowledge of the underlying investment. For example, a profit of $10 million produced from net assets of $100 million is much better than if the net assets were $500 million. Therefore, it is more common to use financial ratios as part of performance measurement. In Chapter 14 we discussed financial ratios. Table 14.1 provides a range of ratios that could be used in performance measurement. Ratios such as expenses as a percentage of sales are commonly used in an attempt to monitor and control the entity's level of expenses. Table 21.1 shows possible financial measures to use for the three types of responsibility centres identified earlier in this chapter.

Table 21.1 Responsibility centres and performance measures

Type of responsibility centre	Factors under management control	Major financial measures
Cost centre	• controllable costs	• costs as a percentage of sales or some other base • analysis of variances of actual costs from budget (see Chapter 15)
Profit centre	• controllable costs • selling prices • output quantity	• profit • gross and net margins • other financial ratios from Table 14. 1
Investment centre	• controllable costs • selling prices • output quantity • investment in assets	• return on investment • return on shareholders' funds • other financial ratios from Table 14.1

NON-FINANCIAL MEASURES

Non-financial measures relate to aspects of performance which are difficult to measure and assign numbers to, but are, nonetheless, important in the assessment of performance. In fact, they may be even more important than the financial measures. Examples of non-financial measures are:

- customer satisfaction
- supplier reliability
- quality of production (or service for a service organisation)
- customer complaints
- employee morale
- delivery time.

While non-financial measures are difficult to measure, questionnaires and surveys are often used to assess items like customer satisfaction and employee morale. It is quite likely that all of us, at some stage, have had an opportunity to complete a survey (like those used in hotels and restaurants) for a product or service. It is also possible to use quantitative measures as an indication of the organisation's success in achieving qualitative outcomes. For example, the number of units rejected as a percentage of the total number of units produced is a way of measuring quality of production and the number of customer complaints can help measure customer satisfaction.

Review exercise 2

Give examples of financial and non-financial measures of performance.

FINANCIAL VERSUS NON-FINANCIAL MEASURES

Which measures are the best and which are most commonly used? Financial measures have traditionally been the most commonly used in business to assess performance. The major advantage of financial measures is that they involve numbers and most of us feel comfortable with numbers because we understand them and believe they are more reliable and objective. In addition, they are also:

LO 5

Identify the strengths and weaknesses of financial and non-financial measures of performance

- easy to calculate
- more efficient in that they require less time to calculate and can be easily verified
- provide a standardised measure in a money-based economy.

Financial measures allow us to compare the performance of business units within an entity and judge one entity against another. For example, it is common in industries to compare key ratios with those for other firms within the industry. ANZ bank compares key ratios, like the percentage of bad and doubtful loans to total loans, across branches in each state within Australia, and with the other banks like the National Australia Bank, Westpac and the Commonwealth Bank.

The major weaknesses with financial measures are:

- the numbers can be manipulated, as discussed in the financial accounting chapters, to report an expected outcome
- inflation can automatically result in some measures increasing with no real increase in the underlying performance
- establishing inappropriate targets can result in ineffective and inefficient performance. For example, a bank set up a reward scheme whereby it awarded bonuses based on the amount of loans approved. As a result, managers relaxed their lending criteria and approved loans that previously they would have rejected. The effect of this was that the amount of loans increased and so, also, did the amount of loan defaults.

Non-financial measures provide insights into aspects of performance that are not reflected by the financial measures; therefore, they allow entities to have a more complete assessment of performance. They take into account the human factor and, because the objective of performance measurement is to motivate employees, this is an important aspect. Other possible advantages are that non-financial measures:

- can be more readily linked to the strategies of the entity
- are often made available more regularly than some financial measures like profit
- are less susceptible to manipulation than financial measures that are based on accounting numbers. For example, some financial measures, such as return on assets, can result in

inappropriate actions by managers to increase this measure in the short term. Actions, such as deferring important maintenance work on machinery, will cause profits to increase but, in the long term, the machine will cost the entity more so the short-term gain is achieved at a long-term cost. This is not to say that non-financial measures cannot be manipulated. For example, performance information that results from non-financial measures used in surveys *can* be manipulated by appropriate question design.

It is a fact that non-financial measures are more difficult to measure and this is a major disadvantage. Other problems with non-financial measures include the following:

- Actions to improve a non-financial measure may conflict, in the short term, with financial measures. For example, an investment in a new machine may improve the quality of production but may also result in an increase in depreciation expense and, as a result, lower profit.
- Because non-financial measures are not expressed in monetary terms, it is more difficult to assess their impact on profits. For example, with regard to increasing customer satisfaction, what is its dollar impact on the net profit?
- The non-financial measures are not as easily integrated into systems which have been based on financial measures.

Most performance assessment systems will use both financial and non-financial measures as a way of rewarding managers and aligning their behaviour with the goals of the entity.

In the next section we examine the balanced scorecard, which brings together both types of measures in a tool that is aimed at improving the overall performance of the entity.

Review exercise 3

What are the strengths and weaknesses of financial and non-financial performance indicators?

ECONOMIC VALUE ADDED METHOD

Explain and apply the Economic Value Added method (EVA®) of measuring performance

The Economic Value Added (EVA®) method of assessing performance is similar to the Residual Income method – although there is some variation in the application of each method. In this book we only discuss and illustrate the EVA® method.

Profit-making companies exist primarily to create wealth for their shareholders. In Chapter 13, we discussed the notion of triple bottom line reporting and the evolving practice of entity's reporting on their social and environmental performance. However, for-profit companies normally pursue TBL reporting with a focus on the need to create shareholder value, as illustrated in the following quote from the Westpac 2004 *Stakeholder Impact Report*:

> For a number of years now, we have been on a journey to embed responsible, ethical, trustworthy business behaviour throughout the company. Why? Because, we believe that by fully integrating corporate responsibility into who we are and the way we operate, we will be a much better business and will be in a much stronger position to sustainably enhance shareholder value.

EVA® is a method of measuring how effectively a company achieves the objective of creating shareholder value. It is another performance measure which, some argue, is more closely aligned to a company's share price. It is a simple measure to apply once you have the required variables. A positive economic value added calculation means that the company is creating wealth for shareholders and a negative economic value added calculation means that the company is destroying shareholder wealth.

EVA® is a simple method to understand and can easily be incorporated into a company's strategy. It could, for example, be included as one of the financial measures in the balanced scorecard (which we discuss in the next section). To calculate the economic value that has been added, we need to solve the following equation:

$$EVA = \text{after-tax profit} + \text{interest} - (\text{cost of capital} \times \text{total capital employed})$$

The most difficult part of the equation is to determine the cost of capital. The cost of capital was mentioned in Chapter 16, but we did not discuss how to calculate it. To measure the cost of capital an entity must:

a   identify all sources of capital

b   determine the cost of each source of capital

c   determine the proportion of total capital of each source

d   multiply B × C for each source of capital

e   sum the results for each source of capital from D.

To illustrate the calculations that are involved for the cost of capital and the economic value added amount, we will use the data in Example 21.1.

Example 21.1 Juliet Co. Ltd

Juliet Co. Ltd
Income statement for the year ended 30 June 20X6

	$
Sales	85 000
Less Expenses	
Material	35 813
Labour	18 000
Production expenses	6 750
Administrative expenses	8 250
Interest expense	1 500
	70 313
Net profit	14 687

To determine the cost of capital, we need to establish the sources of funds. For Juliet, the funds consist of $20 000 worth of loans and $80 000 of shareholder funds. We do not include non-interest-bearing liabilities, like accounts payable, in this calculation. The capital that is employed includes shareholder funds and interest-bearing debt. We use the after-tax cost for debt funds and the required rate of return demanded by shareholders as equity providers for the cost of equity.

Balance sheet as at 30 June 20X6

	$
Current assets	67 500
Non-current assets	42 500
Total assets	110 000
Current liabilities	10 000
Long-term loan (8%)	20 000
Shareholder funds	80 000
Total liabilities and shareholder funds	110 000

Equity providers demand a rate of return on their investment, and the expected return will be based on the company's risk. In Chapter 14 it was explained that the concept of risk consists of business and financial risk. The higher the risk, the higher the expected return demanded by equity providers. The cost of equity capital can be determined by application of the capital asset pricing model – but this is beyond the scope of an introductory accounting textbook. We will assume that the cost of equity is 10 per cent for Juliet and note there are no tax adjustments for equity as payments to equity providers are not tax deductible (unlike interest payment to debt providers). We assume a 30 per cent tax rate.

	Amount	Per cent	×	After-tax cost	=	Weighted cost
Long-term loan	$20 000	0.2		0.8 (1 – 0.3)		0.0112
Equity	$80 000	0.8		0.1		0.08
Total	$100 000					0.0912

This means that the weighted average cost of capital for Juliet is 9.12 per cent.

We can now solve the EVA® equation as shown below for Juliet:

$$EVA = \$14\ 687 + 1500 - (0.0912 \times \$100\ 000)$$
$$= \$16\ 187 - 9\ 120$$
$$= \$7\ 067$$

The positive amount of $7 067 indicates that Juliet Co. Ltd has created wealth for its shareholders in the year 20X6. EVA® offers opportunities for managers to improve shareholder wealth by pursuing the projects that offer the highest value creation for shareholders. They should also look to divest the projects and assets that destroy shareholder value. If the entity is able to lower its cost of capital, it will also add to shareholder wealth.

EVA® is not a static measure, and managers should be calculating it on a regular basis so that they can revise decisions that are in the best interests of creating value for shareholders – because this should result in higher share prices. Alinta Ltd is a company that actively pursues growth in Total Shareholder Returns (TSR) and the use of tools like EVA® enables companies like Alinta to choose investments that will create value for shareholders and thus increase TSR (visit www.alinta.net.au).

CASE STUDY 21.3

MEASURING PROFIT WITH EVA HIGHLIGHTS PERFORMANCE
by G. Bennet Stewart and A. Thompson

. . .

THE EVA Governance System is a proven, practical way to embed these best practices [of good corporate governance] in a company. The foundation of this system is the performance measure known as EVA, or economic value added. EVA is economic profit – profit the way that economists measure it. In simplest terms, EVA is a firm's net operating profit after taxes, or NOPAT, less a charge for using all capital, equity as well as debt. Unlike conventional accounting profit, in which only the after tax cost of borrowing money is subtracted, EVA starts to register 'earnings' only after the shareholders have also been rewarded with a fair return on their investment.

Shareholder value creation is best measured using the concept of net present value (NPV), which is defined as the future cash flows the business can generate, discounted to a present value using the appropriate risk-adjusted discount rate, net of any investments required to generate those cash flows. NPV can also be defined as the present value of future EVA (economic profit). Both methods – cash flow and EVA – will give the same NPV, but the advantage of EVA is that it is a periodic measure of performance.

It is this mathematical relationship between NPV and economic profit that makes EVA the best internal measure of shareholder value creation.

The EVA Governance System fosters long-term value creation. It starts by introducing an EVA orientation into the strategic planning process. Strategies are evaluated in terms of how much value they add to the company's intrinsic value. This is done by estimating the incremental NPV each strategy is expected to contribute. The value maximising set of strategies must be selected. Each selected strategy is then broken into the set of projects that must be executed over time to achieve the strategic outcome. These projects will typically represent major investment, marketing or infrastructure programmes. These projects should then be converted into a series of specific action steps and assigned to individual persons or teams.

The projects will also determine the funding requirements for the strategies, and enable the company to establish a long-term financial strategy. Financing requirements should be dictated by operating plans, not vice versa. Consequently, the company's financial strategy should be tailored to its business risk and the funding requirements of the business plan, and should consider the company's financial objectives, funding needs, dividend policy and market conditions.

This process is iterative and interactive for managers at all levels. As a final check, management will want to be sure that their initiatives will generate EVA sufficient in the aggregate to meet their strategic goals in the near, medium and longer term. Once the plans are concluded the company should document the chosen action plans and the expected results for key metrics and milestones, including the expected contribution to EVA over time, and incorporate them into the performance reporting and management system.

An integral and key element of the EVA Governance System is the incentive compensation plan. It must be designed to align managerial decisions with the interests of the shareholders by linking variable pay to the ⅢⅢ➡

long-term value creation (EVA) goals and targets of the company.

Key features of such a plan include objective, multi-year EVA targets, derived from the value maximising strategies, that set the performance standard required to earn competitive total compensation, and a bonus banking system that defers a portion of the bonus pay-outs.

This has two advantages: First it discourages managers from making short-term decisions that increase their near-term bonus but might be detrimental to the company in the long term. Second, it also helps retain good managers during economic downturns by paying bonuses from the bonus bank.

Progress must be measured against the plan embodied in the selected strategy as the year unfolds, and remedial action taken as required. The strategy should never become static. Action plans and milestones, and even entire strategies must be revised as circumstances dictate. Keeping everyone's incentives tied to creating near-and long-term EVA will help make them more willing to do that.

The EVA Governance System is thus a practical way to enable managers to execute the value-adding strategies and hold them accountable for how well they do this, thereby fulfilling the fundamental corporate objective – increasing the intrinsic value of the company to deliver shareholder value.

Extract from article in *The Nation* (Thailand),
11 November 2002
© 2002 Nation Multimedia Group Public Co., Ltd

COMMENTARY

The article refers to economic value added and economic profit, which recognises that an entity does not add value for a shareholder until the cost of the shareholder's investment is covered. Underlying the concept of economic profit is the notion that shareholders are no better off until the company earns an amount that is sufficient to compensate them for the cost of their investment. Net present value was explained in Chapter 16.

The balanced scorecard

LO 7

Explain what is meant by the term 'balanced scorecard'

In this section, we briefly consider the use of a balanced scorecard (BSC). The balanced scorecard is a tool that focuses on more than just the financial measures of performance. It is a concept first developed by Kaplan and Norton (1992) in some pioneering work published in the *Harvard Business Review* and is defined as a:

> . . . set of measures that give top managers a fast but comprehensive view of the business. The balanced scorecard includes financial measures that tell the results of actions already taken. And it complements the financial measures with operational [non-financial] measures on customer satisfaction, internal processes, and the organisation's innovation and improvement activities – operational measures that are the drivers of future financial performance.

Later in this section we explain the four components of the BSC and how the use of a BSC can enhance the performance of an entity. We will also look at the measures that can be used in each of the four components of a BSC and link the BSC back to the previous sections of this chapter. We do not discuss the ways and methods of developing strategies in this book, although it is important to appreciate that as *measurement motivates, it must be linked to strategy.*

KEY CONCEPT 21.2

BALANCED SCORECARD

'. . . set of measures that give top managers a fast but comprehensive view of the business. The balanced scorecard includes financial measures that tell the results of actions already taken. And it complements the financial measures with operational [non-financial] measures on customer satisfaction, internal processes, and the organisation's innovation and improvement activities – operational measures that are the drivers of future financial performance'. (Kaplan & Norton 1992)

Before we discuss the four components of the BSC, it is important to understand the following types of key performance indicators (KPIs): operating and strategic KPIs, and driver and outcome KPIs.

LO 8

Identify the difference between operating and strategic key performance indicators (KPIs)

OPERATING AND STRATEGIC KPIS

In order to understand the difference between operating and strategic KPIs, imagine that you are sailing a yacht in the America's Cup. You would want to know where you were heading and the most efficient way to get there. Strategic KPIs are steering measures and are concerned with where you are heading. Yachts do not sail in a straight line, so strategic decisions are made about where to go on the course to get the most favourable wind conditions. Hence, strategic decisions are concerned with setting the direction and then changing course if conditions alter and a change in direction is warranted.

The operating KPIs, on the other hand, are sailing measures and are concerned with sailing the yacht as fast as possible once the direction is set, making sure the sails are trimmed and, when the time comes to tack, making sure the exercise is carried out in the most efficient manner. Once the direction is set (strategic), the aim is to keep the yacht sailing steadily in that direction (operating).

Some KPIs may not be easily classified as either strategic or operating, and it is possible for the classification to change. For example, managing the time a customer waits in a queue to be served in a bank would normally be regarded as an operating KPI. However, a major bank in Australia that has been concerned about the bank's public image has actively pursued a strategy of guaranteeing customers will not spend more than a certain time waiting to be served. In so doing, the bank has indicated that the measure of time spent in a queue has assumed a more strategic role in that bank.

DRIVER AND OUTCOME KPIS

Performance measures can also be categorised as 'drivers' or as 'outcomes'. The *driver* measures are those that lead to or cause a change in the *outcome* measures. Traditionally, businesses have concentrated on financial performance measures such as return on assets, return on shareholders' equity, profit margins and many others. These are outcome measures that are used by external parties to assess the

LO 9

Identify the difference between driver and outcome KPIs

performance of the entity. The 'out' in outcomes is a reminder that the measures are used by parties 'outside' the entity to assess its performance. The problem with outcome measures is that they are, in effect, measuring what has happened in the past.

The 'drivers' are the measures that measure the items that will cause a change in the 'outcome' measures. For example, an improvement in delivery time to customers results in increased customer satisfaction, which in turn causes higher profits as repeat business increases. It is the things a business *does*, like improved training for workers, a better quality product or service and so on, which result in improvements in the *outcome* measures.

Review exercise 4

What are operating and strategic key performance indicators?

KEY CONCEPT 21.3

CLASSIFICATION FRAMEWORK OF KEY PERFORMANCE INDICATORS

	Strategic	Operating
Outcomes	Managers and accounting professionals need to monitor these for positive trends and major changes in the longer term.	Managers and accounting professionals need to monitor these through variance reporting for unanticipated changes in the short term.
Drivers	These capture innovation, operational excellence, use of modern technologies and new skill sets. Investment is required.	Management need to allocate sufficient resources to maintain business as usual.

Derived from: CPA Australia, *KPIs in Business*, 2001, p. 36
Reproduced with the permission of CPA Australia.

THE FOUR PERSPECTIVES OF THE BALANCED SCORECARD

LO 10

Explain the four perspectives of a balanced scorecard

The balanced scorecard is a tool that incorporates the various types of KPIs into a sort of map which demonstrates how an entity can improve the *outcome* measures, such as the return on assets, by making improvements in the aspects of its business which *drive* the improvements. The outcome measures should assess how effective the entity has been in achieving its strategy, which underpins the BSC. Case study 21.4 shows how important a company's strategy is in determining its success.

CASE STUDY 21.4

MISSING MEASURE LEAVES NAB FLOUNDERING

J. Parsons

One of the key indicators missing from the National Australia Bank's performance measures is productivity ('It's Australia's biggest but by no means the best', May 12). Not having the benefit of robust total resource productivity measures leaves organisations floundering with simple (and misleading) partial indicators of performance such as sales per employee. This is equivalent to calculating profit by taking the difference between revenue and manpower cost and forgetting about all the other costs incurred. An inevitable consequence is a non-strategic focus on cost cutting, and we know what that means.

NAB has claimed that job cuts are necessary to improve performance and efficiency ('Prove that jobs must go', May 13). This despite numerous studies that have shown that, in the long run, it simply doesn't work. It looks good in the short run though, which is why it is so beloved of those investment analysts whose idea of a long run is 24 hours.

Bank executives and senior management should rightly be concerned about profitability measures such as the cost-to-income ratio, but they should also be interested in what is causing those indicators to move. Total resource productivity is the main driver of financial performance. Why is this so? Because, by creating wealth, improvements in productivity translate directly into sustainable improvements in profitability. The alternative is to grab somebody else's wealth by manipulating prices.

Appreciating the difference between wealth created and wealth redistributed is crucial to understanding the origins of organisational performance and how you manage in order to improve it. And despite all its sophistication, economic value added doesn't make the distinction between wealth created and distributed either. The answer is productivity accounting, an approach that measures the separate contributions to profitability changes of productivity and price recovery.

From examination of the results the bank may well discover more effective ways to improve profitability rather than causing major social disruptions through significant redundancy processes. In addition, all stakeholders would benefit because such an analysis clearly identifies the contributors to and recipients of wealth created through the productivity process and then goes on to quantify the size of their shares. As business values change, the issue of how wealth is distributed among stakeholders (and the transparency of the process) becomes increasingly important.

Finally, because productivity accounting is rigorously locked in to the financial and management accounting systems, it offers an extension to those systems, not a substitute for either. At the same time, by reconciling with the financial figures, it offers a similar level of robustness and lack of ambiguity. Productivity accounting is also entirely consistent with corporate dashboards and can be easily located within performance systems such as the balanced scorecard.

Australian Financial Review, 27 May 2005
© 2005 Copyright John Fairfax Holdings
Limited. www.afr.com
Not available for re-distribution.

COMMENTARY

The article discusses the NAB's decision to cut jobs to save costs. The author argues that the NAB would be better served if it focused on the drivers of future performance instead of cutting jobs. The balanced scorecard is offered as a management tool which can assist in the development of a more effective performance system.

As indicated in Key concept 21.2, a balanced scorecard is a set of measures giving a fast but comprehensive view of a firm from four perspectives:

- *Financial perspective.* From this perspective, the entity asks the question: How do we appear to our shareholders? Key performance indicators such as return on assets and return on shareholders' equity can be used as measures in this perspective. They are referred to as 'outcome measures'.
- *Customer perspective.* Here the entity asks: How do we appear to our customers? Key performance indicators such as customer retention and customer satisfaction measures can be used and are also referred to as 'outcome measures'.
- *Internal business process perspective.* Here the entity asks: What do we need to do within the core processes of our business in order to satisfy our shareholders and customers? Key performance indicators such as delivery time to customers and product quality can be used and are referred to as 'driver measures'. Improvements in this perspective will drive improvements in the customer and financial perspectives.
- *Learning and growth perspective.* From this perspective the entity asks: What do we need to do to develop our employees, work practices and technologies for the future? Key performance indicators such as employee satisfaction and employee training can be used and are also known as 'driver measures'.

It is the non-financial measures in the internal business process, and learning and growth areas, that drive future financial performance. These measures depend on the management of a business asking the following types of questions:

- What does the firm have to excel at to achieve its goals?
- What are critical or core processes impacting on customer satisfaction?
- What are our core competencies?
- How long do we take to develop new products?
- How quickly does the firm move through the learning curve?
- What is the revenue from new products?
- What contributions do employees provide?
- What is the level of morale?
- What is the effect of training?

When a business addresses these types of questions and develops target KPIs in the critical driver areas, this will result in improved customer satisfaction and, ultimately, improved financial performance. Of course, the development of a BSC for an entity, particularly large entities, requires a significant amount of effort in both time and resources. This is because it is important to involve as many people in the entity as possible so that they all 'buy in' to the concept and have some ownership of the final product.

It is important to appreciate that linkages exist in a BSC, as shown in Figure 21.1, below. The objectives and strategies of the entity drive the development of KPIs in each of the four perspectives. However, the achievement of one objective – such as increased productivity through better processes and a more skilled work force – will mean that the entity can produce more goods with the same number of employees. If this is not accompanied by increased sales, then the improved productivity will not be reflected in an improved financial scorecard. Ultimately, managers must translate improvements in the other three perspectives into better financial measures.

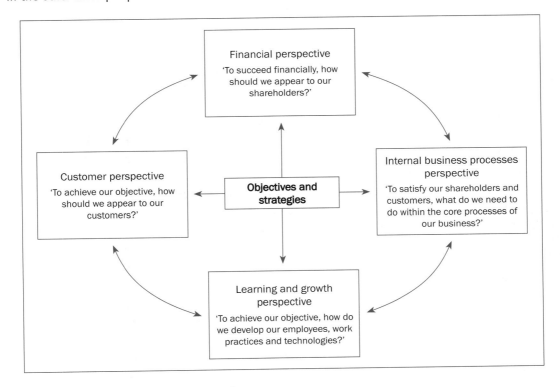

Figure 21.1 Linkages in a balanced scorecard

It is more common to visualise a BSC in a vertical format, as displayed in Figure 21.2, where the drivers in the internal business process, and learning and growth perspectives, drive the outcomes in the customer and financial perspective. Figure 21.2 shows a balanced scorecard, which could apply to a specialty coffee house like Starbucks.

The BSC for Jen's Coffee Escape, for example, would require KPIs in each of the four perspectives and these could be:

- *financial*: sales revenue and level of operating profit
- *customer*: survey of customers
- *internal business process*: speed of service to customer
- *learning and growth*: number of staff who have attended training program.

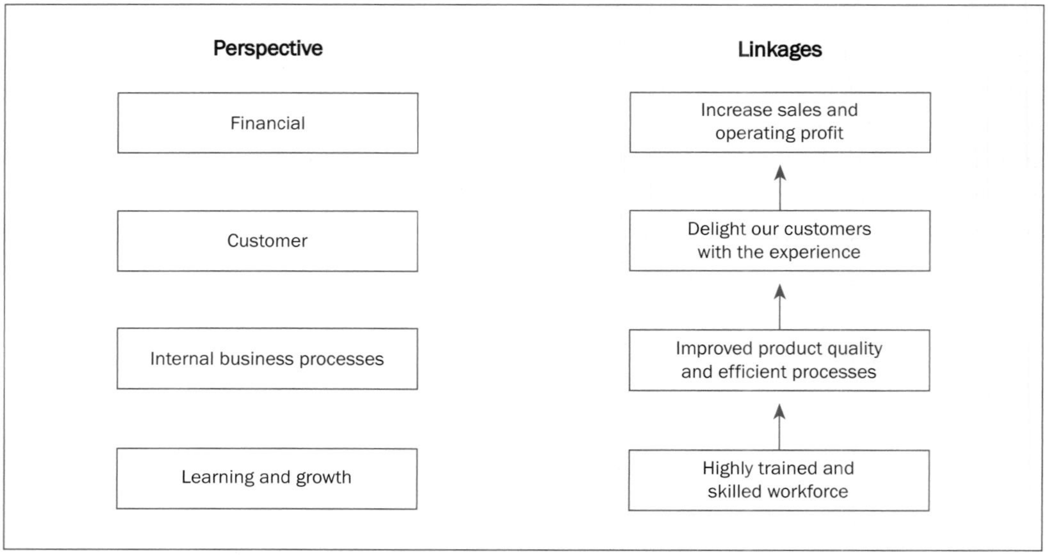

Figure 21.2 Vertically structured balanced scorecard for Jen's Coffee Escape

Review exercise 5

Name two performance measures that are useful in evaluating investment centres.

SUMMARY

LO 1

LEARNING OBJECTIVE 1
Explain the concept of responsibility accounting

Responsibility accounting occurs when an entity is structured into strategic business units and the performance of these units is measured in accounting results. This type of accounting is used to identify and monitor employees in an organisation who incur expenditure and generate income and are, therefore, responsible for these costs and earnings.

LO 2

LEARNING OBJECTIVE 2
Identify cost centres, profit centres and investment centres

A cost centre is a business unit (which could be a function, activity or even an item of equipment) which is liable for certain costs. A profit centre is a business unit which is accountable for both costs and income. An investment centre is a business unit where the manager not only has control over the profits of the unit but also has some discretion as to the amount of investment undertaken by that unit.

LO 3

LEARNING OBJECTIVE 3
Discuss the issues associated with assessing and rewarding performance

A manager's performance needs to be assessed if there is a reward system in place. This assessment is usually based on budget outcomes or previously set goals. The achievement of the reward(s), which can be monetary or share-based, is determined by assessing whether the goals have been met or exceeded.

LO 4

LEARNING OBJECTIVE 4
Discuss financial and non-financial measures of performance

Financial measures are the traditional measures of performance and include net profit, return on assets and return on investment. Non-financial measures are more difficult to quantify and could encompass, for example, customer satisfaction, employee satisfaction, product/service quality or supplier reliability.

LO 5

LEARNING OBJECTIVE 5
Identify the strengths and weaknesses of financial and non-financial measures of performance

Financial measures are easy to calculate, can be easily verified and provide a standardised monetary measure. However, numbers can be manipulated, inflation can increase a result without increasing performance and inappropriate targets can lead to inefficiencies. Non-financial measures are useful to an entity in setting strategies and providing an overall goal. They are difficult to measure and, at times, can be at odds with the financial objectives of an entity.

LO 6

LEARNING OBJECTIVE 6
Explain and apply the Economic Value Added method (EVA®) of measuring performance

EVA® is a method of measuring how effectively a company achieves the objective of creating shareholder value. It is another performance measure which, some argue, is more closely aligned to a company's share price. It is a simple measure to apply once you have the required variables. A positive economic value added calculation means the company is creating wealth for shareholders while a negative economic value added calculation means the company is destroying shareholder wealth. This measure is easy to understand and can easily be incorporated into a company's strategy. It could, for example, be included as one of the financial measures in the balanced scorecard. To calculate the economic value added, we need to solve the following equation:

$$\text{EVA} = \text{after tax profit} + \text{interest} - (\text{cost of capital} \times \text{total capital employed})$$

LEARNING OBJECTIVE 7

7

Explain what is meant by the term 'balanced scorecard'

A balanced scorecard is a set of measures that give managers a comprehensive picture of a business. It includes financial and operational measures. These operational measures can be the drivers of future financial performance.

LEARNING OBJECTIVE 8

8

Identify the difference between operating and strategic key performance indicators (KPIs)

An operating KPI measures day-to-day operations, and is a housekeeping-type measure. Strategic KPIs measure how effectively an entity is achieving its strategic objectives.

LEARNING OBJECTIVE 9

9

Identify the difference between driver and outcome KPIs

The 'driver ' measures are those that lead to or cause a change in the ' outcome measures'. Businesses tend to use financial performance measures, such as profit margins, return on equity and others; these are 'outcome' measures. The 'drivers' tend to alter these indicators; therefore, an improvement in operational excellence will improve an outcome.

LEARNING OBJECTIVE 10

10

Explain the four perspectives of a balanced scorecard

The four perspective are as follows: financial, customer, internal business processes, and learning and growth perspectives. The financial perspective is an outcome measure. The customer perspective is an outcome measure aimed at assessing customer satisfaction. The internal business perspective is a driver measure – such as finding ways of improving business to the satisfaction of customers and shareholders. Finally, the learning and growth perspective is a driver measure aimed at improving work practices, the use of technology, and so on.

REFERENCES

Kaplan, R.S. & Norton, D.P., 1992. 'The balanced scorecard: Measures that drive performance', in *Harvard Business Review*, January–February.

Walsh, P., 2001. *KPIs in Business* in National Workshop Series, CPA Australia.

Westpac., 2004. *Stakeholder Impact Report*, Westpac, Sydney, p. 10.

FURTHER READING

Hansen, D.R. & Mowen, M.M., 2003. *Management Accounting and Control*, 6th edn, South-Western, Mason, Ohio.

REVIEW QUESTIONS

1   Explain what is meant by the term 'responsibility centre'.

2   For what decisions is the manager of a cost centre not responsible?

3   What are driver and outcome KPIs?

4   What is a balanced scorecard?

5   Explain the four perspectives of a balanced scorecard.

6   Why would a firm use a balanced scorecard in evaluating divisional performance?

7   Give some examples of KPIs for each of the four perspectives for a bank.

PROBLEMS FOR DISCUSSION AND ANALYSIS

1   Discuss the concept of responsibility accounting. What does it mean and why is it important in the assessment and rewarding of performance?

2   Indicate, for each of the following independent cases, whether they are best structured as cost, profit or investment centres:

   a   Kellee is head of the marketing and public relations department at Satellite University. The department receives funding from the central administration for teaching and research. The department is allocated funds based on projected expenditures. Kellee is responsible for 10 academic staff and two general staff.

   b   Leigh is head of the school of business located on the campus at Planet University. The school enrols only full-fee-paying students and is responsible for all operating costs and a share of the university's overheads. The university provides a building and teaching venues. Leigh is responsible for 30 academic staff and 10 general staff.

   c   Troy is head of the division of business at Universe University. The division is located in its own building in the city as part of a strategic move by the university. The division enrols only full-fee-paying students and it also conducts short courses for businesses in the CBD. The division is responsible for all capital and operating costs.

3   You are a director of a credit union and you have been appointed to the remuneration subcommittee. One of your first tasks is to consider a bonus for the general manager. You believe that a bonus should be paid based on performance. The credit union has 10 000 members and total assets of $50 million, with $40 million in loans to members. It operates four branch locations and a head office and employs a total of 30 people. You are familiar with using KPIs such as return on assets as a measure of performance. However, the board of directors has a policy of not aiming to maximise profit as the credit union exists for the benefit of its members. Therefore, you consider it to be inappropriate to use return on assets as a measure of the performance of the general manager.

Required

   What other financial and non-financial measures of performance could be used to assess the performance of the general manager?

4   List three performance measures that would be appropriate for the following centres:

   a   an academic department in a university established as a cost centre

   b   a branch of a bank established as a profit centre

   c   a division of a large steel company established as an investment centre.

5   Roy Rogers is the divisional manager in Trigger Enterprises and he is rewarded based on overall divisional return on investment (ROI). Currently, his division produces a 25 per cent ROI. Roy is

investigating an opportunity to expand the plant of his division. The projected ROI for the expansion is 18 per cent and the company's cost of capital is 13 per cent.

Required

Do you think Roy will proceed with the expansion? Discuss the issues involved looking at it from Roy's position and from the shareholders' position.

6 Jack Thomson, the CEO of Thomo Ltd, has been reading about EVA®. Because you have completed your MBA, he asks you to calculate the economic value added amount for the company. You gather the following facts:

For year 20X5

Net profit for the last year	$40 000
Interest expense	$10 000
Accounts payable	$100 000
Long term loans (6%)	$200 000
Shareholders equity	$300 000
Total assets	

You have found that the rate of return on government bonds is 6 per cent, and you estimate that shareholders expect a premium on the government bond rate of 6 per cent. The tax rate is 30 per cent.

Required

a   Calculate the economic value added amount for Jack.
b   Explain what your answer means for the company.

7 Jack Thomson approaches you at the end of 20X6 and asks you to determine if the company has created value for its shareholders for the year. The details are the same as in the question above, except that net profit for the year was $30 000.

8 Determine the economic value added amount for Woodside Ltd for the half-year ended 30 June 2005 from the half-yearly report in Appendix 1 (using the following assumptions):
a   interest cost, 6 per cent
b   equity cost, 12 per cent
c   tax rate, 30 per cent.
   State any other assumptions you need to make.
   Comment on the economic value added result you obtain for Woodside.

9 Explain the differences between strategic, operating, driver and outcome KPIs. Give examples of each of the four types for Jen's Coffee Escape (see Figure 21.2).

10 Eggleton Limited provides a range of professional services to the Australasian business community. An indicator that would not be directly relevant to assessing the market profile and client acceptance of Eggleton Limited in the Australasian business community is:
a   editorial comments in the Australasian financial and business press about Eggleton Limited and the industry in which it operates
b   the ratio of new clients signed by Eggleton Limited (measured in number and dollar value of billings) to client terminations (measured in number and dollar value of fees lost)

    c   the annual budget allowance by Eggleton Limited for expenditure on corporate and service promotion

    d   the average number of complaints lodged by clients of Eggleton Limited per quarter.

        Explain the reasons for your selection.

                        (We acknowledge and thank Peter Robinson, Business School, UWA for this question.)

11 The following KPIs are calculated on a monthly basis for the loans department in a credit union. Classify each KPI as strategic or operating; driver or outcome:

    a   dollars spent on advertising

    b   time taken for loan approval

    c   dollar value of loans approved

    d   number of loan applications received via the internet

    e   number of loans referred to the credit department for non-payment after 60 days

    f   profitability of loans approved

    g   percentage of loans funded out of the total number approved.

12 The list below contains a variety of performance measures that could be used in a balanced scorecard. Classify each measure as financial, customer, internal business process, or learning and growth:

    a   market share

    b   net profit

    c   defect rate

    d   number of employees attending training programs

    e   lead time to delivery

    f   growth in sales

    g   employee morale

    h   number of repeat sales.

13 In Figure 21.2 we looked at a basic balanced scorecard for Jen's Coffee Escape.
    For each of the four perspectives, list two performance measures in addition to those provided in this figure.

14 Recent articles have focused on summary information for running a business and a 'balanced scorecard' approach (using a number of performance measures).

        Explain the following in relation to the sentence above:

    a   The arguments for using the profit measure as the all-encompassing measure of the performance of a business.

    b   The limitations of the profit-measure approach, and of undue dependence on the profit measure.

    c   The problems of using a broad range of non-financial measures for the short-and long-term control of a business.

                        (We acknowledge and thank Peter Robinson, Business School, UWA for this question.)

15 One of Kaplan's recommendations for improving management accounting was the increased use of non-financial performance indicators to control organisational performance.

        Explain and discuss the advantages and disadvantages of using non-financial performance indicators in controlling organisational performance.

                        (We acknowledge and thank Peter Robinson, Business School, UWA for this question.)

Note to instructors: *The following problem is considered more suitable for use in MBA courses. However, undergraduate courses may also find the problem useful.*

16 The generic balanced scorecard, as conceived by Kaplan and Norton (1992), has four perspectives: financial, customer, internal process, and innovation and learning. In contrast, the triple bottom line envisages three forms of performance reporting: economic, social and environmental.

BestWest, the State Government agency responsible for promoting the use of sustainable practices by the Western Australian community, reports the following triple bottom line performance measures:

a   Waste material produced by BestWest as a percentage of total materials used.

b   BestWest operating surplus for the year ending 30 June 20X0.

c   Number of people attending a BestWest workshop promoting the use of environmentally friendly packaging.

d   Number of BestWest employees completing a fitness program intended to improve the physical and mental well-being of agency employees.

e   Percentage of total BestWest revenue received from corporate philanthropists (e.g. Gill Bates the CEO of MacroHard Software) due to the sound environmental management policies promoted by the agency within the business community.

f   Community satisfaction with BestWest that is attributable to the agency's reputation of being a good 'corporate' citizen.

g   Tonnes of waste paper recycled by BestWest in the year ending 30 June 20X0.

h   Percentage reduction in BestWest energy consumption (as measured in Giga Joules and cost per full-time employee) due to the agency's adherence to the targets set in the State Government's Energy Smart policy.

i   The total number of BestWest employees on occupational stress-related sick leave as at 30 June 20X0.

Required

Classify each of the TBL measures into one of the four perspectives of the balanced scorecard. Explain your reasons for each classification.

(We acknowledge and thank Peter Robinson, Business School, UWA for this question.)

17 ElectroWizardry is a small electronics firm that buys circuit boards from overseas suppliers, inserts various electronic devices into these boards, and then sells the modified boards on to local computer assemblers. The owner of ElectroWizardry is concerned because the firm's profits have been well below the budgeted targets for the past few years. For this reason, the services of a consultant have been engaged to identify the sources of the low profit levels. The consultant undertook a detailed study of the firm's processes, and, as a result, determined that 10 per cent of the modified boards were being returned to ElectroWizardry because they were defective. Related to this high defective rate was a low level of customer satisfaction and a diminishing level of sales over the past few years. The consultant's discussions with ElectroWizardry employees led to the conclusions that (i) many employees had had insufficient training in essential skills such as soldering; (ii) some of the electronic insertion diagrams provided to employees were inaccurate; and (iii) approximately 5 per cent of the overseas supplied boards had defects of various sorts, which the employees were expected to correct (but without any extra time being allowed for such corrections).

Required

a   Using the terminology of the balanced scorecard, determine some financial and non-financial KPIs that the firm needs to improve in order to achieve their budgeted profit target.

b   Illustrate your answer in (a) using a vertically structured balanced scorecard similar to the one shown in Figure 21.2.

18 At the end of 20X2, Kanton Enterprises implemented a low-cost strategy to improve its competitive position. Its objective was to become the low cost producer in its industry. To lower costs, Kanton undertook a number of improvement activities such as just-in-time production, total quality management and activity-based costing. Now, after two years of operation, the president of Kanton wants some assessment of the system's achievements. To help provide this assessment, the following information on one product has been gathered:

	20X2	20X4
Theoretical annual capacity*	96 000	96 000
Actual production**	76 000	88 000
Production hours available (20 workers)	40 000	40 000
Scrap (kilograms)	5 000	2 000
Materials used (kilograms)	50 000	50 000
Actual cost per unit	$125	$100
Days of inventory	6	3
Number of defective units	5 000	2 000
Suggestions per employee	2	6
Hours of training	100	400
Selling price per unit	$150	$140
Number of new customers	2 000	8 000

* Amount that could be produced given the available production hours.

** Amount that was produced given the available production hours.

Required

a Compute the following measures for 20X2 and 20X4:

   i   theoretical operating cycle time per unit
   ii actual operating cycle time per unit
   iii labour productivity (output/hours)
   iv scrap as a percentage of total material used
   v   percentage change in actual product cost (for 20X4 only)
   vi percentage change in days of inventory (for 20X4 only)
   vii defective units as a percentage of total units produced
   viii new customers per unit of output
   ix total hours of training
   x   selling price per unit (as given)
   xi total employee suggestions.

b For the measures listed in (a), list likely strategic objectives, classified according to the four balanced scorecard perspectives. Next, classify each measure as a driver or outcome measure. Finally, evaluate the success of the strategy. Would you like any additional information to carry out this evaluation? Explain.

(Adapted from D. Hansen and M. Mowen, *Cost Management: Accounting and Control*, 4th edn, South-Western, Mason, Ohio, 2002, question 14–15, pp. 586–7.)

ETHICS CASE STUDY

THE PRICE OF LEADERSHIP
by Ian Dunlop
Ian Dunlop is an adviser on governance and sustainability
The backlash against excessive executive salaries is just beginning.
Ian Dunlop says we need to rethink the issue.

SENIOR executive remuneration is out of control and present differentials are not sustainable if the credibility of business, and social cohesion, are to be maintained. There is no objection to reasonable reward for genuine performance and results. But what is reasonable? And how much is any individual worth? These are not matters for legislation. The market must resolve them. However, if executives insist on multi-million dollar remuneration when in most instances their financial independence has long since been provided for, one has to question their personal motivation and whether these are the right individuals to be running sustainable businesses.

Leadership particularly at this level brings many entitlements, but also carries obligations to act ethically, not only in regard to business in general but also in regard to self-interest. It should imply an acceptance of the principle of duty whereby, given reasonable remuneration, the individual feels privileged to have the opportunity to lead and, in the interests of the wider organisation, does not have to be driven by further financial incentives.

Further, as anyone with experience in large organisations can testify, it is not exclusively the CEO and a small cadre of senior executives who are responsible for success. Reward structures should reflect this reality. This is not altruistic theory, and none of it obviates the need for a hard-nosed commercial drive among our business leaders. But, sadly, business has demonstrated that performance-based incentives are not producing superior results or responsible outcomes. Time, then, to rethink the entire concept.

Ethics provides the framework to carry out these tasks by defining what is right in relation to the stated values of the organisation. As KPMG's Attracta Lagan argues: 'Being ethical is essentially about accepting our interdependence with each other and taking the other's needs into consideration before acting. It sometimes boils down to an ability to manage the tension between self-interest and what is good for the group or community.'

. . .

Extract from article in *Australian Financial Review*, 11 October 2002

Discuss

a   The article refers to the team effort that is involved in large organisations, and argues successful organisations require good teams and good leaders. When a football team wins the premiership, is it due to the players or the coach or both? The CEO is like the coach of the team. How do we assess the performance of the CEOs of large organisations?

b   Is it reasonable to expect CEOs to moderate their remuneration demands when they have achieved 'financial independence'? Is acting in self-interest unethical?

ANSWERS TO REVIEW EXERCISES

1   A *cost centre* is a business unit (which could be a function, activity or even an item of equipment) whose costs may be attributed to it. A cost centre is appropriate when a manager only has control over costs and not revenues.

    A *profit centre* is a business unit which is accountable for both costs and revenues.

    An *investment centre* is a business unit where the manager not only has control over the profits of the unit but also has some discretion as to the amount of investment undertaken by the unit.

2   Examples of financial measures are total income/revenue, return on assets, return on shareholders' equity, cost per unit. Examples of non-financial measures are customer satisfaction, supplier reliability, quality of production, customer complaints, employee morale and delivery time.

3   Financial measures are easier to calculate than non-financial measures and are more well-known. Financial measures provide standards for comparison across entities. However, financial measures can be manipulated, and inflation causes problems with measures involving dollars.

    Non-financial measures can be more directly linked to strategy, may be more readily available than measures like profit and are less susceptible to manipulation. However, non-financial measures are often more difficult to measure, may conflict with financial measures in the short term and are not as easily understood as financial measures.

4   Operating KPIs measure factors which a business needs to perform on a regular basis to 'keep the ship moving in the right direction' (i.e. the 'business as usual' measures). Strategic KPIs measure factors which help determine the direction in which the business is moving.

5   Performance measures that would be useful in evaluating investment centres are rate of return on investment, return on assets, and net profit.

APPENDIX 1
WOODSIDE HALF-YEARLY
REPORT 2005

WOODSIDE PETROLEUM LTD.

AND ITS CONTROLLED ENTITIES

A.B.N. 55 004 898 962

HALF-YEARLY REPORT

30 June 2005

CONTENTS

DIRECTORS' REPORT
For the Half-Year Ended 30 June 2005

The Directors of Woodside Petroleum Ltd. present their Report and the consolidated Financial Report for the half-year ended 30 June 2005 as follows. The dollar figures are expressed in Australian currency unless otherwise stated.

a) FINANCIAL AND PRODUCTION PERFORMANCE

Financial Performance

The reported net profit after tax (NPAT) of $512.2 million for the first half (1H) 2005 is 31.6% lower than the $748.5 million for the corresponding period in 2004. However the 2004 result included an after tax significant item of $373.7 million which arose from the profit on the one-off sale of Woodside's 40% equity in the Enfield oil development and WA-271-P.

The reported NPAT of $512.2 million includes an unrealised gain on embedded derivatives of $63.7 million (after tax). Gains or losses on embedded derivatives within sales contracts are now recognised under AIFRS. Excluding this impact, the underlying 1H 2005 NPAT (pre embedded derivatives) is $448.5 million, 19.7% higher than the underlying 1H 2004 NPAT (pre significant items) of $374.8 million.

The overall improvement in profit was largely due to increased revenue from higher sales volumes and realised oil prices. Increases were partially offset by the stronger Australian dollar and the higher secondary taxes that resulted from higher revenues.

Revenues from oil and gas operations were $1,231.9 million, up 30.2% from $946.3 million in 1H 2004. With increased production, sales volumes were up 7.5%. During the period the US$ realised oil price increased to US$49.27/boe (up 40.6%), however increases in the average A$/US$ exchange rate to 0.773 (up 5.3%) partly offset the oil price benefits.

An interim dividend of 35 cents per share (cps) fully franked will be paid on 23 September 2005 to all shareholders registered at 2 September 2005 (2004: 27cps fully franked).

Expensed exploration and evaluation of $104.8 million was up 5.1% due to $27.8 million of prior period capitalised evaluation costs being written off following decisions relating to commerciality of capitalised exploration. This was offset by reduced general exploration activity compared to the previous corresponding period.

Depreciation and amortisation expense of $124.9 million was down 12.4% mainly due to lower units of production depreciation rates as a result of the upward revision of reserve bases on 1 January 2005.

Tax expense on operating profit before significant items decreased by $23.6 million to $228.0 million primarily due to lower foreign exploration expenditure. The effective tax rate of 30.8% (2004: 26.3%) is marginally higher given the relatively low tax impact on the prior period's significant item.

At June 2005, net debt was $459.0 million compared to $241.0 million as at 31 December 2004. Total outstanding debt stood at US$800 million, comprising three unsecured US dollar denominated bond issues. As of the reporting date, the Group had US$400 million undrawn borrowing capacity within its bilateral loan and a dual currency US$50 million revolving credit facility.

The Group has prepared its financial statements in accordance with AIFRS for the first time in this Half-Year Financial Report. Comparative figures have been adjusted accordingly.

At 1 January 2005 the impact on total equity is an overall reduction of $189.2 million. There is no impact on the underlying cash flows of the Group and no impact on the Group's loan covenants.

The introduction of AIFRS will however introduce an increased level of volatility to future reported earnings. This will result from the future revaluation of embedded derivatives contained within contracts and exposure to unhedged foreign denominated debt.

Two domestic gas sales contracts have been identified as containing embedded derivatives. These contracts contain pricing mechanisms (a linkage to certain commodity prices) not usually present in sales contracts in the Western Australian domestic gas market. Therefore, the pricing elements of these contracts which change the nature of the contract's risk are separately recorded at fair value with movements reported in the income statement. All other sales contracts, including export LNG, contain pricing mechanisms which are considered usual in their respective markets and therefore are deemed not to contain embedded derivatives.

Production Performance

Production of 29.9 million barrels of oil equivalent (MMboe) was 4.9% higher than the 28.5 MMboe for the previous corresponding period. This was due to:

- higher production for all North West Shelf products.
- lower oil production from the Laminaria-Corallina and Legendre projects (caused by natural field decline), partially offset by first production from the Mutineer-Exeter oil project from the end of March 2005.

In July 2005, Woodside revised the company's full year 2005 aspirational production target upward from 56 MMboe to at least 58 MMboe.

b) CORPORATE MATTERS

Management Changes

In February 2005, the company appointed Ross Carroll as Chief Financial Officer. Mr Carroll, a finance executive with 18 years experience in the resources industry, took up the position in late March 2005.

c) HEALTH, SAFETY AND ENVIRONMENT

Woodside's safety performance during the period improved with the company's Total Recordable Case Frequency (all injuries more serious than first aid cases, including lost time injuries) at 4.5 for each million hours worked. This was a 21% improvement on the rate of 5.7 recorded in the 1H 2004.

Health performance also showed improvement during the period, with Total Recordable Occupational Illness Frequency (based on severity higher than first aid cases) at 0.5 for each million hours worked. We seek to improve our health performance by continuing to increase awareness of health risks and implementing targeted risk programs.

Woodside had 13 reportable environmental incidents to the end of June 2005, compared to 3 in the corresponding period in 2004. Of the 13 incidents, 7 were temporary exceedances of oil-in-water limits. Regrettably, there were 5 reportable oil spills including a leak caused by a flowline fault at the Laminaria field in the Timor Sea in January 2005. An investigation of the cause of the leak was instigated and the affected well has remained shut-in until remedial action can be taken, which is expected in early 2006.

DIRECTORS' REPORT
For the Half-Year Ended 30 June 2005

In April 2005, Woodside released its inaugural Health, Safety and Environment Report which is available on Woodside's website.

d) FINANCIAL RISK MANAGEMENT

Woodside's management of financial risk is aimed at assisting the Company to ensure net cash flows are sufficient to:

* meet all its financial commitments as and when they fall due;

* maintain the capacity to fund its forecast project development and exploration strategy;

* continue to pay dividends; and

* sustain financial ratios which maintain an investment grade credit rating.

Woodside continually monitors and tests its forecast financial position against these criteria and in general will undertake hedging activity only when neccessary to ensure these objectives will be met. There are other circumstances which may result in hedging activities such as the purchase of reserves or underpinning the economics of a new project.

Hedging Impact

The statement of financial performance for first-half 2005 includes a $1.3 million after tax loss on oil price hedging settlements and $0.5 million after tax gains from foreign exchange hedging settlements. This compares with oil price hedging costs of $25.4 million after tax and foreign exchange hedging gains of $11.4 million after tax in first-half 2004.

The implementation of AIFRS has resulted in a $15.8 million after tax gain from foreign exchange hedging settlements being taken to equity as at 31 December 2004 rather than being realised in the statement of financial performance during 2005.

Hedging Position

The 30 June 2005 hedge positions outlined below will impact on Woodside's future reported financial performance in line with the settlement of the hedge and recognition of the underlying hedged item in the relevant future periods.

Currency

As at 30 June 2005, US$ 33 million was hedged using forward exchange contracts with varying maturities out to April 2006 at an average rate of 0.5164 and a mark-to-market valuation gain of $ 20.3 million, compared to a gain of $ 40.1 million at 30 June 2004.

Interest Rate Management

Woodside maintains a diversified funding portfolio with the objectives of spreading its borrowing, maintaining a spread of maturities, and achieving a balance between fixed and floating rate debt liabilities. This balance is achieved through the issue of fixed and floating rate debt and, where appropriate, the use of derivative instruments which consist of primarily fixed-to-floating rate swaps.

e) PRODUCTION AND SALES (Woodside's share unless otherwise stated)

Domestic Gas and LNG

Production and sales volumes of domestic gas for the Western Australian market in 1H 2005 were in line with 1H 2004 volumes. Woodside's share during the period averaged 292 terajoules per day (Tj/d) (1H 2004: 293 Tj/d).

LNG production volume for 1H 2005 totalled 951,203 tonnes (1H 2004: 659,754 tonnes). The 44.2% increase was largely due to the LNG Train 4 start-up in the third quarter of 2004. Sales volume also lifted significantly to 954,691 tonnes, up 50.1% from 636,092 tonnes 1H 2004.

The NWS Venture delivered 99 LNG cargoes in 1H 2005, including 3 spot cargoes, a 47.8% increase on the 67 cargoes delivered in 1H 2004.

Woodside's share of domestic gas and LNG sales revenue during this period totalled $436.6 million, a 37.7% increase on the $317.0 million received for the corresponding 2004 period.

Condensate

Woodside's condensate production from the NWS Venture in 1H 2005 was 6.4% lower at 4,307,122 barrels (1H 2004: 4,603,750 barrels). The reduction was due to the planned cessation of reinjection compression at the Goodwyn platform in June 2004. Woodside's condensate sales volume for the period was also 6.4% lower at 4,353,472 barrels (1H 2004: 4,648,900 barrels). Despite lower condensate production, the company's condensate revenue during the period was 35.3% higher at $294.6 million due to higher product prices (1H 2004: $217.7 million).

The Ohanet joint venture received its full revenue entitlement of $20.8 million for the six months to June 2005, which equates to 671,265 barrels of condensate at US$24/bbl oil[1]. This compares with the $24.6 million and 728,244 barrels reported for 1H 2004.

Crude Oil

Woodside's NWS Venture crude oil production volumes in 1H 2005 lifted by 8.0% to 3,105,752 barrels, compared with 2,876,569 barrels in 1H 2004, due to the tie-in of Wanaea-8 and Lambert-6 infill wells in December 2004. Crude oil sales volume for the period was 8.1% higher at 3,147,346 barrels, (1H 2004: 2,910,656 barrels). Woodside's revenue during this period increased by 44.0% to $209.2 million (1H 2004: $145.3 million) reflecting higher volumes and product prices.

Woodside's Laminaria-Corallina crude oil production for the reporting period totalled 2,160,579 barrels (1H 2004: 3,102,044 barrels). This 30.3% decrease, due to natural field decline and to a number of Laminaria wells being off-line during the period, was partially offset by the additional 16.67% interest in production licence AC/L5 acquired from Shell in March 2005. All wells are now in production with the exception of Laminaria-2, which is expected to resume production in early 2006.

Laminaria-Corallina crude oil sales volume for 1H 2005 totalled 2,179,322 barrels, 21.8% lower than the 2,787,338 barrels for 1H 2004. Higher oil prices offset the volume decrease, resulting in revenue for the period of $127.6 million which was in line with the contribution of $127.4 million in 1H 2004.

Legendre oil production in 1H 2005 was 1,052,848 barrels. This was down 37.0% from 1,672,446 barrels in 1H 2004 due to natural reservoir decline and a planned maintenance shutdown in May 2005. Woodside's Legendre crude sales during the period were 37.6% lower at 979,886 barrels (1H 2004: 1,570,248) and revenue was down 14.6% to $65.4 million (1H 2004: $76.6 million).

The Mutineer-Exeter oil project started production on 29 March 2005, producing 537,654 barrels of crude oil to 30 June 2005 through the FPSO vessel 'MODEC Venture 11'. Woodside's Mutineer-Exeter crude sales during the period were 478,726 barrels, contributing revenue of $30.5 million in 1H 2005.

---

[1] Derived volumes calculated using a 10 year long-term average oil price (currently budgeted by Woodside at US$24/bbl pre-tax)

DIRECTORS' REPORT
For the Half-Year Ended 30 June 2005

LPG

Woodside's share of NWS Venture LPG production in 1H 2005 was 65,431 tonnes, up 4.6% compared with 62,539 tonnes in 1H 2004. This increase was due to the start of dual trunkline operations and LNG Train 4 from Q3 2004. Woodside's LPG sales volume during the period was 11.0% higher at 68,110 tonnes (1H 2004: 61,361 tonnes). Sales volume increases combined with higher product prices lifted LPG sales revenue by 52.1% to $33.3 million compared to $21.9 million in 1H 2004.

The Ohanet joint venture received its full revenue entitlement of $13.9 million for 1H 2005, which equates to 54,657 tonnes of LPG at US$24/bbl oil. This compares with the $15.8 million and 57,316 tonnes that was reported for 1H 2004.

f) REVIEW OF OPERATIONS

AUSTRALIA and the TIMOR SEA

North West Shelf Venture

- Domgas
  Domgas demand was impacted by the ongoing suspension of BHP Billiton's (BHPB) Hot Briquette Iron (HBI) plant in Western Australia but lifted in the second quarter due to strong customer demand. BHPB is expected to make a decision on the plant's future in 2H 2005.

- LNG Train 4
  Two successful shutdowns of LNG Train 4 were completed during the period. The work was done to eliminate an internal leak on the main cryogenic heat exchanger. No further shutdowns are planned for LNG Train 4 in 2005.

- Phase V LNG Expansion Project
  Final investment approval for the $2 billion expansion of the NWS Venture's onshore LNG facilities at its Karratha plant in Western Australia was granted in June 2005. Following the expansion, the NWS Venture onshore gas plant will be one of the largest LNG complexes in the Asia-Pacific region.

  The Phase V LNG Expansion Project includes construction of a fifth LNG train, associated infrastructure and a second loading jetty. The new train will process an additional 4.2 million tonnes of LNG a

year and increase the plant's capacity to 15.9 million tonnes a year.

In June 2005, Woodside awarded the engineering, procurement and construction management contract to the Foster Wheeler Worley joint venture. Engineering and procurement activities are progressing according to plan. Site works commenced in August 2005 and commissioning is due to start around mid-2008, with first LNG cargoes planned for Q4 2008.

- China LNG Supply
  All conditions precedent in the gas sales agreement with the Guangdong Dapeng LNG Company have now been satisfied and the integration of China National Offshore Oil Corporation (CNNOC) into the NWS Venture under the China LNG (CLNG) joint venture continues to plan. In Q2 2006 CLNG is scheduled to supply first LNG to Guangdong in China. CNOOC holds a 25% interest in the CLNG venture with each existing NWS venture participant holding 12.5%.

  Construction of the LNG receiving terminal at Dapeng (Guangdong) is well underway. Terminal and end-user projects are progressing and are expected to be ready for commercial start-up in June 2006.

- Wanaea-Cossack Lambert-Hermes Oil
  The Wanaea-Cossack Lambert-Hermes gas lift project, designed to enhance production from existing assets, is underway and on schedule. In addition, the NWS Venture is planning to drill in-fill wells on the Wanaea-Cossack Lambert-Hermes oil complex in 2H 2005 and 2006. The venture anticipates the Wanaea South well will be drilled in December 2005 and, dependent on appraisal drilling, will be followed by the Cossack South well in mid-2006.

- Goodwyn Low-Pressure Train
  Work continues on significant modifications to process train T200 and utility systems onboard the Goodwyn platform to operate T200 at low pressure. The modifications will allow Goodwyn reserves to be produced at a lower system pressure, enabling higher reserves recovery. The project's start-up timing has been revised to 2H 2006 due to the

limitations of performing modifications while the platform maintains live operations. All fabrication work is now complete and offshore construction works are approximately 80% complete.

- Perseus-over-Goodwyn Gas Project
  This project aims to further develop the Perseus field to enable full utilisation of the Goodwyn platform's capacity as it becomes available. Engineering and procurement activities are progressing well and the project is within budget and on schedule for a 1H 2007 start-up. The first shipment of corrosion resistant alloy line pipe has been loaded for shipment to the pipe coating yard in Indonesia. The topsides preparatory tie-in work has been successfully completed during the scheduled Goodwyn platform shutdown in June 2005.

- Perseus-1B Gas Project
  The Perseus-1B gas project involves the development of the Perseus gas/condensate field from the North Rankin platform via three additional platform wells. Gas production is planned from the first of these wells in Q2 2006, with reliable gas from the third well scheduled for Q4 2006.

- Angel Gas Field Development
  The project received environmental approval from the Department of Environment and Heritage and is progressing to schedule for final project approval in Q4 2005. Contracts have been awarded for critical long lead equipment and tenders have been called for the topsides installation contract. Gas production from the Angel field is expected to start in Q4 2008.

Laminaria-Corallina Oil Project
AC/L5 and WA-18-L – Woodside 59.9% and 66.67% respectively, Operator

In March 2005, Woodside announced the consolidation of its ownership of a key asset with the purchase an additional 16.67% interest in production licence AC/L5, which covers most of the Laminaria-Corallina project, from Shell Development (Australia) Pty Ltd.

DIRECTORS' REPORT
For the Half-Year Ended 30 June 2005

The US$93.3 million transaction had an effective date of 1 July 2004 with the amount paid being reduced by US$4.3 million after adjustments for working capital, cash flow movements and interest. The acquisition was recognised in the financial statements on 11 March 2005 (signing date).

This acquisition also delivered Woodside an additional 16.67% interest in the FPSO vessel, 'Northern Endeavour'. Paladin Oil & Gas (Australia) Pty Ltd, the other participant in the Laminaria-Corallina project, purchased Shell's remaining interests in AC/L5 and its 15% interest in the adjacent exploration permit AC/P8.

Following the purchase, Woodside owns 66.67% of the Corallina field and the 'Northern Endeavour' as well as a 59.9% interest in the Laminaria field, which is unitised over production licences AC/L5 and WA-18-L. Paladin holds the remaining 33.33% of both the Corallina field and 'Northern Endeavour' and the remaining 40.1% of the unitised Laminaria field.

Enfield Oil Project
WA-28-L – Woodside 60%, Operator

The Enfield oil project will include five production wells, six water injection wells and two gas injection wells with flowlines to a disconnectable FPSO vessel. The drilling rig, 'Jack Bates', commenced development drilling in February 2005 and is currently batch drilling and completing the horizontal reservoir sections. Preparation for the next phase, installation of the subsea trees and well clean-up, is underway.

The FPSO vessel 'Nganhurra', which is due for delivery in mid-2006, was successfully launched at Samsung Heavy Industries' fabrication yard in Korea on 2 April 2005 and fabrication of topside process modules is progressing to schedule. The project remains within budget and on schedule to meet a Q4 2006 start-up.

Mutineer-Exeter Oil Project
WA-191-P – Woodside 8.2%

Mutineer-Exeter production started on 29 March 2005 and averaged about 72,000 barrels per day (100% terms) in Q2 2005, including the ramp-up period associated

with start-up activities. Once steady operations were achieved, average rates of about 80,000 to 90,000 barrels per day were recorded. Production is expected to decline during 2H 2005 as water cut increases, at which time submersible pumps will be used to optimise the reservoir performance.

Otway Gas Project
T/30P, VIC/P43 , T/L2, VIC/L23 – Woodside 51.55%, Operator

The Otway gas project over the Thylacine and Geographe gas fields remains within budget and on schedule for a mid-2006 start-up. Work is progressing on the onshore gas plant with earthworks now complete, civil works are well advanced and the erection of structural steel work is underway.

Line pipe coating is nearing completion and the first consignment has arrived in Portland, Victoria. The pipelay vessel is scheduled to arrive at site in late October 2005. Fabrication of the production platform is progressing on schedule for an August 2005 load-out.

Blacktip Gas Project
WA-279-P, WA-313-P, WA-34-R, NT/P57 – Woodside 53.85%, 50%, 35%, 66.7% respectively, Operator

In June 2005, the Blacktip joint venturers received notice from Alcan Gove Pty Ltd terminating the gas sales agreement between the parties. Alcan and the Blacktip joint venturers had entered a conditional agreement in November 2004 on the sale and purchase of 800 petajoules of gas from WA-279-P over a period of about 20 years from 2007. Following the cessation of the Alcan deal, other options are being assessed.

Kipper Gas Fields
VIC/RL 2 – Woodside 30%

In June 2005 , the Kipper project participants signed Memoranda of Understanding (MOUs) to develop the Kipper gas fields in Bass Strait. Under the MOUs, project participants agreed on the key terms and conditions to unitise the Kipper field and to process gas through Esso and BHP Billiton's infrastructure and

facilities in Gippsland. Post unitisation, Woodside holds a 21% interest in the development. Esso Australia Resources will be the operator of the development. Front-end engineering and design is expected to start in 1H 2006 and first gas is planned for 2009.

Pluto Gas Development
WA-350-P– Woodside 100%, Operator

The Pluto gas discovery was made in Q1 2005 and is being appraised in 2H 2005. Preliminary results indicate that the structure may contain a significant volume of gas and options to rapidly develop it for LNG markets are being investigated.

Browse Gas Development
WA-30-R to WA-32-R, R/2 and TR/5; WA-28-R to WA-29-R and WA-275-P – Woodside 50% and 25% respectively, Operator

The 'Atwood Eagle' commenced drilling the Brecknock-2 appraisal well in July 2005. The Calliance-1 and Brecknock-3 appraisals will be drilled and 3D seismic surveys acquired to more comprehensively define the substantial gas resource that is intended for LNG markets.

Woodside is progressing pre-feasibility development studies, including options for offshore and onshore facilities, and site selection studies for the location of an onshore gas processing plant in the West Kimberley in Western Australia. Subject to the outcome of these studies, the additional appraisal and customer negotiations, the first reliable LNG cargo could be delivered in 2011-2014 provided a final investment decision is made around 2008-2010.

Sunrise Gas Project
NT/RL2, NT/P55, JPDA O3-19 – Woodside 26.67%, 35.90%, 27.67% respectively, Operator

Woodside awaits agreement between the Timor-Leste and Australian governments which will conclude arrangements over maritime borders, revenue sharing and the International Unitisation Agreement. The Sunrise joint venturers also require an agreement on fiscal stability.

When fiscal stability has been assured, the joint venturers will be in a position to recommence activities on project design, economics and work on securing markets.

DIRECTORS' REPORT
For the Half-Year Ended 30 June 2005

AFRICA

Algeria

- **Ohanet Operations**

  Woodside Energy (Algeria) Pty Ltd 15%

  Ohanet is run under a Risk Service Contract with Sonatrach (the Algerian national oil company). Under the terms of the contract, the participants receive a fixed rate of return based on product price and volume, limited to a maximum revenue entitlement.

  The Ohanet joint venture received its full revenue entitlement for 1H 2005.

Mauritania

- **Chinguetti Oil Project**

  PSC Area B Chinguetti Exploitation perimeter – Woodside Mauritania Pty Ltd 30.8%, WEL Mauritania B.V. 16.584%, Operator

  The Chinguetti oil project remains on schedule for first oil in Q1 2006. Good progress has been achieved on the drilling and completion activities with installation of the first subsea equipment already having commenced.

  The hull conversion is progressing to schedule in the Keppel Shipyard, Singapore and the turret mooring system was successfully installed on the 'Berge Helene' FPSO in June 2005. Integration of the mooring system and process modules is underway. The project costs may be higher than budget, largely due to changes in the scope of drilling operations.

- **Tiof Oil Development**

  PSC Area B – Woodside Mauritania Pty Ltd 35%, WEL Mauritania B.V. 18.846%, Operator

  Appraisal and studies are continuing on the Tiof oil development opportunity with a feasibility review scheduled for September 2005. A decision on possible further appraisal activity will be made then.

UNITED STATES

- **Alliance with Explore Enterprises**

  In January 2005, Woodside Energy (USA) Inc. (Woodside USA) formed a five-year alliance with Explore Enterprises of Louisiana LLC (Explore) to jointly conduct exploration, acquisition, development and production activities in the Gulf of Mexico. The alliance provides Woodside USA with access to an established and experienced management team.

  For each project, excluding the Midway and Neptune projects, Woodside USA holds 95% of the alliance's combined interests while Explore will hold the remaining 5%. Explore's interest in each project will increase from 5% to 12.5% after Woodside USA has recovered the present value of its invested capital in those projects.

- **Neptune Oil and Gas Project**

  Woodside Energy (USA) Inc – 20%

  Development studies of the Neptune oil and gas field in the Atwater Foldbelt region of Central Gulf of Mexico continued during 1H 2005. Final investment approval for project development was granted in late June 2005.

  The project is expected to begin production in late 2007, initially through seven subsea wells tied to a stand-alone platform, with a design capacity to produce up to 50,000 barrels of oil per day and 50 million cubic feet of gas per day.

- **Midway Gas Project**

  Woodside Energy (USA) Inc – 50%

  Testing of the Midway exploration well, in the Gulf of Mexico on Brazos Area Block A39, was successfully completed in March 2005. The well produced at 10 million cubic feet of gas a day, constrained by a 13/64 inch choke, during a 17 hour flow test. Tieback to a nearby production facility is expected to be completed during 2H 2005.

- **Clearwater Port Development**

  Woodside USA ended its heads of agreement with Crystal Energy LLC for the development of a receiving terminal. While both companies will continue discussions over the supply of LNG to Clearwater Port, Woodside USA will consider the possible development of its own LNG receiving terminal off California.

g) EXPLORATION

AUSTRALIA and the TIMOR SEA

Woodside participated in eight exploration and appraisal wells during 1H 2005, of which five wells encountered hydrocarbons.

In the Carnarvon Basin, the Pluto-1 well (WA-350-P, Woodside 100%) intersected a gross gas column of approximately 209 metres. The Hurricane-1 well (WA-208-P, Woodside 34.03%) penetrated a gross gas column of 76 metres and commerciality is under review. The Plymouth-1 well (WA-27-L, Woodside 8.2%) was a dry hole.

In the Otway Basin, two exploration wells in VIC/P 37(v), (Woodside 62.5%) Halladale-1 DW1 (location Black Watch) and Halladale-1 DW2, each encountered gas. Halladale-1 DW1 intersected a gas bearing interval of 59 metres true vertical depth (TVD) before being plugged back and deviated to the north as Halladale-1 DW2. Halladale-1 DW2 also intersected gas, encountering a gross interval of 21 metre TVD. A third well, Halladale-1 DW3, was then deviated to the northeast as an appraisal well to establish aquifer pressures in the Waarre Formation, downflank from the Halladale gas accumulation.

The Falcone-1/1A well was drilled in WA-271-P (Woodside 60%) in the Exmouth sub-basin and encountered non-commercial hydrocarbons.

In Northern Australia, the Petalonia North-1 well was drilled in AC/P 8 (Woodside 66.67%) without encountering significant hydrocarbons.

Woodside increased its interest in the Timor Sea Production Licence AC/L 5 to 66.67% and the company was awarded the Capella Production Licence WA-30-L (Woodside 15.78%) in the Carnarvon basin.

AFRICA

- **Mauritania**

  Exploration activity focussed on maturing prospects for drilling in 2H 2005 and the completion of the Atar 3D seismic survey (~2,970 km^2) in PSC Area C6.

  In June 2005, Woodside Mauritania Pty Ltd announced that the first three exploration wells for its 2005 exploration drilling

DIRECTORS' REPORT
For the Half-Year Ended 30 June 2005

sequence will target the Sotto and Colin prospects in PSC Area A and the Espadon prospect in PSC Area B.

- **Libya**

  Woodside Energy (NA) Ltd. (Woodside NA) is currently acquiring 2D and 3D seismic in the Sirte and Murzuq basins in onshore Libya.

  Woodside NA was a successful bidder in the Libya EPSA IV round one and was awarded four offshore blocks (Blocks 35, 36, 52 and 53). Woodside NA holds a 55% interest in these blocks and is operator.

- **Kenya**

  Acquisition of the Pomboo 2D seismic survey was completed in Q1 2005. Drilling of the first exploration well will now occur in 2006 due to the unavailability of a suitable deepwater rig in 2005. Woodside Energy Kenya Pty. Ltd. has increased its interest in Kenya Blocks L-5 and L-7 to 50%.

- **Liberia**

  In January 2005, Woodside West Africa Pty Ltd successfully bid for 100% of an offshore exploration block in Liberia. The area, known as Block 15, adjoins Blocks 16 and 17 which were won 100% by Repsol Exploracion SA in what was Liberia's first offshore licensing round.

  Repsol and Woodside West Africa each holds a 50% interest in two blocks immediately west of Liberia in neighbouring Sierra Leone (SL-6 and SL-7) and the two companies now have interests in five adjoining blocks across Sierra Leone and Liberia.

  Woodside West Africa's initial four-year work commitment includes geological and geophysical studies and the acquisition of 600km of 2D seismic and 1600km^2 of 3D seismic.

- **Canary Islands**

  The Royal Decree granting permits 1-9 has been partially annulled by the Supreme Court of Spain, which will have the effect of preventing the venture from conducting drilling operations in the permits. Discussions are ongoing with the appropriate authorities in an attempt to resolve this matter.

UNITED STATES

Woodside Energy (USA) Inc. gained interests in Garden Banks blocks 732/733 and 821/823 (Woodside 50%) and increased its interest in Alaminos Canyon blocks 73 and 117 (Woodside 25%). Mississippi Canyon block 449 and Walker Ridge blocks 37, 81 and 123 were relinquished during the period.

h) OUTLOOK

Production Target Lifted

Woodside has lifted its 2005 production target from around 56MMboe to at least 58MMboe. The higher production target is a consequence of increased contributions from the NWS Venture, the start-up of the Mutineer-Exeter oil field and the increased equity in the Laminaria-Corallina oil project.

The NWS Venture is planning to drill an infill well on the Wanaea oil field which, if successful, could be online by year-end. The NWS Venture's oil production is also likely to increase with the planned reinstatement of Wanaea-1 and Wanaea-7 in Q4 2005. In addition, Laminaria oil production should receive a small increase when Lamniaria-2 comes back online in Q1 2006.

i) DIRECTORS

The names of the Company's Directors in office during the half-year and until the date of this report are as follows:

Mr CB Goode (Chairman)
Mr D Voelte (Managing Director)
Mr R E S Argyle
Ms J R Broadbent
Mr P Van Rossum
Mr D P T de Wit (resigned February 15, 2005)
Mr A Jamieson (appointed February 16, 2005)
Mr E Fraunschiel
Dr P H Jungels
Dr P J B Rose
Mr T N Warren

j) ROUNDING OF AMOUNTS TO NEAREST THOUSAND DOLLARS

The amounts contained in this report have been rounded off under the option available to the Company as specified in Australian Securities and Investments Commission Class Order 98/0100, unless otherwise indicated.

k) REFERENCES TO WOODSIDE

References to Woodside may be references to Woodside Petroleum Ltd. or its applicable subsidiaries.

l) AUDITOR'S INDEPENDENCE DECLARATION

In relation to our review of the financial report of Woodside Petroleum Ltd. for the half-year ended 30 June 2005, to the best of my knowledge and belief, there have been no contraventions of the auditor independence requirements of the Corporations Act 2001 or any applicable code of professional conduct.

Ernst & Young

Jeff Dowling
Partner
Perth
17 August 2005

Signed in accordance with a resolution of the directors.

C B Goode AC
Chairman
Perth
17 August 2005

CONDENSED INCOME STATEMENT
For the Half-Year Ended 30 June 2005

| | Notes | CONSOLIDATED | |
		30 June 2005 $000	30 June 2004 $000
Revenues from oil and gas operations	4(a)	1,231,912	946,253
Cost of sales	4(b)	(394,010)	(337,582)
Petroleum resource rent tax	4(c)	(39,533)	19,529
Gross profit		798,369	628,200
Other income	4(d)	134,760	555,420
Other expenses	4(e)	(176,568)	(145,539)
Share of associates' net profits / (losses)	4(f)	3,350	(3,706)
Profit before tax and finance costs		759,911	1,034,375
Finance costs	4(g)	(19,654)	(18,511)
Profit before income tax		740,257	1,015,864
Income tax expense		(228,023)	(267,385)
Net profit attributable to members of the parent		512,234	748,479
Basic and diluted earnings per share (cents)		76.8	112.3
Dividend per share (cents / share)	6	35.0	27.0

CONDENSED BALANCE SHEET
As at 30 June 2005

	Notes	CONSOLIDATED	
		30 June 2005 $000	31 December 2004 $000
CURRENT ASSETS			
Cash and cash equivalents		617,068	797,140
Trade and other receivables		289,941	375,783
Inventories		48,905	28,758
Other financial assets		20,530	40,034
Other assets		78,060	61,980
TOTAL CURRENT ASSETS		1,054,504	1,303,695
NON CURRENT ASSETS			
Inventories		11,581	11,489
Investments in associates		5,690	2,340
Other financial assets		435,741	92,654
Exploration and evaluation		427,327	378,822
Oil and gas properties		4,090,197	3,520,407
Other plant and equipment		106,010	110,958
Deferred income tax asset		32,818	25,717
Other assets		264	8,519
TOTAL NON CURRENT ASSETS		5,109,628	4,150,906
TOTAL ASSETS		6,164,132	5,454,601
CURRENT LIABILITIES			
Trade and other payables		357,734	316,050
Interest bearing loans and borrowings		3,397	3,397
Income tax payable		126,376	64,483
Provisions		60,468	52,562
Other liabilities		6,858	45,483
TOTAL CURRENT LIABILITIES		554,833	481,975
NON CURRENT LIABILITIES			
Interest bearing loans and borrowings		1,072,680	1,034,772
Deferred income tax liabilities		820,101	729,716
Provisions		325,894	270,237
Other liabilities		100,400	168,097
TOTAL NON CURRENT LIABILITIES		2,319,075	2,202,822
TOTAL LIABILITIES		2,873,908	2,684,797
NET ASSETS		3,290,224	2,769,804
EQUITY			
Issued capital	5	706,491	706,491
Treasury shares		(148,891)	(130,849)
Other reserves		55,864	(7,178)
Retained earnings		2,676,760	2,201,340
TOTAL EQUITY		3,290,224	2,769,804

CONDENSED STATEMENT OF CASH FLOWS
For the Half-Year Ended 30 June 2005

	CONSOLIDATED	
	30 June 2005 $000	30 June 2004 $000
CASH FLOWS FROM OPERATING ACTIVITIES		
Receipts from customers	1,287,681	1,144,253
Interest received – other entities	11,916	8,130
Dividends received – other entities	6,799	7,609
Payments to suppliers and employees	(225,508)	(159,722)
Borrowing costs paid (net of capitalised amounts)	(9,368)	(8,935)
Management and other fees – other entities	8,522	13,250
Royalties, excise and PRRT payments	(175,207)	(155,462)
Income tax paid	(210,520)	(187,735)
Advances to employees relating to employee share plan	(41,958)	(24,920)
Repayments from employees relating to employee share plan	20,316	15,372
Net Cash from / (used in) Operating Activities	672,673	651,840
CASH FLOWS FROM INVESTING ACTIVITIES		
Payments for capital and exploration expenditure	(724,113)	(489,933)
Payments for interests in joint ventures	(110,738)	-
Proceeds from sale of oil and gas properties	-	41,253
Receipt of proceeds from sale of exploration and evaluation	190,182	588,903
Proceeds from sale of other plant and equipment	186	18,963
Payments for investments in other entities	(1,379)	(23,233)
Payments for investments in controlled entities	-	(64,535)
Realisation of foreign exchange difference on receivables	-	46,567
Prepayment of deposit on purchase consideration	-	70,633
Net Cash from / (used in) Investing Activities	(645,862)	188,618
CASH FLOWS FROM FINANCING ACTIVITIES		
Dividends paid	(212,607)	(166,667)
Net Cash from / (used in) Financing Activities	(212,607)	(166,667)
NET INCREASE/(DECREASE) IN CASH HELD	(185,796)	673,791
CASH AT THE BEGINNING OF THE HALF-YEAR	797,140	122,691
Effects of exchange rate changes on the balances of cash held in foreign currencies	5,724	14,525
CASH AT THE END OF THE HALF-YEAR	617,068	811,007

CONDENSED STATEMENT OF CHANGES IN EQUITY
As at 30 June 2005

	CONSOLIDATED						
	Issued Capital	Treasury Shares	Foreign Currency Translation Reserve	Hedging Reserve	Investment Revaluation Reserve	Retained Earnings	Total Equity
	$000	$000	$000	$000	$000	$000	$000
Balance at 1 January 2004	706,491	(137,507)	-	-	-	1,402,712	1,971,696
Woodside Employee Share Plan	-	(7,643)	-	-	-	-	(7,643)
Exchange differences arising on translation of overseas operations	-	-	41,616	-	-	-	41,616
Total income and expense recognised directly in equity	-	(7,643)	41,616	-	-	-	33,973
Net profit for the period	-	-	-	-	-	748,479	748,479
Dividends	-	-	-	-	-	(166,667)	(166,667)
Balance at 30 June 2004	706,491	(145,150)	41,616	-	-	1,984,524	2,587,481
Balance at 1 January 2005	706,491	(130,849)	(7,178)	(1,018)	35,986	2,377,859	2,981,291
Cash flow hedges net of tax	-	-	-	(11,369)	-	-	(11,369)
Hedge of net investment	-	-	-	-	-	-	-
Woodside Employee Share Plan	-	(18,042)	-	-	-	-	(18,042)
Revaluation of available for sale investments	-	-	-	-	27,420	-	27,420
Exchange differences arising on translation of overseas operations	-	-	12,023	-	-	-	12,023
Total income and expense recognised directly in equity	-	(18,042)	12,023	(11,369)	27,420	-	10,032
Net profit for the period	-	-	-	-	-	512,234	512,234
Dividends	-	-	-	-	-	(213,333)	(213,333)
Balance at 30 June 2005	706,491	(148,891)	4,845	(12,387)	63,406	2,676,760	3,290,224

Notes to and forming part of the Financial Report for the half-year ended 30 June 2005

1. BASIS OF PREPARATION OF HALF-YEARLY FINANCIAL REPORT

The half-year financial report does not include all notes of the type normally included within the annual financial report and therefore cannot be expected to provide as full an understanding of the financial performance, financial position and financing and investing activities of the consolidated entity as the full financial report.

The half-year financial report should be read in conjunction with the annual Full Financial Report of Woodside Petroleum Ltd. as at 31 December 2004, which was prepared based on Australian Accounting Standards applicable before 1 January 2005 ('AGAAP').

It is also recommended that the half-year financial report be considered together with any public announcements made by Woodside Petroleum Ltd. and its controlled entities during the half year ended 30 June 2005 in accordance with the continuous disclosure obligations arising under the Corporations Act 2001.

(a) Basis of Accounting

The half-year financial report is a general-purpose financial report, which has been prepared in accordance with the requirements of the Corporations Act 2001, applicable Accounting Standards including AASB134 "Interim Financial Reporting" and other mandatory professional reporting requirements.

The half-year financial report has been prepared on a historical cost basis, except for derivative financial instruments and available-for-sale financial assets that have been measured at fair value. The carrying values of recognised assets and liabilities that are hedged with fair value hedges are adjusted to record changes in the fair values attributable to the risks that are being hedged.

For the purpose of preparing the half-year financial report, the half-year has been treated as a discrete reporting period.

(b) Statement of Compliance

The half-year financial report complies with Australian Accounting Standards, which include Australian equivalents to International Financial Reporting Standards ('AIFRS'). Compliance with AIFRS ensures that the half-year financial report, comprising the financial statements and notes thereto, complies with AASB 134.

This is the first half-year financial report prepared based on AIFRS and comparatives for the half-year ended 30 June 2004 and full-year ended 31 December 2004 have been restated accordingly.

A summary of the significant accounting policies of the Group under AIFRS are disclosed in Note 2 below.

Reconciliations of:

- AIFRS equity as at 1 January 2004, 30 June 2004 and 31 December 2004; and

- AIFRS profit for the half-year ended 30 June 2004 and full year ended 31 December 2004,

to the balances reported in the 30 June 2004 half-year report and 31 December 2004 full year financial report prepared under AGAAP are detailed in Note 11.

From 1 January 2005, the Group elected to take the exemption under AASB 1 'First-Time Adoption of Australian Equivalents to International Reporting Standards' to apply AASB 139 'Financial Instruments: Recognition and Measurement' from 1 January 2005. Accordingly, comparatives have not been restated. For information on previous accounting polices, refer to the 2004 Full Financial Report prepared under previous AGAAP.

2. SIGNIFICANT ACCOUNTING POLICIES

(a) Basis of Consolidation

The consolidated financial statements comprise the financial statements of Woodside Petroleum Ltd. and its subsidiaries ('the Group').

The financial statements of subsidiaries are prepared for the same reporting period as the parent company, using consistent accounting policies. Adjustments are made to bring into line any dissimilar accounting policies that may exist. All intercompany balances and transactions, including unrealised profits arising from intra-group transactions, have been eliminated in full.

Subsidiaries are consolidated from the date on which control is transferred to the Group and cease to be consolidated from the date on which control is transferred out of the Group.

(b) Revenue

Revenues from oil and gas operations

Revenues associated with the sale of oil, liquefied natural gas, liquefied petroleum gas and condensate are recognised when title passes to the customer. Revenues in which the group has an interest with other producers are recognised on the basis of the Group's working interest in those properties (entitlement method) and are reported gross of royalties. Amounts sold under long term 'take or pay' contracts are initially recorded as unearned revenue and taken to the income statement when the gas has been drawn by the customer.

Where revenue is earned under a risk service contract, revenue is recognised when the right to receive payment is earned.

Where revenue is earned under a production sharing contract, revenue is recognised when title to the product passes to the customer and is based on the Group's share of sales relating to oil and gas production that are allocated to the Group under the contract.

Notes to and forming part of the Financial Report for the half-year ended 30 June 2005

2.   SIGNIFICANT ACCOUNTING POLICIES (Continued)

Interest revenue

Interest revenue is recognised as interest accrues (using the effective interest method, which is the rate that exactly discounts estimated future cash receipts through the expected life of the financial instrument).

Dividend revenue

Dividend revenue is recognised when the right to receive payment is established.

Voluntary Change in Accounting Policy

From 1 January 2005, the Group changed its accounting policy in relation to the recognition of revenues from oil and gas operations. The Group now recognises revenues from oil and gas operations under the entitlement method referred to above. Previously, the Group recorded actual sales without adjusting for its working interest. The impact of the change in accounting policy has been retrospectively adjusted for previous reporting periods. Accounting for oil and gas revenues using entitlements methods is common within the oil and gas industry and therefore provides more relevant information. Note 11 quantifies the impact of this adjustment. There is no significant impact on the Group's basic earnings per share.

(c) Exploration and Evaluation

Exploration and evaluation expenditure is accounted for in accordance with the area of interest method. The Group's application of the accounting policy for the cost of exploring and of evaluating discoveries is closely aligned to the US GAAP based 'successful efforts' method.

Exploration licence acquisition costs relating to green-fields oil and gas exploration provinces are expensed as incurred while the costs incurred in relation to established or recognised oil and gas exploration provinces are initially capitalised and then amortised over the term of the licence. Capitalised exploration licence acquisition costs are amortised over the remaining term of the licence.

All exploration and evaluation costs, including general permit activity, geological and geophysical costs and new venture activity costs are expensed as incurred except where:

- the expenditure relates to an exploration discovery that, at balance date, has not been recognised as an area of interest as assessment of the existence or otherwise of economically recoverable reserves is not yet complete; or

- an area of interest is recognised, and it is expected that the expenditure will be recouped through successful exploitation of the area of interest, or alternatively, by its sale.

The costs of drilling exploration wells are initially capitalised pending the results of the well. Costs are expensed where the well does not result in the successful discovery of economically recoverable hydrocarbons and the recognition of an area of interest. Areas of interest are recognised at the field level. Subsequent to the recognition of an area of interest, all further costs relating to that area of interest are capitalised.

Each potential or recognised area of interest is reviewed at least bi-annually to determine whether economic quantities of reserves have been found or whether further exploration and evaluation work is underway or planned to support the continued carry forward of capitalised costs.

Upon approval for the commercial development of an area of interest, accumulated expenditure for the area of interest is transferred to oil and gas properties as Transferred Exploration and Evaluation - Projects in Development.

(d) Oil and Gas Properties

Oil and gas properties include construction, installation or completion of infrastructure facilities such as pipelines and platforms, capitalised borrowing costs, transferred exploration and evaluation costs, and the cost of development wells.

Subsequent costs are included in the asset's carrying amount or recognised as a separate asset, as appropriate, only when it is probable that future economic benefits associated with the item will flow to the Group and the cost of the item can be measured reliably. All other repairs and maintenance are charged to the income statement during the financial period in which they are incurred.

(e) Other Plant and Equipment

Other plant and equipment is stated at cost less accumulated depreciation and any impairment in value.

An item of other plant and equipment is derecognised upon disposal or when no future economic benefits are expected to arise from the continued use of the asset. Any gain or loss arising on de-recognition of the asset (calculated as the difference between the net disposal proceeds and the carrying amount of the item) is included in the income statement in the year the item is derecognised.

(f) Depreciation and Amortisation

Oil and gas properties and other plant and equipment, other than freehold land, are depreciated to their residual values at rates based on the expected useful lives of the assets concerned. The majority of oil and gas properties are depreciated on the Units of Production (UOP) basis using proved plus probable developed reserves taking into consideration that some of the assets have a life greater than current developed reserves. The remaining assets use the straight line approach. The major categories of assets are depreciated as follows:

Other plant and equipment
- over useful life (straight line)

Oil and gas properties (offshore)
- over the life of proved plus probable developed reserves (UOP)

Oil and gas properties (onshore)
- over the life of proved plus probable developed reserves (straight line)

Capitalised leased assets
- over the lower of, useful life and lease term

Notes to and forming part of the Financial Report for the half-year ended 30 June 2005

2.   SIGNIFICANT ACCOUNTING POLICIES (Continued)

(g) Impairment of Assets

The carrying amounts of all assets are reviewed bi-annually, or when there is indication of an impairment loss, to determine whether they are in excess of their recoverable amount. If the carrying amount of an asset exceeds its recoverable amount, the asset is written down to the lower value. Individual assets are grouped for impairment purposes at the lowest level for which there are separately identifiable cash flows. Generally, this results in the Group evaluating its oil and gas properties on a field-by-field basis.

In assessing the recoverable amount, which is determined to be the greater of fair value less costs to sell and value in use, the estimated future cash flows are discounted to their present value using pre-tax discount rates that reflect current market assessments of the time value of money and the risks specific to the asset.

(h) Derivative Financial Instruments

The Group has taken the exemption available under AASB 1 to apply AASB 132 and AASB 139 from 1 January 2005. The Group has applied previous AGAAP in the comparative information on financial instruments within the scope of AASB 132 and AASB 139. For further information on previous AGAAP refer to the Full Financial Report for the year ended 31 December 2004.

The Group uses derivative financial instruments such as oil, foreign currency and interest rate swaps, options, futures and forward contracts to hedge its risks associated with commodity prices, interest rate and foreign currency fluctuations.

Derivatives are initially recognised at fair value on the date a derivative contract is entered into and are subsequently remeasured to their fair value. The fair value of derivative financial instruments that are traded on an active market is based on quoted market prices at the balance sheet date. The fair value of financial instruments not traded on an active market is determined using appropriate valuation techniques.

At the inception of the transaction, the Group documents the relationship between hedge instruments and hedged items, as well as its risk management objective and strategy for undertaking various hedge transactions. The Group also documents its assessment, both at hedge inception and on an ongoing basis, of whether the derivatives that are used in hedging transactions have been and will continue to be highly effective in offsetting changes in fair values or cash flows of hedged items.

For the purposes of hedge accounting, hedges are classified as either fair value hedges when they hedge the exposure to changes in the fair value of a recognised asset or liability, or cash flow hedges where they hedge exposure to variability in cash flows that are either attributable to a particular risk associated with a recognised asset or liability or a highly probable forecasted transaction.

Fair Value Hedges

Changes in fair value of derivatives that are designated and qualify as fair value hedges are recorded in the income statement, together with any changes in the fair value of the hedged asset or liability that are attributable to the hedged risk.

Cash Flow Hedges

The effective portion of changes in fair value of derivatives that are designated and qualify as cash flow hedges are recognised in equity in the hedging reserve. The gain or loss relating to the ineffective portion is recognised in the income statement immediately.

Amounts accumulated in equity are taken to the income statement in the periods when the hedged item will affect profit and loss, for instance when the forecast sale that is hedged takes place.

Hedge accounting is discontinued when the hedging instrument expires or is sold, terminated or exercised, or no longer qualifies for hedge accounting. At that point in time, any cumulative gain or loss on the hedging instrument recognised in equity remains in equity until the forecasted transaction occurs.

If a hedged transaction is no longer expected to occur, the net cumulative gain or loss recognised in equity is transferred to net profit or loss for the year.

Commodity Prices

For derivative financial instruments used to hedge forecast commodity sales which meet the conditions of cash flow hedge accounting, the portion of the gain or loss on the hedging instrument that is determined to be an effective hedge is recognised directly in equity and is released to the income statement in the periods when the hedged item will affect profit and loss. Any ineffective portion is recognised in the income statement. The fair value is determined with reference to forward exchange market rates at the balance sheet date.

Interest rates

Interest rate swaps utilised to manage interest rate exposure are fair valued by reference to the market value of similar financial instruments with movements reported in the income statement. Movements in the fair value of the hedged risk are also reported in the income statement where fair value hedge accounting criteria is met. These movements in fair value of the hedged item offset the movements in fair value of the effective interest rate swap. Any fair value difference between the hedged risk and the interest rate swap at the date of transition to AIFRS is amortised over the maturity period of the instrument.

Foreign currency

For foreign currency derivatives used to hedge firm commitments which meet the conditions for cash flow hedge accounting, the portion of the gain or loss on the hedging instrument that is determined to be an effective hedge is recognised directly in equity and is released to the income statement in the periods when the hedged item will affect profit and loss. Any ineffective portion is recognised directly in the income statement. The fair value is determined using forward exchange market rates at the balance sheet date.

Notes to and forming part of the Financial Report for the half-year ended 30 June 2005

2.   SIGNIFICANT ACCOUNTING POLICIES (Continued)

Embedded derivatives

Embedded derivatives inherent in the Group's contracts that change the nature of a host contract's risk are separately recorded at fair value with movements reported in the income statement.

(i) Provision for Restoration

The Group records the present value of the estimated cost of legal and constructive obligations (such as those under the Group's Environmental Policy) to restore operating locations in the period in which the obligation is incurred. The nature of restoration activities includes the removal of facilities, abandoning of wells and restoring the affected areas.

Typically, the obligation arises when the asset is installed at the production location. When the liability is initially recorded, the estimated cost is capitalised by increasing the carrying amount of the related Oil and Gas Properties. Over time, the liability is increased for the change in the present value based on discount rates that reflect current market assessments and the risks specific to the liability. The unwinding of the discount is recorded as an accretion charge within finance costs. The carrying amount capitalised in Oil and Gas Properties is depreciated over the useful life of the related asset.

Costs incurred that relate to an existing condition caused by past operations, and do not have a future economic benefit are expensed.

(j) Joint Venture Operations

The Group's interest in unincorporated joint venture operations are accounted for by recognising its proportionate share in assets and liabilities from joint ventures. In addition, expenses incurred by the Group and sale of the Group's entitlement to production are recognised in the Group's financial statements on a pro rata basis to the Group's interest.

Investments in joint venture entities are accounted for using the equity method of accounting. Under the equity method, the cost of the investment is adjusted by the Group's proportionate share of the results of the venture.

(k) Borrowing Costs

Borrowing costs incurred for the construction of qualifying assets are capitalised during the period of time that is required to complete and prepare the asset for its intended use or sale. Assets are considered to be qualifying assets when this period of time is substantial (considered to be greater than 12 months). The Group has chosen to specifically exclude assets with a value of less than $50 million and any exploration and evaluation amounts as qualifying assets. The capitalisation rate used to determine the amount of borrowing costs to be capitalised is the weighted average interest rate applicable to the Group's outstanding borrowings during the year.

(l) Foreign Currency

The functional currency and presentation currency of Woodside Petroleum Ltd. and the majority of its Australian subsidiaries is Australian dollars. Transactions in foreign currencies are initially recorded in the functional currency at the exchange rates ruling at the date of transaction. Monetary assets and liabilities denominated in foreign currencies are retranslated at the rate of exchange ruling at balance sheet date. All differences are taken to the income statement with the exception of differences on foreign currency borrowings that provide a hedge against a net investment in subsidiaries with a functional currency other than Australian dollars. These are taken directly to the foreign currency translation reserve until the disposal of the net investment, at which time they are recognised in the income statement.

Foreign subsidiaries and some Australian subsidiaries have a functional currency other than Australian dollars (usually US dollars) as a result of the economic environment in which they operate. As at the reporting date, the assets and liabilities of these subsidiaries are translated into the presentation currency of Woodside Petroleum Ltd. at the rate of exchange ruling at the balance sheet date and the income statements are translated at the weighted average exchange rates for the reporting period or at the exchange rates ruling at the date of the transaction.

The exchange differences arising on the retranslation are taken to the foreign currency translation reserve.

On disposal of a subsidiary with a functional currency other than Australian dollars, the deferred cumulative amount recognised in the foreign currency translation reserve relating to that particular subsidiary is recognised in the income statement.

(m) Leases

Finance leases, which transfer to the Group substantially all the risks and benefits incidental to ownership of the leased item, are capitalised at the inception of the lease at the fair value of the leased property, or, if lower, at the present value of the minimum lease payments.

Lease payments are apportioned between the finance charges and reduction of the lease liability so as to achieve a constant rate of interest on the remaining balance of the liability. Finance charges are recognised in the income statement over the lease term.

Capitalised leased assets are depreciated over the lower of the estimated useful life of the asset and the lease term.

Operating lease payments are recognised as an expense in the income statement over the lease term.

(n) Earnings per Share

Earnings per share is calculated as net profit attributable to members divided by the weighted average number of ordinary shares. There are no factors that dilute basic earnings per share.

(o) Cash and Cash Equivalents

Cash and short term deposits in the balance sheet comprise cash at bank and short term deposits with an original maturity of three months or less. Cash also includes the Group's share of cash held as operator of joint ventures. For the purposes of the Cash Flow Statement, cash and cash equivalents are reported net of outstanding bank overdrafts.

Notes to and forming part of the Financial Report for the half-year ended 30 June 2005

2.   SIGNIFICANT ACCOUNTING POLICIES (Continued)

(p) Trade and Other Receivables

Trade debtors are initially recorded at the amount of contracted sales proceeds. Receivables from related parties are recognised and carried at the nominal amount due.

The Group's share of cash held in non operated joint ventures is classified as a receivable.

(q) Inventories

Work in progress and finished stocks

Work in progress consists of stocks requiring further processing by the Group to convert them to finished stock.

Finished stocks represent hydrocarbon products that are in the form in which they will be sold by the Group. The Group records its share of finished hydrocarbon stocks based on its working interest.

Work in progress and finished stocks are valued at the lower of cost and net realisable value. Cost is derived on an absorption-costing basis and includes direct processing costs and an appropriate portion of fixed and variable overheads. Costs are assigned to finished stock on a weighted average cost of production basis.

Warehouse stores and materials

Warehouse stores and materials represent consumable supplies and maintenance spares expected to be used in production and are valued at weighted average cost. Cost comprises purchase, inspection and transportation costs.

Warehouse stores and materials determined to be obsolete or damaged are written down to net realisable value.

(r) Investments

The Group has taken the exemption available under AASB 1 to apply AASB 132 and AASB 139 from 1 July 2005. The Group has applied previous AGAAP in the comparative information on financial instruments within the scope of AASB 132 and AASB 139. For further information on previous AGAAP refer to the

Full Financial Report for the year ended 31 December 2004.

All investments other than investments in associates (see (s) below) are initially recognised at cost, being the fair value of the consideration given and including acquisition charges associated with the investment.

After initial recognition, investments, which are classified as held for trading and available-for-sale, are measured at fair value. Gains or losses on investments held for trading are recognised in the income statement. Gains or losses on available-for-sale investments are recognised as a separate component of equity until the investment is sold, collected or otherwise disposed of, or until the investment is determined to be impaired, at which time the cumulative gain or loss previously reported in equity is included in the income statement.

For investments that are actively traded in organised financial markets, fair value is determined by reference to Stock Exchange quoted market bid prices at the close of business on the balance sheet date.

(s) Investments in Associates

The Group's investment in its associates is accounted for under the equity method of accounting in the consolidated financial statements. An associate is an entity in which the Group has significant influence and is neither a subsidiary nor a joint venture.

The financial statements of associates are used by the Group to apply the equity method. The investment in the associate is carried in the consolidated balance sheet at cost plus post-acquisition changes in the Group's share of net assets of the associate, less any impairment in value. The consolidated income statement reflects the Group's share of the results of operations of the associate.

Where there has been a change recognised directly in the associate's equity, the Group recognises its share of any changes and discloses this, when applicable in the consolidated statement of changes in equity.

(t) Debt Establishment Costs

Debt establishment costs are carried forward and amortised over the lives of the financing facilities.

(u) Employee Provisions

Provision is made for employee benefits accumulated as a result of employees rendering services up to the end of the reporting period. These benefits include wages and salaries, annual leave and long service leave. Liabilities expected to be settled within twelve months of the reporting date are measured at the amount expected to be paid. Liabilities expected to be settled after twelve months are measured at the present value of the estimated future cash outflow to be made to the employee.

In determining the present value of future cash outflows, the interest rates attaching to government guaranteed securities which have terms to maturity approximating the terms of the related liability are used.

(v) Share Based Payments

The Group provides benefits to employees of the Group in the form of share-based payment transactions, whereby employees render services in exchange for shares or rights over shares ('equity-settled transactions'). Currently, the Group operates two schemes being the Woodside Employee Share Plan ('WESP') and the Executive Incentive Plan ('EIP'). The cost of these equity-settled transactions with employees is measured by reference to the fair value at the date at which they are granted. The fair value of equity compensation is recorded as an expense on a straight-line basis over the vesting period of the related plan. The cost of equity-settled transactions is recognised, together with a corresponding increase in treasury shares, over the period in which the performance conditions are fulfilled, ending on the date on which the relevant employees become fully entitled to the award ('vesting date'). Fair value is determined by using a binomial or Black Scholes option pricing model.

Notes to and forming part of the Financial Report for the half-year ended 30 June 2005

2.   SIGNIFICANT ACCOUNTING POLICIES (Continued)

Remuneration of most employees includes equity based elements which are accounted for as share based payments. The fair value of these elements is recognised over the relevant vesting period. The acquisition of shares as part of these payment structures is recognised as treasury shares until those shares fully vest.

(w) Retirement Benefits

All employees of the Group are entitled to benefits on retirement, disability or death from the Group's superannuation plan. The Group has a defined benefit component and a defined contribution component within the plan. The defined benefit component provides defined lump sum benefits based on years of service and final average salary. The defined contribution component receives fixed contributions from Group companies and the Group's legal or constructive obligation is limited to these contributions.

A liability or asset in respect of defined benefit superannuation plans is recognised in the balance sheet, and is measured at the present value of the defined benefit obligation at the reporting date less the fair value of the superannuation fund's assets at that date. Actuarial gains and losses are recognised immediately as income or expense in the income statement.

Contributions to the defined contribution fund are recognised as an expense.

(x) Financial Liabilities

Borrowings are initially recognised at fair value. Borrowings are subsequently measured at amortised cost. Any difference between the proceeds and the redemption amount is recognised in the income statement over the period of the borrowings using the effective interest rate method.

Trade and other creditors are recognised when goods and services are received, whether or not billed to the Group.

Dividends payable are recognised when payment is due by the Group.

(y) Income Tax

The income tax expense for the period is the tax payable on the current period's taxable income based on the income tax rate for each jurisdiction. This is adjusted by changes in deferred tax assets and liabilities attributable to temporary differences between the tax bases of assets and liabilities and their carrying amounts in the financial statements, and by changes to unused tax losses.

Deferred tax assets and liabilities are recognised for temporary differences at the tax rates expected to apply when the assets are recovered or liabilities are settled. The relevant tax rates are applied to the cumulative temporary differences to measure the deferred tax asset or liability. Current and deferred tax balances attributable to amounts recognised directly in equity are also recognised directly in equity.

Deferred tax assets are recognised for deductible temporary differences and unused tax losses only if it is probable that future taxable amounts will be available to utilise those temporary differences and losses.

(z) Petroleum Resource Rent Tax

Petroleum Resource Rent Tax (PRRT) is considered to be a tax based on income. Accordingly, PRRT is required to be accounted for on the same basis as described in Note 2 (y) – Income Tax.

(aa) Royalties

Royalties under existing regimes are considered to be a production based tax and are therefore accrued on a monthly basis as determined by that month's entitlement to physical production.

(ab) Goods and Services Tax

Revenues, expenses and assets are recognised net of the amount of GST except:
- where the GST incurred on a purchase of goods and services is not recoverable from the taxation authority, in which case the GST is recognised as part of the cost of acquisition of the asset or as part of the expense item as applicable; and

- receivables and payables are stated with the amount of GST included.

The net amount of GST recoverable from, or payable to, the taxation authority is included as part of receivables or payables in the balance sheet.

Cash flows are included in the Cash Flow Statement on a gross basis and the GST component of cash flows arising from investing and financing activities, which is recoverable from, or payable to, the taxation authority are classified as operating cash flows.

Commitments and contingencies are disclosed net of the amount of GST recoverable from, or payable to, the taxation authority.

(ac) Issued Capital

Ordinary share capital is recorded at value of consideration received. The costs of issuing shares are charged against the share capital. Ordinary share capital bears no special terms or conditions affecting income or capital entitlements of the shareholders.

Notes to and forming part of the Financial Report for the half-year ended 30 June 2005

3. SEGMENT INFORMATION

Business Segments
The Group has the following reportable segments.

Primary Reporting - Business Segments

	North West Shelf Business Unit		Australia Business Unit		Africa Business Unit		Group and Unallocated		Consolidated	
	2005 $000	2004 $000	2005 $000	2004 $000	2005 $000	2004 $000	2005 $000	2004 $000	2005 $000	2004 $000
Revenue										
Revenue from oil and gas operations	973,749	701,833	223,529	204,031	34,634	40,389	-	-	1,231,912	946,253
Cost of Sales										
Production costs	(54,728)	(56,659)	(29,717)	(18,313)	(3,787)	(4,181)			(88,232)	(79,153)
Petroleum resource rent tax, royalties and excise	(128,181)	(85,843)	(60,106)	3,064				-	(188,287)	(82,779)
Shipping and marketing	(36,688)	(17,047)	(2,508)	(2,395)	(74)	(70)		-	(39,270)	(19,512)
Depreciation and amortisation	(72,651)	(84,871)	(28,128)	(34,454)	(16,975)	(17,523)		-	(117,754)	(136,848)
Restoration provision	-	239						-		239
Total cost of sales	(292,248)	(244,181)	(120,459)	(52,098)	(20,836)	(21,774)		-	(433,543)	(318,053)
Gross Profit	681,501	457,652	103,070	151,933	13,798	18,615		-	798,369	628,200
Other income	112,084	262	457	484,564	351	434	21,868	70,160	134,760	555,420
Other expenses	(3,535)	(14,671)	(30,944)	(1,838)	(32,395)	(25,638)	(109,694)	(103,392)	(176,568)	(145,539)
Share of associates' net profit/(loss)	4,482	-				-	(1,132)	(3,706)	3,350	(3,706)
Profit before tax and finance costs	794,532	443,243	72,583	634,659	(18,246)	(6,589)	(88,958)	(36,938)	759,911	1,034,375
Finance costs	(6,222)	(6,568)	(2,325)	(789)	(40)	35	(11,067)	(11,189)	(19,654)	(18,511)
Segment results	788,310	436,675	70,258	633,870	(18,286)	(6,554)	(100,025)	(48,127)	740,257	1,015,864
Income tax expense									(228,023)	(267,385)
Net profit / (loss)									512,234	748,479

North West Shelf Business Unit
Exploration, evaluation, development, production and sales of LNG, Domgas, Condensate, LPG and Crude Oil from the North West Shelf Ventures.

Australia Business Unit
Exploration, evaluation, development, production and sale of crude oil, in assigned permit areas and from the Laminaria and Legendre, Exeter Mutineer projects.

Africa Business Unit
Evaluation, development and production from the Algerian Ohanet project and the Mauritanian Chinguetti, Tiof and Banda exploration, evaluation and development.

Group and Unallocated
This segment comprises the activities undertaken by all other business units and corporate costs.

Notes to and forming part of the Financial Report for the half-year ended 30 June 2005

4. PROFIT BEFORE INCOME TAX

Profit before income tax is arrived at after taking into account:

	CONSOLIDATED	
	30 June 2005 $000	30 June 2004 $000
(a) Revenues from oil and gas operations		
Liquefied Natural Gas and Domestic Gas	436,663	316,981
Condensate - NWS	294,573	217,654
Condensate - Ohanet	20,781	24,620
Oil – Laminaria	127,560	127,416
Oil – NWS	209,174	145,264
Oil – Legendre	65,453	76,615
Oil – Mutineer Exeter	30,515	-
Liquefied Petroleum Gas - NWS	33,340	21,935
Liquefied Petroleum Gas - Ohanet	13,853	15,768
Total revenues from oil and gas operations	1,231,912	946,253
(b) Cost of sales		
Cost of production		
Production costs	(85,752)	(72,276)
Royalties and excise	(148,754)	(102,308)
Third party gas	(48)	(2,582)
Insurance	(8,039)	(6,372)
Product inventory movement	5,607	2,077
	(236,986)	(181,461)
Shipping and marketing costs		
LNG shipping	(25,900)	(12,748)
Other liquids shipping	(6,490)	(1,253)
Marketing	(6,880)	(5,511)
	(39,270)	(19,512)
Oil and gas property depreciation/amortisation		
Land and buildings	(4,304)	(4,952)
Transferred exploration and evaluation	(5,643)	(12,025)
Plant and equipment	(97,851)	(109,583)
Marine vessels and carriers	(5,637)	(5,431)
Restoration assets	(4,319)	(4,857)
	(117,754)	(136,848)
Provision for restoration of operating locations	-	239
Total cost of sales	(394,010)	(337,582)
(c) Petroleum Resource Rent Tax		
Total petroleum resource rent tax	(39,533)	19,529
Gross profit	798,369	628,200

continued on next page

Notes to and forming part of the Financial Report for the half-year ended 30 June 2005

4.   PROFIT BEFORE INCOME TAX (Continued)

	CONSOLIDATED	
	30 June 2005 $000	30 June 2004 $000
(d) Other income		
Interest revenue	12,643	15,542
Dividends	241	267
Management and other fees	11,297	13,280
Exchange fluctuations		
Cash balances	5,724	14,563
Other items (including foreign exchange hedges)	-	75,382
	5,724	89,945
Increment in fair value of embedded derivatives	91,041	-
Realised gains on embedded derivatives	13,814	-
Profit on sale of exploration and evaluation assets	-	436,386
Total other income	134,760	555,420
(e) Other Expenses		
Exploration and evaluation		
Exploration	(73,423)	(87,268)
Amortisation of licence acquisition costs	(3,560)	(12,392)
Evaluation	(27,789)	-
	(104,772)	(99,660)
Corporate and business development	(51,861)	(31,067)
Depreciation recovered through other income	(7,191)	(5,743)
Financial instruments no longer specific hedges	(1,389)	(1,129)
Exchange losses	(7,240)	(3,416)
Defined benefit superannuation fund surplus	-	5,314
Net loss on sale of assets		
Oil and gas properties	-	(9,412)
Exploration and evaluation	(4,115)	-
Other plant and equipment	-	(426)
	(4,115)	(9,838)
Total other expenses	(176,568)	(145,539)
(f) Share of associates' net profit/(loss)	3,350	(3,706)
(g) Finance costs		
Interest expense	(30,365)	(28,051)
Borrowing costs (interest) capitalised	19,757	17,560
Accretion expense	(6,938)	(6,112)
Lease interest	(644)	(778)
Other debt servicing costs	(496)	(596)
Amortisation of debt establishment costs	(968)	(534)
Total finance costs	(19,654)	(18,511)
Profit before income tax	740,257	1,015,864

Notes to and forming part of the Financial Report for the half-year ended 30 June 2005

	CONSOLIDATED	
	30 June 2005 $000	31 December 2004 $000
5. ISSUED CAPITAL		
666,666,667 issued and fully paid ordinary shares	706,491	706,491

	30 June 2005 $000	30 June 2004 $000
6. DIVIDENDS		
(a) Dividends Paid during the half year		
Franked final dividend 32.0 cents (2004: 25.0 cents)	213,333	166,667
(b) Dividends in relation to reported periods not recorded as a liability		
Dividends declared after period end		
Franked interim dividend 35.0 cents (2004: 27.0 cents)	233,333	180,000

7. INDIVIDUALLY SIGNIFICANT ITEMS

Items that affect the Group Balance Sheet and Income Statement because of their nature, size or incidence include:

(a)In March 2004, the Group sold a 40% interest in the WA-271-P exploration permit and associated production licence. The effect on profit was as follows:

Proceeds on sale	-	630,085
Cost of assets sold	-	(193,461)
		436,624
Applicable income tax	-	(62,984)
Net profit after tax reported in the income statement	-	373,640

8. CHANGE IN COMPOSITION OF THE GROUP

Since the last annual reporting date, there have been no significant changes in the composition of the Group.

9. CONTINGENT ASSETS AND LIABILITIES

In April 2005 Hardman Chinguetti Production Pty Ltd ('Hardman') filed a writ in the Supreme Court of Western Australia against Woodside Mauritania Pty Ltd ('WMPL'), WEL Mauritania BV ('WEL M BV') and the other joint venture partners in deepwater blocks 4 and 5 in offshore Mauritania ('Area B') seeking a declaration as to how the joint venture partners should share the recovery of certain costs incurred by WMPL and another pursuant to their farm-in obligations ('Farm-in Costs'), from production in Area B. WMPL and WEL M BV are defending the writ. The amount of the Farm-in Costs in Area B in issue for WMPL and WEL M BV is estimated to be USD17m (before tax, not adjusted for timing of recovery from production and subject to clarification by Hardman of its position).

10. EVENTS OCCURING AFTER BALANCE SHEET DATE

Dividends
On 16 August 2005 Woodside declared an interim dividend of 35.0 cents per share fully franked (2004: 27.0 cents per share fully franked).These dividends will be payable to shareholders registered on 2 September 2005 and will be paid on 23 September 2005.

Notes to and forming part of the Financial Report for the half-year ended 30 June 2005

11. IMPACT OF ADOPTION OF AUSTRALIAN EQUIVALENTS TO INTERNATIONAL FINANCIAL REPORTING STANDARDS

Introduction

From 1 January 2005, the Group prepares its financial statements in accordance with Australian Equivalents to International Financial Reporting Standards ('AIFRS'). Due to the requirement to publish comparative information for the previous corresponding period, the effective date for transition to AIFRS is 1 January 2004.

To explain how Woodside's reported income statement and balance sheet are affected by this change, information previously published under Australian GAAP ('AGAAP') is restated under AIFRS in the tables below. These restatements include:

- Table A – Summary reconciliation of Total Equity as presented under AGAAP to that under AIFRS;

- Table B - Summary reconciliation of Profit After Tax presented under AGAAP to that under AIFRS;

- Table C - Reconciliation of Total Equity as presented under AGAAP to that under AIFRS as at 1 January 2004 (Transitional Balance Sheet);

- Table D - Reconciliation of Total Equity as presented under AGAAP to that under AIFRS as at 30 June 2004;

- Table E - Reconciliation of Total Equity as presented under AGAAP to that under AIFRS as at 1 January 2005;

- Table F - Reconciliation of Profit after Tax presented under AGAAP to that under AIFRS for the half year ended 30 June 2004; and

- Table G - Reconciliation of Profit After Tax presented under AGAAP to that under AIFRS for the year ended 31 December 2004.

Transitional Arrangements

The rules for first time adoption of AIFRS are set out in AASB 1 "First-Time Adoption of Australian Equivalents to International Reporting Standards". In general, a company is required to determine its AIFRS accounting policies and apply these retrospectively to determine its opening balance sheet at 1 January 2004 (Transitional Balance Sheet), under AIFRS. The standard allows a number of exceptions to this general principle to assist companies as they transition to reporting under AIFRS. Where Woodside has taken advantage of these exemptions they are noted below.

Summary of Impact of AIFRS

At 1 January 2005 the impact on total equity is an overall reduction of $189.2 million. There is no impact on the underlying cash flows of the Group and no impact on the Group's loan covenants.

Where AIFRS adjustments have a significant or material impact on equity, a description is included in Note 11 (a)–(l).

Notes to and forming part of the Financial Report for the half-year ended 30 June 2005

11. IMPACT OF ADOPTION OF AUSTRALIAN EQUIVALENTS TO INTERNATIONAL FINANCIAL REPORTING STANDARDS (Continued)

Table A – Summary reconciliation of Total Equity as presented under AGAAP to that under AIFRS;

	Explanatory Transition Notes	1 January 2004 $000	30 June 2004 $000	1 January 2005 $000
		CONSOLIDATED		
Total equity under AGAAP		2,433,531	2,991,497	3,170,495
Change in accounting policy*		32,279	6,601	40,322
AIFRS adjustments to equity				
Petroleum resource rent tax (PRRT)	(a)	(246,649)	(202,881)	(195,737)
Employee share plan	(b)	(138,986)	(148,534)	(136,930)
Leases	(c)	5,824	4,954	4,084
Functional and presentational currency	(d)	(109,631)	(66,827)	(110,311)
Borrowing costs	(e)	(67,158)	(48,016)	(28,028)
Provision for restoration	(f)	11,724	10,960	15,745
Investments	(g)	-	-	51,408
Defined benefit superannuation fund	(h)	7,849	13,898	23,419
Embedded derivatives	(i)	-	-	159,521
Financial instruments	(j)	-	-	29,542
Hedge of net investments	(k)	-	-	60,790
Other adjustments		4,274	1,420	(6,547)
Income tax	(l)	38,639	24,409	(96,482)
Total equity under AIFRS		1,971,696	2,587,481	2,981,291

*   The change in accounting policy relates to the Group's change to the 'entitlement' method of accounting for oil and gas revenues. Refer to note 2(b) for details.

Notes to and forming part of the Financial Report for the half-year ended 30 June 2005

11. IMPACT OF ADOPTION OF AUSTRALIAN EQUIVALENTS TO INTERNATIONAL FINANCIAL REPORTING STANDARDS (Continued)

Table B - Summary reconciliation of Profit After Tax presented under AGAAP to that under AIFRS;

	Explanatory Transition Notes	CONSOLIDATED	
		6 months ended 30 June 2004 $000	Year ended 31 December 2004 $000
Total profit after tax under AGAAP		724,633	1,083,631
Change in accounting policy*		(25,679)	8,043
AIFRS adjustments to profit after tax			
Petroleum resource rent tax (PRRT)	(a)	43,768	50,912
Employee share plan	(b)	(1,905)	(4,602)
Leases	(c)	(870)	(1,740)
Functional and presentational currency	(d)	1,188	6,498
Borrowing costs	(e)	19,142	39,130
Provision for restoration	(f)	(764)	4,020
Defined benefit superannuation fund	(h)	6,049	15,570
Other adjustments		2,854	(10,821)
Income tax	(l)	(19,937)	(45,348)
Total profit after tax under AIFRS		748,479	1,145,293

*   The change in accounting policy relates to the Group's change to the 'entitlement' method of accounting for oil and gas revenues. Refer to note 2(b) for details.

Notes to and forming part of the Financial Report for the half-year ended 30 June 2005

11. IMPACT OF ADOPTION OF AUSTRALIAN EQUIVALENTS TO INTERNATIONAL FINANCIAL REPORTING STANDARDS (Continued)

Table C - Reconciliation of Total Equity as presented under AGAAP to that under AIFRS as at 1 January 2004 (Transitional Balance Sheet)

	Explanatory Transition Notes	AGAAP 31 December 2003 $000	Change in accounting policy & reclassifications $000	Effect of transition to AIFRS $000	AIFRS 1 January 2004 $000
CURRENT ASSETS					
Cash and cash equivalents		177,601	(55,121)[2]	211	122,691
Trade and other receivables	(a)	260,878	92,943[1,2]	(15,011)	338,810
Inventories		14,007	(5,543)[1]	1,520	9,984
Other financial assets		73,123	-	(2,290)	70,833
Other assets	(a),(h)	11,342	-	21,999	33,341
TOTAL CURRENT ASSETS		536,951	32,279	6,429	575,659
NON CURRENT ASSETS					
Other receivables	(b)	307,252	-	(128,537)	178,715
Inventories		18,264	-	(466)	17,798
Investments in associates		9,096	-	953	10,049
Other financial assets		106,034	-	(21,052)	84,982
Exploration and evaluation	(d)	653,518	-	(24,932)	628,586
Oil and gas properties	(c),(d),(e),(f)	2,985,154	-	(2,941)	2,982,213
Other plant and equipment		137,910	-	3,284	141,194
Deferred tax assets		649	-	-	649
Other assets	(b)	27,471	-	(17,604)	9,867
TOTAL NON CURRENT ASSETS		4,245,348	-	(191,295)	4,054,053
TOTAL ASSETS		4,782,299	32,279	(184,866)	4,629,712
CURRENT LIABILITIES					
Trade and other payables	(a)	335,783	-	(18,635)	317,148
Interest bearing loans and borrowings	(c)	-	-	3,397	3,397
Income tax payable	(a)	100,992	-	16,349	117,341
Provisions		55,064	-	-	55,064
Other liabilities		86,747	-	(140)	86,607
TOTAL CURRENT LIABILITIES		578,586	-	971	579,557
NON CURRENT LIABILITIES					
Interest bearing loans and borrowings	(c)	1,068,376	-	9,326	1,077,702
Deferred tax liabilities	(a) - (l)	455,090	-	208,235	663,325
Provisions	(f)	156,552	-	94,505	251,057
Other liabilities		90,164	-	(3,789)	86,375
TOTAL NON CURRENT LIABILITIES		1,770,182	-	308,277	2,078,459
TOTAL LIABILITIES		2,348,768	-	309,248	2,658,016
NET ASSETS		2,433,531	32,279	(494,114)	1,971,696
EQUITY					
Issued capital		706,491	-	-	706,491
Treasury shares	(b)				(137,507)
Other reserves	(d)	-	-	-	-
Retained profits		1,727,040	32,279[l]	(356,607)	1,402,712
TOTAL EQUITY		2,433,531	32,279	(494,114)	1,971,696

(1) The change in accounting policy relates to the Group's change to the 'entitlement' method of accounting for oil and gas revenues. Refer to note 2(b) for details.

(2) Relates to a reclassification of balances between cash and other receivables (refer note 2(o)).

Notes to and forming part of the Financial Report for the half-year ended 30 June 2005

11. IMPACT OF ADOPTION OF AUSTRALIAN EQUIVALENTS TO INTERNATIONAL FINANCIAL REPORTING STANDARDS (Continued)

Table D - Reconciliation of Total Equity as presented under AGAAP to that under AIFRS as at 30 June 2004

	Explanatory Transition Notes	AGAAP 30 June 2004 $000	Change in accounting policy & reclassifications $000	Effect of transition to AIFRS $000	AIFRS 30 June 2004 $000
CURRENT ASSETS					
Cash and cash equivalents		761,442	49,604 [2]	(39)	811,007
Trade and other receivables	(a)	559,415	(27,406) [1,2]	(47,754)	484,255
Inventories		20,014	(1,751) [1]	1,977	20,240
Other financial assets		50,035	-	(4,252)	45,783
Other assets	(a),(h)	19,530	-	65,662	85,192
TOTAL CURRENT ASSETS		1,410,436	20,447	15,594	1,446,477
NON CURRENT ASSETS					
Other receivables	(b)	138,769	-	(138,769)	-
Inventories		11,756	-	272	12,028
Investments in associates		2,309	-	721	3,030
Other financial assets		120,550	-	(22,914)	97,636
Exploration and evaluation	(d)	346,584	-	(71)	346,513
Oil and gas properties	(c),(d),(e),(f)	3,277,965	-	(568)	3,277,397
Other plant and equipment		119,008	-	-	119,008
Deferred tax assets		179	-	-	179
Other assets	(b)	95,704	-	(16,344)	79,360
TOTAL NON CURRENT ASSETS		4,112,824	-	(177,673)	3,935,151
TOTAL ASSETS		5,523,260	20,447	(162,079)	5,381,628
CURRENT LIABILITIES					
Trade and other payables	(a)	297,664	13,846 [1]	(29,192)	282,318
Interest bearing loans and borrowings	(c)	-	-	3,397	3,397
Income tax payable	(a)	128,518	-	27,534	156,052
Provisions		56,714	-	260	56,974
Other liabilities		134,320	-	(1,793)	132,527
TOTAL CURRENT LIABILITIES		617,216	13,846	206	631,268
NON CURRENT LIABILITIES					
Interest bearing loans and borrowings	(c)	1,158,748	-	8,191	1,166,939
Deferred tax liabilities	(a) - (l)	492,512	-	178,643	671,155
Provisions	(f)	164,380	-	65,586	229,966
Other liabilities		98,907	-	(4,088)	94,819
TOTAL NON CURRENT LIABILITIES		1,914,547	-	248,332	2,162,879
TOTAL LIABILITIES		2,531,763	13,846	248,538	2,794,147
NET ASSETS		2,991,497	6,601	(410,617)	2,587,481
EQUITY					
Issued capital		706,491	-	-	706,491
Treasury shares	(b)	-	-	(145,150)	(145,150)
Other reserves	(d)	-	-	41,616	41,616
Retained profits		2,285,006	6,601 [1]	(307,083)	1,984,524
TOTAL EQUITY		2,991,497	6,601	(410,617)	2,587,481

(1) The change in accounting policy relates to the Group's change to the 'entitlement' method of accounting for oil and gas revenues. Refer to note 2(b) for details.

(2) Relates to a reclassification of balances between cash and other receivables (refer note 2(o)).

Notes to and forming part of the Financial Report for the half-year ended 30 June 2005

11. IMPACT OF ADOPTION OF AUSTRALIAN EQUIVALENTS TO INTERNATIONAL FINANCIAL REPORTING STANDARDS (Continued)

Table E - Reconciliation of Total Equity as presented under AGAAP to that under AIFRS as at 1 January 2005

	Explanatory Transition Notes	AGAAP 31 December 2004 $000	Change in accounting policy & reclassifications $000	Effect of transition to AIFRS $000	AIFRS 31 December 2004 $000	Effect of transition to AIFRS 1 January 2005 'step change'[3] $000	AIFRS 1 January 2005 $000
CURRENT ASSETS							
Cash and cash equivalents		732,163	66,779[2]	(1,802)	797,140	-	797,140
Trade and other receivables	(a)	420,074	(19,849)[1,2]	(24,442)	375,783	-	375,783
Inventories		31,071	(3,217)[1]	904	28,758		28,758
Other financial assets	(j)	43,428	-	(3,394)	40,034	(1,665)	38,369
Other assets	(a),(h)	16,322	-	45,658	61,980	(525)	61,455
TOTAL CURRENT ASSETS		1,243,058	43,713	16,924	1,303,695	(2,190)	1,301,505
NON CURRENT ASSETS							
Other receivables	(b)	127,814	-	(127,814)	-		
Inventories		11,489	-		11,489	-	11,489
Investments in associates		1,619	-	721	2,340	-	2,340
Other financial assets	(g),(i)	120,311	-	(27,657)	92,654	210,929	303,583
Exploration and evaluation	(d)	389,266	-	(10,444)	378,822	-	378,822
Oil and gas properties	(c),(d),(e),(f)	3,517,400	-	3,007	3,520,407	-	3,520,407
Other plant and equipment		109,180	-	1,778	110,958	-	110,958
Deferred tax assets		25,717	-	-	25,717	60	25,777
Other assets	(b)	23,681	-	(15,162)	8,519	-	8,519
TOTAL NON CURRENT ASSETS		4,326,477	-	(175,571)	4,150,906	210,989	4,361,895
TOTAL ASSETS		5,569,535	43,713	(158,647)	5,454,601	208,799	5,663,400
CURRENT LIABILITIES							
Trade and other payables	(a)	328,772	3,391	(16,113)	316,050	-	316,050
Interest bearing loans and borrowings	(c)			3,397	3,397	-	3,397
Income tax payable	(a)	51,024	-	13,459	64,483	-	64,483
Provisions		52,679	-	(117)	52,562	-	52,562
Other liabilities	(j)	46,294	-	(811)	45,483	(36,945)	8,538
TOTAL CURRENT LIABILITIES		478,769	3,391	(185)	481,975	(36,945)	445,030
NON CURRENT LIABILITIES							
Interest bearing loans and borrowings	(c),(j)	1,027,749	-	7,023	1,034,772	21,937	1,056,709
Deferred tax liabilities	(a) - (l)	527,047	-	202,669	729,716	89,835	819,551
Provisions	(f)	189,119	-	81,118	270,237	-	270,237
Other liabilities	(k)	176,356	-	(8,259)	168,097	(77,515)	90,582
TOTAL NON CURRENT LIABILITIES		1,920,271	-	282,551	2,202,822	34,257	2,237,079
TOTAL LIABILITIES		2,399,040	3,391	282,366	2,684,797	(2,688)	2,682,109
NET ASSETS		3,170,495	40,322	(441,013)	2,769,804	211,487	2,981,291
EQUITY							
Issued capital		706,491	-	-	706,491	-	706,491
Treasury shares	(b)		-	(130,849)	(130,849)	-	(130,849)
Other reserves	(d),(g),(k)		-	(7,178)	(7,178)	34,968	27,790
Retained profits		2,464,004	40,322[1]	(302,986)	2,201,340	176,519	2,377,859
TOTAL EQUITY		3,170,495	40,322	(441,013)	2,769,804	211,487	2,981,291

(1) The change in accounting policy relates to the Group's change to the 'entitlement' method of accounting for oil and gas revenues. Refer to note 2(b) for details.

(2) Relates to a reclassification of balances between cash and other receivables Refer note 2(o).

(3) Relates to first time adoption of AASB 139 'Financial Instruments: Recognition and Measurement' from 1 January 2005.

Notes to and forming part of the Financial Report for the half-year ended 30 June 2005

11. IMPACT OF ADOPTION OF AUSTRALIAN EQUIVALENTS TO INTERNATIONAL FINANCIAL REPORTING STANDARDS (Continued)

Table F - Reconciliation of Profit after Tax presented under AGAAP to that under AIFRS for the half-year ended 30 June 2004

	Explanatory Transition Notes	AGAAP Half-Year ended 30 June 2004 $000	Change in accounting policy* $000	Effect of transition to AIFRS $000	AIFRS Half-Year ended 30 June 2004 $000
Revenue from oil and gas operations	(c)	994,446	(29,470)	(18,723)	946,253
Cost of sales	(a),(b),(c),(d),(e),(f)	(368,885)	3,791	27,512	(337,582)
Petroleum resource rent tax		(24,239)	-	43,768	19,529
Gross profit		601,322	(25,679)	52,557	628,200
Other income		768,154	-	(212,734)	555,420
Other expenses	(d),(h)	(359,148)	-	213,609	(145,539)
Share of associates' net profits / (losses)		(3,475)	-	(231)	(3,706)
Profit from continuing operations before tax and finance costs		1,006,853	(25,679)	53,201	1,034,375
Finance costs	(c),(e),(f)	(29,066)	-	10,555	(18,511)
Profit before income tax		977,787	(25,679)	63,756	1,015,864
Income tax expense	(a),(c),(e),(f),(h),(l)	(253,154)	-	(14,231)	(267,385)
Net profit attributable to members of the parent		724,633	(25,679)	49,525	748,479

*   The change in accounting policy relates to the Group's change to the 'entitlement' method of accounting for oil and gas revenues. Refer to note 2(b) for details.

Table G - Reconciliation of Profit after Tax presented under AGAAP to that under AIFRS for the year ended 31 December 2004

	Explanatory Transition Notes	AGAAP Year ended 31 December 2004 $000	Change in accounting policy* $000	Effect of transition to AIFRS $000	AIFRS Year ended 31 December 2004 $000
Revenue from oil and gas operations	(c)	2,158,641	5,718	(39,517)	2,124,842
Cost of sales	(a),(b),(c),(d),(e),(f)	(811,706)	2,325	57,335	(752,046)
Petroleum resource rent tax		(47,500)	-	50,912	3,412
Gross profit		1,299,435	8,043	68,730	1,376,208
Other income		844,670	-	-	844,670
Other expenses	(d),(h)	(595,295)	-	2,250	(593,045)
Share of associates' net profits / (losses)		(4,684)	-	(231)	(4,915)
Profit from continuing operations before tax and finance costs		1,544,126	8,043	70,749	1,622,918
Finance costs	(c),(e),(f)	(61,915)	-	28,217	(33,698)
Profit before income tax		1,482,211	8,043	98,966	1,589,220
Income tax expense	(a),(c),(e),(f),(h),(l)	(398,580)	-	(45,347)	(443,927)
Net profit attributable to members of the parent		1,083,631	8,043	53,619	1,145,293

*   The change in accounting policy relates to the Group's change to the 'entitlement' method of accounting for oil and gas revenues. Refer to note 2(b) for details.

Notes to and forming part of the Financial Report for the half-year ended 30 June 2005

11. IMPACT OF ADOPTION OF AUSTRALIAN EQUIVALENTS TO INTERNATIONAL FINANCIAL REPORTING STANDARDS (Continued)

(a) Petroleum Resource Rent Tax (PRRT)

AASB 112 'Income Taxes' extends the scope of tax effect accounting to encompass all taxes on income, including Petroleum Resource Rent Tax (PRRT). Under AGAAP, the Group accounted for PRRT on an accruals basis. Under AIFRS a deferred PRRT liability or asset is recognised for the differences that have accumulated between the PRRT tax base of assets and their accounting base. These differences arise from the earlier deductibility of expenditure for PRRT when compared with expense outcomes under the Group's accounting policies for exploration and evaluation and oil and gas property assets. These taxable temporary differences will reverse as each project generates PRRT assessable income. The impact at the end of each transitional period results in an increase in deferred tax liabilities and a reduction in retained earnings.

(b) Employee Share Plan

From 1 January 2005, AASB 2 'Share-based Payments' requires the Group's Employee Share Plan to be treated as share-based compensation. Under this approach the principal amount of the interest-free, limited-recourse loans to acquire shares, are reclassified from receivables to a separate class of shareholders' equity (Treasury Shares). Dividends paid on shares issued under the share plan, to the extent they are retained to repay the loans, are offset against that separate class of shareholders' equity.

Share-based compensation is measured as the value of the option inherent within shares issued under the Share Plan, granted to the employee and is expensed over a 5 year period.

Woodside has elected to adopt the AASB 1 transitional arrangements which allow companies not to fully retrospectively apply AASB 2 'Share-based Payments'. Under the terms of the transitional arrangements, the cost of the shares issued under the share plan after 7 November 2002, which had not vested at the relevant reporting date, has been recognised in the income statement.

(c) Leases

Under AIFRS, service contracts which include the provision of equipment must be analysed to determine whether they contain leases. Any leases identified are to be accounted for in accordance with AASB 117 'Leases'. Review of the Group's contracts has identified one case which is assessed as containing a finance lease required to be reported on the balance sheet. This results in the fair value of leased assets being capitalised into oil and gas properties and the remaining balance of the lease liability being reported as interest bearing loans and borrowings. The impact on retained earnings in the transitional period reflects the replacement of lease payments expense with interest and depreciation charges.

Under certain LNG transportation agreements, the Group leases transportation assets under a back-to-back operating lease arrangement. Under AIFRS, the group is now required to net these revenues and expenditures. The impact on retained earnings is nil.

(d) Functional and Presentation Currency

As required by AASB 121 'The Effects of Changes in Foreign Exchange Rates', the Group has determined that the functional currency of its major Australian operating subsidiaries is Australian dollars and the majority of the Group's foreign subsidiaries is US dollars reflecting the economic environment in which they operate. The presentation currency of the Group continues to be Australian dollars. Assets and liabilities of subsidiaries with a foreign currency as their functional currency are translated into Australian dollars at each period's closing rate and any exchange movements are recorded through the foreign currency translation reserve (FCTR). The impact at the end of each transitional period includes the reduction of oil and gas properties and exploration and evaluation expenditure in relation to foreign operations where assets are now translated at closing rates compared to historical rates under AGAAP.

The Group has elected to apply the exemption in AASB 1 under which the cumulative

translation for all foreign operations represented in the FCTR is transferred to retained earnings at 1 January 2004.

(e) Borrowing Costs

The Group has elected to capitalise borrowing costs on qualifying assets ie. assets which take a significant period of time (greater than twelve months) to construct. The Group have chosen to specifically exclude assets with a value of less than $50 million and any exploration and evaluation amounts as qualifying assets.

Borrowing costs includes interest, however, foreign exchange differences on borrowings are now expensed. Consequently, the carrying value of oil and gas properties has been reduced by net foreign exchange losses that had previously been capitalised on qualifying assets.

(f) Provision for Restoration

Under AIFRS, at the commencement of a facility's operation, the present value of restoration obligations is recognised as a non-current liability and the cost of future restoration is capitalised as part of the relevant project. The capitalised cost is depreciated over the life of the project and the provision is accreted periodically as the discounting of the liability unwinds. The unwinding of the discount is recorded as a finance cost. The impact at the end of each transitional period is to reduce restoration provisions reflecting the difference between the previously recorded future value under AGAAP and the present value recorded under AIFRS.

(g) Investments

Under previous AGAAP, investments in equity securities were held at cost. Applicable from 1 January 2005, AASB 139 'Financial Instruments: Recognition and Measurement', requires investments in equity securities that have readily determinable fair values to be classified as either held for trading or available for sale and carried at fair value. Unrealised gains or losses on investments held for trading are reported in the income statement and for

Notes to and forming part of the Financial Report for the half-year ended 30 June 2005

investments classified as available for sale are reported in shareholders' equity. The Group's investments are classified as available for sale reflecting the intention to hold these investments rather than trade in them. Movements in fair value are dependent upon movements in the share price of investments. The impact as at 1 January 2005 was to increase other financial assets and investment revaluation reserve for the difference between the fair value of investments and historical cost.

(h) Defined Benefit Superannuation Fund

The Group is the sponsor of a superannuation plan with a defined benefit fund and a defined contribution fund. Under previous AGAAP, cumulative actuarial gains and losses on the defined benefit section were not recognised on the balance sheet. At the date of transition, an asset is recognised in the provision for employee benefits and is measured as the difference between the present value of the employees' accrued benefits at that date and the net market value of the superannuation fund's assets at that date. The impact at the end of each transitional period was to increase other assets for the surplus superannuation fund assets and to record the related gain in the income statement.

(i) Embedded Derivatives

The Group has taken the exemption available under AASB 1 to apply AASB 139 'Financial Instruments: Recognition and Measurement' from 1 January 2005. AASB 139 requires the identification, recognition and measurement of derivatives embedded within contracts entered into by a company. Embedded derivatives that introduce risks and characteristics not closely related to the risks and characteristics of the Group's contracts are separately recorded at fair value with movements reported in the income statement. In reviewing existing contracts to determine the extent of any embedded derivatives, two gas sales contracts have been identified as containing embedded derivatives. The fair valuation of these contracts will reflect the long-remaining term of these contracts and the estimated future changes in benchmark commodity prices and

the AUD/USD exchange rate. As a consequence there will be volatility in future reported earnings. The impact as at 1 January 2005 was to increase other financial assets by the fair value of the embedded derivatives and to increase retained earnings.

(j) Financial Instruments

The Group has taken the exemption available under AASB 1 to apply AASB 132 'Financial Instruments: Disclosure and Presentation' and AASB 139 'Financial Instruments: Recognition and Measurement' from 1 January 2005. The standards require all financial instruments to be initially recognised at fair value. Subsequently, certain financial instruments, including derivatives, must be remeasured at fair value with movements in the fair value of derivatives taken to the income statement. Where cash flow hedge accounting requirements are met, the effective portion of the hedge is taken to equity. Gains or losses that are recognised in equity are transferred to the income statement in the same year in which the hedged firm commitment affects the net profit and loss, for example when the future sale actually occurs. Where hedges are ineffective for accounting purposes, reported results may be more volatile. The impact as at 1 January 2005 reflects the released profit of the mark-to-market position of hedges identified as being ineffective.

(k) Hedge of Net Investments

Under AIFRS, US dollar borrowings have been assessed as not meeting the requirements for hedge accounting of revenue, due to changed designation and effectiveness requirements. Under previous AGAAP, US dollar borrowings had been designated as a hedge of US dollar sales revenues. Therefore, as at 1 January, 2005 the amount deferred as an exchange gain or loss on the US dollar debt has been taken to retained earnings. Subsequent to 1 January, 2005, US dollar borrowings have been designated as hedges of net investments in the Group's subsidiaries with a US dollar functional currency. Exchange differences that arise on the borrowings designated as a hedge are

recorded through the foreign currency translation reserve. The exchange differences arising from US dollar borrowings not designated as a hedge have been recorded in the income statement. Financial impacts are dependent upon movements in the Australian to US dollar exchange rate, and the level of US dollar exposure.

(l) Income Tax

Under previous AGAAP, income tax expense was calculated by reference to the accounting profit after allowing for permanent differences. Under AIFRS, any difference between the carrying value of an asset or liability and its tax base is recognised as a temporary difference. Prior to transition to AIFRS, permanent differences were not included in calculating deferred tax balances.

DIRECTORS' DECLARATION

Directors' Declaration

In accordance with a resolution of the directors of Woodside Petroleum Ltd., I state that:

In the opinion of the directors:

a) the financial statements and notes of the consolidated entity for and as at the half-year ended 30 June 2005 are in accordance in accordance with the Corporations Act 2001 ("Corporations Act") including:

   i.   section 304 (compliance with accounting standards) of the Corporations Act; and

   ii. section 305 (true and fair) of the Corporations Act; and

b) there are reasonable grounds to believe that the company will be able to pay its debts as and when they become due and payable.

On behalf of the Board

Charles Goode AC.
Chairman

Don Voelte
Chief Executive Officer

Perth, 17 August 2005

INDEPENDENT REVIEW REPORT TO MEMBERS OF WOODSIDE PETROLEUM LTD.

Scope

The financial report and directors' responsibility

The financial report comprises the condensed balance sheet, condensed income statement, condensed statement of changes in equity and condensed statement of cash flows, accompanying notes to the financial statements, and the directors' declaration for Woodside Petroleum Ltd. (the company) and the consolidated entity, for the half-year ended 30 June 2005.

The consolidated entity comprises both the company and the entities it controlled during the half-year.

The directors of the company are responsible for preparing a financial report that gives a true and fair view of the financial position and performance of the consolidated entity, and that complies with Accounting Standard AASB 134 "Interim Financial Reporting", in accordance with the *Corporations Act 2001*. This includes responsibility for the maintenance of adequate accounting records and internal controls that are designed to prevent and detect fraud and error, and for the accounting policies and accounting estimates inherent in the financial report.

Review approach

We conducted an independent review of the financial report in order to make a statement about it to the members of the company, and in order for the company to lodge the financial report with the Australian Stock Exchange and the Australian Securities and Investments Commission.

Our review was conducted in accordance with Australian Auditing Standards applicable to review engagements, in order to state whether, on the basis of the procedures described, anything has come to our attention that would indicate that the financial report is not presented fairly in accordance with the *Corporations Act 2001*, Accounting Standard AASB 134 "Interim Financial Reporting" and other mandatory financial reporting requirements in Australia, so as to present a view which is consistent with our understanding of the consolidated entity's financial position, and of its performance as represented by the results of its operations and cash flows.

A review is limited primarily to inquiries of company personnel and analytical procedures applied to the financial data. These procedures do not provide all the evidence that would be required in an audit, thus the level of assurance is less than given in an audit. We have not performed an audit and, accordingly, we do not express an audit opinion.

Independence

We are independent of the company, and have met the independence requirements of Australian professional ethical pronouncements and the *Corporations Act 2001*. We have given to the directors of the company a written Auditor's Independence Declaration, a copy of which is included in the Directors' Report.

Statement

Based on our review, which is not an audit, we have not become aware of any matter that makes us believe that the financial report of the consolidated entity, comprising Woodside Petroleum Ltd. and the entities it controlled during the half-year is not in accordance with:

(a) the *Corporations Act 2001*, including:

(i) giving a true and fair view of the financial position of the consolidated entity at 30 June 2005 and of its performance for the half-year ended on that date; and

(ii) complying with Accounting Standard AASB 134 "Interim Financial Reporting" and the *Corporations Regulations 2001*; and

(b) other mandatory financial reporting requirements in Australia.

Jeff Dowling
Partner
Ernst & Young

Perth 17 August 2005

Registered Office

Woodside Petroleum Ltd.
240 St. George's Terrace
PERTH   WA   6000
   Ph: +61 8 9348 4000
   Fax: +61 8 9348 4142
Requests for information on the Company can be directed to the Company Secretary.
Woodside Website: http:\\www.woodside.com.au

Share Registry

It is important that shareholders notify the Share Registry immediately in writing, if there is any change in their registered address:

The Share Registry is Computershare Investor Services Pty Limited, located at:

Level, 2 Reserve Bank Building
45 St George's Terrace
Perth Western Australia 6000
Telephone: 1300 557 010
Facsimile: +61 8 9323 2033
Email: perth.services@computershare.com.au
Website: www.computershare.com

APPENDIX 2
PRESENT AND FUTURE VALUE FACTOR TABLES

Table 1: Future value of $1 = (1 + R)^n$

n	0.25%	0.5%	0.66%	0.75%	1.0%	1.5%	1.75%	2.0%	2.5%	3.0%	3.5%	n
1	1.002 50	1.005 00	1.006 67	1.007 50	1.010 00	1.015 00	1.017 50	1.020 00	1.025 00	1.030 00	1.035 00	1
2	1.005 01	1.010 03	1.013 38	1.015 06	1.020 10	1.030 23	1.035 31	1.040 40	1.050 63	1.060 90	1.071 23	2
3	1.007 52	1.015 08	1.020 13	1.022 67	1.030 30	1.045 68	1.053 42	1.061 21	1.076 89	1.092 73	1.108 72	3
4	1.010 04	1.020 15	1.026 93	1.030 34	1.040 60	1.061 36	1.071 86	1.082 43	1.103 81	1.125 51	1.147 52	4
5	1.012 56	1.025 25	1.033 78	1.038 07	1.051 01	1.077 28	1.090 62	1.104 08	1.131 41	1.159 27	1.187 69	5
6	1.015 09	1.030 38	1.040 67	1.045 85	1.061 52	1.093 44	1.109 70	1.126 16	1.159 69	1.194 05	1.229 26	6
7	1.017 63	1.035 53	1.047 61	1.053 70	1.072 14	1.109 84	1.129 12	1.148 69	1.188 69	1.229 87	1.272 28	7
8	1.020 18	1.040 71	1.054 59	1.061 60	1.082 86	1.126 49	1.148 88	1.171 66	1.218 40	1.266 77	1.316 81	8
9	1.022 73	1.045 91	1.061 63	1.069 56	1.093 69	1.143 39	1.168 99	1.195 09	1.248 86	1.304 77	1.362 90	9
10	1.025 28	1.051 14	1.068 70	1.077 58	1.104 62	1.160 54	1.189 44	1.218 99	1.280 08	1.343 92	1.410 60	10
11	1.027 85	1.056 40	1.075 83	1.085 66	1.115 67	1.177 95	1.210 26	1.243 37	1.312 09	1.384 23	1.459 97	11
12	1.030 42	1.061 68	1.083 00	1.093 81	1.126 83	1.195 62	1.231 44	1.268 24	1.344 89	1.425 76	1.511 07	12
13	1.032 99	1.066 99	1.090 22	1.102 01	1.138 09	1.213 55	1.252 99	1.293 61	1.378 51	1.468 53	1.563 96	13
14	1.035 57	1.072 32	1.097 49	1.110 28	1.149 47	1.231 76	1.274 92	1.319 48	1.412 97	1.512 59	1.618 69	14
15	1.038 16	1.077 68	1.104 80	1.118 60	1.160 97	1.250 23	1.297 23	1.345 87	1.448 30	1.557 97	1.675 35	15
16	1.040 76	1.083 07	1.112 17	1.126 99	1.172 58	1.268 99	1.319 93	1.372 79	1.484 51	1.604 71	1.733 99	16
17	1.043 36	1.088 49	1.119 58	1.135 44	1.184 30	1.288 02	1.343 03	1.400 24	1.521 62	1.652 85	1.794 68	17
18	1.045 97	1.093 93	1.127 05	1.143 96	1.196 15	1.307 34	1.366 53	1.428 25	1.559 66	1.702 43	1.857 49	18
19	1.048 58	1.099 40	1.134 56	1.152 54	1.208 11	1.326 95	1.390 45	1.456 81	1.598 65	1.753 51	1.922 50	19
20	1.051 21	1.104 90	1.142 13	1.161 18	1.220 19	1.346 86	1.414 78	1.485 95	1.638 62	1.806 11	1.989 79	20
21	1.053 83	1.110 42	1.149 74	1.169 89	1.232 39	1.367 06	1.434 54	1.515 67	1.679 58	1.860 29	2.059 43	21
22	1.056 47	1.115 97	1.157 40	1.178 67	1.244 72	1.387 56	1.464 73	1.545 98	1.721 57	1.916 10	2.131 51	22
23	1.059 11	1.121 55	1.165 12	1.187 51	1.257 16	1.408 38	1.490 36	1.576 90	1.764 61	1.973 59	2.206 11	23
24	1.061 76	1.127 16	1.172 89	1.196 41	1.269 73	1.429 50	1.516 44	1.608 44	1.808 73	2.032 79	2.283 33	24
25	1.064 41	1.132 80	1.180 71	1.205 39	1.282 43	1.450 95	1.542 98	1.640 61	1.853 94	2.093 78	2.363 24	25
30	1.077 78	1.161 40	1.220 59	1.251 27	1.347 85	1.563 08	1.682 80	1.811 36	2.097 29	2.427 26	2.806 79	30
35	1.091 32	1.190 73	1.261 82	1.298 90	1.416 60	1.683 88	1.835 29	1.999 89	2.373 21	2.813 86	3.333 59	35
40	1.105 03	1.220 79	1.304 45	1.348 35	1.488 86	1.814 02	2.001 60	2.208 04	2.685 06	3.262 04	3.959 26	40
45	1.118 92	1.251 62	1.348 52	1.399 68	1.564 81	1.954 21	2.182 98	2.437 85	3.037 90	3.781 60	4.702 36	45
50	1.132 97	1.283 23	1.394 07	1.452 96	1.644 63	2.105 24	2.380 79	2.691 59	3.437 11	4.383 91	5.584 93	50
60	1.161 62	1.348 85	1.489 85	1.565 68	1.816 70	2.432 20	2.831 82	3.281 03	4.399 79	5.891 60	7.878 09	60

Table 1: (Continued)

n	4.0%	4.5%	5.0%	6.0%	7.0%	8.0%	10.0%	12.0%	15.0%	20.0%	n
1	1.040 00	1.045 00	1.050 00	1.060 00	1.070 00	1.080 00	1.100 00	1.120 0	1.150	1.200	1
2	1.081 60	1.092 03	1.102 50	1.123 60	1.144 90	1.166 40	1.210 00	1.254 4	1.322	1.440	2
3	1.124 86	1.141 17	1.157 63	1.191 01	1.225 04	1.259 71	1.331 00	1.404 9	1.521	1.728	3
4	1.169 86	1.192 52	1.215 51	1.262 47	1.310 79	1.360 48	1.464 10	1.573 5	1.749	2.074	4
5	1.216 65	1.246 18	1.276 28	1.338 22	1.402 55	1.469 32	1.610 51	1.762 0	2.011	2.488	5
6	1.265 32	1.302 26	1.340 10	1.418 51	1.500 73	1.586 87	1.771 56	1.973 8	2.313	2.938	6
7	1.315 93	1.360 86	1.407 10	1.503 63	1.605 78	1.713 82	1.948 72	2.210 7	2.660	3.583	7
8	1.368 57	1.422 10	1.477 46	1.593 84	1.718 18	1.850 93	2.143 59	2.476 0	3.059	4.300	8
9	1.423 31	1.486 10	1.551 33	1.689 47	1.838 45	1.999 00	2.357 95	2.773 1	3.518	5.160	9
10	1.480 24	1.552 97	1.628 89	1.790 84	1.967 15	2.158 92	2.593 74	3.105 8	4.046	6.192	10
11	1.539 45	1.622 85	1.710 34	1.898 29	2.104 85	2.331 63	2.853 12	3.478 5	4.652	7.430	11
12	1.601 03	1.695 88	1.795 86	2.012 19	2.252 19	2.518 17	3.138 43	3.896 0	5.350	8.916	12
13	1.665 07	1.772 20	1.885 65	2.132 92	2.409 84	2.719 62	3.452 27	4.363 5	6.153	10.699	13
14	1.731 68	1.851 94	1.979 93	2.260 90	2.578 53	2.937 19	3.797 50	4.887 1	7.076	12.839	14
15	1.800 94	1.935 28	2.078 93	2.396 55	2.759 03	3.172 16	4.177 25	5.473 6	8.137	15.407	15
16	1.872 98	2.022 37	2.182 87	2.540 35	2.952 16	3.425 94	4.594 97	6.130 3	9.358	18.488	16
17	1.947 90	2.113 38	2.292 02	2.692 77	3.158 81	3.700 01	5.054 47	6.866 1	10.761	22.186	17
18	2.025 82	2.208 48	2.406 62	2.854 33	3.379 93	3.996 01	5.559 92	7.690 0	12.375	26.623	18
19	2.106 85	2.307 86	2.526 95	3.025 59	3.616 52	4.315 70	6.115 91	8.612 8	14.232	31.945	19
20	2.191 12	2.411 71	2.653 30	3.207 13	3.869 68	4.660 95	6.727 50	9.646 3	16.367	38.338	20
21	2.278 77	2.520 24	2.785 96	3.399 56	4.140 56	5.033 83	7.400 25	10.803 8	18.821	46.005	21
22	2.369 92	2.633 65	2.925 26	3.603 53	4.430 40	5.436 54	8.140 27	12.100 3	21.645	55.206	22
23	2.464 72	2.752 17	3.071 52	3.819 74	4.740 52	5.871 46	8.954 30	13.552 3	24.891	66.247	23
24	2.563 30	2.876 01	3.225 10	4.048 93	5.072 36	6.341 18	9.849 73	15.178 6	28.625	79.497	24
25	2.665 84	3.005 43	3.386 35	4.291 87	5.427 43	6.848 47	10.834 71	17.000 1	32.919	95.396	25
30	3.243 40	3.745 32	4.321 94	5.743 49	7.612 25	10.062 65	17.449 40	29.960 0	66.212	237.376	30
35	3.946 09	4.667 35	5.516 02	7.686 08	10.676 58	14.785 34	28.102 44	52.800 0	133.175	590.668	35
40	4.801 02	5.816 36	7.039 99	10.285 71	14.974 45	21.724 52	45.259 26	93.051 0	267.862	1 469.771	40
45	5.841 18	7.248 25	8.985 01	13.764 61	21.002 45	31.920 44	72.890 48	163.987 6	538.767	3 657.258	45
50	7.106 68	9.032 64	11.477 40	18.420 15	29.457 02	46.901 61	117.390 85	289.002 1	1 083.652	9 100.427	50
60	10.519 63	14.027 41	18.679 19	32.987 69	57.946 43	101.257 06	304.481 64	897.596 9	4 383.999	56 347.514	60

Table 2: Present value of $1 $= \frac{1}{(1 + R)^n}$

n	0.25%	0.50%	0.66%	0.75%	1.0%	1.5%	2.0%	2.5%	3.0%	3.5%	n
1	0.997 51	0.995 02	0.993 38	0.992 56	0.990 09	0.985 22	0.980 39	0.975 60	0.970 87	0.966 18	1
2	0.995 02	0.990 07	0.986 80	0.985 17	0.980 29	0.970 66	0.961 16	0.951 81	0.942 59	0.933 51	2
3	0.992 54	0.985 15	0.980 26	0.977 83	0.970 59	0.956 31	0.942 32	0.928 59	0.915 14	0.901 94	3
4	0.990 06	0.980 25	0.973 77	0.970 55	0.960 98	0.942 18	0.923 84	0.905 95	0.888 48	0.871 44	4
5	0.987 59	0.975 37	0.967 32	0.963 33	0.951 46	0.928 26	0.905 73	0.883 85	0.862 60	0.841 97	5
6	0.985 13	0.970 52	0.960 92	0.956 16	0.942 04	0.914 54	0.887 97	0.862 29	0.837 48	0.813 50	6
7	0.982 67	0.965 69	0.954 55	0.940 94	0.932 71	0.901 02	0.870 56	0.841 26	0.813 09	0.785 99	7
8	0.980 22	0.960 89	0.948 23	0.941 98	0.923 48	0.887 71	0.853 49	0.820 74	0.789 40	0.759 41	8
9	0.977 78	0.956 10	0.941 95	0.934 96	0.914 33	0.874 59	0.836 75	0.800 72	0.766 41	0.733 73	9
10	0.975 34	0.951 35	0.935 71	0.928 00	0.905 28	0.861 66	0.820 34	0.781 19	0.744 09	0.708 91	10
11	0.972 91	0.946 61	0.929 52	0.921 09	0.896 32	0.848 93	0.804 26	0.762 14	0.722 42	0.684 94	11
12	0.970 48	0.941 91	0.923 36	0.914 24	0.887 44	0.836 38	0.788 49	0.743 55	0.701 37	0.661 78	12
13	0.968 06	0.973 22	0.917 25	0.907 43	0.878 66	0.824 02	0.773 03	0.725 42	0.680 95	0.639 40	13
14	0.965 65	0.932 56	0.911 17	0.900 68	0.869 96	0.811 84	0.757 87	0.707 72	0.661 11	0.617 78	14
15	0.963 24	0.927 92	0.905 14	0.893 97	0.861 34	0.799 85	0.743 01	0.690 46	0.641 86	0.596 89	15
16	0.960 84	0.923 30	0.899 14	0.887 32	0.852 82	0.788 03	0.728 44	0.673 62	0.623 16	0.576 70	16
17	0.958 44	0.918 71	0.893 19	0.880 71	0.844 37	0.776 38	0.714 16	0.657 19	0.605 01	0.557 20	17
18	0.956 05	0.914 14	0.887 27	0.874 16	0.836 01	0.764 91	0.700 15	0.641 16	0.587 39	0.538 36	18
19	0.953 67	0.909 59	0.881 40	0.867 65	0.827 73	0.753 60	0.686 43	0.625 52	0.570 28	0.520 15	19
20	0.951 29	0.905 06	0.875 56	0.861 19	0.819 54	0.742 47	0.672 97	0.610 27	0.553 67	0.502 56	20
21	0.948 92	0.900 56	0.869 76	0.854 78	0.811 43	0.731 49	0.659 77	0.595 38	0.537 54	0.485 57	21
22	0.946 55	0.896 08	0.864 00	0.848 42	0.803 39	0.720 68	0.646 83	0.580 86	0.521 89	0.469 15	22
23	0.944 19	0.891 62	0.858 28	0.842 10	0.795 44	0.710 03	0.634 15	0.566 69	0.506 69	0.453 28	23
24	0.941 84	0.887 19	0.852 60	0.835 83	0.787 56	0.699 54	0.621 72	0.552 87	0.491 93	0.437 95	24
25	0.939 49	0.882 77	0.846 95	0.829 61	0.779 76	0.689 20	0.609 53	0.539 39	0.477 60	0.423 14	25
30	0.927 83	0.861 03	0.819 27	0.799 19	0.741 92	0.639 76	0.552 07	0.476 74	0.411 98	0.356 27	30
35	0.916 32	0.839 82	0.792 50	0.769 88	0.705 91	0.593 86	0.500 02	0.421 37	0.355 38	0.299 97	35
40	0.904 95	0.819 14	0.766 61	0.741 65	0.671 65	0.551 26	0.452 89	0.372 43	0.306 55	0.252 57	40
45	0.893 72	0.798 96	0.741 56	0.714 45	0.639 05	0.511 71	0.410 19	0.329 17	0.264 43	0.212 65	45
50	0.882 63	0.779 29	0.717 32	0.688 25	0.608 03	0.475 00	0.371 52	0.290 94	0.228 10	0.179 05	50
60	0.860 87	0.741 37	0.671 21	0.638 70	0.550 45	0.409 30	0.304 78	0.227 28	0.169 73	0.126 93	60

Table 2 (Continued)

n	4.0%	4.5%	5.0%	6.0%	7.0%	8.0%	10.0%	12.0%	15.0%	20.0%	n
1	0.961 53	0.956 93	0.952 38	0.943 39	0.934 57	0.925 92	0.909 09	0.892 86	0.869 57	0.833 33	1
2	0.924 55	0.915 72	0.907 02	0.889 99	0.873 43	0.857 33	0.826 45	0.797 19	0.756 14	0.694 44	2
3	0.888 99	0.876 29	0.863 83	0.839 61	0.816 29	0.793 83	0.751 31	0.711 78	0.657 52	0.578 70	3
4	0.854 80	0.838 56	0.822 70	0.792 09	0.762 89	0.735 02	0.683 01	0.635 52	0.571 75	0.482 25	4
5	0.821 92	0.802 45	0.783 52	0.747 25	0.712 98	0.680 58	0.620 92	0.567 43	0.497 18	0.401 88	5
6	0.790 31	0.767 89	0.746 21	0.704 96	0.666 34	0.630 16	0.564 47	0.506 63	0.432 33	0.334 90	6
7	0.759 91	0.734 82	0.710 68	0.665 05	0.622 74	0.583 49	0.513 16	0.452 35	0.375 94	0.279 08	7
8	0.730 69	0.703 18	0.676 83	0.627 41	0.582 00	0.540 26	0.466 51	0.403 88	0.326 90	0.232 57	8
9	0.702 58	0.672 90	0.644 60	0.591 89	0.543 93	0.500 24	0.424 10	0.360 61	0.284 26	0.193 81	9
10	0.675 56	0.643 92	0.613 90	0.558 39	0.508 34	0.463 19	0.385 54	0.321 97	0.247 18	0.161 51	10
11	0.649 58	0.616 19	0.584 67	0.526 78	0.475 09	0.428 88	0.350 49	0.287 48	0.214 94	0.134 59	11
12	0.624 59	0.589 66	0.556 83	0.496 96	0.444 01	0.397 11	0.318 63	0.256 67	0.186 91	0.112 16	12
13	0.600 57	0.564 27	0.530 32	0.468 83	0.414 96	0.367 69	0.289 66	0.229 17	0.162 53	0.093 46	13
14	0.577 47	0.539 97	0.505 06	0.442 30	0.387 81	0.340 46	0.263 33	0.204 62	0.141 33	0.077 89	14
15	0.555 26	0.516 72	0.481 01	0.417 26	0.362 44	0.315 24	0.239 39	0.182 70	0.122 89	0.064 91	15
16	0.533 90	0.494 46	0.458 11	0.393 64	0.338 73	0.291 89	0.217 63	0.163 12	0.106 86	0.054 09	16
17	0.513 37	0.473 17	0.436 29	0.371 36	0.316 57	0.270 26	0.197 84	0.145 64	0.092 93	0.045 07	17
18	0.493 62	0.452 80	0.415 52	0.350 34	0.295 86	0.250 24	0.179 86	0.130 04	0.080 80	0.037 56	18
19	0.474 64	0.433 30	0.395 73	0.330 51	0.276 50	0.231 71	0.163 51	0.116 11	0.070 26	0.031 30	19
20	0.456 38	0.414 64	0.376 88	0.311 80	0.258 41	0.214 54	0.148 64	0.103 67	0.061 10	0.026 08	20
21	0.438 83	0.396 78	0.358 94	0.294 15	0.241 51	0.198 65	0.135 13	0.092 56	0.053 13	0.021 74	21
22	0.421 95	0.379 70	0.341 84	0.277 50	0.225 71	0.183 94	0.122 85	0.082 64	0.046 20	0.018 11	22
23	0.405 72	0.363 35	0.325 57	0.261 79	0.210 94	0.170 31	0.111 68	0.073 79	0.040 17	0.015 09	23
24	0.390 12	0.347 70	0.310 06	0.246 97	0.197 14	0.157 69	0.101 53	0.065 88	0.034 93	0.012 58	24
25	0.375 11	0.332 73	0.295 30	0.232 99	0.184 24	0.146 01	0.092 30	0.058 82	0.030 38	0.010 48	25
30	0.308 31	0.267 00	0.231 37	0.174 11	0.131 36	0.099 37	0.057 31	0.033 38	0.015 10	0.004 21	30
35	0.253 41	0.214 25	0.181 29	0.130 10	0.093 66	0.067 63	0.035 58	0.018 94	0.007 51	0.001 69	35
40	0.208 28	0.171 92	0.142 04	0.097 22	0.066 78	0.046 03	0.022 09	0.010 74	0.003 73	0.000 68	40
45	0.171 19	0.137 96	0.111 29	0.072 65	0.047 61	0.031 32	0.013 72	0.006 10	0.001 86	0.000 27	45
50	0.140 71	0.110 70	0.087 20	0.054 28	0.033 94	0.021 32	0.008 52	0.003 46	0.000 92	0.000 11	50
60	0.095 06	0.071 29	0.053 54	0.030 31	0.017 26	0.009 88	0.003 28	0.001 11	0.000 23	0.000 02	60

Table 3: Future value of $1 per period $= \dfrac{(1 + R)^n - 1}{R}$

n	0.25%	0.5%	0.66%	0.75%	1.0%	1.5%	2.0%	2.5%	3.0%	3.5%	n
1	1.000 00	1.000 00	1.000 00	1.000 00	1.000 00	1.000 00	1.000 00	1.000 0	1.000 0	1.000 0	1
2	2.002 50	2.005 00	2.006 67	2.007 50	2.010 00	2.015 00	2.020 00	2.025 0	2.030 0	2.035 0	2
3	3.007 51	3.015 03	3.020 04	3.022 56	3.030 10	3.045 23	3.060 40	3.075 6	3.090 9	3.106 2	3
4	4.015 03	4.030 10	4.040 18	4.045 23	4.060 40	4.090 90	4.121 61	4.152 5	4.183 6	4.214 9	4
5	5.025 06	5.050 25	5.067 11	5.075 56	5.101 01	5.152 27	5.204 04	5.256 3	5.309 1	5.362 5	5
6	6.037 63	6.075 50	6.100 89	6.113 63	6.152 02	6.229 55	6.308 12	6.387 7	6.468 4	6.550 2	6
7	7.052 72	7.105 88	7.141 57	7.159 48	7.213 54	7.322 99	7.434 28	7.547 4	7.662 5	7.779 4	7
8	8.070 35	8.141 41	8.189 18	8.213 18	8.285 67	8.432 84	8.582 97	8.736 1	8.892 3	9.051 7	8
9	9.090 53	9.182 12	9.243 77	9.274 78	9.368 53	9.559 33	9.754 63	9.954 5	10.159 1	10.368 5	9
10	10.113 25	10.228 03	10.305 40	10.344 34	10.462 21	10.702 72	10.949 72	11.203 4	11.463 9	11.731 4	10
11	11.138 54	11.279 17	11.374 10	11.421 92	11.566 83	11.863 26	12.168 72	12.483 5	12.807 8	13.142 0	11
12	12.166 38	12.335 56	12.449 93	12.507 59	12.682 50	13.041 21	13.412 09	13.795 6	14.192 0	14.602 0	12
13	13.196 80	13.397 24	13.532 93	13.601 39	13.809 33	14.236 83	14.680 33	15.140 4	15.617 8	16.113 0	13
14	14.229 79	14.464 23	14.623 15	14.703 40	14.947 42	15.450 38	15.973 94	16.519 0	17.086 3	17.677 0	14
15	15.265 37	15.536 55	15.720 63	15.813 68	16.096 90	16.682 14	17.293 42	17.931 9	18.598 9	19.295 7	15
16	16.303 53	16.614 23	16.825 54	16.932 28	17.257 86	17.932 37	18.639 29	19.380 2	20.156 9	20.971 0	16
17	17.344 29	17.697 30	17.937 61	18.059 27	18.430 44	19.201 36	20.012 07	20.864 7	21.761 6	22.705 0	17
18	18.387 65	18.785 79	19.057 19	19.194 72	19.614 75	20.489 38	21.412 31	22.386 3	23.414 4	24.499 7	18
19	19.433 62	19.879 72	20.184 24	20.338 68	20.810 89	21.796 72	22.840 56	23.946 0	25.116 9	26.357 2	19
20	20.482 20	20.979 12	21.318 80	21.491 22	22.019 00	23.123 67	24.297 37	25.544 7	26.870 4	28.279 7	20
21	21.533 41	22.084 01	22.460 93	22.652 40	23.239 19	24.470 52	25.783 32	27.183 3	28.676 5	30.269 5	21
22	22.587 24	23.194 43	23.610 66	23.822 30	24.471 59	25.837 58	27.298 98	28.862 9	30.536 8	32.328 9	22
23	23.643 71	24.310 40	24.768 07	25.000 96	25.716 30	27.225 14	28.844 96	30.584 4	32.452 9	34.460 4	23
24	24.702 82	25.431 96	25.933 19	26.188 47	26.973 46	28.633 52	30.421 86	32.349 0	34.426 5	36.666 5	24
25	25.764 57	26.559 12	27.106 08	27.384 88	28.243 20	30.063 02	32.030 30	34.157 8	36.459 3	38.949 9	25
30	31.113 31	32.280 02	33.088 85	33.502 90	34.784 89	37.538 68	40.568 08	43.902 7	47.575 4	51.622 7	30
35	36.529 24	38.145 38	39.273 73	39.853 81	41.660 28	45.592 09	49.994 48	54.928 2	60.462 1	66.674 0	35
40	42.013 20	44.158 85	45.667 54	46.446 48	48.886 37	54.267 89	60.401 98	67.402 6	75.401 3	84.550 3	40
45	47.566 06	50.324 16	52.277 34	53.290 11	56.481 07	63.614 20	71.892 71	81.516 1	92.719 9	105.781 7	45
50	53.188 68	56.645 16	59.110 42	60.394 26	64.463 18	73.682 83	84.579 40	97.484 3	112.796 9	130.997 9	50
60	64.646 71	69.770 03	73.476 86	76.424 14	81.669 67	96.214 65	114.051 54	135.991 6	163.053 4	196.516 9	60

Table 3 (Continued)

n	4.0%	4.5%	5.0%	6.0%	7.0%	8.0%	10.0%	12.0%	15.0%	20.0%	n
1	1.000 0	1.000 0	1.000 0	1.000 0	1.000 0	1.000 0	1.000 0	1.000	1.000	1.00	1
2	2.040 0	2.045 0	2.050 0	2.060 0	2.070 0	2.080 0	2.100 0	2.120	2.150	2.20	2
3	3.121 6	3.137 0	3.152 5	3.183 6	3.214 9	3.246 4	3.310 0	3.374	3.472	3.64	3
4	4.246 5	4.278 2	4.310 1	4.374 6	4.439 9	4.506 1	4.641 0	4.779	4.993	5.36	4
5	5.416 3	5.470 7	5.525 6	5.637 1	5.750 7	5.866 6	6.105 1	6.353	6.742	7.44	5
6	6.633 0	6.716 9	6.801 9	6.975 3	7.153 3	7.335 9	7.715 6	8.115	8.754	9.93	6
7	7.898 3	8.019 2	8.142 0	8.393 8	8.654 0	8.922 8	9.487 2	10.089	11.067	12.92	7
8	9.214 2	9.380 0	9.549 1	9.897 5	10.259 8	10.636 6	11.435 9	12.300	13.727	16.50	8
9	10.582 8	10.802 1	11.026 6	11.491 3	11.978 0	12.487 6	13.579 5	14.776	16.786	20.80	9
10	12.006 1	12.288 2	12.577 9	13.180 8	13.816 4	14.486 6	15.937 4	17.549	20.304	25.96	10
11	13.486 4	13.841 2	14.206 8	14.971 6	15.783 6	16.645 5	18.531 2	20.655	24.349	32.15	11
12	15.025 8	15.464 0	15.917 1	16.869 9	17.888 5	18.977 1	21.384 3	24.133	29.002	39.58	12
13	16.626 8	17.159 9	17.713 0	18.882 1	20.140 6	21.495 3	24.522 7	28.029	34.352	48.50	13
14	18.291 9	18.932 1	19.598 6	21.015 1	22.550 5	24.214 9	27.975 0	32.393	40.505	59.20	14
15	20.023 6	20.784 1	21.578 6	23.276 0	25.129 0	27.152 1	31.772 5	37.280	47.580	72.04	15
16	21.824 5	22.719 3	23.657 5	25.672 5	27.888 1	30.324 3	35.949 7	42.753	55.717	87.44	16
17	23.697 5	24.741 7	25.840 4	28.212 9	30.840 2	33.750 2	40.544 7	48.884	65.075	105.93	17
18	25.645 4	26.855 1	28.132 4	30.905 7	33.999 0	37.450 2	45.599 2	55.750	75.836	128.12	18
19	27.671 2	29.063 6	30.539 0	33.760 0	37.379 0	41.446 3	51.159 1	63.440	88.212	154.74	19
20	29.778 1	31.371 4	33.066 0	36.785 6	40.995 5	45.762 0	57.275 0	72.052	102.443	186.69	20
21	31.969 2	33.783 1	35.719 3	39.992 7	44.865 2	50.422 9	64.002 5	81.699	118.810	225.03	21
22	34.248 0	36.303 4	38.505 2	43.392 3	49.005 7	55.456 8	71.402 8	92.502	137.631	271.03	22
23	36.617 9	38.937 0	41.430 5	46.995 8	53.436 1	60.893 3	79.543 0	104.603	159.276	326.24	23
24	39.082 6	41.689 2	44.502 0	50.815 6	58.176 7	66.764 8	88.497 3	118.155	184.167	392.48	24
25	41.645 9	44.565 2	47.727 1	54.864 5	63.249 0	73.105 9	98.347 1	133.334	212.793	471.98	25
30	56.084 9	61.570 6	66.438 8	79.058 2	74.460 8	113.283 2	164.494 0	241.532	434.744	1 181.88	30
35	73.652 2	81.496 6	90.320 3	111.434 8	138.236 9	172.316 8	271.024 4	431.663	881.168	2 948.34	35
40	95.025 5	107.030 3	120.799 8	154.762 0	199.635 1	259.056 5	442.592 6	767.088	1 779.090	7 343.95	40
45	121.029 4	138.850 0	159.700 2	212.743 5	285.749 3	386.505 6	718.904 8	1 358.224	3 585.128	18 281.31	45
50	152.667 1	178.503 0	209.348 0	290.335 9	406.528 9	573.770 2	1 163.908 5	2 400.008	7 217.716	45 497.19	50
60	237.990 7	289.498 0	353.583 7	533.128 1	813.520 4	1 253.213 3	3 034.816 4	7 471.641	29 219.992	281 732.57	60

Table 4: Present value of $1 per period $= \dfrac{1 - \frac{1}{(1+R)^n}}{R}$

n	0.25%	0.5%	0.66%	0.75%	1.0%	1.5%	2.0%	2.5%	3.0%	3.5%	n
1	0.997 51	0.995 02	0.993 38	0.992 56	0.990 10	0.985 22	0.980 39	0.975 6	0.970 9	0.966 2	1
2	1.992 52	1.985 10	1.980 18	1.977 72	1.970 40	1.955 88	1.941 56	1.927 4	1.913 5	1.899 7	2
3	2.985 06	2.970 25	2.960 44	2.955 56	2.940 99	2.912 20	2.883 88	2.856 0	2.828 6	2.801 6	3
4	3.975 12	3.950 50	3.934 21	3.926 11	3.901 97	3.854 38	3.807 73	3.762 0	3.717 1	3.673 1	4
5	4.962 72	4.925 87	4.901 54	4.889 44	4.853 43	4.782 65	4.713 46	4.645 8	4.579 7	4.515 1	5
6	5.947 85	5.896 38	5.862 45	5.845 60	5.795 48	5.697 19	5.601 43	5.508 1	5.417 2	5.328 6	6
7	6.930 52	6.862 07	6.817 01	6.794 64	6.728 19	6.598 21	6.471 99	6.349 4	6.230 3	6.114 5	7
8	7.910 74	7.822 96	7.765 24	7.736 61	7.651 68	7.485 93	7.325 48	7.170 1	7.019 7	6.874 0	8
9	8.888 52	8.779 06	8.707 19	8.671 58	8.566 02	8.360 52	8.162 24	7.970 9	7.786 1	7.607 7	9
10	9.863 86	9.730 41	9.642 90	9.599 58	9.471 30	9.222 19	8.982 54	8.752 1	8.530 2	8.316 6	10
11	10.836 77	10.677 03	10.572 42	10.520 67	10.367 63	10.071 12	9.786 85	9.514 2	9.252 6	9.001 6	11
12	11.807 25	11.618 93	11.495 78	11.434 91	11.255 08	10.907 51	10.575 34	10.257 8	9.954 0	9.663 3	12
13	12.775 32	12.556 15	12.413 03	12.342 35	12.133 74	11.731 53	11.348 37	10.983 2	10.635 0	10.302 7	13
14	13.740 96	13.488 71	13.324 20	13.243 02	13.003 70	12.543 38	12.106 25	11.690 9	11.296 1	10.920 5	14
15	14.704 20	14.416 62	14.229 34	14.136 99	13.865 05	13.343 23	12.849 26	12.381 4	11.937 9	11.517 4	15
16	15.665 04	15.339 93	15.128 48	15.024 31	14.717 87	14.131 26	13.577 71	13.055 0	12.561 1	12.094 1	16
17	16.623 48	16.258 63	16.021 67	15.905 02	15.562 25	14.907 65	14.291 87	13.712 2	13.166 1	12.651 3	17
18	17.579 53	17.172 77	16.908 94	16.779 18	16.398 27	15.672 56	14.992 03	14.353 4	13.753 5	13.189 7	18
19	18.533 20	18.082 36	17.790 34	17.646 83	17.226 01	16.426 17	15.678 46	14.978 9	14.323 8	13.709 8	19
20	19.484 49	18.987 42	18.665 90	18.508 02	18.045 55	17.168 64	16.351 43	15.589 2	14.877 5	14.212 4	20
21	20.433 40	19.887 98	19.535 66	19.362 80	18.856 98	17.900 14	17.011 21	16.184 5	15.415 0	14.698 0	21
22	21.379 95	20.784 06	20.399 67	20.211 21	19.660 38	18.620 83	17.658 05	16.765 4	15.936 9	15.167 1	22
23	22.324 14	21.675 68	21.257 95	21.053 31	20.455 82	19.330 86	18.292 20	17.332 1	16.443 6	15.620 4	23
24	23.265 98	22.562 87	22.110 54	21.889 15	21.243 39	20.030 41	18.913 93	17.885 0	16.935 5	16.058 4	24
25	24.205 47	23.445 64	22.957 49	22.718 76	22.023 16	20.719 61	19.523 46	18.424 4	17.413 1	16.481 5	25
30	28.867 87	27.794 05	27.108 85	26.775 08	25.807 71	24.015 84	22.396 46	20.930 3	19.600 4	18.392 0	30
35	33.472 43	32.035 37	31.124 55	30.682 66	29.408 58	27.075 60	24.998 62	23.145 2	21.487 2	20.000 7	35
40	38.019 86	36.172 23	35.009 03	34.446 94	32.834 69	29.915 85	27.355 48	25.102 8	23.114 8	21.355 1	40
45	42.510 88	40.207 20	38.766 58	38.073 18	36.094 51	32.552 34	29.490 16	28.833 0	24.518 7	22.495 5	45
50	46.946 17	44.142 79	42.401 34	41.566 45	39.196 12	34.999 69	31.423 61	28.362 3	25.729 8	23.455 6	50
60	55.652 36	51.725 56	49.318 43	48.173 37	44.955 04	39.380 27	34.760 89	30.908 7	27.675 6	24.944 7	60

Table 4 (Continued)

n	4.0%	4.5%	5.0%	6.0%	7.0%	8.0%	10.0%	12.0%	15.0%	20.0%	n
1	0.9615	0.9569	0.9524	0.9433	0.9345	0.9259	0.9091	0.8929	0.8695	0.8333	1
2	1.8861	1.8727	1.8594	1.8333	1.8080	1.7832	1.7355	1.6901	1.6257	1.5278	2
3	2.7751	2.7490	2.7232	2.6730	2.6243	2.5770	2.4868	2.4018	2.2832	2.1065	3
4	3.6299	3.5875	3.5460	3.4651	3.3872	3.3121	3.1698	3.0373	2.8549	2.5887	4
5	4.4518	4.3900	4.3295	4.2123	4.1001	3.9927	3.7907	3.6048	3.3521	2.9906	5
6	5.2421	5.1579	5.0757	4.9173	4.7665	4.6228	4.3552	4.1114	3.7844	3.3255	6
7	6.0021	5.8927	5.7864	5.5823	5.3892	5.2063	4.8684	4.5638	4.1604	3.6046	7
8	6.7327	6.5959	6.4632	6.2097	5.9712	5.7466	5.3349	4.9676	4.4873	3.8372	8
9	7.4353	7.2688	7.1078	6.8016	6.5152	6.2468	5.7590	5.3282	4.7715	4.0310	9
10	8.1109	7.9127	7.7217	7.3600	7.0235	6.7100	6.1445	5.6502	5.0187	4.1925	10
11	8.7605	8.5289	8.3064	7.8868	7.4986	7.1389	6.4950	5.9377	5.2337	4.3271	11
12	9.3851	9.1186	8.8633	8.3838	7.9426	7.5360	6.8136	6.1944	5.4206	4.4392	12
13	9.9856	9.6829	9.3936	8.8526	8.3576	7.9037	7.1033	6.4235	5.5831	4.5327	13
14	10.5631	10.2228	9.8986	9.2949	8.7454	8.2442	7.3666	6.6282	5.7244	4.6106	14
15	11.1184	10.7395	10.3797	9.7122	9.1079	8.5594	7.6060	6.8109	5.8473	4.6755	15
16	11.6523	11.2340	10.8378	10.1058	9.4466	8.8513	7.8237	6.9740	5.9542	4.7296	16
17	12.1657	11.7072	11.2741	10.4772	9.7632	9.1216	8.0215	7.1196	6.0471	4.7746	17
18	12.6593	12.1600	11.6896	10.8276	10.0590	9.3718	8.2014	7.2497	6.1279	4.8122	18
19	13.1339	12.5933	12.0853	11.1581	10.3355	9.6035	8.3649	7.3658	6.1982	4.8435	19
20	13.5903	13.0079	12.4622	11.4699	10.5940	9.8181	8.5135	7.4694	6.2593	4.8696	20
21	14.0292	13.4047	12.8212	11.7640	10.8355	10.0168	8.6486	7.5620	6.3124	4.8913	21
22	14.4511	13.7844	13.1630	12.0415	11.0612	10.2007	8.7715	7.6446	6.3586	4.9094	22
23	14.8568	14.1478	13.4886	12.3033	11.2721	10.3710	8.8832	7.7184	6.3988	4.9245	23
24	15.2470	14.4955	13.7986	12.5503	11.4693	10.5287	8.9847	7.7843	6.4337	4.9371	24
25	15.6221	14.8282	14.0939	12.7833	11.6535	10.6747	9.0770	7.8431	6.4641	4.9476	25
30	17.2920	16.2889	15.3725	13.7648	12.4090	11.2577	9.4269	8.0552	6.5659	4.9789	30
35	18.6646	17.4610	16.3742	14.4982	12.9476	11.6545	9.6441	8.1755	6.6166	4.9915	35
40	19.7928	18.4016	17.1591	15.0462	13.3317	11.9246	9.7790	8.2438	6.6417	4.9966	40
45	20.7200	19.1563	17.7741	15.4558	13.6055	12.1084	9.8628	8.2825	6.6542	4.9986	45
50	21.4822	19.7620	18.2559	15.7618	13.8007	12.2334	9.9148	8.3045	6.6605	4.9995	50
60	22.6235	20.6380	18.9293	16.1614	14.0392	12.3766	9.9672	8.3240	6.6651	4.9999	60

GLOSSARY

AASB (Australian Accounting Standards Board) (Chapter 2) The body responsible for setting accounting standards in Australia.

AASB Accounting Standard (Chapter 2) The standards issued by the Australian Accounting Standards Board.

ABC (activity-based costing) (Chapter 17) A costing method which tries to capture the change in technology by apportioning overheads into product costs on a more realistic basis, taking account of the activity and transactions that drive the cost. The focus in ABC is on managing activities instead of costs.

absentee owners (Chapter 14) The shareholders in large businesses.

absorption costing (full costing) (Chapter 17) The method whereby the cost of inventories is determined so as to include the appropriate share of both variable and fixed costs, the latter being allocated on the basis of normal operating capacity. (AASB 102)

absorption of overheads (Chapter 17) The term used for the process of sharing out indirect costs to products.

absorption rate (Chapter 17) An absorption rate is normally used to charge out overheads to units of production on an equitable basis. It is determined by dividing the total overheads of a production cost centre by the level of activity.

account (Chapter 2) A device used to provide a record of increases and decreases in each item that appears in a firm's financial statements.

accounting (Chapter 1) The process of identifying, measuring and communicating economic information to permit informed judgement and decisions by users of the information.

accounting profit (Chapter 12) The amount of profit as determined by the application of Accounting Standards and Concepts.

accounting rate of return (Chapter 16) A method of project evaluation which involves dividing average net profit by either average book value of investment or total initial investment.

accounting system (Chapter 1) A collection of source documents, records, procedures, management policies and data-processing methods used to convert economic data into useful information.

accounting theory monograph (Chapter 2) A series prepared by various authors which explores conceptual matters of relevance to the development of accounting standards.

accrual basis (of accounting) (Chapter 2) The method of accounting whereby income and expenses are identified with a specific period of time, such as a month or year, and are recorded as incurred, along with acquired assets, without regard to the date of receipt or payment of cash.

accruals (Chapter 8) Amounts owing at a point in time, the amounts of which are not known with any certainty.

aged debtors analysis (Chapter 8) An analysis that is prepared by management and examines debts in terms of how old they are in order to reach a decision on the probability of receipt of payment.

allocated (Chapter 17) In the context of product costing, a cost that can be directly traced to a cost centre.

amortise (Chapters 9) To systematically write off a portion or all of an asset over a period of years. This normally applies to intangible assets.

annuity (Chapter 16) A stream of equal cash flows received or paid over a number of periods.

apportioning (Chapter 17) In the context of product costing, this term describes the sharing out of overhead costs that cannot be directly traced to a cost centre.

assets (Chapters 2, 4, 9) Resources controlled by the entity as a result of past events and from which future economic benefits are expected to flow to the entity. (AASB *Framework*, para. 49)

audit (Chapter 2) The examination of a company's general-purpose financial reports by an independent external observer (the auditor) to ensure that they present a 'true and fair' representation of the company's financial status. The auditor's findings are presented in the auditor's report.

audit committee (Chapter 13)　A subcommittee of the board of directors and is part of the corporate governance of a company. Its roles depend on the company, but, in general, its role is to ensure that the financial statements have been reliably prepared and verified.

auditor independence (Chapter 2)　The auditor must be independent of the client for whom the audit is conducted so that he/she is able to express a truly objective opinion about the financial statements.

auditor's report (Chapter 2)　A report required by the *Corporations Act 2001*, prepared by an auditor and included with a company's financial statements, stating whether the company's financial statements comply with the requirements of the *Corporations Act*, whether they provide a true and fair view of the state of affairs of the company, and whether they are in accordance with applicable accounting standards.

average cost (Chapter 7)　A method of inventory valuation where an average cost is calculated by dividing the total costs of goods available for sale by the number of units available for sale. Two variations of the average cost method are moving average and weighted average.

avoidable cost (Chapter 19)　A cost that will not have to be paid if a company does not proceed with a decision; for example, delivery of a special order. Such a cost is relevant and should be included in the decision.

bad debts (Chapter 8)　Credit sales of a business for which the cash is not collected due to the debtor(s) not paying. Two ways in which this non-payment can be accounted for are by the direct write-off method and the provision for doubtful debts.

balance sheet (Chapters 1, 4)　A statement that shows all the resources controlled by an entity and all the obligations due by the entity at one point in time.

balanced scorecard (Chapter 21)　'A set of measures that give top managers a fast but comprehensive view of the business. The balanced scorecard includes financial measures that tell the results of actions already taken. And it complements the financial measures with operational measures on customer satisfaction, internal processes, and the organisation's innovation and improvement activities – operational measures that are the drivers of future financial performance.' (Kaplan, 1992)

bank overdraft (Chapters 4, 10)　A common source of short-term funds whereby a business negotiates with a bank to establish a limit to which the business can write cheques that will be accepted even though there is no money in the account. Normally, an overdraft can be terminated by the bank at short notice.

board of directors (Chapter 13)　The board is an important corporate governance mechanism. Its role is to represent shareholders and create value for shareholders.

break-even chart (Chapter 18)　A method used in CVP analysis which illustrates the relationship between cost, volume and profits by plotting these variables on a graph. The break-even point and areas of profit and loss can clearly and quickly be identified, enabling management to establish the effects of changing one of the variables.

break-even position (Chapter 18)　The sales volume at which income and total costs are equal, with no net profit or loss.

budget (Chapters 16, 20)　A short- and long-term plan of action for the future operating activities of a business, expressed in monetary terms.

budget period (Chapter 20)　The timeframe of the budget – normally one year. The reason for choosing this period relates to the periodic reporting requirements for published accounts regulated by law.

budget process (Chapter 20)　The sequence of operations that are necessary to produce a budget for a particular organisation. The operations depend upon the type of organisation and its perceived requirements for planning and control.

budgetary control (Chapter 20)　This describes the use of budgets as a control mechanism. For example, actual performance can be compared with the budget to identify any deviations so that management can take corrective action.

business entity principle (Chapter 4)　This states that transactions, assets and liabilities that relate to the entity are accounted for separately. It applies to all types of entities, irrespective of the fact that the entity may not be recognised as a separate legal or taxable entity.

business risk (Chapter 14) The risk resulting from factors in the uncertain commercial environment affecting the operations of a business. Also referred to as commercial risk, business risk is a function of many variables and differs from industry to industry.

capital budgeting (Chapter 16) Analysis of proposed investments in assets with a long life.

carrying value (Chapter 9) *See* written-down value.

cash (Chapter 12) Cash on hand and cash equivalents.

cash equivalents (Chapter 12) Highly liquid investments that are readily convertible to cash on hand which a company or an economic entity uses in its cash management function on a day-to-day basis; and borrowings which are integral to the cash management function and which are not subject to a term facility.

cash flow statement (Chapter 12) A financial statement showing the cash inflows and cash outflows for an accounting period.

cash flows (Chapter 12) Cash movements resulting from transactions with parties external to the company (or economic entity).

cash on hand (Chapter 12) Notes and coins held, and deposits held at call with a bank or financial institution.

common-size statements (Chapter 14) A financial statement in which the amount reported of each item in the statement is stated as a percentage of some specific amount also reported in the statement.

company (Chapter 11) An entity incorporated, or taken to be incorporated, under the *Corporations Act* (*Corporations Act*, section 9). It is recognised as a separate legal entity.

compound interest (Chapter 16) Interest based on principal plus interest previously earned.

conceptual framework (Chapters 1, 2) A set of interrelated concepts which define the nature, subject, purpose and broad content of general-purpose financial reports.

conservatism (Chapter 2) The concept of conservatism applies to the practice of understatement of income or assets and/or maximum recognition of expenses or liabilities.

consolidated financial statements (Chapter 12) The name given to the financial reports prepared on behalf of an economic entity which enable users to examine the performance and financial position of both the parent entity on its own and the combination of the parent entity and the other entities it controls.

contra account (Chapters 7, 9) An account that is deducted from a related account.

contribution margin (Chapter 18) Equal to the sales revenue less the variable costs.

control (Chapter 12) The capacity of an entity to dominate decision making, directly or indirectly, in relation to the financial and operating policies of another entity so as to enable that other entity to operate with it in pursuing the objectives of the controlling entity. (AASB 127)

corporate governance (Chapter 13) Mechanisms such as the board of directors and audit committees which exist to provide some assurance to the absentee owners that the management of a company are accountable for their actions and to minimise agency costs in respect of their management.

correlation (Chapter 18) In a general sense, correlation denotes the interdependence between quantitative and qualitative data. In a narrower sense, it describes the relationship between two or more measurable variables.

cost centre (Chapter 21) A business unit, which could be a function, activity or even an item of equipment which can be held responsible for certain costs.

cost estimation (Chapter 17) Relates to methods that are used to measure past (historical) costs at varying activity levels. These costs will then be employed as the basis to predict future costs that will be used in decision making.

cost function (Chapter 18) A graphical representation of the relationship between a dependent cost variable y and an independent cost variable x, where the vertical axis is the dependent cost variable and the horizontal axis is the independent cost variable. Points are plotted on the graph to produce a cost function. The function may be linear or non-linear.

cost object (Chapter 17)   A product, service, customer, process, activity or any object for which costs are measured and assigned.

cost of a non-current asset (Chapter 9)   Includes: (a) all reasonable and necessary costs incurred to place the asset in a position and condition ready for use; and (b) all costs incurred which enhance the future economic benefits of the asset beyond those initially expected at acquisition.

cost of capital (Chapter 16, 21)   The minimum rate of return required of a project before it is accepted.

cost–volume–profit (CVP) analysis (Chapter 18) A technique used by organisations to help them make decisions by examining the interrelationships between cost, volume and profits.

creditor (Chapters 1, 8)   A person or entity to whom a debt is owed.

current cost (Chapters 2 and 3)   The cost of replacing an asset.

curvilinear regression (Chapter 18)   A regression which is not linear.

debentures (Chapter 10)   The term given to a secured transferable loan instrument that can be listed on the stock exchange. Debentures can be secured over specific assets, or by way of a floating charge over all assets.

debtors (Chapter 8)   Also called accounts receivable, debtors arise when a business sells goods or services to a third party on credit terms.

dependent variable (Chapter 18)   In a cost function, the dependent variable is expressed as variable y and is the cost to be predicted – the total cost for an activity.

depreciable amount (Chapter 9)   The historical cost of a depreciable asset, or other revalued amount substituted for historical cost, in the financial report, less, in either case, the net amount expected to be recovered on disposal of the asset at the end of its useful life. (AASB 116)

depreciable asset (Chapter 9)   A non-current asset having a limited useful life. (AASB 116)

depreciation expense (Chapters 2, 3, 5, 9) An expense recognised systematically for the purpose of allocating the depreciable amount of a depreciable asset over its useful life. (AASB 116)

differential costs (incremental costs) (Chapter 19) The differences in costs and benefits between alternative opportunities available to an organisation. It follows that when a number of opportunities are being considered, costs and benefits that are common to these alternative opportunities are irrelevant to the decision.

direct costs (Chapter 17)   A cost that is traceable, and thus attributable, to a product.

direct write-off method (Chapter 8)   A method of accounting for bad debts where the amount owing by the debtor is eliminated when it is determined the debtor will not pay. The debtor's balance is reduced and the other side of the transaction is the recognition of an expense.

directors' report (Chapter 2)   A report required by the *Corporations Act*, prepared by a company's directors and included with the company's financial statements, providing information including the directors' names, activities of the company, profit or loss for the year, amount of dividends, review of operations and many other matters in relation to the company.

directors' statement/declaration (Chapter 2) A statement required by the *Corporations Act*, signed by at least two directors and included with a company's financial statements, outlining whether, in their opinion, the income statement and the balance sheet present a true and fair view, whether the company will be able to pay its debts as they fall due, and whether the financial statements comply with applicable accounting standards.

discounting (Chapters 3, 16)   Present value of a sum to be received in x period given y interest rate.

dividend cover (Chapter 14)   Number of times the net profit after tax covers the ordinary dividend payment.

double-entry bookkeeping (Chapter 6) The system developed for recording accounting information based on the concept that every transaction affects two or more components of the balance sheet (accounting) equation.

driver KPIs (Chapter 21) Measures of performance that drive or influence the success of an entity.

due process (Chapter 2) The name of the process that has been designed to allow all interested parties maximum opportunity to comment on proposed accounting standards.

economic consequences (Chapter 1) The impact of accounting policy changes on the economic position of various parties affected by the change.

economic value (Chapter 3) The value of the expected earnings from using an item, discounted at an appropriate rate to give a present-day value.

economic value added (Chapter 21) EVA = after tax profit plus interest – cost of capital × total capital employed

efficient markets hypothesis (Chapter 14) A market is efficient if it reacts immediately and without bias to reflect new information in asset prices.

entity (Chapters 1, 12) A fictional or notional being, such as a business, club, company or partnership, in respect of which financial transactions occur and accounts are kept.

equity (Chapters 2, 4) The residual interest in the assets of an entity after deduction of its liabilities. (AASB *Framework*, para. 49)

equity investors (Chapter 4) The ordinary shareholder in a company, or the owner or partner in a sole proprietorship or partnership.

ethical (Chapter 1) Behaving in an honest and morally correct manner.

expectation gap (Chapter 2) The difference between what an auditor is required to do and what is expected by users.

expenses (Chapters 2, 5) Decreases in economic benefits during the accounting period in the form of outflows or depletions of assets or incurrences of liabilities that result in a decrease in equity, other than those relating to distributions to equity participants. (AASB *Framework*, para. 70)

exposure draft (ED) (Chapter 2) A document circulated by the IASB and AASB to interested groups for comment and amendment before a standard is produced.

factoring (Chapter 10) The process whereby amounts that are owing by debtors are sold to a collection agency.

feasible region (Chapter 15) Where the boundaries of the activity spaces of each group involved with an organisation overlap – that is, the acceptable activity is common to more than one group.

FIFO (first in, first out) (Chapter 7) A method of inventory valuation based on the artificial assumption that the first goods bought are the first ones sold. The inventory held at the end of the period is assumed to be that purchased most recently.

final dividends (Chapter 11) Dividends proposed by the directors at the annual general meeting. The shareholders can approve the dividend or lower it, but they cannot raise it.

finance lease (Chapter 10) A lease which effectively transfers from the lessor to the lessee substantially all the risks and benefits incidental to ownership of the leased property. (AASB 117)

financial accounting (Chapter 1) That part of an accounting system that tries to meet the needs of various external user groups.

financial risk (Chapters 5, 10, 14) The risk that a business might not be able to repay borrowed funds or interest as they fall due.

financial statements (Chapter 1) The means of conveying a concise picture of the profitability and financial position of the business to management and interested outside parties. The most widely used financial statements are the balance sheet, the income statement, the statement of changes in equity and the cash flow statement (plus the notes attached to the statements).

finished goods (Chapter 7) Goods that have been through the complete production or assembly cycle and are ready for resale to the customer.

fixed assets (Chapter 4) A term previously in use to describe those assets of an entity which were acquired with the view to be held by the entity, for the purpose of generating income over a number of years. Today, fixed assets are commonly referred to as non-current assets.

fixed charge (Chapter 14) In relation to a creditor, a fixed charge means the creditor has a charge against specific assets and normally holds a mortgage or other security over the asset.

fixed costs (Chapters 17, 18)   A cost is fixed if it does not change in response to changes in the level of activity within the relevant range of activity.

floating charge (Chapter 14)   In relation to a creditor, the security over the assets does not relate to a specific asset but to all assets in general.

***Framework* (Chapter 2)**   The *Framework for the Preparation and Presentation of Financial Statements* issued by the IASB and the AASB.

franked dividends (Chapter 11)   Dividends paid by a company which have been subject to company taxation.

FRC (Financial Reporting Council) (Chapter 2)   The Financial Reporting Council is responsible for the priorities, business plan, budget and staffing arrangements of the AASB but is not able to influence the AASB's technical deliberations.

full costing (absorption costing) (Chapter 17)   The full cost of a product consists of the direct and indirect costs of production.

functional-based cost accounting system (Chapter 17)   An accounting system that classifies all costs as either variable or fixed in relation to changes in the volume or units produced.

general-purpose financial report (Chapter 2)   A financial report intended to meet the information needs that are common to users who are unable to command the preparation of reports so as to satisfy, specifically, all of their needs.

goal congruence (Chapter 15)   The alignment of organisational goals with the personal and group goals of the individuals within an organisation.

going concern (Chapters 1, 2)   The assumption that a business will continue to operate in the future without any intention to liquidate or to significantly reduce its scale of operations.

goodwill (Chapter 9)   The future benefits from unidentifiable assets.

group (Chapter 12)   The term applied to a parent company and its subsidiaries for which consolidated financial statements are prepared. The group is an economic entity and not a legal entity.

GST (Goods and Services Tax) (Chapter 12)   An indirect tax on goods and services.

hire-purchase (Chapter 10)   A financial institution buys an asset and hires it to the prospective buyer. Ownership remains with the financial institution until the hirer makes the final payment.

historic cost (Chapter 3)   The cost incurred by an individual or entity in acquiring an item, measured at the time of the originating transaction.

IAS (International Accounting Standards) (Chapter 2)   Standards issued by the IASB prior to January 2002.

IASB (International Accounting Standards Board) (Chapter 2)   The body responsible for the development of International Accounting Standards.

IFRS (International Financial Reporting Standards) (Chapter 2)   Standards issued by the IASB from January 2002. An IFRS includes all new IFRSs, previously issued IASs and interpretations of these standards.

impairment test (Chapter 9)   An impairment test specifies that, when the carrying value of an asset is higher than its recoverable amount, the asset must be written down to its recoverable amount.

income (Chapter 2)   Increases in economic benefits during the accounting period in the form of inflows or enhancements of assets or decreases of liabilities that result in increases in equity, other than those relating to contributions from equity participants. (AASB *Framework*, para. 70)

income statement (Chapters 1, 5)   A financial report listing the income, expenses and net profit or net loss of a business (entity) for a time period.

income tax expense (Chapter 12)   The aggregate amount included in the determination of net profit or loss for the period in respect of current and deferred tax. The term 'tax income' is used to describe this amount where it is a net credit. (AASB 112)

independent projects (Chapter 16)   The acceptance or rejection of one project has no effect on other projects.

independent variable (Chapter 18)   In a cost function, the independent variable is expressed as variable x and is the level of activity.

indirect costs (overhead costs) (Chapter 17)
Costs that cannot be easily and conveniently
identified with a particular product.

intangible assets (Chapter 9) Non-current assets
which lack physical substance and are not used for
investment purposes.

interest (Chapters 1, 16) A charge made for the
use of money.

interest cover (Chapter 14) The number of times
net profit before interest and tax covers the interest
payment.

interim dividends (Chapter 11) Dividends
declared and paid part way through the accounting
period in anticipation of a final profit.

internal control (Chapter 12) The procedures and
processes in place within a business to safeguard all
assets including cash.

internal rate of return (Chapter 16) The rate of
return which discounts the cash flows of a project
so that the present value of cash inflows equals the
present value of cash outflows.

inventories (Chapter 7) Goods, other property
and services: (a) held for sale in the ordinary course
of business; (b) in the process of production for
such sale; or (c) in the form of materials or supplies
to be consumed in the production process or in the
rendering of services. (AASB 102)

investment centre (Chapter 21) A business unit
where the manager not only has control over the
profits of the unit but also has some discretion as to
the amount of investment undertaken by the unit.

irrevocable contract (Chapter 2) A legal or
formal agreement made between two or more people
that cannot be changed without incurring significant
penalties.

just-in-time management (Chapter 7)
A management technique designed to lower the costs
of holding high levels of stock.

KPIs (key performance indicators) (Chapter 21)
Measures (financial or non-financial) used to assess
the degree of success in achieving certain targets of
performance.

lease (Chapter 10) A contractual agreement
between two parties whereby one party (the lessee)

obtains the rights to use an item, such as a machine,
in exchange for a series of lease payments to the
other party (the lessor).

lenders (Chapter 14) Persons or organisations
which permit the temporary use of money; for
example, in return for payment.

lessee (Chapter 10) The person or company
obtaining the rights to use leased property.

lessor (Chapter 10) The owner of the property
which is leased out.

liabilities (Chapters 2, 4) A present obligation
of the entity arising from past events, the settlement
of which is expected to result in an outflow from
the entity of resources embodying future economic
benefits. (AASB *Framework*, para. 49)

LIFO (last in, first out) (Chapter 7) A method of
inventory valuation based on the assumption that the
last goods bought are the first sold. Ending inventory
is assumed to consist of the cost of the earliest units
purchased.

limited-by-shares company (Chapter 11)
This class of company restricts the liability of
members (shareholders) to a specified amount.

linear cost function (Chapter 18) A linear cost
function is a straight-line cost function which can be
mathematically expressed as $y = a + bx$ where y is
the total cost to be predicted; a is a constant (or fixed
cost); b is the cost that will be the same for each unit
of activity and, therefore, as the activity varies so will
the cost (this cost is known as 'variable cost'); x is
the level of activity measured in units of output.

liquidity (Chapters 1, 14) The ability of a business
to satisfy its short-term obligations. Liquidity refers
to the ease with which assets can be converted to
cash in the normal course of business.

long-term finance (Chapter 10) For periods
greater than one year, and often more than 10 years.

make or buy decision (Chapter 19) The decision
made by an organisation which must choose
between, on the one hand, making a product or
carrying out a service using its own resources,
and, on the other hand, paying another external
organisation to make the product or carry out the
service for it.

management accounting (Chapters 1, 15)
That part of an accounting system that tries to meet the needs of management and internal users.

marginal product (Chapter 19)   The change in output (production) associated with a unit change in one of an organisation's scarce resources, such as labour.

marginal return (Chapter 19)   The contribution or economic value of a marginal unit of a particular scarce resource used by an organisation in the production of a specific product.

master budget (Chapter 20)   The budgeted income statement and balance sheet, representing a summary of the individual functional budgets of the organisation as a whole.

materiality (Chapter 9)   Broadly, an item can be said to be material if its non-disclosure would cause the accounts to be misleading in some way.

materiality test (Chapter 2)   Assesses whether omission, misstatement or non-disclosure of an item of relevant and reliable information could affect decision making about the allocation of scarce resources by the users of the general-purpose financial reports of an entity.

medium-term finance (Chapter 10)   Not strictly the case, but generally finance for periods of one to 10 years.

mortgage loan (Chapter 10)   A loan which is secured by real property such as land and buildings.

multiple regression (Chapter 18)   The regression of a dependent variable on more than one independent or predicted variable.

mutually exclusive projects (Chapter 16)
Where the acceptance of one project results in the rejection of the other project.

net present value (Chapter 16)   The figure that results from discounting all cash flows of a project at a minimum rate of return and summing the resultant present values.

net realisable value (Chapters 3, 7)   The estimated proceeds of sales less, where applicable, all further costs to the stage of completion, and less all costs to be incurred in marketing, selling and distribution to customers. (AASB 102)

non-cancellable lease (Chapter 10)   A contract which cannot be cancelled allowing a person or entity to use or occupy property in return for rent.

non-current assets (Chapters 4, 9)   All assets other than current assets. (AASB 101)

non-current liabilities (Chapter 4)   Liabilities which are not current liabilities. (AASB 101)

non-redeemable preference share (Chapters 10, 14)
Preference shares which cannot be redeemed out of the company's profits or out of the proceeds of a new share issue.

normal costing (Chapter 17)   Where the cost of a product is determined using the actual costs for direct costs and a predetermined rate for the allocation of indirect costs.

objective of financial statements (Chapter 2)
The provision of information about the financial position, performance and changes in financial position of an entity that is useful to a wide range of users in making economic decisions.(AASB *Framework*, para. 12)

operating cycle (Chapter 4)   The average period between the purchase of merchandise and the conversion of this merchandise back into cash.

operating decisions (Chapter 15)   Decisions that focus on the efficient use of the resources available to a firm in the short term.

operating KPIs (Chapter 21)   Measures of performance that relate to normal operating matters.

operating lease (Chapter 10)   A short-term lease under which most of the risks and rewards associated with ownership of the property remain with the lessor.

opportunity cost (Chapters 19)   The opportunity cost of a resource is normally defined as the maximum benefit which could be obtained from that resource if it were used for some alternative purpose. If a firm uses a resource for alternative A rather than B, it is the potential benefits that are forgone by not using the resource for alternative B that constitute the opportunity cost. The potential benefits forgone, the opportunity cost, are a relevant cost in the decision to accept alternative A. The opportunity cost reflects the cost of the most valuable alternative given up.

ordinary shareholder (Chapters 10, 14) A person holding a class of shares that have no preferences relative to other classes.

outcome KPIs (Chapter 21) The measures of performance of an entity from an external viewpoint.

over-recovery of overhead (Chapter 17) The difference between the actual overhead cost and the estimate on which the absorption rate is based. The difference is classified as period income in the income statement because it is not identified with any of the units of production produced during the year.

parent entity (Chapter 12) One which controls another entity.

partnership (Chapters 1, 11) The relationship which exists between persons carrying on a business in common with a view to profit. (*Partnership Act 1891*, section 1(1))

payback (Chapter 16) The time required to recover the initial investment.

performance evaluation system (Chapter 21) A system to evaluate the performance of individuals in an entity; often used as a basis for the determination of rewards.

period costs (Chapter 17) Costs that relate to the period in question. They are recognised in the income statement in the accounting period when they are incurred and cannot justifiably be carried forward to future periods because they do not represent future benefits, or the future benefits are so uncertain as to defy measurement.

periodic method (Chapter 7) A method of accounting for inventory where an accurate record of purchases is kept and an annual inventory count is conducted to establish the cost of goods sold during a period. This annual inventory count is carried out at the balance sheet date; thus, the inventory figure in the balance sheet represents a snapshot of the inventory level at that particular point in time.

perpetual method (Chapter 7) A method of accounting for inventory that operates at the point of every sale: the inventory records of a business are updated every time a sale occurs. The perpetual method is applied by entities with sophisticated computer systems and by certain types of businesses in which it is easy to keep track of inventories.

planning and control (Chapter 15) Planning involves the determination of objectives and the means by which to attain them. The control process is the means of ensuring that the plans are achieved.

preference shareholder (Chapters 10, 14) One who holds a class of shares which receive preferential treatment over ordinary shares; for example, preference in dividend distribution.

prepayments (Chapter 8) Prepayments are payments made in advance for goods and/or services.

present-day value (Chapters 3, 16) The value today of a given amount or item.

principle of duality (Chapter 4) The basis of the double-entry bookkeeping system on which accounting is based. It states that every transaction has two opposite and equal components.

product cost (Chapter 17) The cost of producing an item. When firms manufacture only one product, the process of product costing is straightforward. When firms manufacture more than one product (multi-product firms), the process of product costing can be complex. Two approaches used in determining product costs in multi-product firms are variable costing and absorption costing.

production budget (Chapter 20) An estimate of the number of units that will be manufactured by an organisation during the budget period.

production cost centre (Chapter 17) A department where the manufacturing activity physically takes place.

profit (Chapter 3) The difference between the wealth at the start and at the end of a period, profit is income less expenses. It is a measure of flow which summarises activity over a period.

profit centre (Chapter 21) A business unit which is accountable for both costs and income.

provision for doubtful debts (Chapter 8) A contra debtors' account which shows the estimated total of future bad debts.

qualitative (Chapter 1) The nature or characteristics of information.

quantitative (Chapter 1) The amount or size of information.

realise (Chapter 5) Convert to cash or a legal claim to cash.

recognise (Chapter 5) To record an item in the financial statements.

redeemable preference share (Chapters 10, 14) Preference shares that can be redeemed out of the company's profits or out of the proceeds of a new share issue.

reducing-balance method (Chapter 9) A method of depreciation which results in a decreasing depreciation charge over the useful life of the depreciable asset. Depreciation expense is calculated for each period through the application of a predetermined depreciation rate to the declining undepreciated cost of the asset, called the written-down value or book value. The following formula, in theory, is used to determine the annual depreciation rate:

$$\text{depreciation rate} = 1 - \sqrt[n]{\frac{r}{c}}$$

where n = estimated useful life (in years), r = estimated residual value, and c = original cost (in dollars). In practice an approximation, such as doubling the straight-line rate, is used.

regression analysis (Chapter 18) A sophisticated method of cost estimation which involves making a number of observations from past cost behaviour and statistically analysing the data to produce a line of best fit through plotted cost points on a graph. Patterns of behaviour can be identified from the linear regression model and conclusions drawn about the correlation between cost and the activity being analysed.

relevance (Chapter 2) For financial information to be relevant it must influence the economic decisions of users by helping them evaluate past, present or future events, or by confirming or correcting their past evaluations. (AASB *Framework*, para. 26)

relevant range of activity (Chapter 18) The levels of activity that a firm has experienced in past periods. It is assumed that in this range the relationship between the independent variables will be similar to that previously experienced.

reliability (Chapter 2) The reliability of financial information is determined by the degree of correspondence between what that information conveys to users and the underlying transactions and events that have occurred and been measured and displayed. Reliable information is free from material error and bias, and can be depended upon by users to represent faithfully that which it either purports to represent or could reasonably be expected to represent. (AASB *Framework*, para. 31)

replacement cost (Chapter 3) The amount that would have to be paid at today's prices to purchase an item similar to the existing item. The cost has come about as a direct result of the decision to use a resource for a purpose not originally intended and the need to replace the resource.

reporting entities (Chapter 2) Entities (including economic entities) for which there are users who rely on the financial statements as their major source of financial information about the entity. (AASB *Framework*, para. 8)

reserves (Chapter 11) Amounts set aside out of profits and other surpluses which are not designed to meet any liability, contingency, commitment or diminution in value of assets known to exist at the date of the balance sheet. Reserves do not equal cash.

residual value (Chapter 9) The residual value of a non-current asset is an estimate of the net amount recoverable on ultimate disposal of the asset when it is no longer viable to use in the business.

responsibility accounting (Chapters 15, 20, 21) An approach used to monitor performance whereby personnel in an organisation who incur expenditure and generate income are identified and made responsible for these costs and income.

responsibility centres (Chapters 15, 20, 21) The various decision centres throughout an organisation, normally departments or divisions, recognised in the responsibility accounting management approach. The manager's knowledge of the centre places him or her in an advantageous position within the organisation to ensure that budget targets are achieved.

revenues (Chapters 2, 5) Gross inflows of economic benefits during the period arising in the course of the ordinary activities of an entity when those inflows result in increases in equity, other than increases relating to contributions from equity participants. (AASB 118 , para. 7)

sales budget (Chapter 20) The conversion of the sales forecast for a budget period of an organisation into detailed information concerning the products or services that it is anticipated will be sold.

secured lender (Chapters 10, 14) Someone who has a legal charge over the assets of a business and can claim those assets if the business does not repay or service the loan in accordance with the agreement.

service cost centre (Chapter 17) Those decision centres that are primarily engaged in servicing the production function, but are not directly involved in the production activity.

short-term finance (Chapter 10) Finance for a period of less than one year.

simple interest (Chapter 16) Interest based on original principal only.

sole trader (Chapter 11) A one-owner business.

solvency (Chapter 14) The ability of a business to repay borrowed funds or interest as they fall due. An insolvent firm is unable to meet its commitments.

spare capacity (Chapter 19) An organisation which has enough resources available to make another product or component, without affecting the production of other products, is said to have spare capacity.

standards overload (Chapter 2) A problem concerned with the time and costs involved in preparing general-purpose financial reports which must comply with a large number of Accounting Standards.

statement of changes in equity (SOCE) (Chapter 5) The purpose of the SOCE is to report all changes to equity that are taken directly to the equity section of the balance sheet, together with the profit or loss for the period. Therefore, this shows the total changes to the equity for the period.

stewardship (Chapter 1) The need to protect a firm's economic resources (normally referred to as assets) from theft, fraud, wastage, and so on.

stock exchange (Chapter 1) A market for the buying and selling of stocks and shares in which supply and demand governs price.

straight-line method (Chapter 9) A method of depreciation which allocates an equal amount of depreciation to all the periods over the useful life of the depreciable asset. The depreciation charge for each period is determined by dividing the cost of the asset, less the estimate of any residual value at the end of the asset's life, by the useful life of the asset.

strategic decisions (Chapters 15, 21) Decisions that determine the long-term policies of a firm and are necessary if the firm is to meet its objectives.

strategic KPIs (Chapter 21) The measures of performance that are concerned with how well an entity is achieving its strategies.

subsidiary (Chapter 12) An entity which is controlled by a parent entity.

sunk costs (past costs) (Chapter 19) Costs which have been paid or which are owed by a firm. The firm is committed to paying for them in the future.

T account (Chapter 11) Under the traditional approach to accounting, this was an account format shaped like the letter T. Debits are recorded on the left-hand side and credits on the right-hand side.

tax-effect accounting method (Chapter 12) Accounting for the temporary differences between tax values for assets and liabilities and their respective values for accounting purposes.

tax-payable method (Chapter 12) The accounting method for calculating income tax expense, where taxable income is multiplied by the tax rate to give income tax expense.

taxable income (Chapter 12) The amount of profit, as determined by the Tax Commissioner, on which the current income tax liability is calculated.

temporary differences (Chapter 12) The differences between the tax balances and accounting balances of assets and liabilities.

trade credit (Chapter 10) The finance that is available from suppliers selling goods on credit.

trend analysis (Chapter 14) A technique commonly used in financial statement analysis to assess a business's growth prospects.

trial balance (Chapter 11) The preparation of a statement which lists all the financial accounts and their respective debit or credit balances to ensure the equality of debits and credits made to the accounts.

UIG (Urgent Issues Group) (Chapter 2)
A subcommittee of the AASB, responsible for the interpretation of accounting standards to give timely guidance.

unavoidable cost (Chapter 19) A cost which will be incurred regardless of whether or not a decision (e.g. the delivery of a special order) is accepted or rejected. Therefore, the cost is irrelevant to the decision.

under-recovery of overhead (Chapter 17)
The difference between the actual overhead cost and the estimate on which the absorption rate is based. The difference is classified as a period cost in the income statement because it is not identified with any of the units of production produced during the year.

units-of-output method (Chapter 9) A method of depreciation that relates depreciation to use rather than to time. It is appropriate to use for an asset where usage will materially affect its lifespan. The depreciation charge is determined by dividing the cost of the asset, less the estimate of the asset's residual value, by the estimated number of output units expected from the asset during its estimated useful life. Output units can be expressed in numerous ways; for example, kilometres or operating hours. The result of the calculation is a depreciation rate per output unit which, when multiplied by the number of units used or produced during the period, gives the depreciation expense for a period.

unrealised gain (Chapter 2) A gain which is yet to be realised by way of a transaction. For example, an increase in the value of an asset represents an unrealised gain until the asset is sold, at which time the gain would be realised.

unrealised loss (Chapter 2) A loss which is yet to be realised by way of a transaction. For example, a decrease in the value of an asset represents an unrealised loss until the asset is sold, at which time the loss would be realised.

unsecured creditor (Chapters 10, 14) Someone who does not have a legal charge on the assets of a business.

unsecured note (Chapters 10, 14) A debt instrument which is not secured by a charge over property.

useful life (Chapter 9) For a non-current asset, the time period the asset is expected to be used to produce goods or services.

user group (Chapter 14) The different classes of people for whom financial statement analysis is being undertaken.

value (Chapter 3) An item's equivalence in money.

variable costing (Chapter 17) Only variable production costs are included in variable costing.

variable costs (Chapter 18) Costs that are the same per unit of activity within the relevant range of activity; therefore, total variable costs increase and decrease in direct proportion to the increase and decrease in the activity level. The activity level depends upon what is being measured; that is, production output or sales output.

wealth (Chapter 3) A static measure representing a stock at a particular point in time.

work in progress (Chapters 7, 18) Products and services that are at an intermediate stage of completion.

worksheet (Chapter 6) An arrangement of columns on a sheet of paper, used by accountants to gather and organise the information from which financial statements can be prepared.

written-down cost (Chapter 3) The historic cost after an adjustment for usage (commonly referred to as depreciation).

written-down value (carrying value or net book value) (Chapter 9) The cost of a non-current asset less the total depreciation to date.

INDEX

Numbers in **Bold** indicate key concept; numbers in *italic* indicate newspaper article